The
ITALIAN INQUISITION

The
ITALIAN
INQUISITION

CHRISTOPHER F. BLACK

YALE UNIVERSITY PRESS
NEW HAVEN AND LONDON

Copyright © 2009 Christopher F. Black

All rights reserved. This book may not be reproduced in whole or in part, in any form (beyond that copying permitted by Sections 107 and 108 of the U.S. Copyright Law and except by reviewers for the public press) without written permission from the publishers.

For information about this and other Yale University Press publications, please contact:
U.S. Office: sales.press@yale.edu   www.yalebooks.com
Europe Office: sales@yaleup.co.uk   www.yalebooks.co.uk

Set in Arno by IDSUK (DataConnection) Ltd

Library of Congress Cataloging-in-Publication Data

Black, Christopher F., 1941-
  The Italian inquisition / Christopher F. Black.
    p. cm.
  Includes bibliographical references and indexes.
  ISBN 978-0-300-22062-9
  1. Inquisition–Italy. 2. Italy–Church history. I. Title.
  BX1723.B53 2009
  272'.20945–dc22   2009013404
A catalogue record for this book is available from the British Library.

10 9 8 7 6 5 4 3 2 1

Contents

Preface		*vii*
Acknowledgements		*xii*
Glossary		*xiv*
Maps		*xvi*
Chapter 1	The Establishment of the Roman Inquisition in 1542	1
Chapter 2	The Roman Holy Office and Local Tribunals	19
Chapter 3	How the Tribunals Worked	56
Chapter 4	How the Inquisitors Worked	102
Chapter 5	The Carnesecchi Moment	123
Chapter 6	Diverse and Changing Targets	131
Chapter 7	Censorship	158
Chapter 8	Inquisitors, Accused and Witnesses	208
Chapter 9	The World of Witchcraft, Superstition and Magic	231
Chapter 10	Conclusion	255
	Appendix: Tables of Types of Accusations and Cases	260
	Abbreviations	266
	Notes	267
	Bibliography	298
	A Brief Reading Guide	298
	Full Bibliography	299
	Index	314

Preface

THE TOPIC OF 'THE ITALIAN INQUISITION' (WHICH IN PRACTICE COVERS several inquisition systems, as we shall see), might seem dark and unattractive, but it is not as gruesome as myths and prejudices might suggest, nor does it resemble Francisco de Goya's distorted artistic images of the late stages of the Spanish Inquisition. The subject presents intellectual challenges in the face of very diverse evidence, which can lead to a study of wide aspects of social as well as religious history. It brings out the quirkiness of human nature and bizarre philosophies, which can have their own amusement value, and titillation. The subject has new topicality, whether considering world politics and the clash of religious beliefs, fears (justified or not) of 'the enemy within', or debates about due legal process and the merits and disadvantages of different legal systems, and the use of torture. Torture under the early modern Inquisitions was for the most part more selective, milder physically and less gruesomely imaginative than what is practised in most modern states, or accepted through 'rendition'.

The amount of evidence that can be used (despite huge losses of records in the nineteenth century) is considerable, and has recently been extended by the opening to scholars in 1998 of the central archive of the Roman Inquisition. While revivifying debate and controversy this in part justifies an interim report and analysis, from somebody not totally enmeshed in Inquisition history – and accustomed, for good and ill, to discussing 'Italy' – and the Roman Church's response to the varied calls for 'reform', internal as well as non-Italian, on a wide scale.[1]

My book is intended as an overview of the current knowledge produced by international scholars, with some input from my own excursions into a few of the archival resources extant. Archives in some twenty Italian cities and towns could have been utilised, but also those in Spain, Dublin and Malta. Mindful of Adriano Prosperi's criticism of foreign historians who have pontificated on the Spanish and Italian Inquisitions without direct study of their records,[2] I have emphasised the details from some of my own forrays into archives in Bologna, Florence, Rome and Venice. My approach is probably affected by having been brought up in the Anglican tradition, but having liberal Catholic relatives in Britain and the USA. Unlike Delio Cantimori and his early followers, or

Massimo Firpo now, I do not consider that the failure of an Italian Reformation was disastrous for the development and modernisation of Italy, nor that the victory of the Catholic Church almost alone impeded Italian unification and democratisation. The diversity of reform movements within Italy and the multiplicity of political states rendered a Protestant victory almost impossible. No single state, no prince or republican oligarchy was powerful enough to impose an Italian Reformation; and too much might have been lost by a total break with the traditional Roman Church. A strict Calvinist victory would have been no more welcomed by most people in Italy than the strictest Catholicism. Traditions of lay Catholicism, localised religious loyalties and sceptical anti-clericalism would have been very hard to suppress. The new Roman Inquisition, as shaped dogmatically by Gian Pietro Carafa and Michele Ghislieri (later popes Paul IV and Pius V), prevented the possible establishment of a humanist reformed Catholicism, an Erasmian or Valdesian (followers of Juan de Valdés) version, tolerating flexible approaches to Salvation, without abolishing papal leadership and the apostolic succession.

Despite this dark side to the Roman Inquisition, I follow Adriano Prosperi and Simon Ditchfield in arguing that it became also a creative and educative force, contributing to a common Italian culture by the nineteenth century. As one of Prosperi's seminal books has argued (and demonstrated), 'the fundamental question in the Italian situation became, evidently, that of persuading and convincing, not that of conquering'; in this the new confessional procedures, missionary work and the work of the Inquisition (closely linked to the procedures of confession) led to 'persuasion', that a new Catholicism was acceptable, beneficial and appealing.[3] Positive contributions and persuasion also came from religious art, music, liturgical ceremony. On the negative side inquisitorial damage done through book censorship and reinforcing habits of dissimulation was considerable.

The complexity of this topic is governed by the consideration that we are not dealing with a single, centralised 'Italian Inquisition'. The main institution is what is generally called the Roman Inquisition, or Holy Office – a permanent institution established from 1542 under the Pope, building on medieval inquisition practices and more temporary 'inquisitions'. Because Italy was not politically united (see Map 1), it proved impossible to operate a uniform inquisition system throughout the peninsula, and arrangements had to be made with the different states. But – depending on your definition of 'Italy' – a second inquisition system was involved to a greater or lesser extent: the Spanish one. The Spanish Inquisition had been inaugurated in 1478, gradually covering Castile and Aragon (which had been united under one monarchy through the marriage in 1469 of Ferdinand and Isabella). Although sanctioned by the Papacy, this was essentially a state institution responsible to the king of Spain. The islands of

Sicily and Sardinia were part of the Kingdom of Aragon, and tribunals were there established. When, by 1559, the Spanish had fought for and won control of the Kingdom of Naples and the Duchy of Lombardy, conflicts arose over whether the inquisitions there should be 'Spanish' or 'Roman'. The Spaniards failed to install their Inquisition, though as we shall see they impeded a proper operation of the Roman Inquisition in the Kingdom/Viceroyalty of Naples.

In the sixteenth and seventeenth centuries distinctions between 'Italy' and 'Spain', 'Italians' and 'Spaniards', could be fuzzy, as a recent book of essays on *Spain in Italy* emphasises.[4] Many Spaniards infiltrated most mainland states as well as the islands, especially among the aristocracy; the Spanish influences on the Italian reform movements were forceful especially through the Valdesian movement, mysticism more generally and early Jesuit attitudes. Sicilians, though under Spanish domination, could see themselves as 'Italians'.[5] Discussion of inquisition developments in the islands of Sicily and Sardinia encourages a comparison with the Spanish systems. Malta had been under Spanish control, but passed to the political control of the Knights of St John in 1530 and eventually an inquisition tribunal answerable to Rome was established there in 1561.

The chronological coverage of this book is 'early modern', essentially from the early sixteenth to late eighteenth centuries, starting with the foundation in 1542 of the central administration of the Roman Inquisition under papal supervision in Rome. This is variously seen by scholars as a 'new' Inquisition, a 'renewal' or 'revision' of the existing papal Inquisition. For me it is essentially new, because of its permanency as a central bureaucratic organisation. Its foundation was influenced by the prior operations of the Spanish Inquisition, and it did draw on the pre-1542 inquisitorial activity on the mainland, what I call the 'medieval' Inquisition, or what some call the 'Episcopal Inquisition'. The 'medieval' or 'episcopal' inquisition system persisted – notably in the Kingdom of Naples, where neither the Spanish nor the Roman structures could be formally established, and maybe in the independent Republic of Lucca. Under the full Roman Inquisition bishops could persist as guardians of the faith, variously working in cooperation with inquisitors, or impeding them. The story continues through to the eighteenth century, to the formal closures, or withering away of activity. My coverage of this century is briefer for reasons of knowledge and space but it emphasises what has emerged from the opening of the ACDF (Archivio della Congregazione per la Dottrina della Fede), which has revealed full records of the Congregation of the Index.

The inquisitions are considered from several viewpoints: their legal procedures, the evolution of centralised bureaucracies, which reinforced greater social and intellectual control by Church and States. We will tell the story of how high theological heresies with their many different strands were confronted, and largely overcome, within Italy. Chapters 2 and 5 discuss in detail the handling of the Italian reformers by the Inquisition, as the Roman Inquisition evolved, revealing struggles between hardliners and some more emollient popes and cardinals. My priority is analysis of the inquisitions' workings, not of the diverse Italian reform movements and their fates. Chapters 3 and 4 reveal how tribunals and inquisitors operated on broad fronts. Chapter 5 on the Carnesecchi Moment, featuring the much-publicised condemnation and death of a leading heretic in 1567, marks to some extent the watershed, witnessing the culmination of the main defences against the threats of high theology, a victory for the more unbending Cardinal inquisitors. From then on the Roman Inquisition could broaden its scope of heretical and quasi-heretical targets, but become more educational and less punitive. Chapter 6 and the Tables indicate the shifting targets. In that chapter and in the following ones I discuss some of the types of cases that lay behind the statistical entries. The overall strategy of my discussion in this second half of the book is to reveal the sorts of beliefs and practices considered by the inquisitors, and their reactions in questioning and punishing. The individuals who appeared before them were there not just as a result of the inquisitors' fixations and mind-sets, but those of a wider society. We can detect the behaviour and beliefs of blasphemers, of people attempting magic (and their victims), of Christians, Jews and Muslims in contact with each other, of pedlars of false beliefs and those seen as 'living' or 'pretend' saints. Chapter 7 considers many issues of censorship, how the inquisitions sought to curb the propagation of dangerous and misleading ideas, whether of deep theology, philosophy and science, or of immoral literature.

Analysis of interactions between inquisitors, accused and witnesses – the focus of Chapter 8, but evident in other discussions – is predicated on my view that in reading the records we are dealing not just with a top-down system of domination, and an acceptance that inquisition records and their 'evidence' can provide aspects of truths perceived by the 'victims'. This also means that historians can utilise the records for wider studies of social and cultural history, as the consideration of superstition and magic in Chapter 9 further illustrates. In reading my case studies, their possible value for social history more generally should be considered as well as their exemplification of inquisitorial activity – for instance, taking incidental details and not the inquisitors' immediate targets, and considering the relationships of neighbours.

Like Carlo Ginzburg and Anne Schutte, I consider one can hear something of an authentic voice in witnesses and accused, especially when the discourse is shifting away from a questioner's central target. Some replies could clearly surprise inquisitors and go beyond their preconceptions, and their strategic planning (if any). A respondent might well be distorting his or her 'true beliefs' when telling tales to a tribunal to minimise dangers, mitigate real or alleged behaviour and appearances; but the story itself and the language used *may* be useful evidence of a wider mental outlook. Understanding the nature of an inquisition tribunal, its rules, the assumptions of its documentation and, on the other side, the contexts in which witnesses and accused could respond, can lead to a better appreciation of the religious and social world in the early modern period. 'Hearing the voices of those subjected to control from above, though never easy, is not impossible.'[6]

John Tedeschi – 'the godfather of the current image' – has produced clear and forceful corrections to past 'Black Legend' attacks on the Roman Inquisition. His illustrations of inquisitorial attempts to follow due processes, and to educate as well as punish, have had a major impact on my approach. Tedeschi emphasised that the Roman Inquisition 'was not a drumhead court, a chamber of horrors, or a judicial labyrinth from which escape was impossible', to which Schutte legitimately adds, 'it offered the best criminal justice available in early modern Europe'.[7] This 'best' does not mean that illegality, brutality, corruption and other human failings were absent – as what follows also shows; nor that we endorse the moral view that deviations from a religious norm, the reading of dubious books or talking about them, should have been severely punished. In correcting the black legend, I hope to avoid endorsing a 'pink' or 'grey' one.

My growing enthusiasm for researching and discussing the inquisitions led to a draft text of nearly 200,000 words. Purging this to meet the publishing realities of Yale University Press has meant that many illustrative examples have been sacrificed, as well as certain themes and topics. Virtually all Italian quotations from archival sources have been eliminated, though I hope many will appear later in specialist articles. Meanwhile dedicated scholars who miss such sources should feel free to e-mail me and I will try to satisfy them with helpful quotations: C.Black@history.arts.gla.ac.uk

ACKNOWLEDGEMENTS

THE OBVIOUS FIRST ACKNOWLEDGEMENT IS TO HEATHER MCCALLUM who pressed me back in 2004–5 to undertake this book when I had other plans for writing in my retirement. Working on this project has proved very stimulating and much more enjoyable than anticipated, outweighing the inevitable frustrations and pressures when working to a tight schedule; hence the inflated first draft! I am grateful to Heather for accepting a compromise on its length. A little decoding enabled me to detect the hand of Simon Ditchfield behind a most helpful reader's report on the initial proposal, an additional benefit after some years of mutual support and friendship. He has continued to inform, stimulate and comfort me as the book has been written – and un-written! I am indebted to Nick Davidson and Richard Mackenney who long ago first introduced me to Venice's old Archivio di Stato and the riches of its inquisition records, used for my other books.

Andrea Del Col has had a considerable influence through his books and articles, but also from some encouragement and advice when we met in Montereale Valcellina (Friuli) back in 1999. His magisterial study *L'Inquisizione in Italia dal XII al XXI secolo* of 2006 appeared most opportunely as I concentrated fully on researching for this book that autumn. In Friuli I received the kind hospitality of Aldo Colonnello and guidance from him on that fascinating area. Aldo runs the Circolo Culturale Menocchio, and he has also sent me relevant books sponsored by that organisation. Stephen Bowd's work and conversations alerted me to some fifteenth-century activities in northern Italy, especially in Brescia, which affected my attitude to the late 'medieval' Inquisition, and transitions to 'early modern' Inquisitions. My introduction to the Maltese Inquisition is indebted to Frans Ciappara, who has kindly provided me with copies of his own work.

For facilitating dedicated research into this book in Bologna and Rome in 2006–7 (as on several occasions since 1975), I am most grateful to Alberto Melloni and his staff for favoured treatment in the Istituto per le Scienze Religiose, Bologna, and its splendid library; to the staff of the manuscript room in the Biblioteca Comunale dell'Archiginnasio, Bologna; to Monsignor Alejandro Cifres and his staff for allowing an abnormally long continuous stint in the ACDF in Vatican City in June–July 2007. I commend the efficiency, helpfulness and pleasant atmosphere of these institutions for maximising research time.

As with my other books I have received from numerous other friends and contacts their advice and encouragement, supplies of books, offprints, archival references, conference invitations, hospitality, and penetrating or embarrassing questions as work progressed. These include for this book in particular, as well as those individuals already mentioned (with apologies for any inadvertent omissions): Simonetta Adorni-Braccesi, Tricia Allerston, Alexandra Bamji, Elizabeth Black, Maria Bortoluzzi, Sarah Cockram, Sam Cohn, Natasha Costantinidou, Niki Dialeti, Mario Fanti, Irene Fosi, Gigliola Fragnito, Costas Gaganakis, David Gentilcore, Jenny Greenleaves, Vincenzo Lavenia, John Martin, Adelina Modesti, Mary Moran, Stefania Pastore, Georgios Plakotos, Adriano Prosperi, Camilla Russell, Nicholas Terpstra, Jane Wickersham and Danilo Zardin. Mike Shand has again helped with the maps.

GLOSSARY

Abitello	penitential garment worn after condemnation as a heretic; more often awarded under the Spanish than Italian Inquisition.
Alumbrados, Illuministi	those who followed a Spanish mystical approach, believing in a passive union with God, an abandonment of self, and the irrelevance of the institutional Church and all sacramental paraphernalia.
Auto da fé/Auto	'act of faith'. Public ceremony parading those condemned for serious heresy, and/or naming these in their absence. More common under the Spanish than the Roman Inquisition.
Beata/o	(a) person officially considered blessed, as stage towards canonisation, (b) a *beata*, especially in Spain, was a woman popularly deemed holy, especially in healing and prophesying
Busta	in archival references (with 'b.' as abbreviation), a bundle of documents.
Contado	the district of rural areas and small towns dependent on a major city.
Converso	Jew converted to Christianity; less derogatory than *marrano*. Also called neophyte, *anusim* (Hebrew). Can also mean lay brother.
Familiari	paid and/or privileged supporters of the local Inquisition.
Foro interno, foro esterno	forum or procedure judging matters of conscience (*interno*), the internal court of confession, spiritual penance, reconciliation; and the physical offence (*esterno*), resolution by public abjuration and reconciliation.
Gonfaloniere	literally standard-bearer, for an urban district, as in Florence; but more widely in Tuscany, the equivalent of the *Podestà*.
Marrani/Marranos	converts from Judaism or Islam; often abusive (as 'pigs'), assuming not genuine converts.
Pievano/Piovano	parish priest, mostly used when he headed a church with a baptismal font (*pieve*), with dependent lesser churches and/or other priests. *Piovano* is normally used for the head of Venetian parish churches (usually collegiate).
Podestà	administrative and judicial city official, usually a foreigner.
Processo/i	inquisitorial investigation(s), from taking up a denunciation; may or may not include a formal accusation and trial. The word may refer to the transcript of the proceedings. I have sometimes used 'process' in these restricted senses.
Spirituali	term used for Italian evangelical reformers interested in, but not necessarily committed to, Lutheran and other northern Protestant

	ideas, but more likely Valdesian; likely to follow the doctrine of salvation by faith alone (*sola fide*). Associates of cardinals Contarini and Pole used the term about themselves.
Theatines	Order of Clerks Regular of Theatines, named after Gaetano da Thiene (d.1547), bishop of Chieti. It derived from the reforming Oratory of Divine Love. Its first superior was Gian Pietro Carafa.
Valdesi/Waldensians	followers of a French medieval heresy involving the merchant Waldo, stressing vernacular Bible reading and apostolic poverty; surviving in northern Italy, Calabria and Puglia; then linked with Calvinists.
Valdesiani/Valdesians	followers of Juan de Valdés.
Visitation	official episcopal or apostolic delegate's inspection of churches and chapels in a diocese.

Map 1: The States in Italy in 1559

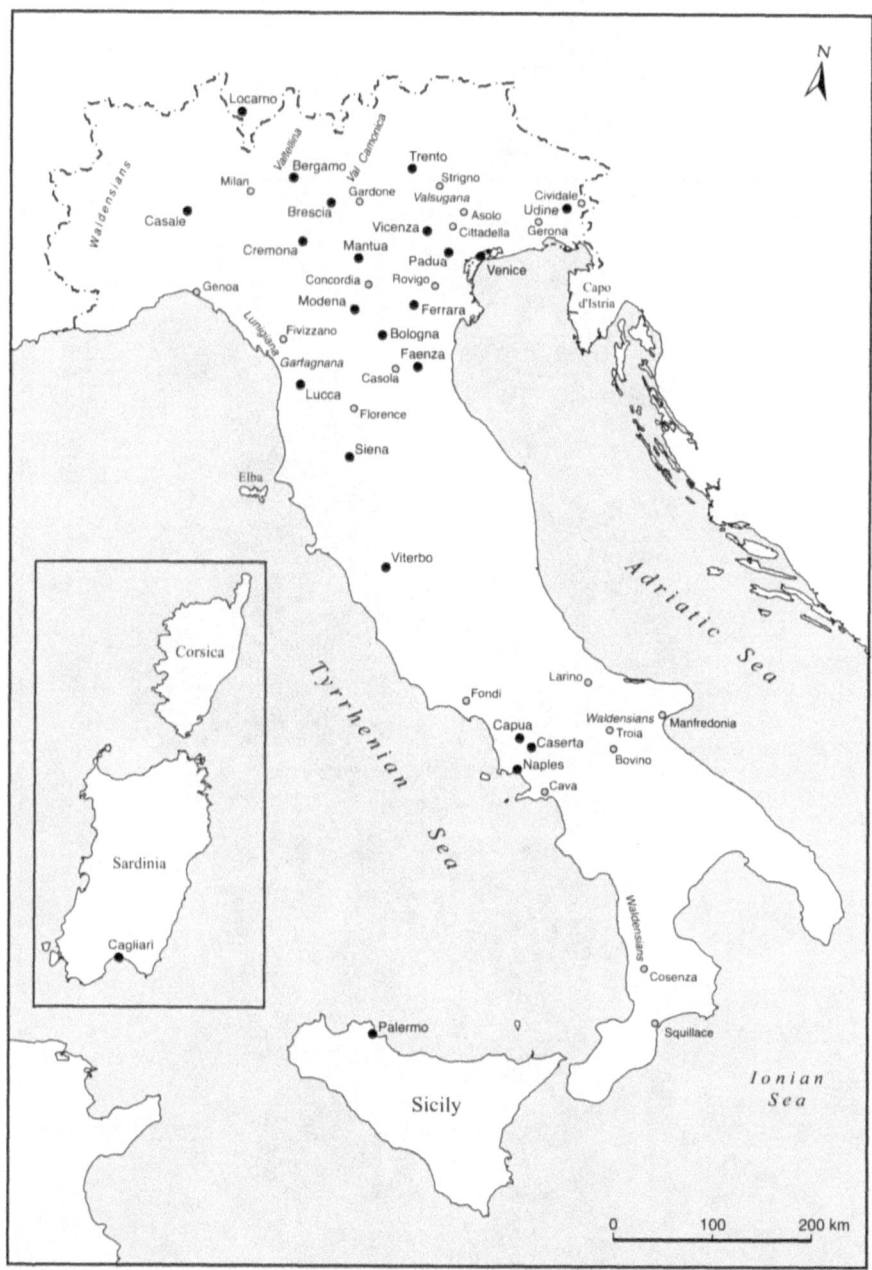

Map 2: Location of Groups of Protestant Sympathisers, 1530s–50s (• main centers ○ smaller groups)

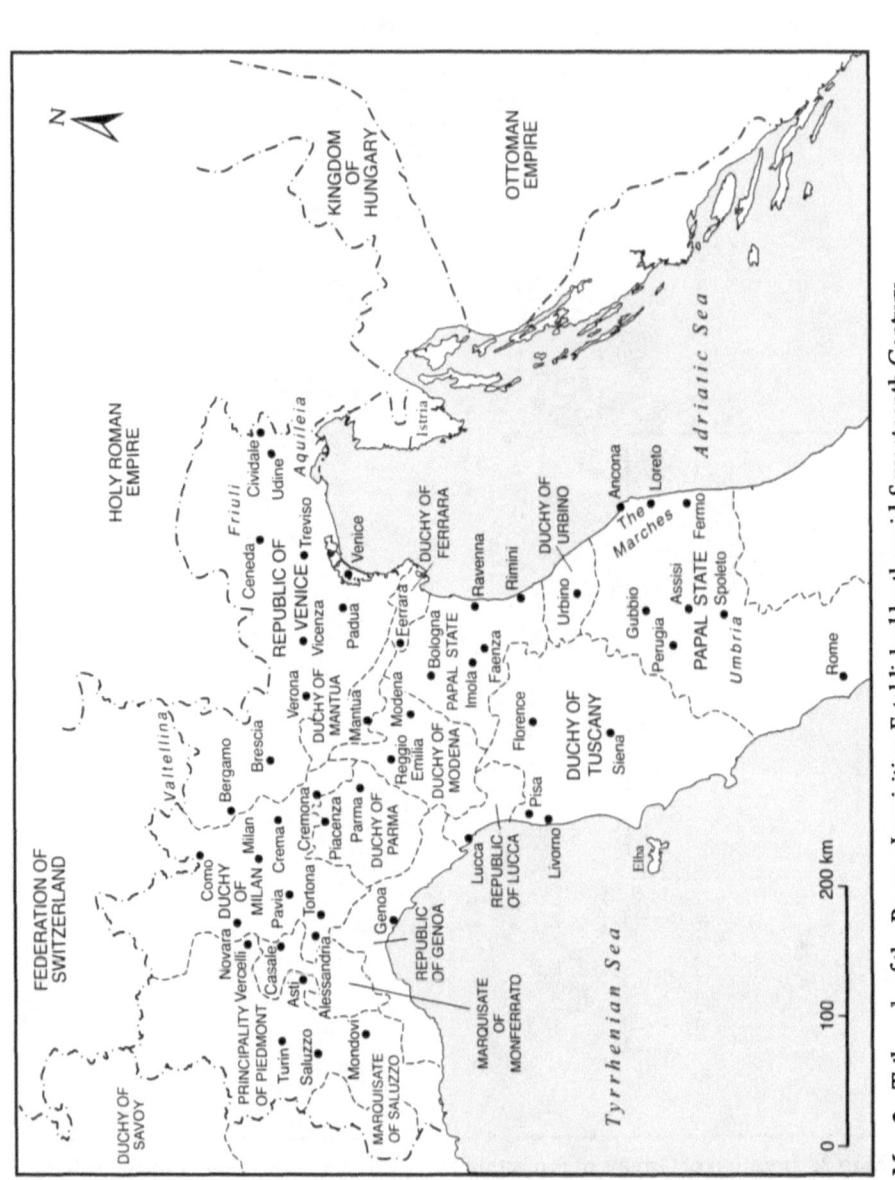

Map 3: Tribunals of the Roman Inquisition Established by the mid-Seventeenth Century

CHAPTER 1

THE ESTABLISHMENT OF THE ROMAN INQUISITION IN 1542

THROUGHOUT THE MIDDLE AGES INQUISITORS HAD BEEN PERIODICALLY appointed to deal with particular heresies in confined areas of Europe. In 1542 Pope Paul III (Alessandro Farnese) decided to have a centrally organised, permanent institution based in Rome, the Holy Office of the Inquisition, to coordinate activity against the growing threat of Protestant heresies within Italy. The immediate background, nature and basic procedures of medieval inquisitions affected the Roman Inquisition's early operations, and attitudes towards local inquisitors. Likewise the new Italian institution was affected by the pre-existing Spanish Inquisition, which partly stimulated the creation of the Roman one. The adverse reputation of the Spanish Inquisition had, and has, influenced views on the Italian Inquisition, even though there were significant differences between their operations, targets and casualties.

The Church faced many religious crises in Italy by the 1530s. Substantial calls for internal reform, building on longstanding anti-clericalism and anti-papalism, had been shown from the 1490s, with Fra Savonarola's movement in Florence (leading to his execution in 1498), the development of the Oratory of Divine Love in Genoa and then Rome, the challenges for reform in the 1511 Church Council in Pisa, and the Fifth Lateran Council, 1512–17. Theological rethinking, partly anticipating Luther, took place among some Benedictines and, more notably, among some Venetian patricians such as Vincenzo Querini (or Quirini) and Tommaso Giustiniani in the Camaldolese Order, and the future Cardinal Gasparo Contarini with his friend Paolo Giustiniani. Luther's writings and ideas, especially on salvation by faith rather than works, had a gradual influence from 1518, but the threats of northern Protestantism were matched by the impact of the Spaniard Juan de Valdés who had fled to Naples and encouraged a hybrid and eclectic movement, Valdesianism, as discussed below. The combined threats of northern and southern reform groups led to the establishment of the Holy Office under papal leadership.

What Is the Inquisition?

The institutional bodies known as inquisitions derive from the Latin word *inquisitio* meaning 'enquiry'. The word referred to a legal investigative process carried out by a magistrate figure seeking evidence from witnesses. His investigation could start on the basis of an anonymous accusation, or the general reputation (*fama*) of a person. The 'inquisition' might or might not lead to a formal trial, which would feature an encounter between a combative accuser and a defendant before a magistrate and sometimes a jury; in the early medieval period, trials could be conducted with various kinds of ordeals or tests. The inquisitorial kind of investigation was developed in the middle ages by Church courts and ecclesiastical officials, firstly as a replacement for ordeal tests, but then especially from the 1220s and 1230s for formally appointed inquisitors to pursue heretical Cathars as part of their major investigative powers across other jurisdictions. Over the centuries secular courts in many parts of Europe took over the inquisition procedure. The inquisition could be a non-confrontational investigative process, leading to a 'fair' trial or decision-making process. It could also become grossly unfair and unjust when torture was brought into the equation, notably introduced for such issues as heresy and witchcraft when 'witnesses' and other evidence were lacking; it became designed to ensure confessions, and the naming of accomplices or teachers of heresy.[1]

The use of a non-combative *inquisitio* in the early modern period has been highlighted in a recent study of the procedures of the Venetian tribunal of the Avogaria di Comune, when testing whether certain women were suitable for marriage into the elite noble class. In secular adaptations of inquisitorial procedure, as in Tuscany, an accuser played a more active role than the judge, who was more an arbiter than the inquisition judge.[2]

The inquisitorial trial method was developed while attempting to defeat the Cathars' heresies. 'Heresy' (Greek *hairesis*) had meant simply the choice of doctrines different from those of the main Church, either through rejection of it or through proposing a new doctrine not yet approved. In the western Church this came to be seen as both sin and crime, meriting serious punishment. The Cathars, originating in Bulgaria as a branch of the Bogomils (a dualist sect) from the tenth century, became the most feared heretics in the west, because they appeared as an alternative organised Church, founded on the New Testament but with divergent and dangerous views: for example on reincarnation; the creation of the world by an evil force; the belief in adult baptism for only a select few (the *perfetti*, perfect), who would give up property, sexual relations and most foods. Such threats to the western Church deserved intense prosecution, with torture needed in the absence of 'witnesses'.

Canon and civil lawyers gave varied opinions as to whether civil or religious leaders should have the prime responsibility for eradicating such heresies. Facing perceived reluctance by princes to curb heretics, from 1198 the Church under Pope Innocent III took fuller control, through bishops, with or without the backing of learned friars concentrating on enquiries into heresy – who came to be known as inquisitors. These friars were commissioned by the Pope, and given fullest jurisdictional powers in the target area allocated to them. The Order of Preachers, or Order of Dominicans (papally recognised in 1217), came to be the preferred source for recruiting inquisitors, thanks to St Dominic Guzman's driving force.[3] The Dominicans received the best theological training. However, Franciscans were also appointed as inquisitors, though their theological and legal training was less intense. Local bishops could also enquire into heresy without benefit of inquisitors (and sometimes resenting the latter as intruders into episcopal duties of pastoral care). The secular arm of princes and city councils was to implement death sentences for the Church (a policy established at the 1215 Lateran Council), but it was also expected to pursue heresies and heretics. This again generated jurisdictional conflicts between Church and State. These divisions between and among those judging and controlling the true faith persisted into the sixteenth century.

The history of the medieval inquisitions is characterised by some excessive zeal in rushing to harsh enquiry, backed by the prompt use of torture to elicit confessions and the names of heretical associates. Although an *inquisitio* was supposed to be triggered by an outside accusation, or denunciation by unforced witnesses, many cases were clearly conducted by pro-active heresy hunters, and triggered by torture-induced allegations. As a foretaste of a reactive, protesting attitude in the sixteenth century, arguing for *inquisitio* by due process, and as an introduction to procedures used later in complex cases, we can cite from a now famous case. In 1599 Domenico Scandella known as Menocchio, a miller (among other activities) from Friuli, was on trial for a second time. He has been made famous by Carlo Ginzburg's book *The Cheese and the Worms*, whose title derives from Menocchio's idea that the earth had started like fermenting cheese, and angels and men emerged from it like worms. Besides his strange cosmological theories challenging divine creationism, Menocchio had at various times questioned the Trinity, the sacraments, ecclesiastical authority, had possessed or borrowed prohibited books and had an Italian vernacular Bible without licence.[4] Towards the end of his second trial he asked for a defence lawyer. Unable to finance one of his own choice, he was allocated a court lawyer, Dr Agostino Pisenti, who provided a stalwart defence based on legal texts and the Bible. He sought to stress to the inquisitor Girolamo Asteo of Pordenone the fundamental nature of 'inquisition':

> In criminal cases one proceeds either through inquisition or accusation. If through the former, which is adopted to cleanse cities of evil men, the judge can proceed when he receives strong information from honest people who are not in themselves under suspicion, ... [I]f the judge becomes aware of a crime, he should not proceed against it until a denunciation and claim of defamation should arise against it. 'No one is ever condemned without an accuser, according to a saying by our Lord: "If no one accuses you woman, nor will I condemn you"'

[John: 8.3]. . . . But where there has been no denunciation, the judges should abstain from investigating, except in the case of grievous crimes. One should not investigate frivolous cases because then we would be prosecuting peccadilloes rather than crimes and God condemns those mean judges who investigate improperly. . . . In the trial formed by the Holy Office of the Inquisition against the aforesaid Domenico, nowhere is any proof adduced by any denouncer substantiated by the word of a least two witnesses . . .[5]

Pisenti was valiantly trying a purist legal line to undermine the validity of this particular trial. Medieval churchmen considered 'heresy' as more than a peccadillo, and it often was difficult to secure witnesses. In part the procedures of the post-1542 Roman Inquisition, backed by new written manuals, were reverting to a more legalistic framework as desired here by Pisenti. Inquisitors tried to ensure that accusers were not malicious but honest, that evidence or opinion was corroborated, and that justice was tempered with mercy. After Menocchio's first trial in 1583–4, he abjured, was fairly mildly punished (despite been judged a heresiarch, a dangerous teacher of heresy) and soon allowed back into the community. Denounced as relapsed, and allegedly continuing to teach or influence others with heretical beliefs, he was deemed by the Franciscan inquisitor Fra Asteo as more dangerous than Pisenti claimed. Contrary to a previous interpretation Friulian officials were not inclined to be lenient now, and he was condemned to death in August 1599. The Holy Office in Rome apparently was not consulted over the sentence, being informed after the event, noting simply that he was a relapsed heretic, and thus consigned to the secular authorities. Variations in conducting the *inquisitio*, and clashes of views, will become obvious as this book progresses.

The Medieval Inquisition: Prelude to the 1542 Roman Inquisition

This book is not concerned with the long history of the medieval Inquisition, but some information and comments on the situation in the last century or so before the Roman Inquisition should help our understanding of the latter's evolution, and the extent of continuity and discontinuity between the Inquisitions. The period of the second half of the fifteenth century has been rather neglected in Italian inquisition studies, based on an assumption that the earlier assaults on Cathars and Waldensians (followers from 1173 of the merchant Waldo, or Waldes, of Lyon, dedicated to apostolic poverty and vernacular Bible reading), who had infiltrated Italy, had proved 'successful'. However the Waldensians still thrived. We know some witch-hunting took place (under ecclesiastical and secular judges). Given archival destructions of many kinds, few records survive concerning actual inquisition trials. Modena provided the only significant exception, with cases surviving from 1495–1500 and 1517–23, some of which have been fruitfully studied. The records for a thorough investigation of six female witches (*masche*) in Rifreddo and Gambasca (near Saluzzo) present the stereotypical concept of witches who have sex with the Devil, embark on missions to do harm, perform dances and so forth.[6]

Recently, light has been shone on the Dominican inquisitors in northern Italy in the later fifteenth and early sixteenth centuries, profiling about a hundred who served as inquisitors between 1474 and 1527.[7] Franciscans were appointed as inquisitors in some areas, notably in the Veneto, but these cases remain hazy. The northern Italian Dominicans were initially attached to three provinces: the 'conventuals' in the Provinces of St Peter Martyr and St Dominic, the reformed Observants in the Congregation of Lombardy (created 1459). Inquisitors were appointed from all three provinces, but steadily the Congregation of Lombardy came to dominate. The number of inquisitorial districts grew, but with constant reconfigurations, notably to fit political boundaries. The appointment of inquisitors before 1542 was largely the responsibility of the provincial ministers, or Generals of the Dominican and Franciscan Orders (though occasionally the Pope might make a personal appointment). Once appointed the inquisitors received their powers by papal authority, and were responsible to the Pope rather than the nominating Order. This nominating procedure continued in some places after 1542, despite the Congregation of Cardinals having the chief nominating responsibility.[8] Pre-1542 inquisitors were not single-minded inquisitorial practitioners, but often multi-tasking members of the Dominican Order. Some held the title of inquisitor for many years but were busy on many other duties, and little or nothing is known of their own inquisitorial activities. Profiles of those appointed inquisitors indicate their education (crucially, in academically lively Bologna and Pavia), their moves around convents, their office-holdings, teaching posts, periods as priors and provincials (heads of a religious Order in a province), as Master of the Sacred Palace (*Maestro del Sacro Palazzo*) in the Vatican, Rome, and their writings. For many, being named as inquisitor seems part of a career move, or a recognition of other roles, and practising as an inquisitor was a minor activity – if active at all. A few can be shown to have been directly or indirectly influential through inquisitorial vicars in brutal witch-hunting, especially in the Alpine valleys.

Michael Tavuzzi argues that the earlier conventual inquisitors, often appointed to their native areas, knew local non-diabolic magic practitioners, and were fairly lenient towards them. The development of the reformed Observant Congregation of Lombardy, which appointed inquisitors of wider experience and education – changing from 'deferential courtiers to dogged constables'[9] – was the catalyst for more dire persecutions, as diabolic aspects became more widely suspected. Inquisitors' experiences of investigations and confessions led to (rather than being derived from) theories, tracts and subsequent trial assumptions, as found in

Silvestro Mazzolini's *De Strigimagarum daemonumque mirandis* (1520) or inquisitorial vicar (in Modena) Bartolomeo Spina's *Quaestio de strigibus* (1523). We witness a growing 'professionalisation' of inquisitors, feeding into the post-1542 Roman Inquisition. This contributed to a greater scepticism about witchcraft allegations.

Despite limited surviving evidence Tavuzzi provides a useful picture of inquisitorial activity against Waldensians, Judaisers and particularly witches. Pressures to persecute Waldensians largely came from political rulers, for example from Saluzzo and Monferrato, and Duchess Iolanda of Savoy in 1476, who were ready to deploy soldiers. Inquisitors often followed lukewarmly, as they did over Judaisers in Genoa in the 1490s when the city panicked over the influx of Marranos (converts from Judaism or Islam) fleeing Spain. In contrast some inquisitors vigorously persecuted witches either directly or by superintending vicars: notably Niccolò Constantini who covered the regions of Vercelli, Ivrea and Novara between 1460 and 1483, and was allegedly responsible for the burning of 300 male and female witches; his successor from 1483 to 1505, Lorenzo Soleri, whose witch-hunting experiences at Bormio in the Valtellina supposedly informed Heinrich Kramer's notorious anti-witch book, the *Malleus Maleficarum* (1486); and Girolamo da Lodi, inquisitor of Brescia from 1518 to 1526, whose campaigns in the Val Camonica between 1518 and 1521 aroused the ire of secular officials in Brescia and Venice. Tavuzzi's *Renaissance Inquisitors*, Appendix 2, provides a grim calendar of witch persecutions and burnings. Some inquisitors like Constantini, or Modesto Scrofa for Como in the 1520s, blatantly disregarded judicial procedure and constantly used torture, as did many others. In one campaign at Sondrio in the Valtellina, between August and September 1523, Scrofa seems to have organised thirty-four trials. He routinely used torture, which evinced confessions conforming to diabolic witchcraft stereotypes, leading to the burning of at least six witches and much confiscation of property. A local chronicler condemned Scrofa for greed, which eventually led to his expulsion by Sondrio's secular authorities. However one of his vicars (a local man) continued with at least one case, condemning a male witch to death.[10]

We sometimes know more about active inquisitorial vicars, and other clergy, when they pursued alleged witches. Facing a particular perceived crisis over witches, many vicars might be employed; from eight to ten were used by the Inquisitor of Como in the 1520s for witch-hunting. Such vicars were not necessarily Dominicans but might be recruited from local secular clergy, after some legal training.[11] Their persecuting enthusiasm, fuelled by confessions derived from torture, could lead to local opposition. The inquisitorial vicars involved in a well-known persecution in the Val Camonica between 1518 and 1521 incurred opposition from Brescian and Venetian lay authorities. The *podestà* (civil judge) of Brescia, Giovanni Badoer, wrote to the Venetian Council of Ten about the Dominican inquisitors and their vicars:

> They are, to speak frankly, overdressed peasants (*rustici trasvestiti*), who have devoured their shame, as well as their conscience. I say this of the greater part of those who are here, and this because the decent friars don't want to come to this city, knowing that they are looked upon worse than Jews on account of their squabblings and bad behaviour. . . . On account of their friars' cloaks, they permit themselves every enormous and nefarious crime . . . confident that the laity and the temporal lords, as they claim, have no jurisdiction over them.[12]

The Venetian government eventually stopped this persecution, which had been instigated by inquisitor Girolamo da Lodi, appointed in 1518. It followed earlier persecutions in the Val Camonica (as in 1485–7, and in 1510–11 under the more famous inquisitor Silvestro Mazzolini da Prierio [called Prierias], who was to publish on witch hunting). Albanians were blamed for importing witch practices and introducing sabbats. Initially the Bishop of Brescia, Paolo Zane, backed Girolamo da Lodi and vicar Lorenzo Maggi. The bishop provided his own clergy to assist during the first persecutions in 1518, when his diocesan team appeared more zealous than the Dominicans. The casualty figures were disputed at the time: Badoer estimated sixty-two executions (forty of them women), while the famous Venetian diarist Marino Sanudo, who copied much of the documentation, calculated sixty-six (fifty-six of them women). Interventions and enquiries came from the papal nuncio, from other bishops as papal commissioners, but more trials took place until 1521 when Venice called a halt.[13]

Brescian hostility to Dominicans had a wider context. In the late fifteenth and early sixteenth centuries civic and secular religious pride meant Brescians contested Venetian political control and clerical domination. In 1505 a major internal dispute erupted over the expense and organisation of funerals. A statute to control expenditure jeopardised the income, and pride, of the Dominican convent, which threatened to refuse absolution to those observing the statute. In a war of words an anonymous humanist pamphlet, *Defensio statuti Brixianorum de ambitione et sumptibus funerum minuendis* (*A defence of the Brescians' statute for reducing the rivalry and the expense of funerals*) appeared (recently tentatively attributed to Elia Capriolo, a local pious nobleman). This *Defensio* produced a powerful condemnation of Dominican behaviour, greed, lack of true Christian values, whether over alms or funerals; but it also attacked their long-standing assaults on supposed witchcraft, especially in the Val Camonica, where they tortured, terrorised and demonised old women. When the city tried to curb one aspect of Dominican greed, it was argued, the Dominicans resorted to using papal powers to bully the city:

... in order to satisfy your uncontrollable lusts, frightening a people of pure and simple faith, who fear God and the Church, with all the dreadful bogies of excommunication. Your aim is that this terror may shock them into casting themselves and everything they own at the feet of you greedy and haughty people, who give yourselves such airs by using a certain title of the Inquisition – a title weighty in itself, and rightly established by our forebears long ago, but now weak and hollow thanks to you – or rather, lucrative, for according to popular gossip you use it for profit. You use the office (such is your vanity and pride) almost as a kingdom and, lest it lie idle, you seize from the Valcamonica certain old women who are stupid and frozen in a kind of mental daze, and you interrogate them about their faith, the Trinity, and other such topics. You bring in scribes and drag out proceedings; you conduct examinations under torture so that, by inflicting pain and torment on women who are admittedly little different from brutish beasts, you may appear as guardians of the Christian faith.[14]

The local Dominicans did not bow to this attack, as the later events just cited indicate. The post-1542 Roman Inquisition had to face up to such reputations of the Dominicans – who were still deemed the best providers of inquisitors – and so assert more control from Rome.

Dominican witch-hunting caused a stir elsewhere. When Antonio da Casale was inquisitor for Parma and Reggio (1508–13), he struggled to bring about the burning of witch Lucia Cacciarda in 1510 (opposed by the *podestà* and bishop's vicar), but with the French Governor of Lombardy's support he finally succeeded with a *live* burning, deemed unprecedented in recent memory. As inquisitor in Como (1513–15) he had thirty heretics, presumed witches, burned. When Girolamo Armellini da Faenza was inquisitor for Parma and Reggio province (1518–26), he became involved in hunting witches in Mirandola (1522–3), alerted by the lord, Giovanni Francesco Pico, to supposed large witch gatherings on the Secchia river bank. A 'lascivious old priest' was burned in late 1522, and at least six persons in 1523. When Pico's subjects protested he wrote a Latin tract in defence of his and the inquisitor's actions; this was translated and published (as *Libro della Stregha*) in 1524 by the Dominican historian and humanist Leandro Alberti.

Alberti was to become inquisitor in Bologna from 1544 to 1546 and 1550 to 1551, but he had been involved with the Inquisition there as vicar or censoring consultant since at least 1533; he thus provided continuity between the old and new inquisitional systems. He had been taught theology in Bologna by Giorgio Cacatossici da Casale, who at various stages between 1502 and 1515 was an active inquisitor in Cremona, Piacenza, Crema, Bergamo and Brescia; Cacatossici evinced particular alarm at the prevalence of witchcraft in Cremona and Piacenza, and met strong opposition from local clergy and laity who considered such cases beyond the legal competence of inquisitors. Alberti had some sympathy for Dominican supporters of Girolamo Savonarola in Mirandola and Bologna, and signs of support appeared for the mood of the popular but soon banned *Beneficio di Cristo* (1543, *Benefit of Christ*), to which his friend Marcantonio Flaminio had contributed. Alberti found time to write histories of Bologna and a major *Description* of Italy (*Descrittione di tutta Italia*, 1550) based on extensive travels (1525–8) through the whole peninsula. This book was the focus of a major conference in 2004, making Alberti one of the most studied inquisitors of the period because of his all-round contributions.[15] Paolo Giovio showed mixed feelings about this ambivalent inquisitor, privately referring to him in 1543 as *'dolce cosmografo e brusco inquisitore'* ('good-natured cosmographer and harsh inquisitor').[16] Silvestro Mazzolini da Priero had been another influential and, according to Alberti, entertaining teacher. These influences may have bolstered Alberti to become a forceful inquisitor in his turn, but he seemingly shifted from witch-hunting to the more serious problem of theological reform heresies, including those of the Anabaptist leader Pietro Manelfi, whose confession he received.[17] The complexity of interests and attitudes of these men helps explain the ambivalent, sometimes emollient, inquisitorial approaches to the more learned sympathisers of the new theological debates.

The above 'medieval' examples are variously relevant for what will be said about the Roman Inquisition. Witch-hunting leading to death sentences declined considerably under the new post-1542 system. Obviously this was affected by changing fears, of Lutheranism, Valdesianism and Calvinism. Unlike most of the aforementioned medieval inquisitors, those under the Roman Inquisition were centrally appointed and kept under supervision by the popes and cardinals as the Congregation of the Holy Office developed. The local inquisitors were now appointed essentially for inquisitorial activity, serving full time as long as they held the office. Torture was not often used, and officially it required sanction from Rome. Manuals counselled scepticism about denunciations (which might derive from malice), and about claims of actual diabolic intervention. The new inquisitors, especially Dominicans, had to combat the reputation for cruelty, corruption and anti-episcopacy of some of their predecessors.

The Spanish Inquisition

Spain produced the first of the 'modern' Inquisitions, a centralised and permanent organisation in contrast to the local episcopal *ad hoc* organisations. The foundations were laid between 1478 and 1480.[18] The 'Catholic Kings', Ferdinand of Aragon and Isabella of Castile, uniting their two major kingdoms in Iberia in 1469 with other dependent territories such as Sicily and Sardinia, were intent on ensuring the Christian reconquest over the Jewish and Muslim religions. Pressures were exerted for Jews to convert to Christianity, but then concerns arose over the sincerity of converts, and possible treasonable subversion of royal power. The old inquisitorial localised activity could not cope. The Dominican prior of Seville, Alonso de Hojeda, persuaded the royal couple that only a permanent Inquisition could control the threats posed by Jews and heretical converts. A papal Bull from Sixtus IV on 1 November 1478 sanctioned the appointment of inquisitors on a long-term basis, and gave the Spanish Crown the power to appoint and dismiss future inquisitors. By September 1480 Dominican inquisitors were commissioned under these new rules, and the modern Spanish Inquisition was essentially established. Gradually tribunals were created in different parts of Castile and Aragon. Their spread through Castile was bitterly opposed by many. In 1488 a new Council for Castile, the *Suprema*, was created as a coordinating body, with an Inquisitor-General as president. The first Inquisitor-General, already appointed in 1483 for Aragon, Valencia and Catalonia, was the notable and notorious Fray Tomás de Torquemada. The development of the Spanish Inquisition on the Spanish mainland, however, is not the concern of this book. It should be emphasised that the Spanish Inquisition was responsible to the Crown, was in essence a department of State; the popes had very limited control or influence, and Sixtus IV soon regretted the extent of the powers he had delegated over heresy. Already in April 1482 he had complained in a Bull of the inquisitors' abuses of power, cruelties, unjustified imprisonment, torture – motivated by greed not 'zeal for the faith and the salvation of souls'.[19] But it was too late; the papacy never regained control or a moderating influence.

The early decades of inquisitional activity in Spain were undoubtedly brutal. The first *auto da fé*, which involved the burning at the stake of six persons, took place on 6 February 1481. Alonso de Hojeda was the leading preacher, and he set a precedent for a long history of such assertions of the faith being thus defended. Hojeda died soon after in a plague epidemic.[20] The expulsion from 1492 of Jews who would not convert to Christianity and be designated *conversos*, and the subsequent hounding of *conversos* to ensure they did not relapse, created huge social tensions, especially in urban areas. Advantage was taken by old Christians, led by landed aristocrats, to persecute or undermine urban aristocrats and their supporters who had often had links with Jews in past centuries. Many communities and political forces opposed the inquisitional activities, and intrusions into other jurisdictions, which at times created conditions of civil war. Eventually by the 1530s and 1540s the Spanish inquisitional system settled down to being a more controlled organisation, with greater attention to due legal processes. The notoriety of this grim period resonated outside Spain, and encouraged the resistance to the creation of Spanish-linked tribunals in

Lombardy and the Kingdom of Naples when Spain's political control of them was ratified in the 1559 Treaty of Cateau-Cambrésis (see Map 1).

Inquisition tribunals were established in Sicily (1487) and Sardinia (1492) as part of the Aragonese Crown, and Torquemada named the inquisitors, though with limited recorded action at first. Sicilian leaders hotly protested against the 1492 order to expel Jews.[21] The Sicilian and Sardinian inquisitors came under the control of the *Suprema*, receiving orders from there until the eighteenth century. Arguably, however, there was a little more influence from Rome than on the Iberian mainland, directly or through bishops.

The prior establishment of the Spanish Inquisition affected that of the Roman Inquisition. It inspired Gian Pietro Carafa (later Pope Paul IV) after diplomatic experiences in Spain, to promote a forceful centralised Inquisition based in Rome. But Pope Paul III and others were determined not to lose control to secular princes or republican governments, as in Spain. Fear of persecution in Spain drove various reform-minded Spaniards to head for Naples, notably Juan de Valdés who helped promote an Italian hybrid reform movement.

The New Heresies and Early Attempts to Combat them in Italy[22]

From the 1490s Italy was enlivened and challenged by many proponents of religious reform, whether in terms of theology, of philanthropy, or opposition to moral corruption. Some of this was generated by the French invasion of Italy in 1494 when Charles VIII tried to establish a claim to the Kingdom of Naples against the Spanish. Italy faced international war intermittently until the Cateau-Cambrésis peace settlement of 1559, when Spain under Philip II was recognised as ruler in the Kingdom of Naples, Lombardy, Sicily and Sardinia. The disruptions of war, with major impacts on civilian populations (coupled with plagues and epidemic diseases, including syphilis), posed challenges to be met by lay men and women, and clerics, in new philanthropic measures especially to assist orphans, children and women in danger, and victims of syphilis. The psychological effects of political and physical upheaval provoked more fundamental religious thinking, coupled with anticlerical opposition to corrupt Church leaders, as seen in the example of Fra Savonarola in Florence (burned at the stake in 1498, though more for political than theological reasons) and his Dominican followers. The Sack of Rome in 1527 by imperial troops also generated religious angst and rethinking. The Ottoman Turks posed threats and challenges, with Sultan Suleyman seriously contemplating seizing Rome and organising raids on the southern Italian coast. The Ottoman threat distracted the Papacy and the Holy Roman Emperor Charles V from confronting Luther and Zwingli, and the northern Reformation.

At the turn of the fifteenth and sixteenth centuries various individuals and groups within Italy were involved in analysing both conventional theological positions (by rethinking St Paul's teachings and St Augustine's interpretations) and the state of the Church and authority, linked to failures of leadership. Issues of salvation by faith and works, of concepts of predestination and of the active and the passive life, were under discussion, as among Venetian patricians such as Tommaso Giustiniani, Vincenzo Querini and friends. Their Church reform ideas entered the public domain when these two named figures composed a *Libellus ad Leonem X* for the fraught Lateran Council of 1513. More quietly issues of salvation were aired, as by their associate Gasparo Contarini. The humanist atmosphere by the 1490s, notably in Florence, Venice, Padua and Naples, had produced considerable philosophical and religious intermingling of challenging ideas, debates about Neo-Platonism, new approaches to Aristotle (as more Greek texts became available) and a rethinking of St Augustine. Classical textual criticism fostered biblical textual criticism. Italians came to lead the way in producing vernacular translations of the Bible, especially that of Antonio Brucioli (who published in instalments until he finished his work in 1551).

This atmosphere was conducive to a reception in Italy of Erasmus' work, and of his contacts, after he visited Venice first in 1508. However, Erasmus became better known in Italy only after Luther had made his mark, Italian translations of Luther's writings appearing from 1518. The impact of Luther can be detected as early as 1523 in correspondence between Gasparo Contarini and Paolo Giustiniani especially over the issue of justification.[23] Contarini and his circle interacted with, and influenced members of, the Benedictine Cassinese congregation, such as Gregorio Cortese, Teofilo Folengo and Isidoro Chiari, who were rethinking St Paul's teachings in various ways. Influenced also by Lutheran views was Marcantonio Flaminio, a member of the Oratory of Divine Love that had grown from the 1490s (in Genoa, then Rome) as a philanthropic confraternity promoting good works, asceticism, but also frequency of communion. While Flaminio headed towards the Protestant reform movements, others of the Oratory helped the growth of Catholic reform movements and new Orders like the Theatines, with which the theologically conservative or 'intransigent' Gian Pietro Carafa was associated.[24] Debates over theology and practical moral reform so generated in Italy pointed in many directions.

'Lutheran' ideas were increasingly debated in Italy in the 1520s and 1530s, though not necessarily with a deep knowledge of Luther's actual writings. Erasmus and then Philip Melanchthon were better known by then, and their works were more likely to be unearthed in later decades in the hunts for prohibited books. But the audience in 1528 for the Venetian dramatist Ruzzante's Carnival play *La Moscheta* knew that Luther had stirred up debate over free will and predestination, in conflict with Erasmus.[25] A crucial disseminator of new ideas was the *Sommario della Sacra Scrittura*, a digest of Lutheran ideas, originally produced in the Netherlands. Its Italian translation (probably first in Genoa in 1534, with at least six editions to follow) popularised the doctrine of salvation by faith. It was a casualty of the burning of Lutheran books in the Piazza Maggiore of Bologna on 31 March 1538, to which Alberti, then attached to the Dominican convent there, may have contributed.[26]

The new ideas were propagated at two main levels, in two ways. Among the elite, letters, poems, exchange of texts and personal contacts spread the debate; while a wider audience listened to preachers who, in a long tradition of public preaching about social and moral reform, insinuated Lutheran concepts of faith and salvation. To add to the northern influences of Erasmus and Luther was the impact in the 1530s of Juan de Valdés as an exile from Spain. He was the brother of Alfonso de Valdés, secretary to Charles V, and had absorbed Erasmian ideas when studying at the university of Alcalá de Henares, when Erasmus was still favoured at court. Juan had also absorbed various Spanish mystical ideas, especially from Pedro Ruiz de Alcaraz. In 1529 Valdés published a kind of catechism, *Diálogo de doctrina cristiana*, which also cited Luther's work.[27] Spanish opinion turned against Luther, then Erasmus, and alleged *converso* influences on the mystical, *alumbrado*, traditions and approaches to God (the spirit will help reveal the divine secrets hidden in the Bible, and assist a closer direct relationship with God). Juan de Valdés avoided the Spanish Inquisition by fleeing to Rome, and then to Naples.

Valdés attracted many supporters, personally and through manuscripts that were circulated, until his death in 1541. His *Alfabeto cristiano* (Venice 1545), possibly co-authored by Giulia Gonzaga, was probably his most important work. The Valdesians combined teachings from Erasmus, Luther and Calvin, Spanish mystical contemplation, and added native Italian glosses, pointing in different directions that could lead to minor suspicions or accusations of serious heresy. The Valdesian influences on the Italian intellectual and cultural world, clerical and secular, were considerable. Reforming bishops might warm to Erasmian scholarly criticism and Lutheran or Calvinist approaches to justification by faith, but be warier about undermining clerical authority and pastoral leadership. Among those influenced by Valdesianism who will appear in this book as under threat from the Inquisition we should name Bernardino Ochino, the Capuchin General and astounding preacher who fled in 1542 to Switzerland, like Pier Martire Vermigli (a Lateran canon regular, who later appeared in England as Peter Martyr). Those who remained in Italy and came under investigation with varying fortunes included: Pietro Carnesecchi, Giulia Gonzaga, Mario Galeotta, Bishop Vittore Soranzo of Bergamo, Archbishop Pietro Antonio di Capua of Otranto. Reginald Pole, later Cardinal in England, twice deemed likely to be elected Pope – and also close to trial by the Inquisition on the eve of his death, thanks to Cardinal Carafa's fears – assisted the spread of Valdesian ideas when based in Viterbo. His friends included the great painter and sculptor Michelangelo Buonarroti and the poet Vittoria Colonna (who also was to attract close attention from the new Inquisition).[28]

Marcantonio Flaminio, who had become part of Pole's group in Viterbo, joined the Benedictine Benedetto Fontantini da Mantova (an admirer of Valdés' *Alfabeto cristiano*), and revised a draft text by Benedetto to produce in 1543 the *Beneficio di Cristo*, which counts as the bestseller of the Italian Reformation. This text expounded the doctrines of justification by faith and of predestination, bringing in some ideas from Calvin's *Institutio christianae religionis*.[29] Essentially a product of the Viterbo circle – or 'a collective effort with deep and broad roots'[30] – the publication of *Beneficio di Cristo* was probably promoted by cardinals Pole and Morone. While modern scholars have debated with some verve and acrimony about the influences on this book, especially from Calvin, it seems best to take it as a product of Italian reform thinking that could borrow from pre-Lutheran spiritual reform and self-criticism, Luther, Valdés (as debated within Italian circles) and Calvin. It illustrates the non-dogmatic open-mindedness or eclecticism of many Italians interested in religious reform. The unwillingness to commit completely to one new school of reform – for which Calvin was to castigate Italians who fled to Geneva as well as those who remained in Italy as dissimulating and cowardly Nicodemists – helps explain why Italian states did not produce a successful 'Italian Reformation'. Initially the *Beneficio* seemed favoured as an acceptable response to the Protestant reformers as well as meeting perceived Italian needs; tens of thousands of copies were printed within a few years. However with later editions by 1547, and with the Tridentine decree *De justificatione* effectively ending a doctrinal compromise with Lutheranism, it was seen as the chief propaganda work for 'Lutheranism'. The book was hunted by inquisitors, who engaged in strenuous efforts to remove copies from bookshops, libraries – conventual and private – until it was seemingly eliminated by the mid-seventeenth century, and so deemed a 'success' for the censors. Possession of this book was used in many trials through to the seventeenth century as a proof of heretical inclinations.

By the early 1540s in Italy, Church reform ideas that might prove heretical in terms of traditional Catholic teaching had been selectively taken up by significant groups at different levels of society. The intransigents such as Cardinal Gian Pietro Carafa faced the challenges they posed by creating a permanent, centralised Inquisition. Crucially (in terms of implementing the Inquisition as well as curbing proselytising), powerful ecclesiasts were interested in, and partial promoters of, new heterodox ideas, without necessarily wanting a break with papal authority and the creation of a new Church. These included the already mentioned cardinals Pole and Morone; Cardinal Prince Bishop of Trent

Cristoforo Madruzzo, Patriarch of Aquileia Giovanni Grimani, cardinals Ercole Gonzaga and Pietro Bembo; bishops (or soon to be bishops) Vittore Soranzo (Bergamo), Pietro Antonio di Capua (Otranto), Pier Paolo Vergerio (Capodistria), Giacomo Nacchianti (Chioggia) and Giovanni Tommaso Sanfelice (Cava dei Tirreni);[31] leaders of religious Orders such as the Augustinian Girolamo Seripando, the Benedictine Gregorio Cortese, the Dominican Tommaso Badia. They were joined by leading nobles and patricians who could protect religious dissenters and impede inquisitorial activity, among them members of great Roman families like Ascanio Colonna and Camillo Orsini; Vittoria Colonna as a sponsor in Rome and Viterbo; Galeazzo Caracciolo, marchese di Vico; Giulia and Eleonora Gonzaga (away from the Gonzaga home base of Mantua); Giovanni Rangone, a noble in Mantua; Giovan Andrea Ugoni in Brescia. Patrician families in Modena that also made that city a centre of reform debate included the Carandini, Molza and Sadoleto, and the city's notable Accademia. In Lucca similar roles were played by the Burlamacchi and Balbani. Valdesianism was spread through the Kingdom of Naples by baronial families as in Capua, Cava, Caserta, Larino and little Puglian enclaves.[32]

Venice had in some respects paved the way for Luther in quiet theological debate thanks to Vincenzo Querini and patrician associates, but given its cosmopolitan trading position and its centrality in the new printing industry, the debates were taken up by merchants, clergy, artisans and artists – as with groups around the painter Lorenzo Lotto and the goldsmith/poet Alessandro Caravia.[33] Other key places within the Republic's territory that by the 1540s had revealed Protestant-inclined groupings included Bergamo, Padua, Rovigo, Udine and Vicenza. Besides these cities, those that were seen as most 'infected' by the 1540s, with reform spreading right down the social order to artisans' groups, included Siena, the target of Bernardino Ochino's preaching (1537–40); Bologna, where Martin Bucer's influence was added to Erasmus' in the early 1530s. Ochino had 'infected' Sicily by preaching there on 'the benefit of Christ' in 1539–40. Parts of Calabria and Puglia had retained allegiance to the old medieval Waldensian heresy. In 1532 some leaders from there met northern Waldensians in Chanforan (Angrogna valley), and made common cause with the Genevan followers of Guillaume Farel. The real alarm about the spread of these ideas was not to come, however, until the 1560s. All this indicates the extent to which interest in Lutheran, Calvinist and Valdesian ideas had spread, and were apparent in the early 1540s when the Roman Inquisition was established in response to Cardinal Carafa's call to action. By the mid-1550s the geographical distribution of supposed heresies was even greater (see Map 2).

Local inquisitors (Italian and Spanish), bishops and some secular authorities had already taken some action against the new heretics. As propagators of

Lutheran ideas in sermons, Augustinians were among the first to be processed, such as Fra Geremia da Tripedi in Palermo in 1529, followed by Alessio Casani da Fivizzano in Florence, imprisoned in 1530 but pardoned by Pope Clement VII. According to his own memoirs Fra Alessio had been given a chest filled with fifty 'Lutheran' books by his superior Agostino da Fivizzano, who had studied in Paris in the 1520s. Possibly the most notable of these Augustinian preachers was Giulio della Rovere (or da Milano), who was tried in Venice in 1541 after his Lenten sermons hinged on *sola fede, sola gratia* and *sola Scriptura*. He underwent a long investigation by the nuncio Giorgio Andreassi, the inquisitor Fra Paolo Filomella da Venezia and the Patriarch's Dominican delegate Fra Andriano da Venezia. Rovere was sentenced to a year's imprisonment, but in February supportive patricians helped his escape from prison and flight to the Grisons, where he became a pastor and missionary in the Valtellina until his death in 1581. During the 1530s in Venice the apostolic legate through his auditor and inquisitor had tried a number of suspects including a carpenter, three nobles from Pirani and a friar, Agositino da Treviso (who was pardoned in Rome).[34]

Giovanni Buzio da Montalcino, regent of studies in the friary of San Francesco, had created a scandal in Bologna over free will and predestination, which led to the first *processo* against him in 1538. Although some of his writings were found to be heretical and he was condemned to death, he was sent to Rome on papal orders, and absolved before the Master of the Sacred Palace (the chief of book censorship). Reinvestigated from 1550, he was again condemned to death as a relapsed heretic, and the Pope could not prevent this sentence being carried out in the Campo dei Fiori, Rome, on 4 September 1553.[35]

Cardinal Gian Pietro Carafa and the 1542 Bull

Some other local tribunals such as those at Modena and Venice showed a growing awareness of the threats of new heresies, and took some action. The failure of attempts at reconciliation during the conference at Ratisbon (Regensburg) in Germany in April 1541 created alarm and pushed the more intransigent leaders in Rome to seek coordination between local inquisitors. In July 1541 Paul III gave cardinals Gian Pietro Carafa and Girolamo Aleandro the authority to organise the centralised control of inquisitorial activity. Privileged exemptions of certain laity and clergy from inquisitorial investigation were removed, except for bishops. Cardinal Aleandro's death on 4 July 1542 led Paul III to bring in others to balance the intransigence of Carafa: cardinals Pier Paolo Parisio, Bartolomeo Guidiccioni and Dionisio Lauerio as traditionalists, and cardinals Giovanni Morone and Tommaso Badia as ones more sympathetic to some reform ideas, and ready to consider dialogue with Lutherans and Valdesians. Then on 21 July 1542 the Pope issued the Bull *Licet ab initio* as the basis on which these six cardinals could centralise inquisitorial activity under cardinals in Rome. Morone was taken off this commission to operate in his bishopric of Modena, a scene of much reform debate – and practical reforms of abuses. He was replaced by Juan Alvarez de Toledo, which added the experience and attitudes of a Spanish inquisitor to those already dominant in the hands of Cardinal Carafa, whose diplomatic experience in Spain buttressed his authoritarianism as the prime mover in the Roman Inquisition. Intriguingly, Carafa had initially defended Erasmus against his theological opponents in Louvain, only to become his opponent later.[36]

In the eyes of the Roman authorities the above scenario of controversial ideas on Church reform, whether theological teaching or organisation, spelled major danger that needed addressing by a centrally controlled campaign through a reconstituted Inquisition, as well as episcopal activity. That the Roman Church was seriously endangered, and that an Italian Reformation was narrowly bypassed (thanks to inquisitional authoritarian rigour led by Carafa and later Michele Ghislieri, as Cardinal inquisitors and then popes), might be doubted. As Silvana Seidel Menchi has argued, Italian Protestantism was a 'non-event' and 'marginal phenomenon', to which no state committed itself, whether under a prince or corporate elite (unlike in many German states, England or Scotland). Even in the cities most affected by the new ideas, like Venice or Lucca, only about 0.2 per cent of the population might be fully committed, and only 2 per cent inclined towards Protestantism.[37] Undoubtedly, knowledge of and enthusiasm for new religious ideas would have grown had the inquisitorial system not been developed beyond its 'medieval' structure. Expansion of interest in Protestantism seems to have increased over the first fifteen to twenty years of the Roman Inquisition. But as has been suggested and will be further indicated in the next chapter, competing versions of 'Protestantism' were on offer; and many of those interested were prepared to pick and choose, mix and match. Had that religion been allowed to prevail – especially if 'ecumenical' views on agreeing to differ over salvation by faith, on predestination and on the cult of saints had been accepted – the end result would more likely have been a strengthened and intellectually livelier Roman Church than a Protestant one.

Many dynamic ecclesiastical leaders were attracted by some of the new theological thinking or were ready to tolerate discussions (especially until the sessions of the Council of Trent decided on certain key issues between 1545 and 1563); they included Giovanni Morone, Reginald Pole, Ercole Gonzaga, Vittore Soranzo, Giovanni Grimani, Pietro Bonomo and Pier Paolo Vergerio. Many wanted to reform within the overall Roman structures, to have the theological debates among the well-educated, both clerical and lay people. Some of these leaders of course ended up being prosecuted, or forced to flee like Vergerio. However, others who remained in post were alarmed when popular preachers spread ideas dangerously from pulpits, to have these ideas then discussed in the workshops and taverns of their major cities. This elite attitude divided the reform movement; also it meant that some of these bishops preferred to handle the situation as pastoral leaders (including disciplining preachers), and not have new inquisitors interfering. Many of those interested in Protestant ideas remained discrete, declined to act as leaders or to form solid conventicles. As Giulio da Milano wrote in 1540 ahead of his trial: 'the Christians of Italy are like dead, dispersed limbs without a head, without direction, for the Italian churches are neither congregated nor regulated according to the Word of God.' He attacked others for Nicodemist behaviour, hiding new views under a façade of conformism, and urged martyrdom rather than flight. Given that many Italian 'reformers', especially Valdesians and *spirituali* followers of Pole, agreed with some Lutheran, Melanchthonian or Calvinist ideas but not others, and had hopes of reform within the Roman Church to which they had 'an unfailing will to remain faithful', not 'coming out' is understandable.[38] This lack of serious sect formation made the task of the Papacy and Inquisition easier – though it did not prevent inquisitors avidly questioning, and sometimes torturing, to ascertain the existence of coherent heretical sects.

CHAPTER 2

THE ROMAN HOLY OFFICE AND LOCAL TRIBUNALS

THE ROMAN INQUISITION DATES LEGALLY FROM THE BULL *LICET AB INITIO* issued by Pope Paul III on 21 July 1542. This was in response to several crises over religious belief and discipline in north, central and southern Italy, which were influenced by both 'foreign' (non-Italian) and Italian thinkers, writers and activists, of social levels from artisans upwards. The existence of a centrally organised Inquisition in Spain set precedents. Cardinal Gian Pietro Carafa, who is often seen as the architect of the Roman Inquisition, had had knowledge of the Spanish Inquisition as a diplomat in Spain. As we study the situation in 1542 and subsequently, we find ourselves dealing with 'renewal' and novelty, with continuity and revolution. The language of historians varies considerably over the degree of change and revolution. John Martin has recently added 'refurbishing' and 'revamping' to the descriptive vocabulary.[1]

Although there was little change inherent in the 1542 Bull, by the 1560s and 1570s we have a radically different Inquisition: a centrally organised bureaucratic structure reaching out to most of Italy through official tribunals, or in the Kingdom of Naples through less formal 'medieval' episcopal inquisitors, who nevertheless experienced greater control from Rome. The development of the central organisation was contentious – between hardliners or intransigents, and the more emollient popes and cardinals. The creation of tribunals throughout Italy was seldom smooth, as both bishops and secular rulers showed some distrust. The inquisitions operating in Sicily, Sardinia and Lucca, though not directly part of the Roman Inquisition, are included here for convenience as 'Local Tribunals'. They were not immune from Roman intervention.

The Foundation Bull and Early Activity in Rome

The Bull *Licet ab initio* contained no new dispositions, but built on old rules and approaches. A first step towards central control had come in 1532 with the appointment of a single overarching inquisitor for Italy. The Bull established a commission of six cardinals operating under the Pope. Adriano Prosperi argues forcefully that this group was immediately in a much more powerful position to fight heresy, with full powers to name other ecclesiasts to proceed against suspects elsewhere. The six cardinals were in control, though the Pope reserved to himself powers of absolution and reconciliation. Pope Paul III was allocating powers to cardinals, creating 'a purely ecclesiastical body (*ente*), inserted with full title into the structure of the papal Curia'. Given the way that Cardinal Carafa in particular took control and pursued the accused, this Pope and some later ones came to regret their loss of supremacy in this matter. This new body had the dual purposes of coordinating repression and acting as an appeal institution. It was the foundation of the Cardinalate Congregation structure to be developed over the next decades.[2]

Although the Holy Office (as it became known) and its inquisition tribunals came to dominate, and is our focus, it should be stressed that rival tribunals also asserted their rights and roles: those of the bishops (who had a longer history of enquiring into matters of faith); papal nuncios (ambassadors but also with ecclesiastical powers); ancient central bodies such as the Penitenzieria (Penitentiary, concerned with matters of internal conscience, *foro interno*, and appeals against penitential punishments); and secular courts which might claim rival authority over physical and moral offences, including the governor's court in Rome itself. Later other Congregations, such as those for Rites, challenged the Holy Office and the Congregation of the Index. We are dealing with jurisdictional pluralism.[3]

The Cardinal committee's early central operation is not well documented; its first surviving meeting record, *verbale*, was apparently in 1548. By then four cardinals were dominant: Carafa, Juan Alvarez of Toledo, Francesco Sfondrati and Marcello Cervini. They had a small group of collaborators as *consultores*; a *fiscale* (for financial and administrative control), his deputy and the *Maestro del Sacro Palazzo* (Master of the Sacred Palace, a key figure in book censorship). However, the committee was almost immediately taking action in response to the flight of Bernardino Ochino and Pietro Martire Vermigli, looking for their followers. Six legal processes for heresy were on their way to Bologna within six months of the commission being founded.[4] The small group of personnel was inadequate for the increasing workload from 1548. The early stages followed Paul III's attitudes, influenced by people like Giovanni Morone and Girolamo Seripando, and saw the Inquisition operate with moderation and mildness. The Inquisition changed under Carafa's iron fist ('il pugno di ferro del Carafa'), according to Agostino Borromeo. The Pope probably slowed the pursuit of Pietro Carnesecchi, Reginald Pole and Giovanni Morone, to the disapproval of Carafa, who notoriously hounded them once he was Pope Paul IV (1555–9).

During Paul III's last year (1548–9), the central Inquisition conducted ninety-two investigations (into fifty-five lay persons and thirty-seven ecclesiasts); these were either formal tribunals or simply investigatory. Some under investigation were bishops, including Pietro Antonio di Capua, archbishop of Otranto, and bishops Giacomo Nacchianti of Chioggia and Pier Paolo Vergerio of Capodistria. Vergerio fled Italy on hearing he was being investigated, and was declared contumacious. He had had plenty of protectors in Capodistria, including Venetian patricians, like the *podestà* (lay magistrate) Donà Malapiero, who had sought to minimise Vergerio's contentious beliefs and their impact. His beliefs were investigated in Venice between June 1546 and June 1547, and reported to Rome. Not until 8 July 1550 was it there decided to burn Vergerio in effigy. Cardinals Carafa, Cervini and Sfondrati alone made such key decisions, but they asked Cardinal Ciocchi del Monte to coordinate enquiries in Venice, with the aid of the notable secretary to the Council of Trent Angelo Massarelli, which led to the questioning of fifty-three witnesses. After a decision to arrest. Nacchianti on 20 November 1548, he was detained in Rome, in the Dominican house at Santa Maria sopra Minerva, which became a major centre of the Inquisition. Nacchianti was suspected of harbouring Lutheran ideas on scripture and tradition, and various sessions discussed his views but by August 1549 he seems to have been deemed innocent and released so that later he was active at the Council of Trent, though he remained fearful of re-arrest. Apparently inquiries continued about him in Chioggia in October 1549. Nacchianti died there in 1569.[5]

Twenty-nine of the ecclesiasts investigated who were not bishops were regular clergy, and only six secular. To exemplify early procedures we can cite Paduano Grasso, a conventual minor who was teaching in his Franciscan Order's Studio in Venice. In January 1549 the results of investigations were fed to the Master of the Sacred Palace. Grasso was then imprisoned in a cell in his Roman convent of Santi Apostoli, forbidden to correspond with or speak to others, except for a clerical brother with whom he ate. Two weeks later he was allowed free circulation within the convent. Having called on Dominicans as consultants, on 12 March cardinals decided to inflict spiritual penalties, but also to make Grasso retract by preaching in S. Maria dell'Anima and refuting what he had previously believed and expressed in his books (unspecified), which could be reprinted with corrections. In 1550 this Franciscan published in Venice his *Concilium Pauli*, previously published in 1542 and 1545.[6]

The 1542 Bull did not envisage book censorship specifically, but the commission could hardly avoid it. On 12 July 1543 the Pope issued an edict affecting booksellers in Rome and elsewhere, through the customs control of the Papal State. It threatened heavy penalties for selling or trading in prohibited books. It only mentioned two specific texts – Bernardino Ochino's *Prediche* (Sermons), and a *Pasquilli in ecstasi*, which might have meant Celio Secondo Curione's *Pasquillus extaticus*. On 7 May 1549 the Roman bookseller Francesco Tramezzino and some colleagues appeared before the cardinals, and they asked to be given a list of banned books from which they could work. One appreciates their problem since no papal Index of Prohibited Books yet existed. The cardinals appointed as consultant the Dominican *maestro* Teofilo (Teofilo Scullica da Tropea in Calabria), who was entrusted by Carafa with compiling a suitable register, which would be deposited in Tramezzino's bookshop. He was to be responsible for communicating with his colleagues. Teofilo was designated thereafter as *sottoinquisitore* or *subdelegato*, and was to be succeeded by Michele Ghislieri (later Pope Pius V).[7] Soon two Dominican consultants were asked to examine indexes of banned books already produced in Paris and Louvain (Belgium), and to bring Rome's own lists up to date. The key consultant was Egidio Foscarari, *Maestro di Palazzo*, later bishop of Modena (1550–64), who was active in a number of later Inquisition cases at the centre and periphery, and was inclined to seek reconciliation rather than condemnation. Under Paul IV's paranoid regime in June 1557 Foscarari came under suspicion, along with others associated with Morone, though without a formal *processo* being set in motion. With Paul IV's death in 1559 and the election of Pius IV (Giovanni Angelo de' Medici) he was absolved, along with Morone, Di Capua and Carnesecchi.[8]

These cases indicate that attitudes in Rome in the early stages of the Roman Inquisition were fluid, relationships tense and procedures inefficient. The election of Pope Julius III (Ciocchi del Monte) in 1550 had produced other tensions, and some bureaucratic consolidation of the Congregation as a power centre with considerable autonomy from the Pope. The Pope distrusted Carafa and his severity, and was aware of Carafa's attack in conclave against Cardinal Reginald Pole, essentially vetoing his election. The Pope was early on reported to be 'up to his eyes with the inconstancy and fantasies' of Carafa, and his 'annoying nature'.[9] According to Girolamo Muzzarelli, consultant to the Congregation and the Pope's confidant, Julius was 'continually irritated against the Office of the Holy Inquisition', which he saw as acting 'through malignity and through envy of the papacy'. So the Pope ordered that there should be no dispositions made in the Holy Office against cardinals, or other leading prelates such as bishops, without His Holiness first knowing.[10] According to one Holy Office member, Carafa 'had many times contradicted Pope Julius III on Inquisition matters and shown him that it was not necessary to proceed *freddamente* (dispassionately)'.[11]

The papal attitude was shown when Julius III ordered the release of Vittore Soranzo, bishop of Bergamo, in May 1551 from Castel S. Angelo, in the midst of the Congregation's *processo* against him. He abjured on 9 September 1551 in the Palazzo Apostolico before the Pope, who absolved him from ecclesiastical censures, though he did not readmit him to episcopal duties in Bergamo. Among those present were Cardinal inquisitors Carafa, Alvarez da Toledo, Girolamo Verallo (recently appointed by the Pope); also commissioners Michele Ghislieri and Gaspare Dotti (lieutenant to the Congregation), and Girolamo Muzzarelli as *Maestro del Sacro Palazzo*. Soranzo admitted to having argued and upheld views in a Lutheran way. The Pope had probably pressed Soranzo to give a full confession so he could be absolved. But Carafa probably insisted that he should not be returned to his bishopric though retaining his title.[12] The Republic of Venice strongly backed their bishop of Bergamo (one of its key cities), which helped the papal position. Soranzo produced a number of confessions for the Pope in an attempt to secure a compromise and release – an early example of plea-bargaining. The Pope wanted to mitigate the punishment, and avert a condemnation that would indirectly involve Pole, Morone and others as part of a network of vulnerable thinkers. This was the apex of the secret political and religious conflict between the Pope and the Holy Office.[13]

Both Pope and dominant Cardinal inquisitors pursued policies unbeknownst to each other. Without papal awareness the inquisitors were investigating leading figures such as Pole and Morone, but also Valdesians. This policy was facilitated when on 3 June 1551 the cardinals expanded their team by naming two new *commissari*: Gaspare Dotti, a priest and doctor of two laws, and the inquisitor of Como, whose name was left blank by the notary but was in fact Michele Ghislieri, and who was detailed to investigate printed books.[14] The Pope, said Girolamo Muzzarelli, secretly kept documents 'in the room where he slept . . . in a small box above the small table, where he had the summaries of other *processi* he had had from me'. These probably related to cases concerning Vittore Soranzo, Giovanni Grimani and Pietro Antonio Di Capua, bishop of Otranto. The Pope kept Morone informed of investigations against him, giving him copies of records, as Morone's own deposition confirmed.[15]

The cardinals on the Congregation at this stage could mix harshness and comparative mildness, seemingly on their own account. For example a priest called Apollonio Merenda had been arrested in Naples, as a Valdesian, and sent to Rome in the summer of 1551. Three years of investigation led to abjuration, perpetual imprisonment at the will of the 'Most Reverends' – not the will of the Pope, just of the cardinals. Unusually, Merenda was released after six months, with the proviso that he did not leave the city without permission. But in the same session involving this benign gesture the cardinals ordered the capture of Mario Galeota, one of the most active Valdesians in Naples. Furthermore, the Pope was unable to protect a key Bolognese figure from the death sentence demanded by his cardinals, the previously noted Giovanni Buzio da Montalcino, regent of studies in San Francesco, Bologna. The relevant congregation sitting on 8 August 1553 reported that all five cardinals present (Carafa, Alvarez de Toledo, Verallo, Puteo and Pighini) unanimously decided to turn him over to the secular authorities for execution.[16] Years later, in 1578, a Bolognese weaver, Giacomo Saliceti, returned from long absences in Mantua and Venice (where he was investigated), and was soon denounced for not believing in indulgences or Purgatory. He attested to the influence of Buzio's sermons forty-five years before. Saliceti was hanged and burned as relapsed in April 1579. This suggests Buzio had been complicit in a wide range of heresies, and had had some impact, which the cardinals would have seen as justifying their death sentence in the face of papal misgivings. Buzio was the first person to be executed in Rome for heresy under the new Congregation's orders in 1553: a landmark event.[17]

The Roman Congregation and Regular Activity

The Pope was head of the Congregations. The Congregation of the Holy Office (the Inquisition) or select members thereof met up to three times a week. The Pope presided over at least one meeting, for the most crucial decisions on prosecutions and sentences, and gave guidance on what instructions to send to local inquisitors, collectively or individually. From the 1560s the Holy Office was housed in the Palazzo del Sant'Uffizio, south of St Peter's piazza, though many of its activities took place at Santa Maria sopra Minerva, the Dominican headquarters. The Pope was not necessarily in a dictatorial position, and might be dominated by, or at loggerheads with, the inner clique of Cardinal inquisitors. Cardinals might be members of several congregations and have different priorities and interests; membership of the Congregation for the Regulars or the Congregation for the Bishops might either provide information beneficial to the Inquisition or set up conflicting loyalties, defending bishops or abbots and their claimed jurisdictions from undue inquisitorial investigation locally. A Cardinal Secretary played a key role in ensuring that suitable summaries of cases and issues were available for the Pope and attending cardinals, and that correspondence went back to local inquisitors. Cardinal Santoro fulfilled this role between 1587 and 1602, giving the highest priority to the Congregation of the Holy Office, and dying at his desk.[18]

By the 1560s the Roman Congregation of the Holy Office had settled into a basic pattern of activity.[19] Two formal congregations were usually held towards the end of the week; the first was led by the active Cardinal inquisitors, whereas the second was presided over by the Pope, who might arrive part-way through the proceedings. The meetings might be in the papal palace, in the Inquisition's own palace, or in that of a dominant Cardinal such as that of the Cardinal of Pisa (Scipione Rebiba), or, in the mid-1560s, Cardinal Francisco Pacheco. Later Clement VIII (Ippolito Aldobrandini) ordered that all Congregation meetings should be in the Apostolic palace or Quirinale, and not in cardinals' houses, except for minor meetings about book expurgations.[20] Only three or four cardinals might attend the 'congregations of cardinals' without the Pope, as a hard core of dedicated inquisitors; more might attend when he presided. Confidence and experience doubtless led those who met on 14 December 1565 to declare that during the papal vacancy (*sede vacante*), they had full powers to act, and to address letters written to the Pope in this role.[21] As inquisitorial cardinals were quite likely to distrust a Pope, this was an ideal opportunity to act alone (though the papal vacancy was short this time). About ten other persons were listed as attending, in the *Decreta* volumes, with their contributions sometimes specifically recorded. Non-Cardinal members on a regular basis included the Master of the Papal Palace, the Governor of the City (important for prisoners kept in Castel Sant'Angelo, and possibly in the Tor di Nona), the *Commissario*

Generale (probably the key bureaucrat behind the scenes), the *Fiscale* (for finances), one or more procurators fiscal (legal), the *stampa assessore* (at this stage the specialist on prohibited books, before the separate Congregation of the Index was created in 1572), and some others who might be consulted on theological or legal matters. The Father General of the Dominicans or his vicar was the most frequent attender from the religious Orders.[22] Some sessions are stated as following a visit to the prisoners; the minutes merely list names in most cases, but occasionally record a decision or recommendation for somebody. A meeting on Saturday 28 June 1565 (involving just three cardinals, but with eight others assisting), listed fifty-four prisoners visited (many from Bologna), with comments on only two: prisoner no. 30, D. Julius, originally from Piacenza but sent from Bologna to have his case remitted to the Pope, while new arrangements were made for the imprisonment of no. 51, Mario Galeota, a Neapolitan and a Valdesian who greatly concerned the Congregation in the 1560s.[23]

Some sessions with or without the Pope could be full and varied. Most of the reporting in the 1560s is very cryptic, noting that letters and memorials were read; the matter might be referred to a particular Cardinal, to interview an accused or witness informally or to compose a reply; the *fiscale* might be asked to investigate. Some clear decisions were recorded but much was left pending. However, a leading Inquisition Cardinal would be writing (or getting the scribes and notaries to write) numerous letters, which would be sent around Italy, and perhaps other Catholic countries.

A meeting could occasionally be confined to one issue, as with reading the long *processo* of a major case, like Mario Galeota's. More unusually, on 3 July 1567 the Pope, four cardinals and ten others were faced with the decision of what to do with a heretic who had died in prison. Five of the non-cardinals gave opinions that were noted, no record being made of the cardinals' views, leading the Pope to declare that the body should be exhumed, pulled apart (*tirandendum*) and burned. The man's goods were to be confiscated and submitted to the Holy Office in Rome. The marginal difference in views was about the business of confiscation. The procurator fiscal said *de iure* property should be confiscated, but the Pope should decide its subsequent allocation.[24]

A session could have a greater variety of business, as that of Saturday 6 July 1566, which was presided over by the cardinals of Trani (Bernardino Scotti) and Pisa (Rebiba), as well as Francisco Pacheco and Gian Francesco Gambara.[25] Nine others were listed, including the later prime inquisitor Giulio Antonio (Santoro), archbishop of Santa Severina. Eleven memorials were read: against some was written *nihil ordinatum* (nothing ordered), against others *nihil resolutem* (nothing resolved) was the comment. In most cases the issue was not indicated. With Giovanni Gallo, servant of the late Don Pompeo de Montibus, the commissioner was ordered to seek all of the late Pompeo's possessions (kept in Castel S. Angelo), and sell them to satisfy others' claims. In response to a memorial from Ancona about two Jews, the cardinals decided they should remain prisoners until the cause was expedited. A convicted Piedmontese heretic should serve some Roman hospital assigned by Cardinal Gambara. Various people from Venosa (Kingdom of Naples) should be taxed for expenses, conceded remission and committed to the vicariate and chapter of Venosa. Finally, the congregation came to vote about a Don Dionisio Gallo, and one Fra Tranquillo, and whether they should be tortured. The views of the non-Cardinal consultants show divergent opinions on whether the examination with or without torture should be concerning the man's 'faith' or just whether he was 'inimical'. No decision was recorded.

The cryptic judgements are better understood if one knows that Dionisio Gallo was a bizarre and quixotic character, and under arrest by the Venetian tribunal. Originally from France, he had become a famous prophetic preacher, considering himself anointed by the Virgin and destined to bring about reform of the Church by returning the Pope and corrupt high clergy to moral ways. He bombarded the Pope with letters saying that Venice would lead the reforms. After some spectacular and popular vituperative preaching in Rome from January 1566, Dionisio had been imprisoned and investigated by the Holy Office. He was questioned about his writings, then released on 15 February and told he could live in Rome, provided he remained silent about clerical reform and assembling princes to discuss reform. He soon left for Florence, then for Venice, where he was again arrested by the Inquisition in June, and investigated for fourteen months in grim prison conditions in the Ducal Palace, as reported in letters he wrote afterwards. Eventually it was decided he was guilty of holding public assemblies against the tribunal's orders. He had, however, committed offences 'not from error of intellect but from a certain disturbance of the soul, agitated by certain disquieting humours' – so he was not responsible. This verdict probably reflects earlier qualms in Rome about torture in his case. In August 1567 Dionisio was banished from the Venetian Republic.[26] Behind the other cryptic notes here lay very important, long-running cases or worries, such as those concerning the bishops Policastro (Nicola Francesco Missanelli) and Alissani, with the latter being sent under guard to the hospital of Santo Spirito as sick.[27]

Moments in other sessions cryptically refer to memorials and pleas about the aforementioned Mario Galeota. Eventually complete sessions were devoted to reading his trial records, on 13, 20, 23 July, and more reading was done after a few other items on 16 and 27 July. The congregation on 30 July decided he should be given paper so he could write his defence. Three of the four cardinals attended all sessions, but Cardinal Trani missed two. The session on 27 July also decided that two books by Dionisio Gallo should be given to the Master of the Palace; and a memorial from an Englishman, John Harry, was read arguing that Cardinal Morone should be treated as a good Catholic.[28]

Dependent Tribunals and Central Control

In contrast to the expanding systems of the Spanish and then Portuguese Inquisitions, the spread of the Roman Inquisition's control through dependent tribunals and officials was complicated and unsystematic. Many obstacles impeded development, notably jurisdictional, political and financial. Within the Papal State the creation of tribunals was comparatively simple from the legal-political aspect, but the effectiveness of actual implementation depended on cooperation between bishops and city governments, and in reality jurisdictional battles could be long and fraught, and the inquisitions could not monopolise religious controls, notably when bishops and their vicars had delegated inquisitorial duties.[29] Elsewhere the Papacy had to negotiate with the sovereign rulers, whether princes or republics, most of whom wanted some leverage over the working of a tribunal and the degree of control from Rome. In some cases this was a marginal supervision or recognition that there should be some consultation with the secular arm, other than for executing those found guilty of heresy. In other cases, notably in Venice, the answer was a kind of Church-State system of power-sharing. Within the Italian peninsula the Republic of Lucca refused to allow a secular Roman Inquisition tribunal, but established its own inquisitorial office to control heresy. In the Kingdom of Naples the Roman Inquisition had essentially to operate like the old medieval episcopal Inquisition. Outside Italy proper the Roman Inquisition had linked tribunals in Avignon (part of the Papal State), Malta (under the Knights of St John), and in parts of the Venetian empire, Capodistria and Zara. Later offices existed in Chios (Genoese possession), Besançon (Spanish controlled), Carcassonne and Toulouse (French), Annecy (Savoy) and Cologne.[30]

Establishing a complete list of tribunals and sub-tribunals for mainland Italy is difficult. The following seem to have been operative at the end of the sixteenth century, or to have been added later (at dates stated): Adria, Alessandria, Ancona, Patriarchate of Aquileia (but meeting in Cividale, Portogruaro, or Udine), Asti, Bergamo, Bologna, Brescia, Casale Monferrato, Ceneda, Cividale, Como, Concordia, Crema (1614), Cremona, Faenza, Fermo (1631), Ferrara, Florence, Genoa, Gubbio (1631–2), Imola, Mantua, Milan, Modena (1598), Mondovì, Novara, Padua, Parma, Pavia, Perugia, Pisa, Reggio Emilia (1598), Rimini, Saluzzo, Siena, Spoleto (1685), Tortona, Treviso, Turin, Venice, Vercelli, Verona, Vicenza (see Map 3). Up to 1598 inquisitorial officials operated in Modena and Reggio Emilia as vicarial sub-delegates to Ferrara and Bologna respectively rather than in direct relationship with Rome. Also, it is unclear when one should count a sub-delegated inquisitorial official, with a notary and odd helpers, a formal tribunal as with Modena or San Miniato in Tuscany.[31]

In the Papal State Province of Romagna initially the inquisitor of Bologna presided; under him Faenza had an inquisitorial office from 1547. In 1567 the

Faenza inquisitor became inquisitor for Romagna. In the dependent bishoprics of Ravenna, Cesena, Forlì, Bertinoro, Cervia, Sarsina and Imola the bishop's vicar was delegated also to act as a commissioner and judge for the Inquisition, though he might also have a commissioner or vicar from the central Romagna inquisition. This doubling of vicars could cause confusion and conflict (and subsequently confusion in documentation). In Imola (where the first heresy case dates from 1551), apparently the inquisitorial vicar generally prevailed over the bishop's vicar; but a bishop of Imola like Rodolfo Paleotti in 1612, in advice to confessors tried to define, and limit, the competence of the Inquisition. Imola, which had a number of staff and should be seen as a largely self-sufficient tribunal, had at least 742 *processi* from 1551 to 1700.[32] Establishing the number of Inquisition vicariates under the main inquisitor is also difficult. The Bologna inquisitor seems to have had up to seventeen vicariates at some point in the seventeenth century.[33]

A formal tribunal was not essential for the Roman Inquisition to take action in the provinces, especially in the early years. Sometimes when an incipient inquisitorial tribunal had too 'liberal' or weak an inquisitor in Rome's eyes, a roving representative might intervene. In Modena, for example, between 1544 and 1554 the Holy Office processed about seventy persons, largely when Bishop Morone was being investigated. When activity was at a peak Francesco da Michalis, bishop of Casale Monferrato, and the Dominican Fra Girolamo da Lodi were appointed apostolic commissioners to investigate and try accused individuals. In another D'Este state, Ferrara (fief of the Papacy), where the French duchess Renée (Renata) was a Calvinist sympathiser, the inquisitorial cardinals initially proceeded via a vice-legate in 1547 against the baker Fanino Fanini da Faenza, with some cooperation from the duke who, after long delays, accepted Fanini's execution in August 1550 as a relapsed heretic. This action received publicity across Europe. By then a Dominican inquisitor Fra Girolamo Papini was installed, but also a Fra Michele (Ghislieri), as a special commissioner was in Ferrara, under whom the Benedictine visionary and prophet Giorgio Rioli (better known as Siculo) was pursued, tried and strangled in prison in May 1551. Siculo was an impenitent who had refused at the last minute to abjure at a solemn ceremony in front of the duke, despite for long being an advocate of dissimulation, and arguing that abjuring was not a sin against the Holy Spirit. The Roman cardinals under Carafa had attempted to have Siculo tried in Rome. The duke was able to resist this, but ultimately unable to prevent an execution. Although Papini in this case was the regular inquisitor, it seems that Ghislieri was applying pressure on behalf of the Roman Congregation, probably because Papini had earlier recommended Siculo's writings. As we have seen, Ghislieri, a heretic-hunter much trusted by Carafa, was a special commissioner for the Cardinal inquisitors, and as such had greatly endangered himself trying to nail Vittore Soranzo, bishop of Bergamo, who had much popular support in that city.[34]

Although the central Congregation after 1542 had the responsibility for inquisitorial appointments, in practice the heads of religious Orders continued to name inquisitors in local tribunals in the medieval fashion. The Dominicans in Milan did not cede this role to the central Congregation until 1587, nor in Parma until 1588; the General of the Conventual Minors in Florence did not cede his role until 1572, and then under much protest. In Ancona the Dominicans and Conventual Minors nominated the inquisitor until 1565, but although the Congregation took over, we still find the Dominican General nominating inquisitors in 1569 and 1580.[35] Rather than see this as reflecting weak central control, it might be interpreted as a willingness on the part of the Roman cardinals to trust the Dominican Order to select suitable local appointees. Rome had to ratify the choice.

The Franciscans had provided inquisitors in some areas in the fifteenth century, notably in the Veneto. After 1542 a number of tribunals were handed over to Dominicans: Venice from 1560 under Pius IV's orders; the province of Romagna in 1567; the districts of Verona, Vicenza, and the provinces of Treviso and Ancona in 1569.[36]

Tuscany

As the new Inquisition was established in the growing absolutist state of Tuscany under Cosimo I de' Medici, the duke faced little opposition. A reputation for cooperation was sealed with Cosimo's agreement finally to allow Pietro Carnesecchi to be extradited for trial (and eventual execution) in Rome, in return for recognition as a Grand Duke and freedom from scrutiny for some of his other dubious associates. The Florentine inquisitor could establish his tribunal and operate through the Medici state, provided he kept the duke and his court informed, and provided the Cardinal inquisitors communicated properly via the papal nuncio. Given that political and religious dissent could go together, the duke was ready to see tight inquisitorial control if he was kept informed. He expected the state police to be used as enforcers, and to control who would be imprisoned. Cosimo would not allow the Inquisition to be as intrusive as the Spanish Inquisition, making it clear that Carafa's proposals to attack Jews as usurers, or enthusiastically to seize the property of accused individuals, were unacceptable. He also expected to be allowed to send somebody from one of his secular courts, such as the Otto di Guardia, to attend investigations alongside the inquisitor, as in the 1551–2 case of Lodovico Domenichi, poet, writer and publisher of works favouring women and their writings, and of Calvinist works. Finally, the inquisitor for Tuscany and his leading vicars and deputies were to be chosen from the duke's approved churchmen.[37]

Piedmont

Piedmont was extremely vulnerable to heretical intrusions from the north, which might build on the remnants of Waldensian and Cathar heresies of previous centuries. Under such circumstances rulers of the House of Savoy such as the Duke of Piedmont, Emanuele Filiberto (recognised to be in control by the Treaty of Cateau-Cambrésis in 1559) were ready to accept Roman inquisitorial activity in Piedmont, though less so in French Savoie. For Piedmont the basic conditions of acceptance were that the papal nuncio should be the link between the central Congregation and the Turin government, and that the inquisitors throughout the province should similarly use the nuncio to secure approval for important action. In March 1570 the Cardinal of Pisa, Scipione Rebiba, warned an inquisitorial commissioner that 'in cases of importance they should not move to do anything' without the nuncio's participation.[38] Campaigns to eradicate heretics in the mountain valleys were coordinated through him. The more militant campaigns came to be moderated in 1560 under the influence of the Jesuits, led by Antonio Possevino (from Mantua). Duke Emanuele Filiberto signed a peace treaty at Cavour in June 1561, allowing some Waldensian communities to live unmolested. The nuncio, Francesco Bachaud, was prepared to do deals with non-Catholics. However, when the Pope's young nephew Cardinal Carlo Borromeo took an intolerant attitude, Cardinal Ghislieri was then sent with fullest powers to his titular diocese of Alessandria, but also to others as general *sopraintendente* over all matters concerning heretical preaching, thus competing with the nuncio. Generally the Waldensians managed to evade capture and trial under this and subsequent inquisitorial activities, fleeing to sanctuaries in the mountains or to Geneva. The effectiveness of the Inquisition may also have been impeded by the fact that episcopal courts retained fairly strong jurisdictional control and limited the links between confessors and inquisitors (though this remains to be studied).[39]

Later the House of Savoy led the way in increasing impediments to inquisitorial activity by asserting State control against the Church, especially under Vittorio Amedeo II. His attitude was indicated by the forceful expulsion of three inquisitors at twenty-four hours' notice (in Saluzzo 1698, Turin 1708, Alessandria 1709), largely because he disliked the named inquisitors or the way they were appointed. After the expulsion of the inquisitor of Alessandria in 1709, Rome ceased nominating an inquisitor there, employing only lesser vicars, responsible to Turin. The duke's officials also tried to ensure that they had a secular official sitting with the Inquisition tribunal, a practice that had apparently been dropped in the late sixteenth century. The state largely took over censorship.[40]

Venice and the Venetian Republic

The central Venetian tribunal[41] and its work is the best known of the tribunals, because of the survival of so much of its archival material and its availability to scholars from the mid-nineteenth century. This survival was affected by the fact that the secular Republican government was more closely involved with the tribunal's affairs than governments in other states. Consequently, when the Venetian Republic fell to the French in 1797 its archival records were treated as 'secular', and were later absorbed into the State archive – not destroyed or left to neglect, as in many other states.

Following the establishment of the Roman Inquisition in 1542, the Republic had been wary of allowing activities by the Inquisition within its territory. Many Venetians – nobles, merchants, clergy and artisans – had shown interest in Church reform, and in religious debate (and some had preceded Luther and Zwingli on some doctrinal issues connected with faith and salvation). The city contained many non-Roman Catholics – Jews, Greek Orthodox, Muslims and converts of some dubiety – who were important to its economy. Too rigorous an intrusion by inquisitors might be damaging. Inquisitors had operated intermittently here in the medieval period (though evidence of this is limited), and according to the scholar and controversialist Paolo Sarpi this practice ceased in 1423, only to be revived in 1540. This is slightly misleading in that nuncios had launched inquisitorial processes earlier, with Venetian clerical cooperation. In 1533 a certain Antonio *marangone* (carpenter) had shown himself to be a boastful Lutheran, causing such offence to some neighbours in the parish of San Giacomo that the newly arrived nuncio Girolamo Aleandro started an investigation, leading to an inquisitorial trial and a sentence of life imprisonment. Antonio had had his artisan supporters. He possessed prohibited books and a vernacular Bible, and he denied the eucharist and free will. The tribunal consisted of the nuncio, an inquisitor (Fra Angelo, a Franciscan Minor), the Patriarch's vicar-general and five other ecclesiasts. Antonio was condemned to perpetual imprisonment, but it is not clear how long he actually served. The nuncio then concerned himself with rumours of heresy up in Istria, and started to pursue Pier Paolo Vergerio.[42]

Then, in 1540–1, Nuncio Giorgio Andreassi with inquisitor Paolo Filomella proceeded against Fra Giulio della Rovere (or Giulio da Milano), who abjured and was sentenced to a year's imprisonment in 1542. Secular officials played no positive part, and Andreassi complained that leading gentlemen of the Republic were protecting Giulio. Thanks to them he managed to flee to Geneva in 1543 and declared himself a Calvinist.[43] When from 1542 Rome pressed the Venetians to act against the known and suspected heretics in Venice, it received little help. Doge Francesco Donà, one of the more forceful Doges of the century, was wary both of the Papacy under Paul III and of the Holy Roman Emperor, Charles V. International politics in the 1540s ensured the Venetians wavered between pro- and anti-imperial policies, with temptations to make arrangements with Henry VIII of England, the French and the Schmalkalden League against Charles V. But in 1547 Henry VIII and Francis I of France died, and the weight of opinion in the Roman Senate moved towards confronting Protestant heresy, pushed by strong diplomacy from Nuncio Giovanni Della Casa. A decree of 22 April 1547 announced the establishment of a new magistracy, *Tre Savii sopra eresia*, three wisemen to deal with heresy. They were to be elected by the Doge and *Collegio* to help the papal legate (or nuncio), the Patriarch of Venice, and the inquisitor with 'the formation of trials'.[44] Thus was born the Venetian Inquisition tribunal, and Nuncio Della Casa moved swiftly to win the cooperation of the three secular nobles. The nuncio remained a key judge of faith in the Republic (like his counterparts in Turin, Naples and Florence).[45]

The Venetian tribunal thus was headed by three clergy and three secular Venetian nobles. The balance is somewhat misleading. The bias was 'Venetian', in that the Patriarch was invariably a Venetian noble (named by the Senate for papal approval), often with a senatorial or diplomatic background before late ordination. About half the inquisitors came from Venice or other parts of the Republic's territory. However, while the Patriarch and the nuncio could send deputies to attend investigations and trials, the three lay noblemen, often referred to as *assistenti*, seem not to have done so. Current knowledge indicates that it was rare, especially in later years, for all three to attend investigative sessions, and that they only did so appearing for the conclusion of a full trial. Much of the inquisitional activity took place in San Domenico in Castello, discouragingly away from the centre, with its own prison cells, though key trial sessions could be held in the Doge's Palace (with nastier prison cells at hand, especially before the improved New Prisons were completed in about 1604).[46] Should all three *assistenti* insist on attending all sessions of a key trial, it could cause major delays, as nuncio Ludovico Beccadelli complained in 1551. The attendance of one was the norm. These assistants do not usually feature expressly in the formal questioning as recorded – often the notary just writes 'questioned', without indicating the questioner. Evidence seems lacking on how much *assistenti* participated in background preparation, in decisions on following up denunciations, on whether to seek Rome's permission to torture or in discussions on sentencing policy. Denunciators and witnesses might address letters to the *assistenti* rather than the inquisitor.[47] The cases against the printers Valvasense and Batti in 1648, for printing and trading in prohibited and unlicensed books, show that Piero Sagredo, described both as *procurator* and *assistente*, heard evidence from, and questioned, printers as witnesses and experts; the *procurator di S. Marco* Antonio da Canale was a leading figure in organising witnesses and then questioning the accused.[48]

Some individuals served as an *assistente* many times, thus providing accumulated knowledge: Giulio Contarini di Zorzi (d. 1578) was eleven times a *savio dell'eresia* between 1553 and 1571, and was involved in a number of the cases against Judaisers, including beginning the now noted Adamo Righetto case (1570–3).[49] Later in that case, after Righetto had asked for a copy of the record to prepare a defence, he was told: 'The *signori clarissimi assistenti* are here present by the orders of the Most Excellent Council of Ten, and they represent that Council, and in this matter of issuing indictments and permitting defences the Holy Tribunal proceeds in the same manner as the Council'. It is not clear whether the inquisitor made this point, or one of the *assistenti*. The tribunal's composition on that day was not recorded.[50] In tense conflicts in 1765–6 between Nuncio Francesco Carafa, who was battling to uphold the powers of the religious members of the tribunal, and the *Savi all'Eresia*, who defended secular rights and controls, the latter complained that the inquisitor would arbitrarily schedule the audiences and the calling of witnesses to inconvenience the laymen and dilute their involvement in cases.[51]

Some nuncios cajoled and praised some notable assistants: Nuncio Giovanni Antonio Facchinetti in 1566 lauded Girolamo di Marin Grimani (assistant 1560–62, 1565–7) as 'very devoted to the Apostolic See and protector of ecclesiastical things'. In routine cases the nuncio was often represented by his auditor for criminal affairs, who might become as active as the inquisitor. Rocco Cataneo, canon of Pola, valuably served successive nuncios from 1550 until 1562.[52]

That a lay patrician assistant might help an accused from the same social order is evidenced by the 1616 case of Cristoforo Canal, accused of refusing to fast on Fridays and blaspheming, including saying 'Roman pontiffs are pigheads and goatherds'. This phraseology had been used in pamphlets during the Interdict of 1606–7. The assistant to the court, Agostino Nani (who had been ambassador to Rome at the beginning of the Interdict crisis), defended Canal, saying he had not intended heresy, and that he was reputed to be 'not completely sane of mind'.[53]

The first inquisitor under the new dispensation was Fra Marino (Venier) da Venezia, a Franciscan (nicknamed *Zotto*, the Lame); he had been inquisitor under the old dispensation from 1544, so provided continuity after 1547. He is seen as a 'mediator'. From 1544 to 1550 he brought twenty-four processes (involving thirty-five people) to completion; seemingly about 150 persons were denounced, with little or no follow-up. He apparently avoided torture, preferring to wear down an accused by persistent questioning, as with a tailor Francesco Poetin da Vicenza in 1550, who had argued against the value of confession, the need for fasting, lighting of candles for the dead and papal authority, and who freely discussed the New Testament with fellow tailors and friends. He seems not to have been intimidated by the inquisitor; whether he agreed to confess and abjure because partly convinced by the inquisitor, or whether he calculated that, if he did so, he would achieve a light sentence and be able to continue his protestant beliefs surreptitiously, cannot be known. Fra Marino's court treated him mildly: public abjuration, report once a month to the Inquisition, confess and communicate in his parish church, or another as licensed by his priest. Only if he avoided these conditions would a more serious sentence to the galleys come into force, with confiscation of property, and thereafter permanent banishment from Venice.[54] It is presumed Francesco Poetin fulfilled the mild conditions.

One of the earliest cases brought to a verdict ended, unusually, with a declaration of innocence. A Conventual Franciscan Bonaventura Clozio da Casalmaggiore was investigated in 1547 after suggestions that his sermons were irregular. Witnesses praised his preaching, did not indicate he was deviant, though some said he started to sing the introit to the Mass for the dead from the pulpit, which was irregular for a preacher. Fra Bonaventura was imprisoned in Padua, then questioned in Venice by Fra Marino, and the tribunal agreed that the accusations arose from rivalry with another preacher. So he was freed, having been a prisoner for about three months. A harsher approach was taken in 1548 against a Judaiser, Aaron di Rafael Francoso from Sarzana in a *contado* (district) of Siena (with numerous aliases), who had been baptised four times in various cities (Venice, Modena, Ferrara and at an abbey in the Polesine), receiving small payments for these 'conversions', and being licensed to beg from Christians. He had occasionally taught Hebrew to scholars. He very quickly abjured before all active members of the tribunal, and was sentenced to twenty years in the galleys with the usual payment to sustain his life (but with a threat of hanging if he tried to escape), and then banishment. Surprisingly he survived the twenty years, and was then given a safe-conduct by the Patriarch to return to Venice in February 1568.[55]

Consequences followed from Fra Marino's general mildness; he himself was put under inquisitorial investigation from the autumn of 1551. Two early witnesses, a Dominican and a Franciscan, Fra Angelo da Venezia (who may be identified as a Fra Angelo serving as inquisitor in 1533–4), claimed among other things that Fra Marino had often bad-mouthed the Congregation of the Inquisition. As a censor in 1543 he had licensed a vernacular version of a work by Luther (probably *Dechiaratione de li dieci commanti*), and in 1547 as inquisitor he licensed Erasmus' paraphrases of St Matthew's Gospel. He was also accused of 'covering up for heretics', and of supporting the suspect Bishop Pier Paolo Vergerio. As Anne Schutte has argued, Fra Marino was more a Venetian than a Roman, inclined to be indulgent towards high-ranking Venetians and to Franciscans of various kinds. Venetian secular authorities generally backed him, but the investigation dragged on until 1561, when Fra Marino appealed to Doge Girolamo Priuli. He stressed his great loyalty to the Republic and the Christian cause, his commitment to Christian charity, and to ensuring that there was Venetian input and that the Roman

Tribunal did not fully dominate proceedings. The government secured the case's closure through its ambassador in Rome, with Fra Marino having a public purgation (2 December 1561) and being allowed to resume taking divine services.[56]

Fra Marino, following nuncio Della Casa's leadership, had laid the foundations of the Venetian tribunal, and secured a general local policy of fairly emollient prosecution of heresy, leaving room for reconciliations and mitigated punishments. His conduct probably contributed to Rome's policy that inquisitors should be Dominicans not Franciscans. The revelations by the Anabaptist Pietro Manelfi in October 1551 to the Bolognese inquisitor Leandro Alberti that an 'international' Anabaptist council had met in Venice in 1550, revelations that were passed by Rome to the Venetian tribunal, goaded the Republic into a tougher stance against theological heretics, especially given the radical social implications of some Anabaptist teaching. The Republic struggled, with mixed success, to ensure that Venetian inquisitors came from the Republic's territory.

Another important inquisitor during the Inquisition's foundation period was Fra Felice Peretti da Montalto (active from 1557 to 1560), later Pope Sixtus V; he was the last Franciscan appointee to Venice's central tribunal (though Franciscans served in subsidiary offices within the Republic). Fellow Franciscans had conspired against Peretti as too inquisitorially enthusiastic, and because he was a foreigner from Grottomare (near Ancona) also in charge of studies at the Frari convent! These factors contributed to the shift towards using Dominican inquisitors. Peretti was also very unpopular with the Venetian secular authorities, especially over his threats to the Venetian printing industry through rigid censorship. He had started processes without consulting the lay assistants. He fled Venice on Paul IV's death in August 1559, and the government forbad his return. As a sop to the new Pope Pius IV the Republic agreed that the Inquisitor-General in Venice should be a Dominican. In the autumn the Council of Ten still complained that the tribunal was 'neither just nor intelligent', and in June 1561 warned the nuncio not to bring in new procedures.[57]

The lay assistants linked up with the Council of Ten, the most powerful Venetian government committee, whose backing was needed for arrests of important accused, any extraditions to Rome and for executions. Although the Venetian Republic and the Papacy had many conflicts through the early modern period – over territorial borders, taxation of ecclesiastical property, loss of land to tax-exempt Church properties, and international allegiances – it could be argued that unexpectedly reasonable cooperation over matters inquisitorial was established with the 1547 settlement, and the resolution of issues between 1557 and 1561. The correspondence between Venice and the Roman Congregation was active and mutually beneficial much of the time.[58]

The Venetian inquisitor (or Inquisitor-General as he was sometimes called from Fra Peretti onwards) and the nuncio had overall charge of inquisitional matters throughout the Venetian Republic. The Patriarch and his vicar-general, as well as the lay assistants, were concerned with the Venetian diocese. The Council of Ten also oversaw potential or actual inquisitional matters throughout the Republic, affecting decisions on whether certain cases would be tried in secular courts, by episcopal courts or the Inquisition tribunals and on whether cases should be transferred from a local tribunal to the central Venetian one. Some cases were allowed to be taken to Rome. The principle of having secular assistants or observers was accepted by the Church leaders, so other tribunals within the Republic followed suit. The Brescia and Bergamo tribunals (started 1548) had two city rectors (*Rettori*) and two lay doctors (of law) involved. The Council of Ten in 1557 nullified a sentence passed by the Bergamo tribunal because no lay rector had been present.[59] While the Roman Congregation might send special commissioners to work on processes in the mainland dioceses in more complicated cases, the Holy Office's involvement in routine inquisitional matters there seems limited. By the later 1550s inquisitional offices seem to have been operating in Belluno, Bergamo, Brescia, Concordia, Feltre, Nicosia, Padua, Rovigo, Spalato (Split), Treviso, Verona, Vicenza and Udine. Grendler counts fourteen inquisitors in the Republic by 1645, adding to the above offices Adria, Aquileia (Concordia and Udine), Capo d'Istria, Ceneda, Crema and Zara (in Dalmatia), but losing Feltre (?), Nicosia and Spalato.[60]

Outside Venice itself the best records are for the Patriarchate of Aquileia. The once great Roman city of Aquileia was now reduced to a village, and the Patriarchate's main centre was Udine, where a tribunal was established in 1556–7. Here an operational system developed in which the episcopal vicar-general worked closely with the inquisitor, and arguably ran the organisation with superior powers (contrary to the proper canonical position), with the patriarchal Curia providing notaries and other officials, and keeping the inquisition archive. (The archive is still housed in the arch-episcopal palace in Udine.) The Patriarchate's territory stretched to parts of Styria, Carniola, Carinthia and Gorizia, which were politically ruled by the prince-bishop of Bamberg or the Habsburgs; here the inquisitors could hardly operate, though such areas could feed heretics into 'Italy'.[61] This problem greatly worried Giacomo Maracco, the first vicar-general, who proved a lively investigator of claims of heresy in the Friuli area, and who hunted those holding prohibited books and eating prohibited meats (taken as a prime indicator of pro-reform enthusiasm). He was involved in the attempts to capture Bishop Pier Paolo Vergerio, who was seen as the key to much heresy in the area.

Significant numbers of people became involved in hunting heretics, especially vicars attached to local churches throughout the Friuli region. But the pursuit was then accompanied by jurisdictional conflicts – whether between rival ecclesiastical jurisdictions or between these and secular feudal ones – over who would control the accused and handle further investigations. In particular, authorities in

Cividale, led by the Venetian supervisor (*provveditore*) and backed by the city council, claimed independence from Udine, and argued that inquisitorial proceedings against suspects there should be held in Cividale. This led to the appointment, through the inquisitor in Venice, of another inquisitor to try Cividale cases in 1559. The canons of the chapter of Cividale also proved a stumbling block to the vicar-general in his inquisitorial role, partly because at least two of their number were under suspicion. When one of these canons gave way and recognised the vicar-general's authority, he was 'benignly' absolved. This Cividale conflict had later repercussions when the Patriarch himself, Giovanni Grimani, was denounced as a heretic and pursued by the Cardinal inquisitors.[62]

Another troublesome border area, Bergamo, further illustrates the complexities of getting new inquisitorial activity launched. While Bishop Vergerio was a problem in Friuli and Istria, as noted earlier it was Bishop Vittore Soranzo who was the suspect in the Bergamo region. Surviving correspondence shows that the Roman Congregation was very active from a distance, and used an apostolic vicar-general, Giovanni Battista Brugnatelli, to launch *processi* of faith as 'the long arm of the Roman Holy Office' from 1557; inquisitors were under his leadership and authority but they met opposition from Venetian rectors and city judges who supported Bishop Soranzo. 'I am in a purgatory, not to say in hell,' declared Brugnatelli, complaining of his cramped conditions and lack of support. But an illustrious noble ambassador, Achille Brembati, denounced Brugnatelli as lacking any concept of pastoral care, and declared he was there rather 'for the destruction of the universal Church in this city and territory and has these operations to acquire reputation and aggrandise himself with these means, not being able to do so through virtue and good works'.[63] Following Soranzo's condemnation and death in 1558 and the appointment of a new bishop (Alvise Lippomano), whom the Pope wanted in Rome, a new vicar-general took charge of the diocese. This time, however, the Cardinal inquisitors worked more closely with the local inquisitors than with the vicar-general – though he could be the decisive force in some difficult cases. As Del Col has noted: 'The relations between apostolic vicar and inquisitor and the local state authorities were very bad, continually harmed by suspects, rudeness, jurisdictional conflicts, injuries, enough to paralyse procedural activity (March 1557, July 1557, November 1558).' The situation was worsened by financial difficulties, and by the all-important notaries often being disloyal and leaking information to the suspect who could thus take evasive action.[64]

Bergamo city authorities, such as the rector, expected laymen to work with the inquisitor, and when the latter in 1595 attempted to try laymen without lay participation, the Venetian government threatened to summon him to Venice. Cooler tempers prevailed. The Pope and Congregation consulted through the ambassador (the eminent Paolo Paruta), leading to an apology from the inquisitor and a retrial with lay participation.[65]

Lombardy and Milan

The state of Lombardy–Milan was a jurisdictional battleground. Politically it was ruled by the Spanish Crown, operating through governors. As early as 1541 Governor Alfonso d'Ávalos (Marchese di Pescara) had arrested and tried for heresy some students from Pavia University, and similar *processi* followed in places like Como and Cremona. He had had some sympathy for Bernardino Ochino, and his wife for Juan de Valdés, but he followed orders from Charles V. Plenty of churchmen, notably Franciscans and Augustinians, were interested in ideas for reform, which may help explain why it was the state authorities rather than the Church that pursued heretics in the 1540s. These secular officials were the harsh ones who employed forceful torture (as in Casalmaggiore in 1547), not episcopal vicars or inquisitors attached to bishoprics. Reactions were mixed, and conflicts many-sided. When an inquisitor in Como attempted his own campaign, he was opposed by the bishop's auxiliary, and by similarly unconsulted civic councillors. When this inquisitor arrested a priest for heresy in 1549 he faced opposition from the Como cathedral canons. When the forceful Michele Ghislieri, succeeding as inquisitor there, seized twelve sacks of prohibited books coming from Poschiavo, the canons put up so much opposition that he had to leave Como. Conflicts continued throughout the 1550s as more Protestant sympathisers were revealed, and Calvinist support seemingly grew. But if inquisitors took the initiative, as in Cremona in 1550–1, the local civil judge, the *podestà*, and others tried to moderate the pursuit of suspected heretics who were fleeing to the Grisons and Geneva, and persuade the Milan Senate to take the trials away from inquisitors and episcopal vicars. The unfortunate inquisitor of Cremona, lacking practical power, was reprimanded by the Roman Congregation for trying to mollify the Senate. The destruction of documents in the eighteenth century leaves us unsure of the subsequent steps.[66]

After the 1559 peace settlement of Cateau-Cambrésis, Philip II of Spain wanted a branch of the Spanish Inquisition to operate in Milan, as for the Viceroyalty of Naples. A Church–State solution like the Venetian one was ruled out, and in the early summer of 1563 Philip II planned a Spanish tribunal, as Cardinal Archbishop Carlo Borromeo informed the Council of Trent in August. Borromeo strongly, and successfully, resisted such proposals, though Pius IV at one point seemed to succumb to Spanish pressures. A violent popular protest in Milan in 1563 changed his mind. Another Spanish attempt in 1566 also failed.[67] Following his papal uncle's death (December 1565), Borromeo could settle fully in Milan and from 1566 organise an inquisitorial system under his own surveillance, fairly certain initially of the Congregation's backing. But as usual his combination of enthusiasm, harshness and inflexibility caused conflict. While Borromeo had his struggles with Spanish officials in Milan, he also was later frequently at loggerheads with different persons and congregations in Rome; and he was not always in harmony with the Cardinal secretary (Scipione Rebiba, Cardinal of Pisa) and fellow Congregation cardinals, or the inquisitors in Milan and other Lombard cities. Impatient at the slowness of inquisitional activity he brought borderline cases to his own curia. In 1569–70, Borromeo – one of the leading campaigners against witchcraft and a firm believer in the sabbat – had a number of women originally from Lecco arraigned for witchcraft (*stregoneria*); he condemned six to death after one had died in prison. The Milan Senate protested, and was backed by the Roman Congregation, which challenged the standards of proof used in Borromeo's court. To his annoyance the women were saved from the fire.

Later, in 1583, Borromeo was more successful. As apostolic visitor to the Val Mescolina bordering on the Grisons and trying to convert a large Protestant population, he detected witchcraft. He gave a delegate inquisitorial powers leading to the indictment of 106 persons (mainly women). Here local civil authorities in the valleys supported him. Thirty-two women confessed, and nine women with one man were condemned to death, with seven *streghe* eventually being burned alive. The Roman Congregation and well-trained inquisitors were not involved, and the outcome was typically harsher. Simultaneously the Inquisitor-General, Fra Giulio Ferrari da Cremona, preferring re-education to punishment, was apparently primarily concerned in the Grisons with the interaction of Catholics and non-Catholics, especially those trading through the zone, and he tried to ensure proper Catholic worship for as many as possible, and that feast days be observed.[68]

Until his death in 1584, Borromeo had to deal with worries from Spain and Rome about serious Protestant threats from supposedly numerous cells and individuals. Lombardy was extremely vulnerable to Protestant infiltration from the Grisons, the Valtellina and Val Chiavenna with its links to Geneva. There were transit routes across Italy from Savoy to the Veneto, with the threat exacerbated by the Huguenot desire to recruit support – religious and military – from within Italy, especially in the 1570s. Given Spain's vulnerability as it struggled on several fronts, and its need for supplies to be sent from the Kingdom of Naples and from Lombardy up the Spanish Road to bolster its defence of The Netherlands, political and religious fears commingled. Hence Spanish representatives in Lombardy might more vehemently denounce and accuse 'heretics', possibly exaggerating the amount of genuine support for reform. Those Italians wanting to oppose Spanish rule might use 'religion' to secure support to undermine political authority. Italian rivals could easily use denunciations to the Inquisition for non-religious purposes. Italians militarily useful to the Spanish, but religiously suspect, could escape inquisitional processes by appealing to a secular Spanish official, as in the Nicola (or Niccoló) Cid case of 1565–71. He bribed his gaolers to report court proceedings to him. The political tensions undermined the efficiency of the Inquisition. Local Inquisition officials in Milan or Cremona connived to allow accused, such as Cid eventually, to escape from the Inquisition's prisons.[69]

Lucca

The Republic of Lucca avoided the imposition of a Roman Inquisition tribunal, but produced its own institution to curb heresies. Lucca was seen as a hotbed of heretical debate and intrigue, among artisans and patricians alike, and the sense of crisis there had encouraged the creation of the Holy Office in Rome in 1542.[70] The Republic's leaders were anxious to maintain their independence in political and economic matters from against the Medicean Duchy of Tuscany, and in church affairs from the Papacy. The latter had a long battle to establish an Inquisition tribunal linked to Rome, a struggle which was intensified by Cardinal Gian Pietro Carafa from the winter of 1550. To forestall this, the Republic had in May 1545 instituted its own Office on Religion (*Officio sopra la Religione*); headed by one Gonfaloniere di Giustizia, it had three citizens elected by the city's General Council. They were to investigate those discussing heretical matters, even as a joke or in banter, and those reading or possessing dubious books, which should be submitted to their confessor (and avoid the bishop's vicar). The city fathers wanted to control heresy, but initially not through the episcopacy because it might then link up with the Roman Inquisition. A civilian judge, the *podestà*, would deal with those not complying, and any fines would go to the Misericordia hospital system. Bernardino Ochino and Pietro Martire (who had been a major converter in the city) were named as damaging heretics. In 1542, the bishop of Lucca did secure the arrest of Celio Secondo Curione, another influential supporter of reform, which led to further denunciations, and protests by reformers.[71]

In 1555 Cardinal Carafa, now Pope Paul IV, told the Lucchese agent in Rome that he feared the wrath of God would strike the city for its inveterate religious errors. However, reluctant to offend the Republic, he advised caution in dealing with possibly suspect nobles. Developing respect for the office of Lucca once it worked with the bishop, as it came to do, he admitted that 'the spiritual arms were little feared where not backed by the secular arm and its help'.[72] Thus Lucca operated under a somewhat medieval-type inquisitorial system, with bishops and the secular councils trying to cooperate, and keep Rome at a distance. Lucca was the only Italian state to have a state tribunal for crimes against the faith. The bishop tightened control in Lucca from 1558, with processes against upper-class dissidents, leading to a well-attended *auto da fé* where seven abjured and others were burned in effigy. A policy of destroying records every five years has, however, inhibited our knowledge, but apparently no heretic was executed in the Republic of Lucca, though a number of capital sentences were issued (twenty between 1566 and 1570, and four in 1580, with treason as a factor). A complete confiscation of property was seldom effected.⁷³ Evidence discovered for about twenty heresy cases processed up to 1572 indicates they were mainly of ordinary merchant citizens, some of whom clearly had commercial links with Geneva and Lyon, where they might have been directly involved in religious discussions.⁷⁴ The full office membership was seldom involved, often only the *gonfaloniere* and two or three others participating. They acted like ecclesiasts in enquiring about matters of faith. While presumably lacking theological expertise, their membership could include jurists. Torture was used in only two of these cases – but then repeatedly. Some accused regularly perjured themselves. A certain Pompeo in 1564 deposed that while in Lyon he had never dealt with people over religious matters, and never went to sermons by Calvinists (*ugonotti*). Later in a discourse written for his sons he frankly stated that in 1562 in Lyon he had regularly attended such sermons, 'and the Lord through this sowed the seed that till now I have retained in myself hidden and unfruitful'. Through the century Rome attempted to circumvent Lucca's 'independence', and curb its alleged remaining Calvinist affiliations. At times the Roman system operated from the fringes, with the nearby inquisitor of Pisa spotting the persistence of Calvinism in Lucca and arresting suspect Lucchesi passing through his district.⁷⁵

In Lucca accusations concerning magic and superstition were largely handled by the civic system, through the General Council and *podestà*. Some appear fairly classic cases of demonology, with sabbats, night flying, unguents and so forth. Torture for such cases was more persistently used than under a Roman Inquisition tribunal. Crezia di Agostino Mariani, who had been a witness in a 1571 case, ended up being the only woman tried as a full witch (*strega*). Against all norms, at the age of eighty-five she was frequently and severely tortured (using the trestle, *cavaletto*), from which she died, so the death sentence was carried out on her cadaver. Bishops tried to downplay harsher public attitudes, and argue that 'magic' belief was largely medicinal and practical, and not serious diabolism.⁷⁶ For the abnormal situation in Lucca we find complex relationships between a civic 'Inquisition' and other city courts, the Roman Inquisition and the bishops. The Lucchesi appear harsh in cases of magic and superstition, but in those of reform theology they might do little more than 'go through the motions' to appease Rome, while allowing the accused to escape.

The Kingdom of Naples

In the Kingdom of Naples by the mid-sixteenth century there was a stand-off between Philip II and the Spanish system on the one side, unable to secure permission from the feudal superior – the Papacy – to have a branch of the royal Spanish Inquisition, and, on the other side, the Papacy unable to obtain the facility by the *de facto* secular power of Philip II to operate its Roman Inquisition system openly. The Kingdom did have certain inquisitorial mechanisms linking the Congregation of the Holy Office to archbishops and bishops, who had commissioners and other officials with inquisitorial authority, rather like the old medieval systems. But as Pierroberto Scaramella shows, at least until the 1580s diverse people at various levels contested who should be called 'inquisitor', and not just those candidates delegated by Rome.[77]

The Roman Holy Office might send a *commissario* to the Viceroyalty. This title was first given to Scipione Rebiba, on 30 May 1553 when he was *vicario* at the court of the archbishop of Naples; he was later Cardinal of Pisa and supreme inquisitor. Otherwise there were *ad hoc* appointments of Religious, usually Dominican, to sort out local problems, using both violent and pastoral approaches. For example the Dominican Luca dell'Iadra, lecturer in the convent of Maddaloni, was entrusted with a vast anti-heretical campaign in the *Valdesi* (Waldensian) settlements in the spring of 1558.[78] The second model was to delegate powers to vicars of episcopal courts for which the bishop was normally residing in Rome (very common among the numerous, and poor, southern sees). In the battle against the *Valdesi*, Orazio Greco, the *vicario* of Cosenza and bishop of Lesina, received such authority.

A third approach was to delegate somebody to tour a vast area, again subject to episcopal authority. Already in 1554–5 Basilio da Castelluccio, a priest, was given this task in the *terra* of Faeto in Puglia, in *ultramontane* communities. He denounced to the bishopric of Troia a *perniciosissima* situation, since 'all men, women, and children are heretics'; the local vicar (a Florentine) exacted a hundred ducats in penalties, 'but left the heretics as before'.[79] The area was under the Count of Biccaro. Basilio provided an interesting report, recollected in tranquillity. These heretics were from Provence (*di natione provenzani*, in other words, Waldensians), sharing opinions with Luther. Seven years earlier they had been tried and found guilty of heresy by a secular *commissario*, backed by a Jesuit; but all that happened was they were condemned to wear the penitential tunic, *abitello*, men and women. When threatened again they said they were Catholic or were willing to convert. Basilio noted their boldness, and astuteness when challenged; he pointed to a key problem, that these Waldensians were scattered throughout three bishoprics (small and poor). The main population was poor, most were '*idioti*' (uneducated), not inherently heretical but easily won over by the *provenzani* heretics, when little contrary teaching was provided. Here the *commissario* was conducting an observation mission, rather than one of punishment or re-education.[80]

A more inquisitorial offensive came from a fourth approach using Jesuits under various titles to eradicate the '*peste ereticale*'. In 1552 in Naples Father Nicolàs Bobadilla arrested and tried Fra Sisto da Siena for saying during a sermon: 'Christ is the adopted son of God, according to his humanity' (Fra Sisto may have been a converted Jew). Bobadilla founded the first Jesuit Company in the city. The Jesuits moved against the *Valdesi*, their intervention made more effective by power given to them by the Roman Congregation. Bobadilla boasted after a mission in Calabria: 'I go purging the diocese [of Monteleone]. I make the world tremble, partly through castigation through justice, partly with good [*lo bono*].'[81]

Various Church figures and royal officials might cooperate, especially against the Waldensians, and against links with Geneva. In March 1552 in Capua, the archbishop's *vicario* (in the absence of Archbishop Fabio Arcella) initiated the vast *processo* that led to the condemnation of 53 of 117 accused. Sitting with him was the governor of the city, and a secular judge. Torture was immediately used to extract key evidence about associates (*complices et socios*). A similar mix of judges was provided in 1552 in a case against iconoclasts. The secular judge was the key signatory, including for torture sessions, until a month later when the archbishop was back and present. Another extensive Capuan investigation in 1563 saw the governor present, informing the Viceroy. But in 1561 in Calabria, during another anti-*Valdesi* campaign, the archbishop's notary warned that the presence of secular members might prejudice the case.

When the Dominican Valerio Malvicino was active as an inquisitor, he was officially backed by both the Pope and the Viceroy; Scaramella sees him as the architect of the 'crusade' against heretics in Calabria, while Euan Cameron judged: 'Malvicino's assault can well be regarded as *one of the last thoroughly medieval-style raids* on a Waldensian community [my emphasis].' There was some fighting against Spanish soldiers at San Sisto and Guardia. Eighty-six persons were executed in June 1561, by having their throats cut. Children under fifteen were scattered among other families to be brought up as Catholics. When Malvicino was not present the *vicario* of Cosenza acted as *commissario* for the Roman Inquisition. The archbishop of Cosenza's court notary explained that in the tribunals they had the balance of the spiritual authority from the archbishop, and the temporal from the Royal *Audienza*: as a result, he went on, dealing with the key Waldensian towns of Guardia and San Sisto, they have got five 'Lutherans' (as he called them) from Guardia in prison, along with the teacher who came from Geneva to teach 'the false doctrine'.[82]

The calibre of those delegated to be inquisitors varied, but some forceful people emerged, like the Dominican Giulio Pavesi (one of the first vicars), Giulio Antonio Santoro (later a dominant hardline Cardinal member of the Congregation of the Index), or Don Carlo Baldino. Pavesi had distinguished himself in violent anti-heretical activity; he was dedicated to the Congregation, 'becoming for Rome a true and proper oracle about matters of faith crimes', from whom Cardinal Seripando sought advice.[83] Confronting the problems of the *Valdesi* in Calabria, Seripando wrote to Cardinal Alessandrino (Michele Ghislieri) that it was hard to find people there who were not infected with heresy, and that, to combat this, extreme action from the secular arm was needed; that 'it will not be sufficient provision to capture ten or twenty, but overall it will be necessary to burn them'. In 1561 he instructed that those who presented themselves 'spontaneously', should be reconciled, but others burned. Fra Malvicino told Ghislieri that if all could not be exterminated, at least some should be. This was the prelude to a policy of massacre by the secular authorities, until the Jesuits recommended that education was preferable to killing.[84] We have in Pavesi a hardline inquisitorial figure, but one who was a refined humanist, who also had links with leading Valdesians judged to be sympathetic to some ideas that were condemned as heretical; these figures included Giulia Gonzaga (a key supporter of Juan de Valdés from 1536) and Giovanni Francesco Alois (also an early disciple of Valdés,[85] and influenced by Pietro Martire Vermigli and Marcantonio Flaminio, author of the bestselling *Beneficio di Cristo*).

Alois was a nobleman from Caserta, with great estates around it; he was hospitable and protective of many who discussed religious ideas from several different viewpoints. St Paul's Epistles were the focus of these discussions. Alois first abjured in 1552, and was finally executed in March 1564 as a relapsed heretic following trials in 1562 and 1563–4. He had been arrested in Naples in late 1562, but sent to Rome for trial. He was ready in 1562 to name eleven Neapolitan archbishops and bishops who were induced to embrace '*opiniones luteranes*' and provided damaging evidence about other notable alleged heretics such as Vittore Soranzo and Pietro Carnesecchi. He was burned in the Piazza Mercato, Naples, before a large crowd, and was reported by Cardinal Santoro as being very contrite. Afterwards there was rioting against ecclesiastical and secular authorities who had executed this respected man.[86]

Pavesi's case indicates that in the mid-century period an inquisitor might have some sympathy with certain 'new' religious ideas, and/or with others of intellectual calibre and social standing who discussed them with some discretion. Also, some thought in the 1540s and 1550s that the ideas of Valdés and his followers (*Valdesiani, spirituali*), which mixed Spanish illuminism with some elements of Lutheranism and Calvinism, might become acceptable to the Roman Church. However, the Waldensians (*Valdesi*) were a different matter; they were viewed as largely ignorant lowly persons from remote areas, but infected by foreigners from northern Italy, Provence and Geneva, and some of their leaders were seeking a close alliance with Calvinists. Therefore, it was easier to argue they should be exterminated.

By the 1560s the Kingdom of Naples had a whole range of 'heretics' for the 'Inquisition', the bishops and secular authorities to confront (or ignore): '*Luterani*' loosely defined, *Valdesiani*, *Valdesi*, Anabaptists. Scaramella likens this situation to that in Poland, both for the diversity of dissenters and for the ability of feudal lords to offer protection to heretical groups, even the more radical and

threatening. Beatrice Carafa could defend a *Valdese* settlement in her territory, as could the Spinelli family in Calabria. One could add that Giulia Gonzaga protected intellectual Valdesians in her lordship at Fondi as well as Naples. Clearly, Alois for some time could foster and protect what the above quotation on confessional practice suggests was a developed sect. Although the Roman crowd might celebrate his burning, it triggered anti-Inquisition riots in Caserta and Naples. Cardinal Santoro (originally from Caserta) had to cope with the latter between 1559 and 1564 as the inquisitorial *commissario* as well as, initially, vicar to the bishop of Caserta. Although some progress in control that was pleasing to Rome was to follow, in 1577 the Roman Inquisition was complaining that the Marchese of Cerchiaro, Giulio Pignatelli, was consistently impeding the work of inquisitors, and set a bad example to his vassals.[87]

From the 1580s the Roman Congregation's *de facto* control over matters of faith in the Kingdom of Naples was probably more standardised. Its cardinals linked with, and operated through, episcopal courts, much as they did with inquisitorial tribunals in central and northern Italy. They were determined that episcopal and archiepiscopal courts, when dealing with matters of faith, kept the Holy Office well informed and took advice, just as elsewhere the local Inquisition tribunals should. Much credit for this system, which lasted until the eighteenth century, was due to Don Carlo Baldino, appointed by Pope Gregory XIII in 1585 to the newly reinstituted office of *commissario* or *ministro delegato della Inquisizione*, which he held until his death in 1598. Originally from the Salerno diocese Baldino had been a canon, a lecturer in canon law at Naples university (1567 till 1591), then from 1571 a consultant to the Roman Congregation on criminal matters. As *commissario*, and also from 1591 as archbishop of Sorrento, he fostered correspondence between the Roman Congregation (especially through Cardinal Santoro), the archbishopric of Naples and the extended episcopal networks in the Kingdom. He could instigate his own *processi*, though archbishops and bishops took more initiatives here. In the known cases in Naples between 1585 and 1607 the archbishop's court initiated 345 heresy *processi*, and the Roman ministers only 48. The *commissario* and successive Rome-appointed ministers may have been best in dealing with the many small dioceses. On 30 March 1598 during a papal audience Cardinal Santa Severina read a brief epistle from Carlo Baldino, then on the verge of death, who wrote asking for a papal blessing and plenary indulgence 'after having been a servant of the Holy See for thirty years very honourably and praiseworthily, as much in matters of the Holy Inquisition and in other tasks'. The Pope then expressed sorrow at hearing of his death.[88]

Malta

Malta in the middle ages was considered part of Sicily,[89] politically and economically. In 1530 Charles V allocated it to the Knights Hospitaller of St John, homeless since having been driven out of Rhodes by the Ottomans. Ultimately their responsibility was to the Pope. While the Order of St John had members from many countries, its main language was Italian, which was increasingly imposed on the indigenous Maltese dialects, which were not written down until the nineteenth century. Within the Order French were the chief rivals to Italians.[90]

From 1561 Malta had an Inquisition system linked to the Congregation in Rome, initially through the bishop. By 1574 the island had its separate inquisitor firmly established, with a rather limited tribunal in terms of personnel and resources, which lasted until 1798. Technically Malta was a fief of the King of Naples (and this was to become a major issue in the eighteenth century), but here we are dealing with an island complex run by the Hospitallers. On their arrival in 1530 they drove out some nobles, taking control of the government. This Maltese tribunal features disproportionately in the history of the Roman Inquisition, partly because inquisitors serving in Malta subsequently played key roles in Rome, and partly because of the range of activities and problems that Maltese inquisitors encountered. Problems derived from Malta's geographical location and economic functions linking with the Muslim world of North Africa, with Jewish communities moving between the Ottoman world and Christian areas, and slaves on all sides to be rescued and (re)converted. Additionally, the surviving archival material is rich, in terms of denunciations and cases and for its many-sided correspondence, especially eighteenth century. With the capture of the island in 1798 by the French under Napoleon Bonaparte, orders were given by the bishop and erstwhile inquisitional consultants to burn the Inquisition's archives, or at least the most recent ones, to avoid embarrassing use of certain cases by the revolutionary anti-clerical French. Financial and other complications ensued; and most of the material survived, if in great disarray, to enter the public archive – after the bishop had in fact helped preserve it in 1800–1.[91]

Between 1574 and 1798 some sixty inquisitors served in Malta. Of these two became popes: Alexander VII (Fabio Chigi, inquisitor 1634–9; Pope 1655–67) and Innocent XII (Antonio Pignatelli, inquisitor 1646–9; Pope 1691–1700). Twenty-five others became cardinals, eighteen bishops. Only six ended their career there, through death or old age.[92] The appointees tended to be of high social status, partly because they had to deal with the high-born leaders of the Order of St John, partly because they played a dual role as the Pope's representative and inquisitor. Some eighteenth-century appointees complained of social boredom on the island, though Ciappara finds some of this exaggerated.[93] The turnover of appointees was not that rapid, and if the prospects for a good career were high, life there was tolerable.

Malta had witnessed activity by the medieval Inquisition. When in 1561 the Pope appointed Bishop Domenico Cubelles as the Roman inquisitor for Malta, he was appointing the last of the medieval pro-inquisitors. Secular officials opposed him, wanting their own inquisitors (as in Lucca). The situation was resolved in 1574 when the Pope sent Pietro Duzina (or Dusina) of Brescia as an apostolic visitor to test how Tridentine reform was progressing. Also appointed as inquisitor, he had greater investigative powers and jurisdiction than the bishop, Martino Royas. Thereafter the bishop's role in matters of faith was minimal, and merely consultative; the inquisitor became the direct representative of the Pope, holding a dual role. As vicar-general, then Holy Office assessor in Naples from 1571 to 1574, Duzina had been a rigorous pursuer of heretics, and judaising women in particular, and was close to Pius V. But he had been expelled from Naples after a jurisdictional conflict with lay officials.[94] Bishop Gargallo was supposed to pay a subsidy of 400 ducats to the Inquisition. When he refused he was exiled by the Pope for two years, and the inquisitor administered the diocese in his absence.[95] The Inquisition became the leading force for controlling heresy, disciplining and educating a populace that Frans Ciappara judges to have been particularly ignorant and immoral. The Hospitallers were not involved in the selection of inquisitors, though they might occasionally have made a suggestion. The inquisitors operated out of a fairly substantial palace created in the port city of Vittoriosa (called Birgu before 1565),[96] next to the church of St Lawrence where they were formally installed, which by about 1619 had become a well-protected 'island' to ensure secrecy. Prisons in the palace or in nearby buildings were not very secure for much of the period. From 1625 the inquisitors also had a substantial country palace near Girgenti.[97]

The Inquisition needed to defend itself against bishops and the Order in a three-sided conflict over jurisdictions, which could be violent. In 1599 and 1600 attacks by the Order on the Inquisition's jurisdiction led to some officials being wounded. In the early seventeenth century a knight, Charles of Aymede, murdered the Inquisition's notary. Having mitigated the Inquisition's powers, the Pope agreed with Grand Master Alof de Wignacourt that the Order's tribunal should try Aymede; he was deprived of his habit, and allegedly strangled in the courtyard of the inquisitor's palace.[98]

Lacking a large police force, the Maltese inquisitors initially relied on local informants, but these proved reluctant to speak out, unless about unpopular and immoral Hospitallers against whose rule the Inquisition became the main bulwark. Although the number of *familiari* grew, supposedly to inform on heresy and immorality, the main attraction was the accretion of privileges and prestige – especially as part of the noble entourage surrounding nuncios. From the mid-eighteenth century the Hospitallers, turning the tables, gained some popularity as opponents of the Church, whether represented by bishops, Jesuits (expelled in 1768), or the Inquisition. The Inquisition remained until 1798, but confined itself more to serious matters of faith than immorality. Generally, the Maltese inquisitors had had a wider remit than many elsewhere, often intruding into the affairs of weak bishops. Inquisitional activity remained high in the eighteenth century, especially because of Malta's mixed religious and ethnic population at the centre of trading routes (see Appendix Table E).[99] Investigations were often protracted due to the great need for interpreters. This was an issue in the notorious case in 1658 of two English Quaker ladies, Katherine Evans and Sara Cheevers. They had arrived in Malta on a Dutch ship, dressed as Franciscans, trying to get to Alexandria. They were arrested and imprisoned for nearly five years by the Inquisition, though at some point this became house arrest with the English consul James Watts as the investigation continued. Problems of language and of taking oaths prolonged their case. They were eventually released on a petition to the Inquisition by a new English consul (Alphonse des Claus); Rome was consulted and agreed.[100]

The multicultural mix on Malta probably added to the continuing high prevalence of cases of superstition, and sacrilege. The tribunal had less trouble over books and censorship. The island had a printing press briefly in 1642, but it was soon closed, not to be re-established until 1756. What the small literate group on the island imported was watched, as also was what passed through on foreign ships or was in the hands of English Protestants and others with Enlightenment interests.[101]

The Spanish Branches: Sicily and Sardinia

Branches of the Spanish Inquisition were established in Sicily in 1487 and in Sardinia in 1492, with inquisitors named by Inquisitor-General Torquemada. Initially, limited action was apparent. Local powers were hostile to such intrusion, and notably in Sicily to the 1492 policy to expel Jews who would not convert. *Conversos* came under attack from 1500, but the inquisitors were initially cautious over executions. An Inquisition based within the Viceroy's palace was established in Palermo in 1510 and the death sentences and *autos da fé* increased, with about seventy people killed in Palermo *autos* between June 1511 and January 1516. The Sicilian Parliament in 1513 and 1514 complained about the abuse of torture to induce false confessions that were then rescinded; but protests were ignored by Viceroy Juan de Moncada and the inquisitions. The death of King Ferdinand II of Sicily in January 1516, however, produced riots, then a fuller insurrection with news in March of the death of Cardinal Francisco Jiménez de Cisneros, the Inquisitor-General since 1507. Viceroy Moncada and inquisitor Mateo Cervera were forced to flee, the palace was sacked and prisoners of the Inquisition were released.[102] The new king of Spain, Charles I, eventually restored some order and the Inquisition returned to Sicily, backed by 7,000 soldiers. The battle over the royal anti-*converso* policy, over jurisdictional rights between Inquisition, bishops and secular courts continued for decades in Sicily, with periodic riots or revolts, while *autos* and executions continued. King Charles (later Holy Roman Emperor from 1519 as Charles V) expanded the remit of the Inquisition first against Lutherans and Calvinists, and then from 1532 against witchcraft. By 1542 the new First Inquisitor, Arnaldo Albertini from Valencia (also bishop of Patti), had fully re-established the Inquisition in Sicily as an almost untouchable institution, backed by privileged institutionalised *familiari*.[103]

By the mid-sixteenth century the Sicilian tribunal was headed by the First Inquisitor, assisted by two others, a notary taking records while another registered confiscations; additionally, a secretary or two, prison officials, *familiari*, and outside advisers as needed. The inquisitors here, in contrast to those under Roman supervision, were jurists rather than theologians, though they received theological advice from advisers (*qualificatori*). Unlike Roman inquisitors, Sicilian ones were frequently also bishops. Those not having dual roles might have a closer involvement in trials than many under the Roman inquisitional system, but they might also have to contend with other inquisitors. Torture seems to have been used more frequently, and with less control over its timing or brutality. The prison conditions, as notoriously in Palermo, were dire, leading to many suicides and deaths from starvation. Public *autos* were very common whereas mainland Italian ones were few.[104]

Public participation in the *autos* suggests a degree of local support for the Inquisition and its pursuit of heresy. Willingness to be *familiari* might suggest support, except that the associated exemptions, privileges and immunities were probably the prime motivations. These factors do not disguise the strong opposition at times from the elites in the Sicilian Parliament, from viceroys (who were sometimes Italian not Spanish) and local communities. Henry Lea suggested that inquisitorial brutality and corruption over confiscations may have increased the support of nobles for heresies. Violent opposition by Sicilians in 1543 prevented the adoption of the Spanish practice of hanging the *sanbenitos* (tunics signifying condemnation of heresy) in the local churches, which would perpetuate public shame for the accused's family.[105] Bishops who were not also inquisitors could add to the complexity of jurisdictional battles. They or secular magistrates might side with those accused by the Inquisition. Although inquisitors might lose some battles, and various 'privileged' persons escape their clutches, through the sixteenth century they steadily increased their control of a widening range of offences – magic and superstition, bigamy and blasphemy, as recognised in a papal Bull of 1554. Bigamy was a hotly contested issue in 1555 and one in which Viceroy Juan de Vega took considerable interest, remitting it to Emperor Charles V. While he ruled that this offence should be handled by bishops, local inquisitors continued trying bigamists and getting them to abjure at *autos*.[106]

The inquisitors in Sicily, all drawn from Spain and part of the mainland career structures, were forceful representatives of an imperial regime and not integrated into the local society. Francesco Renda stresses the foreignness of the system, its creation of fear and terror: it 'contributed solely to repress and destroy'; '. . . with an absolute lack of control that would moderate or mitigate action, the inquisition abused its power, humiliated, mortified, overwhelmed, but did not conquer, did not create converts, nor form consciences, nor exercise hegemony. It was a power without a soul, which entrusted its fortunes to the pedagogy of fear.'[107] As my book indicates, such harsh and damning comments cannot be applied to the Roman Inquisition, or the mixed system in the Kingdom of Naples. Despite four centuries of Spanish domination, Sicily remained Italian – argues Renda – or at least non-Spanish.

The War of the Spanish Succession from 1701 disrupted Spanish control over Sicily and its Inquisition. In 1738 Pope Clement XII made the Inquisition autonomous, with the Bourbon King Charles of Naples proposing candidates for Inquisitor-General to the Pope. Inquisitorial activity diminished significantly, though followers of the Quietist Miguel de Molinos were pursued. When Domenico Caracciolo, marchese di Villamarino, became Viceroy in 1781 he followed his Enlightenment enthusiasms, fostered when he was ambassador to France, setting about undermining the roles of the Inquisition and then securing a decree in March 1782 from King Ferdinand III of Sicily abolishing the Sicilian Inquisition. Properties and incomes were seized. On royal orders, documents (notably details of *processi* and about *familiari*), images and *sanbenitos* of the condemned were burned on 27 June 1783. Three old women accused of witchcraft were released.[108]

The Sardinian tribunal, established in 1492, was first based in the archbishop's palace in Cagliari. Its development and operation were seriously impeded both by the island's poverty, which limited its staff (only five members in 1522), and by episcopal opposition, though some bishops were made inquisitors.[109] Inquisitor Leandro Alberti, in his *Descrittione di tutta l'Italia*, which in its second volume included the islands as part of Italy, stressed the poverty, un-Christian behaviour and ignorance of Sardinians, complicated by their multilingualism and clerical ignorance.[110] Here in the sixteenth century Jews and *conversos* presented few problems. When Protestant threats appeared, as they did only rarely, offenders were considered more seriously, as with the Cagliari groups discussed below. In the 1590s the Huguenot Gaspar Poma invented a Jewish past to secure a lighter sentence, declaring 'if I had said I was a Protestant they would have punished me more vigorously'.[111] Converted Muslims, *moriscos* (about 18 per cent of those charged over the period 1540–1700) and those accused of magic (21 per cent) were significant targets. The *Suprema* from 1527 strongly encouraged the Sardinian inquisitor to combat witches (*bruxas*), initially with preaching and indoctrination rather than trials (though that soon changed).¹¹² A degree of opposition to the Inquisition is reflected in many cases (25 per cent) classified as 'acts against the Holy Office'. Inquisitor Alfonso Lorca in 1571 wrote to the Inquisitor-General that the Sardinian populace 'abhors the inquisition more than hell'. Later in 1579, when he was archbishop of Sassari, he complained that Sardinians were totally untrustworthy as officials of the Inquisition: they lived without laws, and in fact 'they are ill-inclined and enemies of the Holy Office ... and above all are supreme enemies of the Spanish nation and very attached to the French and Italian [nations]'.¹¹³

Bishops opposing inquisitors and seeking to protect their jurisdictions could successfully solicit papal help, as did Archbishop Salvator Alepus of Sassari in 1538 to ensure that a bishop could be present in a *processo* alongside the inquisitor; and Archbishop Anton Canopolo of Oristano secured papal authority to conduct heresy trials without the inquisitor. Some inquisitors with royal backing achieved their victories against episcopal interventions. The Inquisition was moved to the city castle in Sassari in 1563 in a bid to separate it from episcopal controls and frustrations. Later, when inquisitors were sometimes judged excessively offensive to episcopal rights and roles, archbishops and bishops secured the *Suprema*'s support, and had the powers of the inquisitors curbed.

Sardinia was somewhat influenced by new ideas of reform, Erasmianism and Calvinism, as in the case of members of the erudite and internationally travelled Arquer and Gallo families. The experience of Sigismondo Arquer from Cagliari is worth noting. His learned father Giovanni Antonio became an adviser to Viceroy Antonio de Cardona. Some nobles who resented the Viceroy's attempt to curb their abuses persuaded the Inquisition's *commissario*, Pietro Vaguer, to arrest Giovanni Antonio in 1543 for necromancy, as an indirect attack on the Viceroy. Arquer was held for thirteen months in the Inquisition's gaol before he was released as innocent (and rewarded by Prince Philip of Spain). The misuse of inquisitional denunciations for political-social purposes was always a danger. Sigismondo studied canon and civil law at Pisa University, then theology in Siena. The treatment of his father seemingly encouraged his pursuit of religious novelty. He travelled widely and met reformers in the Grisons, Zurich and Basel. At Sebastian Münster's suggestion he wrote a history of Sardinia, well used in Leandro Alberti's *Descrittione d'Italia*. Sigismondo was an Erasmian enthusiast, and opponent of the Spanish Inquisition, but he was able to win Philip II's support. In 1563 he was denounced in Sardinia as a Lutheran, and investigated by inquisitor Diego Calvo and Archbishop Antonio Parragues de Castillejo of Cagliari; the latter cleared him, but the inquisitor continued investigations. Then Sigismondo was implicated in the trial of a Valencian nobleman Gaspar Centelles (whose family had large estates in Sardinia), executed as a 'Lutheran' in 1564. Sigismondo had failed to burn incriminating correspondence with Gaspar, which showed his knowledge of works by Valdés and German Protestants. He was investigated at length, with torture, until burned at the stake in 1571.[114]

More dedicated Calvinists in the same period included the brothers Nicola (a physician) and Giovanni Gallo di Iglesias. Francesco and Gervaso Vidini escaped in time to Geneva and avoided inquisitorial persecution. In 1590 at an *auto da fé* in Sassari three Piedmontese artisans were condemned for spreading heretical ideas. One, Ambrogio Veraldo, was certainly a convinced Calvinist (influenced in Lyon), and was sentenced to the galleys. Two others abjured and were then banished from the island.[115]

In 1578 Sardinia was allocated a second inquisitor. Inquisition finances improved from the end of the sixteenth century (sponging off episcopal incomes), though the stipends were claimed to be the lowest in the Spanish inquisitional system. At various points in the seventeenth century money was lacking to pay inquisitors, or recruit a suitable notary. Numerous *familiares* and *comisarios* were, however, added as privileged adherents. Periodically the *Suprema* commissioned an inquisitorial visitation to establish conditions and problems in Sardinia, and seek resolutions – especially where jurisdictional controversies with royal officials or bishops were involved. The best-known visitation was that in 1596–8 by a member of the Barcelona tribunal, Pedro de Hoyo. He moved on to be an active inquisitor in Sicily, especially interested in claims about witches flying at night. Other noted visitations showing Spanish interest and control were in 1640, 1665 and 1696, which revealed defects in inquisitors' behaviour, and those of the numerous *familiares*.[116] In three areas of Gallura in the early seventeenth century 500 persons belonged to the Inquisition in some guise or other, with various titles. Often the inquisitor, given public hostility around him, wanted to ensure a suitable bodyguard. The Sardinia tribunal was the first to be suppressed, in 1708, when the island came under the control of the Habsburg Charles VI.

Papal involvement in policies in both Sardinia and Sicily could be accepted by the Spanish kings. We find this in the issue as to whether sodomy should be tried by secular or Inquisition courts. In the 1590s the Viceroy and elite Sicilians secured Clement VIII's veto against transferring all sodomy cases to the Inquisition. Henceforth only *familiares* so sinning would be tried there (and many were), but sentences passed on the most serious cases were sent to Rome for ratification.[117] In Sardinia in 1593 Archbishop Antonio Canopolo of Oristano secured Clement VIII's support that he, rather than the inquisitor, should try a priest for solicitation while confessing a penitent. This archbishop was also ready to claim the right to try a Holy Office familiar accused of sorcery by invoking the devil.[118] So bishops and inquisitors in their conflicts could turn in several directions to have their positions ratified – to the Pope and to Spain, whether the Holy Office *Suprema* or the Royal Council.

Later Developments of the Roman Inquisition: the Inquisition Style

In 1572 the chief tasks of book censorship were made the responsibility of a Congregation of the Index, an offshoot of the main Holy Office Congregation. As Chapter 7 below will show, the two congregations had complex relationships, sometimes acrimonious, with each other and the Master of the Sacred Palace.[119]

The 1580s arguably witnessed a new phase in the history of the Inquisition. Sixtus V considerably reorganised and expanded the Cardinalate congregational system in a form of central government, with fifteen congregations existing in 1588 (new or reconstituted). While the Congregation of the Holy Office retained pre-eminence, others became powerhouses for groups of cardinals.[120] Since the Pope had direct links with all congregations, he could use some to counteract the Holy Office or the Congregation of the Index if he was at loggerheads with them. However, the Holy Office could also impede the work of other congregations, such as that of Rites if it suspected persons suggested for beatification to be bordering on heresy. This power of veto was formalised from 1615.[121] The proliferation of congregations probably complicated the life of local inquisitors, especially as their range of activities (and types of offender) expanded, and more jurisdictional rights were at issue.

From the 1580s the struggles between inquisitors and bishops over control of matters of faith shifted in favour of inquisitorial pre-eminence, or to beneficial cooperation. Forthright episcopal opposition and intransigence seem less in evidence (though clashes were not eliminated). The use of inquisitorial vicars in smaller towns as deputies to the main tribunal became more widespread, and more acceptable to bishops and archbishops. Neapolitan bishops also had to accept more officials linked to the Inquisition. Through to the 1620s the remoter bishops showed greater cooperation with the Roman Holy Office, and then were prepared to publish edicts issued by it.[122] However, conflicts were never eliminated, as a large Holy Office file devoted to conflicts over the issuing of general edicts in the mid-seventeenth century testifies.[123]

Centralising control was facilitated following the Inquisition Congregation's 1593 decision to create a proper archive in the Inquisition Palace (Palazzo del S. Uffizio), followed by campaigns to ensure local inquisitorial archives were created (if not already in place), and properly maintained. Instructions from Rome, whether particular or general for several tribunals, were to be archived.[124]

By the early seventeenth century an 'Inquisition style' may be detected, overtly discussed and promoted – as Francesco Beretta has emphasised – by Cardinal Gian Garzia Millini under Paul V.[125] This involved mastering, and combining, ecclesiastical and civil law, doctrines of theology and canon law, and the Holy Office's jurisprudence. This brought together theory and practice. The ultimate role of the Holy Office was to condemn and excommunicate heretics, and possibly have them turned over to the secular authorities for execution, if they had voluntarily with their intellect adhered to a specific heresy. The developed inquisitorial style was, however, both to embrace a wider range of lesser offences and also less damning ranges of condemnation and reconciliation. It stressed that for somebody to be condemned to execution as an impenitent heretic the alleged doctrinal propositions attributed to the accused must be formally heretical. But other propositions might be deemed 'erroneous'; they might be indirectly heretical (*haeresim sapiens*) and close to heresy, or be rashly opposed to the theological consensus, but not so as to endanger faith. Or they could be offensive to the ears of the faithful (*piarium aurium offensiva*), without leading to 'suspicion of heresy'. This hierarchy of offences encouraged subtler consideration of theological and practical error, and an expansion of jurisdiction. Theologians might be more fully consulted to secure opinions that would justify inquisitors covering an issue because it was doctrinally suspect at some level. While this system encouraged inquisitorial remits to be more pervasive, and particularly over writings that might be censored, two other consequences could follow. Theological discussions behind a case could be more controversial, and hence lengthier. It also encouraged the tribunals to order the offenders to 'retract' their propositions, rather that formally 'abjure' them. While of course this meant a book might still be banned, or subjected to partial censorship, its author suffered no physical or spiritual punishment and, where relevant, could continue his ecclesiastical career.

The Closure of Italian Inquisition Tribunals

The ending of local Inquisition tribunals came at various stages in the eighteenth century. Some were closed abruptly, others withered away into virtual inactivity before a formal closure. Some tribunals, such as at Modena and on Malta, had a great spurt of activity before their demise.[126]

The Sardinian tribunal was the first to close, in 1708 when the island was occupied by anti-Spanish allies in the War of the Spanish Succession; when the House of Savoy took over in 1718 the inquisitorial role returned to the bishops, though representatives of the Roman Congregation may also have been active. In Sicily in 1739 an Inquisition tribunal independent of Spain was established in Palermo. The Bourbon King of Naples proposed names of inquisitor-generals to the Pope, and took some interest in what archbishops and bishops did 'in the way of the Holy Office', in matters of faith.[127] This tribunal was abolished in 1782 by Viceroy Domenico Caracciolo. In the Duchy of Milan the closure process was that of slow death from 1771, gradually starving the tribunals of staff and resources, not replacing inquisitors and vicars when they died or resigned; as in Milan itself with the death of Fra Gian Franco Cremona in March 1779. The Congregation was told of the closure of the tribunal in Como in May 1782. The last Lombard inquisitor was that in Crema; the French Cisalpine Republic abolished the post in August 1797, arresting the Dominican office-holder. The Venetian tribunal system drifted to a halt, with the last documents of the Venetian inquisitor being dated 1794. Some mainland convents that had housed inquisitors, as in Udine, Capodistria and Verona may have continued some activity until the Napoleonic governments closed such convents in 1806.

The Tuscan system also witnessed a slow diminution of activity; it lost control of book censorship in 1743, had heavy lay and princely involvement from 1754, and then was totally suppressed by Peter Leopold's decree on 30 November 1786. The Parma and Piacenza tribunals were closed in 1778–9, though briefly revived in 1780 in a deal between the duke and the Roman Congregation. In that year the office in Reggio Emilia was merged with Modena, which itself closed in 1785 with the death of an old inquisitor, Orlandi. Malta lost its last inquisitor, Giulio Carpegna, in May 1798, under French occupation, and the French closed the Bologna tribunal in July 1798. Some trial documents were destroyed, lost or ceremonially burned as in Rome under the 1798 Republic. By various means the Maltese archives were saved from proposed destruction and, thanks to the British occupiers in 1814, passed to the bishop; they are substantially intact today. French actions in 1798 also effectively ended the Piedmontese system, and that of Genoa, whose tribunal had been heavily restricted by state vetoes and interventions since the mid-seventeenth century.

The truncated Papal State saw the continuation of some tribunals directly linked to the Roman Congregation. After Avignon returned to French control in 1791, this meant nine tribunals. The nineteenth century saw some revival of inquisitorial activity, and notably attempts to censor Catholics' reading, but that is another story.

This chapter has outlined the development of the post-1542 Roman Inquisition at its centre and through dependent tribunals in north and central Italy, and Malta. There could be significant variations in inquisitional operation between states. Roman controls operated indirectly in the Kingdom of Naples, and more tangentially in Sicily and Sardinia. Episcopal concern with policing matters of faith persisted in many areas. In describing the institutional growth of the Inquisition, examples of most kinds of cases and of accused, and their various fates, have been illustrated as a foretaste of fuller explanation and analysis to come.

CHAPTER 3

How the Tribunals Worked

While the establishment of the inquisitional tribunals presented complications, the operation of inquisitorial investigations moved more smoothly according to procedural rules developed by the better practitioners in the later medieval period, the use of old or new manuals, and with the assistance of newer, more professional inquisitors and theorists. The post-1542 tribunals developed legal procedures, followed basic rules and patterns. Full-time inquisitors and their assistants, facing more numerous and more complex cases, needed to follow clearer pathways for their own advantage and convenience. The systematisation helped them, but more controversially it could perhaps also ameliorate conditions for those accused who learned to work the system. The current discussion is about how the system or systems worked; how the inquisitors proceeded through the investigations; how the accused and witnesses might respond. Concepts of heresy and rules of procedure affected questioning processes, the admission of witnesses and evidence, the uses of torture, and what kinds of confession, abjuration and expiation were acceptable. Conditional on these factors were the sentences that could be imposed. Here we discuss the courtroom procedures in theory and basic practice. Outside conditions that affected the operations and operators will be the focus of the subsequent chapter.

The Outline of the Process

A new inquisitorial process (*processo*) usually started with an external denunciation (or delation),[1] though some originated internally resulting from another case, or were triggered by a reference from another tribunal or from the Congregation in Rome. Bishops and their vicars, as longstanding judges of the faith, also received denunciations, or became suspicious of heresy during a visitation, and then passed on information to their local inquisitor (with or without continuing cooperation). The external denunciation by non-professionals might be written, anonymous or signed, or made orally by somebody coming to an inquisitorial official, upon which a notary would make a record. Juridically the 'delator', who provided the allegation and information, was not an 'accuser' since he did not have to prove a case against the accused;[2] that was the role of the tribunal. The Roman Inquisition tribunals seldom had officials proactively seeking heretics, unlike the Spanish system where their own paid officials or voluntary *familiari* would look for and report on rumoured offenders, and so launch a case.

People increasingly denounced themselves, as confessors pressured penitents to report themselves to the Inquisition before being granted absolution. Inquisitors in sermons, or other preachers, issued edicts of faith or a general call for members of the parish who thought they might be suspected of heresy, or knew others in such a position, to approach the Inquisition. This was more standard in the Spanish than Roman systems. Some self-denounced ahead of a possible denunciation by another party. Bishops, parish priests and inquisitors encouraged this, suggesting it would more readily lead to absolution and light punishment. By the seventeenth century some approached the Inquisition to clear their names, or seek a return to the Catholic fold, having been a Calvinist in France, a Muslim in the Turkish empire, a Judaiser within Italy. Delators might be close relatives, who feared for their own implication in offences, or desired to save their relative's soul. Many delators were neighbours, who denounced in vengeance, because a superstitious practice they had sought (for medicinal and love-magic purposes) had gone wrong, or because a disaster such as the death of a child or animal needed to be blamed on somebody – some evil practice.

Rules of secrecy governed all those involved. Injunctions were issued to those appearing as accuser, witness or accused, that they should keep silent about what had transpired before the inquisitor or his officials. Secrecy also applied to outsiders assisting the court, such as legal and theological consultants. People might be required to take a formal oath of silence. This oath-taking was strongly resisted in the Venetian Republic, especially under the influence of Paolo Sarpi in the early seventeenth-century.[3]

Once a denunciation had been recorded, a tribunal official needed to decide whether action could be taken. In the case of anonymous delations naming no witnesses, no action would be taken, unless the individual denounced could be clearly identified and the accusation was potentially of high-level heresy. It was unusual for the accused to be immediately interrogated. The Venetian Inquisition files contain numerous single-sheet delations without further comment, though we do not know whether a messenger, notary or other individual was sent to make some discreet enquiries. Sometimes an unpromising denunciation was kept, and then later a more helpful denunciation against the same person triggered action. If potential witnesses could be identified they might be summoned for questioning, even if only by a notary. Depending on the results of these questionings the inquisitor, with or without wider consultation, decided whether to summon the accused for interrogation, under arrest or not. The process could stop at this stage, if the person investigated gave plausible answers, or if he or she could indicate that the original denunciation derived from neighbourly malice. It was standard procedure to ask the investigated person to name enemies; if one or more of them conformed to the name of a denouncer or denouncers (whose identity was not initially revealed to the investigated person, if at all), the denounced individual could be sent away, with a warning to keep silent about the investigation. Alternatively, the denounced person might at once confess to error, plead ignorance, lack of understanding, put him or herself at the mercy of the court, and end up with an admonition and minor spiritual penalties. As in the case of Giorgio Moreto, the tribunal might stop short of a full formal accusation, establish that the accused had misbehaved in various ways, and arrive at a punishment, without calling on the accused for a formal response and defence; so also resolving the case quite quickly – with cautions, inhibitions and suspended sentence.[4] This can be seen as the 'summary' *processo*. If 'due process' were followed a formal trial should not be initiated on the testimony of only one witness, but this did not preclude lengthy 'protective custody' which might induce a confession and pleas for mitigation. Arguably, Giordano Bruno's prolonged investigation (see pp.182–5) was conditioned by the Venetian and initially the Roman tribunals' views that they only had one acceptable witness/accuser, with too much tainted third-hand gossip.[5]

Failing such quick results, the accused might be subjected to prolonged questioning in one or several sessions; more witnesses could be called, or earlier ones re-questioned. Some cases were abandoned or left pending. If the case reached the stage of multiple questioning then it became a trial proper, or 'formal *processo*', with formulated accusations put to the accused, who would then be clearly on the defensive. He could ask for favourable witnesses to be called to clear his name. Very occasionally the court allowed a confrontation between the accuser and accused, as noted below in the Gostanza da San Miniato case (see p.67), where the accuser at once apologised for telling lies about an erstwhile friend, out of fear.

Accused individuals who proved stubborn in the eyes of the court could be threatened with torture, more rarely have it imposed, to elicit an admission of heretical conduct or beliefs, and/or the naming of accomplices in a heretical conventicle or gathering of witches. The Congregation in Rome was meant to be consulted over the use of torture and serious punishments. If the accused remained firm in the face of torture, the court could decide to end the trial, accepting innocence from the most extreme accusations, with the accused probably agreeing to confess something, so leading to a mild sentence or caution. Alternatively, the accused was left in prison to determine whether he changed his mind, or until Roman officials recommended a different strategy. After accusations that heresy had been voiced in sermons, or written down in books, the court might take advice from theological advisers on the extent of guilt, though their opinions and recommendations were not usually entered into the record. When the court decided the trial should be resolved, the accused might be allowed a defence lawyer. His role was essentially to plead mitigating circumstances, not to cross-examine the adverse witnesses, or undermine supposed factual evidence. He could call character witnesses in favour of the accused. Having read or heard read the notarised copy of the proceedings (usually without witnesses' names), the accused, with or without assistance, could prepare some challenging questions for the inquisitor to put to those witnesses. The inquisitor or a deputy might travel to question named defence witnesses (expenses which the accused might have to pay).[6] Surviving whole cases show that many defendants waived the offer of defence, and put themselves contritely at the court's mercy – sometimes a beneficial strategy.

Decisions on a case leading to a verdict could be largely conducted by a single inquisitor, or be informed by several others locally, whether or not further guidance was sought or given by the Congregation in Rome, or the Spanish *Suprema* in the cases of Sicily and Sardinia. The Roman inquisitors, mostly Dominicans, could presumably draw on advice from fellow Dominicans in the convent where they were based. The wealthier and busier tribunals had consultants to advise on theological or canon law matters as part of a large staffing network. Some inquisitors in dealing with Rome cited a local congregation of consultants who had given opinions. Sometimes they gave opinions favourable to an accused and his defence, as in the 1607 Flaminio Rinaldo case involving inquisitors from Bologna and Ferrara.[7] In mainland Italy consultants came from a range of backgrounds, religious and secular, especially when universities were at hand. In Sicily, where inquisitors' backgrounds were in canon law rather than theology, in the sixteenth century they apparently turned to '*qualificatori*' with a masters degree in theology from a Dominican training. In the seventeenth century they also used Theatines (who were established in Palermo from 1602 and dominated by Genoese) as extra consultants.[8] It is difficult to judge the extent and helpfulness of the consultative process leading to tribunal judgements, since the consultants' advice was seldom recorded in the *processo*. Their reports might, however, survive in background files, as instructively in the Galileo case as several experts reported on his *Dialogue* in 1633.[9] Expert opinions on books and manuscripts appear in the Congregation of the Index's records. Authors under suspicion for dubious or heretical ideas could challenge the opinions of theological consultants, and even the right of the cardinals in congregation to base verdicts on them, as the Capuchin Giacinto Averoldi of Brescia did in a lengthy case from 1600.[10]

As a case became more serious the accused endured lengthy imprisonment, under very variable conditions. Local tribunals often lacked proper prison accommodation, as inquisitors complained, so they relied on secular prisons, cells in convents, or rooms in an episcopal palace. The Venetian tribunal did not have its own prisons until 1580.[11] Security was often lax, and gaolers could be accommodating, allowing escape, out of sympathy or for money. Gaolers could also spy on prisoners, overhear conversations, and inform the court. Here one man's experience illustrates several points: that of Adam Righetto of Portuguese origin (alias Enriques Nuñes, further discussed below and in Chapter 6), accused of Judaising. He had been brought in 1570 from Ferrara to Venice, where he was first imprisoned in the debtors' prison of the San Giovanni in Bragora district between the Arsenal and San Marco. During his lengthy stay and delays between interrogations he had the company of other prisoners, and fairly friendly gaolers, with whom he gambled, and who could escort him to shops. In 1572 when the city celebrated the naval victory of Lepanto against the Turks the gaolers enabled prisoners to escape. Righetto went to Ferrara, where he was recaptured and returned to his Venetian prison. In the summer of 1573, suffering from fever and swollen legs, he was allowed to spend a few weeks in a room in the Doge's Palace. (According to Dionisio Gallo's letters the prison conditions he endured in the Ducal Palace were grim, and he suffered from antagonistic fellow prisoners.[12]) To avoid paying special warders there Righetto asked to be moved to one of the new state prisons in San Marco, where he had learned prisoners could wander freely in corridors – if they paid the gaolers. The court agreed to his request, thinking he would be secure there. On 20 August 1573 the gaolers went off to watch a public hanging in the Piazza San Marco. Righetto, not locked in a cell, walked out, not to be seen by the Venetian Inquisition again (though the Lisbon inquisitors may have held him in 1578). The Venetian tribunal possibly decided they had had enough of him, and conceivably assisted with his escape, as the case dragged on without Rome expediting it.

The final stages of consolidated accusations, partial or full admission, pleading for mercy, or stubborn contestation, and then sentencing, were complicated, and could be misleading. Sometimes negotiation and plea-bargaining were conducted behind the scenes. Sentencing could involve release to the secular authorities (meaning death), life imprisonment, or the galleys. A short time later, depending on the accused's reaction, a formal alteration might be made to a limited number of years in prison, house arrest, confinement in a convent, the galley instead of death, or banishment. As already indicated in the case of Moreto, a suspended sentence might be imposed, and the accused released and watched for good behaviour. Other individuals (as in cases involving supposed superstitious practices) were cautioned, sent away and told they would be watched.

Summary versus Formal Procedures; 'Spontaneous Appearances'

The majority of denunciations or accusations that led to a conclusion were subject to summary procedure rather than a full formal trial. Summary procedures generally followed from a 'spontaneous appearance' (*spontanea comparizione*) by an individual, or when those persons whose appearance had been demanded made a quick admission of guilt, or when a plea of ignorance and a submission to the mercy of the inquisitor were accepted. The procedure used depended on what evidence the tribunal felt it could make use of for a full trial, its view of the seriousness of the individual's offence, and whether through formal procedures the accused could be induced to name names; and it probably depended on financial, personnel resources and the current case-load.

Some early 'spontaneous appearances' were dramatic, and had wide-ranging consequences. Possibly the most significant was that of Pietro Manelfi, a leading Anabaptist who in October 1551 presented himself to the Bolognese inquisitor Leandro Alberti, declaring that he wanted to return to the Catholic fold. He was a former priest from the Marche who had become a sort of Anabaptist 'bishop'. The death sentence in March against another Anabaptist 'bishop', Benedetto del Borgo, in Rovigo, may have frightened Manelfi into self-denunciation ahead of a possible summons. Manelfi was urged to talk; and he did. Naming many names he revealed a considerable network of Anabaptists and Lutherans he had encountered, or heard about, when travelling to places such as Venice, Vicenza, Rovigo, Ferrara, Istria, Ravenna, Imola, Florence, Pisa, Lucca, Cittadella, Modena and Padua. Having revealed names (though some would be hard to identify), he was absolved and received penances – as suitable for someone who presented himself voluntarily. The disturbing evidence of the networks of Lutherans and Anabaptists was passed to Rome, where Manelfi was sent for further debriefing. Whatever the shock over the extent of heretical networks, the Papacy benefited. The Master of the Sacred Palace, Girolamo Muzzarelli, was sent to Venice with ammunition that finally persuaded the Republic to establish an effective Inquisition tribunal. Manelfi had 'revealed' that an international council of Anabaptists had met in Venice in September 1550. Given the political 'communist' elements in Anabaptism this alarmed republican leaders. Manelfi seemingly exaggerated the numbers and international nature of the Venetian gathering, and may not have been present himself. But his disclosures produced a greater inquisitorial campaign within the Venetian Republic and elsewhere. The triggering of arrests produced further revelations, including information about Valdesians in the Kingdom of Naples who were in contact with northern heretics, such as Lorenzo Tissano (discussed below, pp.75–6). The Manelfi revelations strengthened the determination of the intransigent cardinals to act forcefully, and ensure local inquisitors traded information.[13]

The concept of 'spontaneous appearances' developed from Julius III's briefs in 1550 allowing confessors to abjure privately those appearing voluntarily (initially with heretical books), in both forums, *interno* and *externo*, without abjuration; and for somebody making a voluntary confession before the inquisitor for crimes of opinion to be abjured privately.[14] 'Spontaneous appearances' increased after the Council of Trent (1545–63), as confessors pressurised the penitent to report suspect actions or thoughts to the local Inquisition official.[15] Denunciations were encouraged by sermons and printed edicts published on church doors and in other public places, which followed formulae issued from Rome starting in 1607. Some highlighted specific heresies and erroneous behaviour to be reported or self-denounced.[16] However, the major trigger could be the pre-Easter confession, and the parish priest's duty to compile the 'state of souls' (*status animarum*) register listing parishioners who could and should receive the eucharist. The parish priest or confessor should refuse absolution for certain 'reserved cases' (for absolution by bishop, Pope – or inquisitor). It could turn the parish priest into the local policeman.[17] The penitent could expose himself or herself to public process, shame and punishment, or appear 'spontaneously' before an inquisitor to clear the conscience (*per discarico di coscienza* being a set phrase). This could lead the inquisitor to conduct a sacramental confession in a strict sense, or a combination of that and a judgemental process, but in secret (as *foro interno*) – or a full trial. In most circumstances abjuration was private, and penalties before absolution were spiritual and fairly private (*in foro conscientiae*), rather than physical or public penances (*foro esterno*).

The idea of spontaneity was hypocritical if in the context of obligatory Easter confession, though in other circumstances somebody fearing a public delation might prefer to appear voluntarily ahead of it, thereby limiting the likely punishment(s). The norms of spontaneous, voluntary appearance applied in the south where bishops were acting as inquisitors. The system broke the confessional seal between penitent and confessor. It turned the sacrament into a more punitive system, for the initial penitent, or others. This was particularly so when the penitent in confession named others – as with cases of magic and superstition – and was told to report them to the inquisitor before obtaining absolution. Although the person appearing spontaneously might then – if partially complicit in an offence – be leniently received, others were exposed to inquisitorial investigation. Yet even in the eighteenth century, protests against coerced voluntary appearances seem almost nonexistent.[18]

The summary procedure, however triggered, usually had the attractions of excluding other witnesses, defence – and torture. It normally led to private absolution and abjuration, and to salutary penances (extra prayers, fastings). So physical suffering and public shame were limited. Voluntary appearances received opposition and criticism from those who thought they led the Inquisition to give light sentences, when bishops or secular authorities considered the accused should receive harsher punishment. In the seventeenth century this was especially true with moral issues and superstitious practices. One such moral issue was that of the sexual relationship between Christians and Jews, which exercised the minds, and maybe consciences, of bishops of Mantua in 1636 and especially 1684. The bishops challenged the Inquisition's jurisdictional claim to try all such cases, implying that the offenders were being marginally punished or just warned. This was because many appeared 'spontaneously', even if the inquisitor's police (*birri*) had picked them up in the hostelry under suspicious circumstances, which almost automatically led to minor penalties. Jews in Mantua had learned to use the Christian Inquisition court, and the art of 'spontaneous appearance' to their advantage.[19]

Del Col looked closely at the types of procedures in the records for Aquileia-Concordia.

	Formal	Summary	Information & denunciation	Total
1557–1600	324 (46.75%)	80 (11.54%)	289 (41.70%)	693
1601–50	75 (6.80%)	559 (50.73%)	468 (42.47%)	1,102
1651–1700	26 (3.45%)	471 (62.63%)	255 (33.91%)	752
1701–50	5 (1.47%)	249 (73.45%)	85 (25.07%)	339
1751–98	0	183 (73.20%)	67 (26.80%)	250
Total	430 (13.71%)	1,542 (49.17)	1,164 (37.12%)	3,136

In Naples a less rigorous assessment suggests that in the second half of the sixteenth century formal cases amounted to over 59 per cent of the total, informal 14 per cent, information/denunciation 27 per cent; for the first half of the sixteenth century the figures were 34 per cent, 12 per cent and 54 per cent respectively. However, the Modena tribunal records apparently indicate that in the eighteenth century only 29 per cent of cases started from voluntary appearances. Del Col suggests that this was because the tribunal had a succession of proactive inquisitors. He also notes that for the Sicilian tribunal of the Spanish Inquisition, in which 77 per cent of cases involved people 'converting' from Islam to Christianity, the sentencing was mild (with capital sentences few); this possibly was linked to the high number of voluntary appearances leading to summary *processi* (487, versus 553 formal trials).[20] In the busy Maltese tribunal between 1743 and 1798, of the 1,467 persons appearing, 936 (63.8 per cent of cases) involved voluntary appearances, though many of the individuals had been pressed by priests refusing absolution.[21]

Recording and Reading the 'Evidence'

Interpreting the investigative process depends on understanding the records of the *processi* that survive to be read, the nature of the dialogues between inquisitorial questioners and those questioned, and what lay behind the recording of those dialogues. Understandably the written accounts are not an exact record of the formal proceedings, but this does not render them useless as evidence of attitudes and techniques. The questioning followed certain rules, partly governed by manuals. The responders were not necessarily helplessly cowed and frightened. We may be reading stories fashioned by witnesses and accused who understood, or thought they understood, certain rules of the game. Some of the answers may have been 'rehearsed', anticipating a line of attack, even aided by court officials, the recording notary, or the inquisitor, as for a kind of plea-bargaining.

With *processi* records we gain a better idea of the mentality of the witnesses and accused than of the court questioners. Notaries tried to minute, verbatim, the replies to the questions (making allowances for linguistic problems, discussed below), even the exclamations under torture. This record is usually in the vernacular, though some of the well-educated accused used Latin. Some early cases were reported in the third person, in Latin (as with medieval Inquisition records). The court's questioning was differently reported; often in third-person Latin, and regularly we only have *'interrogatus'* ('he was asked'), or *'Ei dixit'* ('said to him'). The Venetian tribunal, however, was more likely to summarise the question, and in Italian. It is thus very difficult to know how questions were phrased, whether there were elucidations of what the question meant, before the witness or accused replied. Very occasionally the question is given in first-person Italian, suggesting a quick (emotional) reaction to the previous answer. The notary might indicate (in Latin or Italian) that the accused replied with some emotion, gesture, or after a pause.

Most historians of the Inquisition assume that during the formal questioning the inquisitor was the questioner, but this is not so stated. In some tribunals the 'court' might just be the inquisitor and his notary. But where you have a formal tribunal consisting of many individuals, as most notably in Venice, the position is less clear. The record usually states who is present. Anne Schutte has suggested that although the inquisitor might have been the main questioner, others like the nuncio, Patriarch, their deputies or even a lay assistant might have taken over, without the notary so specifying. The notary in the case of Suor Mansueta in 1574 did record that the identity of the questioner had changed.[22] So caution is needed in assessing an individual inquisitor's attitude and strategies. That the identity of the questioner could change may also help explain why the questioning could shift away from a topic, when we might think a reply should still have been sought.

Final sentences were not necessarily recorded with the account of the questioning. It is hard to work out the actualities of carrying out a sentence, and how far petitions, or practical realities, mitigated the punishment. Other records report sentences, but cannot be matched by *processi* records to show what led to them.

Notaries and their Records

Notaries were crucial to the work of the inquisitors, being involved in virtually all procedures from recording original witness statements and denunciations, through the formal investigations and trials, to sentencing. They were also involved in routine correspondence and administrative chores for the tribunal. They remain, however, largely unknown and understudied figures. We must assume they came with general notarial training to work for inquisitors then developed some expertise in inquisitional procedures and lore. They could provide continuity from one inquisitor or vicar to another, and help brief the newcomer. Their linguistic competence must have been considerable, as they had to operate in Latin, a standard Italian and in one or more dialects from which generally they translated into standard Italian as witnesses spoke. Many copies of *processo* documents might have to be written to be sent away, given to local interested parties, or to the defence. Whether lesser scribes, laymen or friars from the convents were brought in for such purposes is an open question; issues of secrecy and confidentiality would have been involved. In the case of the witches of Soraggio in 1607, the local inquisitorial vicar, when sending his witness transcripts to the Modena inquisitor, indicated that a fellow Franciscan had made the record because his notary was sick with fever.[23]

Whether copies of *processi* that we have were seriously altered versions of what had originally transpired – censored, as opposed to just having names omitted or meanings changed by forms of translation and grammatical clarification, or being specified as a shortened version – also remains an open question. That records might be altered, embellished, modified according to the immediate purpose of the documentation at a given stage in the development of a *processo*, has been carefully shown by Andrea Del Col for some Friuli records. In the case of the miller Menocchio Scandella there are some changes in wording between redactions of the trial records, whether unintentional by a copyist, in correcting an obvious mistake, or deliberate in the light of later testimony. In some sessions questions were written out, but no answers given: whether because the question was never answered, or the answer was confused or unintelligible; or whether because a copyist could not read the notary's writing, or the answers were later deemed irrelevant or inconvenient for further transmission. At a session on 19 July 1599 the questioner and Menocchio discussed what had been said at the 12 July session about prophets erring, but the surviving record for 12 July says nothing on that topic.[24]

That investigative records could be more seriously doctored and censored in seventeenth-century Venice is clear from a study of files from the *Inquisitori dello Stato* (not to be confused with the secular members of the Inquisition tribunal) and Council of Ten. The *Inquisitori dello Stato*, a sub-committee of the Ten, investigated plots and treason, controlled spies or chased foreign ones. These records were manipulated according to what needed to be retained privily, or what was to be passed to others, as to the Collegio committee. The archive had two functions, 'remembering and concealing'. This secular system involved many more persons, who changed roles rapidly, so control of secret information, or 'spinning', was more essential than for the ecclesiastical Inquisition. But that the latter might significantly manipulate its records is a consideration worth further analysis.[25] It would be interesting to know whether many individuals served both as *inquisitori dello Stato* and inquisitorial *assistenti* in their careers.

Venetian evidence indicates that occasionally an interpreter assisted the court; as with Fiorenza Podacataro, a Greek-speaking member of a noble Cypriot family, who spoke no Italian or Latin, and who was trying to gain acceptance as a Catholic, having lived as a Muslim for over twenty years following her capture at the fall of Nicosia in 1570, and marriage to an Ottoman official in Bulgaria. An interpreter participating in tribunal affairs might be in a good position to coach similar Balkan and eastern Mediterranean outsiders in giving evidence, and handling questioning, and possibly affect the court discourse.[26]

When we do have surviving investigative and trial records from the notaries, we need to be wary of assuming they are in the form taken down when witnesses and accused were being questioned. Nicholas Davidson's long experience of the fullest collection of such records in Venice decades ago induced him to give pertinent warnings about them and notarial practice.[27] He deduced that what survives was more often a reworked version from original notes, especially when we have a record with few crossings-out and with fairly coherent grammar, which not many scared witnesses would have managed. How far this led to major editing – with omissions or additions – is unclear, given that Davidson found few cases where an early draft and later copy survived. Crossings-out may not be a guide to the closeness to the original tribunal questioning. When years ago I chanced on a version of the questioning of the painter Paolo Veronese over a painting of the Last Supper the version appeared refreshingly clear and neat, but with crossings-out; these struck me as due to careless copying rather than the result of a notary trying to follow the question-and-answer session. Handwriting style suggested a copyist who was not a notary.[28] The omission of names in transcripts suggests we have a version designed to be shown to the accused (if literate), or his defence lawyer. In the *busta* containing the records of the investigation of the printer Francesco Valvasense in 1648, two versions appear; one leaves out names.[29]

The occasional appearance of a comment *'inter alia dixit'* ('among other things he said') shows that not everything said was recorded – presumably when the inquisitor or notary decided it was not helpful. Omitting unhelpful comments from a version to be passed on could be considered more suspect. The Bergamo rectors expressed their concerns to the Council of Ten in Venice in 1551 that inquisitor Michele Ghislieri, in investigating Bishop Soranzo, was ensuring the record omitted the evidence of those witnesses who were not saying what he wanted them to testify, but for those who were against Soranzo 'all was written'. The notary might have coached witnesses ahead of the formal session. The record for a young Greek carpenter questioned in January 1587 over blaspheming at Christmas contained both a passage of chaotic, rambling explanation (blaming the wine for his Christmas misbehaviour) and a coherent, more formal passage, transcribed as he was kneeling, admitting wrong doing and that he deserved to be castigated if he blasphemed again. This suggests coaching.[30]

The record of Gostanza Libbiano da San Miniato's investigation was written down in Italian, questions and answers. The notary often indicated the question fully, though in the third person. He also made comments on reactions by the accused or witnesses. When Gostanza was being questioned on 24 November 1594 he recorded how she kept on kneeling, with arms out stretched. At one point he notes that in replying on her knees she turned to the Padre Vicario to confirm she had invented her story for fear of torture. When on the same day Lisabetta, an alleged accomplice, was being questioned, and told that she had been accused and referred to the Holy Office for serious crimes, the notary recorded that she crossed her hands, showed shock by closing her mouth, and clasping her shoulders then said, 'I don't know that I have done anything'. He glossed another reply she gave, 'being shocked and surprised' (*Et stupendosi et meravigliandosi, disse*). Gostanza was then brought in for a confrontation between the two women. The notary records that she went down on her knees again to ask often Lisabetta's forgiveness for telling lies about her; and again he notes her kneeling on the ground with arms crossed. She wept and turned to Lisabetta to ask pardon for deceiving her. Lisabetta was then exonerated by the tribunal.[31] Gostanza was later released as a mad fabricator of stories, to be discussed in Chapter 9.

One valuable legal manual, by Marc'Antonio Tirabosco, directly advised court officials to observe the reactions of suspects, their gestures and facial expressions, and not just listen to words. This may have reflected the practice of some inquisitors and their notaries.[32] In a 1697 Bolognese case involving four women who had attempted a little love magic, or distortion of the use of prayers, the notary stressed that one wept, and showed the greatest grief. This may have helped produce a minor sentence of warnings and penances.[33]

How far a notary interfered during an investigation is also opaque, though one suspects he could elaborate while explaining or translating the inquisitor's questions. Since a notary probably had more local knowledge than the inquisitor, he could provide supplementary information. In discussing the case of Abbot Alessandro Ruis and his former concubine in 1573, Guido Ruggiero notes that the notary 'moralised' in the margin of his transcript: 'Cecilia lived in the house of the accused [Abbot Ruis] and in diverse places without her mother and she was not married.'³⁴ Most notaries were laymen. Various tribunals found it hard to recruit able and honest ones. In 1561 Pius V stated this as a widespread problem, and authorised inquisitors to seek recruits from the religious Orders and secular clergy.³⁵ Some inquisitors and their vicars sought to obtain benefits and recompense for the notaries and other officials when pleading with Rome for better resources or rewards.

Archiving the material and storing it must have been the notaries' responsibility. They might well serve much longer than an inquisitor, his vicar or fiscal, and so were able to combine written recording with their memory of old cases and procedures. The extent to which the tribunals drew on past records, and how they managed them, remains little known. As for the major suspects such as Carnesecchi, Morone, Pole and Soranzo, their leading enemies, based in Rome with its higher level of funding and more organised staff, were deliberately piling up evidence to trap them. With lesser suspects in local tribunals, the situation was presumably more complex, and haphazard. Venetian inquisitors matched up records on certain suspect families over several years, such as the Lutheran Cerdoni family from Dignano.³⁶ More revealing is the inquisitor of Mantua's performance in 1684, when the issue of who should try Jews and Christians involved in (forbidden) sexual relations – designated *commercio carnale* – arose. Much documentation was almost immediately produced in April by the notary and inquisitor, dating back to 1636. To show the history of the tribunal's involvement in this type of case (and the virtual absence of episcopal or other clerical concern), inquisitor Fra Bassano Gallicciolo produced two *Compendi* commenting on 201 denunciations between 1598 and 1635. These were presented to the Roman Congregation.³⁷ This seems an impressive feat of records finding (given that it is totally improbable the cases were filed under type of offence, or that such a cross-index existed then), and being able to give a quick summary of who and what was involved, and the outcome. Occasionally the entry admits some doubt about a possible follow-up, but an effort had been made.³⁸ This exercise – presumably unusual – seems testimony to an archival system, well kept by notaries over a long period, with the last notary joining the inquisitor in an impressive piece of documentation.

Manuals

Inquisitors had potentially a whole range of manuals and treatises to help them conduct cases. Increasingly these were printed, but circulated manuscript guides remained useful. Most were in Latin, but some in Italian or Spanish. Medieval manuals had existed, notably that by Nicholas Eymeric (*Directorium inquisitorum*, written in 1368, printed in Seville in 1500, and Barcelona in 1503), which had a lasting impact into our period, especially through a revised edition by

Francisco Peña (printed from 1571). As a reviser of several editions Peña gained from wide experience, as consultant to the Congregation of the Index, an auditor of the *Ruota* (an appeal court) and as member of the Congregazione dei Beati, involved in processes that led to canonisation. His direct knowledge from Holy Office affairs is less clear.[39]

The Italians used manuals and histories of the inquisitorial processes written by Spanish experts; some of the latter such as Diego (or Iacobo in Italy) de Simancas and Peña served in Italy. Simancas' works were published in Rome and Venice. A lesser known long-serving inquisitor (of twenty years) in Palermo, Luis de Páramo, may have had some influence in mainland Italy.[40] Similarities of attitude have been detected between him and the Piacenza inquisitor Umberto Locati (*Judiciale inquisitorum*, Rome, 1568), who saw the punishment of Adam and Eve as acts of the Inquisition.[41] In terms of historical precedent he argued that God was the initiator in quizzing Adam as the first heretic; that Moses was another key influence on juridical process (as Simancas also argued); and that Christ who was sent as a lawgiver was the greatest of the inquisitors. Simancas took Greek and Roman law as the foundations rather than the Bible. The Páramo argument also fed the attitude that inquisitors were papal delegates, as part of the apostolic charge. This was a medieval idea, but was a key to the position in Malta under the Roman Inquisition.

The manuals dictated general attitudes towards heresy and heretics. De Simancas' *De catholicis institutionibus* of 1575 stressed that 'a heretic is not one who lives improperly but one who believes improperly', though in practice ways of living had to be taken as some guidance to belief. The Peña edition of the *Directorium inquisitorum* of the same year elaborated:

> Two conditions must obtain before one is considered a heretic in the proper and complete sense. The first is if one holds in the intellect or the mind erroneous views concerning the faith, and this is the beginning of a disposition towards heresy; the second is if one stubbornly clings to these errors in the will or the affect, and this act fulfils or completes the heresy. These two conditions, that is, render one a heretic in the full sense of the term.[42]

This explains much of the questioning by inquisitors, who looked for intentionality and inner belief, and the degree of understanding of those questioned. Different views could be taken of actions, with varied sentences, according to verdicts on the intention and comprehension of the accused.

As the Roman Inquisition was being established, those seeking a hardline punitive approach towards heretics, including burning them, could look to the Spanish Franciscan Alfonso de Castro's *De iusta haereticorum punitione* (Venice, 1549). For him death was a just punishment for heresy, though he also advocated missionary educational activity to re-Christianise remoter areas, as in Navarre and Galicia. His work condemning heretics was praised by Tomaso Garzoni in the chapter on heretics and inquisitors in his widely published *Piazza universale* (1585): 'a famous man of letters, who has composed a most beautiful work against all heresies old and new, many times printed and reprinted', whose arguments and reasons can be used against 'the asinine pride of these universal archbuffoons'.[43]

A much-used manual was Eliseo Masini's *Sacro Arsenale, overo prattica dell'Officio della Santa Inquisizione*, which was produced in at least ten editions, regularly updated, from 1621 to 1730. His experiences as an inquisitor in Ancona will be discussed in Chapter 4. His manual was prepared as he was serving as inquisitor in Genoa. This gave model questions and answers, showing how questions for different types of cases could be formed, how the accused might reply, and be re-questioned, and what an abjuration should look like. He tended to show consideration for the accused and witnesses, giving them chances to explain themselves. At the end he provided a summary of advice and warnings for inquisitors.[44] Probably the chief competition came from Cesare Carena's *Tractatus de Officio Sanctissimae Inquisitionis* (1631), which went through several editions. Although Andrea Errera assesses him as possibly harsher than Masini, Carena was insistent that people should not be condemned for heresy without real proof of guilt, 'as clear as mid-day light', given the serious consequences.[45] In the late seventeenth century vicars and other inquisitorial officials were issued with a procedural manual, Fra Tommaso Menghini's *Regole del tribunale del Sant'Offitio*, initially for Ferrara 'as a light for vicars of his juirisdiction' (with four editions printed, 1683–1702). His particular concern were cases of blasphemy, prophecy and superstitious medicine, and he suggested what might be included under such headings. He emphasised the bureaucratic procedures to be followed in taking up such cases, how testimonies should be gathered and confessions handled.[46]

Some manuals seem to have circulated quite widely in manuscript before being printed, and others were not printed in the period; notably the *Prattica di procedere nelle cause del S.Offizio*, attributed to Desiderio Scaglia from Brescia, who was inquisitor in Pavia, Cremona and Milan, before being named *commissario* to the Holy Office by Paul V. According to Tedeschi this is an informal work, and many copies were scattered throughout Italy and abroad. Desiderio's Dominican nephew Deodato Scaglia also composed a *Prattica di procedere con forma giudicale* (with only one copy found by Tedeschi, dated 1637 and dedicated to Cardinal Francesco Barberini). Both Scaglia served as bishop of Melfi, an interesting overlap of careers. Both devoted attention to handling cases of magic and superstition, and warned strongly against being deceived by names of other participants given by a witch under investigation.[47]

Evidence on the use of manuals is limited, though we receive some insights into what was recommended or believed to be in regular use. In 1573 the Holy Office in Rome told a Bolognese inquisitor he should act 'as the Simancas [book] counsels and teaches well'.[48] In 1608 the Modenese inquisitor licensed the printing of a *Breve informatione del modo di trattare le cause del S.Officio* for the benefit of his dependent inquisitional vicars, which according to the 1668 Bolognese edition of Carena's *Tractatus* enjoyed success, and was used by other tribunals.[49] An inventory taken in October 1658, when one Pisan inquisitor handed over to another, listed among other books the Eymeric-Peña *Directorium*, Prospero Farinacci's *De haeresi*, Umberto Locati's *Praxis iudiciaria* and a copy of the *Malleus Maleficarum*.[50] On his death in 1783 the library of the Belluno inquisitor Fra Francesco Antonio Frigimelica da Padova included copies of Eymeric and Masini manuals, Paolo Sarpi's account of the Venetian Inquisition and Cardinal Francesco Albizzi's reply to it; and two copies of the Index of Prohibited Books (editions unspecified).[51]

Denunciations

Denunciations or delations by third parties (as opposed to self-denunciations, or cases picked up by Inquisition officials, or following leads from ongoing cases) had many motives: a wish to clear the conscience, having been witness to suspicious activities; the exercise of revenge for perceived malicious acts by another; the worry for the salvation of a relative or friend; or the forestalling of a possible accusation against oneself by taking the initiative and being the accuser and not the accused.

Delators might suggest they were reporting to clear their conscience, '*per scarica la coscienza*'. The anonymous denouncer of Cristina Collarina in May 1625 more elaborately started, 'I a private person, moved by the zeal to honour God; as a good and Catholic Christian'; he (or she) wanted to complain about 'a wicked and iniquitous woman, deserving the most burning fire for her diabolic activities [...]'; these included various forms of witchcraft ('*striganie et scongiuri*'), leading to a death, incest and sex with Jews.[52]

Tribunals were fully aware that denunciations might be part of family squabbles, conflicts between different clergy and monks, employers and employees, with attempts to prepare witnesses to back the accusation. Hence a standard question to an accused: 'Do you have any enemies?' There might be some truth to a denunciation, but also inventions and bids to frame somebody. In 1566 the Venetian Girolamo Badoer denounced an advocate who had employed him, Giovanni Fineti, because of meat-eating on fast days, suggesting heresy. One named witness told the court Badoer had approached him to testify against Fineti, threatening violence if he did not; up to eight other 'witnesses' were so approached. The Venetian tribunal was told in 1572 by Marc'Antonio d'Armanno – admittedly as part of his defence – that a group of Venetians were earning fees by agreeing with delators to give false witness.[53]

A delator might be in an official position, if serving on a civil court or with the police, when deciding that a person under accusation was not just an ordinary criminal, but also a religious offender. Giorgio Moreto first appeared before the Venetian Inquisition in 1589, where he was investigated for several alleged offences as a Christian within the Ghetto, because a deputy constable of the *Cinque della Pace* (Five Justices of the Peace) passed on the complaints, seeing Giorgio's behaviour as more than a matter of law and order, and breaking Ghetto rules. The constable's delation ends: '... this I have made known to your lordships so that, having had the truth, you may give me something to help me live and support my family, and commend myself to your favour.'[54] Here was an expectation of direct financial gain, or of promotion, but whether he was rewarded is unclear.

Experience of the Venetian archives indicates that many denunciations were not followed up, because they were anonymous, they lacked names of witnesses or other indications of evidence, or they were likely to be of malicious intent. For example, in June 1571 the office received a single-sheet denunciation against a concubinal parish priest, a *piovano* (of Sant'Angelo presumably), a case of great shame and scandal. It was written by somebody unused to writing and spelling, though aware that the tribunal had lay members. It was annotated that the Sacred Tribunal would not admit it, because it was not signed and gave no indication of the delator's identity.[55] In contrast, the anonymous denunciation against Cristina Collarina was initially pursued, because witnesses were carefully named for the various alleged offences, though the tribunal delayed from May to December 1625 before hearing witnesses. The first cited and interviewed witness, advocate Nicolo de Elmis, may well have been the anonymous delator, judging by details of the initial denunciation and Nicolo's replies. The tribunal, having heard several witnesses, seemingly closed the file, without questioning Cristina.

Confessions and Confessors

Many investigations started with self-denunciations, or people reporting suspicious persons, because they had been sent by their confessor or parish priest – under pressure. The 'confessor' might be a professional itinerant confessor, or their local parish priest. Absolution might have been withheld until this person had reported to the Inquisition, perhaps adding that the denunciation was also to unburden his or her conscience.

Currently historians argue how far the pressure of the confessional contributed to inquisitorial activity, and the combinations of confessors and inquisitors produced a highly repressed and fearful society.[56] A key debating issue was – and remains – the role of confession, and the code of secrecy. Some inquisitors, bishops and theologians argued that in the case of a suspected major heresy a confessor was obliged to report to the Inquisition what had been confessed or hinted at, if the confessant did not report himself. Others strenuously defended the secrecy of the confessional. This might be on grounds of sacramental principle, though it was also an argument favouring those bishops and their vicars who wished to preserve episcopal autonomy and resist inquisitorial intrusions into their work of pastoral care. As Wietse De Boer has emphasised in studying Archbishop Carlo Borromeo's regime in Lombardy, the episcopacy and Inquisition could be in strong competition over confession and the salvation of souls: 'The Milanese archbishop enlisted his confessors in a comprehensive ritual and pastoral offensive aimed at conquering souls, changing public conduct and, ultimately, transforming the entire social order.'[57]

Few bishops were as intense in purpose and activity as Borromeo. The extent to which heresy and quasi-heretical accusations, and the resulting 'control', ended up with the bishop or the inquisitor must have varied considerably according to locality, power relations between bishop and inquisitor, and the relationships between confessors and the diocesan system. Many parish priests and confessors remained ignorant or were lax despite post-tridentine reforms. The very nature of the confession and the sacrament of penance inhibits any clear judgement. Confessors may have quietly ignored dangerous confessions, or chosen to remit cases of conscience to the bishop, rather than push the penitent towards the Inquisition. Sometimes bishops might fight for their rights against inquisitors, but decide to send cases suspected of deep heresy to the inquisitor anyway, as in Sicily and Sardinia.

In January 1559 the Holy Office under Paul IV followed the Spanish Inquisitor-General in instructing confessors that they should not absolve penitents who adhered to heresy, or possessed prohibited books, unless they had first gone to an inquisitor or their bishop and declared themselves penitent, revealed their offence officially, and named any accomplices. Furthermore, confessors who did not comply would be severely castigated by the Holy Office. This functionally changed the confessional process. Paul IV had earlier recognised the problem of respecting the secrecy of the confessional. Concerning a case in August 1557 he had said: 'The *Santissimo* expressly prohibited the examination of a confessor with a view to making him reveal the content of the confession, even with the authorisation of the penitent, and decreed that such interrogations should give no word in this or any other tribunal, because they would shame and prejudice the sacrament of penance.'[58] The 1559 instructions emphasised a view that heresy was a mortal sin as well as a crime, turning the Inquisition tribunal into an internal forum (*foro interno*) as well as an external court (*foro esterno*).

But the pressure was on the confessant to denounce himself. It 'deprived sacramental confession of any protective value and left the field open to inquisitors and their will to know'.[59] How far confessors continued to protect penitents and maintain secrecy is obviously unknowable.

A confessor might directly break confessional secrecy, as opposed to denying absolution until the penitent self-denounced to the inquisitor. Fra Giusto da Camaiore appeared in 1562 before the Lucca Office of Religion, presided over by *gonfaloniere* Matteo Gigli, and having taken the oath of silence said he was ready to testify that 'Catherina di Piero Del Cuoco . . . in San Francesco had said how a son of Domenico Da Cotrone used to sweep through the house with an image of San Rocco.' Catherina then confirmed that 'it was true that before Easter she had been confessed by fra Giusto from San Francesco and being questioned on the article of her confession and being asked if there was anything rumoured by anybody . . . said that she had learned from certain women . . . how a son of Domenico Da Cotrone, weaver, one day possessing a figure of San Rocco with a broom (*scopa*) . . .'.[60] Her alleged offence (not fully spelled out in this account) seems a trivial case of superstitiously misusing a saintly image, and the priest was reporting the episode at fourth hand. The priest seems to have been prompting gossip through the confessional, so going beyond his remit.

Ultimately, to the inquisitorial mind the confessor and the inquisitor had different mentalities and roles, which should govern their relationship. As inquisitor Michele Ghislieri wrote to the Jesuit Cristoforo Rodriguez in 1563 when dealing with Waldensians in Puglia and Calabria:

> I alert again Your Reverence that the person of the confessor is one, that of the judge another: the confessor believes everything that is told to him; the judge has always to suspect the accused's (*reo*) truth, and especially in this kind of causes (*in hoc genere causarum*).

The Inquisitor-General distrusted the potential leniency of confessors in matters heretical. He had issued strict orders to confessors that they should not absolve heretics, but refer them to the inquisitor (and not the bishop). The distinction in his letter also reflected the gulf between the Dominican inquisitorial judgemental mentality and that of the confessionally minded Jesuits, who were inclined to seek accommodation, even compromise. Rodriguez was in reality acting as an inquisitor for Rome, but in the guise of an episcopal vicar in deference to the Spanish monarchy. He joined other Jesuits like Nicolò Bobadilla and Alfonso Salmerón in trying to resolve the Waldensian conflict through private reconciliations and missionary work. Despite Ghislieri, Rodriguez went on to offer secret penance to some Waldensian heretics in San Ginesio, and secure quiet abjuration. When Ghislieri tried to have some of them imprisoned in the Holy Office prisons, Rodríguez went to secure papal support for his policy.⁶¹

The inquisitorial mind often insisted on a distinction between the *foro interno* (the private court of confession, spiritual penance, reconciliation), and the *foro esterno* (public court of abjuration and reconciliation). In the medieval period absolution by confessors and bishops could protect the sinner or criminal from further penalties. The Spanish inquisitors were followed by the post-1542 Roman leaders who sought to secure inquisitorial investigation leading in cases of heresy to a public reconciliation. Considerable debate continued at theoretical level throughout the sixteenth century. But this attitude was more clearly expressed in the *Sacro Arsenale*:

> The heretic absolved in the court of conscience (*foro della coscienza*), even by the Roman Pontiff himself, if he is then accused in the public court (*foro esterno*), he cannot escape the penalties due to heretics; though through the penalty proposed in the *foro interno* he satisfies God and is reconciled: the penalty of the *foro esterno* relates to the public vendetta and the satisfaction of the *Repubblica*.⁶²

The move to the *foro esterno* of the Inquisition tribunal meant, if nothing else, that accomplices and influences might be ascertained, leading to an eradication of the heretical 'infection'. Confessors who felt under pressure to refuse absolution for what seemed heretical, but were reluctant to do so, could alleviate their conscience, and protect the penitent from the more rigorous investigation and sentences by guiding that individual to present him or herself to an inquisitor 'spontaneously'.⁶³

Court Confessions and Admissions

Many of the confessions leading to abjurations were a logical outcome of the investigative process, essentially forged by the question-and-answer interchanges, and dictated from above. Sometimes a confession was, however, a more genuine expression from the accused, which could surprise, and educate, the inquisitors. In 1552 Lorenzo Tissano, or Tizzano (alias Benedetto Florio), Neapolitan but a Paduan medical student, provided a personally written confession, at the Venetian tribunal's request, in which he supposedly recounted 'all the errors and heresies which I have held in the past'. 'In order to distinguish better among my opinions which have been diverse, I distinguish them in a threefold manner: the first I will call Lutheran; the second I will call Anabaptist; and the third, since I know of no name more fitting, I will call diabolical.' He revealed that his 'Lutheranism' – with views on grace, works and predestination to the fore – had been acquired via Valdesians in Naples, when he was chaplain to Giulia Gonzaga. Then he had moved to rejecting Christ's divinity as the son of God, with Christ being just one of Mary and Joseph's children. From Francesco Renato he formed the view that the Messiah was yet to come. The 1551 arrest of the Anabaptist Pietro Manelfi and his revelation of contacts had frightened Tissano, who fled Padua where his friends had been arrested, and wandered homeless before returning to Padua and eventually deciding to seek absolution from the inquisitor there (Geronimo Girello), so he could renew his medical studies. He made one detailed confession whose significance prompted Girello to inform Venice, and from there Rome. Tissano was then requested to write out the fuller narrative. This added to the Inquisition's knowledge of the contacts of a whole variety of heretics interconnecting and feeding each other ideas (from Naples, the Grisons, Venice, Ferrara, etc.). Manelfi's evidence to the Bolognese inquisitor about Tissano's ideas (knowing him as Binedetto, or Benedetto Florio) largely matched Tissano's self-revelation. Inquisitors in Bologna, Ferrara, Venice and Rome shared information following Manelfi's disclosures, but the extent to which it involved Tissano's disclosures is unclear, and so, therefore, is the extent to which his 1552 narrative confession was revelatory or confirmatory.[64]

Tissano in his confession also raised the issue of dissimulation among those doubting or challenging orthodox beliefs. He expressed his own frustration over not knowing the stances of those he encountered, or which beliefs they really challenged:

> I was not able to gather from them whether they believed these things or not, because they are very cautious individuals, who don't make their views known ... and about Fra Girolamo, for example, I wouldn't know how to tell you what he has resolved, because he seems very inconsistent, and that which he seemed to believe one day, he doubted the next.

Fra Girolamo (Capece) and others may well have genuinely dithered over beliefs, especially as in this fluid period they were exposed to different new ideas circulating from various parts of Italy and further afield. It was also a warning to the inquisitors that they faced a culture of dissimulation among the suspect, making it hard to delve into the 'true' beliefs of the accused and witnesses. Later questioned by the inquisitor, Tissano exemplified his point with reference to the bishop of Pozzuolo:

> He used to talk to me about these Lutheran and even Anabaptist opinions, and I would answer him, and tell him what I believed, and at times he would remain quiet, and at times he would laugh about it, and I just don't know how to judge if

he accepted or consented to these things or not, because he is a person who is always joking and bantering in such a way that one cannot gather what it is he feels in his soul.[65]

Although Tissano was ready to bare his soul, the inquisitors faced a much harder task with others in a climate of dissimulation. The wider cultural climate in Italy had fostered dissimulation, through popular writings by individuals such as Baldassare Castiglione (*The Courtier*, 1528), then Giovanni della Casa (*Galateo*) – as nuncio, a promoter of the inquisition in Venice – and Stefano Guazzo (*Civil Conversation*). In his 1537–8 *Treatise on Prudence* the scholarly nobleman Bartolomeo Carli Piccolomini from Siena stressed that a person should 'project an impressive image of himself, training himself to be all things to all men, while at the same time preserving his own inner freedom and remaining detached from the world despite his dealings with it', and the reformed Christian should 'conform to what others [do] on the outside but internally to do whatever the spirit inspires [one] to do, addressing everything to Christ'. Piccolomini, who died in about 1539 and so did not have to test himself against inquisitorial investigations, had been converted to Valdesianism by Ochino's sermons in Siena, and had encouraged Aonio Paleario to propagate his ideas for reform in Italian.[66]

Inquisitors could be mediators rather than judges and accept the idea of plea-bargaining, as found in the case of Pietro Gelusio, an apostate Dominican from Spoleto, before the Venetian tribunal in 1556. In Basel he had been influenced by Zwingli, he had protected a condemned Capuchin, and advocated heretical ideas in a Spoleto nunnery. The inquisitor saw a memorial for confession drawn up by Gelusio, and in a letter (not surviving) suggested that this was too damaging if entered into an official trial record. He proposed a more circumspect confession, leaving out the most incriminating aspects. Judging by the simpler confession that ensued, Gelusio was merely sent into exile.[67] Another Venetian tribunal case involved Franzino Singlitico in 1550, who was brought up in the Greek Orthodox faith and mainly resident in Cyprus. He had previously abjured before an inquisitor on Cyprus (Fra Lorenzo da Bergamo), who told him not to defend Luther or Melanchthon. The initial questioning by the nuncio's auditor in Venice was firm and uncompromising. But when the inquisitor Fra Marino da Venezia took over on the second day, he suggested a compromise formula for their dispute as to where authority lay for resolving matters of faith, and how 'Christian Church' might be glossed. Removing specific references to bishops and popes, the inquisitor suggested different wording, 'congregation of faithful Christians', and 'that part learned in sacred scripture admitted by Christ to the ministry of the sacraments'. He thus avoided reference to the doctrine of 'scripture alone' (supposedly held by the accused), or scholastic tradition (the Catholic orthodox position). The inquisitor allowed the accused to remain ambiguous about papal authority. On this basis Singlitico was ready to submit himself to (an unspecified) Holy Mother Church.[68]

Defence

Those accused of heresy could receive legal assistance for a defence, and significantly more so than under medieval inquisitions. Manuals used in both the Italian and Spanish inquisitorial systems (for example, those written by Peña and Carena) gave advice on defence strategies. A defence lawyer should not persist in defending an accused he believed to be knowingly and unrepentantly guilty of heresy. He might have duties to the court rather than to the client; according to a Congregation decree of June 1564, he should tell the court if he found out the names of accomplices of the accused.[69] However, he could also help challenge accusations, credibility of witnesses, and unmask illogical arguments. He could plead for mitigation, as on grounds of the accused not fully understanding that the supposed offences were heretical, and prepare humble apologies. By the seventeenth century the Roman tribunal might allow the accused to suggest up to three names of his or her preferred lawyers.

The lawyer as well as the accused might be hampered by not knowing the names of the accusers and informers. Witnesses could be seriously harassed and threatened by supporters of the accused, justifying the tribunals' attempts to keep identities secret. Some of those released had to take an oath not to molest their accusers. In 1583 Cardinal Savelli authorised the Florentine inquisitor to release Cosimo Tornabuoni (held under house arrest), and let him move freely through the city, provided he obeyed a decree 'not to offend the witnesses'; the inquisitor could use this as a precedent for future releases.[70] Tomaso Garzoni alleged in his popular *Piazza universale* that the populace impeded informers and tribunal officials trying to curb heretics, and this had happened to him. He appears to have acted as an exorcist, and so may have been involved in inquisitional activities. He had some extravagant language about heretics of all periods, and called on readers to support the inquisitors.[71] Should the accused be released he might be attacked by his accusers, a danger fully recognised by the Congregation, as in a 1626 letter to the bishop of Conversano. Eliseo Masini admitted that secrecy disadvantaged the accused's defence: 'Because the capacity for defending himself which we grant to the accused is somewhat deficient, since we do not inform him who the accusers are, it is necessary that the evidence for conviction be absolutely clear and beyond doubt.'[72] This understanding might have led to some acquittals.

Sometimes the court officials were ready to indicate who delators or witnesses were, to the annoyance of the central Inquisition authority. A spokesman for the Congregation wrote to the inquisitor in Verona in May 1626:

'I will not omit to warn you that these my most Illustrious Lords are astonished that contrary to the style (*stilo*) of the tribunal, the names of denouncers and of witnesses have been manifested to the criminal (*reo*), by asking him if he knows Francesca, Achillina, Agnese and if ever in confession he has dealt with dishonest matters with them.' The Congregation might also warn other inquisitors to be careful about removing names from copies of the notarial court record given to the accused and his lawyer.[73] Occasionally, however, the court was allowed to reveal identities and arrange a confrontation between accuser and accused, as with the *benandante* Giovanni Sion in the face of conflicting accounts of who had attended a sabbat.[74]

Evidence of the use of defence lawyers can be found in a variety of cases, from the famous and learned to the poor and obscure. Cardinal Morone benefited from a team of lawyers, as did Bishop Pier Paolo Vergerio of Capodistria. Camillo Renato (Lisia Fileno) in 1540 in Ferrara had a doctor of both laws and recognised *consultor* to help him, though he himself had access to a learned library to help write his own *Apologia* as a defence. Tommaso Campanella, the utopian philosopher and alleged revolutionary, was defended by a leading jurist in his 1601 trial in Naples. When the case of Flaminio Rinaldini was transferred from Bologna to Rome in 1608, Cardinal Arrigoni asked the former city's inquisitor to forward the defence file prepared by advocate Domenico Medici for Rinaldini. Medici was also a *consultor* to the Inquisition; and it was not normally approved that a *consultor* should additionally act for the defence.[75] The now well-known Jew, Righetto, who 'sailed by two rudders, Christian and Jewish, according to the waters', could secure legal services before the Venetian tribunal. Benedetto Bariselli, doctor of both laws, was instructed 'he may without fear of incurring censures or other penalties extend his protection to Righetto'. But Righetto remained active in his own defence, which sometimes took a different line from his advocate's. Bariselli dealt forcefully with witnesses, and worked to get the case expedited when Rome was causing delays.[76] Other examples of documented defences include that of Domenico Scandella (Menocchio) in his second trial in Friuli in 1599, some of the *benandanti* also in Friuli, and a witch in 1588 in Triora (Genoa), who had a legally trained friar as a defence lawyer.[77]

In Menocchio's second trial (July 1599) his lawyer (Dr Agostino Pisenti), who had been found by the court since Menocchio had requested a lawyer but could not afford one of his own choosing, deployed quotations from legal authorities and the Bible as one approach; he also made emotional appeals highlighting Menocchio's age (sixty-seven), ill-health, ignorance and simplicity, arguing that justice should be tempered with mercy. Pisenti challenged the nature of the accusations and (lack of)identity of the accuser, the lack of proof for allegations (so the accused must be absolved); in criminal cases 'proof needs to be clearer than the light at mid-day' as many legal texts (cited) declare; no accusation was backed by two witnesses; 'no crime has been verified'; witnesses contradicted each other, and much was hearsay. From Menocchio's own testimony all that can be deduced is 'his simplicity and ignorance, and all this exempts him from punishment and from justice', and 'the pure simplicity and unambiguous ignorance of the defendant emerge from his various interrogations'; and 'God does not desire the death of the sinner, but rather his conversion and life'. Unfortunately, further accusations appeared after this defence, whereupon Menocchio and Pisenti abandoned the defence strategy, pleading for mercy. The tribunal, meeting in Portogruaro, disdained mercy, and he was executed locally in August 1599 under the Venetian governor's supervision. Rome was informed afterwards, seemingly not consulted on the sentence. Pisenti defended in several other trials.[78]

Defence lawyers could help bring in expert opinion and witnesses in controversial instances of alleged witchcraft in medical cases. In four Venetian cases sufferers from syphilis improbably blamed witchcraft rather than sexual activity for their suffering. In 1624 the prostitute Angela Castellana, so badly affected by syphilis that she had to live by begging, charged the notorious *strega* Bellina Loredana, now aged seventy and also impoverished, with bewitching her, when anointing her with, or giving her, oil. The defence lawyers secured Bellina's acquittal on this charge, using the 'experience' and public knowledge that prostitutes generally died of the (French) disease, and Angela was a prostitute. Angela died in the hospital of SS Giovanni e Paolo during the year-long trial. One lawyer declared:

> For her entire life [she] was a public prostitute making her body available to everyone: and because of this she was already for many years full of the French disease sores [*gomme*] and other incurable diseases; [in hospital] she died miserably because of these aforesaid illnesses not for another [reason], as is usual for similar prostitutes, and this is well-known and obvious, and thus the truth.

However, the lawyers could not clear Bellina of eight other charges and she was found guilty of 'sorcery, magic and diabolical operations', for which she was sentenced to an hour in the pillory in Piazza San Marco, and three years in prison. In another case of the 'French disease' in 1624, Andrea Marcello accused his ex-lover Camilla Savioni of giving him the disease and epilepsy by witchcraft; several doctors with divided opinions were employed as 'expert witnesses', but their evidence led to Camilla's release.[79]

One defence strategy was to discredit adverse witnesses, whether this was done by a lawyer or by the accused. This could occur when the accused and witness were allowed to confront each other, as in the Gostanza of San Miniato case of 1594. In 1588 Giovanni Battista Capponi took advantage of the opportunity partially to discredit a bookseller from Santi Apostoli who had sold him prohibited books, suggesting the bookseller had foisted these on him without Capponi realising their danger. However, this did not stop Capponi being put to torture later. The tribunal eventually reacted against his bold courtroom games (he had previous experience of a trial in Padua), as when he named enemies in various stages (possibly benefiting in part from a poorly edited copy of the *processo* that left names for him to see!), and told him: 'even though you think by these means to discredit the witnesses against you, you only reveal yourself to be an evil man, in confessing that everyone hates you – a thing that can only arise from your evil and criminal ways; and so general objection to the witnesses is unworthy to be considered.'[80]

Torture

Contrary to the myth of the Roman and Spanish Inquisitions, physical torture was sparingly used, at least once the Spanish system was well established and guidelines produced, which were then taken up by the Roman Inquisition. The latter was more circumspect in sanctioning torture, with local tribunals meant to secure permission from the Roman Congregation to impose it. Secular courts were more likely to apply unregulated torture. In the fifteenth century proverbially most thieves faced torture, though the records of its occurrences in secular courts were sketchy. They were less concerned than the inquisitors when death resulted, though public anger could erupt.[81] The basic guidelines for the inquisitions, as set down by Diego Simancas or Eliseo Masini, were that torture should only be used when a defendant denied guilt without being able to disprove the case against him or her, in the face of damning evidence (coming from at least two sound and reliable witnesses); or when the court seriously doubted the sincerity and completeness of a confession and the naming of accomplices. Masini stated that the main purpose was to ascertain the true intention behind the accused's deeds or expressions. Roman Inquisition officials seemed less keen to follow Peña's belief that torture was a very suitable weapon in cases of alleged occult practices, where witnesses were wanting. Masini warned that anything said under torture had to be confirmed later, free from the torture room, or it was invalid.[82] If the confession was then retracted, with the claim it had only be made out of fear and pain, the inquisitor faced dilemmas whether to repeat the torture, decide the person was innocent, or continue questioning more subtly. An overall assessment of the use of torture is difficult given the loss of full investigative and trial records for most tribunals.

The manuals warned against premature and excessive use of torture. The Roman Congregation reprimanded local officials who misused torture, and would discount evidence so obtained, or through torture applied without their permission. Masini ruled: 'Never commence with torture but with the evidence.

It would be iniquitous and against all human and divine law to expose anyone to torment without weighty evidence.'[83] According to Carena an inquisitor should take the counsel of clerical and lay advisers attached to the tribunal, on torture as well as on sentencing policies. Masini went on:

> to proceed safely the inquisitor must first propose to the congregation of *Consultori* of the Holy Office the accusation and defence *processo*, and with learned and mature counsel (although their vote should not be decisive but only consultative), be so governed and always operate. Or should the case be grave and difficult, he should consult the sacred and holy Tribunal of the Holy and Universal Roman Inquisition, and from there await the resolution.[84]

Consultations could considerably lengthen a case – and add to a form of psychological torture. In receiving information, the Roman Inquisition wanted the evidence of both questions and answers in Italian, not Latin, and 'with the very words for substantial matters from the witnesses and the accused'.[85] Cardinal inquisitors felt themselves obliged to take advice from consultants in Rome before replying to a local tribunal's query. The Pope himself might make the crucial decision at the weekly meeting of the Congregation over which he presided. To a query from Bologna in 1572, the Cardinal of Pisa replied: 'The case of Pavolo Vasellaro was raised in Congregation and seen by the *consultori*, and the general opinion concluded that he should be firmly tortured (*dare di buona corda*) to clarify whether he truly relapsed, and if the things that are against him had been said by him with evil intention.'[86] Against a Neapolitan bigamist Antonio Frezza, whose case was moved to Rome, Pope Paul V in 1607 ruled: 'he should be tortured concerning his intention and if nothing resulted, he should abjure *de vehementi*, and be condemned to the triremes for five years.'[87]

Some inquisitorial officials could be overhasty in introducing torture, as with Gostanza of San Miniato, accused of witchcraft in 1594, who was brought straight into the torture room for questioning, and soon subjected to it. This may have been because the investigation had started under the bishop's vicar, and the inquisitorial vicar involved was newly appointed.[88] Cardinal Santoro in 1594 wrote forcefully to the Sienese inquisitor that whatever the Sienese 'style' (*stilo*) on torture had been, 'the universal style of office of the Holy Inquisition' was that in cases of superstition there should not be rigorous examination (torture), until after the defence had been heard. The poor should be provided with a defence lawyer. This Cardinal was trying to moderate the policies towards witchcraft and sorcery, and he stressed the need for '*charità*' in the Inquisition's style.[89]

Many stages normally existed before an accused was put to a full physical torture, as Maurice Finocchiaro appositely stressed when dealing with the ongoing debate as to whether Galileo was 'tortured'. During his inquisitorial investigation in 1633 Galileo was ordered to be subject to 'rigorous examination' – a standard euphemism for 'torture'. The stages leading to the use, say, of the *strappado*, could be: interrogation under the threat of physical torture; being shown the torture room and the relevant instruments; disrobing the accused as if he were to be tortured; linking the accused to the instrument; finally using it. The physical application could be mild, moderate or severe (and limited to half an hour unless the Congregation authorised up to an hour, as occasionally happened). At any stage the process could be halted according to the cooperative reaction of the accused. The modern consensus is that Galileo was verbally threatened with torture, but not physically touched.[90] His age, poor health and his renown would have inhibited serious torture, and various people in Rome were ready to organise a 'deal' with Galileo for a reduced sentence, compromise confession and light punishment (see also, pp.190–2, below).

The form of torture (*tormento*) normally used by the Italian Inquisitions (Roman and Sicilian) was the *corda* or *strappado*. (*Corda* might also, confusingly, mean the use of a rope whip as punishment.) The victim had his hands tied behind his back, which were then attached by a rope to a pulley, enabling him or her to be hoisted up – to be held there or dropped and re-hoisted if not giving satisfactory answers to the questions, or admitting guilt. This punishment could seriously damage the shoulders in particular. According to Inquisition manuals, such as Masini's, stone weights should not be attached to the feet as used in secular courts; nor should there be excessive jerking. The Roman Inquisition was anxious to ensure torture did not lead to 'death on the rope', which had happened earlier under secular justice.[91] Under Roman rules the victim was normally questioned in the presence of the inquisitor, a representative of the bishop or a lay member of the court, and a notary to record questions, answers, imprecations and cries of agony (recorded as 'Oihme!, Oihme!', for example). In Sicily more persons might attend, such as consultants, as seen in a transcript of the 1555 torturing of one Pellegrina Vitello, accused of using magical practices with a mirror and symbols written on paper. Throughout her half-hour torture she insisted she had told the truth and had nothing to add, frequently saying 'I know nothing'.[92] According to Bernardo da Como's *Lucerna inquisitorum haereticae pravitatis* (Rome, 1584, edited by Peña) as well as Masini, excessive torment should be avoided. If innocent, the victim should not suffer bodily defects and should be able to enjoy their subsequent freedom, and if deemed guilty should be in a position to receive the due punishment (which would not usually be death).[93] It is hard to ascertain the damage suffered by those hoisted by the *strappado*. A fire that scalded the feet might be less harmful for a man likely to be sentenced as an oarsman to the galleys than injury to the shoulders.

Other torture methods were employed, though normally if bodily defects impeded the preferred *strappado* method. Masini noted the use of fire (rarely used because of its great danger) applied to bare feet, coated in pork fat; *stanghetta*, feet pressed between two metal concave dies (*taxillos concavos*); *cannette*, hands and fingers pressed. In 1635 the Roman Congregation criticised the Vicenza inquisitor for using the fire torture, and ordered that it should not be repeated. Finger-pressing (by tightening cords between fingers), called *sibille*, was used on the young painter Artemisia Gentileschi, to see whether her testimony that she had been raped by another artist was true. However, she was being tortured in the Roman governor's court, where torture was more widespread, and had volunteered to be so 'tortured' to prove her truthfulness. I have not read of such volunteering in Inquisition cases. Thumbscrews, the favoured method against witches in the Duchy of Lorraine for example, seem absent in the Italian Inquisitions.[94]

We know of the use of the *stanghetta* on Pietro Antonio da Cervia in Bologna in June 1567, because he was too infirm to undergo the *strappado*. The *stanghetta* was applied to his right foot. When the *corda* was deemed inappropriate, this method was used in at least eight cases in Malta between 1743 and 1798 including on a woman accused of sorcery.[95] When Giovanni Morone was under investigation his *maestro di casa* don Domenico Morando was frequently questioned; and on 11 October 1558, during his eleventh session, he was tortured on his left foot for about twenty minutes. Constantly shouting he was dying, he insisted he had told the truth and knew no heretics, and would accuse none unjustly. This method of torture was used given his age and because a doctor considered the *corda* might 'ruin or kill him' (*se guastassi o crepassi*). The preliminary questioning took place in the torture room and then the torturing was done in the presence of Cardinal Alessandrino (Ghislieri)'s assessor G.B. Bizono, and the procurator fiscal, Sebastiano Atracino, who seem to have shared the questioning.[96]

The nastiest method of torture used in Italy seems to have been the *veglia*, but almost entirely by secular courts. It involved something like the *strappado*, together with 'a form of triangular wooden sawhorse with sharpened point, and sleeplessness': the Judas cradle. This is what was inflicted on Tommaso Campanella in Naples, for thirty-six hours in June 1601, with a brief respite. This, however, was presided over by local ecclesiastical judges, not proper Inquisition officials – though Campanella was to be imprisoned later by the Inquisition in Rome. In Naples he succeeded in maintaining the defensive appearance of madness, meaning he could not be sentenced to death. The *veglia* torture was considered a suitable method to test claims of madness – though we might judge it a sure road to madness.[97] More mildly, severe fasting was imposed instead of other physical tortures, as on two Augustinian nuns in Piacenza in 1578, who ratified earlier admissions of offences.[98]

Doctors or surgeons were meant to visit the chamber to ensure the equipment was suitable and could be used properly, and the accused was fit enough to withstand the type of torture and avoid serious lasting injury or death. They might return to apply medicines at the end of the ordeal. Bishop Giovan Battista Scanaroli, originally from the Modena area, wrote *De visitatione carceratorum* (Rome, 1655), which became a key work on penal procedures generally. A section devoted to torture declared that doctors should remain present during the session, ensuring it was not excessive and life threatening. Under the Spanish tribunals torture was more frequent and less controlled, whereas notaries in the Palermo Inquisition tribunal complained that 'nowadays the *corda* is applied with such slight reasons it is a disgrace'.[99]

Torture was sparingly used in the Venetian inquisitional system, and rarely on women.[100] It was used in only five magic and witchcraft cases between 1550 and 1650, and in only three Judaising cases, all in the 1580s, designed to elicit names of associates, and in Francisco Dies' case to blow his cover and reveal his true origins. Also an aggressive Christian associating with Jews was tortured in 1588. Giovanni Battista Capponi, aged twenty-one, having confessed to irreligious activities and heretical speeches, was then tortured at the Roman Inquisition's command so that he would reveal accomplices and the origins of his heresies. With fire under his feet he cried out: 'What cruelty to try to extract from me thus a thing not in me to tell.' Denounced for heretical speeches by other prisoners in the Rialto gaol, he blamed discussions with Jews (with whom he probably traded) for his beliefs. He was sentenced, judged 'vehemently suspect of heresy' to five years in the galleys; to say five Pater Nosters and Ave Marias daily, and seven penitential psalms weekly.[101] When in Venice in 1584, under strong threats of torture, Merina Perighi resolutely refused to admit to charges of practising love magic, the tribunal decided against its imposition – and sentenced her to six hours in the pillory as a '*strega et herbera*'.[102] A cleric accused of witchcraft, Fra Felice Bibone, was tortured by *strappado* in 1588. Judged by a nearly full tribunal, with two *assistenti* involved, he was accused of having assisted (by misusing the Host) a Paolina de Rossi in her attempt to use love magic to win back her noble lover Battista Giustinian. The notary records Bibone calling out: 'Ohime. Jesus Lord God I've said the truth, the Host was not consecrated, do you want me to say what isn't so'; 'Oihme, I've said the truth.' When he was again hoisted up he declared: 'I didn't do it, I'm dying, Oihme, mamma mia, oihme.' He had denied Paolina's story when they were (unusually) put face to face, but torture did not break him.[103]

One of the cases where the accused suffered from lengthy torture was that of Niccolò Franco, erstwhile friend of the satirist Pietro Aretino. Franco was tried in Rome in 1569–70 for libels against Paul IV and his Carafa family. Contrary to guidelines he was tortured once early on in the trial in September, then on four days in February 1570, for an hour or more on each occasion. He was later hanged.[104]

Showing the accused the instruments of torture might be enough to induce a confession. An early example was Pietro Vagnola from Siena, living in the Venetian Republic, investigated first in Rovigo in 1547, then in Venice, for a variety of Protestant views. Interviewed in Rovigo by the nuncio's auditor in January 1548, after several witnesses had been heard, and hearing the charges, Pietro admitted to some Protestant beliefs, and to having discussed the faith with rustics, but denied he had challenged the divine authority of priests. The court, unhappy about this, had the instruments of torture shown to him – and he at once changed his position, and abjured. He was further questioned in Venice by inquisitor Fra Marino da Venezia, readily abjuring a second time, and after a sermon by the inquisitor he made a public recantation, to the public's great joy. Whether this was a Nicodemist tactic in order to avoid pain is an open question.[105]

Withstanding torture, especially more than one session, could persuade a tribunal that the accused was not guilty of heretical acts or intentions, leading to release or minor sentences for unintended heresies. However, robust resistance to torture might not be enough if the court felt it had sufficient evidence from other procedures, as noted by both Carena and Masini. If inquisitors were trying to elucidate evidence and guilt between a group of accused, they were advised to start with those they judged the weakest, and women – even though a medical view held that women were better able to withstand the *strappado*. In March 1594 Cardinal Santa Severina advised the Florentine inquisitor, who was investigating monks accused of desecrating images in their own church: torture was to be applied, 'beginning by giving the *corda* to whichever of them from whom you will judge it easiest to discover the truth'.[106]

As an example of the Roman Inquisition condemning the misuse of torture by a local tribunal we have the case of three women (prostitutes) who had appeared in Pistoia before the Florentine inquisitor's vicar and the bishop's court. Under torture they confessed to sacrilegious and sorcerous acts:

> Firstly the evidences against the aforesaid women are very light and weak, being founded on the deposition of Menichina likewise a prostitute, who other than through her confession is revealed to be an enemy of the said Spinetta and Calochina. . . . Secondly the said prostitutes and Zino . . . had not given their defences, and had been placed under torment, and more than once each, and had very much varied in their confessions. Whence it is our opinion that for the confessions they made about the said offences it is not really possible to come to any safe and well-founded resolution, and the aforesaid matters can be doubted as having been done, and [admissions] extorted through torments, or from fear . . .

So the Florentine inquisitor should personally control the trial in Pistoia.[107]

Torture was not meant to be imposed if the accused was disabled or too young. In some cases a local tribunal would not proceed with torture recommended by Roman officials because a local doctor ruled the accused was physically unable to withstand it. Conversely, Roman officials might criticise the local tribunal for torturing somebody who was disabled or too young. In January 1626 the Congregation criticised the Modena inquisitor's treatment of one accused of being a heretic, 'subjecting him to the *corda* while he had an impediment in his arm, making him abjure in public ... giving him a higher grade of abjuration than fitted the quality of the propositions to trick him (*burla*)', and he was a minor of seventeen years.[108] In the case of Francesco Vidua of Verona, in April 1580, a letter addressed directly to the accused by the bishop of Verona and an inquisitor read: 'not being able by way of torments to remove the presumptions and suspicions held against you, and that because of the indisposition of your body, we have decided to come to ... sentencing'. Francesco had denied the value of confession, of Jubilees and suffrages, and the existence of Purgatory.[109]

Inquisitors were well aware of the unreliability of torture for eliciting truthful information or true confessions. Eymeric's view, repeated in subsequent manuals, was that 'torture is a fragile and dangerous thing and the truth frequently is not obtained by it. For, many defendants because of their patience and strength are able to spurn the torments, while others would rather lie than bear them, unfairly incriminating themselves and also others.'[110] This did not stop the use of torture, but it seems to have been used less, and then less harshly. In his famous attack on torture in the mid-eighteenth century (when its use even in secular courts had diminished), Cesare Beccaria stressed that 'a test ... carried out on the sufferer's muscles and sinews ... is a sure route for the acquittal of robust ruffians and the conviction of weak innocents'.[111]

The formal decision by the Inquisition to use physical torture did not normally come quickly, given the procedural rules and the need for organisation. By then a guilty person trying to create diversions might conjure up the names of other suspects that could be given with some safety – because they had fled, or their names were assumed to be known to the tribunal anyway – or work out the least damaging admission to make. Pietro Carnesecchi may have tried this. He hoped his seemingly voluntary appearance before an inquisitor in 1566 would lead to a short, gentle investigation, confession and absolution (avoiding torture and a death sentence). When the Pope and Congregation decided on an intense investigation and trial and called for torture, his claims of serious illness led to two doctors being called to declare him fit for the *corda*, which was used at two sessions. He was left strung up for a quarter of an hour or more, but gave no new information.

Evidence of resolute resistance to torture and the maintenance of innocence is available. Margarita, called La Mora da Casale, charged with sorcery (*lamia*) in Novara in June 1581, was imprisoned but denied all, 'was sufficiently tortured according to expert advice, confessed nothing further but always persisted in her denial, and under the same advice was released and dismissed'.[112] Three of the four witches put to extreme torture in the 1607 Soraggio trials, two women (one aged eighty) and a man, resolutely insisted on their innocence in denying any involvement in witchcraft and attendance at sabbats. The fourth, a woman, died of illness before she could be tortured.

If an accused stoutly resisted torture and maintained his or her innocence, then a case existed for release. In the later 1650s Cardinal Barberini reprimanded the inquisitor's vicar in Malta, Antonio Tolossenti, for proceeding to condemn Francesco Leante after Leante stoutly maintained his innocence during torture: 'It cannot be recognised what foundation the said Vicar [Tolossenti] has had to abjure the said person, who has not confessed nor been found guilty, and when all the suspicions remained purged through the torture, it was not possible to condemn him to that punishment of standing at the door of the church.'[113]

Abjuration and Sentences

Convictions were administered at various levels, which affected the severity of punishment. The accused might be found guilty of non-heretical transgressions (a sort of 'not guilty' verdict); there may be slight suspicion of heresy, mild suspicion, vehement suspicion, strong suspicion, or, at worst, suspicion of formal heresy.

Somebody sentenced to abjure lightly, *de levi*, did so in a private ceremony in the inquisitorial or episcopal building; and the punishments were likely to be penitential rather than physical. Those abjuring *de vehementi* or *de formali* were humiliated publicly in a church (at a major service), on the steps of the cathedral, or at an *auto da fé*, with a public reading of the accusations and sentence. The last and most serious category tended to apply to the relapsed, and might be followed by execution.[114] The verdict in Galileo's case was at the level of 'vehement suspicion of heresy'.[115]

The *auto da fé* as a major public occasion publicising the condemnation of heresy had a limited life under the Roman Inquisition in the 1550s and 1560s. Pius V was an enthusiast for such publicity, which took place mostly in Rome. The first *auto* seems to have been on 6 June 1552 when seven Lutherans were displayed in yellow tunics (*abitelli*) and reconciled before a large crowd, but not executed. On 21 March 1553 eleven Lutherans were paraded at an *auto*. One was later hanged and burned on 4 September, namely, Giovanni Buzio da Montalcino who had preached heresy in Naples. His books were burned at a separate event. News of his fate spread through Europe, and he was treated as a Protestant martyr. These events probably made reformers in Italy more cautious and fearful. The most spectacular *auto* in mainland Italy was probably that for Pietro Carnesecchi on 21 September 1567. He was subsequently executed, but the earlier *auto* on 22 June involving another significant heretic Mario Galeotta, an admirer of the *Beneficio di Cristo* book, and another Valdesian friend of Giulia Gonzaga, was a public humiliation without executions but instead a five-year prison sentence. Several *autos* took place in some other cities riddled with heresy, such as Mantua and Casale (1568–9), and Naples (1564 and 1571). At the last twelve women of Catalan origin were paraded in yellow *abitelli*; they had 'lived secretly for many years like Jews (*alla giudaica*) and committed many excesses', according to a chronicler.[116] Thereafter large-scale public humiliations were few under the Roman Inquisition.

Sicily presented a different case. Francesco Renda and Maria Sofia Messana have both recently attempted to trace all *autos* held on the island, their locations and the numbers of people involved. According to Messana there were 211 *autos* from 1501 to 1744, 186 of them in Palermo, 10 in Messina, with 15 in other places or in an unknown place. In Palermo the *auto* might be held at the cathedral, San Domenico, or in the various major *piazze*. In the early years they occurred most frequently, but diminished from the mid-seventeenth century with none in the years 1662–5, 1671–7, 1681–7, 1691–4, 1696–1700, 1704–12 and 1738–43. The most active years were 1513 with 6 separate *autos*, and 1648 with 4, involving 136 persons. The number of condemned is usually not known, nor the number executed. On the 19 May 1549 there were 21 sentences, with 3 'relaxed in person' (executed) and 5 condemned in effigy.[117] Those condemned in effigy were persons sentenced but absent through death or flight. Renda estimates that 210 were handed over to secular authorities for execution in the first half of the sixteenth century, 42 in the second half, and only 12 in the first half of the seventeenth. There were burnings in 1724 and 1732. For those condemned in effigy the figures were 286 in the first half of the sixteenth century, 33 in the second half and 3 in the first half of the seventeenth century. Of the 265 deaths, 202 were men, 63 women (see Table D, p.264 below). No capital sentences were carried out between 1659 and 1723. Even under the more brutal Sicilian system the *autos* were primarily shaming exercises. Unlike the Roman inquisitors and politicians, the Sicilian inquisitors (Spaniards) and viceroys did not see a downside to public condemnations and gruesome executions carried out under the glare of full publicity. Of the 588 persons handed over for execution in person or in effigy, 471 were condemned as Judaisers (primarily in the early period), 76 as Protestants (many of them foreigners), 11 for 'various heresies', 19 as Islamists and only 11 for other offences.[118]

'Every unrepentant, executed heretic marked a political defeat, not a victory.' Brad Gregory emphasises that there was a duty to be intolerant on the one hand, that there was a willingness to kill, but that in practice Catholics and Protestants were reluctant to execute those accused of heresy, unless it involved an overt sedition. Clergy were often anxious to save the accused from execution. On the other hand some accused were intent on being martyrs, with a duty not to succumb to compromises or recant. 'Authorities asked specific, litmus-test questions about religious teachings and practices. If one wilfully denied an article of Christian faith in response, heresy was manifest. In this sense men and women executed for their persistence were not "made" into heretics.'[119]

The Inquisition could impose a whole range of punishments, from death sentences of varying degrees of cruelty, through imprisonment, a term as a galley oarsman, banishment, fines, to minor religious penances. Contrary to the myths, the Roman Inquisition imposed few death sentences (in contrast with secular courts). 'Life imprisonment' (*carcere perpetuo*) very rarely meant that, but somewhere between three and eight years (and that might in effect become only house arrest). Simancas' 1573 *Enchiridion* stated: 'these penalities of perpetual imprisonment are customarily remitted after three years'.[120] Renda's analysis of the punishments awarded by the Sicilian tribunal, 1500–1750, indicates that of 3,192 individuals given non-capital sentences 989 were sentenced to the galleys, 703 to prison, 157 to seclusion in a convent or monastery, 98 to service in a hospital, 908 to public floggings (100 or 200 blows), 154 to public shaming, 718 to banishment or exile, 1,596 to confiscations of property, 1,502 to abjuration *de levi*, 342 to abjuration *de vehementi* and 287 to the penitential *abitello*. In many cases two or more punishments were involved; flogging was added to many sentences of prison, the galleys (for 425 individuals), or exile. Abjuration *de levi* accompanied floggings (636 cases) or prison (166), etc. The period for the galleys ranged from a year to perpetuity (in 31 cases), with 3 years (257) and 5 years (267) being the commonest. In prison sentencing the specified period usually ranged up to 10 years with unspecified years in 68 cases, under 5 years in 127, but perpetual imprisonment in 87 cases. The extent to which these sentences were made effective is a great unknown, here and with other sentencing.[121]

When death sentences were imposed they could undoubtedly be cruel, involving mutilation, burning, hanging, or drowning (the preferred method in Venice). An amelioration might be that the person was strangled or hanged before mutilation or burning, with burning alive seen as the worst fate. Fra Bartolomeo Fonzio, an active publicist for reform, and of great concern to the Council of Ten, was in 1562 sentenced to be strangled in prison, and then his body hung and burned between the two pillars in St Mark's Square, the sentence for criminals; but the Inquisition acted in advance to have him drowned at night in the open sea. It had other unrepentant Protestant advocates of reform drowned in the 1560s.[122] Whether executions were public or private involved considerations not only about the convicted person and their family's shame, but also public policy. A public execution could be a salutary warning, as intended with Fonzio. But it could also give publicity to certain heresies better not publicised (as Fonzio's inquisitors might have feared), or provide an opportunity for the condemned to advertise their own beliefs. In 1600 Giordano Bruno was gagged to prevent his making a speech before being burned in Rome.[123] His burning alive would have been a horrendous event, though that in 1595 of a Scot, Walter Merse, was even worse, when he was clothed in a shirt of pitch so he would not die so quickly. His crime was to have shouted out opposition to the concept of the Eucharist during a Mass in Rome.[124]

Outside interventions and protests could affect the nature of an execution. In 1568 Marco Magnavacca (originally from Bologna) was condemned to death by the tribunal for anti-clericalism and anti-trinitarianism in Modena. The city council petitioned the Duke of Ferrara to intervene and secure 'compassion for the miserable wife and his five little children unable to earn a living'. And, if carried out, the execution should not be a public spectacle that might shame the city. On Rome's recommendation Magnavacca was strangled at night in prison, with his body burned in the public piazza next day. He was the only one executed out of a large group of anti-clericals and anti-trinitarians in Modena who were tried in 1567–8. Although some managed to flee, three were sent to the galleys, twelve to perpetual imprisonment (probably not strictly upheld), others to minor penalties, while many benefited from Pius V's concessions in February 1568 to those who had presented themselves to the authorities 'spontaneously'.[125] Others connected with Magnavacca were tried in Bologna under Antonio Balducci; two were sentenced to death, and others to perpetual imprisonment, including a painter Marcantonio Gazzani, who had presented himself 'spontaneously'. Again some fled, notably Gasparre Canossa, who was still an active propagandist in 1608.[126]

In the early years of the Roman Inquisition worries were expressed about the cruelty of punishments imposed or threatened, especially by opponents of Cardinal Carafa's policies, whether over gruelling investigations or death sentences. In 1545 Girolamo Seripando, a famous reforming Cardinal, expressed fears about the harshness of Carafa, who lacked humanity. In 1557 Cardinal Morone (of course a sufferer from Carafa's paranoia) attacked the increasing rigidity of inquisitorial methods used in Rome and elsewhere. A humbler accused, Ambrogio Castenario, a smith from Udine and tried in 1568, argued that 'it was never possible to find in the New Testament that God had ordered that anyone should die for the faith'.[127]

If the death sentence was avoided, a sentence to the galleys (a preferred sentence in the view of the Roman Inquisition for ecclesiasts committing serious heresies) might be seen as a slow death sentence, though many did survive. The Venetian Council of Ten in 1559 ruled that those guilty of doctrinal heresy should not be sent to the galleys, because they might there seek to spread their ideas. Nuncio Giovanni Antonio Facchinetti in 1568 tried to countermand this; the galley sentence was suitable for those deserving such a harsh penalty short of death. (It needs stressing that oarsmen on the Venetian ships were not necessarily criminals, but often poor men who had been contributed under government orders as quotas from the guilds, who would then support their families at home.) Once somebody was in galley service a reprieve or remission may have been harder to secure than with a 'life imprisonment' sentence. Sometimes popes and their agents struggled to secure release when time was up, when the prisoners were on non-papal galleys, for example when they were sold to the Neapolitan navy.[128]

Before being put on the galley the culprit might have his sentence changed in the light of health or family circumstances, and possibly some paid another to serve the sentence instead, as seemingly did Carlo Chiavello, spice dealer from Savona, in 1581, when the Genoese inquisitor handed down a twenty-year galley sentence. Chiavello appealed to the Pope, on grounds of his health, age and family responsibilities (seven children, including four females). In a letter to Cardinal Savelli the inquisitor contested some of Chiavello's claims, including that he was old (only about forty), and suggested that as he was rich and traded with Seville and Barcelona, including in wines: 'Let him buy a Muslim slave to row for him. He has the means to do it.' He stressed that Carlo Chiavello was part of an extensive family and group of heretics, had learned heresies in his youth from his master, and had married a Milanese woman with heretical connections. Chiavello had been accused since 1578, among other things, of denying the real presence, the existence of Purgatory, the value of holy images and pilgrimages, that the Pope was the Vicar of Christ; Chiavello had derived ideas from prohibited books. He had confessed after torture. His sentence also included perpetual exile from the Republic of Genoa and the whole Ligurian coast.[129]

Life imprisonment (*carcere perpetuo*) seldom meant that. Canonists treated this as a three-year sentence. *Carcere perpetuo irremissibile* meant eight years, and *immurato* (immured) indicated confinement to a cell only, while in other cases the convicted might be able to move around a building, contacting others. (Past historians stressing Inquisition cruelty wrongly treated phrases like '*essere immurato perpetuamente*' as meaning complete immuration, bricking-up, for life.) Imprisonment was expensive, and many tribunals had no prison of their own but shared one with episcopal or secular authorities, as some complained. Those imprisoned were meant to have financial or food contributions from family and friends. The wealthy could make their sizeable cells quite comfortable, especially in Rome. But elsewhere alternative concepts of 'imprisonment' or substituted sentences were tempting for the inquisitors. Pardons could be given within a few months. Those sentenced to imprisonment might soon be transferred to a monastery or nunnery (where the confinement could vary from isolated ascetic harshness to a fairly lax regime). The 'prison' might soon be the person's own house, or that of a protector – Galileo was soon in the palace of the archbishop of Siena. The 'pretend saint' Cecilia Ferrazzi, sentenced to seven years in prison, was transferred after about two to the care of Cardinal Barbarigo. Those under 'house arrest' might have this widely stretched to a large surrounding locality, having provided some sum in surety.[130]

As in the secular world, prisons were used more for holding persons pending trial and sentencing than as places for post-conviction punishment, though the two kinds of prisoners might coexist. The Roman Congregation took a regular interest in the prison population and conditions.[131] Of those under investigation some were held in Castel Sant'Angelo, in the Holy Office prisons, or in a convent. The Puglian Valdesian Mario Galeota, investigated in 1564–8, seems to have moved from Castel Sant'Angelo to the Holy Office in February 1566, then to a convent in June. He was finally told he could be released to his property outside Naples in May 1568.[132] Antonio Carracciolo, marquess of Vico, when under investigation was allowed to leave prison for his own house on a huge surety of 10,000 *scudi* in December 1565. However, he was ordered back to Castel Sant'Angelo in February 1566, with orders that he should not be allowed to wander in the city without licence, which he had been doing.[133]

As cases considered in later chapters will indicate, much of the sentencing was to fasting, penances, public humiliations in front of church doors with a sign indicating the offence, whipping through the streets (as for practitioners of superstitions) and the saying of extra prayers or psalms.

Roman Intervention on Sentencing

The Roman Congregation and local tribunals consulted, and clashed, over the use of torture. Similarly consultations took place over sentencing, and conflicting views emerged, before and after sentencing, sometimes because of the way the accused had been treated under investigation, with or without full torture. The validity of confessions obtained locally could be challenged, and the outcome modified to the benefit of the accused. Sometimes revisions took place when Roman officials saw documentation sent for review with a proposed sentence. Appeals against the local tribunal's declared sentence were occasionally taken to Rome, where the sentence might be modified, or the case retried.

Having reviewed the case against a Bolognese woman, Maria de'Gentile, a suspected witch who had confessed she had caused somebody's death, in May 1591 the Roman Congregation replied in the name of Cardinal Santa Severina: 'having come to the opinion that she should not be released to the secular court [and potential execution] ... because there are too many contradictory elements in her confession to homicide which do not agree with the evidence presented in the trial record', the Congregation recommended banishment from Bologna for a while.[134] The case of Bartolomeo Betti also shows careful

Roman scepticism. He had undergone a lengthy trial in Ferrara in 1606. On 29 July 1606 Cardinal Pompeo Arrigoni told the Bologna inquisitor that the Roman Inquisition judged that officials in Ferrara had extracted confessions by improper methods (*con mali modi*), and that Bologna should run a re-trial. On 29 June 1607 Cardinal Pompeo Arrigoni recommended that the Bolognese inquisitor give Betti a light prison sentence, and obtain a financial security of his choosing for Betti 'not to offend witnesses'. Betti was subsequently released, but he had, evidently, spent a considerable time under scrutiny and in prison through two trial procedures.[135]

The alteration of sentencing conditions could involve discussions with Roman officials. For example, we have the long-drawn-out correspondence between the Bolognese inquisitor (Fra Paolo Vicari da Garessio) and Cardinal Arrigoni in 1607–8 over whether a canon, Costanzo Oradino, should be released from prison to house arrest with nephews. He had abjured in 1587 and 1605, had served ten years in prison (in a convent), and was now eighty-two, 'decrepit and paralytic'. The Roman Congregation wanted to know about his behaviour in prison, whether he was truly repentant. When informed of his satisfactory behaviour, it let the Bologna tribunal decide whether Oradino should stay in the convent at liberty within it, and attend choir (but not celebrate, if he were a priest), or be released to his nephews' house. The latter choice was accepted, provided he only left to hear Mass in the nearest church. Arrigoni indicated that petitions and letters were discussed in the Congregation and comments made there, and that he did not act alone as the leading cardinal.[136]

Abitello *or* Sanbenito

The sentencing of heretics to wear a special garment (*abitello* in Italy, *sanbenito* in Spain, often a yellow tunic) to signify their condemnation is one of the best-known aspects of Inquisition history, since prints are reproduced in books on the inquisitions from Phillipp van Limborch's famous 1692 *Historia inquisitionis* (dedicated to the archbishop of Canterbury) onwards. Paintings by Francisco de Goya show heretics with these garments in the final stages of the Spanish Inquisition. These visible indicators were more common in Spain than in Italy. After the death of a convicted man under the Spanish system, the *sanbenito* might be put on display in his local church, as a mark of family dishonour unto the third generation. Local opposition restricted its use by the Sicilian tribunal.[137]

Some correspondence between Rome and Mantua and Bologna in the 1560s–1570s shows different opinions about the topic, as the condemnation of protestant heretics reached a peak. In 1568 Mantuan merchants and others sentenced to wear the *abitello* petitioned to be excused from this, as they risked starvation. Others were refusing to do business with them. The Roman

Inquisition reached a compromise. The guilty need not wear them, but their *abitello* should be on public display, with their full names attached. In Bologna in November 1569 a certain Marcantonio Basenghi (a wealthy member of Pompeo da Loiano's group) returned to the city after a long trial in Bologna, then Rome. Within a few days he unfortunately happened to meet inquisitor Balducci, who asked why he was not wearing his *abitello*. Basenghi said he did not think he now had to wear it. Balducci consulted Cardinal Rebiba. It took until June 1571 for a clear decision, when a letter from the Cardinal implied Basenghi had been granted a dispensation from wearing it. The Cardinal insisted that Balducci gave full publicity to the names of those who had been sentenced in Rome. So people could be known as heretics, but not have to display a daily reminder.[138] Within a few months Basenghi was allowed to travel freely within Italy, but no further.

In 1573–4 letters from the Cardinal of Pisa heading the inquisitors of the Congregation to Bologna dealt with Girolamo Guastavillani's wearing of the *abitello*. This nobleman, a member of Girolamo Vittori's Valdesian group, who had among other things denied the real presence of Christ, the need for confession, the efficacy of venerating the saints, and challenged papal authority, had endured months in prison in Bologna and Rome between 1566 and 1568, before abjuring. Initially he was sentenced to perpetual imprisonment in a cell, though the cardinals stressed this could be mitigated. They returned his confiscated property and then confined him to the *contado* of Bologna, where he was to wear the *abitello*. In response to a request that this garment should now be abandoned, in September 1573 the Cardinal of Pisa ruled that Guastavillani could go about the *contado* without wearing it, but he was still not allowed to return to the city itself.[139] Another nobleman of the group, Antonio Ludovisi, who had allegedly judged the Mass to be a business affair and a lazy act ('*una mercantia e una poltronaria*'), who had denied Purgatory, the value of suffrages for dead souls, and the need for confession, also had his wearing of the *abitello* reviewed – eventually in his favour in 1574, with support from the inquisitorial vicar. However, his '*carcere perpetuo*' had in fact lasted six years, rather than a more standard three.[140]

Diverse Procedures and Punishments under One Inquisitor

Unanimity on procedure and punishment was not to be expected between inquisitors, but a single inquisitor might act very divergently as well, as can be illustrated from Fra Antonio Balducci (or Balduzzi) da Forlì's dynamic period as inquisitor in Bologna, 1560–72, a crucial time in the suppression of Protestant groups across Italy. A Dominican since 1539, he fully established the Inquisition base in and next to San Domenico church and convent, where he improved the facilities, including suitable prison accommodation in 1563. Confiscations of possessions belonging to accused persons gave him a tolerable financial base by

1567, facilitating the creation of more prisons, and an essential increase in his staff. He served as Prior of San Domenico between 1567 and 1569, and as Provincial of the Lombard Dominican province (which embraced Bologna) between 1571 and 1573, though he moved to Rome part of the way through. From this background he could derive theological support and advice.[141]

Balducci was assiduous in following up old suspicions, and in investigating new groups. For the most part he had the active co-operation of the bishop's vicar-general, and the support of Bishop Gabriele Paleotti, and there was a lively correspondence with the Inquisition cardinals, especially Cardinal Rebiba of Pisa. During the crucial period from 1566 to 1569, twenty persons were condemned to death (but eleven *in absentia*), five to the galleys, and about thirty were reconciled after abjuration. Many fled ahead of arrest, or escaped while under investigation. Inquisitor Balducci was inclined towards a mild approach, with Bishop Paleotti's approval – to try and secure recantations and abjurations, and re-education, rather than imposing the harshest punishments. This particularly applied to the socially less influential offenders. With noble or professional accused he was inclined to proceed cautiously, to avoid local political trouble. Balducci and Paleotti tried informal talks to obtain easy confession and reconciliation with some suspects (including the Vittori and Ercolani families and associates), an unorthodox procedure that Balducci tried to justify to the Roman Inquisition. The pressure from Rome was for him to be harsher. The Inquisition there found Paleotti not forceful enough, and became angry when it was believed he had warned Girolamo Vittori that his Valdesian group was under suspicion, and let him escape from Bologna. Balducci defended his bishop, and helped scotch the allegation.

In dealing with Rome, Balducci seemed torn between defending the Bolognese nobility as generally faithful, and explaining that given the networks of family relationships it was hard to make progress against the few who were heterodox, though ultimately families were prepared to disown heretical relatives. The Roman Inquisition tried to have the more prestigious accused sent to Rome, where they were subjected to long, harsh sessions in prison and slow procedures, with severe punishments at the end. The first to take this path to Rome were the brothers counts Astorre and Nicolò Ercolani imprisoned by Balducci on 1 January 1567 as part of the Vittori sect, and (after posting a large sum in caution money) escorted towards Rome within two weeks. Following harsh imprisonment they abjured, and were finally allowed back to Bologna in May and November 1569 respectively.[142]

Balducci's relative mildness changed when he dealt at length with the rich Sienese nobleman Diofebo Spannocchi, who proved to be one of the most obstinate heretics and militant Protestant campaigners. Balducci eventually subjected him to many sessions of torture to make him reveal his contacts. Spannocchi confirmed some names put to him, but avoided naming others. Midway through

Balducci reported (26 April 1568) to Rome that Spannocchi 'was remaining very pertinacious in his errors and still with offensive words against the Roman Church, which I have with extreme patience tolerated. . . . God may convert him, but I believe it will not be through us.' He even suggested to Rome he should use a French method of torture, a bundle of wood on his neck, during a public sung High Mass. Eventually Spannocchi did abjure publicly and was sentenced to the papal galleys.[143] Spannocchi's contacts had included a wide range of people, male and female, including two blind beggars (Pietro the Florentine and Astorre Albertazzi). For the two latter Balducci wrote to Rome, seeking a rapid decision on further action, given their poor health, and the grim conditions in the full prison, where nearly all his prisoners had fallen ill during the year. Roman officials delayed two more months before recommending perpetual confinement in a convent both for the blind, and for the females unless families were prepared to keep them. Male associates were to go to galleys.[144] In March 1572 correspondence with Rome dealt with an unnamed blind man (but Pietro), held in the convent of S. Proculo. Cardinal Rebiba wrote that the Roman Congregation had decided he would be better off at home under his wife's care, especially as the convent was finding it financially and otherwise burdensome to keep him.[145]

Balducci would probably have argued that his mixture of soft and harsh approaches had produced, overall, beneficial results. Sects had been unmasked and destroyed, the more intransigent severely punished – or driven out of Italy. In 1572 Balducci moved to Rome as a *commissario*. From here he remained in contact with his successor to whom he indicated that the time of torture should be properly noted, that it was suitable to show some accused the *corda*, but not to use it; that the canons regular of San Salvatore, suspected of heresy, would be better treated by pacification (re-education) than castigation. From the late 1540s a group of canons was busy reading and discussing the Scriptures, Pauline epistles and some heterodox book. One member was Teseo Aldrovandi, brother of the later famous naturalist Ulisse Aldrovandi. The canons were linked with private houses where lay groups had similar discussions, including that of the Aldrovandi and Lelio Sozzini. The canons again caused alarm in 1571, as Balducci wrote to Cardinal Rebiba in March, though he was in part relying on an old deposition he had found in the archive. Ulisse was questioned by the inquisitor and argued this was about events twenty-two years before, and he did not recall them. Presumably this led Balducci to take a moderate line when advising from Rome. Since Ulisse had good relations with Paleotti, who was friendly to Balducci, the latter probably did not want to create a stir that would encourage the real hardliners in Rome who distrusted Paleotti and Morone. Ironically, in September 1571 the canons were petitioning to be relieved from the costs and efforts of holding prisoner Gostanzo Gozzadini and the priest don Bernardino Cavallini (the latter being blind), who had abjured in 1567.[146]

Death Sentences

The numbers of persons actually executed by the Roman Inquisition were low by the standards of capital punishment in wider society, though the loss of records for many tribunals prevents a full estimate. In general one might judge that a higher percentage of convictions led to execution in the 1550s–1560s than later. This was not just because of the development of more tolerant and forgiving attitudes, centrally and locally, but also because of the consideration that the early targets involved significant advocacy of Protestant ideas, and subsequently more cases of superstition (See Chapter 6 and Appendix). A significant number of death sentences were not carried out: some accused were convicted *in absentia*, some escaped (with the connivance of warders or others), other sentences were commuted by the Roman Congregation, or under local political pressure.

The records for the tribunal of Aquileia and Concordia for 1544–99 demonstrate the disparity between death sentences and actual executions. We know of fifteen capital sentences passed. In eight cases (including three females) they were *in contumacia*: the women had evaded the court at some point, and one fled between condemnation and execution due to be carried out by the *luogotenente* of Udine. The first case (concerning Ieronimo or Girolamo Venier, 1544) was annulled in Venice (he had a noble name!). One died a natural death, though seemingly his body was hanged just the same. So in all only four were executed – two in Udine, one in Portogruaro (Domenico Scandella, or Menocchio) and one sent to Rome (Alessandro Iechil da Bassano). In two further cases the trial was held in Udine, but the final condemnation and execution were held in Rome.[147] That Menocchio's death sentence was carried out by the *Podestà* was at the insistence of the cardinals in Rome, and contrary to the local tribunal's wishes.

Attitudes differed about publicising death sentences and their implementation. The Spanish Inquisition gave them considerable publicity through their lavish *auto da fé* celebrations. Although Rome went through a phase of using such publicity in the later 1550s and 1560s, enthusiasm was diminished. When the new Inquisition moved to executions in the early 1550s, European-wide publicity followed. The execution in Ferrara in August 1550 of Fanino Fanini, a peripatetic baker from Faenza who spread Calvinist ideas, was immediately reported in a printed account, and further publicised by the revised edition of Francesco Negri's *Tragedia del libero arbitrio*, a leading influence on evangelicals. Adriano Prosperi sees Fanini as the first true proto-martyr for Italian reform. Jean Crespin included Fanini in his list of martyrs, published in Geneva in 1560 to inspire fellow Calvinists. In 1552 Ortensio Lando from Lucca (an enthusiastic Erasmian, leading anticlerical and utopian writer, who encouraged reliance on Scripture, and faith not works) published a catalogue of modern executions for religious reasons since Savonarola (*Catalogo dei moderni morti per fuoco*). He ended with the Anabaptist Benedetto d'Asolo (or del Borgo), executed in Treviso on 17 March 1551.[148] How far such news deterred the ambivalent from committing themselves to the cause of reform, and drove hardliners into exile, is hard to judge. Caponetto sees Fanini's publicised fate as inspiring other evangelical reformers in Faenza and neighbouring towns. The publicity encouraged Genevan Calvinist calls for exemplary martyrdoms. Balanced against the efficacy of a few executions as warnings was the consideration that publicity which outlined the accusations could spread those same ideas. The publicity about these cases contributed to a black legend about the Roman Inquisition, which might be seen as exaggerating its cruelty and mortality rate.

It should be noted that Fanini was a relapsed heretic, having been tried and abjured in Faenza in 1547. When he was tried in 1549 the Inquisition cardinals had ordered his execution, but it was delayed under pressure from Duchess Renée (Renata) of Ferrara, who was a Calvinist sympathiser. Duke Ercole finally bowed to Rome and fear of being seen as a protector of heretics. Under the Roman Inquisition death sentences tended to be for repeat offenders.

Staffing

The main tribunals in Italy were not sufficiently well staffed to achieve their overall aims: to eradicate heresy and encourage correct belief and behaviour. They needed help from other church officials, whether willing or under pressure, paid or unpaid.[149] They relied on the public for denunciations, as well as parish priests and confessors pressurising people to self-denounce. Complications arose because the inquisitions could have a considerable number of other staff and hangers-on for other purposes. This was particularly so with the Spanish Inquisition from early on, and with Malta under the Roman Inquisition later. Best known are the Spanish 'familiars', or *familiari* and *familiares*. These were men, paid or voluntary, who took pride in assisting the Inquisition tribunals, in spying on neighbours (especially if they were considered 'converts' rather than Old Christians) and actively looking for offenders. Service was rewarded by privileges, tax and jurisdictional exemptions; by the benefits from properties accumulated by the tribunals (from confiscations or even testamentary donations); and by 'prestige' in being recognised as a 'good Christian'. So attachment to the Inquisition might swell its numbers of staff significantly, but not increase the efficiency and efficacy of the *religious* campaign. The Sicilian link between the Inquisition and its supporting society has been seen as a forerunner of the modern Mafia. The tribunals of the mainland Roman Inquisition generally did not follow this pattern as they had few *familiari*, but Malta was closer to the Sardinian and Sicilian models. Here the *familiari* acted as an armed guard for the inquisitors, and their property.[150] Generally secular rulers needed to count and curb the exempt hangers-on, whether of the bishops or inquisitors.[151]

Modena illustrates the expansion of tribunal staff through the seventeenth and eighteenth centuries. When Modena initiated an independent tribunal in 1598 its finances and personnel were tiny. In terms of covering the territory, including mountainous areas, the solution was linked with the episcopal vicarial and *pieve* system. A 1612 inventory indicates that in the mountainous province of Frignano, the Congregation of the Pieve of Pellago with nine churches had three rectors who were also vicars for the Holy Office, while the Pieve's leading rector was authorised to receive denunciations; another rector was titled a *commissario* of the Holy Office, and another was a notary for it. All such rectors were native, possibly impeding authoritarian control, though some denounced relatives. By 1622 the central Modenese tribunal had the inquisitor, his vicar, twelve consultants (four each of theologians, canonists and lawyers), eight ministers (executive officials), twelve *familiari* – voluntary helpers possibly embracing members of the confraternity of the Crocesignati. (The number of notaries is not clear.) The whole inquisitorial territory was divided into forty congregations, each with a vicar, a notary and a messenger. So the Modenese Inquisition comprised 152 persons, who received concessions of patents, approved by the Roman Congregation, which might guarantee certain privileges and protection. The numbers of such patentees seemed to peak at 197 in the 1760s. Between 1700 and 1785 the tribunal was looking at about forty cases a year, probably predominantly those concerning superstition and book censorship. The number of staff seriously active has not yet been calculated; most would be combining inquisitorial roles with diocesan, educational, legal or wider notarial duties.[152]

The *vicari foranei* appointed to supervise significant areas for the inquisitor and/or bishop may have paid more attention to the wider benefits and prestige coming from their patents than to the efficiency of their activities. The Venetian government at various stages raised issues with nuncios and Rome about 'incompetent' vicars, as in 1640, 1693, 1708–9, 1747 and notably 1766. They were accused of manipulating or coaching denunciators and witnesses, and variously evaded laws and restrictions on roles. In 1766 the secular authorities (*Savi dell'Eresia*) judged that the dangers of heresy throughout the whole Republic were not enough to justify so many patented officials serving the Inquisition. They saw no reason why the inquisitor of Bergamo, taking up questions of censorship, should maintain about twenty vicarial officials in his territory. Reforms were introduced by the Senate, such that mainland tribunals should always meet with a lay assistant present, in episcopal palaces, where archives should be centralised.[153]

In the hunt for heretics through Lombardy, evidence exists for networks of spies and more overt informers, working for the Crown, archbishop and inquisitors in the 1560s–1570s. The provost of Lecco was subsequently paid in 1573 for his work as an informant on heretics in and around the Valtellina, according to the Cardinal of Pisa. Archbishop Borromeo praised Franciscan preachers for similar assistance in Pluvio and Morbegno; possibly they had physically helped to capture suspects.[154]

Staff who were properly recognised and patented could expect to be exempt from certain taxes, and to be free of prosecution by other courts. The tribunals were expected to discipline their own members, but not leave them to the mercy of secular or episcopal courts. Also, servants of the Holy Office expected their superiors to take action, in court or through other means, if they were 'insulted'. As the statistical tables in the Appendix show, 'offending the Holy Office' was a classified and significant offence (at least in the eyes of the Inquisition). Correspondence to and from the Congregation in Rome indicates that privileges and exemptions were taken very seriously, and an inordinate amount of time must have been consumed in settling minor infringements and upsets far away, as well as in establishing major jurisdictional principles.

Volumes of documents in the central archive of the Holy Office show battles went on for years over what taxes and customs dues could or could not be paid by those attached to local tribunals. Given the number of patentees, the impact of exemptions could be deemed significant for communal treasurers. A bulky file relates to the struggle by Fermo city to get officials of the Inquisition working in the Porto of Fermo to pay taxes.[155] A minor privilege could be hotly and lengthily defended: in August 1698 the community of San Lupidio in the Fermo diocese complained to Rome that a muleteer, Francesco Peccapelo, a patentee of the Holy Office, claimed exemption from the *gabelle* and *dazii* imposts, which were paid by others in the commune. The exemption claimed was not only for himself, but for those goods he carried for others. The inquisitor in Fermo, Fra Giovanni Francesco Orselli, having checked with the inquisitorial vicar in San Lupidio, suggested that documentation supported the muleteer more than the commune; he added that Peccapelo rendered good service to the Holy Office with fidelity and promptness, that he was one of the most deserving of the patentees in this jurisdiction which was very scattered, and very poor, and so a claim like his should be supported by the cardinals. In other words the tax exemptions could balance the meagre pay for jobs with the Holy Office. The Inquisition tribunals were not paid for directly by local communities. They could subsidise by having to accept some tax exemptions.[156]

This chapter has given some idea of how the inquisitorial tribunal system worked, with guidance from manuals, how it dealt with operational problems and how practices varied. We can now turn to the specific activities and environments of multitasking inquisitors, and the conditions that influenced their variable behaviour.

CHAPTER 4

How the Inquisitors Worked

Having explained and illustrated the general procedures of tribunals and the ways in which cases were handled from denunciation to sentencing, we can now consider how the inquisitors and their staff worked on a wider basis, their problems and preoccupations as they tried to carry out their duties. Detailed consideration of the experiences of a few inquisitors based on recent archival research should illuminate what must have been the life of many. Inquisitors had to deal with the central organisation of the Congregation of the Holy Office, later also that of the Index; they had to work with or against bishops and their diocesan systems, and within the state political environment already indicated. Within the various states local power struggles with laity or clergy could impede efficiency. Alternatively, inquisitors could receive cooperation and loyalty from other clergy in their jurisdiction, from inquisitors and officials elsewhere, from *familiari* and members of confraternities. Limited financial resources and unskilled staff impeded inquisitorial work, for which suspects must have been grateful.

Running Tribunals and Wider Activities

Offices of the Inquisition had to be organised and financed, and the inquisitor and other officials had more preoccupations than just chasing and trying heretics and badly behaved Christians. Our knowledge of the finances of the Roman Inquisition is limited, though some accounts for the tribunal in Ferrara can be instructive.[1]

The finances of Italian Inquisition tribunals were probably always fairly precarious, unlike for some Spanish tribunals and Spanish central organisation, where confiscations from accused and condemned heretics provided a major income. The inquisitor for the D'Este state of Ferrara in 1556 and 1557, the Dominican Camillo Campeggi from Pavia, noted the meagre income, the reliance of Dominican inquisitors on their convents, and argued that the inquisitors should be able to confiscate the property of heretics to fund their activities. Contrary to the Modenese perception of an accused man before his court in 1566, namely that Dominicans were gaining much from confiscations, this was not true. Campeggi argued that besides ameliorating their poverty with confiscations, inquisitors should seek help from wealthy confraternities pledged to assist the Inquisition (though not doing so). Confiscated property was usually returned to those who repented, as most did. Accounts survive for Campeggi's period in office, and that of his successor Paolo Costabili (1568–72), with some references to earlier financing. The regular income came from renting out a few properties, some pious donations and a levy on Ferrara's Jews. Confiscated property might help cover costs while the accused were investigated, but it did not increase long-term assets.

Expenses mostly went on the essentials of conducting the Inquisition's business, equipping offices and cells, corresponding with Rome and other cities, chasing and moving suspects, enabling the inquisitors and Campeggi's active vicar Niccolò del Finale to travel to question suspects. The inquisitor and officials seemingly lived, very modestly, off the convent's income. Payment for a boat trip on the Po river with Dominican novices was a rare sign of relaxation. While prisoners were largely paid for by relatives, charitable payments went to poor prisoners. We find entries on the costs of torture equipment, and moving it if necessary for use outside the Dominican convent, or erecting scaffolds for executions or burning prohibited books, and a pulpit for a penitent to make a public abjuration. Payment was also made for ointments or something similar to treat somebody after torture, or a sick prisoner. Some money was spent on paintings: religious ones for the Inquisition rooms, but also paintings of individuals condemned and executed in person or effigy, for publicity purposes; several were by Bartolomeo Cavra. When one accused was found to be innocent, some embarrassment ensued for the inquisitor who had to repay what had been charged for his capture. Expense accounts demonstrate Costabili's vigour in pursuing heretics, mainly followers of Giorgio Siculo; and some brutal executions, as of the notable and popular physician Francesco Severi da Argenta (beheaded and burned on Rome's orders, as relapsed), rendered Costabili unpopular, so his travels were precarious and required extra guards.[2]

The Bolognese tribunal relied heavily on an agreed allocation from the archbishop's diocesan income (*mensa*), which had implications for cooperation between the two upholders of the faith. Intermittently, correspondence with Rome indicates that pressure was needed to ensure this was paid, and at a suitable cash rate in relation to the notional money of account written in the contract. From this income the Bolognese tribunal then had to make a subvention to the one in Modena. Money from confiscated properties played an important role.[3] This might be from properties held for only a few years before restitution, as with the landed properties of the Vittori family and their Valdesian friends, or from a property not handed back, such as the Aquila mill in the city, confiscated from a painter, Peregrino (or Pellegrino) Righetti, executed as a relapsed heretic in 1567. This mill was still providing income in the eighteenth century. Negotiating contracts with tenants and share-croppers of properties would have taken some time and effort on the part of Inquisition officials. An interesting contract of 1572 where rent was paid in produce throughout the year indicates that the inquisitor and his assistants had contributions to a healthy diet – eggs, poultry, pigs, lamb, fresh and dried grapes, oranges.[4]

The inquisitor and his staff had extensive administrative duties, and had some expertise in wide-ranging financial matters. In the light of this they might be entrusted with more social activities, especially if well ensconced in a large Dominican convent, as in Bologna. For example, in the eighteenth century the inquisitor in Bologna joined with the Prior of San Domenico in dispensing dowries for poor Bolognese citizens, resulting from the will of Dottore Rinaldo Duglioli, professor of Medicine at Padua, in February 1734 in which he had left them as fiduciary heirs (ahead of his death in 1739). Each girl was chosen by the Prior, the inquisitor and the oldest *maestro* in the convent.[5]

I have found detailed accounts for the tribunal in Ancona for 1612, compiled for Rome's benefit in pleading for help given a significant shortfall in income over expenditure. Notably the income came from rents, the sale of produce from possessions under the tribunal's control and various outside contributions. The human and institutional interest derives from the detailed listings of expenditure, on the inquisitor's barbering and tonsuring, his modest clothing, office costs, travel expenses by horse or on foot (when he might be accompanied by a youth), extra wine for medicinal purposes. The inquisitor Giovanni Maria da Bologna had the personal attention of Fra Eusebio ('*mio converso*', my lay brother), who not only organised his medicinal wine but his laundry and other services. He and other helpers received pre-Christmas bonuses. Charitable donations went to helpers when they were ill, but also to three Moorish women (*Moresche*) and two English converts.[6]

Fra Elisio Masini as Inquisitor in Ancona

Elisio Masini is best known for his production of his well-used *Sacro Arsenale* manual, but he was also an active inquisitor in places like Ancona, Mantua and Genoa. Letters preserved by the Congregation in Rome from his period in Ancona in 1608 (February to November) are a useful guide to issues and problems faced by one exemplary inquisitor and illustrate relations between a local inquisition and the Roman cardinals.[7] Masini was clearly energetic over these few months, both in Ancona and in investigating witnesses and problems in other places under his jurisdiction, such as Osimo and Rocca Contrada.[8] When Masini arrived Cardinal Carlo Conti, bishop of Ancona, sent a letter of recommendation to Cardinal Pompeo Arrigoni (who clearly knew little of Masini) as head of the Roman Congregation: 'I can promise the best success from this office, on all matters, and he will be seen and assisted by me, especially in serving Your Illustrious self.' Masini's correspondence with Arrigoni shows some respect beyond the conventional courtesies, as when in May he expressed warm greetings on the latter's safe return from Benevento.[9]

Masini operated with a local Congregation which, though the full number is not clarified, contained two doctors of law whom he praised when Cardinal Arrigoni asked questions about them. He favourably reported their assistance, for example, in the case of Annibale Ferri from Monte del'Olmo, denounced for swearing by the *potta* (cunt) of St Paul, and many other offences. He followed their advice in having Annibale 'whipped a little', and given salutary penances.[10] He was protective of his staff, especially notaries (as in Osimo, Macerata and Ancona), and he pressed for greater rewards and emoluments for their heavy tasks; in the case of his long-serving financial official (*fiscale*), Masini asked for beneficial patronage to help with his large family responsibilities. For the notary in Osimo he asked Cardinal Arrigoni to secure him a canonry.[11] Masini did not show huge initiative or troublesome self-will, but sought advice from Rome. Concerning various jurisdictional problems outside Ancona, he pressed for the Roman Congregation's assistance.

Some of Masini's letters covered a variety of issues, others were single-purpose. He would sometimes send more than one letter to Arrigoni on the same day.[12] Much of the correspondence accompanies documents being sent about ongoing or completed processes, while he is also assuring Roman officials he will endeavour to track down suspected persons whom they think might pass through his jurisdictional territory. This was not easy, and the pursuit of individuals could concern successive inquisitors, as Masini noted on 23 November. He had used 'the greatest diligence' on diverse occasions to know where to find Alessandro Voglia from Camerino, formerly *podestà* of Montenovo, to proceed against him, 'as your letters to my predecessor ordered'. He had recently heard Voglia was dead but had wished to confirm this, so he wrote to the bishop of Camerino, who informed Masini that Voglia's wife wore widow's clothes, and all other evidence confirmed that he was dead. 'He was indicted for matters of Necromancy, and fled.' 'I will give a full account of this to my successor who I am expecting this coming week.'[13]

Eliseo Masini's first surviving letter from Ancona, dated 14 February and addressed to Cardinal (Giovanni Garcia) Millini, raised two key issues that might be particular to a port like Ancona: bigamy and foreign Protestants.[14] He had discovered in the criminals' prison a certain Giorgio da Tira (Tyre), originally from the Levant, who was indicted for having two living wives. On judicial examination Masini confirmed that being enslaved in the Levant a Donna Marulla from Messina became enamoured of him, and proposed they should marry, with a dowry of 60 *scudi* to be used to achieve freedom; to liberate himself from captivity he accepted the deal, and married her. So liberated he took her to Pescara where five months ago he left her infirm. And Giorgio's first wife, called Lucia is here in Ancona, where she has always stayed in the absence of her husband. I told [the Governor] that this case pertained to the Holy Office.

The governor at once agreed, and promised to hand over the prisoner quickly, so Masini let matters proceed; but he had heard that the *luogotenente* for criminal matters was issuing processes for Giorgio's defence. The inquisitor also noted that he had heard that morning from Cardinal Conti, informing him about some English merchants who had arrived in this port. Allegedly 'many times on prohibited days they are accustomed to eat meat in public, also in the company of Catholics; I have myself had a little of the odour of this.' Two English *bertoni* (large sailing ships) were in port, with grain to sell. As Lent was near, Masini was worried, and wanted instructions from Rome on what to do. The Congregation on 21 February annotated the letters to say that the Inquisition banned the English from eating prohibited foods, whether secretly or in the presence of Catholics.[15]

On the bigamy case Masini later informed Arrigoni that he and the bishop, Cardinal Conti had agreed to send Giorgio to the bishop of Pescara, where Marulla was presumed still to be without knowing Giorgio's marital status, possibly for that bishop to resolve the case, but with the Congregation's involvement. But Masini, showing some sympathy for the wife in Ancona, seemed reluctant to handle this transfer, considering his office should keep its distance and commenting cryptically: 'I don't want to do this myself, thinking it very much more convenient that this information should come from the sacred Congregation, rather than the inquisitor as a private person.'[16] The outcome is not revealed, but the case shows a degree of cooperation between two jurisdictions, both of which had an interest in bigamy issues.

Ancona was a meeting place of different religions and the background to a potentially very serious case discussed in a letter of 19 November. Masini's court was investigating Fra Angelo Impoccio from Ascoli, a lay Capuchin, indicted for formal heresy, for what he had said in his Order's convent of Corinaldo. One evening after supper by the fire, he proclaimed that 'the Turks, the Jews and all other Infidels can save themselves without baptism, and he did not agree with good doctrine of some priests of his Order who said this opinion was heretical'; these priests had tried to correct him. He remained obstinate. According to witnesses he held his opinion firmly, but he responded that he had only said such things in a spirit of disputation, and had apologised to his father confessor the next day. Masini opined this might represent a common defect of the (less educated) lay friars. Fra Angelo was imprisoned, and Masini awaited orders from Rome on how the case should be completed.[17]

Among other issues during Masini's term as inquisitor in Ancona, he asked advice on how to handle a persistent heretical blasphemer (including in Osimo's cathedral), who cheated on his wife and whose stepson followed him in blaspheming.[18] In September Masini visited Rocca Contrada to follow up several matters at Rome's suggestion, hunting suspects, securing the release of somebody from prison, detecting prohibited books in bookshops and at customs controls, and inhibiting innkeepers and hoteliers from breaking fasting rules. Rocca Contrada was on a significant trading route that attracted both legal and illegal activities.[19] Prohibited books and censorship were of particular concern in the aftermath of the 1606–7 Venetian Interdict crisis. Masini found himself investigating Trivisano Bertolotti, a bookseller in Venice who had come to Ancona to deal with the bookseller Francesco Manoletto. Bertolotti had a woodcut portrait of Fra Fulgentio Manfredi, an anti-papal supporter of Sarpi. A copy (about 5 × 3 inches) is still attached to the file: Fra Fulgentio is portrayed in a central oval holding a crucifix in the right hand and the left resting on a skull. The inscription says he is aged forty-four. Below the oval are piles of books, an hourglass and inkpot. Below these is the Latin inscription: *Si fulmen fulgens fulgur,* FULGENTIUS *ergo/Fulgidius emisso fulmine fulgur erit.* This was a play on his name, as bringer of lightning and thunder. On the back of the sheet is handwritten '*Ritrato del Apostata*' ('portrait of an apostate'). Masini promised to search for other copies in circulation, and round them up. He was also continuing efforts to track down Fra Girolamo Crosta from Osimo, a noted challenger of papal authority whom the Roman Congregation wanted pursued.[20]

Like other inquisitors Masini had jurisdictional problems with local bishops, if not the Cardinal bishop in Ancona, as shown in a long letter of 17 April. This took up issues raised with his predecessor by the bishop of Recanati concerning the expedition of cases under his jurisdiction. A case involved a certain Donna Quintilia di Bartolomeo from Isola di Fano, an inhabitant of Recanati, but who was imprisoned in Ancona, and sent home 'by vote of my congregation without a penalty or penance, finding nothing proved against her.' But the bishop of Loreto and Recanati wrote that his counsellors had different opinions, and his doctors of law claimed a relevant order from the sacred Congregation; 'but I cannot find anything relevant in the archive'. The claim seems to be that such persons should be returned to the place of the alleged offence, and so to the Ordinary (bishop), and not be investigated by an inquisitor in Ancona. The bishop seemingly wanted such cases investigated by his court, and not in convents where the Holy Office operated (via vicars). Masini asked for this to be resolved, and to have peace (*quiete e tranquillita*) when serving his tribunal.

His successor, Archangelo Calbetti da Recanati, was to have similar jurisdictional conflicts with the bishop of Macerata.[21]

In one of his last cases Masini raised interesting issues of imprisonment and bail securities, which have not been much discussed by historians. He explained the case of Francesco di Vincenza da Montemarciano and his Sienese wife Livia, imprisoned in 1607 in Ancona's Palazzo Criminale at the behest of the Holy Office. Masini's predecessor had them conditionally released on security of 200 and 300 *scudi* respectively for not leaving the city and territory of Loreto without licence. But Francesco went to many, many places without licence, particularly to Macerata, where his wife also visited, 'to use there her secrets and remedies on a poor sick girl', but with little effect, as the girl died. The treatment had involved many superstitious procedures. Both husband and wife came and confessed, were indicted and imprisoned for a second investigation. This raised the fiscal problem of the security bonds. Civil proceedings were taken against Cristoforo Monaldi from Pesaro, an innkeeper in Loreto, who had given security for Livia. Nothing remained to do except give *sentenza*, but first Masini needed Rome's formal opinion. Cristoforo said he wanted to petition for a lesser sum. Consultants debated whether this sum was too low. Masini did think Monaldi should not go without penalty. The cardinal was asked to make recommendations.[22]

Masini moved to take up his post as inquisitor in Mantua. He had written on 9 October 1608 that he had received the patent for his appointment sent by Cardinal Arrigoni. He rendered thanks to him and his colleagues for favours and graces received, and awaited the new inquisitor to whom he would give full instructions verbally and in writing, indicating the uncompleted cases, and handing over records and property. He promised on his arrival in Mantua to make an inventory of writings and property, to compare with the previous ones, 'as you command'. However, he remained busy in Ancona, as his successor Fra Calbetti did not arrive until 27 November. By 7 December Calbetti wrote that he had personally taken instructions and information from Masini, had already been away from Ancona to take witness statements in Senigaglia and had celebrated a Mass at San Agostino in Montecchio.[23]

Calbetti was soon at work on the Fra Girolamo Crosta case. He reported receiving letters from the inquisitor of Perugia, where Girolamo was now detained, who said that Girolamo had appeared in Rome before the Holy Congregation, and had been absolved. Calbetti asked whether this was true, so as to know what to do next.[24] Communications about cases were clearly problematic, but inquisitors around north-central Italy made considerable efforts to track itinerant troublemakers.

A different issue of communications was raised by Calbetti at the end of his longer stint in Ancona, ending in June 1611 (after two years and seven months there, as he firmly noted, and overall eleven years as servant of the Holy Office).

He had found it a strain to tour his inquisitorial jurisdiction, having to travel on horseback over mountains on many occasions – as the Holy Office well knew. He stressed he was now old, and corpulent. He was delighted to accept the priorate of the Convent of Del Bosco (San Michele in Bosco, above Bologna), which had been his great ambition. He was, however, pleased that he had been able to serve 'a holy Congregation of such quality', for those eleven years. Unlike Masini, Calbetti did not personally hand over to his successor, but departed hurriedly for Bologna. His successor, Fra Giovanni Maria da Bologna, was admittedly delayed a few days – by excessive heat! He was grateful, for the written instructions and details left for him.[25]

Opposition and Impediments

Inquisitional jurisdiction and operations were challenged on many sides, by state governments, local legal officials such as the *podestà*, by bishops and their vicars. Beyond legal quibbles, the inquisitors and their officials could face considerable abuse and physical threats, even murder. Two Dominicans linked to the Mantuan Inquisition were assassinated on Christmas Day 1567, as part of the hostility to the inquisitorial campaign against Endimio Calandra, former secretary to Cardinal Ercole Gonzaga and serving Duke Guglielmo, and as revenge for burned Protestants. For the Pope 'this is the path of martyrs, . . . their souls have gone straight to heaven'.[26] On Christmas Day 1549 in Como Cathedral, when a friar tried to read out a declaration of the Inquisition against heretics he was drowned out by bells and driven from the Cathedral. In 1550 Como crowds, including children encouraged by clergy, verbally abused and expelled the hardline inquisitorial commissioner Michele Ghislieri. Ghislieri was also threatened in Bergamo when he was pursuing Vittore Soranzo. An Observant Minor, Aurelio Griani d'Urcisioni provided a horse to facilitate Ghislieri's departure. As Pius V, Ghislieri later rewarded Fra Aurelio by conferring a diocese on him in November 1570. The interconnection of these events was noted by Cardinal Giulio Santoro in his concistoral diary.[27]

When Ferrante Gonzaga, the younger brother of Cardinal Ercole, was governor in Milan in 1552, he declared himself ready to hunt heretics and prohibited books, but on several occasions he backed those who opposed the activities of inquisitors. He supported the governor of Piacenza's attempt to stop the inquisitor from arresting and trying a false preacher who was attacking the Catholic Church, and his noble supporters. When combating Lutheranism among local nobles and merchants, the inquisitor in Cremona, Giovanni Battista Chiarini, was confronted by an armed gathering of gentlemen who invaded his convent, calling him names and issuing death threats. Seeking support and protection from Governor Gonzaga, the local governor and the *podestà* (whose prison should be used), Chiarini was told he would only get this if he ensured full consent after consulting with the *podestà* and the bishop's vicar before making arrests, and kept the Senate fully informed.[28] Anti-heresy campaigns required cooperation and power sharing.

Jurisdictional conflict between Inquisition and episcopacy could turn violent. In Pisa in 1581 the Franciscan inquisitor Francesco Pratello and other Franciscans were the recipients of a violent verbal tirade and some blows from a gang of between sixty and a hundred ecclesiasts, including Cathedral canons, who were defending the archiepiscopal vicar's jurisdictional claims, and protesting the inquisitor's lack of consultation especially when pursuing accused clerics. This confrontation ended with them singing the *Requiem aeternam* for the inquisitor – who declared them excommunicated. Replying to the inquisitor's questions as to why he should, and how he could, allow such abuse of himself and the Holy Office, the vicar, Cesare Nuzzi, replied: 'What Inquisitor? What Holy Office? I am the Inquisitor and Holy Office.' The vicar was immediately summoned to Rome by the Congregation, and ordered to apologise to Pratello. This inquisitor, and his successor, pursued the policy of minimal consultation with the diocese over matters of faith. When the archbishop's vicar was invited to attend the public abjuration at the end of a trial for *magia*, he wrote angrily to say he would not attend since he had not been shown the documents in the case. The inquisitors were being precariously tactless, or unreasonable.[29]

Whatever the impediments and frustrations, clerics who took on the role of an inquisitor or his vicar could consider themselves to have gained power and effectiveness. When Francesco Montichiari, episcopal vicar of Fivizzano, became an inquisitorial vicar for the Florentine tribunal in 1625, he declared: 'As the bishop's vicar I did as much as I could, but now with a more fearful arm (*con braccio più tremendo*) I hope with God's help to extirpate everything [heretical]'. He promised he would immediately gather together the confessors and press them not only to observe the recent Bull against solicitation, but to observe the edicts against superstition and blasphemy. But with the position came harder work. He wanted assistants to act for him in remoter places, and a general guidance on what penances to impose, so as to avoid having to write to the inquisitor for each case.[30]

One might expect that an inquisitor would at least receive support from fellow Dominicans in the convent where he was based. Fra Giacomo Figino, inquisitor of Casale Monferrato (1624–30), made clear his problems at length to the Roman Congregation in 1628; he had to contend with opposition from a former inquisitor (1603–16), Benedetto Rota (or Ruota) from Mantua, now residing in the same Dominican house.[31] The heart of the matter was that Casale, under the Gonzaga Dukes of Mantua, was dominated by the Grand Chancellor Triano Guiscardi (or Viscardi), a soldier but also a leading literary figure. Figino reported him as having a bad reputation within the faith – others had sensed he was a heretic since 1610. But Rota worked amicably with Guiscardi, protected him from investigation, and had resisted pressures from Rome to eradicate or discourage Protestant German-Swiss brothers, who were trading in this state with the duke's approval. Rota, who was retired, impeded Figino's inquisitorial actions, encouraged Rome to refuse an increase in staffing (Figino only had a notary) and wrote testimonials for certain persons accused by Figino. Rota was popular with most in the convent, who elected him prior at one point. So Figino seemingly achieved little to curb pro-Protestant activity. The Roman Congregation, mindful of the politico-geographical sensitivity of Casale (which passed to French control in 1630 with Guiscardi's assistance), was not helpful to Figino.

As Albrecht Burkardt stresses, this was not the only example in the period of conflicts between inquisitors and the convent in which they were based. In 1619 the Dominican prior in Como complained to Rome about the inquisitor's interference in conventual affairs, and the Franciscan prior in Crema clashed with his inquisitor (the archbishop of Pisa was asked to mediate). The inquisitors were entering a convent as outsiders; the regular members may have established long-term relations with the urban community and political leaders, and didn't want such contacts to be disturbed. The average Dominican or Franciscan might also be jealous of those appointed inquisitor in a career that might lead to a high-profile role as a commissioner working from Rome. A long-serving inquisitor who wished to avoid challenges might of course be accommodating to both conventual brothers and local secular forces.[32]

The Inquisition in Ancona, and Relations with Bishops

The sampled correspondence from the Ancona Inquisition shows several irritants in relations with the various bishops whose diocese fell within that territory. We have noted that Eliseo Masini had problems with the bishop of Recanati. His predecessor, Fra Giovanni Paolo da Cremona, had been the target of a major complaint from the bishop of Osimo, Antonio Maria Gallo, who in December 1606 complained to Cardinal Arrigoni about Fra Giovanni Paolo's lack of consultation with him or his vicar over, for example, the use of torture or whipping of diocesans. He wanted the Cardinal's advice so he could have better 'consideration of his honour and reputation, and provide an opportune remedy for this fact, and mortify who deserved it'. This bishop came from a powerful Osimo family with past feudal power, so was especially likely to resent inquisitorial intrusion.[33]

Masini's successor, Archangelo Calbetti, had trouble with the bishop of Macerata. In April 1610 this bishop complained to Cardinal Millini about the inquisitor in Ancona arresting and imprisoning in Ancona some of his diocesans when they were outside his diocese, 'which is contrary to custom, and should not be a subterfuge to take cases from me', and asked the Cardinal not to permit such a subversion of his episcopal responsibilities. He also wanted to know whether a Canon Cornelio had been replaced as the inquisitorial vicar in Tolentino (in his diocese). It becomes clear in later correspondence that Fra Calbetti had appointed Cornelio (Servio) without the bishop's agreement. The bishop claimed he had published authority to support his case. He concluded his letter with the view that the inquisitor 'had little thought [or, did little thinking], and shows himself very contrary to usual practice', and he calls for reason and equity. The Roman Congregation annotated the letter on 21 April to say Don Cornelio should not be removed from his position.[34] Inquisitor Calbetti had previously written to Cardinal Millini about his struggles with the bishop's vicar, noting that the Congregation had on several occasions ruled that inquisitors took precedence over bishops' vicars in matters pertaining to the Holy Office. He had seen this declaration in the tribunal at Piacenza, 'and this I saw practised while Inquisitor there, and also in Modena; and I understand this is observed in Milan'. He asked the Cardinal to send a copy of the relevant decree to the bishop. The Congregation's annotation on the letter stressed that inquisitors took precedence; and this was to be communicated to Cardinal Bishop Conti of Ancona (with the possible implication that he would bring the bishop of Macerata into line).[35]

Acrimonious correspondence continued, with more ructions over who should control violent clergy, including canons (notably Servio). Fra Archangelo at one point stressed that the *Commissario Generale* and the vicar-general would confirm that 'I have had no confrontation with the other Reverend bishops subject to my jurisdiction'. He had appointed vicars across his whole area of authority without others objecting. The confrontation seems to have ended when the inquisitor left to be prior in Bologna.[36]

In 1613-14 Bishop Imperiolo of Iesi attacked the inquisitional system in Ancona, contesting who controlled lesser officials; which notaries served whom; whether work done for the Inquisition in the bishop's palace meant the bishop had superiority; also what changes of relationship were implied if local inquisitional congregations met in the bishop's palace, rather than in the Dominican convent where the inquisitor was based. Sharing notaries and officials in a small diocese seemed sensible, but episcopal pride and private interests were at stake. In January the inquisitorial vicar in Iesi, Vincenzo Maria da Bologna, reported to Cardinal Millini the bishop's abuse of the inquisitor in Ancona, but also threats to imprison him over a woman he had in his custody. She turned out to be the wife of the bishop's bailiff (*balio*). 'I will not go on to tell you the impertinences and filthy words he said, so as not to offend your Illustriousness' ears, but say that he gave me till the next day to release the woman, or he would have me imprisoned.' The bishop noised this confrontation through the city, so people would not appear before him (the vicar), either because the Holy Office was now held in low esteem or from a great fear of the bishop, 'since he is known by all as an unstable man who disregards reason and words'.[37] That same day the bishop wrote to the Roman Inquisition that he was grateful for an order that if inquisitional matters were being formally discussed in his episcopal palace they should be discussed in his presence, or regulated through his vicar. He assured his most Illustrious Reverend that in many ways he worked for the good of his people.[38] He later defended himself, denied being abusive in words or threats, or revealing secrets of the Inquisition. The problem of the bailiff's wife was one of only partial consultation by the vicar. The latter may have been resentful because the bishop had denied him a licence to give certain sermons. Bishop Imperiolo assured the Roman Congregation he was loyal. Former inquisitor Calbetti told Rome that in his time he had held congregations in Iesi, in the Dominican convent not the episcopal palace; and the bishop had sent his vicar, as records would show. Again what followed is unclear from the surviving files.[39]

A full study of such correspondence from many areas in Italy would doubtless produce very similar letters, as different jurisdictions came into conflict and personalities clashed. It was clearly difficult for many active bishops with wider responsibilities to accept the authority of a more secretive inquisitorial system.

Wider Support and Cooperation from Episcopal Systems

We have already noted both opposition and assistance from the episcopal diocesan systems, and there seems no clear pattern of practice or developments. A legacy from the medieval inquisitions was that bishops and inquisitors should agree about the use of torture, though in our early modern period the Roman Inquisition was also to be consulted. Probably the early decades of transition saw more tension between bishops and inquisitors, especially where a diocese had had some degree of episcopal-led inquisitional activity before 1542. Some bishops like Giovanni Morone and Egidio Foscarari in Modena, or Ercole Gonzaga in Mantua, were anxious to control some heresies but also to persuade and convert suspects, moderate the situations ahead of any intransigent inquisitorial activity, and leave open some theological points not yet resolved by the Council of Trent.[40] In the diocese of Novara the bishop's tribunal played a significant role in suppressing heresy and witchcraft over a long period.[41] At the Council and thereafter episcopal attitudes towards confession and reservation of cases could foster opposition to inquisitorial interference. Bishops who served longer in the same place might also be more aware of, more susceptible to, local power politics than inquisitors who tended to move more often, and so be more wary of pursuing certain suspects. A manual (*Prattica*) from the early seventeenth century, attributed to Cardinal Desiderio Scaglia, stated that inquisitors and bishops could act independently over citation, apprehension, imprisonment, establishing the informational process and absolving decree; but they had to cooperate over punishment, torture and sentencing.[42]

Under the Spanish, Sicilian and Sardinian inquisitional systems some people served as both inquisitor and bishop, but the inquisitor (or inquisitor-bishop) could face jurisdictional conflicts with other bishops. In actual *processi* in Sicily bishops or their deputies were likely to be involved at all stages, including torture, absolution or condemnation. But the bishops could be torn between instructions from Rome and the political realities of the Viceroyalty.[43] In the Roman system the degree of episcopal consultation and involvement was much more variable.

However, we have also recorded inquisitors and episcopal vicars making common cause, as with inquisitor Balducci, Bishop Paleotti and his officials in Bologna. One of Balducci's helpers was a canon of San Petronio and bishop's vicar (from March 1566), Cristoforo Pensabene. Originally a notary, he became a doctor of both laws. He had had a phase of religious disquiet (unclarified), which resulted in a secret abjuration in 1540. He then joined the leading confraternity of Santa Maria della Morte, and from 1555 became one of its specialist spiritual comforters for those condemned to death by the civic courts, comforting some thirty condemned individuals over twenty years. He was charged with reforming the city's Torrone prison. He offered to help the Holy Office as a procurator fiscal, and served from 1561. Given Pensabene's apparent dedication to the Holy Office, Cardinal Ghislieri discounted his earlier religious doubts, and let him serve the tribunal as well as be the bishop's vicar. His brother Lorenzo was one of the inquisitor's notaries in 1568.[44]

With this diverse background Pensabene came to investigate a number of cases for the Inquisition and the bishop (for which copies of some investigations in 1567–9 survive).[45] An interesting example was that of Giulio Panzacchi and his sister-in-law Isabella. The main target of investigation, being undertaken by Balducci, was Alessandro Panzacchi, Isabella's husband and Giulio's brother. From a rich Bolognese notarial family, Alessandro Panzacchi had become a spendthrift adventurer, a soldier and an itinerant bookseller, but had recovered his financial position. He was clearly part of quite widespread sets of heterodox individuals, in Bologna, Cento and Modena. He had first been tried in December 1566 as the accomplice of the trimmer Marco Magnavacca, a fugitive from Modena, who valued sermons but not the Mass; he had been retried and executed as relapsed. Alessandro Panzacchi had abjured after a partial confession, but was now being reinvestigated by Balducci who had deeper suspicions about his views on the Eucharist, and about his accomplices. Alessandro Panzacchi was eventually condemned to death in October 1567.[46]

Balducci entrusted to Pensabene the investigation of Alessandro's relatives and their contacts who had resided in, or visited, his house. Pensabene questioned Giulio Panzacchi and Isabella in September 1567: about how far Giulio was an intermediary for his brother with people outside Bologna, and how much Isabella knew of her husband's beliefs and activities.[47] They claimed they knew nothing about Alessandro's views until he was arrested, when they visited him in prison. Pensabene apparently established that Giulio then informed contacts from Cesena and Cento, including some being tried in Ferrara, hoping they would not name Alessandro, but one became a key informant against him. Following Pensabene's questioning, Giulio Panzacchi and Isabella were released to house arrest, on a high bond of 500 *scudi*, having confessed to helping Alessandro once he was imprisoned.[48] Pensabene seemed content not to push further on their own beliefs. The family was able to recover what had been confiscated from Alessandro, claiming that all or most of it derived from Isabella's dowry, and so was not legally confiscated from her husband. In dealing with the Panzacchi, besides Balducci and Pensabene in Bologna, the inquisitors and episcopal vicars of Modena and Ferrara were involved, and the cardinals on the Roman Congregation were kept well informed, ratifying the death sentences and giving verdicts on confiscations.[49] A cooperative mission proved successful – for the authorities.

Interchange between Local Tribunals and Rome

The post-1542 Inquisition system generated a considerable correspondence between local inquisitors and leading cardinals on the Congregation. The records of the central archive have now reinforced what was known from correspondence surviving in local archives, as in Bologna. A decree from Cardinal Alessandrino, Michele Ghislieri on 18 June 1564 demanded frequent and speedy communication.[50] The Roman Inquisition expected consultation over local appointments, summaries or full transcripts of ongoing processes, consultation about whether to torture and about final sentences. By contrast the Congregation – besides issuing general orders and instructions, demanding information and replying to queries – would relay information received from other tribunals, congregations, ambassadors, bishops, etc.; it would notify them that it was suspicious of various people, seek help in tracking them, request local officials to be on the lookout for some who might be travelling out of Italy. The Congregation of the Index also generated consultative correspondence, and both centre and locality tried to keep track of new publications, ensure pre-publication control, organise expurgations, chase dealers in forbidden books, or raid bookshops and libraries.[51] Letters between Bologna or Ancona and Rome took about five days. Once an issue was put before a meeting of the Cardinal inquisitors, a reaction might be written and signed by the principal Cardinal inquisitor, and sent within a day or two. Delays tended to be between when a letter reached Rome and when the issue was being presented to the Congregation and the Pope. The essential secrecy of this correspondence was stressed, as by Cardinal Scipione Rebiba to the Bolognese inquisitor Angelo da Faenza in 1575: on matters concerning the Holy Office 'do not write or give notice to anybody else but me, even if a person from the same Holy Office, or even to the father *commissario*; and do not omit to observe this always.'[52]

The Roman office of the Inquisition had a long memory and good records. It might seek information from a local tribunal years after an initial problem, as in 1591 when Cardinal Santoro (in the light of some new occurrences) wrote to the Bolognese inquisitor Giovanni Antonio da Foiano for the 1575 *processo* records against the physician Giovanni Angelo Oddoni. Oddoni was a member of an Erasmian group, about whom there had also been correspondence in 1575, when his movements in the Kingdom of Naples were being tracked. At that time the Bolognese inquisitor was informing the Holy Office in Rome, which consequently wrote to the Viceroy of Naples to get Oddoni arrested.[53]

The nature and tone of letters from Rome to local inquisitors could vary considerably. Some letters were cryptic, dealing with a single issue, reporting what had happened at a Congregation meeting, or asking for information. Others covered a whole range of topics. Some letters could be bluntly reprimanding, others affectionate and encouraging. Antonio Balducci had moved from his post as an inquisitor in Bologna (1560–72) to Rome as an inquisitorial *commissario* (with Cardinal Pisa as 'mio *patrone*'). In February 1574 he wrote reprimands to officials left in Bologna, including the vice-inquisitor Giacomo da Lugo, because they had only provided part of the *processo* record for the case of Giovanni Antonio Pero da Chiavenna, already condemned once and burnt in effigy. The Roman Inquisition lacked the principal part of that case; diligence must be used to find the rest (and Balducci even cited the volume number where it should be found). The situation was complicated since an inquisitor had just died, and the vicars were probably intent on safeguarding inquisitorial property and monies. Balducci had just warned them to be careful over these, adding there should be no defects and that nothing should happen to cause grief to the illustrious cardinals.[54] The late inquisitor, Innocenzo Morandi, had been urged by Balducci to show more effort and diligence, including when writing his own letters. When Morandi pleaded injury, Balducci caustically commiserated: 'I am sorry about the hurt finger which prevented you from writing, especially if it was a bed warmer sickness [*male di scalda letta*] that kept you as I suspect; oh well, patience.'[55]

A sampling of the Roman Holy Office's dealings with inquisitors in Bologna under Cardinal Pompeo Arrigoni between 1606 and 1608 reveals several different tones and attitudes, from the helpful and encouraging to the tart, as he sought overall justice, *giustizia*. In February 1607 Arrigoni was concerned with the length of time a case involving a Flaminio Rinaldini was taking. He and the Roman Cardinals were upset that consultants to the Holy Office had been consulted, and then began to defend the accused. Arrigoni had been instructed to tell the inquisitor in Bologna that 'The Consultants of the Holy Office must not undertake the task of defending the accused processed by the Holy Inquisition.' The inquisitor must avoid this for the future. He should clearly set a limit to the period for defence, and not allow the accused maliciously to delay further, but 'proceed expeditiously with due ends of justice. So be warned to exercise the office with maturity and prudence, not allow the accused, or their procurators, to act or speak with little concern for the office and with prejudice to the cases; and so carry this out in the future.' In a subsequent letter Arrigoni warned the inquisitor not to avoid executing the previous written instructions, and to remember 'to exercise and deal with the cases of the office with that dignity, prudence and resolution as suitable, and limit the actions and words of the accused and their procurators'. The inquisitor so addressed was Paolo Vicari da Garessio, who served until 1643 (refusing the offer of the Neapolitan bishopric of Nocera dei Pagani), and died in office in the odour of sanctity.[56]

Cardinal Arrigoni soon encouraged the Bolognese Inquisition to put the Rinaldini case to the local congregation of consultants, expedite the case according to justice and keep him informed if any problems arose. The reports came to him in September, and he briefly noted the Congregation in Rome would consider them, and give instructions, before lamenting the slowness of another case, that of Bartolomeo Betti, 'which renders it immortal, with little service to justice, and grave expense and ruin to that family. And may you be healthy.' In January Cardinal Arrigoni had taken the Betti case away from the inquisitor of Ferrara and handed it to the Bologna tribunal: 'because the means used by that Inquisitor who formed the process was very displeasing [to the Congregation], and it considered that Betti's confessions were extracted through the imprisoned Fra Cesare Cacina from the Servite Order and other illicit means.' So Betti should be re-examined, 'if your Reverence does not get the suspect to maintain the confessions made in the first process, and sends the first copy of the Betti record and what he will adduce in his defence, so it may be possible to expedite the case.'[57]

Frustrations and tensions could be shown when local inquisitors faced overall Church policy that seemed to ignore local realities. Making large gestures and heavy threats could be counter-productive. The inquisitor of Venice at the conclusion of the Interdict crisis was bold enough to make this point. Writing to Cardinal Scipione Borghese he advised: 'May I point out in all humility that, whatever happens in dealing in any kind of negotiations . . . it is not convenient to publish here any new censure as absolute, because it would produce contrary effects, due to people's lack of devotion, the clergy's unfaithfulness, and the power of rulers.'[58]

Surviving published correspondence from Roman to Neapolitan tribunals shows a whole range of consultation on all sorts of cases. Between 1563 and 1625 the leading Cardinal inquisitors in Rome who sent instructions or requested information were Michele Ghislieri (1563–5), Scipione Rebiba (1568–77), Giacomo Savelli (1577–87), Giulio Antonio Santoro (1588–1602), Camillo Borghese (1602–05), Pompeo Ar(r)igoni (1605–12) and Giangarzia Millini (1612–25). They were sending four to five letters a month to the archbishops or their vicars. Many letters dealt with exchange of dossiers about the accused, either those who were moved between the two tribunals, or where Rome's verdict was desired; but the letters are not very explicit about the cases. A fair number of letters dealt with matrimonial matters, marriage annulments and dispensations, and bigamy. For example archbishop di Capua was pressed to check whether Ferrante from the Abbruzzi, called il Rosso, and Margarita della Vecchia understood when they married that his first wife was still alive, and that this was a formal heresy; the archbishop could put both to the *corda* to ascertain this, if he thought fit.[59]

The Roman Inquisition might sanction or suggest a change of punishment, as when Cardinal Santoro in 1595 recommended that the sentence to the galleys for Giovanni Maria Rosso should be cancelled as not suited to the heresy, and he should pay 100 *scudi* to a pious cause instead. In March 1596 he agreed (after several petitions), a sentence of ten years in the galleys for Giuliano Musella da Casamassima (Bari) for necromancy and incantations, on the grounds that he had to support a wife, and marry off a daughter. He had other daughters and a 'useless family'. He had been condemned five years before, but implementation of a sentence was complicated because Rome was worried about his possible links with Sicilians coming to Naples, and so copies of the case were sent to the Sicilian inquisitor seeking assistance. By March 1593 Rosso was seemingly on a galley. Given the grave age of one Angela Leona, Cardinal Savelli left it to archbishop Annibale di Capua's prudence, but suggested that he see whether punishment with the *corda* or other physical punishments were too much. Angela had been accused of reverting to Jewish practices (mainly concerning eating), not respecting the Cross and encouraging others to copy her.[60]

Some tantalising topics are mentioned, as when Cardinal Savelli and Archbishop di Capua spent some time tracking a Beatrice Portella, an old and fat Spanish woman indicted in Rome in July 1579 as a leading instructress in confining the devil in a carafe. She left Rome and Savelli asked the archbishop to look out for her as she was seeking her son in Naples, and imprison her. The indictment record was forwarded, and further details to help identify her were sent in attached documents. She was in prison there in November 1579, but somehow fled Naples, only to be noted in prison in Rome by April 1580, when

Savelli requested the investigation records from Naples so he could complete the case. Details of the case and what the devil-in-the-bottle exercise involved have sadly not been traced. Santoro in February 1594 advised about the treatment of a Giovan Domenico di Mastro Giovanni, alias Gran Turco from Bitetto, and how he should abjure, being vehemently suspected of apostasy from Jesus Christ to the devil. He had abjured in Rome, and this should be repeated in Naples before archbishop di Capua's tribunal, with the sentence read out. An authentic sealed copy should be sent to Rome.[61]

Most of the letters from Cardinal inquisitors to the archbishops of Naples and their vicars were crisply polite. But a certain testiness becomes apparent in Santoro's letters to Archbishop Annibale di Capua concerning a Spaniard Giovanni di Silva, from the Order of San Giovanni Gerosolimitano in 1594–5, because the archbishop had apparently preempted the Roman Congregation's intended actions by a premature excommunication.[62]

The Support of the Lay Confraternity

Some of the patented official members of the inquisitorial tribunals might be members of lay confraternities.[63] The extent to which other lay people in confraternities, which were supposedly dedicated to helping the inquisitors, were of use as spies and informers is not known, at least as far as the Roman Inquisition system was concerned. Confraternities dedicated to Peter Martyr, a martyred inquisitor, had existed in the medieval period; some of these remained in name into the sixteenth century. They were joined by new Crocesignati societies (so named from the emblem of the Cross on their tunic, and special crosses they carried in procession), under Dominican leadership and sometimes based in the same Dominican house where the local inquisitor was based, as in Bologna. Scattered evidence indicates that similar confraternities existed in the sixteenth century that were linked to local inquisitors, and were deemed to be valuable to them – in Milan (a S. Pietro Martire fraternity), Como, Cremona, Pavia, Modena, Rimini, Faenza, Imola and Florence. In 1562 the S. Paolo confraternity in Turin was reported to be active in hunting heretics. Some of these fraternities came to consist exclusively of noblemen, as in Milan and Como, again suggesting that status and prestige for lay brothers (and possibly the inquisitor, as he was accompanied on major processions by them) were more important than the giving of information. The elevated social status of confraternity members could lead them to challenge an inquisitor who wanted to supervise their internal activities, as happened with the Santa Croce confraternity of Cento in 1677, who resisted the inquisitor from Bologna.[64]

The 1595 printed statutes of the Mantuan Crocesignati in most respects conform to those of many post-Tridentine confraternities, especially in devoting initial chapters to office-holders and their duties, and concluding with an extensive list of Indulgences that could be earned.[65] It was made clear that the inquisitor was the founder and continuing *capo* (head) of the company. Surprisingly, this Crocesignati also had female members, *Sorelle*, though clearly (and typically for those confraternities admitting women), being lesser members they were not office-holders. Their function, as far as the statutes reveal, was to help visit the sick who were dying, and stay with them if family support was unavailable. Processions were clearly important, where they showed their support for the inquisitor to whom they took vows, and they received ceremonial crosses. The statutes do not mention special duties to report suspected persons. A philanthropic approach, guided by a reference to the seven acts of mercy, is more evident than any hostile 'neighbourhood watch' scheme.

Non-religious sentiments could also encourage people to join the Crocesignati fraternities, where they could enjoy privileges similar to those enjoyed by appointed officials of the Holy Office, as already discussed. For example, confraternity members under scrutiny might claim to avoid regular secular jurisdictions, and place themselves under the Inquisition's own court. The inquisitor of Ancona in 1611 told Rome he would ensure that the new privileges for the Crocesignati would be properly recorded in the archive, and it would be published.[66] The following year in relation to a minor dispute the officials of the Crocesignati fraternity in Ancona wrote to Cardinal Millini as presiding Cardinal of the Congregation 'that [the inquisitor] at the time should be our judge for our Company, and that outside his tribunal there should be no recognition (of rival jurisdictions)'.[67] The company could expect an inquisitorial tribunal to favour their cause against secular outsiders; and the cases need have nothing to do with religious matters of the true faith.

Direct subjection of these confraternities to the Holy Office was challenged at times by bishops trying to fulfil Tridentine rules of visitation governing confraternities. A lengthy dispute started in 1659 over on offshoot of the Mantuan Crocesignati in the parish church of Goito, and whether the curate or the inquisitorial vicar should preside and control proceedings. Life in a confraternity was at times halted by such disputes. Inquisitorial control and administration seem to have been lax, giving the curate and bishop a case for intervention. The documentation revealed earlier disputes, and problems rumbled on until at least 1678, though the Holy Office's jurisdictional and administrative control was essentially backed. The documentation then submitted showed that these disputes were widespread. Precedents were quoted for archbishops and bishops elsewhere over time claiming control over Crocesignati societies, or taking a practical lead in reform – for example the archbishop of Turin's decrees in 1598, or the archbishop of Ravenna's vicar and his claims to visit the confraternities in October 1601. We find notes of serious controversies between bishops and inquisitors over visitations, as in October 1623 in Rimini, and regular trouble with the bishops of Cremona from 1624 to 1659. It was made clear that the bishop could make a visitation, but that the vicar of the Holy Office should be involved in executing any orders, and that the inquisitor was the legitimate *capo*. Cardinal Millini confirmed this on 18 April 1626 in dealing with Cardinal Bishop Campori.[68]

Given the time, energy, money and ill-feeling that these confrontations generated – as seen from fuller evidence for the above Goito episode – the practical and better legal position would have been to have added to a decision from Cardinal di Santa Severina to the then inquisitor of Faenza, 8 October 1588, a ruling that the Company of the Croce was a branch (*membro*) of the Inquisition, but that the bishop or vicar could visit, if the local inquisitor was informed. The episcopal system was generally better organised and funded for visitations than were the largely underfunded Inquisition tribunals.

The Crocesignati and members of similar confraternities might provide a suitable noble entourage for the inquisitor in public ceremonies, but otherwise they could create problems rather than serve the cause of the true faith.

Sicilian Problems and Confraternities

Given the vulnerability of Spanish inquisitors in Sicily the support of a confraternity might have been more necessary. The operation of the Inquisition here through means other than fear was not helped by the Spanish inquisitors and imported bishops having a low opinion of the Sicilians, regarding them as lying, deceitful and unreliable. According to the archbishop of Cagliari, 'In this island it is much easier to find a hundred witnesses to prove a lie than two to prove a truth'. Sicilians themselves judged that many denunciations reflected vendettas rather than true accounts.[69]

Inquisitors in Sicily were career men from Spain, not part of Sicilian social networks, and better trained in law than theology. The main Palermo tribunal generally had two or three inquisitors at the same time. They might also be bishops, but could be in conflict with other bishops, though those bishops or their vicars were more part of the inquisitional process than on the mainland. They could face opposition from viceroys, as from the Italian Marco Antonio Colonna, prince of Tagliacozzo (Viceroy from 1577 to 1584), admiral of the victorious Spanish and Italian fleet at the 1571 battle of Lepanto against the Ottoman empire. He was able to establish a Concordat (1580) that somewhat controlled inquisitorial abuses outside strict matters of faith, though the inquisitors won some jurisdictional battles against competing civil claims.[70] Given frequent, often violent, hostility from local communities, the inquisitorial team needed bodyguards and support from *familiari*.

The Sicilian tribunal probably had a stronger armed police force through its *familiari* than the Roman Inquisition, and it penetrated into remoter parts of the island. Most of the *familiari* were Sicilian not Spanish, with their own local interests — and local knowledge.[71] However distrustful, the Spanish inquisitors had to rely on this Sicilian support. Confraternities were formed in an attempt to bind some *familiari* close to the anti-heretical work of the Inquisition. The first major one was the Compagnia dei Bianchi, founded in 1541 with a primary duty to assist those condemned to death, and performing this comforting task for three days before execution. This was followed by the creation of a rival in 1565, the Compagnia della Vergine dell'Assunzione, which had more to do with those about to appear at an *auto*. In 1570 under Theatine guidance the Compagnia della Pesca del Pesce, or di San Pietro Martire, was founded for *familiari*, including a wider spiritual remit for members; as participants in public processions associated with the inquisitors, they carried a green Cross, other crosses and standards. The Santa Maria della Consolazione or della Pace was established in 1580 as an alternative organisation for *familiari*. As with the mainland Crocesignati societies, these appealed to nobles, and may have curbed their opposition to inquisitorial jurisdictions. As elsewhere, confraternal anti-heresy activities remain obscure. Francesco Renda sees the Compagnia di San Pietro Martire acting as a kind of Masonic lodge for the baronage.[72]

This chapter and the previous ones have established the diversity of the inquisitorial systems as established through different Italian states; how the investigative and condemnatory processes worked; the complexity and diversity of the tasks that inquisitors and their assistants faced, sometimes aided by bishops and others but in other circumstances impeded. Before turning to attempts to quantify the types of offences tried, and how these changed over time, one famous case will receive special consideration both to illustrate some procedural points already made and because to some extent it marks the end of one phase, the concentration on high theology, allowing tribunals to broaden their remit. This is the case of Pietro Carnesecchi.

CHAPTER 5

※

THE CARNESECCHI MOMENT

THE FINAL TRIAL AND HIGHLY PUBLICISED EXECUTION IN 1567 OF PIETRO Carnesecchi has been singled out as a crucial moment in the history of the Roman Inquisition. For the intransigents in Rome it signified the removal of a key lay nobleman from the Valdesian movement that developed in Italy itself. The publicity warned that theological equivocation or forms of Nicodemism were no longer to be treated with sympathy, even if the perpetrator had powerful political supporters. Coupled with other high-profile condemnations and *auto da fé* spectacles, the period of the late 1560s marks the end of the serious threats by reformers to Rome's conservative doctrines and authority, especially when post-Tridentine positive Catholic reforms and teachings were moving ahead and winning back allegiances. While Valdesians, Lutherans and Calvinists might periodically be unearthed and punished in the decades ahead, the Roman Inquisition could pay greater attention to the suppression of more mundane errors, superstitious practices and immorality. To some extent re-education could replace harsh repression. Looking at the Carnesecchi case at this point in our story will pull together some threads from the previous chapters, curtain off some old contests and enable us to open up new scenes of inquisitional activity. The discussion will allow some personalisation of interactive lives of reformers. The revelations and admissions by Carnesecchi at his final trial provided the Roman Congregation with a historical memorial of the evolution of Italian theological ideas through various movements with which he had been connected, and evidence against many *spirituali* alive or dead. The puzzled and irritated inquisitors in the process had to confront his 'labyrinthine cunning and brittle falsehoods'.[1]

Pietro Carnesecchi, a Florentine nobleman born in 1508, began his career in the Roman Curia thanks to the patronage of Giulio de' Medici, who was Pope Clement VII from 1523 to 1534. Carnesecchi was among those who were influenced by Juan de Valdés and his circle (1539–42), and then by those in Reginald Pole's group in Viterbo.[2] As a friend of the religious and secular elite, male and female (in Florence, Naples, Viterbo and Venice), he had survived previous investigations and trials by carefully arguing in his own defence, and through the support of powerful friends. He first presented himself to the Inquisition in

1546, but friends had the investigation stopped and Paul III absolved him. After a spell at the French court Carnesecchi moved to Venice and, while there, with Paul IV in pursuit, he was condemned in Rome in 1557 as a heretic. The local tribunal was not pressed to pursue him, and his trial records were happily destroyed by the Roman crowd who attacked the Holy Office archives on Paul IV's death in 1559 out of general hostility to both the Inquisition and the Pope and his family. Under Pius IV another trial was launched in 1560–1, but Carnesecchi was eventually absolved again from the earlier charges, after considerable conflict within the Holy Office.[3]

Pius V (Michele Ghislieri) proved a most dangerous opponent of the surviving *spirituali*, of whom Carnesecchi was the most prominent. Carnesecchi was finally entrapped by his close friendship with Giulia Gonzaga, a leading patron and promoter of Valdés and his writings.[4] When she died in 1566, her papers were seized from the accommodation attached to a Franciscan convent in Naples where she and her entourage had lived. The writings included some of Valdés' own work, Marcantonio Flaminio's incomplete 'Apologia del Beneficio di Christo' and crucially 228 letters sent to her since 1547 by Carnesecchi. These were handed over to the Congregation in Rome, and became the foundation of the fatal trial against him.

The letters exchanged between Carnesecchi and Giulia Gonzaga had been fairly guarded on religious views, had used ciphers especially to disguise names and had often referred to one another in the third person. Carnesecchi destroyed most of his incoming correspondence, Giulia did not. He relayed her a warning in June 1558 from Cardinal Pietro Bertano of Fano: 'Donna Giulia needs to watch out, otherwise she could fall into the net', and so she should leave Italy. Carnesecchi showed some awareness of his own danger in April 1559: 'This time I have spent long in writing... because it may be that I will be unable to write any more during my lifetime, as there is a risk of being burned (*bruciato*) in Rome before departing for the next life'. He had earlier suggested that he and Giulia might die together because of their friendship:

> And certainly, my lady, friendship is a wonderful thing, particularly when it is born from honest causes and grows and is confirmed with the years and with judgement, and to the end is founded in God, as one can truly say is that which exists between these two [i.e. themselves]. May God bless them and grant them the grace to be able to live and die together according to His holy desire.[5]

Why Donna Giulia did not destroy the letters is unclear. She may have thought that the Valdesian way might prevail if Pole or Morone were elected Pope, and the correspondence might testify to her and Carnesecchi's support for Valdés' teaching or that she was safe as a noblewoman in a Neapolitan convent. Both realised the threats posed by Gian Pietro Carafa as Pope Paul IV and his domination of the Inquisition, and its 'monsters' as Carnesecchi called them in 1556, but he rejected Giulia's advice to flee to France when she heard that the Roman Inquisition was angling to get him out of Venice.[6] She, however, raised the issue of an early death along with him, to which Carnesecchi's letter of 7 January 1559 seemed to respond.[7] From about June 1557 they informed each other about the arrests and harassments of mutual friends among the *spirituali*, such as Giovanni Morone, Tommaso Sanfelice (bishop of Cava), Vittore Soranzo (bishop of Bergamo) and Egidio Foscarari (bishop of Modena). Carnesecchi named cardinals Scipione Rebiba, Giovanni Reumano, Michele Ghislieri and Virgilio Rosario as leading the Congregation's pursuit.

> So, in this way the temporal war has finished, and it seems a spiritual one has begun, so that the world does not have to remain withdrawn (*otioso*), and there will always be an occasion to exercise the spirit and the flesh. There is no doubt that God permits all of this with just judgement (if obscure to us), and that from everything he will draw his glory for the edification and profit of his elect ones.[8]

Giulia cajoled friends to stop Carnesecchi being formally processed. Summoned to Rome, he pleaded serious illness: 'finding myself . . . indisposed because of a sore around the pudenda which caused me to pass water with immense pain, and as well as sciatica that prevented me going to Rome either by horse or by any means without evident danger to my health.' The local Venetian inquisitor accepted this. The Pope lacked sympathy but could not have him extradited, so he was condemned as contumacious, and burned in effigy in Rome.[9] 'Your Ladyship has heard how Carnesecchi has finally lost the battle with the Pope and how the sentence was published in Venice.' But the Venetian authorities, whether or not knowing his hiding place, did not proceed against him, showing limited enthusiasm for Paul IV's hard line. Giulia recommended that they both stay and not leave Italy, despite warnings against both.[10]

The promulgation of Paul IV's Index in January 1559 rendered the possession of works by Valdés illegal. This made Giulia Gonzaga's position much more dangerous since she guarded his writings, and was a known distributor of his *Alfabeto cristiano*, including to Queen Catherine de' Medici in France via Carnesecchi. This was a dialogue based on actual conversations between Valdés and her, which she probably co-authored (though keeping her name off the title page). She and Carnesecchi consulted on whether she should send her collection of Valdés' writings to Rome, destroy them, or preserve them. Writing in the third person in a heavily ciphered letter, he advised her 'to be directed by one's conscience and satisfy it in everything'; it would be a sin to act against conscience so 'I say keep them, which is what I desire and firmly hope she will do, for I am in no doubt that indeed she would not be committing any greater sin by burning them.... But it is necessary to have another consideration, advising herself with human prudence and governing herself as she will judge to be more secure and expedient.'[11] While the death of Pius IV temporarily relieved the pressure in 1565, and Giulia died in 1566 before another Pope trained in the Inquisition could target her, the preservation of the Valdés writings along with the letters about them doomed Carnesecchi.

On the opening day of the *processo* in the Palace of the Holy Office in Rome, 6 July 1566, Carnesecchi admitted: 'I have had notice already over many days and weeks what the Inquisition has done about the letters and writings of *signora donna* Giulia Gonzaga, who died two months ago in Naples, and because of those that I could come to some harm, but I have not wished to change my position because of this'. But he wanted to give some satisfaction and account of himself, 'to reconcile myself entirely with God and the holy Church'. Especially given that he was sorely afflicted and could not sleep well, he asked to be able to write out the whole truth, which he could do in about two days.[12] He had started by saying that if it seemed he was appearing by force, in fact he would have come voluntarily, 'because I thought that Our Lord called me through you to exonerate my conscience and to restore my infirm soul to health', and noted the paternal charity of his inquisitors, 'which till then was partly not known, and partly dissimulated for a certain respect for the honour of the world, thinking it enough for me to repent internally and to have confessed before to God and to his penitentiaries, confessors and ministers on the occasion of the Jubilee conceded from time to time by Sanctity of past popes, and indeed by Pope Pius IV.'[13] For some accused the supposed voluntariness might have secured a rapid outcome. However the court, involving four cardinals as questioners – G.F. Gambara, Francisco Pacheco, Scipione Rebiba and Bernardo Scotti – did not agree to this quick solution, but instead subjected Carnesecchi to a year's interrogation, until the sentence was read on 16 August 1567.

Proving that Carnesecchi's beliefs were heretical was not the only aim of the court, or even the main one. It wanted him to confirm the damaging evidence of the letters and clarify the beliefs and activities of his friends and associates, dead and alive; these included the conciliatory organiser of the final stages of the Council of Trent, Cardinal Morone, who was still deeply suspect to the Pope and others, and possibly another secret protagonist of reform. Massimo Firpo and Dario Marcatto argued that the aim of the court was to use Carnesecchi's evidence 'to contribute to a true and proper rewriting of recent history'; to confirm that Valdés, Ochino, Vermigli, Spadafora, Gelido, Pole and Morone (who wisely kept quiet and out of Rome during this trial) were heretics; and to support the view that the Inquisition over the past quarter century had been the only bulwark against the infiltration of heresy at the top-most levels of the Church.[14] By March 1567

Carnesecchi himself acknowledged the inquisitors' aims in one of the secret letters he sought to smuggle out from prison, to Bartolomeo Concini:

> The pretext for using such vigour is to make known their conviction that I did not tell them everything that I could have or should have told them in my [earlier] trial. But the truth is that they want me to talk about the affairs of others, and especially of those friends and masters of mine, both alive and dead. And because I do not have to say truly those things they wish to know.

This passage was quoted at him in the trial over these letters, on 7 April 1567. It came from the postscript to a long letter that had sought the help of Concini, the Medicean agent in Rome, in getting support from the Medici both over this investigation, and over confiscated properties and incomes. Carnesecchi also singled out the Spanish Cardinal Pacheco as 'more terrible and austere' than his colleagues, 'which I believe however comes from the natural severity of that nation in similar matters'. The postscript was written in anger that he was now being threatened with torture, which 'God knows is wrong, having confessed spontaneously much more than they have against me. . . .'[15]

Carnesecchi tried to confine himself to admitting that he was a follower of Valdés' teachings when they were not condemned, and that he strayed beyond those positions only in the short term. He did his best to shield Giulia Gonzaga and other friends, avoiding naming names or giving information that he reckoned the court did not know, and just confirming what he suspected it knew. However his equivocations, and his comments that Giulia Gonzaga adhered closely to Valdesian views only before they were fully condemned, or that she was not talking to particular members of her entourage, or visitors, about religious matters, were readily tested by the inquisitors, armed with his letters on which he was now asked to comment. The letters before him contradicted his denials about knowing, or knowing much about, her friends, servants and visitors, and their discussions.[16] The inquisitors did not need witnesses to testify against Carnesecchi; his letters essentially condemned him.

Failing to provide enough extra information, Carnesecchi was tortured (using the *corda*) first on 21 April 1567 after doctors ruled that, contrary to his claims, he was fit to undergo torture without risk of death. Protesting that tying his hands was enough, he noted that Christ had been tied to a column. Led to the rope he started reciting Psalm 50, '*Miserere mei Deus*' ('God have mercy on me'). Once hoisted up he started crying out, and called for vinegar (as Christ was given). He pleaded he could say no more, then: 'I have no more in my body. My Lord, I thank you. Oyme, do you want more? Kill me, Kill me. I die, I die.' His cries and protests continued with him calling out that they were killing him, and pleas for mercy. Questioned again, he replied that what he had said about others was true, that he could say no more, and he lapsed into silence. After being lowered and allowed to sit, he responded: 'I have said all I knew, and if you don't believe it God is the one who will harden your heart to not believe me for my greater penitence.' Brought back to court on 23 April, Carnesecchi told the inquisitors he had nothing further to say, he remembered nothing he had not already said. He had no more names to give.

Torture was again ordered. Carnesecchi admitted he deserved punishment for his sins, including 'for the irreverence and immodesty used in my letters when I mentioned the holy memory of Paul the fourth. Which I confess to be worthy of punishment, but not so serious and bitter as this'. Once hoisted up again, he uttered similar cries and pleas as on the first occasion, adding that he did not wish to die without confession or communion. When about to faint, vinegar was put on his face. Pressed again about whom he had named, he declared he would not commit perjury. Brought down, he was asked if he wanted time to think further about the truth, but he vehemently declined. He was not going to lie by adding to, or subtracting from, what he had already said, and 'I would die a thousand times than lie once.'[17] His next appearance before the Inquisition, on 24 April, was in relation to a supplementary trial – for breaching the Inquisition's secrecy rules by smuggling out of prison several letters addressed to leading figures who might help him, such as his nephew Marcantonio Divizi da Bibbiena and Cosimo I de' Medici (whose attempts to mitigate his position failed).[18] This would not have helped his reputation among the cardinals dominating the Inquisition. The final stages of the main trial, involving a little more questioning without satisfactory answers, processes of confession and pleas for mitigation, the preparation of the sentences on this 'impenitent heretic, falsely converted', took until 16 August.[19]

If the inquisitors failed to secure as much information from Carnesecchi as they expected, they made much of his final sentence and death. He became the focus of an *auto da fè* on Sunday, 21 September 1567, in Santa Maria sopra Minerva, before virtually all the normally resident cardinals (though Morone had left Rome just before), and many other cardinals and senior clergy. Reading the sentence against him took two hours; his noble demeanour during this process was praised by the master of ceremonies. Although eighteen persons were sentenced at the *auto*, only two received capital sentences – Carnesecchi and a conventual friar, Giulio Maresio from Belluno. Carnesecchi was executed on 1 October in front of a sizeable crowd at the bridge in front of Castel Sant'Angelo (as opposed to execution in the Campo dei Fiori, the more normal location); he was beheaded before his body was burned, since he was a recognised nobleman.[20]

Besides being a promoter of Valdés' ideas and books, Carnesecchi had admitted to being a reader of the works of Luther and Bucer from the 1540s, then accepting Luther's ideas on justification. In 1546 Carnesecchi was alleged to be 'one of the principals in Italy . . . of that [Lutheran] sect'.[21] He had also read

Calvin's *Institutio Christianae religionis*. The inquisitors found it hard to secure Carnesecchi's views on confession and transubstantiation (about which he admitted to doubts in Naples in 1540); 'And finally you believed in all the errors and heresies contained in that book, the *Beneficio di Cristo*, and in the false doctrine and institutions of the above mentioned Juan de Valdés, your master.'[22] The list of high-powered people condemned as heretics, or deemed highly suspect, with whom Carnesecchi had conversed and corresponded was extensive. They included Giulia Gonzaga, Ochino, Flaminio, Vermigli, Galeazzo Caracciolo from early days in Naples, and some again in Florence; later Morone, Pole, Apollonio Merenda, Alvise Priuli, Vittore Soranzo. The religious views of his contacts when he lived discreetly in Venice are unclear, but probably significant; his social circle included powerful patricians such as Andrea da Ponte (who allegedly organised a *ridotto/reduto*, or meeting group for religious discussion), Agostino Tiepolo, Bernardino Loredan, and three individuals who were to abjure: Marcantonio da Canal, Carlo Corner and Alvise Malipiero. The condemnation of Carnesecchi stressed that he lodged, fed and financed many religious refugees, and helped many escape abroad, especially to Geneva.[23] Under the rules of the game he was clearly a widely influential and active proselytiser, though not a heresiarch through the printed word – which might have saved him under a different Pope.

The condemnation and execution of Carnesecchi was a well publicised event, and it carried, probably intentionally, several messages to the wider world. It warned the highly intellectual and educated doubters and challengers to orthodoxy (with Cardinal Morone to take note) that they could no longer weasel their way to avoid condemnation. The preamble to the thirty-four clauses in the final condemnation of Carnesecchi referred to '... your excuses and many variations and *tergiversationi* in which you show yourself hard and difficult in freely confessing your false opinions against the holy Catholic faith'. He had strung along inquisitors, evaded them since 1546, secured a pardon from an emollient Pope, and absolution in 1561 from the Congregation. Cardinal Michele Ghislieri (who was party to the 1561 absolution of Carnesecchi), now turned Pope Pius V, would not have found the subsequent revelations from seized letters amusing and worthy of charity. That the Congregation did not harken to the pleas from those like Cosimo I de' Medici, to whom Carnesecchi had written from prison, indicated that they were no longer willing to accept outside political protection of heretical nobles, at least on such deep theological matters.

In the lengthy public condemnation of Carnesecchi the Inquisition essentially defined the parameters of orthodoxy and heresy, and reviewed the whole history of heretical reform. This was possibly more potent than the Council of Trent's efforts to consolidate doctrine, leading Simon Ditchfield to suggest this was an 'inquisitorial turn'.[24]

Carnesecchi's treatment contrasts with that of Mario Galeota, a friend with a rather similar heretical profile. Galeota had abjured at an *auto da fé* on 22 June 1567 in Rome. He was sentenced to five years' imprisonment away from Naples, his main centre of operations. In relation to the 1559–64 troubles in Naples inquisitor Giulio Santoro declared that Galeota was 'one of the authors of tumult, previously investigated, and a disciple of Valdés'. Santoro pressed Ghislieri to have Galeota tried in Rome. He had supplied Giulia Gonzaga with copies of Valdés' works, some of which he had translated into Italian (including his *One Hundred and Ten Divine Considerations*, at Giulia's request) and had them printed. In June 1561 Carnesecchi had asked Giulia to send Galeota a copy of the sentence from his 1561 trial, and his absolution, 'that he may know I am an Israelite', and to urge him to have less fear about greeting mutual friends; 'I do not doubt that he is rejoicing with all his soul over this, my honoured liberation.' (This letter surfaced at Carnesecchi's trial.) From August 1564 Giulia was keeping Carnesecchi informed about the arrest and investigation of Galeota. She speculated as to whether he had been betrayed by one of his servants, or because the Viceroy was hostile. Or some false friend had told lies, which led her to condemn the inquisitorial methods in acting on denunciations: 'everyone can arbitrarily cause harm to whomever he pleases, without that person knowing against whom he is to defend himself'. (This letter was also submitted at Carnesecchi's trial.) In 1566 Galeota admitted he had been taking ideas from the *Beneficio di Cristo*, especially that 'faith alone justifies and saves man'. He had denied the existence of Purgatory, the value of monastic vows, the intercession of saints and that good works gave merit. His books had been seized, but according to Giulia the inquisitors found that none was prohibited, and she believed he had never had any prohibited books. Galeota was not worried about the banning of works by Valdés and the *Beneficio*, or the confiscation of his books. Earlier he had declared: 'I do not care at all, because I have in my head that which no one can take from it, and if they prohibit me from reading they cannot make me remove it from my soul.' The aftermath of his sentencing to prison is not clear, but by May 1571 he was leading a normal life in Naples. He died in 1586.[25] In 1568 another powerful associate of the *spirituali*, the Modenese nobleman Endimio Calandra, who was closely associated with the Gonzagas, abjured publicly. He was banished, lost his benefices and was obliged to provide 200,000 stones to build new prisons for the Inquisition.[26]

With Carnesecchi's death the Roman Inquisition was relieved of the most high-profile and influential remaining Valdesian in Italy. Other reform leaders, Galeota in the south, Calandra and Dionisio Gallo in the north, were less painfully silenced. A number of impressive *autos da fé* were held up until 1570, in Rome and elsewhere as in Faenza, Naples and Mantua to curb lesser heretics – but with few executions. Probably less fearful of the spread of heresy, inquisitors could diversify their activities.

CHAPTER 6

※

Diverse and Changing Targets

THE SPANISH INQUISITION WAS DESIGNED AT FIRST TO MONITOR AND CONTROL inhabitants of Spain who had converted to Christianity from Judaism and Islam; the Sicilian and Sardinian tribunals shared these targets. By contrast, the creation of the centralised Roman Inquisition was planned primarily to confront various forms of Protestant heresy, when local responses had been inadequate or nonexistent. The targets then changed and became more diverse, as the Appendix of Tables demonstrates. This chapter will summarise the stages of transition and diversification in the targets from the 'medieval' phases through to the eighteenth century, comment on the Tables, and then illustrate what areas more specifically were targeted, especially some of the more intriguing topics like blasphemy, clerical solicitation, the supposed pretence of sanctity, especially by women, and relationships across faith divisions. Two key areas of concern that were more prominent will receive fuller analysis in later chapters: censorship, the magical arts and superstition. The sections dealing with Jewish and Muslim converts and their relations with Christians are substantially detailed (though the numbers of incidents is not vast) because the cases illustrate wider points about reconciliatory as well as negative inquisitorial action, social sensitivities as well as prejudices, diverse sentencing policies and inquisitorial conflicts with bishops. They also illustrate some intriguing inter-religious, inter-ethnic and sexual relations.

In the last stages of 'medieval' inquisitorial activity, as evidenced in northern Italy in the later fifteenth and early sixteenth centuries, the focus was on witchcraft and superstition, and the punishments were heavy persecution and the free use of torture. Contemporaneously, as noted, the Spanish Inquisition was established to superintend those from a Jewish or Muslim background who had been converted, mostly forcibly, to Christianity. To some extent a class war of landed aristocracy against urban aristocracy, with the latter suspected of long term contacts with Jews, worsened the persecutions. This campaign involved much torture, cruelty and miscarriage of justice. Sicily and Sardinia were affected by the campaign. In the 1520s and 1530s the Spanish tribunals turned on Lutherans, Erasmians and *Alumbrados* (or *Illuministi*), who followed a Spanish mystical approach, believing in a passive union with God, an abandonment of self, and the irrelevance of the institutional Church and all sacramental paraphernalia. Prosecutors saw similarities between *Alumbrados* and converted Jews (*conversos*), or Jewish sympathisers, as in the pursuit of the *beata* Isabel De La Cruz and Francisco De Osuna and their followers from 1519. Initially Erasmus had had court supporters around King Charles (Carlos) I (later Emperor Charles V), but from about 1519 this waned, then was reversed. Prosecutors started confusing Erasmian and Lutheran ideas (knowing less about the latter).[1] The Spanish hostility towards Erasmus to some extent influenced the scepticism of the Roman Inquisition about or hostility towards him, though the assault on Erasmus' writings was less intense.[2]

Sicily's first Lutheran victim seems to have been as late as 1547: Heremio de Tripedibus, an Augustinian friar from Maratea, first tried in 1539, was executed as relapsed in 1547 for bringing into his Order Lutheran and Valdesian ideas from Naples. The first inquisitor involved then, Bartolomé Sebastian, was launching a major campaign against Lutherans, worried by the importation of heretical books into the island. Nine Sicilian Lutherans were among the sixty-one condemned at the *auto da fé* of 13 February 1547, and twelve Lutherans (nine of them Sicilian) at the next *auto da fé* on 22 December. They were of several social classes, both secular and religious. The number actually executed is not clear. A leading Genoese merchant Giorgio Costa was condemned in 1549. Between 1547 and 1635 (when the persecution of 'Lutherans' seemingly ended) about 180 were condemned, including 80 Calvinists and 40 Anglicans; many were unlucky English and French sailors seized from their ships.[3]

From the 1530s to the 1560s Church and political leaders in Naples, then in Rome, worried about the influence of Juan Valdés, as already noted. In the 1560s the Kingdom of Naples and Rome were very frightened of the old Waldensian movement, for it had linked up with Genevan Calvinists as well as northern Waldensians. From the beginning the Roman Inquisition focused on the influences of reform both from the north (Lutheran, Zwinglian, Melanchthonian and Anabaptist) and the south (Valdesians). To some extent the anxieties about witches, superstitions and magical arts diminished.

By the late 1560s and 1570s, as already indicated, the main threats from northern Protestantism, home-grown Valdesians and Waldensians were overcome. As the available statistics suggest, the Italian tribunals, Roman and Spanish, moved more to investigating magical arts, superstitions, misunderstandings and misuse of sacraments and sacramentals, as well as sexual misconduct. The eating of 'prohibited meats' could indicate adherence to Protestant viewpoints, or be merely a continuation of medieval opposition to the dietary rules of the Church. Continuing cases of blasphemy against the Virgin and Saints might suggest deep-seated adherence to reform and opposition to the cult of Saints, or just the anger and frustration expressed by people when their prayers failed. Depending on local state and ecclesiastical attitudes, offences such as bigamy, sodomy and bestiality might be examined by the Inquisition, an episcopal court, or the local magistracy. Of what modern historians call generically 'sex crimes', it can be noted that 'sodomy' in the past had been treated as the worst and had been bracketed with heresy.[4] Venice had its secular court for blasphemy whereas other states did not. In the seventeenth century priestly solicitation of women, and occasionally men, in the confessional or when visiting the sick, became a concern for the Inquisition and bishops as an abuse of the sacrament.

Another growing worry in the seventeenth century was the propagation of ideas about mystical union with the divine, mental prayer and the pursuit of spiritual perfection. Two key movements, of the *Pelagini* and the Quietists, came under attack. To some extent linked with these ideas was the problem of claimed 'living saints' (mainly female though not exclusively so) and whether they were consciously fraudulent, or misled by human supporters or the Devil. The official Church was seen to be challenged by people withdrawing from normal parochial or conventual religious life, not accepting male hierarchical authority and leadership. The numbers of cases involved were not huge, but they attracted much attention in some local tribunals, and in the central Holy Office in Rome. The general classification 'Prohibited Books' hides subdivisions. Some owners of such books showed continuing interest in northern reformers, others were trying to evade the post-1596 ban on vernacular editions of the Bible, or parts thereof, while some were reading about astrology and new scientific ideas. In the eighteenth century the Congregation of the Index has been shown to have had intense worries about 'enlightened' ideas and the importation of anticlerical books, and even immoral novels – in French as well as Italian and Latin.

The Tables of Accusations, Cases and Sentences

The Tables produced in the Appendix can suggest trends over the period of our investigation. The compilation is fraught with difficulties. Statistics in some ways are more complete for the Spanish tribunals than for those in mainland Italy, and there those for Venice and Friuli are the fullest. Compilers past and present have used different criteria and definitions. The raw statistics are based on surviving records of denunciations and self-denunciations, not on completed cases.

Classification into types of accusation is likewise fluid, as Anne Schutte stresses in her comments on the famous Index 303 in the Venetian State archive, a nineteenth-century index of Inquisition cases compiled by Giuseppe Giomo and Luigi Pasini between 1868 and 1870.[5] While this Index is a very valuable tool for those of us working on the records of the Holy Office, its limitations need to be noted. The indication of a case's target is based on the key initial factor in the original denunciation or accusation. In complicated investigations other interesting charges might arise not noted in the Index, likewise extra persons not originally cited. Sometimes a vague classification might be given of general heresy (*eresia in generale*); while *luteranismo, calvinismo* and *giudaismo* are loosely used as definitions, not indicating the direction of a person's change of allegiance. Somebody brought up a Calvinist, or having experienced Calvinism outside Italy, who then wished to be recognised as a Catholic was viewed differently from a Catholic-born Venetian accused of dabbling in Calvinist doctrine. *Luterano* could be used all over Italy to cover deviance from Catholic orthodoxy; the accused might be more influenced by Valdés, Melanchthon or Anabaptists. In Table A, which compares the central Venetian tribunal with the one in Friuli, records for Venice allow for a distinction between heresies, whereas for Friuli some confusion may exist between 'apostasy from the faith' and 'diverse heretical propositions'. Some inquisitors might use a charge of possessing prohibited books rather than 'Lutheranism', as being easier to prove. With cases of magic and 'witches', the terminology differed considerably between the Venetian tribunal and others, and the alleged activities could be very variable. They overlapped with 'abuse of sacraments', which could vary from getting talismans baptised or misapplying holy oil to soliciting in the confessional. 'Atheist' and 'sodomite' could be thrown around as terms of abuse in general society, and so affect some classifications of supposed wrongdoing. In Antonio Rocco's case both accusations might have been accurate, though the Inquisition and the Council of Ten might have found it easier to concentrate on sodomy than on Rocco's supposed denial of the soul's immortality. Rocco was a student of Cesare Cremonini, the Paduan professor and friend of Galileo, often accused of denying the immortality of the soul, as we shall note later.[6]

Overview of Inquisitional Accusations and Death Sentences

Andrea Del Col has attempted an overall quantification of the number of persons accused, glossing and adding to previous tables and calculations in light of the opening of the Roman Holy Office archive.[7] He estimates that the number of accused would have been at least 200,400 over the whole period of our study, but may have been as high as 300,000. These refer to denunciations and recorded information, not completed cases. For the Naples area about 47 per cent of cases reached the stage of a formal process, 13 per cent had summary proceedings, and 37 per cent remained as denunciations and information. For the records in Udine (including cases from Aquileia and Concordia) the comparable break-down (until 1645) is 20 per cent formal processes, 40 per cent summary and 40 per cent denunciations. Del Col argues that for Italy the number of of formal processes would have been between 51,000 and 75,000.

A regional break-down for the best-documented tribunals reveals the following:

> *Venice*: 1541–1794.   3,479 accused (but records are missing for 1592–1615, suggesting about 4,400 overall; Tedeschi and Monter give 3,592)
>
> *Udine* (Aquileia and Concordia): to 1798.   3,136 accused. (Tedeschi and Monter give 2,453, to 1786)
>
> *Modena*: 1541–1784.   5,464 accused (with Ferrara cases added from 1599)
>
> *Siena*: 1580–1787.   6,893 accused, with 6,279 after 1600
>
> *Naples*: 4,390 accused (trying to calculate for missing periods. Tedeschi and Monter give 3,038)
>
> *Sicily*: See Appendix, Table D

In the break-down of periods of intensity Venice was most active 1566–90, Udine 1596–1610 and 1641–55, Modena 1601–40 and Siena 1716–50. For Siena the records up to 1580, preserved in Siena itself, are patchy; the post-1580 records are in the ACDF. The figure for Modena (plus Ferrara) in the seventeenth and eighteenth centuries would be 5,034, to be compared with 1,973 accused in Venice for the same period.

The discrepancies between the numbers of accusations and self-denunciations triggering some record, and those that were actually investigated, can be considerable and may be misleading for judging the impact of the inquisitions. Table E concerning Maltese arrests and convictions in the later eighteenth century reveals 148 people sentenced. But under four inquisitors covering 35 of those years, 1,467 penitents appeared at the tribunal, 936 of them being 'self-denouncing'. Only 51 were detained, and a number of these were soon released. No sentence was given for another 322, and most sentences were spiritual.[8]

Del Col estimates that under the Roman Inquisition about 1,250 executions were carried out (with Avignon adding 855 death sentences, some not implemented). Research has been difficult on this topic because of the loss of case records. Del Col considers that the old figures for executions in Rome (which comprised many accused individuals across Italy from cases started elsewhere) may be significantly under-recorded: 98 deaths in the sixteenth century, 28 in the seventeenth century and 2 in the eighteenth century, totalling 128. The Venetian tribunal issued 26 death sentences (3 not implemented); Udine 15 (10 not implemented); Bologna 29–30 at least (11 not implemented). Ancona carried out 25 executions by burning in 1556, nearly all *marranos* who had been admitted in the 1530s to improve the port's economy, but now seen as Judaising – a dire example of Paul IV's anti-Semitism.⁹ About half the death sentences were for adherents of reform, and 150–200 for actions of damaging witchcraft (*maleficia*).¹⁰

The Spanish Inquisition is estimated to have instigated 200,000 cases, with 12,100 death sentences (6 per cent). The figures for the Portuguese Inquisition are more in question, but one calculation gives 31,353 formally completed cases (1536–1794), with 1,250 executions in person and 630 in effigy (total 6 per cent). In contrast the execution rate for the Roman Inquisition was between 1.6 and 2.4 per cent, depending on which estimated total one takes from above.¹¹ In considering the balance between major and minor heresy in Spain, it has been suggested that in the period 1560–1614 under tribunals in Aragon there were 7,985 cases tried of major heresy (including *moriscos*, *conversos*, *alumbrados* and Protestants), and 8,039 tried of minor heresy; for Castile the figures were 4,923 and 6,963. For the longer and less active period 1615–1700 the figures for Aragon were 2,244 and 5,959, while those for Castile were 3,052 and 3,178, again showing some shift towards the lesser heresies.¹²

The inquisitions in Italy and Iberia featured significant numbers of denunciations for magic and superstition – loosely called 'witchcraft' – but few leading to serious punishment, let alone executions, though a proper calculation of death sentences for witchcraft has not been attempted. After the late fifteenth- and early sixteenth-century witch-hunts in northern Italy discussed earlier, Italy endured few scares over witches or nationwide witch-hunts. This contrasts with much of the rest of Europe, where inquisitorial methods coupled with a liberal use of torture under untrained magistrates could lead to horror stories, even if figures have often been grossly exaggerated. A sceptical and balanced assessment has suggested 110,000 prosecutions for witchcraft across Europe, with 60,000 executions. With that one can point to localised paranoid witch-hunts such as in Bamberg with about 300 executions (1625–31). Over a longer time scale the English county of Essex between 1560 and 1672 tried 291 witches, executing 74; Scotland between 1563 and 1727 tried 402 and executed 216; Geneva between 1537 and 1662 tried 318, executing 68, though the nearby rural Pays de Vaud executed 90 of 101 tried between 1537 and 1630.¹³

Blasphemy

The Holy Office's increasing attempts to control blasphemy varied geographically according to how much other courts, religious and secular, were involved and how far other matters were deemed more serious. Blasphemy could be seen as the rowdy expression of violence, often associated with sacrilege as in the past, or as an indirect way of showing adherence to Protestant ideas, as over the cult of saints. In Rome itself the Congregation noted the prevalence of blasphemy among clergy, notably those in religious orders.¹⁴ Venice had its own separate office, the *Esecutori contra la Bestemmia* (Council against Blasphemy),[15] but a number of cases of heretical blasphemy and swearing were investigated by the Venetian inquisitional tribunal. As with other offences the testimony of friends and neighbours played a variable role.

As in earlier periods, much of the swearing was by the 'arse' (*culo*) and 'cunt' (*potta*) of the Virgin, Christ and Saints. In October 1608 our exemplary inquisitor Eliseo Masini dealt in his local Congregation of consultants in Ancona with Annibale Ferri dell'Olmo, who confessed to blaspheming by the '*Potta di S. Paolo*', which they decided deserved a little whipping and salutary penances. Masini thought the Roman Congregation should know about this judgement.[16] In 1646 Giovanni Paolo Sorratini was accused of swearing by the '*puttana* [whore] *di Dio, puttana di Signore, potta di Dio, Sangue* [blood] *di Dio*'. It was noted that he was reputed to be a thief and cheat; the accusation of blasphemy might have been seen as a better way of controlling him than with a secular charge. Similarly when Francesco Mattei, vice-chancellor to the Patriarch of Venice, was accused in 1653 of blasphemy, the accusers may have been trying to stop legal cases he was trying to bring against them (since 1642). His real or alleged blasphemies included that the Magdalene was Christ's mistress; that St John had a whore (*Bardassa*); that Turks praying to Mohammed could win victories against Christians; that the Devil gained everything, God nothing; and that Venetian saints like St Girardo Sagredo were unbelievable, and just nobles. Numerous witnesses were called and backed some of these allegations at length, including a priest who had stayed in Mattei's house in 1647–8. Notes about the legal battles contained in the file may have persuaded the inquisitor to take no further action.[17] Also, the inversion, distortion or parody of prayers was probably common. The inquisitor in Bergamo prosecuted a mercenary in 1624 for saying '*Sancte Calvine, ora pro nobis*', substituting Calvin for the Virgin.[18]

In 1697 Nicolo Busi of Cento was denounced to the Inquisition for scandalous words and blasphemies, by his brother-in-law (Thomaso Pasqualino of Cento), whom he had disturbed along with his wife at midnight by banging and blaspheming. Here the main offending phrases were '*Cospetto di Dio*' ('In the sight of God', or possibly more in the spirit of 'In your face, God'), and '*Sangue di Dio*' ('Blood of God'), said in the public street outside the house. Thomaso had recommended Nicolo to say Our Fathers and Ave Marias as atonement, and was told to go to the Devil. Asked about his brother-in-law's reputation, Thomaso said he was generally 'held to be a vicious and rabid man', and was a regular blasphemer. The deposition was signed in a good hand. The inquisitor in Bologna said this information should be sent to the vicar in Cento, to issue warnings to Busi.[19] When in the same tribunal Andrea Quaderti from Del Rio (a mercer aged forty) was denounced for the second time for similar swearing during dice games, he ended up with corporal punishment and penances. When players had tried to curb him he had said: 'I want to blaspheme when I want, and scorn Christ, who will not allow the Devil to come and take me away.'[20]

Blaspheming was often noted in the context of other activities which were deemed offensive by the Church: when people were drinking, playing dice and cards (as with Andrea Quaderti above). In this respect a Fra Cherubino Arcangelo d'Urbino, a Dominican priest aged sixty-seven, writing from Cagli to Cardinal Pinelli at the Holy Office, complained about the amount of blaspheming against God, the Virgin and Saints, 'without fear, and the blasphemies are so execrable that they frighten those who hear them, and this vice reigns not only among the laymen, but also among secular clergy, and ordained priests, to the scandal of the good'. His complaint was triggered by hearing a few days earlier a certain Don Andrea Druda, a Cathedral canon who was playing cards in a gentleman's house. On losing, he used every kind of blasphemy, crying: 'Christ, Christ, you caused my loss, I don't know what stops me breaking your arms.' A fellow Dominican had just preached against this vice, and Fra Cherubino saw no reason why gentlemen and priests of whatever standing should escape punishment. He recommended that Druda be questioned, to see whether he did break the arms of a crucifix. Fra Cherubino wanted this matter pursued, alerting the Roman Inquisition that there was no Inquisition in Cagli, not even a prison to put such delinquents.[21] It is notable that such offences were deemed important enough to warrant another local tribunal, which didn't materialise.

Solicitation and Other Sexual Offences by Priests

As the Tables in the Appendix indicate, from the seventeenth century a growing concern with 'solicitation' manifested itself, for example in Venice, Friuli and Sicily. This offence was an abuse of the confessional, when priests molested confessing penitents, whether in or around the confessional box while in church, or in private houses if confessions of the sick were being heard at home. Most such molestations involved female penitents, though occasionally there were male victims. The offence varied from suggestive remarks, to fondling, to full intercourse. While we would classify many cases as rape, some could involve the willing participation of the girl or woman concerned. Given the intimate circumstances of a confessional situation, proving such allegations was difficult, and so cases were dismissed or left on file. The allegation could be made as a ploy, by third parties, to discredit a parish priest or confessor. Convicted priests might receive quite light sentences. In 1623 some friars of San Francesco di Paolo in Venice denounced another of their number, Fra Giovanni Antonio Gervasio, for soliciting several women in confessionals. A certain Paulina at least seemed complicit; the case was dropped, probably because she failed to appear to give evidence against him.[22]

Earlier, in 1592, another friar minor of St Francis de Paula in Venice, Agostino Altomonte da Brissignano, was denounced by four women for sexual abuse in confession, or at home in one case when the woman was sick. He had kissed them with tongue in mouth, touched their *vergogna* (shame), had them handle his erection and claimed his ejaculation would cure the sick woman. The tribunal conducted a fairly lengthy investigation, hearing the women as witnesses. It elicited that the convent had many tensions, rivalries between brothers, that many beautiful women frequented the convent. When questioned, Agostino claimed that the women were prostitutes and concubines of his fellow brothers or others; that Fra Cola was responsible for taking goods (*robbe*), not him, which led to hatred between them. The tribunal appointed a defence lawyer. The continuing case, which heard many witnesses (including some eminent clerics in Agostino's defence), investigated financial irregularities, sexual misconduct, animosities at the convent, and the friar's dubious views on Purgatory, Hell and Heaven. The Roman Inquisition and local theology experts were consulted. A full court (all *assistenti* present) decided that nothing had been sufficiently proved to have Agostino judged a heretic, or suspected of heresy, so they absolved and dismissed him. This showed that a case of solicitation could be fully investigated by a tribunal, evidence well taken, and a defence lawyer secure an acquittal by casting doubts. It involved good story-telling, whether true or invented. Well-attested animosity on the part of the female accusers undermined their graphic descriptions. How many among them were guilty of sexual immorality remains unclear. Agostino was given the benefit of the doubt, but he had to endure more than ten months of harsh detention.[23]

Cases of solicitation should be seen in a wider context of the sexual relations between priests and parishioners, and mixed attitudes in the sixteenth century to priests having concubines and young, unrelated 'housekeepers'; the latter were increasingly singled out, often unfairly, for suspicion. A free and easy attitude by priests to sexual relations might be linked to their other genuine challenges to orthodoxy. A complainant against a priest over sexual matters might rightly or wrongly add other allegations to make a better case. Alternatively, a tribunal starting on one offence might bring in other vices or erroneous beliefs, as some Venetian cases in the 1750s have shown.[24]

Miscellaneous Misconduct

As the Tables in the Appendix suggest, a whole range of misbehaviour and misconduct that might be dubiously part of the Inquisition's remit in terms of heresy could lead to denunciations, and variable punishments. Impeding the activities of the Inquisition's officials, betraying secrets and obstructing justice were all offences.

Disrespect for popes, cardinals, higher clergy – without being blasphemous – could lead to trouble, interpreted as a challenge to the authority of the Church. In 1573 a young flour porter, Dominico Longino, was reported to the Venetian tribunal for regularly singing a vulgar song or songs, about buggery between the Pope and Cardinal Colonna. The court was provided with a copy. One fellow fariner who had heard him several times declared he deserved to be burned alive. When questioned (before the legate, Patriarch, inquisitorial *commissario*, auditor, vicars and one lay assistant), Dominico admitted to singing the song for a year and half, having learned it from children when little. He reported that a certain *fonzegher* (storeman) was his enemy. The storeman had reported him to the night watch (*Signori di Notte*) for stealing flour, and he had copied down the song while Dominico was singing it. Dominico had not been to confession this year, but last year in Friuli. He had never taken communion, 'because the Devil controls my brain'. He was imprisoned while other witnesses were heard, but after a couple of weeks the tribunal released him without any more punishment, taking into consideration this imprisonment, his youth, his ignorance and *insipienna* (stupidity) – and that the song had some history. However, should he sing the song again, or teach it, he would serve a year rowing in the triremes.[25]

Even fairly light-hearted mockery of clergy and religious ceremonies could cause alarm. In 1582 some journeymen mercers in rented accommodation in the Venetian parish of San Luca were seen wearing paper hats, and playing around with religious objects, such as a censer, candles and religious paintings. A nosy noblewoman living opposite noted these, and one garmented youth bowing to another while holding a censer. A network of informants and gossips relayed the observations to the Patriarch and papal legate, setting the Inquisition tribunal in motion. Many witnesses were called to give a picture of the activities of these journeymen (sometimes with others like the landlord's teenage son), simulating the cardinals, the Pope, and preparing to say vespers. The tribunal did not accept that this was just amusing game-playing to pass the time (as the defence claimed), but serious mockery and an assumption by laymen of clerical roles. Consultants were brought in, but gave divergent opinions over whether the journeymen should 'abjure as formal heretics or *de vehementi* or *de levi*'. A Jesuit, Martino Fornario, saw them acting 'out of frivolity and ignorance', but Pietro Vendramin, a noble canon lawyer who had edited an inquisitor's manual (1575), ruled they should abjure *de vehementi*. Another suggested torture or the threat of torture to ascertain the real intentions of these journeymen. The harshest critic, Desiderius Guido, forcefully recommended formal abjuration without further ado. The reconvened tribunal then asked the accused whether they believed all men were priests, though their dressing up hardly conformed to the Lutheran teaching implied by this question. The tribunal of four (Patriarch Giovanni Trevisan, inquisitor Angelo Mirabino, the legate's auditor and one *assistente*) decided the three leading journeymen should abjure as being strongly suspected of heresy. They were set a schedule of penances, confessions, recitations of psalms or the rosary over the following year. Abjurations and sentencing were in the parish church at High Mass. The journeymen might have been imitating the Feast of Fools or another topsy-turvy ritual sanctioned in the past, and creating a little spectacle of their own when the major mercers' guild did not embrace them. By 1582 respectable Venetian neighbours of substance and the Inquisition were largely intolerant of carnival-type foolery in a city with many immigrants who might get involved with alien religious goings-on beyond simple anticlericalism.[26]

Conversions and Reconciliations

From the later sixteenth century tribunals and officials of the Roman Inquisition could be part of several processes of education and re-education, of conversion and reconciliation. Their treatment of many cases of 'superstition' involved a process of educating the accused in correct Christian beliefs and practices, with minor punishments for past misdeeds. When the Tables in the Appendix list cases dealing with Judaisers, Muslims, Calvinists and the Greek Orthodox, they are lumping together people who were being persecuted and punished, but also some who were negotiating their way into an acceptable Catholic position. As immigrants (voluntary or enslaved) they could be converting to Catholicism for the first time. Others may have been baptised but then lived as Jews, Lutherans or Calvinists, or been circumcised when living in Ottoman lands but now wanted to be 'good Catholics'. Their position could be negotiated through a 'spontaneous appearance' before the inquisitor. Jesuits and Capuchins cooperated in this negotiation procedure. Two Lutheran Saxon shoemakers, having been converted by Jesuits, approached the Venetian tribunal in 1639 to be certified as good Catholics. Similarly, in 1646 an Italian who had fought in France and been attracted to Calvinism, along with a French soldier, having passed through the hands of Capuchins asked to be reconciled to the Catholic faith. In 1638 the Florentine inquisitor was approached by Emanuele Lobo, who asked to be allowed to live as a Christian in Tuscany without fear of persecution; he was a circumcised Jew from a Lisbon family, allegedly forcibly circumcised as a sick youth on his father's orders.[27]

Jewish Converts, Judaisers and Jewish-Christian Interactions

A significant number of cases in the sixteenth century coming before the Venetian and Neapolitan tribunals concerned Judaisers; that is, persons born

Jewish but baptised (forcibly or willingly), often called *conversos* or *marranos*, or those converted to Judaism who were accepted back as Christians, but who then were suspected of not behaving as true Christians. Jews who were never baptised were technically not subject to the Inquisition, but in practice some were investigated if they were too closely involved with Christians (as in the case of sexual relations), and a threat to the latter's beliefs and morals. Anti-Semitism increased in Italy in the fifteenth century, encouraged by some Franciscan preachers. Jewish communities from time to time were expelled from certain cities or states, but never totally banned from Italy (unlike from Iberia and Sicily). Venice inaugurated in 1516 the formal system of a Ghetto to enclose Jews in a particular part of the city; this was partly to counteract some demands for total expulsion, and to recognise that some Jewish families could be economically beneficial to the Republic, especially in trading with the Ottoman empire, which had a fairly tolerant attitude towards Jews. The creation of the Venetian Ghetto, expanded by 1633 to three sections, in practice provided a fairly secure area for Jews to practise their religion, and express cultural vitality. Formal ghettos were created in other cities such as Rome (1556), Ancona, Florence (1570), Siena (1571) and Verona (1599); more followed in the seventeenth century (Bologna, Cremona, Ferrara, Modena, Padua and smaller towns or villages). Elsewhere small groups of Jewish families could congregate in unstructured areas of a city. While physically structured ghettos, with high walls and gates, could lock Jews in at night and Christians out, all of them – even in Rome, Venice and Florence – were permeable, as modern research emphasises.[28]

So in fact Jews and Christians could fraternise at all social levels, over interdependent commerce, moneylending, second-hand dealing; over Jewish medical expertise, and language scholarship; over medicinal and love-magic techniques, and sex. Some of these common interests could concern the inquisitors. Catechumen confraternities and houses, aided by Capuchins and Jesuits, campaigned to secure conversions of Jews (and Muslims) to Christianity; they operated in cities like Venice (Pia Casa dei Catecumeni) and Rome (Casa dei Catecumeni). A growing anti-Semitism spread through Rome from the seventeenth century and it increased into the nineteenth, producing brutality in the Roman Casa to enforce conversions. Policies of seizing Jewish babies and forcibly placing them with Christian families were encouraged by the Cardinal vicar of Rome. The Holy Office strongly encouraged denunciations of Judaisers, sowing distrust and undermining local Jewish-Christian interdependence on the Ghetto borders, but from the later seventeenth century it tried to exert restraint on the Casa's brutality. The attitudes of Venetian inquisitors towards Jews were milder and more accommodating.[29]

Sometimes the financial inducements led to some persons 'converting' several times, according to witnesses denouncing them to the inquisitors.

Iseppo (Giuseppe) Bon (alias Moses Israel and Francesco Maria Leoncini) was tried in Venice in 1636–7 after being denounced (by a rich merchant convert Andrea Nunciata, formerly Abram Teseo) for 'trafficking in the holy religion, with great scandal to the holy faith'. He had been baptised in Rome, Vicenza and Bologna. Iseppo was sentenced to public penance and seven years in the galleys, or twelve years in a close prison. Iseppo and Nunciata informed on a certain Elias of Rome, who traded there in converts from all over Italy; and allegedly brought from Livorno four 'Jewesses become Christians' to Venice, to sell them as slaves in the Levant.[30]

Relationships between Jews and Christians in and outside the Venetian Ghetto can be illustrated with the interesting case in 1587 of a physician's widow, Valeria Brugnaleschi, and her daughter Splandiana Mariano. They were investigated for sorcery, having used incantations, diabolic objects and an *inghistera* (a clear glass flask) of holy water to conjure devils, in order to discover stolen property; and they used love concoctions involving semen. Sometimes they cooperated with Jews, both in the Ghetto and outside it. Valeria lived in the Ghetto for two years, teaching Jewish girls to read and write, and talking with them about the Old Testament. A self-proclaimed 'good Christian' declared that Valeria believed 'the faith of the Jews is better than ours and that it pleases her more because they observe it better'; this was a view shared by others who encountered Jews, and Muslims. Valeria and her daughter were sentenced to a public whipping, pillorying and five-year exile, 'for love magic, witchcraft and bean-casting'.[31]

An admirer of Judaism or somebody converting to it could be a Nicodemist, as with Laura Raguante (or Raguantes) in Naples who converted to Judaism, but continued to attend Mass for three years without confessing or receiving communion, as a 'cover'. She had been converted, 'taught by other judaising women to believe the old law was better than our evangelical law, and that was saving the soul and the evangelical was not good'. She was tried in 1579/80 under Archbishop Annibale di Capua of Naples. Previously she had been convicted for heresy and apostasy from the Catholic faith. Now she was sentenced to wearing the *abitello*, to penances, confession and receiving the sacraments four times a year, and perpetual imprisonment (*carcere perpetuo*, but it was stated this could be mitigated).[32]

Admiration by a Christian for Jews and their behaviour was vocally expressed by Giovanni Battista Capponi while in the Rialto prison, who was reported by fellow prisoners in 1588. He revealed himself to be fascinated by the unorthodox, by possessing prohibited books, discoursing with Jews on his travels. He informed a notary taking evidence: 'the law of the Jews was better than ours, because the law was given to the Jews by God himself and to us by the apostles only.' He had said that Christ was not the true Messiah, and his miracles had been aided by the Kabbalah. The Inquisition treated Capponi more as a loudmouth than a serious heretic who posed a danger by infecting others. He was convicted as 'vehemently suspect of heresy', and sentenced to five years in the galleys and penitential prayers. On Rome's orders he had been tortured to elicit any teachers of the heresies or contacts. He gave nothing away: 'What cruelty to try to extract from me thus a thing not in me to tell'. He did, however, end up admitting the general charges to lighten his sentence.[33]

The Venetian situation was complicated when the government and local tribunal adopted the policy that Jews who had been forcibly converted to Christianity, in Iberia particularly, could decide to live and practise in the Venetian Ghetto as Jews. This could be a headache for the Inquisition, especially where an extended family was involved, when some offspring decided to be Christians, and so were free to roam through the city, and others to be Jews. It could add to the complications of identifying allegiances. Those involved in international trade could find it convenient to be Jewish in Salonica and other parts of the Ottoman empire, and Christian in the Venetian Republic; to 'sail by two rudders', in the words of the Jewish consul to the Levantine Jewish community in Venice, Chaim Baruch (or Chayn Saruc), who castigated the behaviour of such converts in the 1570s. These complexities emerged in the very full case of Gaspare Ribeiro (or Gasparo Ribiera), of Portuguese origin, who was tried in 1580–1. When Baruch was questioned in January 1580 by the inquisitor about Ribeiro ('my mortal enemy', because of lawsuits involving large sums), he declared: 'I took that Gaspare for a Marrano, and we think of Marranos as ships that have two rudders.... For a ship to have rudders means that with one rudder it sails with one wind, and with the other with another wind.' In September he clarified: 'a Marrano, as I said, is one who sails with two rudders, because he is neither Jew nor Christian.'[34] Gaspare had alternated between the two faiths when trading internationally, though he gave the impression to some of finally settling down as a good Christian, supporting and serving a confraternity of the Holy Sacrament. His daughter Violante adamantly wanted to be a Christian, as had emerged years earlier in 1569 before the Inquisition when she noisily protested that her brother João was trying to force her to marry a Jew. Gaspare himself died in prison while under investigation, and was denied a Christian burial.[35]

Another heavily investigated Venetian case was that of Filipe, or Felipe, de Nis (alias Soloman Marcos) and his family, arrested in October 1585 as crypto-Jews living in the parish of S. Leonardo. The Inquisition, the state and Rome via the nuncio were concerned about their involvement with unconverted Jews in the Ghetto, and with networking between Jews and converts, due to the international ramifications.[36] Details were elicited about the family's activities, dress, eating habits; their observation or lack of observation of ceremonies and rituals, whether Christian or Jewish; their travelling to Portugal wearing black hats to avoid identification there as Jews, but appearing as Jews to Jews. Some of the family seemed to attend neither Christian nor Jewish services as they moved between identities. Investigations were made of who among them was circumcised, and when (as a child or adult). One servant witness, Francisco, close to Felipe senior (who mainly took the line he was a Jew), proved not to be circumcised. There were doubts between experts whether Felipe senior himself was circumcised. New experts declared that, judging by a callus, he had been circumcised as an adult, not as a child. Felipe replied that the callus was due to a medical operation not an adult circumcision. Stories by various persons changed regularly. A witness against Francisco was made to confront him, then Francisco was tortured to reconcile different stories.[37] Eventually the tribunal was convinced Felipe senior had been born of baptised parents, and was himself baptised in Porto. For a long time Felipe stuck to his claim to be Jewish, but then appeared dramatically in June 1586 to declare that in prison 'God has enlightened me and I beg for your mercy'. He may have been influenced by a defence lawyer's view that his case was indefensible. Felipe asked to confess – as he had often done in Portugal and San Tomè, an island off the west African coast. He wanted to return to Christianity, as did a couple of other prisoners. He was sentenced to life imprisonment, but this was then interpreted as compulsory confinement within Venice, and bail of 1,700 ducats. His wife, Felipa, and other members of the family who had fled to Salonica, returned to Venice in late 1588. In a private session the inquisitor accepted Felipa and a servant's confession and reconciliation to Christianity, heard a formal abjuration and imposed penances.[38] From the viewpoints of the Inquisition and the state (and the modern historian) the long de Nis and Ribeiro cases revealed a lot about the Jewish and Judaising communities, and probably warned powerful families criss-crossing the religious borders to be more circumspect. However, Venice resisted the request of the Roman Inquisition to investigate Felipe in Rome, to ascertain even more about contacts with the Portuguese in Rome, and secure control over them. Such a move might harm Venice's economic interests by alarming other trading families 'sailing by two rudders'.

As a test of Jewish or Muslim adherence, circumcision posed problems for the Inquisition. Inquisitors were slow to summon doctors to investigate the accused, and doctors could not always agree whether somebody had been circumcised, and when. Adult circumcision was deemed proof of apostasy. Sons from Iberian Jewish families might have had circumcision delayed until they were in a more tolerant area (such as Ferrara, or within the Ottoman empire).[39] The practice of Muslim circumcision (*khitan*), then as now, allowed that this could be performed not just after birth, but when the boy was older. The social celebrations could, and can, be impressive and joyful. This may have affected a Christian's willingness to convert when in Muslim territories.[40]

Distinguishing between Jew and convert, identifying those who were behaving in a way appropriate to their faith, was fraught with difficulties, and there was much questioning of witnesses in Venetian tribunals to try and sort out the reputation of those who were reported as suspect. Neighbours were questioned on the way people dressed, whether the men shifted from the Jewish red hat to the Christian black hat (as the above-cited Andrea Nunciata allegedly did), or hid the yellow badge of the legitimate Jew; whether women did their hair in a perceived Jewish fashion; whether a supposed convert raised his hat in front of a holy image or when the sacrament was being carried through the streets to the sick; whether he knelt at the sound of the bell chiming the Ave Maria or hid in a shop to avoid the required action; on what people ate and when; whether burials deviated from the normal Christian way of wrapping the body in a linen sheet; whether individuals had been seen at church services or confessing.[41] Witness statements indicated that the terms *marrano* and *luterano* were used interchangeably by native Catholics, as both would break the fasting laws for Friday and Saturday. *Marrano* could indicate a religiously suspicious person. In the Ribeiro (Ribiera) case a neighbouring woman, Margharita Vitrario (wife of a bailiff to the Inquisition), testified: 'many times I heard Gasparo Ribiera shouting at Giulia his servant. And leaning over Gasparo's house balustrade she said of old Gasparo: This Lutheran, he eats meats on Friday and Saturday. And at that time I did not know what it meant to say Lutheran, and I laughed.' Later Giulia allegedly added to Margharita: 'My dear, these *Marrano* dogs, these traitors eat meat on Friday and Saturday.' The scribe of the Sacrament confraternity of Santa Maria Formosa, Matteo, when testifying as a defence witness to Gasparo's contributions to the confraternity as a *gastaldo* (steward), was asked what he thought of a Portuguese who was apparently a Christian, but secretly married his son to a Jewess. He replied: 'I would believe him a bad man (*tristo*), and worse.' Matteo testified that Gasparo was known in the parish as a *marrano* or 'the *marrano*'. Asked if he had more to say for or against Gasparo, Matteo answered: 'If I knew anything I would say it, because I do dislike those sorts of person, Lutherans and similar ones.'[42]

The cases brought against Judaisers were primarily about outward conduct, avoiding Christian duties, but seldom involved accusations that they blasphemed, openly disrespected Christians or debated theological positions. It was an unusual accusation in 1555 when alleging Elena de Freschi Olivi had shouted during Mass in S. Marcilian while the priest was saying the Credo: 'You lie in your teeth, you are a bastard, son of a harlot.'[43] In 1674 Tomas Butierz was denounced for challenging the story of the Magi, whom he judged to be merely wizards. In 1641 Emmanuel Fernandes, a black man and former slave from Goa, allegedly argued that 'it was Moses that remedied Adam's sin', not Christ.[44]

A voluntary conversion from Judaism to Christianity for someone coming into a port could appear easy, if he or she approached the Inquisition. In 1612 the inquisitor of Ancona informed the Roman Congregation via Cardinal Millini that a Giacob, son of the late Samuele Coen from Saphet in Galilee, a *Hebreo*, had appeared before him, and 'sworn by oath in the presence of witnesses that he wishes to become a Christian'. The inquisitor had sent him to the confraternity of the Sacrament, which customarily in this city had the care of such petitioners, and the confraternity would take the necessary measures. Because Giacob wished to be baptised in Rome, he had asked for a letter of recommendation from the inquisitor, who duly provided it. In this case the confraternity of the Sacrament was the organ for instructing the would-be convert, rather than the special Catechumen organisations noted above.[45]

Sexual Relations between Christians and Non-Christians

From time immemorial all three monotheistic religions had showed distrust of the sexual attitude and behaviour of those from other faiths, and discouraged inter-faith sexual relations. Food habits and hygiene might also be interconnected, which further discouraged or prevented social and sexual intercourse. This was particularly true of parts of early medieval Iberia where all three faiths might be presiding, where they partially interacted and developed myths about each other that could be passed on as the Jews and Muslims were driven out of Iberia. Jews and Muslims were inclined to see Christians as heterosexual predators and promiscuous. Christians saw Muslims as inclined to sodomy and what we now call pederasty. But Muslims in Spain could equally attack Christian priests, supposedly celibate, as either sodomites or womanisers. For Jews and Muslims the Christians were unclean in their food habits, and their men were uncircumcised; to which Christians replied that they had been cleansed through baptism.[46] Whatever the more complex realities, these attitudes induced the Inquisition and other authorities to ban or discourage sexual and close social relationships between Christians and those of other faiths. The Inquisition should not theoretically exercise jurisdiction over Jews (as opposed to Jews who had been baptised), but they could and did if Jews were suspected of having sex with Christians. Such intimacy might pervert true belief. For those cities and smaller towns that had Jewish and Muslim communities in post-Tridentine Italy, inter-faith sexual relations featured in denunciations and investigations – as in Venice, Friuli, Mantua and Malta. Existing case classification makes it hard to establish the size of the problem, and the seriousness with which it was treated, or not.

Sexual relations between Christians, Jews and Judaisers are noted in a number of Venetian cases, though that was not the main issue as far as inquisitors were concerned. Jews clearly frequented Christian prostitutes outside the Ghetto. Christian women might not recognise a Jew even during sexual relations, as one witness in the Adam Righetto (Enriques Nuñes) case stated. At the

Florentine court (where Jews were welcomed by the grand duke and duchess), Righetto behaved as a Christian courtier in the way he dressed, ate and showed his awareness of Christian prayers; 'and he slept and had to do with Christian women, who would never have taken him if they had thought him a Jew'. The court received written evidence from some Portuguese witnesses including Alvaro Caçeres, who wrote of Nuñes' (Righetto's) escapades in Madrid in 1567. Nuñes and a friend had invited courtesans to a banquet, and this was ruined when one courtesan during lovemaking with Nuñes suddenly screamed and told him to go to the Devil, when she saw he was circumcised (*deschapelhado*).[47] The existence of longer-term relationships is less documented. In the multifaceted denunciation of the *strega* Cristina Collarina, she was alleged to have had a Jewish lover, and love letters supposedly sent by him in Ferrara were produced in court.

Some insights can be derived from data accumulated by or for the inquisitor of Mantua, Bassano Gallicciolo, in 1684–5, when the bishop challenged the Inquisition's right to try cases involving Jewish-Christian sexual relations without episcopal participation or knowledge. The inquisitor explained to the Roman Inquisition the background in an *Informatione*.[48] On 19 April 1684 David Norlengo, a *hebreo*, had appeared spontaneously before the Holy Office accusing himself of sexual misconduct. But on 29 April a *processo* was begun against him in the episcopal court for the same offence, to which the inquisitor objected. Claims and counterclaims followed via notaries over who should try Norlengo. Gallicciolo copied a letter from Cardinal Barberini, 26 July 1636, saying the then bishop would be ordered not to molest those appearing before the inquisitor in Mantua for carnal relations between Jews and Christians. This led the inquisitor and his notary to compile two dossiers (*Compendi*) to ascertain how cases of Jewish-Christian relations – 'carnal commerce' – had been handled in the past. For the period of eighty-seven years between 1598 and 1684 (inclusive) Gallicciolo gave summary notes (from 2 to about 50 lines) on 201 *cause*: 42 processed, 103 *sponte comparenti*, while those cases begun but not completed for lack of proof, or because persons fled, numbered 56 (so only receiving 2 or 3 lines of comment).[49] Only in three cases was the episcopal court involved.

A picture emerges of a significant number of Jewish males involved with Christian women, mainly but not always of ill repute. The Mantuan ghetto was clearly permeable. The Inquisition police were proactive, snooping around Christian hostelries. They could spot Jews, who if just sitting next to a Christian woman might be hauled off to the tribunal office for questioning. On several occasions a short time in prison turned the claim of a Jew and a Christian merely knowing each other, but without a sexual relationship, to a full confession of sex.[50] Jews denounced fellow Jews for relations with Christian women, but such denunciations were not always accepted as accurate.[51] Punishments, when they were applied, were variable and seemingly inconsistent, as one would expect when many different inquisitors were involved. At the end of the second *Compendio* Fra Gallicciolo emphatically stressed to the Roman Congregation the quality of many named inquisitors who had served Mantua over the eighty-seven years, including Eliseo Masini, whose manual *Sacro Arsenale* was still esteemed. The sentences included salutary penances for the Christian women deemed offenders; mere warnings to both sides to behave, to be ready to appear again 'as and when' (*toties quoties*); for Jews not to have Christian women in their houses, and Christian women not to allow Jewish men to enter theirs. These sentences were administered on pain of prison, the galleys, or fines if the injunction was breached. Confinement for a period was another resolution – in the house or in the ghetto. Inquisitors showed some emollient consideration for accused pregnant women.[52]

After the inquisitor in Mantua had made his case by producing his records of what his predecessors had done, the bishop's representatives would report on a few cases of Jewish-Christian relationships that had been pursued by the episcopal court. Seven *cause* had been expedited since 1597: the first in 1654, and last resolved in 1672. The final case was in 1677 when the accused fled from prison (a repeat offender, Moise Norsa),[53] to be recaptured by the ducal police, which led to a controversy with the secular courts over where the trial should continue.[54] The 1684 Norlengo episode seems another episcopal test of jurisdictional rights, with the Inquisition as the contender. Various file notes pointed out that the episcopal court had processed Jews for other offences, not involving sex with Christians. It seems that the Roman Inquisition eventually backed the inquisitor over the bishop. Interestingly, Jews appeared willing to utilise the Inquisition's rules and customs of voluntary appearance – possibly to avoid harsher treatment by episcopal or secular courts.

This inquisitorial preoccupation with Jewish-Christian relations in Mantua has been examined at length not just for to reveal prurient interest in sexual relations between the two religions, but also for the light it throws on varying sentencing policies by the Inquisition in relation to one type of offence; on inquisitorial leniency with considerations of the circumstances of the accused; and on jurisdictional conflicts between inquisitor and bishop.

Muslim Converts

Conversions between Christianity and Islam were in both directions. They involved both enforcement and sometimes comparatively free choice, more especially from Christianity to Islam than the opposite, though for social rather than strictly religious reasons. Christians might be captured by the Turks in the naval conflicts, or as they traded through the Mediterranean, then be enslaved and remain within the Ottoman empire for years. They might voluntarily convert to Islam or be forcibly converted. The Ottoman expansion in the eastern Mediterranean from the sixteenth century, to the detriment of the Venetian empire, meant that Muslim rule embraced those whose background had been Roman Catholic but also Greek Orthodox. They might be pressurised to convert to Islam as a way of escaping slavery and of making a reasonable livelihood in the Ottoman empire. A few seem genuinely to have been attracted by Muslim beliefs and behaviour. Those who returned to Italy, whether rescued from slavery, recaptured by Christians when serving on Ottoman ships, travelling back freely as traders, or deciding as soldiers to change sides and serve the Venetians for example, had clearly to plead forced circumcision and conversion. They could seek to be reintegrated into Christian society utilising the courts of the Inquisition, which was comparatively lenient towards Christians who had turned Turk and wished to return to Catholicism.[55]

Like Jews, Muslims might be forced to accept baptism in states dominated by Christians, notably under Spanish rule (including Sardinia and Sicily), or leave for the Muslim world. The main preoccupation of the Iberian inquisitions from the outset was with the problem of the genuineness of conversions from Judaism and Islam to Christianity, and this problem never disappeared even if its priority diminished. In the case of the Roman Inquisition such dubious Christians were not a high priority in comparison with those Christians showing Protestant sympathies, and those indulging in superstitious practices. However, for some tribunals the genuineness of conversions to Christianity was of significance, and more attention was paid to the issue over the period of the Inquisition, as Tables A, C, D, E reveal for Venice, Naples, Sicily and Malta. Although the Tables record Mohammedan/Muslim cases as 'denunciations', this is misleading. Often we are dealing with a negotiated settlement with the local Inquisition over conversion (or reconversion) to the Catholic faith, from Islam (as also from Greek Orthodoxy), and not a punitive exercise.[56]

The Neapolitan inquisitors, but to a greater extent the tribunals of the Roman Inquisition in Malta, Venice and Friuli, had to deal with interactions with the Muslim Ottoman empire, as there was a considerable amount of movement of people around the Mediterranean and into the Balkans. A few Christians making contacts with Muslims on Malta or in the Friuli border areas were attracted by Muslim beliefs and behaviour, and considered conversion, only to be arraigned by the Inquisition. The central Roman Inquisition, and some tribunals – especially in port cities such as Ancona, Venice, Naples, Valletta and Livorno – had to deal with such cases of apostasy. At least by the early 1580s Rome's focus was on this topic: 22 of the 81 recorded sentences for the period January 1582 to December 1583 were for apostasy to Islam.[57] As the Tables show, this issue was an intermittent concern throughout the period. In Malta 281 (9.2 per cent) of the charges brought before the tribunal between 1744 and

1798 involved apostasy (primarily from Islam), in contrast to 116 accusations (3.8 per cent) for allegedly affiliating with Protestants.[58]

The Maltese islands being situated on crucial trade passages between mainland Italy, Sicily and north Africa meant that there was considerable voluntary and involuntary contact between Christians, Muslims and Jews. The Maltese Inquisition, and occasionally those in Venice and Friuli, had to deal with people who had experience of all three monotheistic religions. Recent studies – notably by Giuseppina Minchella, P.C. Ioly Zorattini, Georgios Plakotos, Frans Ciappara and Giovanni Ricci – have highlighted the degree of religious interchange in these areas. They throw light on Mediterranean social-economic history, and on the roles of tribunals of the Inquisition.

The Roman Inquisition gave guidance in the seventeenth century to those tribunals most likely to be dealing with conversions between Islam and Christianity or vice versa, aware of the pressures of conflicts, official and unofficial, in the Mediterranean world, and the capture of slaves. Letters of instructions were sent out to some tribunals and copied to others, as when the Venetian tribunal filed a copy of an instructional letter to the inquisitor in Adria. For example, a manuscript manual was circulated entitled 'Prattica per proceder nelle cause del Sant Uffitio ... come sponte comparenti'. Written some time after 1617, it has been attributed to Desiderio Scaglia, who served as inquisitor in Pavia, Cremona and Milan. It gave some priority to apostates from Islam:

> They have performed acts of apostasy from the faith, such as serving in the army of heretics, going forth with Turks to plunder Christian populations and lands, having been circumcised by Turks, raising the right hand's forefinger and reciting the words Ailala, which refer to Mohammed himself, entering in mosques to pray, living according to the Muslim rites ... consuming meat on fast days in order to show that they conform to the customs of Muslims.

Having guided the inquisitors towards what to expect, the manual stated that such persons should be treated as *sponte comparenti*, and their intentions ascertained:

> As far as the *sponte comparenti* are concerned, attention should be paid to what they testify, both to the facts and their intention. ... And having found their answers about their intentions satisfying, the Holy Office bypasses torture but not the abjuration, because abjuration is not an act of punishment but a declaration of not having had a less than Catholic intention and of wishing to live and die Catholic [which] has its place also with them.[59]

In Venice those of non-Catholic origin – whether slaves from the Ottoman empire or Jews from Europe – who wanted to convert would undergo education and conversion via the Casa dei Catecumeni (established in Venice in 1557, following Rome's Jesuit foundation of 1543). Those brought up Catholics or Orthodox, who had then been converted to Islam (willingly or under coercion) and then sought reintegration into the Catholic faith, could negotiate this through the Venetian Inquisition.[60]

An interesting location for inter-faith conversions was the centrally planned fortress town of Palma (or Palmanova), created in the 1590s to defend the Venetian Republic's north-eastern borders against the Turks and Habsburgs. This was part of a wider area involving Istria and Dalmatia, where people might move voluntarily or under social pressures between orthodox Catholicism, schismatic Greek Orthodoxy, Islam, Lutheranism and Calvinism, especially as population movements were in practice fluid across political ones. Some individuals might try three religious flavours, like the soldier Martino Goich da Sebenico (Catholic, Greek schismatic and Lutheran), tried and abjured in 1607 in Udine, who revealed many heretical associates.[61] The Palma garrison in this area defended itself against both Turkish and Habsburg armies, and controlled the borders when plague threatened to stop goods and people crossing from Turkish lands where authorities took no measures to curb the spread of pestilence, unlike the fairly ruthless Venetian health officials. The Venetian army recruited widely and was ethnically considerably mixed. Through the seventeenth century its soldiers travelled widely in conflicts against the Turks, notably in the defence of the Dalmatian coast and Crete (Candia). Significant numbers of Venetian soldiers were captured, enslaved or bonded, and converted to Islam. Escaping or being freed and re-appearing in Venetian territory, they came before tribunals of the Inquisition seeking reconciliation and a return to the Christian faith. Giuseppina Minchella's study of about ten apostasy cases in Palma between 1605 and 1652 suggests that the inquisitors viewed the apostasy sympathetically, and facilitated the repentant reconciliations.[62] The court had problems testing the stories these apostates told about their becoming Muslims in foreign lands. Inquisitors tended to accept that conversions to Islamic practices were made under dire pressure, and that some individuals might have had no way of resisting circumcision, head shaving or eating the wrong food at the wrong time. To achieve 'conversion' some might have been burned by fire, or threatened with this, and beaten mercilessly. One claimed that after three years as a slave he was made drunk by his uncle before being circumcised, and made to say all sorts of things he did not understand in Turkish.

A Croatian named Giovanni, brought up by Christian parents in Turkish Voinich (or Vojnik, north-west of Zagreb) until he was nearly twenty, had a complicated story to tell. He was taken away by Turks and pressurised to convert ('*a farmi far turco*'). He resisted threats and persuasions, until he was held over a spit, so with his mouth but not his heart he became a *turco*. In the language used at the time, to become *turco* meant to become Muslim; a *turco* or *turca* was a Muslim man or woman, whatever their ethnic or geographical origin.[63] Giovanni then lived as a 'Turk' for thirty years, marrying and having two children. He ended up as a soldier, arrived in Venetian territory at Marasca, and was taken kindly (*amorevolmente*) by a certain captain (seemingly a Venetian recruiting mercenaries) in a boat with his soldiers to these parts.[64] According to their stories, others were 'rescued' by such captains. One wonders how unhappy Giovanni had been as a Muslim Turk, and whether the bid for acceptance as a Christian was to facilitate a new military career with a new state – without his family.

Clearly the Turks/Muslims used both force and inducements (food, money, social mobility) to 'convert' Christians they captured or who came to them voluntarily. The Inquisition provided a path back to a Christian life, and officials in north-eastern Italy were indulgent over previous behaviour in Ottoman-controlled lands. In a number of cases people had converted from Greek rites to Muslim to Catholic, as with Alessandro Sclender (a 1639 case). Brought up under Greek Orthodoxy for fourteen or fifteen years before being seized by Turkish forces and made to apostasise, his replies to the inquisitor stressed that as a Muslim he had always wanted 'to live and die in the Catholic and Christian faith'. Now in the Palma fortress he had the chance, and he converted voluntarily.[65] Both petitioner and inquisitor seemed ready to proceed via various fictions, without much questioning of the differences in religious 'law' and theology.

These stories indicate that there was a soldiering community who crossed several geographical and religious boundaries with limited questioning. In the story-telling it is hard to assess the relative roles between coercion, blandishment, job opportunities and genuine attraction involved in conversions. In reconverting or converting to Catholicism, these soldiers had facilitators who were likely to be Venetian or Friulian nobles or Capuchins, and a public baptismal ceremony celebrated such an event. Correspondence with the Roman Congregation indicates that a certain Piero Leon was responsible for converting many Turkish soldiers, that their baptisms were ratified by the inquisitor, and that the cardinals were pleased with this work, but expected to be kept informed. In 1670 an inquisitorial report was sent to the Roman Congregation about conversions between 1643 and that date. Besides conversions of Calvinist and Lutheran soldiers, it listed thirteen Turkish soldiers.[66]

Problems of 'Living Saints' and 'Perfetti'

In the seventeenth century inquisitors were much exercised by a small number of cases of persons – usually female – who had a reputation for living saintly lives, but whose genuineness was contested. Some were condemned for 'pretend sanctity' (Appendix Tables A and B) while others were judged genuine.

'Pretence' and 'pretend' (when used as a translation of *pretesa*) can be misleading if they imply conscious deceit. Different manifestations of sanctity were demonstrated or claimed: physical signs such as the stigmata on their hands, or side wounds like Christ's. Many reported ecstatic visions, while others seemed to have miraculous healing powers, which might occasionally have links with practical philanthropy, living a saintly life in the world.[67] Inquisitorial attitudes towards locally appreciated *sante vive*, living saints, were affected by fears of wider spiritual movements involving some withdrawal from the world into mystical experiences, and the pursuit of spiritual perfection, based on 'silent prayer'. New promotions of mysticism in the seventeenth century, notably by the Pelagini (*pelaginismo*, rather than Old Pelagianism), and Quietism, alarmed the Papacy and the Sicilian Inquisition (see Appendix, Table D). The Church in general worried about the mystical visions and private prayers of such individuals, because they removed them from ecclesiastical supervision, education and control. Much confusion existed, and still exists, between Pelaginism, Quietism, pseudo-mysticism and affected sanctity, with people being considered '*perfetti*' or as aiming for some spiritual perfection.[68] The retreat of females from male clerical control was particularly worrying. Also of concern was that the saintly and ecstatic shaded into sexual experiences, fostered or not by admiring male supporters, especially confessors.

Quietism was the movement inspired by the Spaniard Miguel de Molinos (formally condemned in 1687), which 'had to do with reading books that taught how to achieve the prayer of quiet and consequent annihilation of will, not with actions and somatic signs indicating holiness'.[69] Molinos spent many years in Rome but had an impact across Europe. His most influential book, *Guía espirituel que desembaraza el alma* (1675) was produced in twenty editions within the first six years, with translations into Latin, Italian, French, Dutch, German and English. In 1682 Cardinal Francesco Albizzi prepared a report on Molinos and his works for the Inquisition, arguing that he followed on from the Spanish mystical tradition of the *Alumbrados* (the Illumined), against which the Spanish Inquisition had long campaigned, not least because early sixteenth-century advocates were associated with Jewish *conversos*. Molinos and his works were formally condemned in 1687, after many witness statements were thrown at him about obscene acts.[70] Quietists were then pursued all over Italy. The Pelagini by the 1680s were linked to this undesirable evolution of mysticism. They started as devotees of Giacomo Filippo Casolo, based in the Milanese church of Santa Pelagia, but their impact spread to Brescia, Bergamo and the Val Camonica, causing much inquisitorial worry and activity from the 1650s. At the core of the movement was the belief in silent prayer as personal devotion, unguided, and leading to union with God – but also ecstatic prophesying after silent prayer, preaching (including by women) and philanthropy. A notable trial was that by the Milanese inquisitor of the Milanese nobleman, the alchemist and physician Francesco Giuseppe Borri, as a leading promoter of Pelaginism, along with some 'apostles'. Sentenced to death but escaping, Borri was burned in effigy in Rome's Campo dei Fiori.[71]

Besides those possibly connected with these wider spiritual movements there were individual women publicly held to be 'saintly', because of reported visions and ecstatic experiences, and charitable acts. Often they were publicised by spiritual advisers rather than being self-promoting, like Maria Janis (tried in Venice in 1662–3) or Angelia Mellini (tried in Bologna in 1698).[72] In 1668 the *pievano* of Santa Trinita in Venice, Francesco Vincenzi, clearly fell in love with the illiterate Antonia Pesenti, who saw visions before a Byzantine painting in his church which supposedly induced miracles. A few women were almost certainly frauds, or marginally deceitful like Maria Janis. Some such women were themselves worried whether divine blessing was involved, or diabolic deception. The dubiety over saintly or devilish input is exemplified in the 1628 investigation of Suor Giglia di Fino (1601–?), a tertiary nun in Gravina (Puglia) who earned a public reputation as a 'saint' through her ecstatic experiences, visions, healing activities and prophecies. She was supported by her 'guardian angel' who directed her activities, and executed some of her healing activities.[73]

A census of cases by Anne Jacobson Schutte identified ninety-five persons involved in cases about claims of sanctity in Italy between 1581 and 1781 (some investigated by ecclesiastical bodies other than the Inquisition); sixty of them were female, and thirty-five male. In the case of the men a number were cited as supporters of the females, rather than as 'saintly' in their own right; however, I deduce that twenty-one may have been at the centre of 'living-saint' claims. Details on many of them are very sketchy. The cases were spread across Italy: ten were investigated mainly in Rome, fourteen in Venice, fifteen in Naples, four in Siena (between 1714 and 1722), with the others scattered from Udine and Mondovì to Benevento and Squillace.[74] Three persons were tried by the tribunal of the Spanish Inquisition in Palermo, two of these being the only accused known to have been executed for 'pretence', by burning at the stake on 6 April 1724: Maria Geltruda, a Benedictine tertiary and Maria's supporter, Fra Romualdo. Maria was also considered a Quietist.[75] Andrea Del Col has now suggested that about 120 cases of 'claimed sanctity' (*pretesa*) were investigated by the Holy Office between 1580 and 1758, as more cases have been identified. A fair number of them involve male mysticism, with miracles claiming healings and prophecies, while the women were more involved with internal mysticism, assisted by confessors.[76]

The testing of 'pretend' versus genuine holiness by inquisitors was often thorough and lengthy. Alfonsina Risposa, a Franciscan tertiary who allegedly saw visions and received the stigmata, was investigated by the Neapolitan vicar-general from 1581 for ten years, and was confined in a nunnery before Rome decided against a full trial. Another Neapolitan, Giulia di Marco, who seemingly combined spirituality and sexual licence, attracted much public support fostered by a priest and a lawyer, and Jesuits. After eight years the Holy Office with Theatine encouragement condemned Giulia and her two male supporters to life imprisonment.[77]

The care and rigour of inquisitorial investigation of 'pretence' cases are illustrated by the experienced inquisitor Agapito Ugoni who, when inquisitor in Venice (1652–63), was involved wholly or in part in some now well-known cases. He was a patient, probing and circumspect inquisitor. He took over the case of Maria Janis, originally from a Brescian village, and a teacher of Christian doctrine to a confraternity of the Holy Belt alongside a priest Pietro Morale, who then became her promoter and travelling companion. Reported in Venice, she was suspected of heresy in claiming to live off the bread of the Eucharist alone, as instructed by the Virgin. An inquisitor in Bergamo who was also involved in the enquiries suggested she was influenced by the Pelagini, but Ugoni ignored this suggestion. Eliciting that she occasionally had other food to eat, Ugoni eventually had her sentenced to imprisonment at the tribunal's discretion. Without requesting it, she was soon released to the mendicant hospital and obscurity. Ugoni also investigated Francesco Vincenzi, a priest, and Antonia Pesenti, showing due scepticism towards the activities of an exorcist who considered she was possessed by a demon of lust. He was more interested in the nature of an admitted ceremony between them suggesting a spiritual marriage. Both declined the use of lawyers, and relied on the court's mercy. They were found guilty in March 1669 as 'vehemently suspect' of heresy. She was sentenced to live with an honest woman and was kept separate from Vincenzi, who was given an unspecified prison sentence. But he died in 1676 still as the *piovano*.[78]

Ugoni was also involved in the case of Cecilia Ferrazzi, a sickly spinster with eating disorders who saw visions, and who from the 1650s ran (without apparent male assistance) homes for girls and women in danger (with some 300 in her care in 1664 when she was arrested). The arrest followed complaints from relatives of girls in her care who wanted them released (possibly for prostitution), and she opposed this. Her well-publicised visions had been of concern to the Patriarch for some time. Ugoni investigated her for eighteen months, calling some 300 witnesses. He allowed her to dictate her own story to a friar. Cecilia probably had the genuine doubts she admitted to over whether her visions were real or the Devil's deception.[79] A crucial turning point was when Father Giorgio Polacco, a leading confessor to Benedictine nuns, the Patriarch's vicar over female religious and a noted exorcist, who had been an earlier supporter of Cecilia, changed his mind and reported to the tribunal that she was not genuine. The tribunal's view of her as a manipulator was affected by the revelation that she had portraits painted of herself by at least three different artists. These were then seen altered in her house as cult objects, to look like St Teresa, the Madonna of the Seven Sorrows with stigmata, while a third showed her carrying a female saint. The first two were found and seized by the inquisitor, who established that the original artists were not responsible for the 'saintly' alterations. According to witnesses Cecilia's girls were made to adore or serenade the paintings.[80] In September 1565 Cecilia was found 'lightly suspect' of heresy, guilty of *affettata santità*, and condemned to seven years in prison. She appealed to the Congregation in Rome, which took two years to decide that she should be transferred to house arrest under the care of Cardinal Gregorio Barbarigo, a notable reforming bishop. She was completely released by the Roman Inquisition eighteen months later, after the combined pleading of the Cardinal and the Venetian government.

Cardinal Barbarigo and the exorcist Polacco provide interesting links with another 'living saint', Angela Maria Pasqualigo. She was a patrician, who rejected marriage. Like Cecilia she helped vulnerable girls, though in a less structured way. She was allowed to found a Theatine nunnery, and in 1647 became a strictly enclosed nun there. She earned a reputation as a 'great heroine', according to her Theatine biographer Giovanni Bonifacio Bagatta. Polacco was asked to test whether she was genuine – and found her to be so. Her claim to survive off bread of the Eucharist alone was upheld. Maria Janis' request to be 'tested' in the same way was rejected. When Pasqualigo was asked to comment on Cecilia, she declared her a fraud. Class prejudice?[81]

The later pages of this chapter have indicated the nature and diversity of denunciations that lay behind certain key classifications in the Tables in the Appendix. The stories elucidate the approaches, lenient or otherwise, towards different offences, the kinds of punishment meted out if taken to full condemnation. Some harshness towards 'pretend saints' who seem involved in mystical movements contrasts with leniency towards those crossing religious boundaries. Inquisitors in Italy could positively facilitate conversions, reconversions and reconciliations. They paid attention to individual social circumstances, as with the Jews and Christians in Mantua. The stories in the records of the Inquisition, even if fictionalised, can illuminate social relationships across many cultural areas. The fear that lay people, especially women, were eluding clerical supervision and leadership governed central Roman and some local inquisitorial operations.

CHAPTER 7

Censorship

CENSORSHIP OF WRITTEN AND VISUAL MATERIAL HAD A LONG HISTORY, AND IN the period of our study the inquisitions shared control with governments, universities, leaders of the religious Orders and other clergy. As printing expanded from the end of the fifteenth century, many authorities considered it imperative to exercise their control ideally before publication, but thereafter by formal condemnations, which would be easier to enforce if indexes of prohibited books could be circulated. Such lists were initially produced locally for the more immediate environment. Eventually the Spanish and Roman Inquisitions published the most authoritative and complete printed indexes for wide application in the Catholic world. Historians dispute the extent to which the inquisitorial control of book publication seriously damaged cultural developments in the Iberian and Italian states; whether by seizures and burning, bowdlerisation of texts, or an inducement to self-censorship so that certain kinds of books and tracts were never written, notably in areas of 'new science'. Peter Godman suggested that the Congregation of the Index under Cardinal Agostino Valier in the 1590s conjured up 'a spectre of uncertainty far more fearsome that the Holy Roman and Universal Inquisition and more threatening than the Index of Prohibited Books. The name of that spectre is self-censorship.' Recent work has highlighted the damage done in Italy by the curb on vernacular translations of the Bible, especially after the 1596 Clementine Index. Inept cutting and rewriting of works by the great Italian medieval and renaissance writers was promoted or approved by (in Godman's extreme view) 'the incompetents, bunglers, and boneheads of the Index', despite Cardinal Roberto Bellarmino's more rational efforts.[1] Lay and clerical writers outside the inquisitorial profession could willingly contribute to censorship, seen as 'improvement'.

Old arguments that the Inquisition forced Italian scholars (including Jesuits who had provided leading contributors to the new sciences) out of the forefront of philosophical and scientific knowledge (especially after the Galileo affair), while the Spanish Inquisition prevented Spaniards from entering the field at all, have recently been modified. Jesuits – especially German ones, but also including Italian colleagues – found ways of discussing and teaching their controversial ideas through hypothesising, by ranking theories as more or less probable, or by summarising them as if to refute them. In this they were more subtle than Galileo had been. They did, however, have to tread very carefully over atomistic theories that might affect Eucharist doctrines – an issue raised also by Galileo's writings. Spaniards might avoid some more theoretical debates, but contribute much to the spread of information on nature and the wider world of their huge empire.[2]

Book Censorship and Indexes

Both secular and ecclesiastical authorities soon realised that printed books could be dangerous in various ways; and the idea of drawing up lists of books to be seized and destroyed, or confined to a few licensed readers, soon spread. But the problems of keeping up with the production of books and pamphlets were considerable. While the Papacy was slow to produce its own Index of Prohibited Books (1559), it considered censorship early on. In 1487 Innocent VIII's Bull *Inter multiplices* entrusted bishops with censorship, and the Master of the Sacred Palace was to give guidance in Rome. Later the Inquisition had to face these competitors for control. In 1515 the Fifth Lateran Council brought in inquisitors (where they existed) as censors,[3] not that this led to much coordinated activity. However, if a particular title was targeted, such as the *Beneficio di Cristo*, which initially seemed to be a good seller, it could be all but eliminated.

In the early sixteenth century book censorship was entrusted to the Master of the Sacred Palace. His main role had been as regent master of the Studium Romanae Curiae, founded in 1244–5, which organised teaching of theology, canon and civil law for the Curia, and awarded degrees. The Master from the Dominican Order fulfilled other functions around the papal palace, including selecting preachers for major liturgical occasions and consistories. He had to vet the sermons in advance, for content and length. With that background Leo X decided in May 1515 that the Master should be the official book censor for Rome, charged with vetting pre-publication texts, granting or withholding the imprimatur. The first person appointed Master with this additional role of censor was Silvestro Mazzolini da Prierio, who was also designated inquisitor for the Roman tribunal in Santa Maria sopra Minerva. He prepared the first official reply to Luther's ninety-five Theses in 1519.[4] The censoring duties of the Master increased, his control of papal court preaching remained, his connection with Studium teaching diminished, then ceased. When the Congregation of the Holy Office developed and took on tasks connected with the Index of Prohibited Books and other controls over books, the Master of the Sacred Palace was also involved *ex officio*. Egidio Foscarari (Master from 1547 to 1550) was entrusted with preparing an Index of prohibited books.[5] This involvement continued with the creation of the separate Congregation of the Index. The Master could be more active than the Congregation itself in the early years, when it seemed to slumber, and he dealt mostly with local inquisitors over problematic publications.[6]

As already indicated, the Congregation of 1542 gradually took on responsibility for producing lists of prohibited books and checking on those holding them, with some of their staff having a remit to cover these matters. A Bull of 29 April 1550 rescinded past licences to read or possess books dealing with Lutheran heresies; licences could only be given to inquisitors and *commissari* concerned with combating 'depraved heresies', for a limited time. The cardinals ordered all Roman booksellers to submit lists of what they possessed, with threats of heavy fines; otherwise they would be treated as supporters of heretics.[7] The Congregation sent out orders that its delegates, of whatever kind, should search bookshops and libraries in convents, churches and even private houses, and destroy what they knew to be forbidden (the works of those already declared heretics, and works on existing local indexes). Surviving records are few, so the effectiveness of the edicts or letters is unclear.

On becoming Paul IV in 1555, Gian Pietro Carafa soon made it clear that works of key writers like Erasmus and Niccolò Machiavelli should be burned, and that *favole* (fables, or fiction generally) should likewise be suppressed.[8] This was a forewarning of what would be banned in his 1559 Index.

When the first full papal Index of Prohibited Books to be applied through Italy appeared in 1559, it was immediately seen as essentially representing Paul IV's own strict attitudes. It met with major protests which were to be voiced when the Council of Trent reconvened (after his death), in 1562. By then indexes had been produced in Milan (by the Senate, 1538), Bergamo (1539), Paris (1544 and 1556 by the Sorbonne theology faculty), Louvain (three between 1546 and 1558), Venice (1549, by the nuncio, and 1554); by the Portuguese Inquisition (1547, 1551), and the Spanish (three between 1551 and 1559). All these probably helped Paul IV and his assistants.[9]

The more moderate Pius IV who became Pope in 1559 made it clear he wanted a 'liberalisation' of the Index, heeding the Council of Trent's worries, and wishing to restrain the Inquisition; in 1561 he brought back the bishops as local censors, where Paul IV had tried to exclude them. The bishops at Trent were asked to help produce the new Index, but it did not appear until 1564, after the (hurried) closure of the Council. The bishops and inquisitors were to have equal responsibility for censorship, including the new policy of expurgation, while bishops organised pre-publication licensing.[10] The current limited evidence for the 1560s to the 1580s, and the greater evidence on the aftermath of the 1596 Clementine Index, support the Inquisition's accusation that bishops were haphazard in chasing prohibited books, and local inquisitors not much better. Exceptions existed. In Siena in the 1560s following the new Index, the inquisitor Fra Geremia da Udine and then Pietro da Saronno conducted a purge on booksellers and libraries. Prohibited works by Erasmus, especially the *Adages*, were found, and some minor prohibited texts. Some sellers spent time in prison, then underwent salutary penances, largely for ignorance of the rules and indexes. However, in December 1569 the inquisitor organised the burning of a large pile of confiscated books.[11]

Detailed book control in Rome itself at this point, in terms of chasing copies of existing books, seems to have been a lower priority than the pursuit of major heretics, except when books were connected with such high heresy issues and the leading accused. Another area where book control in terms of seizures and burning was limited was Sicily, and this possibly remained the position. The number of prosecutions in Sicily for prohibited books was meagre, possibly because literacy was lower than in mainland Italy. For Sicily the Supreme Council allowed the Tridentine Index to be used rather than the Spanish versions.[12]

Pius V, elected Pope in 1566, appointed a commission in 1571 to revise the 1564 Tridentine Index; under Gregory XIII in September 1572 this became the Congregation of the Index, with Guglielmo Sirleto dominating, and it essentially formed a subsection of the Congregation of the Holy Office, with a supposed separation of roles. The Master of the Sacred Palace linked the congregations, being *ex officio* a member of both. He also had some competence over expurgating non-heretical works, and publicised rulings of the Congregation of the Index. Gigliola Fragnito endorses the complaint of Cardinal Paleotti, a member of the Index himself, at a session in 1583 that the Masters of the Sacred Palace were offhand and careless in instructing local inquisitors. Thereafter the Index exercised more control over the Master's lists, and what was distributed. The Master's work from the 1590s to the 1600s shows greater dedication and tenacity in an increasingly complex position of censorship, but many disputes and tensions existed between Masters and long-serving secretaries to the Congregation of the Index (notably Paolo Pico, officiating 1591–1613) – over keeping archives and libraries (and where), producing lists of emended titles, and coordinating censors' reports from various places. Master Giovanni Maria Guanzelli from Brisighella was declared a 'bungler' and 'fool' for mishandling expurgatory censorship: 'before being kicked upstairs', he had issued somebody a licence to read Machiavelli. This was rescinded by the Inquisition.[13]

Sixtus V, in his modernisation of Church government on the basis of revised and new Congregations in 1588 (forming fifteen Congregations), raised the profile of the Congregation of the Index. More powerful cardinals now led it, tried to give it major control over censorship and reduce interference by the Congregation of the Holy Office. However, the continuing preparation of the next Index (not published until 1596, the 'Clementine'), and its rigorous implementation, produced three-cornered struggles between the two congregations and the Master of the Sacred Palace (and through him the Pope).[14] In 1600 Pope Clement VIII explained the relationship between the Congregation of the Holy Office and that of the Index to Cardinal Cesare Baronio: that of the Index controlled book authors, printers, sellers and readers, but not heresy, which was under the Inquisition. Given the broad definitions of 'heresy', this gave massive room for the Cardinal inquisitors to interfere with the work of the Index, with inquisitor Giulio Santoro leading the way by ensuring he had supportive members on the Index.[15]

Diaries of meetings for 1607 up to 1620 reveal that the Master of the Sacred Palace was usually present, even when other consultants were not called, so being the only member who was not a Cardinal. Augusto Brasi, the new Master in August 1607, showed himself an active proponent and reporter. On 24 November 1607, for example, he considered the petition of the Florentine 'Nation', or Fraternity, in Rome for the reading of old editions of Giovanni Boccaccio's works, and led a discussion as to whether Giambattista Marini's *Opera Poetica* contained obscenities. On 3 December 1609 he was alerted by Cardinal Bellarmino that an edition of Matthew Paris' *Historia Anglicana* was full of heresies.[16] Some documents suggest that the Master had a final say over expurgations, and might not take them back to a full committee. Cardinal Santoro challenged that role, as when dealing with some Hebrew texts, claiming his own right to finalise corrections.[17]

Permissions for individuals to read prohibited books, especially in order to respond to them, or correct them, were granted; locally by bishops, their vicars and inquisitors, and centrally by the congregations or the Master of the Sacred Palace. Permits granted in Rome from 1561 to 1600 often concerned authors and works in cases where local authorities had some doubts about their status. Virtually no requests concerned books that had never been censored, but notably titles involving medicine and anatomy, astrology, medical astrology, divinatory arts, natural history, botany and 'simples', and natural philosophy that had been queried before.[18] Requests for licences even came from Englishmen as the battles over the true faith continued: on 14 December 1565 the Holy Office dealt with requests to read prohibited books (unspecified in the minutes) from Father Egidio, from the diocese of Bath and Wells, and Thomas Fernan from the Salisbury diocese. The requests were remitted to their ordinaries for consideration. The Congregation conceded licences, however, to the noble master of law Cesare Spetiano and the Dominican father Cesari to read prohibited books (unspecified).[19]

The Indexes and their Targets

The 1559 Index condemned books and authors in three classes: 606 authors were prohibited completely (for existing works, and any that might appear later), as heresiarchs; 126 individual books of named authors; and 332 anonymous works, featuring astrology and magic most prominently. Infelise and Del Col, working through problems of duplication and other errors, calculate that in reality the numbers were 499, 117 and 288 respectively, totalling 904. To these were added two lists: 45 Bibles and New Testaments prohibited, and of 61 publishers banned. These publishers were German and Swiss, Francesco Brucioli being the only Italian. The three classes were maintained for the Tridentine 1564 version (1,168 books and authors), and the 1596 Clementine Index (which added 1,143 new headings).[20] The 1596 Index helpfully provided rules for future classification and censorship, and crucially publicised clear procedures for having works temporarily prohibited, until amended or expurgated: titles were annotated *nisi expurgentur, nisi corrigantur, donec expurgentur*. (The idea of expurgation had been gradually but rather messily developed since the mid 1550s.)[21] This meant that offending words or passages in existing copies could be blacked out, for licensed reuse, or that an agreed expurgated text could become the basis for a new edition. Certain persons could be licensed to hold prohibited copies to prepare acceptable versions or counter-blasts against heretical publications. Bishops and their vicars, printers and booksellers, were expected to have copies of the Index to ensure prohibited publications were not produced and sold in new editions, or old ones possessed. A consultation of copies of the Index makes one sympathetic for those trying to use them, in identifying authors or titles. A 1632 reprint of the 1596 Index included a somewhat chaotic supplement, dated 1624, of decrees and edicts, usually from the Master, with a 1606 condemnation of works by Paolo Sarpi and other Venetians involved in the Interdict controversy. Also it added a *Monitum* (Advice) of 1620 on how to amend the work of Copernicus, prepared by Francisco Capiferro, a Dominican, with chapter and page references. Finally it had an appendix (*Elenchus*), as a massive alphabetical cross-referencing system, with notes of alternative spellings (e.g. '*Eyden vide Heyden*'), making it a 679-page volume. Capiferro produced the *Elenchus* as a private venture, rather than one officially for the Congregation after he had ceased to be its secretary (1615–27).[22] Pleas of ignorance by arraigned booksellers about what was prohibited may be well understood. The Congregation and bishops sometimes provided more user-friendly lists indicating titles that most concerned them.

The succession of Indexes obviously increased the numbers of listed titles as the world of printing expanded, but also because the target areas widened. The 1559 and 1564 Indexes targeted the major theological writers and books challenging the traditional teachings of the Church; both foreigners and the indigenous population. The 1559 Index, governed by Carafa's horror at what he had found being published and read in Venice when he was there (1527–32) after the Sack of Rome, shocked many Church leaders. Its unworkable severity led to calls during the 1562–3 sessions of the Council of Trent for a softening of condemnations. The 1564 Index did allow, for example, some works of Savonarola and Erasmus to be rehabilitated; the former's pastoral works and the latter's humanist scholarship were much prized by some bishops, Dominicans (especially for Savonarola) and lay scholars. Thereafter popes, the Holy Office and congregations of the Index considered more fully the total banning or expurgation of books on astrology and magic, on subversive political and legal theory, and fictional literature that allegedly corrupted morals.

The steps to the next major papal Index of 1596 were complicated and contentious. There were competing views from the two relevant congregations, of the Holy Office and Index, and the Master of the Sacred Palace (Bartolomeo de Miranda), who served both congregations (and was closer to the ear of the Pope). In addition, disagreements arose between cardinals serving on the congregations. Cardinal inquisitors prevented the publication of an Index in 1590 under Sixtus V, and another version in 1593, after they had actually been printed.[23] The 1596 Index's appearance was in doubt right up to its definitive promulgation on 17 May 1596. The main running was made by the Congregation of the Index (with secretary Paolo Pico dominating the talks), but other cardinals from the Holy Office, and Cardinal Santoro in particular, were demanding harsher prohibitions. Santoro led the campaign, backed by the procurator fiscal Marcello Filonardi, to ban vernacular translations of the Bible (including selections thereof) and the Talmud, and was able to pressurise Pope Clement VIII to sanction the harsher policies. Clement VIII had promulgated the Index on 27 March, but been forced to withdraw on 7 April by the Holy Office, which argued that some of their published decisions had been 'omitted'. So an *Observatio* was added, reinstating bans on vernacular Bibles, expurgated editions of the Talmud, and on Jean Bodin's self-amended *Six Livres de la République*, which the Congregation of the Index and Pope had considered permissible.[24]

This Index and its implementation also imposed greater central control over local censorship, book-hunting and the newly articulated policy of expurgations; so undermining the powers of bishops, and local inquisitors. The Holy Office (meaning essentially Cardinal Santoro) was adamant that bishops should no longer have the freedom to permit persons locally, such as theologians, to consult copies of vernacular Bibles – which both the Congregation of the Index and Pope had still thought permissible. Because the Holy Office was adamant about eradicating Italian Bibles, the post-1596 book-hunting was far more intense than before. This had serious effects on the gathering in and destruction of much more literature in all fields that had escaped previous supervision. Bishops, priors and local inquisitors were not necessarily pleased with such intrusions. On the other hand some southern episcopal synods meeting immediately after, as in Salerno (1596), Santa Severina and Amalfi (1597), backed a new rigorous censorship with episcopal aid, as did Archbishop Alfonso Gesualdo of Naples. Royal support followed.[25]

The two key targets of the 1596 campaign will be discussed below. Detailed consideration of the impact of censorship through the Indexes in all fields cannot be undertaken here, but a few points should be made, and a few examples given.[26] The cultural world was affected by what from the past was banned outright, what was affected by rules on expurgation, what was not published because refused a licence (or imprimatur) and what was never written for fear of censorship (the great unknown). Positively, however, censorship could encourage authors to produce new works of a different orientation, especially in areas of religious devotion and learning. Also a certain amount of literature was printed and circulated unlicensed, and evaded censorship for decades, existing today under false covers and frontispieces.

Leaving aside the main teachers of heresy, well-known and previously treasured authors had their original works banned or seriously amended or bowdlerised, among them Ariosto, Boccaccio, Boiardo, Castiglione, Dante, Machiavelli, Petrarch and Pietro Aretino.[27] Through the sixteenth century the various Indexes, including local lists, built up an attack on the wider literary scene and on the popular Italian books of the literate. 'Obscenity' in classical and modern works had been under attack from Savonarola onwards, but the concepts of unacceptable literature were expanded (though with some ebb and flow through the Indexes as some works were readmitted, with or without corrections). The first attacks on what had been seen as more acceptable literature seem to have come with a 1552 local Index printed in Florence in 1552, which included works by Ortensio Lando and Poggio Bracciolini's *Facezie*. A list compiled in Rome in 1557 included Aretino's *Raggionamenti* (or *Sei giornate*), discussing among other matters the arts of whores and lascivious nuns; the 1559 Index imposed a ban on all Aretino's works. From then on the indexers attacked many types of literature under general rules, 'dishonest' or 'lascivious' songs, comedies, madrigals and 'amorous letters'. By 1576 the office of the Sacred Palace was telling the inquisitor in Bologna to forbid publication of 'comic stories and other vulgar books or ones about love', just as in Rome where such books were being destroyed, and booksellers banned from selling them. When the 1596 Index gave guidance on expurgation (a chapter on 'De correctione librorum'), the censors were to look out for attacks on churchmen and princes and their good reputation, anything offensive against Church rituals, and obscene or rude images and engravings.[28]

A concern about 'love' in popular dialogues, romances and poetry dealing with that topic, affected publications by authors such as Veronica Franco, Sperone Speroni, or Niccolò Franco. A growing worry about works that advocated duelling has been detected, which affected books by noted writers such as Andrea Alciato and Girolamo Muzio (whose other works might be perfectly acceptable). This influenced, although temporarily, pending emendation, discussions about noble and gentlemanly behaviour, and the '*scienza cavalleresca*'. Changes to Castiglione's *The Courtier* were partly dictated by comments on duelling and honour.[29] Among other less obvious targets were certain kinds of prayer books and spiritual works, even new religious stories, when they advocated mental prayer and private spirituality divorced from orthodox clerical leadership.[30] Specialised legal texts were added to the list of works to be amended, including by leading foreigners like François Hotman and Charles Du Moulin (or Dumoulin), expertly published in Venice for a wide European market. They supposedly supported resistance to and challenges against authority, the advocacy of temporal against ecclesiastical power, or had unacceptable views on usury and commercial practices. The approach to Dumoulin who attacked the Roman Curia, and policies about taxations, was another example where the two congregations involved had divided opinions.[31] In criticising the Inquisition, Paolo Sarpi commented: 'under the colours of faith and religion, prohibited and condemned with the same severity are the authors of books in which the authority of the councils and bishops is defended against the usurpations of the Roman court'.[32] Naturally the Indexes added the increasing numbers of texts dealing with astrology and associated ideas of magical influences on humans (another topic involving disputes between those on the Index and the wider Inquisition),[33] astronomy, physical sciences and controversial philosophy.

Versions of the Index were produced throughout the seventeenth and eighteenth centuries. Those Indexes of 1664 and 1681, prepared by the then secretaries for the Congregation, allowed for more local discretion, and changed the format to a simpler alphabetical structure. The 1707 version for Clement XI considerably increased the number of authors and titles to about 11,000 entries, where the 1596 Index had contained 2,100.[34]

Implementing Index Policies

Laxness and inefficiency in activating censorship policies have already been noted in passing. The effectiveness of central control was affected by local attitudes and a willingness to fulfil orders from Rome, as well as by sheer practicalities. The determination of the Holy Office that the 1596 Index should be executed with rigour, especially in connection with vernacular Bibles, was still frustrated by impediments. The Holy Office lacked the manpower at the local tribunals to do all the work; the participation of the bishops and their subordinates was needed, and the Congregation of the Index preferred the bishops to local inquisitors for this task. The Kingdom of Naples had inevitably to rely on the ordinaries, given the unofficial status of inquisitors there. Elsewhere there were more diocesan districts than inquisitorial tribunals, which often did not really cover remoter areas. Bishops were told to create their own local 'congregations of the index', with local scholars to vet texts. With their long-term local knowledge, bishops might be better at seeking out likely possessors of prohibited books, clerical, conventual and lay, than the more peripatetic inquisitors. Bishops could also give greater publicity to their attacks by having seized books burned outside their cathedral. With archiepiscopal and inquisitorial cooperation Naples Cathedral featured book burnings on the feast of Saints Peter and Paul (29 June); a rare list of what had been gathered in 1610 survives, including the Bible or parts of it in translation, works on astrology and free will, titles by Cornelius Agrippa and Erasmus.[35] The bishops often had safer facilities for storing confiscated books pending their emendation or burning. However, convents and monasteries (whose libraries might well contain dubious and illegal works) often claimed exemption from both episcopal and inquisitorial jurisdiction. Central demands for such institutions to produce lists of their library holdings were delayed until 1604. Where bishops did have jurisdiction, and did not have inquisitors at hand to pressurise them, or support their initiatives, they might desist from investigating the libraries of powerful local persons and institutions. In 1597 a Dominican, Giovanni Battista Antonelli, complained that the extensive circulation in the Kingdom of Naples, and notably in the Abruzzi, of 'most pestilential books' was because the bishops 'sleep', and are unwilling to 'draw enmity upon themselves'.[36]

The Roman cardinals were themselves prepared to protect some libraries and their dubious holdings, and modify rules about licensing. This applied to the splendid library of Prospero Podiani in Perugia which, after many complications, became from his donation in 1582 the basis of the city's Biblioteca Augusta. In the 1590s and 1600s it proved a valuable lending library for bishops, lesser secular clergy, the major religious houses and laity (in Rome as well as Perugia and other Umbrian towns). They borrowed works by Erasmus, Cornelius Agrippa, Melanchthon, Jansenius, among others. Podiani was licensed to hold prohibited books thanks to support from Pope Gregory XIII's bastard son Giacomo Buoncompagni, Duke of Sora, sometime captain-general for the Church, who established links with the Congregation of the Index. He was instrumental in persuading the historian Carlo Sigonio to reach a compromise with the censors, and had himself the rare privileged as a layman of receiving licences in 1576 to read many prohibited works on diverse topics, 'for recreation and practice in the liberal arts'. Some in the Congregation realised that allowing these holdings in such a library could give scholars much needed access to otherwise almost inaccessible texts; this assisted the selective censorship of Erasmus' works.[37]

In areas where people were keen to come forward with their list of books, the volume of work for inquisitors and bishops could be daunting. The long-serving inquisitor of Bologna, Giovanni Antonio Spadini (1585–98), complained thus in March 1597, having issued 1,500 printed copies of the Index and found that amount inadequate:

> Almost everyone (because they do not know how to apply the Rules of the Index or for some other reason), has brought a list of all the books that they keep at home. Thus I have gathered around four thousand lists of books . . . and since the beginning

of Lent together with four other intendants I have been in audience from morning to evening for this purpose, and I have not yet dealt with a thousand lists.[38]

A letter of 24 May 1596 from the Mantuan inquisitor Domenico Istriani da Pesaro to Cardinal Agostino Valier of Verona also indicated the strain of trying to implement the new Index. Istriani stressed the difficulty of providing enough copies of the Index, which disgusted many people in the city and surrounding area. He wanted permission for the Mantuan printer to produce copies, rather than the Roman printer look to his temporal gain; and this would save costs of transporting copies from Rome. Supplying copies for all parish priests, convents and booksellers would be hugely expensive; as well as copies of the 'Conclusions' to be pinned up in the usual places. He struggled with receiving and checking all the books that were offered up, and scrutinising lists of books entering and leaving the city. How could he publish his Index without the means to implement it, and cope with the whispering against it? Many priests had urged him to suspend implementation until Rome resolved the printing problems. Istriani then raised difficulties about expurgating law books in particular. Many scholars were reluctant to undertake this, and when they did they were unpaid. Could he have the expurgation done privately? On 6 June he assured the Cardinal that the Duke of Mantua was always ready to help the Holy Office. Ahead of securing the duke's permission to publish the Index, Istriani and the episcopal vicar had written to all the rectors in the diocese to publish the prohibition against reading vernacular Bibles. Many had already consigned copies to the Inquisition.[39]

Some bishops and inquisitors proved enthusiastic and effective at seizing and destroying prohibited books, especially in the late 1590s. The Paduan inquisitor in April 1597 boasted to Cardinal Valier that he had burned twenty-nine sacks of books, and was praised for 'the great zeal you have shown in burning such a large quantity of books assuming that in this you have by notarial act performed the usual ceremonies'. The Cardinal wondered whether the texts involved had been suitably listed and publicised, as a warning to other possessors. The Holy Office wanted books publicly burned for 'good edification', but also wanted lists compiled to know what had been possessed and was being destroyed. Burning was 'for the satisfaction of the people', claimed the Paduan inquisitor, and the Perugian inquisitor implied that the burning was to show those who had been dispossessed of their books that they were being appropriated. Without seeing the burning they 'are more loath to consign them to the Holy Office or to the ordinary'.[40]

Eliseo Masini was also an enthusiastic book-burner as inquisitor in Genoa. In 1620 he boasted that he had made up for the laxity of his predecessors, and

> Purged this city of Aretinos, the Machiavellis, the Bodins, the Boccaccios and a thousand other filthy authors, of vernacular Bibles, of historical compendiums,

and of innumerable other totally prohibited books, having had public bonfires made, as I did with much edification of the city some years ago, when fully five or six thousand copies of books were burned.[41]

The burning of heretical or offensive books had a long history, sanctioned by St Paul's reported burning in Ephesus of magic books supposedly from Egypt (Acts 19:19), and later notably by Gregory the Great in burning a Palatine library, and by St Dominic in campaigning against medieval heretics. These early episodes were recalled in our period in paint and print, when naturally the pyres were greater with numerous copies of printed texts as well as manuscripts.[42] Cardinal Ghislieri boasted that 10,000–12,000 volumes were burned in Rome on 18 March 1559, demonstrating the new policy of the 1559 Index. Many cities had pyres, though seemingly of varying size. In Florence Duke Cosimo had sanctioned burnings on 15 and 18 March but, in deference to scholars and 'poor booksellers', it should be a 'fire for show', 'more demonstration than effect'.[43] Maerten de Vos, back in Antwerp after a decade in Italy, produced a lively painting, *St Paul in Ephesus* (1568, now Royal Museums, Brussels), in which the saint is depicted supervising the book burning before a large crowd. San Domenico, Bologna, still has the sizeable *St Dominic Burning Books* (1614–16), which would have reminded the local inquisitor and his supporters of their duty; the saint's own book survives the fire – as a good work. A printed version of this painting (by Giuliano Traballesi) circulated in the eighteenth century, clarifying that this was part of the campaign against the Albigensians.[44] The frontispiece for G.A. Gabuzzi's life of Pius V includes a book-burning episode beneath his portrait. The frontispieces of various editions of the *Index librorum prohibitorum* have variations on the theme of burning bad books. The 1711 version brings St Thomas Aquinas into the picture, while the 1786 edition under Pius VI quotes Acts 19:19: 'Multi eorum qui fuerant curiosa sectati, contulerunt Libros, et combussserunt coram omnibus'.[45]

The seizure of books did not necessarily result in their burning. Some texts might be preserved in a library of the Inquisition for future use in censorship and asserting control. Such holdings could offer temptations. Investigations and trials of Salvatore de' Negri, a notable Venetian bookseller of prohibited books, revealed that Fra Bonaventura Perinetti da Piacenza, inquisitor of Belluno in 1628, had earlier as inquisitorial vicar in Padua depleted that tribunal's stock of prohibited books (including allegedly ones by Cornelius Agrippa, Aretino, Machiavelli, and magic books by Pietro d'Abano), by selling them to second-hand dealers for circulation in Padua and Venice.[46]

The policy of holding or suspending publication of books pending correction or expurgation, which the 1596 Index fully ratified, might seem a beneficial compromise between the harsh and more liberal censors, though Paolo Sarpi damned it as a process of castration.[47] Recent scholarship has produced a more jaundiced view of the impact of these censorship procedures. The tiny niggles, as well as significant doubts, that led to the suspension of books pending correction, created a massive quantity of work for correctors. Many suspended works were never released, because the inking-out was not undertaken on existing copies, nor republished in licensed editions omitting offending phrases. Key works were reissued but in bowdlerised versions, almost as new works. Outside central theological and philosophical matters the processes of censorship were affected by a subtle conflict between the literati and inquisitorial friars who did not understand literature.[48]

The expurgation process required considerable manpower, whether in Rome or elsewhere; recruiting suitable censors could be difficult if they were not paid. Academics in universities and monasteries advised on corrections, carried them out, or vetted manuscripts pre-publication, and liaised with local inquisitors or those in Rome. The Congregation of the Index tended to send works of Italian literature to Florence, those on canon law to Bologna, law to Perugia, history works to Milan, medicine and philosophy to Padua (despite the fact that Padua University housed some of the most suspect lecturers, who debated the immortality of the soul), while scattering texts on duelling to Cremona, Parma and Piacenza. The Congregation of the Index tried to persuade scholars that theirs was an honoured enterprise.[49] Some expurgation was simple but tedious: inking out names of heretics, or replacing *coitus* (deemed obscene) by the acceptable words for sexual intercourse, *copula* or *coniunctio*, even in law texts.[50] Other censoring was of course challenging, potentially exciting (but risky if the verdict was not acceptable to Roman inquisitors and leaders), as for those who had to judge Galileo's writings in 1614–15, or 1632–3. While the immediate post-1596 enterprise of censorship secured willing help, complaints grew through the next century about delays, inefficiencies, failure to fulfil duties properly. Florentine academicians were soon being castigated and threatened for not suitably expurgating literary works.

Many probably disliked tampering with books they admired. In October 1602 the Florentine inquisitor wrote to Cardinal Simone Tagliavia d'Aragona (or Cardinal Terranova) that 'no censorship should be expected from here', that he and his team were 'greatly exercised with certain formal heretics and their accomplices', and 'submerged' in preventive censorship. Many other inquisitors probably felt the same. Between 1596 and 1603 Cardinal Tagliavia had to deal with many complaints from inquisitors, bishops and archbishops, and academics about footling corrections, conflicting guidance, time wasted when, say, Padua was producing one set of corrections while another centre might be heading in a different direction. Tagliavia's pestering could produce satisfactory (to him) results, while Bolognese censors who had been tasked with correcting law books and treatises with passages concerning duelling, provided in 1603 extensive lists of amendments to many texts, including by the widely published Andrea Alciato (Alciati) and Paride dal Pozzo. The Bolognese censors involved were a mixture of theologians, a metaphysician (Alberto Diolaiti, a Carmelite) and many jurists, originating from several universities. The censors were not necessarily in agreement; some were unhappy about amending the famous Alciati, and merely changed the tense of certain passages from present to past, to imply past description rather than present prescription.[51]

By the eighteenth century Rome at least had coteries of well-educated censors, backed with good library resources and licences to read otherwise prohibited books. They were ready to give critical reports on new works, and write their own books against the pernicious ideas they were seeking to ban.

With some literary texts correctors set about their work with enthusiasm, and decided they could rewrite passages to improve style, or even add new material or stories. Some pre-Index rewritings had set precedents. Francesco Petrarca's poems were heavily rewritten by another poet, Girolamo Malipiero, and republished in Venice in 1536. He turned *donna* (woman) into *Madonna*, *amore* into *Amore* (implying divine love). He altered 26 per cent of the *canzoni*, and about 17 per cent of the sonnets. Malipiero's version proved very popular through many editions. But in the 1570s some members of the Congregation of the Index still found this version unsuitable, because of terms like *fortuna* and *fato* (fortune and fate) that challenged God's role. *Fortuna* was a word and concept that triggered animosity towards many works, including those by Castiglione, Machiavelli and Montaigne. Castiglione's internationally popular *Il Cortegiano* (*The Courtier*) of 1528 was corrected and 'improved' by a theologian (in Venice, 1584), Antonio Ciccarelli, who also wrote a commentary on Livy in reply to Machiavelli's *Discourses*. He removed unflattering references in *The Courtier* to Alexander VI, hypocritical friars, heretical cardinals, rewrote passages discussing love (blaming neo-Platonic influences which he said were not really Castiglione's). This became the recognised version, though even more puritanically expurgated editions appeared in the nineteenth century. Castiglione's original was hardly known again until the late nineteenth century. A few early 1531 copies survived, some showing signs of inking out by self-censoring owners. In 1587 the Venetian printer Domenico Giglio produced an unexpurgated edition, complaining that others had 'lacerated and spoiled' the original, and this (with other unlicensed editions) may have had some circulation.[52]

Boccaccio's *Decameron* (1348–58) was entrusted to Florentine academicians, leading to major rearrangements, as well as reducing its anticlericalism; so a misbehaving curate became a secular *podestà* (judge); a Cardinal became an aristocratic *gran signore*. The first expurgated edition of the *Decameron* was approved in 1573 by a Master of the Sacred Palace, Tommaso Manrique, only to be rejected (1573–80) by a more austere, anti-poetic Master, the Dominican Paolo Costabili.

Costabili was also to delay the expurgation of *Il Cortegiano* and condemn numerous literary works – poetic, theatrical and musical – as dishonest, lascivious and contrary to faith. A similar approach was made to Luigi Pulci's poem *Morgante maggiore*, copies of which had been burned in Savonarola's bonfires in 1497–8 (along with the *Decameron*) and banned in 1559; it was republished in a bowdlerised version in 1574. Its printer boasted that it was 'more beautiful than ever in everything that it imparts', 'numerous octaves have been entirely removed from episodes in which matters of faith are strewn with comicality', and 'in scabrous passages the names of saints and references to holy things have been removed and replaced with those of "innocent" persons and facts'.[53] This encapsulates the attitude and zeal of those correcting and publishing the 'improved literature'.

A few battles were undertaken to rescue famous authors from total or near total bans. Factions within the Dominican Order tried to rescue writings by Savonarola, whom they considered unjustly condemned in 1498; his value as a spiritual adviser was worth preserving. Others campaigned for Erasmus' texts and the releasing of suspended editions. After the 1564 Index removed him from the total prohibition of 1559, it still banned the *Colloquia* and *Moriae encomium*, allowed some other texts, and withheld others pending correction. Expurgated versions were still being debated by the Index in 1610. Holders of old copies took the verdict 'suspended' as an excuse to retain them and not surrender them to the authorities. Florentines obviously, but also Venetians, were prepared to claim that Machiavelli, a class-one dangerous author in the 1559 Index, had written meritorious works, including his studies of Florentine history, the *Art of War* and even the *Discourses* on Livy – if amended to eliminate attacks on the Papacy. Some inquisitorial cardinals considered it easier to eliminate the illegal editions still being produced (as by Girolamo Calepin, the Venetian printer of the *Tariffa delle puttane*, the list of Venetian prostitutes), if expurgated editions were licensed. Bishop Eustacchio Lucatelli, papal confessor, declared in 1570 that the Inquisition had nothing serious against Machiavelli. In 1587 the censor of the *Discourses* stated: 'I admire his style. Many of the things that are fundamental to the governance of the state ... he treats fully and eloquently that nothing could surpass him. In conclusion this could be republished,' marginally altered. However, in 1596 leading inquisitor Santoro defeated Cardinal Baronio, and Machiavelli remained a banned author.[54]

The frustrations of the expurgation process and pre-publication licensing were considerable. This encouraged unlicensed publication, and the continuing sale of 'suspended' books. At an official level in 1596 Venetian Patriarch Lorenzo Priuli, in a Venice–Rome 'Declaration' of the rules of the Index for prohibited books, permitted texts suspended pending correction to be sold, if so licensed by the local bishop or inquisitor. This 'concordat' and its concessions were an economic godsend for Venetian printers and booksellers.[55]

The censorship processes were not entirely negative in their cultural impact. Favoured religious works from the past were republished, and the range of religious writing expanded to support new devotions. The sixth rule of the 1559 Index encouraged this: 'Books written in the vernacular concerning the good rules of life, prayer, confession and similar matters, if they contain healthy doctrine, there is no reason for them to be prohibited, and likewise sermons to the people delivered in the vernacular.'[56] Women and their devotions were now targeted by writers and publishers. A new spiritual work like the Theatine Lorenzo Scupoli's *Combattimento spirituale* (first published anonymously in 1589) would become a bestseller through the seventeenth century, and is still used for spiritual self-analysis. Realising that book censorship might undermine the literate laity's religious enthusiasm, the Jesuit Antonio Possevino produced a positive Index, of books that could and should be read, as written or with suitable emendations, for the 'cultivation of intellectual faculties', the *Biblioteca selecta* (originally published in Rome, 1593). Some of his recommendations were 'indexed' later by narrower-minded censors. Possevino provided a major guide to expurgators (an activity he approved of, 'to eliminate evil sentiments and thoughts, heresies and dishonesty, and the obscene things'), and gave practical advice to booksellers about selling expurgated books, including doing more corrections of their own, or supplying replacement pages for those excised. For Possevino participation in the creation of an approved library, and the eradication of bad literature, was part of the culture of intellectuals, 'Coltura degl'ingegni' as he entitled the preamble to the *Biblioteca*.[57]

The pre-publication licensing procedures for new books were fraught with problems, again of manpower, time and dedication, of competence and a willingness to cooperate. Pre-publication procedures have been much less studied than the controls after publication. The Indexes offered guidelines, as did general orders from the congregations, but local inquisitors and bishops, with their consultants, who might be formed into congregations, varied in their dedication and attitudes. Some seem to have been more willing to refer cases to Rome than others. Delays in obtaining permission to send texts to the printers could be inhibiting, so could fears of official censure and calls for revision, as by Cardinal Agostino Valier himself; the Congregation's prefect, Cardinal Silvio Antoniano, took care to submit a treatise on Christian education for children to many revisers before entrusting it to his printers.[58] Local inquisitors might show a liberality that the Roman Congregation of the Index found objectionable, as when the Venetian inquisitor Giovanni Domenico Vignuzzi authorised the printing of a book of prayers for the 'Forty-Hour Devotion' (*Il buon giorno overo orationi delle quarante hore*, Venice, 1601, by Ferdinando Buongiorno), though it contained compositions 'impertinent ... and full of new rites', on the grounds that the prayers were to be recited privately, and not in choir or communally. Cardinal

Valier did not accept these justifications and banned the book. It was listed by the Master of the Sacred Palace in 1603 as a work to be expurgated. Valier did praise the author for the humility with which he accepted the suspension, but reprimanded inquisitor Vignuzzi for allowing litany booklets to be published for private worship that were not acceptable for public worship.[59]

The complexities and problems of getting potentially troublesome books licensed are revealed in the extraordinary case of Galileo's *Dialogue on the Two Great World Systems, Ptolemaic and Copernican*. Having received Urban VIII's approval in 1623 to write about the two systems (as hypotheses), Galileo, based in Florence under the protection of the Grand Duke of Tuscany, had completed a text by April 1630. He travelled to Rome to seek publication under the sponsorship of the Academy of the Lynxes (Accademia dei Lincei), led by Prince Cesi (until his untimely death in August 1630), with help from a coterie of supporters in Rome. For official approval he approached the Master of the Sacred Palace, Niccolò Riccardi, who was predisposed towards Galileo, and ready to seek other opinions from potentially favourable censors. Much of the *Dialogue* was found acceptable, but it needed a suitably tactful introduction and conclusion – to avoid the Copernican interpretation being seen as preferred or proved. Galileo left for Florence in June, without full permission to publish his book but with the understanding that Riccardi (having received the favourable opinion of the Dominican Raffaello Visconti, an enthusiast for astronomy, but also astrology and occult sciences) would agree on amendments and suitable 'top-tailing'. He was assisted by Giovanni Ciampoli, the Pope's correspondence secretary, a Florentine with long-standing friendships with Galileo and the Barberini family, and a member of the Academy of the Lynxes. Between 1630 and 1633 plague then intervened, making correspondence difficult and the transmission of books or bulky texts impossible. After much badgering from the Tuscan ambassador, and after much procrastination, Riccardi first agreed to Galileo's book being published in Rome, provided he saw the full text; then he agreed to publication in Florence, subject to the Florentine Inquisition under inquisitor Clemente Egidi and Dominican consultant Iacinto Stefani approving the final text, including preface, conclusions and title, produced in line with papal instructions. Riccardi himself had seemingly never read the whole text, and only a penultimate version of the beginning and end. In February 1632 the printing was completed, with the stated approval of 'the authorities' in Florence. The distribution and sale of copies started, but bound presentation copies did not reach Rome until May, when the quarantine rules for plague control were lifted. In July Urban VIII took offence at the contents, thinking a key speech was poking fun at him and made the Prolemaic case sound poorly defended; and he took offence at the way the book had been published. Riccardi was told to get the Florentine inquisitor to suspend publication; and the issue was put in the hands of the Inquisition in Rome, leading to its summoning of Galileo to

Rome, his questioning and 'trial' under threats of torture as discussed below. Arguably, had Galileo worked more patiently with Riccardi over the final presentation, he could have avoided trouble. But this might have meant a few more years' work, and the old, sick Galileo was anxious for the final publication.[60]

Vernacular Bibles

One of the biggest and most controversial censorship campaigns concerned the use of vernacular Bibles. The decision in the 1596 Clementine Index to ban their use almost totally can be seen as one of the most damaging decisions in terms of Italian religious culture lasting to the present, even if reading in Latin remained moderately widespread among the laity. Italians had been among the first to translate from the Latin Bible into a local language and issue printed editions of at least key parts, with Nicolò Malerbi leading the way from 1471. Modern humanist scholarship was then reflected by Antonio Brucioli, who drew on Greek and Hebrew texts for his 1530 *Nuovo Testamento* and his 1532 full *Bibbia*. Many reprints, with revisions (about seventy versions by 1567), ensured that many more Italians had a deeper knowledge of biblical teaching. Such knowledge could significantly stimulate artists, like Lorenzo Lotto and friends. Archbishop Ludovico Beccadelli, who had been involved in the Tridentine Index, soon after expressed doubts about the policy of banning or curtailing the reading of vernacular Bibles, as being virtually impossible because for long it had been the custom in Dalmatia.[61]

The 1559 Index had curbed the reading of Bibles other than in Latin, unless under licence (primarily given to clergy). From 1567 the open production and publication of Italian versions virtually ceased, though not of clandestine ones printed at home or abroad. As emerged in the debate over the 1596 policy, local inquisitors as well as bishops had in practice been quite tolerant about licensing the reading of biblical texts, as for the Certosa in Pisa, or Siena's Santa Maria della Scala discipline confraternity.[62] After many struggles the 1596 Index not only banned full translations of the Old and New Testaments, popular translations of the Gospels and Epistles, but any books that used extensive quotations from them in Italian. Bartolomeo Dionigi da Fano's popular compendium (*Compendio istorico del Vecchio e del Nuovo Testamento*), which had been allowed to appear from 1586, was now banned. He had produced this partly in response to Venetian gentlewomen who had complained about their difficulty in understanding the history of the old Patriarchs. Some Church leaders like Cardinal Agostino Valier in the 1600s continued to hope (as he wrote to the Mantuan inquisitor) that the ban on such a useful compendium would be lifted, but in vain; the Holy Office remained adamant. Long-standing popular compilations like the *Fioretti della Bibbia* (or *Fiore Novello*), which also contained profane history and mythology (from Ovid's *Metamophoses*), were, more understandably, banned. This would have pleased the reformer Pier Paolo Vergerio, who disliked its allegation that Cain and his son committed sodomy. However, the Bolognese inquisitor in 1576 had to be hard pressed by Master of the Sacred Palace Costabili's secretary to sequester the *Fioretti*. This was a book that the miller Menocchio listed as favoured reading. Saints' lives, texts of plays and mimed representations about saints and biblical characters staged from the fifteenth century (such as *Rappresentazione di Adamo e Isacco*), or poems about St Alexis, were censored.[63]

Copies of the Bible and compendiums were vigorously hunted down, in the face of continuing resistance from clergy and laity. As already indicated, many copies of vernacular Bibles were found and burned in the late 1590s and 1600s – but Eliseo Masini still had plenty to burn in the 1610s. Bibles, and prohibited lectionaries, were still being sold by Curzio Forlano's shop in Ancona, by several Bolognese and Florentine booksellers in 1599. If editions produced in Italy were rarer after 1567, clandestine imports were sought, notably Giovanni Diodati from Lucca's 1607 version of the Calvinist Bible ('improved' in 1641). Two thousand copies were found in Venice in 1608, and many were given to the inquisitor of Aquileia by self-denouncers in Friuli, between 1649 and 1654, along with Lutheran German translations. The Congregation of the Index was ready to sanction sacramental absolution, without further punishment in the *foro esterno*, for those who surrendered prohibited Bibles and compilations, and witnessed their burning. The paucity of full copies of Bibles translated into Italian that have survived in Italy's libraries suggests major success – eventually – for this campaign by the Holy Office.[64]

Public resistance to surrendering other banned religious literature was strong, and harder to counteract by the inquisitors and bishops: the translations of the Psalms, Epistles and Gospels, lectionaries, lives of saints and biblical figures, and the compilations. They might be slighter and easier to hide or disguise than Bibles. They might have more appeal for their owner than a full Bible. Confusion might also reign, given that such items as the paraphrases of the psalms, as by the famous preacher and bishop, Francesco Panigarola, were permitted. Correspondence received by cardinals Agostino Valier and Marcantonio Colonna between 1596 and 1598 reflected protests across the land and in many quarters against the deprivation of religious texts; inquisitors and episcopal officials were variously sympathetic or hostile as they relayed the protests. The inquisitor in Piacenza seemed more sympathetic to pleas from many in his city for a partial reversal of policy about vernacular religious literature than the inquisitor in nearby Milan. Women in convents from Venice, Lucca, Arezzo and Colle Val d'Elsa to Osimo and Molfetta, protested via their bishops or others at the loss of vernacular Gospels and Epistles, the Psalms, *Fioretti di bibbia* and other works. A bishop such as Usimbardo Usimbardi of

Colle Val d'Elsa stressed that his petitioners were good and pious Catholics, so he should be allowed to restore to them such vernacular literature, including the full Bible and *Fioretti*.[65] Conventual libraries remained depleted, and so were the spiritual lives of nuns, unless other copies of such texts were smuggled in later.

Those remote cardinals in Rome were unlikely to accept the liberal or emotional pleas from pastoral carers. Valier was the more dominant Cardinal of the two leaders in the Congregation of the Index, Colonna and Valier, and he was a prolific writer but had little published in his lifetime. He was wary of printing and stressed the need for self-censorship, as shown in his tract *De cautione adhibenda in edendis libris* (*Concerning Caution in Amending Books*). Valier was a patron of Roberto Bellarmino, and influenced him in cautious censorship. Valier, and Colonna, favoured caution over allowing printed vernacular books to circulate in the hands of the less educated.[66]

The Attacks on Jewish Literature

The Church's attack on Jewish culture could be brutal, along with a wider anti-Semitism, but it could reach accommodation over aspects of Hebrew literature – to the benefit of Jews and Christians. An early attack on the Talmud is noted in the book-burning instigated in Brescia by the sermons in 1492 of a leading anti-Semitic preacher, Bernardino da Feltre, also noted for promoting the Monti di Pietà Christian pawnbroking institutions to replace Jewish moneylenders.[67] Some argued that burning the Talmud would remove a major impediment to converting Jews. Hebrew literature was one of the key targets of the Church from the 1550s; this affected Venice, the leading centre for printing, where copies of the Talmud were burned in 1553, as also in Rome's Campo dei Fiori. The state joined forces with the Esecutori contra la Bestemmia (anti-blasphemy officials) and led a wider onslaught in 1568 on Hebrew books, their printers and sellers, who were heavily fined. An estimated 8,000 folio volumes of such works as the *Midhrash* and *Mahazor Sephardim* were burned, while many more were confiscated. This was part of a widespread panic that the Jewish community and Judaisers were supporting the Ottoman Turks. Venetian printers, notably the Giustiniani press, bounced back, and by the 1590s 'the Jews, with the aid of the Giustiniani family, obtained the books they needed'.[68] In 1570 Marc'Antonio Giustiniani had been accused by a priest of printing and trading (including in Cephalonia) in prohibited Jewish books, *mappamundi* with Arabic script, and trying to repair books that had been legitimately burned. The investigations went on until 1575 (by which time Marc'Antonio had died, and his son Antonio was continuing to import chests of Hebrew books), with the Venetian tribunal showing reluctance to investigate too closely, or make searches too quickly – so Antonio had pre-raid warnings. He ended up with a 100-ducat fine.[69]

Christian leaders were ambivalent about Jewish writings, because they realised that Christian scholars needed to read some Hebrew texts, whether for biblical criticism, philosophical and mystical concepts, or medical expertise. The Talmud was the most sensitive text and was essentially banned through the period of this study. The 1564 Index allowed existing copies to be used if the title 'Talmud' was removed, along with blocking out attacks against Christianity. Discussions were held to determine whether an expurgated edition could be authorised for publication. Cardinals Walter Allen and Marcantonio Colonna proposed a preventive translation into Latin, supervised by Christian theologians. These compromise proposals failed. The struggle over the Talmud was then a central theme, alongside that concerning the vernacular Bible, in the debates leading to the 1596 Index. Cardinal Santoro eventually won his victory that the Talmud should be totally prohibited (as the introduction, *Observatio*, to the final published version proclaimed). However, that this was a late victory is indicated by the fact that the body of the text was covered with the words '*donec corrigatur*', 'until corrected'.[70]

However, other Jewish books were subject to expurgation, as had been started at the Conti press in Cremona in 1556. In the 1570s the Congregation of the Index produced rules to allow presses in various cities to censor texts and print them. Most of the censors were converts, and some were well recognised as experts, such as Domenico Gerosolominato (Shmuel Vivas until his 1593 conversion), whose imprimatur is on many books until his death in 1621. He worked in Mantua, Monferrrato, Milan and finally Rome where he taught Hebrew in the College for Neophytes. From 1596 he provided a guide, regularly updated, for expurgation and censorship, the *Sefer Ha-Zikkuk*. Much of the expurgation work was to remove explicit anti-Christian passages, as in some prayer books (the *Mahzorim*), which were the main religious sources for the Ghetto communities.[71] In Rome Cardinal Santoro from the 1570s seems to have presided over an inner congregation for Hebrew books, to some extent independent of the Holy Office and Index congregations; this dealt with problems in the more scholarly texts. The work was slow, intermittent and sometimes fraught with problems when the Master of the Sacred Palace, or Jewish convert scholars, would not fully cooperate. But Piet van Boxel judges the censors' work as meticulous and effective, especially when Cardinal Roberto Bellarmino became a final arbiter instead of Santoro. Bellarmino knew Hebrew, and was well versed in Rabbinic biblical interpretation. Boxel argues that this branch of expurgation activity ended well, with harmony between the sub-congregation and its censors, the Master, Santoro as head of the Holy Office, and Cardinal Guglielmo Sirleto as prefect of the Congregation of the Index. Amnon Raz-Krakotzkin suggests that some 'censoring' of Ashkenazi prayers in practice reflected a voluntary modernisation of Jewish worship in line with Jewish wishes, and that all was not repressive by Christians, nor agreed solely out of fear.[72]

Local Book Hunting and Burning

The congregations of the Index and Holy Office expended energy in creating indexes of what might be published, set up arrangements for pre-publication assessment, licensing and post-publication prohibitions, systems of expurgation and republication. To be effective much effort and diligence were needed to control what was in circulation and read. Battle was waged with printers, booksellers and binders; some 'shops' (*botteghe*) might be involved in all three activities; some might specialise in one, or move between roles. Printers and sellers were meant to be officially licensed; to have a copy of the current papal Index, and sometimes supplementary lists issued by bishops or secular authorities, so that they did not print or sell what was not authorised. They were supposed to have inventories of their own publications and current stock to show representatives of bishops, the Inquisition or a secular official who might raid the premises. Obeying the rules could be very time-consuming and uneconomic, especially for those who were not official printers/sellers for Church and State authorities. So naturally the bookmen had ways of operating around the rules. Cases concerning Venetian bookmen show them operating clandestinely, claiming to be a binder, but printing and/or selling on the side. They disguised illegitimate texts behind a false frontispiece (with or without a few innocent pages), concealing the real author, printer, publisher and place of publication. Binders and sellers could plead ignorance of the real content, saying they did not read the books they handled, as a leading trader in heretical books, Salvatore de' Negri, and his associates alleged.[73]

Officials from the Inquisition, from the episcopacy (even Cardinal Archbishop Carlo Borromeo himself in Milan), or from state organisations (such as the Venetian Bestemmia office), might easily identify some prohibited books and prosecute. Possession of a prohibited book might be enough for a minor punishment. Proving the more serious charge of printing it could be more difficult, as the Valvasense case discussed below shows. When second-hand books were passing through the shop, proving guilt against a claim of ignorance was harder. When minor punishments were imposed, such as religious penances, the main punishment in effect could be the loss of the stock, and a limit on further activity as printer, seller or binder. Some cases against bookmen lasted a long time if the inquisitor wanted to prove heretical intentionality, which would lead to economic disaster for the accused. Some publishers might be sufficiently suspect of illegal publication and selling that other sellers could be banned from holding their works, as happened to the Venetian Roberto Maietti (or Meietti), whose publications were totally banned in Naples in 1608 after a diligent revelatory survey of many bookshops there.[74]

Two second-hand booksellers in Naples, Marc'Antonio Passero (or Passaro) and Marco Romano, suffered from lengthy imprisonment and investigation by the archbishop from July 1574 to May 1575, after the inquisitorial leader, the Cardinal of Pisa, Scipione Rebiba, had ordered a search of their bookshops, houses and any possible hiding places. Passero and Romano had rich collections of prohibited books including works by Erasmus, Savonarola, Aretino, Machiavelli (*The Prince*), Melanchthon, Antonio Brucioli, Suetonius, Ovid, Nicolò Franco and unspecified books in French and English. They were often unbound and not in the best condition. Romano's defence claimed he was a good practising Christian, of good repute (*de bona fama*), even noble, but was ignorant (*persona idiota*), did not know the contents of his books and could not read or write (a ploy used by other sellers); but this last point was denied by witnesses. It was claimed that Passero had regularly taken books to the archbishop's palace to check they were not prohibited, and he had a copy of the Index. The two were eventually released from prison, and their confiscated books were burned publicly in front of their shops. They were banned from being booksellers for a year, and were to continue to lodge pledges for good behaviour.[75]

Because of the higher proportion of surviving case records, we know most about the Venetian book industry and the fraught lives of bookmen there; and that city led the way in publishing, combined with international trading in books. While Naples and Rome could offer competition in terms of printing and bookshops – legitimate or illegal – Venice and its dependent cities like Padua and Vicenza were tempted by the two-way international traffic in books, especially linking with Frankfurt (for its book fair), or Geneva. Hence a significant number of cases, shown in the Tables in the Appendix, of those prosecuted. Friuli at times had high numbers of prosecutions because of the international trade through the mountains. Some bookmen were sentenced to death, but mainly if they were repeat offenders in the international trade, involving books by leading heretics. In 1587 the Venetian tribunal had Girolamo Donzellini, a physician from Brescia, executed for persistent trading in Protestant books since the 1540s, when he was first arraigned in Rome. He had appeared before the inquisitor again in 1560 and 1574, serving two years in prison. The next year Pietro Longo was finally convicted and drowned for trading in heretical works, and possibly for being a committed Protestant (the *processo* does not survive to elucidate this). However, key booksellers in Venice dealing in heretical works escaped death, such as Francesco Ziletti, who was busy from 1570 in his shop at the Pozzo (well), including dealing in Erasmus' works; and Ziletti's Valgrisi relatives, who were printers and sellers through to the 1590s, were fined but avoided serious punishment.[76]

When booksellers faced scrutiny by the Inquisition and still wanted to serve those interested in prohibited books and ideas, whether reform heresies, magical arts or obscenity, they might circulate manuscript copies, based on a printed copy kept secret, or allow them to be copied by hand. Manuscript copies were sold for some time ahead of finding a printer daring enough to risk the wider printed market. These booksellers might also use inns, such as the *locanda* Istriana at Santi Apostoli, whose host testified in 1639 that foreigners came there for 'bad books against the Catholic religion', whether already printed or to be copied there. The books were provided by several dealers including Bartolomeo Gei from Cadoro, who knew Latin and Polish and specialised in magical texts and libertine works (as by Aretino), and was eventually tried in 1656.[77]

Attacks on Philosophers and New Science

Church censorship inevitably sought to ban or modify many works propagating new humanist scholarship as they went into print from the late fifteenth century; aspects of neo-Platonism, Scepticism, debates about the mortality or immortality of the soul, and new approaches to astronomy (and astrology), from Copernicus onwards. Although Protestants (with a greater emphasis on biblical literalism) initially had more problems with Copernicus' views than the Catholic Church, it was the latter that historically has suffered more in reputation for its opposition to the 'new science', and for its condemnation of the works of Copernicus, Giordano Bruno and Galileo in particular; and of course the burning of Giordano Bruno in 1600 and the 'trial' of Galileo in 1633. Lack of space precludes a discussion here of the battles over these great minds. I will confine my discussion to some select points about how the inquisitors handled some leading figures and their works – largely to highlight the complexities and diversities of attitudes and procedures, as they fit into the wider picture of how the Congregations of the Holy Office and the Index, and papal policies, worked.

The Catholic Church had no absolutist view on most of the new philosophies, whether versions of Platonism or Aristotelianism, Scepticism, approaches to nature, or the universe. Except for Atheism proper and outright claims for the mortality of the soul, most new thinking could find some tolerance by leading figures in the Church, especially if the person and text concerned presented the ideas as hypotheses, and not absolute truths. Such were the terms under which Cardinal Roberto Bellarmino was ready in 1615–16 to allow Galileo to continue his investigations despite the protests of Dominicans sticking to conservative Aristotelian and Thomist doctrines. If Galileo had his Dominican opponents, he had the support and help (not always acknowledged) of leading Jesuit mathematicians for many decades. How far friendship towards the new thinkers could protect them and their writings was variable. Bernardino Telesio, who mainly lived in Cosenza though he had been exposed to new mathematical ideas and philosophy at Padua University, was a friend of many high clergy, and a leading critic of Aristotelian views on nature in his *De rerum natura* (1565, with major expansion in 1586). This was examined by the Congregation of the Index in 1593, and then prohibited by the 1596 Index. Francesco Patrizi da Cherso (originally

Franjo Petrić from Croatia) was also influenced by new ideas at Padua University, and was sponsored by Venetian nobles. This led to his being the first professor of neo-Platonic philosophy in Ferrara, and producing his major work *Nova de universis philosophia* (Ferrara, 1591), which among other matters dealt with the metaphysics of light. Clement VIII's nephew Cinzio Aldobrandini invited Patrizi to be professor of Platonic philosophy at the Sapienza in Rome. However, the Congregation of the Index criticised some of his text; he produced a modified version, which failed to satisfy them. The book was suspended pending expurgation in the 1596 Index, but Patrizi died before he could agree on a suitable text.[78]

An internationally more widely known contemporary, Giambattista Della Porta from Naples, faced more personal trouble. He wrote plays (some translated into English, French and Latin), works on cryptography, natural magic, chemistry, magnetism and astrology. In 1560 he founded the scientific Accademia dei Segreti, but inquisitors had this closed down in 1580. He was implicated in the trial of Vincenzo Vitale (from 1574) for necromancy, was tortured, but eventually purged himself in 1587. Cardinal Scipione Rebiba had solicited Viceroy Granvela and Archbishop Mario Carafa's help in securing Della Porta's arrest in June 1574. Meanwhile his *Magia naturalis* (1558, with several translations), which tried to distinguish between sorcery (which he attacked) and natural magic, was banned in various Indexes (Spain in 1583; Rome orders in 1590 and 1593). His *De humana physiognamia* (1586) was suspended in 1596 pending corrections, and his *Chiromantia* was refused a licence for printing in 1610. In that year, however, he was a founding member of the Accademia dei Lincei, which was to promote Galileo's studies. Investigatory processes could be slow when various tribunals in Italy were involved. In April 1592 Cardinal Santoro wrote to the Archbishop of Naples, Annibale di Capua, that he had *recently* learned of Della Porta publishing a book in Venice on *Fisonomia*, which also contained judgements about future matters. Since Della Porta had been indicted in 1578 for necromancy – when he was condemned to purge himself canonically – the cardinals had written to the Venetian inquisitor to stop that book being printed, or anything similar, without the Roman Congregation's permission. Santoro was now asking di Capua to summon Della Porta and warn him not to publish elsewhere. He was now curbed.[79]

Giordano Bruno and Fellow Prisoners

The most notorious casualty of the Italian Inquisition was Giordano Bruno. He might be seen as the last of the great Renaissance visionary figures. A philosopher who studied neo-Platonism, Hermeticism, Copernicanism; magus and astrologer; playwright; master of the arts of memory; international traveller; and possibly international plotter for a new Reformation, under Henri IV.[80] Feared by orthodox Protestants as well as Catholics, he became the idol of Freemasons who erected the impressive statue to him in 1889 in the Campo dei Fiori, Rome, where he had been burned, unrepentant, on 17 February 1600.[81] The final *processo* leading to that point had started in Venice in May 1592. But Bruno had interested inquisitors long before. As a novice he had been denounced to the Neapolitan Inquisition by his superior, for throwing out of his cell images of saints, and discouraging another novice from reading a book of Marian devotion. No process followed. In 1576 his Provincial denounced him as a heretic, for defending Arian heretics and challenging the concept of the Trinity and cult of saints. Before this was pursued Bruno fled to Rome, where he was soon in trouble – allegedly for throwing into the Tiber somebody who had accused him of heresy. News was also coming from Naples that prohibited books, including texts of Saints Jerome and Chrysostom edited by Erasmus, had been found hidden in his cell's latrine.[82] Again he fled, in March 1576, casting off his habit (which he sometimes later resumed, as bizarrely when approaching Calvinist Geneva) and embarking on his peregrinations (including Geneva, France, England, Zurich, Wittenberg, Prague, Tubingen, Frankfurt, Padua and Venice).

Bruno arrived in Venice in 1592, considering it a safer haven than most cities. There were people there interested in being taught about the arts of memory. He was, however, betrayed to the Inquisition by one of his patrician hosts, Giovanni Mocenigo, who eventually provided the only serious, admissible 'evidence' against him. Mocenigo in one letter claimed Bruno was possessed by the Devil – *indemoniato* – and thus was a great danger; though Bruno later claimed that Mocenigo had behaved in such a way as he believed that he had not been taught the arts of memory well enough. Mocenigo may have been angered that Bruno was overattentive to his wife. Bruno was imprisoned by the Holy Office until February 1593. Mocenigo's case against him (the sole basis of the first investigation) included accusations that Bruno had erroneous opinions on the Holy Faith, on Christ (*un tristo*, a rogue, but also a *mago*, magus), the Trinity, Christ's divinity and incarnation, on transubstantiation and the Mass; that he did not believe in the Virgin's virginity, that he believed the world to be eternal, and that there were no infinite worlds that God would maintain; that souls created for the work of nature passed from one animal to another; and that he wanted to participate in divinatory arts. Some others gave evidence supporting these accusations; but the Venetian tribunal showed this was all hearsay, not from listening to Bruno.[83] In answering the charges over various sessions, Bruno told the court much about his life and travels. He made admissions from enjoying the company of women (if not to the extent of Solomon)[84] to having books printed under false imprints. He admitted that he had not overcome doubts about the incarnation, that he could write and speak of matters contrary to faith, but not in true opposition, and speak philosophically, and that he had read forbidden books by Melanchthon, Calvin, Luther and other heretics. Other allegations by Mocenigo he strongly denied, such as discussing theological matters with heretics, or denigrating the sacrament of penance (though he had not himself confessed for sixteen years, and had been refused absolution twice); he claimed to be orthodox over the immaculate conception.[85]

Bruno at times could address the tribunal as if talking to philosophers in Oxford, Paris or Wittenberg, as when answering about infinity, Egyptian Hermeticism and whether the Christian Cross derived (or was 'stolen') from the Egyptian cross.[86] Based on Bruno's formal set of denials, but some recantations, the Venetian tribunal headed for a verdict of salutary penances. However, Roman inquisitors, led by Cardinal Santoro (who may have known Bruno – adversely – in Naples in the 1560s), had other ideas. Having received a copy of the full transcript of the Venetian process, they demanded Bruno be sent to Rome. Initially the Venetian Senate and Collegio declined permission, declaring the local inquisitorial system exercised good justice. However, a papalist faction eventually secured a reversal and a vote for Bruno to be sent to Rome, on the grounds that he was a Neapolitan and not a Venetian. He finally arrived in Rome under escort in February 1593, to be imprisoned in the Tor di Nona prison (not the Palace of the Inquisition).

The lengthy process that followed was governed partly by new accusations which needed to be analysed in Venice and Rome. Many of these came from highly dubious cell-mates in both cities, one being executed and another sent to the galleys before Bruno's case was completed. The evidence of the mentally unstable Capuchin Celestino Arrigoni da Verona, a former prisoner in Venice with Bruno, provided a particularly desirable second witness statement for the Roman tribunal's purposes. The decision to investigate Bruno's writings in 1594 produced two years of delay. The resulting new charges rested largely on reading his *Ash Wednesday Supper*, which contained allusions to Copernicanism, not on the more dubious 'Heroic Frenzies' or 'The Expulsion of the Triumphant Beast', copies of which were not traced! The lengthy final trial against him reflected desires to understand what he believed (or did not), what influenced him and whom he had influenced; but also keenness by some to secure his recantation and an avoidance of a death penalty. Indeed, the leading inquisitor at the Roman tribunal was *commissario* Alberto Tragagliolo, judged to be fair and sympathetic, and keen to reach a compromise – recantation and minor punishment.[87] In this he was backed by Cardinal Roberto Bellarmino; he tried to simplify the situation by reducing the headings to eight propositions, which he hoped or expected Bruno would recant. Bellarmino also probably forestalled the use of torture recommended by certain consultants.

Bruno dithered over what to admit, hinted he might abjure in full to secure a light sentence, but ultimately did not cooperate enough with those wanting him to admit crucial errors. Bruno was reluctant to accept the soul as 'a form of the body in itself and essentially'; and he still had doubts about the value of confession and penance. Bellarmino took these doubts to indicate adherence to the obscure heresy of Bishop Novaziana (or Novatian, anti-Pope, AD 251–68).[88] In September the Roman Congregation finally decided Bruno was an impenitent heretic and deserved death. But still the more emollient inquisitors tried to persuade Bruno to make a deal (as Galileo was to do). They lost, and in January 1600 Giordano Bruno was handed over to the secular authorities following Clement VIII's personal pronouncement: he was to be burned naked at the stake, in public, without prior quick strangulation or beheading. On 17 February Bruno was executed thus, apparently turning his head away from the proffered crucifix. According to later comments Bellarmino was deeply saddened by this outcome, which affected his handling of Galileo in 1614–16.

The official final condemnation of Bruno does not survive, but a witness report recorded later from memory (by Kaspar Schoppe, recently converted from Lutheranism) said that the fourteen accusations indicated Bruno was condemned in public for theological heresies and magical practices, believing in many worlds; that Christ was not God, but a magus and deceiver; that the Holy Spirit was the world's soul; that demons would be saved; and that Holy Scripture was a dream. Bruno's public condemnation was not linked to Copernicus or the new science, even if his *Ash Wednesday Supper* defended Copernicanism.[89] However, Cardinal Santoro may have treated the whole range of accusations made in private against Bruno as an encyclopaedia of all the issues the Holy Office had to confront in this period.[90] High-profile public execution under the Roman Inquisition became rarer and rarer thereafter, and more secretly implemented death sentences also declined in number.

The fate of a fellow prisoner (since May 1594) and a former correspondent with similar views would have alarmed Bruno while his writings were being investigated. On 5 July 1597 the Florentine Francesco Pucci was decapitated in a Roman prison, and his body then burned in Rome's Campo dei Fiori. Studying in Paris and converted to Calvinism, Pucci had later inclined towards Fausto Sozzini; Pucci studied philosophy in Oxford and in the 1580s, like Bruno, had been very interested in supernatural visions, in astrology and alchemy, associated with John Dee and Edward Kelley in London, and Dee again in Prague. In 1587, supposedly inspired by the angel Uriel, Pucci had abjured before the papal nuncio (Filippo Sega) in Prague. Back in Paris he supported Henry of Navarre's politico-religious policies. Pucci himself was hoping to persuade the Pope to accept his ideas about an ecumenical reconciliation of the faiths. Travelling to Rome for this purpose in 1594, he was arrested on Cardinal Santoro's orders after Santoro had heard from the Florentine inquisitor about Pucci's book *De regno Christi*, which he considered had a heretical flavour, though it was dedicated to Bellarmino. All of Pucci's books were 'indexed', and he was condemned as an impenitent and relapsed heretic, having refused the chance to abjure in December 1596. His fate was then settled more quickly because he unequivocally refused to be treated as 'relapsed', he lacked supporters at the papal court, and Santoro seemingly felt no charity towards this peace-loving admirer of Henri IV.[91]

Another famous prisoner who shared some of Bruno's characteristics, behaviour and ideas, but who escaped the death sentence, was Pucci's cell-mate, the utopian philosopher Tommaso Campanella. Similarly a renegade Dominican from the south (Calabria), he had first been accused of heresy in Naples, and condemned to confinement in a Calabrian Dominican house. He fled to northern Italy, did not offend openly in doctrine, and studied medicine in Padua where he started a friendship with Galileo (1592). However, in 1593 he was arrested and extradited to Rome for holding religious discussions with a Jewish convert who had allegedly relapsed. Campanella abjured in S. Maria sopra Minerva in 1595. He returned to Calabria, where he was accused of leading a plot against the Spanish to turn Calabria into a religiously and politically reformed republic, as outlined in his utopian book *Città del Sole* (*City of the Sun*). Tried for heresy and treachery by a mixed church–state tribunal in 1601, he repeatedly suffered torture (the *veglia*), which apparently drove him mad – or he very convincingly acted it. The testimony of one gaoler that he was sound in mind was not deemed enough. This saved him from the death sentence, but he remained a prisoner until 1626 under grim prison conditions (in S. Elmo, then in the Castel Nuovo). However, he was able to write new works, especially after 1608, including a thirty-volume *Theologia*. He was finally released in Naples, only to be imprisoned in Rome's Palace of the Holy Office in 1626 – under mild conditions. Despite his fear of death prophecies, Urban VIII favoured Campanella, an expert in prognostication, and released him in 1629. In 1634 another anti-Spanish plot (supposedly led by Campanella's pupil Domenico Pignatelli, a Dominican) was revealed, and Campanella's extradition to Naples was requested. The Pope refused, and Campanella was enabled to flee to Paris, where he died in 1639 in a Dominican house fully reconciled with the Church, having advocated a universal monarchy under the leadership of France.[92]

Galileo and the Inquisition

Galileo Galilei's interactions with the Roman Inquisition have been a greater and more publicised topic of dispute than anybody else's – frequently misunderstood, and still hotly debated. Since much is available readily in English (including the key documents), my discussion here will be compact, especially on the better known aspects. I will concentrate on what was typical and in the inquisitional style, and what was unusual about his treatment, from 1590–1 when inquisitional interest in him started until he was 'tried' and his *Dialogue on the Great World Systems* was condemned in 1632–3. By the standards of the time and treatment of some others, he could have suffered much worse than being kept under house arrest.[93]

The long-running interest in Galileo was without any dire consequences for forty years. This reflects the controversial nature of his philosophical, scientific and religious views that could offend orthodox Thomist Dominicans and later less orthodox Jesuits. It also reflects the support he managed to win from the Venetian Republic, the grand dukes of Florence, some Jesuit mathematicians, the Roman Academy of the Lynxes, and leading cardinals like Bellarmino and Maffeo Barberini (until personally offended in 1631–2 when Pope Urban VIII). Galileo's reception and treatment reflect conflicting views at the heart of the Church, within and between the two inquisitorial congregations, over philosophical and religious interpretation and analysis.

Galileo's first subjection to inquisitorial interest in Florence in 1590–1 remains obscure, though his mother may have reported him due to his irreligious conduct and immorality. In 1604 denunciations against him in Padua (where in 1592 he had become professor of mathematics) were more serious. An amanuensis, Silvestro Piagnoni (or Pagnoni), who had lived in Galileo's house and left indebted, denounced him 'to clear my conscience and at the command of my confessor' for casting horoscopes, seeing his whorish mistress (*puttana*) rather than going to Mass, reading Aretino's published *Letters* and keeping company with Cesare Cremonini, professor of natural philosophy at Padua University since 1590.[94] Cremonini was the main target of the 1604 denunciations against Galileo, and the Accademia dei Ricoverati (Sheltered) they had founded. Cremonini had been tried in 1599 for propagating Pietro Pomponazzi's theories about the soul's mortality (as expressed in his *De immortalitate animarum*, 1526). Repeated accusations of this kind (as later in 1607, 1608, 1611, 1619, 1626) did not prevent Cremonini serving as professor until 1629, thanks to the protection of the Venetian Senate. He also maintained the outward show of religious orthodox observation. The Roman Inquisition's pleas for further action were ignored.[95] In 1604 Galileo had the same protection, and the inquisitor was discouraged from further enquiries; Galileo benefited from inquisitorial vicar Cesare Lippi, a Franciscan professor of metaphysics who helped him measure a supernova.[96] When Galileo was based in Tuscany the Roman Congregation, while vainly pursuing Cremonini, in 1611 asked for Galileo to be scrutinised in Pisa and Florence. Friends warned him that the Roman Inquisition was trying to entrap him over his theories of the earth's motion.[97]

The next stages are well known. Opposition to Galileo in Florence from some Dominicans grew, especially after the publication of his *Letters on Sunspots* (1613), culminating in Tommaso Caccini's public sermon on 21 December 1614 (on the Book of Joshua), in which he attacked Galileo and other mathematicians for contradicting the Bible; a charge he repeated in Rome in March 1615. According to Caccini, Galileo had challenged the Joshua text, 'Sun stand still upon Gideon... and the Sun stood still'; he believed the sun to be motionless, while his disciples were saying such things as 'God is sensuous because there are in him divine senses', and 'the miracles said to have been made by the saints are not real miracles'.[98] Meanwhile the Dominican Niccolo Lorini had written from Florence to Cardinal Paolo Emilio Sfondrati (member of both congregations), denouncing Galileo's *Letter to Castelli*, a copy of which he sent. This launched investigations in Florence (questioning persons named by Caccini over what Galileo might have said and taught), and in Rome over his actual writings. The key points are that Galileo was never formally questioned, or charged. Inquisitorial enquiries in Florence were perfunctory, and tended to reveal his accusers as ignorant.

In Rome Galileo's writings and his views on the heliocentric system were scrutinised by *consultores* to the Holy Office. On 24 February 1616 eleven of them, with very varied backgrounds, signed a condemnation of two propositions supposedly advocated by Galileo: (1) 'The sun is the centre of the world and completely devoid of local motion'; this was 'foolish and absurd in philosophy, and formally heretical since it explicitly contradicts in many places the sense of Holy Scripture, according to the literal meaning of the words and according to the common interpretation and understanding of the Holy Fathers and the doctors of philosophy'; (2) 'The earth is not the centre of the world, nor motionless, but it moves as a whole and also with diurnal motion'. They all applied the same verdict to this, and added 'in regard to theological truth it is at least erroneous in faith'.[99] Paul V accepted this verdict the next day, and instructed Cardinal Bellarmino to warn Galileo to stop making such propositions. On 26 February Bellarmino issued his now famous warning, or 'Special Injunction', 'henceforth not to hold, teach, or defend in any way whatsoever, either orally or in writing' these propositions – otherwise proceedings would be started. An inquisitional minute of 3 March indicated that Galileo had acquiesced; that Copernicus' *On the Revolutions of the Heavenly Spheres*, and a defence of the Copernican hypothesis by Galileo's Carmelite supporter Paolo Antonio Foscarini (who argued that Scripture supported the heliocentric interpretation), were prohibited and suspended. Copernicanism was not declared heretical. The dominant Cardinal inquisitor, Giangarzia Millini, was a protector of Foscarini according to a friend of Galileo's in Rome.[100] This suspension order would be published by the Master of the Sacred Palace. Galileo's correspondence to friends and contacts indicates he was fairly relaxed about this outcome, and was receiving direct and indirect encouragement from on high to continue, including at a friendly audience with the Pope on 11 March. Rumours began to circulate, however, that Galileo had been tried and condemned in Rome. Bellarmino then did something extraordinary. He issued a 'Certificate' on 26 May, declaring this not to be the case, and that Galileo was being slandered by these rumours; he had not had to abjure, had not had penances imposed, but was merely warned that the Copernican doctrine was 'contrary to Holy Scripture, and therefore cannot be defended or held'. This certificate was a key document (Exhibit B) in the 1633 'trial'.[101] It should be stressed that as a mastermind behind the activities – and inaction – of the Inquisition and the Congregation of the Index, Bellarmino was not averse to modern, on-going scientific investigations, and saw himself as an amateur astronomer. In a famous letter to Foscarini of 12 April 1615, which he expected would be conveyed to Galileo, he made it clear that he could envisage biblical interpretation changing (as over the flat earth view). However, better proofs for a heliocentric interpretation were needed, enquiry or hypothesising on the basis of appearance could continue, provided a Copernican-type view of the universe was not upheld as 'true' in all senses. 'Your Paternity and Mr Galileo are proceeding prudently by limiting yourselves to speaking suppositionally, and not absolutely, as I have always believed that Copernicus spoke.'[102] Bellarmino's unease over Bruno's extreme fate in 1600 may have encouraged him to avoid a crisis over Galileo in 1615/16, and instead make him behave circumspectly.[103]

While subsequent warnings to Galileo, under papal instruction, were more restrictive, he was aware of Bellarmino's open-mindedness. This was shared in part by others like Maffeo Barberini, who welcomed Galileo's 1613 *Letter on Sunspots* and who on becoming Pope Urban VIII in 1623 had friendly talks with him, encouraging the hypothesising about rival astronomical theories.[104] These attitudes may have encouraged Galileo to be more daring in his later speeches and writings, and forget that other inquisitorial officials might be less benign and open-minded. Although he did not encounter serious trouble until 1632, adverse Church leaders within and outside the Inquisition were vigilant scrutinisers of his publications, notably *The Assayer* (*Il Saggiatore*), as he was warned in 1625. The leading Jesuit mathematician, Orazio Grassi, wrote a powerful response to the *Assayer*; and it was also denounced to the Inquisition, possibly by other Jesuits.[105] Two anonymous reports recently found in the Index archive analysed this book for what it said about the movement of atoms rather than the earth, and its implications for eucharistic doctrine on transubstantiation. These reports have fuelled a debate that these implications were the 'real' reason for curbing Galileo when he presented the opportunity. It would be better to try Galileo for disobedience over injunctions and how the *Dialogue* was published, and for an unbalanced support of the heliocentric theory (a debate already in the public domain), rather than risk airing a far more damaging issue concerning transubstantiation, which few knew about or understood yet. Despite the rules of secrecy, a trial of a high-profile figure like Galileo would generate leaks and rumours. These reports may have been prepared with a view to prosecution, but withdrawn on papal orders, when a safer line of attack presented itself.[106]

As already indicated, the procedures and processes leading to the licensing and publication, in Florence, of Galileo's *Dialogue* were complex, and abnormal. The angered Pope decided that Galileo's behaviour, and his writings, should be investigated in Rome. The Pope had fallen out with his secretary Ciampoli, seemingly believing he had plotted with Galileo to satirise him through the '*Simplicio*' character in the *Dialogue*; he had 'put "the medicine of the end" [the Pope's view] in the mouth of the fool and in a place where it could only be found with difficulty', as a commission report in June 1632 later put it.[107] This may have affected the decision that Galileo's investigation should be handled by the Inquisition, not the Congregation of the Index, thus leading to a *processo* in Rome. Pleas by Galileo's supporters that given his age and illness he should be questioned in Florence were rejected by the inquisitional meeting presided over by the Pope in September 1632. So Galileo travelled 'voluntarily' (with a threat of imprisonment if he did not), but due to illness he did not arrive in Rome until 13 February 1633, where he stayed with the Florentine ambassador, Francesco Niccolini.[108]

The questioning of Galileo started on 12 April 1633, probably with the intention of having a brief proceeding leading to a rapid confession and repentance; and silence on key issues.[109] It was affected by standard consultation reports on the *Dialogue*, and by the discovery in the Holy Office archives of a document, now called the 'Segizzi Injunction'. This supposedly indicated that on 26 May 1616, following Galileo's meeting with Cardinal Bellarmino and receiving his admonition, Father Commissary Michelangelo Segizzi (or Seghizzi), on instructions from the Pope and the entire Holy Office Congregation,

> ordered and enjoined the said Galileo, who was himself still present, to abandon completely the above mentioned opinion that the sun stands still at the center of the world and the earth moves, and henceforth not to hold, teach, or defend it in any way whatsoever, either orally or in writing; otherwise the Holy Office would start proceedings against him. The same Galileo acquiesced in the injunction and promised to obey.

Although this document has often been declared a later fabrication, it can be seen as an authentic type of inquisitional document (*imbrevatura*) from 1616, possibly created by Segizzi when he was unhappy at Bellarmino's leniency and friendliness towards Galileo.[110] Segizzi might have been providing a record of what *should* have happened following orders from the Holy Office – *if* Galileo had been obstinate.

Alerted by Ambassador Niccolini that he had to answer the Segizzi injunction, Galileo upset the inquisitorial strategy when he produced his counter-document, Bellarmino's 'Certificate' of 26 May 1616 (Exhibit B, as noted above). The recorded proceedings show confusion on Galileo's part – whether problems with his memory or deceit in the steps that led to his securing permission to publish the *Dialogue* – but also confusion among the tribunal members over the injunction and the certificate and what to mention in accusation and as an agreed abjuration. The consultants' reports, while providing justification for having the publication and dissemination of the *Dialogue* suspended, and accusing the author of heretically and disobediently holding the Copernican theory, were not ideal for a thundering condemnation and heavy penalty. The three consultants were an interesting mix. Father Agostino Oreggi, Jesuit trained, the Pope's personal theologian, was happy to separate theology and physics, was a specialist on the Eucharist, and not a known opponent of Galileo. The Theatine Zaccaria Pasqualigo was another expert on the Eucharist and hostile towards the Jesuits then in Rome. Melchior Inchofer was a leading Jesuit mathematician; he produced the most damning verdict on Galileo's *Dialogue*. Their recorded reports were confined to the *Dialogue*, and whether he had disobeyed instructions. As with Giordano Bruno under Bellarmino, the tribunal avoided throwing the book at Galileo. The consultants almost certainly read more of Galileo's work than those on Bruno's tribunal, and could have concocted more serious charges, as over his atomism, had they chosen. The selection of this mixed trio might suggest that key figures were not intent on a major condemnation of Galileo, instead following a pro-Galileo agenda to concentrate on his disobeying an injunction by upholding the views of Copernicus. This would enable a quick trial, with minimal trouble for Galileo, who could not be totally exonerated given the public scandal over the *Dialogue* and the animosities it aroused.[111]

Among others the Pope's nephew, Cardinal Francesco Barberini, had sympathy for Galileo, having earlier advocated a mere emendation of the *Dialogue*, and a 'trial' by the Congregation of the Index, not the Holy Office. Barberini forbad the threat of torture at one point, and in May indicated to Niccolini that he was aiming at a sentence of light penances:[112] essentially plea-bargaining processes designed to get Galileo to make some admissions over advocating Copernicanism, agree to a degree of silence on other matters, and receive a comparatively light sentence. Indications of bargaining appear in a letter of 28 April 1633 from Commissary General Fra Vincenzo Maculano da Firenzuola to Cardinal Barberini, with the Pope party to this: 'I proposed a plan, namely that the Holy Congregation grant me authority to deal extrajudicially with Galileo.' 'The Tribunal will maintain its reputation; the culprit will be treated with benignity, and whatever the final outcome, he will know the favour done to him.' 'He could be granted imprisonment in his own house.' After some deliberation this authority was granted, but Galileo did not cooperate as much as had been was hoped; he declined an immediate indication of his 'intention' and confession, which could have ended the case within days.[113]

In contrast to the treatment of Bruno and Campanella, that of Galileo was mild. He resided in the Tuscan Embassy until questioning started, then in the prosecutor's own apartment in the Palace of the Inquisition, not in the prison cells; and he was allowed his personal servant. This situation meant that secrecy could not be maintained, the Roman world would soon know what was afoot, which encouraged a speedy resolution, in contrast to the Bruno case. The Pope did order a formal threat of torture on 16 June, to investigate quickly Galileo's 'intentions', when Galileo seemed to upset the bargain. Then on 21 June Galileo said he wrote what he did because he thought he was free to debate the two world systems, 'deeming only to be doing a beneficial service'; 'I do not hold this opinion of Copernicus, and I have not held it after being ordered by injunction to abandon it. For the rest, here I am in your hands; do as you please.' He was informed as follows: 'And he was told to tell the truth, otherwise one would have recourse to torture.' He answered: 'I am here to obey, and I have not held this opinion after the determination made, as I have said.'[114]

The sentence on Galileo, 22 June 1633, pronounced: 'you have rendered yourself according to this Holy Office vehemently suspect of heresy'. This was the second level of condemnation, below formal heresy, and was for holding and believing a doctrine, false and contrary to divine and Holy Scripture. The inquisitors had introduced the idea of heresy at a late stage, possibly illegitimately, through a distorting 'Summary Report'. The 1616 rulings had not judged Copernicanism heretical, only false. This was breaching the bargain, making the verdict more serious.[115] Galileo would be absolved if he abjured 'with a sincere heart and unfeigned faith'. His *Dialogue* would be prohibited by public edict. He was condemned 'to formal imprisonment in this Holy Office at our pleasure', and the recitation of seven penitential psalms weekly for three years. 'We reserve the right to moderate, change, or condone wholly or in part' the sentences. He duly abjured the same day. Whether he was really surprised and shocked at the formal prison sentence, or knew it would be modified, has been debated. Ten cardinals of the Holy Office were present when the sentence was issued on 22 June, but three did not sign: cardinals Gasparo Borgia, Laudivio Zacchia and Francesco Barberini. Nor did the Pope append a signature. This last omission, and the fact that the Congregation of the Index had not issued the prohibition, was noted by René Descartes in a letter to Marin Mersenne in February 1634. It implied that the anti-Copernican stance was not a matter of faith, and attitudes might change, though for a quiet life Descartes would abstain from writing on this topic.[116]

Galileo was released from the Palace of the Inquisition within two days, to the Tuscan ambassador. Although a petition to be allowed to return to Florence under house arrest was refused, he was told he could serve house arrest in Archbishop Ascanio Piccolomini's palace in Siena, supervised by a friend who had backed the *Dialogue* on first reading. There Galileo could recover his health, write to his illegitimate daughter Sister Maria Celeste and utilise a major library for writing what became *The Discourses on the Two New Sciences*. By December

1633 he was allowed to return to his villa at Arcetri outside Florence, close to his daughter in a convent where he was permitted to visit her occasionally, including to see her as she lay dying (March 1634). Officials of the Inquisition in Florence and Rome regularly discussed his confinement and changing conditions, sometimes being liberal, sometimes petty. He could read, write, receive and send correspondence and gifts. Some visitors were allowed after vetting, though topics of conversation might be vetoed. John Milton visited him, as 'a prisoner of the Inquisition'. One correspondent in 1635 (not ignorant of his recent career) was the leading female painter Artemisia Gentileschi, who asked him to help her get payments out of the Medici, just as he had helped her years before. He could go to Mass. In March 1638 Cardinal Antonio Barberini (the Pope's brother) sanctioned his visits to his house in Florence to see doctors, though the Florentine inquisitor was to prevent him moving about the city, or receiving visitors who might have 'discussions about his damned opinion on the motion of the Earth'. Galileo might have been wryly amused that this same Cardinal was ensuring that Caccini's *Ecclesiastical History* was amended. As blindness crept up on Galileo, he completed the *Discourses*, for publication by Elzevier in Leiden in 1638, with a licence from a Jesuit in Vienna. Thus Galileo may be judged to have received light punishment, given what might have been.[117]

Immediately after the 1633 verdict, a frenzied hunt for copies of the *Dialogue* ensued in many cities, with the aid of local inquisitors and bishops; this was the nearest equivalent to the chase for vernacular Bibles in the late 1590s. Officials of the Inquisition were to notify professors of philosophy and mathematics, and warn against perpetuating the ideas of Galileo and Copernicus. Experts were refused licences to read the *Dialogue*. Some pro-Galilean teachers were dismissed, as in Rome and Florence, from the Pious Schools (*Scuole Pie*) run by the Order of Scolopians for poor pupils. However, the Holy Office, judging by Cardinal Antonio Barberini's correspondence, was none too happy with many local inquisitors (such as those in Florence, Ferrara, Faenza, Como and Pavia) for showing insufficient enthusiasm in chasing books and teachers.[118]

The impact of Galileo's condemnation has been contentiously debated ever since. Tuscans declined to panic. The unfortunate inquisitor who had sanctioned the *Dialogue*, Clemente Egidi from Montefalco, was forced to read out the sentence and Galileo's abjuration to an audience in the refectory of Santa Croce; nothing was added, nothing discussed, and no call was made for Florentines to endorse the Roman condemnation. From 1634 its academies elected Galileo's pupils to key offices and Galilean theses were presented at Pisa University. An Olivetan monk assembled Galileo's manuscripts for publication.[119] By the late 1640s Galilean ideas were again being promoted at the Pious Schools. His publications were smuggled back into Venice and Florence. Whatever the initial worries of Descartes and Mersenne, condemnation in

Rome led to the enthusiastic promotion of Galileo's and similar ideas abroad, especially in Protestant countries. Italian scientists like Giovanni Alfonso Borelli could work their way around the condemnation, as by discussing celestial mechanics in terms of Jupiter and its satellites. However, one could argue that scientific leadership in this area shifted north. Where initially Copernicus had been more of a worry to Protestant biblical literalists than to Catholic theologians and philosophers, the public fuss over Galileo by the Roman Church may have encouraged Protestants perversely to take up his condemned ideas.[120]

Venetian Censorship: Politics, Licentiousness and Liberty

Under normal circumstances the Venetian Republic and the Church were overtly fairly cooperative over book production and censorship. Compromises were needed on both sides. Through the period Venice was the prime book producer, serving much of Italy and further afield with all kinds of literature, both academic and popular. Some Venetian printers were ready to provide works to suit Protestant interests (abroad, but also in the city). The secular authorities were prepared to join in condemning to death a few booksellers who were multiple offenders as traders in heretical works. Since some of these works could subvert the established order, political and social, in Venice, the government was prepared to help control such trade and production. But it did not wish to damage economic interests too much. Tension developed when after the Council of Trent the Papacy tried to monopolise the printing in Rome of the major Catholic texts as they were provided in orthodox editions: the Vulgate Bible, Missal, Breviary. When such lucrative standard works were taken away from Venetian printers, their livelihoods were threatened. The resulting compromises led to Church and State operating monopoly and censorship procedures, but without full rigour.[121] Cases against people possessing prohibited books were proportionately higher in Friuli, Belluno and Feltre than under the Venetian tribunal (which also covered the university city of Padua), with its considerably more numerous reading public.[122] This may be explained both by policies of turning a blind eye on the part of inquisitors, their staff and secular assistants on the tribunal, and by a reluctance to denounce neighbours, with worldly wisdom prevailing in the desire to disguise reading and avoid trouble.

The Interdict crisis of 1606/7 brought to a head some long-running confrontations between the Venetian Republic and the Papacy, especially over taxation of clergy, and the alienation through testaments of property into clerical possession, so depriving the State of taxes; and concerning lay jurisdiction over clerical crime. More recently in 1605 Pope Paul V had annoyed the Republic by wanting to test in Rome its top nominee as candidate for the Patriarchate (Francesco Vendramin), for his theological competence, before ratifying its choice. The immediate trigger for the crisis was the arrest by secular magistrates of three notorious offenders claiming clerical immunity (between them accused of rape, parricide and poisonings), whom the Church courts had not arraigned. When the Republic refused Paul V's demand that the accused be handed over to ecclesiastical jurisdiction, he imposed an Interdict, requiring the suspension of religious services, and excommunicated the Doge and Senate. The city with most clergy's support largely ignored the Interdict (though it had some effect on the mainland in the form of a few more compliant bishops), and staged spectacular anti-papal processions. A war of words was launched through books, pamphlets and sermons, raising fundamental issues of the jurisdictional rights of Church and State, Papal Absolutism, secular sovereignty and liberty. The Jesuits were required by the Pope to defend the rights of the Pope to intervene in another state, which they did forcefully through key figures like Cardinal Roberto Bellarmino – though with some reluctance by some Jesuits who thought the Pope too irascible and undiplomatic. The Jesuits were consequently expelled from Venice. The Republic's case was most effectively made by the hugely erudite Paolo Sarpi, who held a doctorate from Padua University and was formerly Provincial and leading administrator of the old Order of Servites (which embarrassingly generally supported papal powers over secular states and princes in matters religious), for which he had taught theology and philosophy. He had contacts with leading philosophers and scientists, including Protestants, throughout Europe, but he had also been a friend of Bellarmino in Rome. He was interested in the early history of the Church before Roman papal power was developed, which provided ammunition for his attacks.[123]

The Interdict debates and propaganda had implications for political theory across Europe. This brought complications over censorship for the Venetian inquisitor. He was in no position to censor works in favour of the Republic which challenged papal authority. The assistants on the tribunal were strictly warned by the Senate that their duty was to the Republic alone.[124] The Senate then appointed five theologians (later increased to seven) to replace the inquisitor as censors for new pamphlets relating to the controversy. It did not take away all censorship from the inquisitor however, as suggested by Alvise Venier, a supporter of Paolo Sarpi. During the Interdict the Congregation of the Holy Office supplanted that of the Index for other censorship matters. According to cryptic diary notes for the Congregation of the Index, this body was back discussing problems of Venetian booksellers by July 1607 (the Interdict having been lifted in April).[125]

The controversy generated a huge number of publications that were beyond the capabilities of secular and clerical authorities to control. The atmosphere encouraged some readers to pursue certain older condemned works. After the crisis many denunciations were lodged with the Inquisition against patricians for reading works by Machiavelli which were officially condemned by both the Index and secular government. The pro-Republican pamphlets had publicised Machiavelli's hostility to papal controls, and printers had produced anthologies, his texts under false covers, and versions of his sayings and ideas in popular barber-shop literature, *Paternosters*.[126] In confronting the Venetian Republic Paul V and the Inquisition Congregation made strenuous efforts to have the local inquisitors elsewhere control individuals and written works supporting the Republic's stance against papal religious authority. The pamphlets circulated uncontrolled outside Venice, generating considerable debate, often detrimental to Church and papal authority – though some were pleased to see the Republic in trouble. The inquisitor in Pavia arrested a Milanese courier for 'speaking in favour of the Venetians during a conversation concerning the present controversies'.[127]

Surviving correspondence from Cardinal Arrigoni for the Holy Office, and one letter from the Master of the Sacred Palace, show regular dealings with the Bolognese inquisitor (Fra Paolo Vicari da Garessio) over the problem of books and pamphlets entering Bologna that favoured the Venetian cause and challenged papal authority, including a work by a French theologian questioning papal power, Jean de Gerson, and a tract from the Venetian Doge. Samples were sent to Rome of what had been discovered; the rest were to be burned.[128] The Cardinal was alarmed that prohibited books on this topic were found in nunneries; in dealing with them the inquisitor should work through confessors and preachers, who should secure the books, and avoid any publicity through a public *bando*. The Cardinal sent a copy of an edict stating the papal case, which the inquisitor should have published in Latin and Italian and displayed in all the usual places. The inquisitor was authorised to give licences to certain legal doctors and canonists from the university to read the *Conseglio* (Opinion) of Padua University in favour of the Venetian Signoria: 'to be able to reply and refute the said *Conseglio*. You are warned to concede licence to intelligent persons, and suitable for refuting the *Conseglio*.' At the same time the Cardinal sent the Pope's permission (*facoltà*) to know about Holy Office matters, previously given to the superiors of religious Orders.[129]

The complications of censorship, and control, in the environment of the Interdict may be seen as affecting a degree of rebelliousness, subterfuge, evasion among printers and booksellers in other cultural areas, and the promotion of libertarian and libertine literature. Insights into the situation, the inquisitors' problems and procedures can be gained by looking at two linked cases from 1648, against the printer Francesco Valvasense (denounced in February), and the bookseller Giacomo Batti (implicated in February and separately denounced in April).[130] Much controversial literature was being written, circulated and printed. Anticlerical and libertine tracts, writings on the mortality of the soul, fiction and poetry bordering on the obscene, were being produced under the influence of the Accademia degli Incogniti (Academy of the Unknown), founded in 1630 by Giovanni Francesco Loredan, whose nobility and prestige offered some protection to writers, printers and publishers. Loredan and the Accademia are probably best known for their involvement with Ferrante Pallavicino, a prolific member of the academy eventually tried by the Inquisition in Avignon, and brutally killed in 1644.[131] The academy also had connections with the famous literary nun Arcangela Tarabotti, who challenged the male patrician society that tyrannically condemned daughters and sisters to the hell of convent life when they had no vocation. Loredan and others of the Incogniti encouraged her writing and involvement in debate through letters, and discussion in the convent *parlatorio* (where visitors could speak to nuns behind grilles), though they could also produce attacks on her. Tarabotti was a key figure involved in the intense debate about the nature, worth and role of women that Venetian presses and writers had been leading since the mid-sixteenth century.[132]

Both Valvasense and Batti printed or sold works by members of the academy or their protégés. Francesco Valvasense from Friuli, now aged twenty-eight, had a printer's shop in the parish of S. Antonino, and was one of several printers working for Loredan and the Incogniti. Valvasense was denounced in February 1648 by a small-time printer of pamphlets, Matteo Leni from Brescia, who knew several of those working for Valvasense and accused him of being the real printer of an anonymous booklet (translated by Orazio Plata), *Che le donne non siano della stessa specie degli huomini* ('That women are not of the same species as men'). This had appeared in 1647, as if printed in Lyon.[133] Leni said many other writings were produced by Valvasense, without licence and under false imprints, including one about the war in Candia. Leni was not sure which bookshops sold such illegal publications, but claimed that Loredan had personally sold Plata's booklet for two *lire*. Leni subsequently pointed to Giacomo Batti, aged thirty-one, as a seller of this misogynist work, to which Tarabotti was to compose a lively analytical reply, *Che le donne siano della spezie degli uomini* ('That women are of the same species as men'), a defence of Eve and claim for female equality that was published under a pseudonym (Galerana Barcitotti) in 1651. She attacked Pallavicino both for antifemale attitudes and anti-papal views in his *Retorica delle puttane* (*The Rhetoric of Whores*).[134] The bookshops of Valvasense and Batti were then raided in 1648, and many unlicensed or prohibited books were found, including several by Pallavicino, and Giambattista Marino's *Adone*.[135] As a major publisher, Valvasense was seen to be the more serious offender, and he faced a long investigation. Batti, more a bookbinder and small-scale bookseller than a printer, had his case heard separately, and he was sentenced sooner.

In April 1648 Batti was separately denounced by a Giacomo Modena, who appeared before the Inquisition 'spontaneously', to clear his conscience and avoid condemnation by it. He claimed that one day he had been approached by somebody trying discreetly to sell a prohibited book, which turned out to be a copy of Giambattista Marino's *Adone*, a long baroque poem. He bought it to read out of curiosity, and kept it for some months, managing to read some of it but not all. He happened to meet the *commissario* of the Holy Office at the door of the San Domenico convent, and raised the issue of holding a prohibited book. He was naturally told to go to the Holy Office to clear his conscience, and he would have certain penances (specified) to undertake. Modena then embarked on a complicated and muddled story of illicit dealings, implicating Batti. Batti faced various sessions before the tribunal, questioned both about his own position and in relation to Valvasense.

Lengthy and complicated questionings of Batti and Valvasense followed. The procurator Antonio Canale seems to have been the prime mover in these cases, especially investigating the books stored by the pair, and finding witnesses among printers, though it is unclear how far he shared the actual questioning with the inquisitor, Giovan Battista Raimondi. These cases seem unusual in the extent to which *assistenti* (or *Savi*), notably Pietro Sagredo, are specifically recorded as playing active roles interviewing witnesses. This may have reflected a view that the printers' offences were more against the State than the Church, and better handled by noble laymen.[136] The assiduous questioning reveals much about the publication, circulation and sale of prohibited books, their purchasers and promoters and the evasion of Church and State controls. Problems about paper identification and fonts were revealed, making it harder to convict an accused of printing a particular work.[137] When questioned about dangerous books by Pallavacino, Batti tried (like other bookmen) to argue that he merely bound texts, and could not read or understand their content. Questioned about Pallavacino's *Retorica*, which contained a chapter 'That fornication is not a sin', and which has been interpreted as an attack on Jesuit rhetoric and mendacity, he commented (despite his earlier comment, above): 'I read no books'. Questioned about Pallavacino's *Corriero svaligiato* (*The Robbed Messenger*), an epistolary novel concerning gentlemen reading and commenting upon letters seized from a messenger, he responded: 'It contains heresies, but I don't know the quality of the heresies.' The inquisitor informed him it contained 'the worst heresies, maledictions against Popes and clerics, from which derive heresies, and praising the worst vice of sodomy many times'. It contained an outrageous attack on Urban VIII, on which nuncio Vitelli in 1641 had commented to the Doge and Collegio: 'I have seen other outrageous works, but this one wounds to an extraordinary degree... authors have been put to death for far less serious publications.... I read it in shock.'[138] Batti was not heavily punished for handling such dangerous works. He was found guilty as 'slightly suspected of heresy' for possessing and distributing prohibited books, and sentenced to three lashes from the rope. But on grounds of illness he was instead made to stand for an hour tied above St Mark's main door in Venice, a rope around his neck, candle in hand, and with a placard saying:

Giacomo Batti, bookseller, for having dared in this very Catholic city of Venice to keep in his shop and sell to others books printed without official permission, containing heretical and pernicious propositions contrary to our holy faith, and, in addition to this he is also a condemned prisoner.

This was followed by house arrest. Batti petitioned for release so he could work again for his extended family, but it is unclear at what point this was granted before he made an application to join his guild.[139]

As noted, Valvasense was deemed a more dangerous bookman, being a major publisher. He suffered longer in prison (pleading 'I find myself buried alive among the miseries of a Prison') while many witnesses were questioned, several of whom also implicated Loredan. Procurator Canale made Valvasense reveal a certain amount about Loredan's connections and activities. Loredan was, however, never arraigned. Valvasense's former employees (whom he had allegedly treated badly), when questioned in Padua and Vicenza, testified that they had helped him print the *Che le donne*, working at night with Valvasense as proof-reader. Many witnesses – noble, professional and artisan – defended him as a good man, and a victim of jealous rivals that included Matteo Leni.[140] Valvasense's own testimony provided a good picture to the tribunal of the variety of books he printed, including works in Hebrew, histories and the Rosary. He admitted to having many enemies – some of them because he did not frequent hostelries like other associates and admitted to falsifying imprints, as giving Gaeta for Venice as a location. He denied printing *L'anima di Ferrante*, and equivocated when questioned about the pamphlet on women, *Che le donne*.

On 5 February 1649 the tribunal gave its verdict that Valvasense was 'lightly suspect of heresy'; he had printed an *Oratione di Carlo Magno* which contained heresies, a *Frammentio storici* on the Candian war under a false name of printer and place (Bologna), and published *Fagotto* without licence. It was also seriously suggested that he had printed the *Che le donne*. All this indicated, they declared, that he believed it legitimate to print heretical books, and those containing propositions inimical to the Catholic faith; printed without the Holy Office's licences, so earning all the censures and penalties according to sacred canons. He had to abjure such heresies; if he did so, he would be absolved from excommunication. He abjured and was suspended from printing at the pleasure of the Holy Office, held in a sealed prison (*preggione serrata*) as deemed necessary; to have to say the Rosary every week for a year. Inquisitor Raimondi and the archbishop of Pisa signed the sentence. The next day Leni, the original delator, was sentenced to three strikes of the *corda*. In March Valvasense petitioned to be granted house arrest, and he was released on 23 March for a surety of 100 ducats, with two guarantors. In July he sent two petitions to be freed from house confinement, so he could support his family. He was also granted this, and allowed to resume working. He faced stringent straightened printing circumstances, but his family continued as important printers through the eighteenth century, specialising in the safer subject of music and *libretti*.[141]

The protection of Loredan and his academy could cover a more dangerous author being published in Venice: Antonio Rocco and his scandalously obscene *Alcibiade fanciullo a scuola* (*Child Alcibiades at School*, published 1650, though written about 1630). A pupil of Cremonini, and a Benedictine monk who became a lecturer on philosophy and moral philosophy in Venice, Rocco clearly debated the immortality of the soul. An anonymous denunciation to the nuncio in 1635 alleged he had preached that the grace of our Lord was in the carnal delight that man receives in the sex act. Several other denunciations followed. In November 1648 a physician from Udine denounced him there to inquisitor Giulio Missini, for discoursing on his sickbed about his soul being mortal, that he would die like an animal; that there was no Purgatory, and infidels could be saved. They discussed the merits of sexual acts, natural and sodomitical. Missini decided to make further enquiries, but no records of such survive. In July 1652 anonymous denunciations to a Cardinal and reported to the nuncio again accused Rocco of preaching about the soul's mortality, and living like an atheist. A 1647 decree of the Congregation banned several of Rocco's books.[142] Despite Rocco's reputation Loredan had been ready to edit and publish *Alcibiade*, having had the manuscript in his house for several years, and had it read to the academy. It had probably influenced Pallavicino's *La retorica delle puttane*.[143]

These cases suggest a considerable amount of illicit publishing and selling of a variety of controversial literature in Venice. Book control was difficult, especially when patricians were complicit. Inquisitors could be tenacious in eliciting information (true or false) but find it hard to pin charges to their satisfaction. The end punishments for bookmen, once petitions were accepted, might not be that severe. Key writers and promoters could escape unpunished, and even remain unquestioned after denunciations or allegations. The interference of the Roman Inquisition, direct or through nuncios, was also resisted. A degree of intellectual and cultural liberty – and libertinism – was preserved in the Republic.

The Enlightenment and Eighteenth-Century Struggles

Recent studies of the ACDF documentation for both congregations have added to our knowledge of the Catholic Church's attack on the Enlightenment and other new thinking in the later seventeenth and eighteenth centuries, beyond what was known to be on the Index and to have elucidated censoring procedures.[144] Patrizia Delpiano argues that '*governo*' is a more appropriate word than '*censura*' to indicate the changing policies and actions; to emphasise attempts, as society became more secularised, to orientate a public of readers (since it was so difficult to stop the flow of prohibited books) in desirable directions through a more dexterous use of communications. Prosecutions for possessing and reading prohibited books seemingly declined from the later seventeenth century, both in Italy and under the Spanish Inquisition, and this was treated more as a minor offence. It was punishable with salutary penances, such as fifteen to twenty days of penitential recitations for the five pains of Jesus Christ, and saying the Credo, as Antonio Dall'Occhio, inquisitor of Aquileia, suggested to a vicar dealing with a penitent reader in the late seventeenth century. Delpiano agrees with Adriano Prosperi that the Inquisition was now less a tribunal for heresy, more 'a tribunal for collective morality'.[145]

Although readers did not suffer much, the books were still heavily scrutinised. The obvious targets were new scientific theories that might encourage materialism and atheism, that would develop atomistic theories (found earlier, as noted, in the case of Galileo), undermining eucharistic ideas; arguments favouring individual thought that would undermine traditional authority and teaching by well-trained minds; freemasonry; challenges to state authority and order; but also a whole range of secular literature that might undermine Christian moral standards and further encourage licentiousness and lasciviousness. Most of the authors we now associate with the new thinking and writing were targeted, whether with total bans, or expurgations. It should be stressed that the Church faced a considerable literature of anticlerical and anti-curial attacks, from 'Catholic' Italians as well as Protestant and Catholic foreigners. These assaults took the form of traditionally lampooning clerical and conventual immorality; attacking conservative approaches favouring old Augustinian and Aquinan theology; attacking new philosophies, or increasingly stressing the need for individual 'freedom'; and increasingly from mid-century, demanding the separation of Church and State. In the last case influential political support was provided, whether from politically conservative Piedmont, or 'enlightened' rulers and reforming ministers in Lombardy, Tuscany and the Kingdom of Naples.[146] Neapolitan printers produced significant works in an anti-curial campaign, which Rome condemned, but found hard to keep out of Roman libraries and bookshops.[147]

Patrizia Delpiano particularly shows that inquisitorial censorship was very active through the period, especially reacting to works imported into Italy, notably from France. She challenges the view that the 'Enlightened Pope', Benedict XIV, significantly reduced controls: plenty of books were still publicly condemned and burned in the 1740s to the 1750s. A French translation (1730, Amsterdam) of Daniel Defoe's *History of the Devil* (1726) was burned in 1743 on the orders of the Inquisition, as it was judged a serious atheistic work. Benedict did admit that some past prohibitions had been excessive and unnecessary. Targets and methods changed. Benedict's regime also fostered self-censorship, with or without discourse between censors and authors (who if near Rome were allowed to defend their positions), and more reasoned approaches to controls over books, improving the quality of the judgements and regulation. Authorial attitudes towards suggestions for changes by censors and the Index of course varied; Baron de Montesquieu declined to change passages in his *Esprits des lois*, so it was prohibited in 1751. The leading Neapolitan scholar and reformer Antonio Genovesi accepted changes to his *Elementa metaphysicae* (Naples, 1743), so it was not 'indexed', and he cooperated with censors over the fourth volume in 1752. He was praised by the Congregation of the Index for his 'docility' and 'religious submission to the Church'.[148]

Under Benedict XIV, and with the new 1758 Index, the reading of vernacular Bibles was again licensed, provided the editions were approved by the Holy See itself. Prohibitions were removed against books that taught about the movement of the earth and the immobility of the sun, at the recommendation of the Jesuit Pietro Lazzeri (sometime professor, then librarian, at the Collegio Romano, and an active consultant for the Index), to avoid derision levelled at the Catholic Church. However, pleas to remove from prohibition key works by Francis Bacon, John Locke, Nicolas Malebranche and Samuel Pufendorf were turned down – as was the petition in favour of Galileo's *Dialogue*. Lazzeri, however, damned Count Giuseppe Gorani's *Il vero dispotismo* (1770), as impious, subversive, offensive to the ears, as not mentioning Christ, and defending Cesare Beccaria's principles against the death penalty. Gorani's book was privately praised by Beccaria's co-reforming friend Pietro Verri for 'a spirit of philanthropy and liberty'.[149]

In the eighteenth century the Congregation of the Index made the decisions on indexing fully or awaiting expurgation. They were based on often lengthy reports from outside censors in Rome (and two or three different ones might be involved); the main Holy Office decided on book burning; the Master of the Sacred Palace was active in issuing (or withdrawing) licences for reading 'prohibited' books. The censors were not mindless fools, and in more intellectual areas could have wide interests, respect some modern scientific developments, though share with other Church leaders the view that reading was a dangerous activity for less-educated laity, notably the youth and females more generally.[150] Several censors in the earlier eighteenth century belonged to the academy of Gli Arcadi, including for example those involved in the censoring of Thomas Burnet's works: *De statu mortuorum et resurgentium* (1720), censored in 1731, and *Telluris theoria sacra* (1681–89), censored in 1739. Here the leading censor was the long-lived Gianfrancesco Baldini, a Somaschian father from Brescia who, having studied theology in Venice, taught philosophy and theology in Rome, and studied numismatics. Burnet had expressed odd ideas on the concept of Purgatory, the complete separation of body and soul, and considered that the soul could think, had a natural conscience of good and evil, and was an incorporeal entity separate from incorporeal God. Hell was interior and not an external phenomenon. He denied transubstantiation. His *Telluris* was criticised for its deformed and monstrous doctrines of a fivefold development of the world from Chaos, ending with a millenarian world for the elect. These separate notions were not judged heretical, but misguided. However, the overall implication was an attack on the beatific vision, and that was heretical, so Burnet's writings should be banned. Baldini was also the leading censor (1734) of Jonathan Swift's *The Tale of a Tub* (1704), in a French version (*Le Conte du Tonneur*, 1734); Baldini thought that this satire on the three monotheistic religions should be burned for undermining all religions. He also censored (July 1738) Francesco Algarotti's *Newtonianesimo per le dame ovvero sopra la luce e i colori* (1737, supposedly published in Naples, but actually in Milan, without licence) for defending Galileo's heliocentrism, especially in Italian rather than Latin, and propounding the idea that the reality of the world, rather than Scripture, could solve the problems of the physical world. Doubtless the very title's target of educating women (*le dame*) was additionally offensive. Others saw Algarotti as morally corrupt, a danger to youth and a promoter of eroticised science, as when he happily described spermatozoa. He had links with Freemasons, such as Tommaso Crudeli in Florence.[151]

These examples illustrate the general points that the inquisitorial system of censorship and control increasingly targeted vernacular scientific and philosophical literature for a wider reading public, including women. Fictional works (often designated *romanzi*), prose and poetry, were seen as corrupting the young and the female. English writers were targeted from the 1730s, usually through French translations that took liberties with the original text, making it more offensive, as with Swift's *Tale of a Tub*. Samuel Richardson's lengthy *Pamela* (1740–1, and in French in 1742) was much attacked, triggered by the inquisitor in Parma alerting Rome (July 1743), having found a copy in a French bookman's collection. The official commentator classified it as obscene. A four-volume Italian translation appeared in Venice in the same year, 1744. It encouraged the seduction of young women by licentious youths. Richardson's later *Clarissa* (1747–8) encouraged 'the odious race of libertins', through the 'wicked and infamous' Lovelace. Novels projected the world of the *philosophes*, some of whom, like Voltaire and Jean-Jacques Rousseau, also contributed novels.[152] The 1760s witnessed the perceived increase in the impact of French *philosophes*, and native Italian contributors to the Enlightenment, the *illuministi*, who made their own propositions. The extent to which they were quickly or slowly condemned, and how, was partly linked to when they were perceived to be dangerous, and whether the publicity of condemnation would do more harm than good. Warnings, especially about fictional works in Italian, might attract purchasers from the clandestine market. The publicised condemnation and ordering of book burnings were often too slow to prevent some wide circulation.

Subsequent adverse decrees might simply whet the appetite of potential readers, and clandestine printers.[153] A burlesque anticlerical poem, *Ricciardetto* (published anonymously in 1738) was 'indexed' in 1739, and proved a bestseller; it had been written by Cardinal Niccolò Forteguerri (who died in 1735).

Book censorship might be governed by concepts of offensiveness far removed from old notions of heresy. For example, Cesare Beccaria's famous 1764 *Dei delitti e delle pene* (*On Crimes and Punishments*), which pungently attacked the use of torture and capital punishment, was 'indexed' in 1766 for using forbidden authors, offering propositions 'that offend religion, piety and Christian ears', and being dangerous because written in Italian. It had already received heavy criticism in Venice.[154] Judgements by censors that works offended Christian ears, or sounded bad (*male sonant*), were taken to mean that they bordered on heresy, though not actually heretical; and this was enough to have them prohibited. This was an attitude earlier backed by Carena's *Tractatus de officio sanctissimae Inquisitionis* (Cremona, 1641), and seems prevalent in the verdicts of the eighteenth century.[155]

The great French *Encyclopédie*, which promptly saw publication in Lucca starting in 1758, obviously challenged the Inquisition. Both congregations were involved and long debates were held, with several consultants from different Orders employed. The Congregation of the Index condemned it in December 1758, and that of the Holy Office in August 1759, later backed by a papal brief from Clement XIII in September. The consultants differed in their overall judgement, with some arguing for a *corrigatur* verdict, recognising that much of the content was very valuable. Intransigence triumphed, as led by the *commissario* of the Holy Office, Pio Sauli, and the Master of the Sacred Palace, Giuseppe Agostino Orsi, who condemned it for:

> the indifference in matters of religion, materialism, fatalism, deism, and unrestrained liberty of thought which are the disease of the present contagious season, and which, as experience shows, easily attacks every kind of person. To this epidemic disease born in countries infected by heresy, and especially in England, and then through many pestiferous books passed into France, and then Italy, although opposed by excellent preservatives, and antidotes in many notable volumes brought to light by persons armed with valour, doctrine, and zeal, the evil has not ceased ...

Other documents repeated the fears that this great work could eradicate religion itself. Proposals for an edition, concentrating on the technical articles and omitting the more philosophical or anticlerical parts, proved acceptable to members of the Congregation of the Index, but not the wider Holy Office participants.[156]

If the condemnations of offensive literature by the Inquisition increased in the mid-eighteenth century, along with greater attempts to secure local cooperation from other states as well as local inquisitors and bishops, the efforts became harder to enforce. It became more difficult to control the clandestine flow of books from France (and from the Netherlands through France), and Venice. The Master of the Sacred Palace, Tomasso Ricchini, lamented this fact in 1766, noting how diplomatic figures and officials in charge of the postal depots cooperated in the clandestine trade. Local inquisitors, as in Mondovi, Bologna or Pisa, bewailed the problems of checking bookshops and postal depots, and so preventing travellers evading customs inspections. The House of Savoy, while wanting strict political censorship, was resistant to Church power and controls, and from 1730s had curtailed inquisitorial censorship over production within the state. The state censorship that was then developed drove local authors to get books printed elsewhere, and then smuggled in. Turin also became a major transit route for Genevan and French books, aided by a network of printers and booksellers originally from Besançon and working in Geneva and the state of Piedmont. From Turin (which had thirty-five major importing bookdealers, *librai*, in 1759) the books went off to Milan, Pavia, Cremona, Reggio, Parma, Padua, Venice and Genoa, even Rome (where five Besançon booksellers have been recorded). So political works by Montesquieu or Voltaire, or fictional literature, entered Italian cities, evading border controls.[157]

Some possessors of prohibited books could still end up severely punished in the eighteenth century. Abbot Giovanni Battista Pinzi, brother of a poet, was charged with others in 1772 in Ravenna with atheism, which he had learned from 'bad books', and for dispersing 'a great quantity of pernicious French books'; unlike his co-accused (who appeared 'spontaneously') he remained impenitent. He was made to abjure publicly in Ravenna and was sentenced to life imprisonment, where he died within a year. His case induced the Roman Inquisition to issue further warnings about how such books and their disseminators could corrupt the weak.[158]

Two highly publicised cases of censorship coupled with harsh treatment of the authors brought the Papacy in general and the Inquisition in particular into international disrepute, and contributed to the demise of the Roman Inquisition. The first case was that of Pietro Giannone, author of the *Istoria civile del Regno di Napoli* (*Civil History of the Kingdom of Naples*), 1723, which asserted the rights of that kingdom against the Papacy, claiming feudal superiority, and attacked clerical privileges; it was published without ecclesiastical licence. It was at once put on the Index, benefiting its publicity, which was further helped by an English translation. Excommunicated by the archbishop and subject to personal abuse in the streets, Giannone decided to leave Naples and headed for Vienna. He spent some years writing and travelling but eventually fell victim to a combined campaign by Carlo Emanuele III of Savoy and Cardinal Alessandro Albani. Tricked while crossing from Geneva into Savoy to receive Easter communion, he was arrested in March 1736, ending up in prison in Turin. The Savoy government did not want to consign him to the Pope. Seeing religious recantation as a path to liberty, he arranged to present himself before an inquisitor 'spontaneously', make a confession and private abjuration. With the Roman Congregation's approval this was arranged with the inquisitorial vicar in Turin, who was first to quiz Giannone on his possible heretical intentions. In practice no real investigation followed, and the proceedings were designed to improve his confession. Neither inquisitorial vicar nor confessor was particularly competent legally. Giannone was awarded spiritual penances, having abjured *de vehementi* and been absolved. He should by the rules have then been released, as was his objective. But Cardinal Albani and the king did a deal that kept him in a fortress until his death in 1748, though he was able to write. He was a critic of the Index, of papal rule, but not of main Catholic doctrines, though others claimed he was a *calvinista*. His writings proved useful for those challenging Church authorities, and the *riformatori* of Padua University were ready to issue licences to read his works.[159]

The second case, that of Tommaso Crudeli, highlighted the growing fear of international Freemasonry, both among Church leaders and authoritarian regimes.[160] The first Italian lodge seems to have been that in Florence, opened in 1729. Although Spain and Portugal witnessed the early persecutions of Freemasons, it was in Florence that a much-publicised case was prosecuted. In 1737 claims were being made, according to public gossip, that Florence had between 2,000 and 14,000 adherents of Freemasonry (*liberi muratori*, or *des Massons*), with some eminent lay and religious supporters, and in June the Congregation received a report about the sect there from the Florentine inquisitor Antonio Ambrogi.[161] Such reports formed the background to Clement XII's Bull *In eminenti* of 28 April 1738, which condemned Freemasonry societies and their members as thieves and foxes in the Lord's vineyard; it ordered them to be prosecuted as heretics.[162] As secretary to the Florentine Lodge, Crudeli was arrested in May 1739 and became the scapegoat for the group, being the only one to be fully tried. Foreigners could flee, or be too influential to be targeted. Crudeli was a writer of sensual and erotic poetry. He was interrogated by the Franciscan inquisitor Paolo Antonio Ambrogi over many months, ending with eighty-nine charges against which he was allowed to make defences. He allegedly denied the validity of scholastic theology, was critical of confessions, and had for long mocked the cult of the Madonna of Impruneta, and said the Madonna should be buggered. In philosophical and religious discussions he expressed many errors against the faith, including stating there was no Purgatory or valid indulgences, that Christ had not given power to St Peter and his successors, that the Eucharist was not the body of Christ. He naturally had read prohibited books, including – he admitted – Gregorio Leti's *Life* of Paolo Sarpi and a translation of Lucretius (which he justified). He stressed in repeated appearances before the court that he had appeared before them 'spontaneously' and made certain admissions.[163]

Despite much support from Crudeli's friends (including among the English community and from the consul, Sir Horace Mann), and some state officials who were ready to countenance attempts to let him escape, and despite retractions by two initial denunciators, murky Church–State dealings worked against him, so he was condemned to perpetual imprisonment. On grounds of his ill-health this was changed later to strict house arrest (with a surety of 1,000 *scudi*) in his home town of Poppi, from which confinement he was released in April 1741. He died in January 1745 from the long-term effects of his imprisonment.[164]

Inquisitorial investigations and prosecutions of Freemasons occurred in Modena at the same time, and subsequently in Livorno, Venice, Udine (where links with magic and sabbats were alleged) and Genoa, while masonic writings were periodically 'indexed'. The London Lodge treated Crudeli as a secular martyr. The Crudeli case generated a considerable correspondence, between Florence and Rome, and from elsewhere. This reflects widespread interest in, and worry about, Freemasons in northern Italy, and the cooperation of local inquisitors in following the spread of the sect's popularity and influence. Within Tuscany the Crudeli episode fuelled calls for freedom of publication from Church control, the lessening of inquisitional activity, and finally contributed to the Inquisition's suppression in 1782. A collection of Crudeli's poems attacking the papal court, seen as helpful to the anti-papal campaign, was printed in Naples in 1746 and almost immediately 'indexed' – probably without much effect.[165]

This chapter has shown the complexity of censorship procedures through the period, which were made more difficult by the division of labours between the two congregations, the Master of the Palace at the centre, the local inquisitors and bishops in the provinces. Enthusiasm for inquisitorial control waxed and waned. Expurgation proved cumbersome, inefficient, and counter-productive; it delayed or inhibited compromise official editions, probably encouraging the markets for clandestine production or imports. Much evasion and subterfuge occurred. The capture of illegal books and detection of their illicit possession were haphazard, and the punishment of offenders variable. The human casualties among major thinkers were fewer than might have been expected; Bruno might have been saved, Galileo could have suffered worse; Campanella endured lengthy imprisonment; Giannone and Crudeli were partly just unlucky. The major casualties might be seen as the reading of vernacular Bibles, and the scientific work by Jesuits after the Galileo affair. The 'books never written', and the importance of self-censorship, are the major imponderables. By the mid-eighteenth century inquisitorial censorship was only spasmodically effective, and well-publicised excesses, as with Giannone and Crudeli, fuelled campaigns for suppression.

CHAPTER 8

INQUISITORS, ACCUSED AND WITNESSES

MODERN HISTORIANS OF THE INQUISITIONS HAVE MOSTLY DEVELOPED A MORE nuanced approach to both the surviving records of investigations, and what can be deduced from records about the relationships between inquisitors (and lesser officials), witnesses and the accused.[1] As the following extract exemplifies, we are no longer dealing just with a record of terms dictated by elite authority to fearful victims.

> Whoever has read a single inquisitorial *processo*, will never forget the initial question that the inquisitor puts to the *reo* (the accused, who must show he is innocent): if he knows, or imagines the reason he is there, the fault is of the accused. At this point, the accused can decide to confess, or to try to defend himself, to deny: but that question has already said that the judge knows. From the first struggles (*battute*), the dialogue between inquisitor and the questioned (*inquisito*) is a conflict, a test of force: especially a test of astuteness. Theological motivations are not lacking: the inquisitor is warned to take account of the nature of the adversary. The devil is the father of falsehood (*menzogna*). The inquisitor, if he wishes to battle with him, must renounce the forthrightness of doves, and learn vulpine astuteness. . . . In the rules of the game belong duplicity and the feigned benevolence of the inquisitor. The accused could at once collapse; but can also refuse to confess. With him one must weave a complicated spider's web. The accused must believe the inquisitor is good and merciful. . . . In the beginning of the process, the judge will use good words with him and pretend to know his faults but sympathise with him; so he requests only confession, and the names of those who taught him heresy.

Here a leading modern interpreter, Adriano Prosperi, combines his own view of much past practice with the guidance offered in Umberto Locati's *Judiciale inquisitorum* (Rome, 1568). Locati goes on to note tricks the inquisitor might use to secure confession: the initial use of comforting words, selective use of witness evidence, moving to threats of long imprisonment, the multiplication of questions to wear down the accused, trapping the accused in contradictions. The inquisitor might also place spies in the prison cell (few accused were in solitary confinement), including former friends of the accused who had already succumbed and confessed. Locati had been inquisitor in Pavia and Piacenza (where he had conducted a harsh campaign), before being made general commissioner of the Holy Office, and Pius V's confessor.[2]

The interactions between inquisitor and accused, and the games played between them, merit closer attention. The interactions were possibly not always as one-sided as Prosperi here stresses, while some inquisitors were not as ruthlessly manipulative as he implies. Some accused could play games to lessen the charges against them, and so the punishments. The dialogue and game-playing could be affected by outside considerations, undermining inquisitorial domination and severity.

Inquisitors' Questioning and Demeanour towards Accused and Witnesses

It bears repeating that the evidence recorded makes it easier to analyse the accused's side of the dialogue, since that is given as an approximation of the verbatim account, while the inquisitorial questioning was usually recorded as a third-person summary, if at all, and often in Latin. The tone of the questioning is hard to judge, whether very threatening or mildly enticing admission and confession – whether leading or open.

Witnesses might tell highly elaborate but improbable stories about themselves as well as others. Some such stories could be very damaging and be life-threatening. The inquisitors could show scepticism, especially when the topic was magic. In the case of Gostanza of San Miniato in 1594, we can detect her concocting a great scenario of the 'city of the Devil'. Because the notary spells out the line of questioning and adds some comments, we can see that her initial questioners, inquisitorial vicar Mario Porcacchi da Castiglione and episcopal vicar Tomasso Roffia, to be hardliners, convinced of the reality of the superstitious medical practice and sabbats, and ready to use torture from the beginning. When the Florentine inquisitor Dionigi da Costacciaro arrived and took over the interrogation, he questioned her well away from the torture room (unlike under vicar Porcacchi), showed some doubts about the veracity of her extravagant claims and tried to reduce her fear. All this may have induced her to withdraw her story of the Devil's world, and apologise to somebody she had named as an accomplice for lying about her from fear of torture. The inquisitor ensured her release and mere banishment from her home village.[3]

In a 1587 Venetian case Elisabetta Giantis gave an elaborate account of trying to entice a lover by magic (as taught by another woman). It involved casting beans, measuring a wall with salt to measure the heart (and so the lover's attitude to her), preparing a mixture including the heart of a bird (metaphor for the penis); then she was taught how to win her lover's heart. Saying 'I understand one must pay the Devil', she took a special candle (bought in the name of the Devil), and totally naked she shone the light to create a dark shadow of herself to make a shadow sister. This shadow sister was to go out dressed with power from Elisabetta and the Devil, to attract Elisabetta's lover, and magically bind his heart to her will. Having heard all this the inquisitor asked: 'Did you have faith and belief in all this witchcraft?' She replied: 'When I saw that my lover came I believed in the witchcraft and that the Devil could change his will. But when he did not come I did not believe it worked.' Her own lack of confidence led her to attribute success to the Devil, not her own attraction. The sceptical inquisitor gave her a chance to deny such belief in the Devil's work (and blame the woman who had taught her magic). But she endangered her position by stressing she believed the magic worked: 'I know that he came to me many times when I did that witchcraft.' She was sentenced to be pilloried and exiled for two years.[4]

Handling a Complex Denunciation: Cristina Collarina

A delator could hurl a whole range of accusations against somebody he disliked. The following case, though with no result, is cited at length because it illustrates also various points about following anonymous accusations, the inquisitorial questioning of witnesses, priorities between different charges and Christian–Jewish relations within Venetian society. Many accusations were made against Cristina Collarina in May 1625, whose anonymous accuser, acting as a good Catholic, was encountered in Chapter 3 (see p.71).[5] For him she was a most serious witch (*solennissima striga*), who cast beans and performed other diabolic deeds as part of love magic; she had sex with Jews, notably with Effrim (Ephraim) Bonforno, with whom she ate meat on Fridays and Saturdays, and went to the Ghetto. She continued sexual relations with another Jew with a black hat (*Capel negro*), called *il Dottore*. She ate meat in Lent without licence. This hellish woman had carnal relations with brothers Augustin and Giacomo Bazetta, and then she used *striganerie* to kill the first to enjoy better the other. She conjured up angels, Cherubim and Seraphim using diabolical words and writings, learned from Bonforno. She practised these things in her room, where she had a locked box above the bed to keep the secrets. Five potential witnesses were named (one man, Nicolo di Elmi; two single women, Caterina *padrona* of the butter and cheese shop, at Santa Maria Madalena, and Isabella *fiorentina*; and a married couple, Paula called la Mora, and her husband Zuane), noting which offences they might testify about. It was also indicated that a priest had some writings from Effrim, as Cristina's lover (*moroso*). Enough witnesses were clearly identifiable for the tribunal to follow up this anonymous denunciation, which alleged a murder.

The tribunal (nuncio, Patriarch [Giovanni Tiepolo], inquisitor and assistant Marco Antonio Cornelio) met on 15 May to read the denunciation, and decided to request information to assist proceedings. On 24 May the inquisitor was instructed to examine the witnesses, given the very secret complaint provided to him, send officials to Cristina's house and search the box near her bed. Formal meetings did not start until 2 December, when the first named witness, Nicolo di Elmi, aged fifty-five and an advocate, was questioned. He had known Cristina about three years, having sex with her because his wife was ill, but not for the last year, having been chastised by God. He had not seen her do witchcraft, but been told about it by the husband (now deceased) of a Caterina, named as a witness. He had advised Nicolo to give up Cristina because as a *striga* she had harmed their nephew. This couple had been Nicolo's clients. He had found a *cordella* (casting rope) in a bag of combs near Cristina's bed; when he questioned her about it she replied that she used it to tell whether things would go badly or not, and angrily she threw it in the fire. He showed the *cordella* outside the room to a Florentine woman, aged about forty, who rented a room (was she the named witness Isabella?). (Had he rescued the *cordella* from the fire?) Questioned, Nicolo then told about a Ferrarese Jew called Bonforno, aged thirty-six, whom he had seen in the house, who came 'with a black hat, so I thought him a Christian', but later found a red hat he hid in her box, 'and she confessed that this Jew had slept with her'. Questioned about eating, Nicolo said that Bonforno, before he knew he was a Jew, had come to Cristina's house, bringing two chickens cooked in an earthen pot (*tecchia*), and another with meat 'cooked in a carnation flavoured sauce'. Cristina told him that Bonforno brought cooked food on other occasions. When asked whether Cristina ate meat on Fridays or Saturdays, Nicolo said she did so last Lent, when ill. Asked if he had letters from the Jew, he said he had some which he would look for and bring, while others he had burned. Some came from Ferrara, but he did not recall the contents. Questioned further whether the Jew sent her letters containing conjurations and incantations, Nicolo said he had once seen her holding a half sheet or entire *foglio*, which contained Jewish-looking characters; he read most of it, but she then violently seized it from him and hid it. It was a prayer for betting (*scommesse*), to help know which noble would win in elections, and similar words. The letter was in Italian (*in volgare*, excluding some Hebrew characters), without signs or crosses. Nicolo found letters in a wooden box. Then he was asked whether Cristina had made anybody die to enjoy another, to which he replied that she had told him she had made one of two brothers Bazetta die so she could intrigue with the other; but he knew no more.

Nicolo di Elemi reappeared before the tribunal on 4 December (with the lay assistant this time being Leonardo Mocenigo); he presented four love letters, which were filed. They seem to be in the same hand, but using different inks; the letter d was always written as D. Two are headed '*vita del anima mia*' ('the life of my soul'), and two '*Cocha mia Dolgisima*' ('my very sad hen' – possibly more vulgar); and all end with '*V.S.Sa*', as substitute for a signature. They are love letters lamenting the distance between Cristina and the Jew, the desire for intimacy, pleading for a letter in return.[6] There was nothing to offend the tribunal – beyond this being a Jewish-Christian love affair.

On 9 December the same members of the tribunal questioned Caterina, widow of Antonio Fereti Gusona, who denied knowing Cristina. She was warned by the inquisitor that the *processo* said she did know her, but she repeated she had never heard of her. However, she said she had relatives called Bazetta, including a *nipote* (nephew), who was killed, but outside the Republic, in a struggle (*farca*) with peasants. He had rented the butter and cheese shop, and had three sisters in the countryside. When questioned she denied knowing Nicolo di Elmi; denied her *nipote* died from witchcraft (*strigane*); it was murder in a *farca*, and she was told he was thrown into the water. He had left Venice healthy, and his father had sent people to collect the body. Two pages of the *processo* were read to her; she had no brain for what was read to her (*non hò havuto cervello*). Her deceased husband had no legal cases with anybody. She made her annual confession at Easter.

The tribunal interviewed Paula, wife of Giovanni Lorenzo, aged forty-three, recently on the household staff of the most illustrious Carlo Contarini. She had known Cristina for four years in Rio Terra, where she also stayed, but had not known her well for the last two. She did not know whether Cristina had eaten meat in Lent, and on Fridays and Saturdays, when ill. She had never seen her do any *striganie*, and – when told to tell the truth or she would be charged and castigated – replied 'I cannot tell what I have not known or seen'. She was told to remain silent about the case outside the tribunal, and took the oath on the veracity of what she had said.

This closed the file, as far as what survives. Cristina seemingly was not questioned, despite the variety and seriousness of the allegations. Named witnesses did not back accusations of witchcraft, and one was adamant that it had not led to the death of a relative. Did the tribunal conclude that the anonymous delator and the first witness, Nicolo, were in fact the same person, seeking revenge because Cristina had a Jewish lover?

Suspects' Approaches to the Inquisition

Suspects who faced the inquisitor knowing they might be in trouble had to decide on tactics, choosing stages between total denial and dissimulation on the one hand, and 'confessing' what they thought the inquisitor might want to hear, hoping for leniency in the outcome, but risking death; or varying degrees of truth and revelation in between.

One of the standard early questions to a suspect was whether he or she knew the remit of the Inquisition. When this was put by the Modenese inquisitor in 1620 to a young notary, Francesco Zarlati, accused of reading prohibited books, he first replied 'Signor, I don't know it, unless you tell me', and when pressed suggested that it dealt with heresy, witchcraft and other ill-deeds (*'contra li Heretici, et per stregarie et altri malefitii'*). The inquisitor then explained it also dealt with blasphemies, superstitious practices – and readers of prohibited books. Whether Zarlati as a trained notary really did not know the full remit of the Inquisition or was feigning ignorance seems unclear. However, the pretence of ignorance was an obvious ploy to secure more lenient treatment. Prosperi considers this may have been genuine ignorance given that the tribunal's remit was constantly expanding, but by 1620 this should have been well known, especially since public edicts ordered to be published by the Roman Inquisition stressed the issue of prohibited books. Zarlati's first answer might have been a careful move to test the waters to see where his investigation might be flowing. When a Pisan peasant, Favilla da Mezzana, accused of blasphemy in 1575, had been asked 'Do you know what causes are treated here?', he had replied, 'Father, no, because I am illiterate'. This might have been a more genuine reaction at that date. He later admitted that blaspheming against God was a great sin and confessed to saying 'Dio becco' ('God the goat' – or 'cuckold').[7]

We can detect something about the possible agonised internal debate over whether to dissimulate, or openly tell the inquisitor one's true beliefs, in the case of Francesco Spiera in Venice in 1547–8, which was presided over by nuncio Giovanni della Casa. Spiera's position was revealed by Bishop Pier Paolo Vergerio who observed his trial – and later exiled himself as a reformer. Spiera was a notary from Cittadella (Venetian Republic), with strong evangelical, Calvinist ideas. According to Vergerio, 'at times he seemed to want to declare his beliefs openly and hide nothing'; but finally 'after a long internal battle, he decided upon dissimulation. He would keep his opinions firmly but secretly in his heart and with his mouth say something else, namely exactly what the legate [or inquisitor] wished him to say.' Spiera was condemned to reconciliation and public abjuration, first in San Marco, then in Cittadella. He died within months of returning home, in misery and despair (after doctors had failed to cure him in Padua), feeling he had betrayed the evangelical cause and mightily sinned in so doing ('... a rare and horrendous spectacle.... He seemed to me, when I saw him, a live man as if in hell'), for which he would never be forgiven. He seemingly attempted suicide, but was prevented by his sons.[8] Once in exile, Vergerio published booklets in Latin, then Italian, publicising Spiera's crisis of conscience. The whole problem raised by Vergerio's account of Spiera, and then by Celio Secondo Curione (the notable humanist, Calvinist and satirical anti-clerical living in Switzerland from 1542), resonated for a long time throughout the

Protestant world, though it was alleged early on by the suffragan bishop of Padua, Giacomo Rota, that Vergerio had invented the story to damage the Church.[9]

Some of those accused opted for martyrdom over Nicodemism or obfuscation, even knowing the cruel capital punishments on offer. Some considered that obstinacy leading to a public execution would give them an opportunity to publicise their ideas, as with Lorenzo Vex, a Lutheran tried in 1566 in Venice, who did not want to be drowned (the more usual punishment for heretics), but burned in the piazza so he could speak out. Others, like the shoemaker Girolamo Venier, condemned to read an abjuration in Udine Cathedral in 1544, altered it to condemn the cruel punishments being imposed. He escaped serious punishment. In 1551 Giorgio Siculo in Ferrara feigned his willingness to abjure, so he could address the crowd with his ideas.[10]

'The strange methods that they adopt in that tribunal of the Inquisition are such that everyone, in order to be released, says not what they know, but what they imagine.' So Giulia Gonzaga, under suspicion as a key supporter of Valdés, wrote to her cousin Ferrante Gonzaga in March 1553. She added a month later: 'Of the things they have said about me, if there were respect or charity and not malignity, I believe they would perforce admire my life rather than the imaginings of others. . . . God knows the truth. I will not crucify myself so much about it, although one cannot do otherwise than suffer from it.' Giulia Gonzaga declared she was a good Catholic, probably genuinely believing this, and that Valdés was likewise and should also be treated as such. She declared in the March letter that if the Inquisition proscribed Valdés' works, she would be obedient.[11] She clearly opposed the Inquisition and its procedures (though she was not personally subjected to them, since initial investigations had been dropped in February 1554). She realised that friends and associates were obfuscating when questioned and tried to second-guess what declarations would secure their release, as her friend Pietro Carnesecchi tried through various processes. She also realised that the ploys of others might distort her position and endanger her. At this point several inquisitors would accept equivocations and ploys, especially when coming from fairly discreet elite *spirituali*, since they themselves had some interest in, even sympathy for, certain Valdesian ideas. The hope and overconfidence that the more sympathetic inquisitorial minds might overcome the intransigent ones may explain why Giulia preserved Pietro Carnesecchi's extensive, very damaging, correspondence to her (see Chapter 5, pp.124–5).[12]

We can highlight an interesting dialogue. As discussed in Chapter 3 (see p.77), Franzino Singlitico da Rodi, normally resident on Cyprus, appeared before the Venetian tribunal in 1550. At the first session he was questioned by the nuncio's auditor, Rocco Cataneo, who seized on the fact that Franzino had previously appeared in Cyprus before inquisitor Fra Lorenzo da Bergamo. Had he abjured?

Singlitico: No, sir, doesn't the whole island know this? Sure, he wanted me to promise not to talk about matters of faith and not to read books from Germany, but I told him I couldn't make nor did I wish to make this promise, because it wasn't in my power to make it.

Cataneo: Did you receive an absolution from Fra Lorenzo?

Singlitico: I did.

Cataneo: Why did you accept it?

Singlitico: I took it because he wanted me to promise him not to defend either Martin Luther or Philip Melanchthon.

Cataneo: Did you keep the promise?

Singlitico: I kept it, because I did not defend either Luther or Melanchthon, but I did defend what I believed to be true . . .

Cataneo: Do you believe that the Pope has the authority to bind and loose and that the indulgences he grants are valid?

Singlitico: If it is an article of faith that one must believe in indulgences, then I believe in them, but, if not, I don't. Also, as far as I know, this matter of indulgences hasn't been fully decided.

Cataneo: But if it is not decided, what do you think about such a passage?

Singlitico: I believe what the Holy Mother Church believes.

In the next session the inquisitor Fra Marino da Venezia took over the questioning, and suggested a formula to fudge what might be meant by this last phrase.[13] Here we have a witness showing some boldness in a second inquisitorial investigation, being evasive (for his own benefit), playing on matters remaining ambiguous before Tridentine rulings. The attitude of 'I will believe what you tell me I must believe' throws the ball back to the inquisitor/auditor. We have two inquisitors, Fra Lorenzo and Fra Marino, in different investigations being mild and accommodating. In reaching a compromise with Singlitico, Fra Marino brought in the Greek Fathers of the Church such as Athanasius and Chrysostom to appeal to Singlitico's Greek Orthodox background.

One ploy for those under questioning was to repeat more or less the exact words of the accusation, but as a denial. This struck me reading a selection of cases of superstition investigated in Bologna in 1697. The technique may have been suggested by the notary. Some of the questioning in these cases was recorded in Italian, not Latin.[14]

Doubtless some of those summoned were prepared to lie and dissimulate to get out of gaol. According to his wife, Alvise Capuano (in Venice, 1580) took this beyond his own position:

He wanted to teach all those imprisoned by the holiest Inquisition how to get out quickly; they should confess all that will be proposed to them, so they will be immediately released. The man who finds himself imprisoned by the forces of justice, especially if in danger of his life, needs to know how to deceive well and simulate to escape these forces, but once outside prison he can believe and do what pleases him.[15]

Most people summoned by the inquisitor probably realised that a complete exoneration by the tribunal was unlikely. Most would judge that their life was not unblemished, that they were not ideal Christians, and that neighbours or priests might find ways to exaggerate defects, so some penitential punishment at least would follow. Although many might give a negative answer to an initial question – for example, 'Do you know why you have been summoned?' – they probably could guess the answer. Faced with such situations one strategy was to speak ahead of pressing questions, admit defects, and boldly give mitigating explanations. This tactic was used by Milanese-born Caterina Erba, denounced in Venice in 1669 by her lover, the nobleman Andrea Renier, to whose family she had come as a wetnurse (after extensive travels, a marriage and a still-born child). A servant told Renier that Caterina had in her own house wax figurines stuck with pins and knotted cords for magical purposes. Renier consulted his confessor, who told him to denounce her to the inquisitor. Renier suggested she had several other lovers and was not very devout. After the said objects had been discovered in her house, she was summoned to the tribunal. Unprompted, she immediately declared:

> I'll tell you the honest truth. This gentleman who kept me, Andrea Renier . . . after he kept me for a year and got me pregnant, left me with not a thing except a little money for the delivery. I gave birth in this house of the midwife Andriana, where that gentleman had put me until I delivered.

Through the midwife she gathered some female supporters, leading to a boatman's wife, Marina, who promised to teach her ways of ensuring that her master/lover and the Renier family would not totally abandon her. Hence the cord trick and figurines, and spells to recite. She used some of them on Renier; the sequel was that he kept her in various houses, fathered four children by her, secured service for her, until he fired her because of rumours of their relationship. She was now pregnant again, she thought. This hardship story and her immediate admission of guilt led the tribunal to sentence her merely to salutary penances, to stay in the city, report monthly to the Inquisition's office, with an attestation of good behaviour from her parish priest. Within days they told her that if public knowledge made it impossible for her to get a position as a servant in Venice, she would be allowed to try in Padua.[16]

The accused and witnesses might arrive with prepared, formulaic answers, in expectation of certain questions. They often started with phrases about clearing their conscience, such as *'per scarico della mia coscienza'*, or *'per sgravo della mia coscienza'* – probably as instructed by their confessor. As indicated elsewhere, notaries might have coached them further (or turned a rambling answer into a formulaic one). Signs of slightly more elaborate coaching can be detected, for example, in the case of Antonia Mingozzi of Medicina (Bologna territory) in 1697, who appeared 'spontaneously' before the archpriest of Medicina who was acting as inquisitorial vicar. She was a servant, aged about twenty-five, of a notary, Alfonso Ranghi. In an argument with the daughter of the house and another servant, Domenico, who had denounced her, she was under suspicion for attacking the idea of Lent, and of fasting, and for believing that Lent had been invented by a *Razzasfonddradona* (ill-born person). On her knowledge of Lent and its origins she replied: 'and now that I fully understand everything from you Signor Archpriest. I humbly ask pardon from his Divine Majesty proposing never more to speak in such a manner against the institutions of the Holy Mother Church, and from now on observe its holy precepts, and think no more of what I have said.'[17] Ranghi was not only a notary, but one linked to the Holy Office, which may have conditioned this and other replies. She signed with a cross, unable to write. She declared she confessed and took communion monthly. This was received favourably by the court, though declaring it would check on her veracity. She received a warning and salutary penances on 27 February – a quick outcome.

Negotiating Reconciliations

As mentioned earlier, notaries may have helped the accused prepare answers, and learn how to say the right thing. This might essentially be a plea-bargaining exercise, to earn a light sentence. This parallels the petitioning processes in French courts, as notably studied by Natalie Zemon Davis.[18]

Tribunals of the Inquisition could be institutions for re-education and reconciliation as well as for punishment and control. This was particularly so for those who wished to be recognised as good Catholics, either having strayed into other faiths, or never having been baptised Catholics, as previously discussed. Georgios Plakotos' work in this area strongly suggests a fairly coherent process of preparing petitions to make the ratification of (re)conversion easy on both sides. Catholics or Orthodox who had become Muslims in the Ottoman empire were advised to suggest that they had outwardly conformed, been circumcised, followed Muslim customs, but in their heart remained Christian. Muslims, or Greek Orthodox, coming to Venice and seeking conversion, often for job opportunities, were probably not perceived by inquisitors or Patriarchs as a threat to the resident population, so an easy 'accommodation' could be negotiated.

Like many seeking reconciliation with the Catholic faith, Giorgio Iuiririch (originally from Dolaz [Dolac] in Bosnia) was a soldier who had voluntarily converted to Islam (enticed by promises of money, gifts and fame) and fought in Ottoman wars. When his master, a vizier to whom he had been sold, died when fighting in Persia, Giorgio joined a mercenary group to plunder Christians in Wallachia and other Black Sea areas. He then decided to go to Venice, probably (like others) to find employment in a Christian army, and so in 1617 faced the Venetian Inquisition, declaring:

> Although I became a Muslim outwardly ... I never moved away from the Christian religion spiritually and from the wish to become a Christian and to die in Christianity. It is true that I frequented the Muslim mosques and sometimes participated in their ceremonies, but I never gave credit to these in my heart ... I never doubted the Christian faith and I never thought that the Muslim superstition was better than the Christian faith.

This sounds like what the tribunal would want to hear, and in the language of inner and outer conformity which would have been prepared in advance with Giorgio, whether by a priest, the notary or even the inquisitor himself. Under questioning Giorgio excused his plundering of Christians in Wallachia and Podolia on the grounds that 'for the most part they were schismatics', namely Orthodox. He probably helped his case by telling the inquisitor that in Sebenico, on his way to Venice, he had taken 'some instruction on the Christian faith and life'.[19]

Martino Velincovich (alias Ossiman) from Koprivnica (then part of the Habsburg's military frontier confronting the Ottomans, now modern northern Croatia) claimed he never understood the language and rites of his Muslim associates over the eight years he was with them in the 1640s, and he always remained faithful to his Christian beliefs, as he told the Inquisition:

> I have never believed that Mohammed was the prophet of God. ... But I have always believed that Christ our Lord is a true God and all that holds the holy mother Catholic and apostolic Roman Church under which I was born.[20]

This again sounds like a well-rehearsed declaration.

Since numbers of people from the Balkans and the wider Ottoman empire born as non-Catholics or living as such appeared before the Venetian (and Maltese) tribunal in similar circumstances, it would seem that knowledge spread that suitable stories could be crafted in appropriate language to secure reconciliation by the Inquisition without too many questions. Those arriving in Venice from the Levant, speaking Greek or Turkish but not a version of Italian, could find residents knowing these languages to help with translating petitions, and possibly their discourse, before the tribunal. This is a grey and hardly studied area. A translator was recorded in use in the case of Fiorenza Podacataro (alias Titiia) in the early

1590s. Born into a Catholic noble Cypriot family, she was captured on the fall of Nicosia, enslaved, married to an Ottoman official serving in Bulgaria, and lived as a Muslim for twenty-two years, declaring to her master from the outset that she was Muslim. When facing the Inquisition in Venice to secure reconciliation as a Catholic she had an interpreter, because she could not speak Italian or Latin. However, she knew Latin prayers. The case they put to the court was that though outwardly Muslim (and as such having to trample the Cross as a ritual gesture), she had secretly continued to say daily the Credo, Paternoster and Salve Regina, in Greek or Latin. Encouraged by a Greek slave (to whom she became entitled as wife to an important Ottoman official), she had baptised her children, 'throwing water on their head and saying "I baptise you in the name of Christ" '. She did not teach them to sign the Cross in case that betrayed their hidden identity. Further making her case her testimony states, 'From all that the Turks said, I only approved what I knew the Christians did believe, such as that God is omnipotent and great, it is not permitted to lie and other similar'. We cannot tell whether we are hearing the record of a devout Christian acting courageously and dangerously in an alien environment, or a fictional narrative styled in cooperation with an interpreter with experience of such 'reconciliation' cases. Either way the tribunal was ready to accept accounts of dissimulation and the need to live double lives. Fiorenza's stance would have satisfied the criteria for a 'spontaneous appearance', with the judgement on intention in the apostasy.[21]

That a prepared deal could be done between tribunal and convert is suggested by the absence of recorded questioning in the court appearance for a number of them; the convert explains his background and circumstances of non-Catholic behaviour, puts himself at the court's mercy – and expects reconciliation.

Accused and Relatives; Accusers and Witnesses

Some accused of fairly serious heresy were denounced by members of their own family. Eliseo Masini in his *Sacro Arsenale* emphasised that members of the family should be admitted as witnesses in heresy cases: 'To prove the crime of heresy in the Holy Office there can be admitted the son against father, father against son, the wife against husband, the husband against wife, the servant against master, the master against servant.' Edicts before and after Masini's writings stressed this duty.[22]

In Venice in the early decades of the Inquisition wives denounced husbands (rather than the reverse), if they were worried about their husbands' religious welfare; or more likely if the wife had come under opposition or attack for continuing to believe in the cult of saints, having holy images in the house, or insisting on fasting. In 1581 the wife of cobbler Francescin da Trieste testified against him (admittedly ten years after they had separated), for taking down holy images she and the children had put up, for saying she should not teach the children to cross themselves, beating her for going to confession and making her cook meat on fast days; but he taught her the Lord's Prayer, which she recited to the tribunal. In a more immediate denunciation, in April 1582 Caterina, wife of Valentino da Lubiana (modern Ljubliana), denounced him because at the past Easter he had spat on her for going to the parish Mass; she added that he had often beaten her.[23]

A peasant from the Modenese village of Spezzano, Matteo Giazzotto, was denounced in 1598 by his wife Lucrezia for blasphemy; and a daughter, Camilla, was also brought in as a witness. The inquisitor had just issued an edict about blasphemy, and this seems to have encouraged Lucrezia. She also said that she had not come before because her priest from the altar had declared that confession should be of one's own sins, not those of others; but the edict had said people should denounce husbands if involved in heretical blasphemy. It emerged under investigation that her parish priest had in fact denied her absolution until she made a denunciation. A Lenten preacher in Spezzano, Fra Leandro da Capugnano, had given publicity to the inquisitor's edict. It was to him she went to make a denunciation, and he took up the questioning of witnesses, acting as an agent of the Inquisition, to save her journeying to Modena. The wife and daughter revealed Matteo as one who also broke fasting rules, and was violent towards them, as when they returned from confession. It was a family in crisis. The outcome is not clear.[24]

In considering a wife's and brother's position we can revert to the Panzacchi case discussed in Chapter 4 (see pp.114–15). From a rich Bolognese notarial family, Alessandro Panzacchi had squandered money in his adventurous youth, then been a soldier and itinerant bookseller, before recovering his finances. He was suspected of links with heretical conventicles in Bologna, but also nearby Cento. While inquisitor Balducci in Bologna was reinvestigating Alessandro in 1567 (having decided an earlier abjuration was incomplete), he asked the bishop's vicar Cristoforo Pensabene to investigate Alessandro's wife Isabella, and his brother Giulio. Isabella stressed her husband's frequent absences, that she wanted to remain at home, and her husband agreed they should 'do their own thing'. She had no knowledge of his alleged wrong beliefs or contacts until told of his imprisonment; and she did not discuss anything but domestic matters when she talked to him at the prison window. She assured the vicar of her own religious devotion, hearing Mass almost daily. She was particularly devoted to the church of San Stefano, and sought indulgences there; such that her husband told her she should stay at home more and say prayers there, and not kiss crosses so much. He confessed and communicated annually, and publicly did special good works. Giulio testified that Isabella was very respectable ('*una donna da bene*'), and like him knew nothing of what Alessandro was accused of. Then

Giulio claimed he had been made sick and very unhappy by his brother, who seemed to want to ruin the life and honour of the whole house. It had made him ill over the past ten months, so he had lost his memory and mind. He said he had no doubt that Alessandro had sinned in matters of faith: Alessandro would not be in trouble if he had not done something outside the bosom (*gremio*) of the Church. Like his sister-in-law, Giulio claimed that Alessandro showed no signs of deviance at home, and had even encouraged him to benefit from the Holy Jubilee, and they had taken communion together. Giulio claimed he had no knowledge of Fra Ambrogio da Cesena before being asked by Alessandro at the prison window to contact him (to make contact with friends from Cento being investigated in Ferrara, to prevent this wider circle testifying against Alessandro), and then asking Isabella to make the contact.[25] The arrest of Fra Ambrogio undid them all.

The 'don't know' and 'can't remember' approaches, along with Giulio's talk that the Inquisition must be right about Alessandro, were suitable from the family's viewpoint, whatever their veracity; and essentially they worked. Their comments about Alessandro confessing and taking communion were potentially beneficial, but the inquisitor in the main trial eventually secured a confession (after at least two torture sessions) from Alessandro that he had expressed heretical ideas about the Eucharist. It emerged that a more notorious heretic from Modena, Pietro Antonio da Cervia, was part of an extensive group with Panzacchi, had soldiered with him and had stayed in his house. Pietro Antonio in his trial said he had read many works about reform with Alessandro while on guard duty in Modena. The only women he had dealt with on such heretical matters were his own wife Laura and Alessandro's sister, and the women in his house where he stayed. In the light of this, neither the inquisitor nor the vicar seems to have challenged Isabella's claim of innocence. Dall'Olio suggests she may have been genuinely orthodox, but under attack from her husband, who did not want her to go confessing to priests, and appearing at Mass.[26] Pietro Antonio had berated Urselina Varanini, the wife of his landlord Pelegrino da Varanini (or Fra Bonifacio), who denounced him, for going uselessly to Mass and told her to pray at home. Varanini told the inquisitor he found Cervia obnoxious (as did others), which may explain his willingness to denounce him. Pietro Antonio implicated his wife (and many others), where Alessandro did not.[27]

Torture: An Inquisitor and Accused in Confrontation

The Balducci investigation of Pietro Antonio da Cervia involved a confrontation under torture. As a follow-up to the discussion in Chapter 3 (see p.84), the record of this trial is useful for understanding how an accused might react, and its possible value. How did the victims react? How efficacious was the torture in securing confessions and the naming of names? Surviving records show that people could withstand the *strappado* torture, without revealing what they did not want to reveal, without telling lies to escape pain. Others clearly did tell lies. Some would tell the inquisitor they would say anything he wanted to avoid pain, but then deny it afterwards because it was not true. The accused in the inquisitional system usually had due warning that torture might be administered, so a strategy might be worked out to confess quickly, or name names of associates (preferably those who were dead, safely escaped, or certainly already known to the Inquisition) to secure a quick relief.

The long-serving Bolognese inquisitor Antonio Balducci has been noted as a moderate in his attitude to torture, so it is somewhat surprising to find him putting Pietro Antonio da Cervia to torture in June 1567, using the *taxillorum* method (pressing his right foot) because he was too infirm for the *strappado* jerking. Pietro Antonio had sung like the proverbial canary, naming many associates, such as soldiers to whom he had read heretical works, and outlining where he had disagreed with orthodox Catholic doctrine – on Sacraments, Purgatory and relics. He had declared to the court that 'nor would I let myself be crippled for others if I knew that they were heretics or suspect of heresy. Nevertheless I am here to receive these torments, since my sins merit these and more. I beseech you to have compassion and mercy on me.' Balducci was not that merciful. He made it clear that questioning under torture would not be about what had already been covered, 'but only for the sake of further truth, and concerning the other accomplices'. Under torture Pietro Antonio began to shout out with loud cries, 'Oh Jesus, Oh Jesus. I have said everything that I know and I have said the truth ... Oh, do you wish me to speak against my conscience. As for those soldiers, as much is true as I have told you in my examination. Jesus help me. Our Lady help me.' Then he answered that he had never been a priest, or been in minor orders, 'what would it be for me to say it. Wouldn't it be better for me, as I wouldn't have committed idolatry by celebrating mass as many times as I did ...'. It was much graver for him to have celebrated without being ordained 'than if I had been ordained and taken a wife'. Under further questioning Pietro Antonio named two soldiers who had agreed with him, while others opposed. Having named them before, he was not increasing the inquisitor's knowledge. The notary did not record further laments. Having been 'under torture for a notable length of time' (unspecified), and since he was saying nothing new, the judges released him. He affirmed the record read to him and confessed. Presumably Balducci and his advisers decided they would learn no more from Pietro Antonio under further pain (because he knew no more or was extremely stubborn and secretive), and the case could be terminated. He was not shown mercy for what he had earlier freely confessed and supposedly repented, or for the many names; he was executed as a relapsed heretic on 5 September 1567.[28]

An Accused Argues Back

Some accused had the confidence to argue with inquisitors, as already noted with Carnesecchi and Bruno for example. The prophet Dionisio Gallo at times took a forceful attitude towards the Venetian tribunal, confident in his beliefs, even challenging it to have him burned.[29]

The Venetian nobleman Filippo Mocenigo (archbishop of Nicosia, 1560–71, until Cyprus fell to the Turks) was subjected to a heresy trial in Rome in 1583.[30] Previous to becoming an ecclesiast, he had had a diplomatic career and was widely travelled. He was first denounced in 1562 for possessing a condemned edition of Ptolemy's *Geografia*, which contained a commentary by the heretic Sebastian Münster, by one of his former travelling companions through Ottoman lands, the Dominican Fra Antonio da Venezia. He had also expressed controversial views on justification by faith. This denunciation seemingly lay on file without further immediate action. A close associate of the utopian philosopher Francesco Patrizi da Cherzo, Mocenigo wrote his own utopian treatise, *Universales institutiones ad hominum perfectionum* ('Universal Institutions for Men's Perfection'), dedicated to Gregory XIII, with a strong plea for colleges of education, where under priests and learned scholars orthodox teaching could be ensured. However, it attacked the Inquisition as led by Cardinal Scipione Rebiba. When he wanted to publish a vernacular treatise, *'Vie et progressi spirituali'* ('On Spiritual Ways and Progress') in 1573, Mocenigo obtained permission from the Venetian inquisitor and Patriarch. However, an adverse report was made to Rebiba, who had the text analysed, with an adverse view leading to the trial in 1583 under Cardinal Santoro. In 1573 Rebiba had also ensured a veto on the proposal that Mocenigo be appointed Patriarch of Aquileia as desired by the Venetians (when his cousin Alvise di Tommaso Mocenigo was Doge).[31] Rebiba argued that once denounced (even if not tried) he was ineligible, and backed by most cardinals of the Inquisition he overcame the view of a leading Jesuit Francisco Toledo, solicited by the Pope, that Mocenigo should be appointed. The Venetian ambassador Paolo Tiepolo reported Toledo as saying: 'The cardinals of the Inquisition proceed too rigorously at times, and at times they are mistaken, falling into most notable error, and he alleged that they had made a most grave one, and he urged His Holiness to free the archbishop from every charge and to grant this satisfaction to the Serenissima.'[32] The Pope then said he wanted the appointment to go ahead 'without having too much regard for the cardinals of the Inquisition', but the Republic withdrew its nomination.

With this background Mocenigo's confrontation with the Inquisition a decade later potentially faced heavy prejudices. The standard Catholic doctrines were not in dispute; rather philosophical questions about first causes, relations between will and intellect, the relationship of body and soul. Don Teófilo da Siena as denunciator thought much of this had implications for teaching on God's freedom of creation and his omnipotence, amounting to denying infinity and the existence of many worlds. According to Elena Bonora's analysis of the interrogation, Mocenigo argued robustly and philosophically with the Cardinal inquisitors, backing his arguments with quotations from Scripture, Saints Thomas Aquinas and Duns Scotus, and many standard commentaries. He was obviously allowed access to books between sessions. He finally agreed that some of his arguments were not always well founded, and that he had claimed to have resolved various issues where Church Fathers had disagreed; that the Pope could not resolve them; but that the authority lay with the Congregation of the Inquisition. This was a tactful admission to make. It seems that the leading inquisitors were able to accept an intellectual discussion with this accused. They objected that he had threatened through his vernacular treatise (which he had had licensed in a dubious Venetian environment) to put issues before less learned men and women. Theological consultants found that Mocenigo had not shown himself suspect of heresy, but he had been obscure and ambiguous, so dangerous. The inquisitorial group – the Pope, cardinals Madruzzo, Santoro and Savelli – declared that manuscript copies of his '*Vie et progressi spirituali*' be seized and destroyed, though a revised version was not ruled out. Mocenigo was absolved and found innocent. The vernacular work was never published.[33]

This example demonstrates that an experienced nobleman could confront top inquisitors, be treated as an intellectual equal though a known opponent of inquisitorial authority who had offended one of the most powerful inquisitors. Mocenigo made the right concessions during interrogation to avoid further trouble.

Inquisitors and the Accused: Status, Reputation and Fama

While the Inquisition might try and condemn the high and mighty of Church and laity, bishops and nobles, as well as unprotected lowly persons, some attention might be paid to social status, the accused's reputation in society and the views of neighbours. Reputation among the lower orders mattered. Mocenigo's background, status and experience affected some of his treatment, as did Carnesecchi's through his early investigations. In cases of 'pretend sanctity' and holy women, the social status of the woman could influence verdicts on genuineness and fraud.

While some intrepid inquisitors such as Gian Pietro Carafa in Rome, or Michele Ghislieri when active in the northern provinces, pursued an alleged serious heretic whatever his or her social status or political position in a locality, many inquisitors must have been more sensitive towards social and political conditions of the accused. Particularly in the early days inquisitors – and supportive or hostile bishops – made distinctions between those of education and intelligence who debated the new ideas in private, and those who entered the public arena through sermons addressed to a wide congregation and, worse, those of lower social rank and education who debated in the wine bars and hostelries. Unfortunately, records do not exist for preliminary negotiations, nor for deliberations between formal interrogation sessions. We seldom hear the direct voice of the inquisitorial questioner during the process. Some indication of the background considerations do emerge from surviving correspondence with the Roman congregations, inquisitors and vicars-general in a city with a secular government, Venice.

The Venetian inquisitor Fra Marino's comparatively mild treatment of an outspoken Lutheran Massimo de'Consorti from Spilimbergo (Friuli) may have been conditioned by the status and social behaviour of the accused. Massimo came from a local noble family, and was sometimes a grain merchant in Pieve di Cadore, where he was first investigated in 1548. One priest witness stated Massimo was a hardened and boastful Lutheran who would say 'I am Lutheran and I wish to die Lutheran, and those who say that Lutherans are not respectable men lie in their throat'.[34] He was only arrested in February 1549, and sent to Venice in July, where Fra Marino and his team interrogated him three times on the basis of a transcript of the Pieve di Cadore witness statements. Massimo fairly quickly admitted he had denied transubstantiation, and saw the Mass as a memorial. He believed that the Host was merely bread, soft like *lasagna*; the Church was the congregation of the faithful and any group of Christians could celebrate communion; the present Church had created a wall to prevent the people learning what the Gospel said. Hesitant about his views on the Virgin (after many witnesses – of lower status – had been heard about this), after initial denials he eventually admitted saying that she would have been honourable (*da bene*) and so given birth in an honourable place, not a stable. He argued he had only said this when hazy with wine (*ofusendo dal vin*). This led to his abjuration on 30 July 1549. Massimo was sentenced to a public abjuration from the pulpit in San Marco, three years' imprisonment in Venice, a 100-ducat fine and perpetual banishment from the Cadore region. His sentence should be publicly announced in Cadore and Spilimbergo.

The sentence was soon modified when Massimo's wife, 'like a deserted widow', petitioned that the cost of paying for his Venetian imprisonment was jeopardising the chances of providing dowries for their six daughters. He was allowed to transfer to a prison in Friuli. It is not clear how long he remained imprisoned. Given his well-attested and admitted theological statements his treatment might be deemed comparatively mild. Fra Marino and his tribunal seemed prepared to accept drunkenness as a mitigating factor. Maybe they considered public shaming of a noble merchant was enough to keep him quiet when out of prison. His replies do not show theological sophistication or close adherence to a particular strand of Protestantism – Lutheran, Zwinglian or Calvinist.[35] But could he have been astute enough to demonstrate muddle, and blame the wine, to befuddle his interrogators, to survive and be a Nicodemist? Fra Marino and the others did not question him over contacts, from whom or what books he learned, whom he taught. But a little evidence suggests he had followers and supporters, at least within an extended family, in Spilimbergo to where he could return. It remains an open question whether Fra Marino was being inept, showing inexperience and naivety at an early stage of the Roman Inquisition; being socially deferential; or indicating some ambivalence over some views Massimo expressed, as his own later interrogation implied.

The status and demeanour of an accused could encourage a lenient and gentle inquisitorial examination of their opposition to a fundamental doctrine such as the real presence of God. In June 1614 canon Forniti of Rocca Contrada wrote to the experienced inquisitor-general of Ancona, Fra Giovanni Maria da Bologna, about a young female penitent he was trying to correct. Questioning her about what she cannot believe, she replied 'that she was not able to believe, and had never believed that in the holiest sacrament of the altar there was the essentials of God, but believed his grace was there'. The canon was having great difficulty convincing her otherwise, 'possibly because of the Devil operating in opposition', but she will return for further discussion 'because he believes very well that her error comes from simplicity, and not from obstinacy or the infection from others'. The canon asked to be allowed to absolve her from sin and censure, 'because it would be impossible to transfer her from here because of her age, the quality of the person and for other respects she is penitent'.[36] The inquisitor consulted the Roman Inquisition, indicating he might delicately get her to reveal herself and her accomplices to the Holy Office, 'promising every secrecy and kindness towards her person'. The canon stated that she 'is a young girl from a household honoured in this land, kept by Father, Mother and brothers with the greatest control that can be imagined, in a way that it would seem impossible that she could be presented in any way in front of the officials of the Holy Office; not being able to set foot out of her own house, except for going to Mass on special feasts, or going to confession; and from what can be believed she would rather choose to go to the Devil's house.' He believed that 'the error derives not from the false doctrine of others, but from simplicity and her own incapacity as a young girl. I write this to Your Illustriousness that you consider ordering what is expedient for this soul's salvation.' The Roman Inquisition took the lenient line, for on 17 July the inquisitor wrote that he would tell canon Fornito he had the power to absolve that young girl, for not having believed that in the Sacrament of the Eucharist was to be found the essentials of God (*'essentialmente Dio'*); that the canon should continue Catholic teaching and impose salutary penances on her.[37]

The secrecy of the confessional was preserved, so the inquisitors in Ancona and Rome had no idea of the girl's personal identity. In considering whether or not she might have been 'infected' from outside, it should be noted that Rocca Contrada was not a backwater; it had booksellers, and inns for travellers whom Eliseo Masini felt needed careful watching.[38]

The company an accused kept was seriously considered by inquisitors. Those under investigation were seldom treated as lone individuals. Somebody holding dubious religious views was assumed to have been influenced by others, and likely to spread those ideas to a network of contacts. Those involved in superstitious practices were similarly assumed to have learned techniques from others; of interest were not only those they directly affected but those to whom they might have taught their skills. A further guide to guilt or innocence could be the known social contacts. Ascertaining social contacts might overcome the problems of dealing with dissimulators and Nicodemists.

As an example of an inquisitor strenuously seeking past and current associations we have the Venetian inquisitor Aurelio Schellino da Brescia's questioning in 1569–70 of the silk-weaver Paolo Gaiano (or da Campogalliano), originally from Modena. He was lengthily questioned about his contacts in Modena as well as Venice; about where and with whom he had worked, the taverns he frequented. Gaiano himself seemed to reinforce the inquisitorial approach when he offered, in return for his liberty, to take the inquisitor around the city to show him a 'world of heretics'. Hitherto in Venice he had tried to be careful about revealing his anticlerical or quasi-Protestant views outside his heterodox network, as he helped Modenese artisans find work in Venice. He had been a Nicodemist, simulating adherence to Catholic beliefs and practices. But to guild members and a tavern clientele he became known as 'Polo luteran'; within what he thought was a private circle he freely denied the existence of Purgatory and devalued the Host. An associate's confessor eventually persuaded him to denounce Gaiano, though this delator may have felt animosity towards Gaiano over financial and trade matters. Since Modena had had a reputation for heterodox views for some decades, this network would have been of particular interest to inquisitor Schellino. In 1549 in Modena, Gaiano had been dangerously open in his evangelical views, spreading them from the barber's chair while being shaved, as well as at his workplace. Tried by Bishop Egidio Foscarari there in 1555, it was revealed he had learned from the *Beneficio di Cristo*; he had declared the Pope to be Anti-Christ, and that 'all faithful Christians are priests'. He had abjured, and presumably moved to Venice (which he had visited as an itinerant worker before) for more surreptitious teaching. In 1569/70 Schellino's questioning of witnesses revealed quite a network of artisan debaters of religious ideas. An *osteria* near the Rialto fishmarket was a more public forum for Gaiano's religious discourse and debates, frequented by Modenese residents in Venice who were there for the long or short term. Witnesses of course distanced themselves from his opinions. But one priest declined to confirm Gaiano held dubious beliefs. The long period of time before he was denounced suggests there was a degree of tolerance or sympathy, provided he was chattering only within his work and social group.[39]

Secrecy was supposedly a key factor in the operation of the Inquisition, but it could not be guaranteed. Rumours and gossip could readily spread and so warn potential witnesses, who might have time to prepare their story ahead of any voluntary appearance before, or visit by, an inquisitor, and decide what attitude to take towards an accused and their associations. This must have been particularly so in densely populated urban areas, where people met to gossip in shops and taverns, or could chatter across narrow streets and, in Venice, canals. This is apparent in 1616 when Pierina Zatta was denounced to the Venetian tribunal. She lived in the crowded Campo di Do Pozzi (Two Wells). As the many witnesses came forward – workers at the Arsenal, ship's-chandlers, and their wives, washerwomen – they showed an awareness of how the investigation was proceeding.[40]

Reputation, or *fama*, played a significant role in inquisitional procedure. Denouncers would make their accusations on the basis of hearsay, common report, gossip, though unlike persecutors of witches in the Duchy of Lorraine for example, Italian inquisitors did not argue that public reputation was enough to try and torture somebody.[41] We have seen Chaim Baruch (or Saruc) basing his view of Righetto (Nuñes) as a *marrano* on public reputation. The accusations in the Rifreddo witch trials of 1495 or the 1607 trials of witches in Soraggio were strongly governed by local *fama*, back to the reputation of grandmothers in the latter situation. One person, passing by another reputed to be a witch, might claim to have immediately felt pain. Inquisitorial manuals warned against relying on hostile *fama*. Masini in the *Sacro Arsenale* said that a woman's general reputation should not be relied upon; nor should one witch's naming of others be taken as a valid accusation.[42] However, inquisitors were prepared to consider wider alleged public repute as the basis for further enquiry. One reason why witnesses were usually questioned before the accused was to clarify differences between personal animosity and 'revenge' (which might get the case dropped), and the public reputation of the accused – whether as superstitious practitioner, foul-mouthed blasphemer, or anticlerical speaker. *Fama* was often a factor noted in inquisitor Gallicciolo's summaries of cases involving Jews and Christians in Mantua, discussed in Chapter 6 (see pp.148–9). A sexual relationship might be 'the common voice and *fama*', or qualified as 'it is known solely from public voice and *fama*'. In contrast a good public reputation might inhibit further investigation, or be part of mitigation. The phrase '*uomo da bene*' was commonly used to suggest a man of good repute, morally and in terms of social position.[43]

Local Fama: the Case of Aurora Gemma and Marco da Domo

A minor irregularity in somebody's behaviour, as of a stranger, could trigger a denunciation, and expand into a quite wide-ranging enquiry as witnesses spread gossip and volunteered hostile information. But it might become too confusing and not lead to a major offensive by the inquisitors. This happened when they probed an allegation of Protestant beliefs made in Venice in April 1625 against the elderly Aurora Gemma and her second husband Marco da Domo, when they were living that year in the village of Sovernigo, near Treviso, but staying in Venice. A male villager considered Aurora to be Lutheran because she wore a red hat in church in the Polish style (*all'usanza Polaca*).[44] This 'caused some malicious gossip that she was Lutheran', as a sympathetic priest put it, 'started by a bad peasant'.[45] Villagers became worried about this, and other issues. Soon the gossip and accusations flowed, against her and her second husband, Marco, then about her first husband. The case was dropped when the parish priest and two others said they held Aurora for a good Catholic. But there was in fact a challenging record in her wider family.

Aurora was literate and had books, including a Polish vernacular Bible; the church rector Sebastiano Dina, however, declared it was a good Catholic one (*buona et catolica*), 'as good as ours', and he did not consider it wrong to read such a vernacular Bible. During the questioning of witnesses a complex picture emerged as perceived by neighbours, but there was also a family past on Aurora's side, which could have generated a more intensive investigation, and trouble. Many felt she and her husband were remiss in their attendance of divine services; they denied Hell and Paradise, and the Trinity. A Hieronyma de Scuti, with whom the couple had lodged, then widened the picture by saying that Marco had told her he had been in Turkey in his youth, without indicating whether he was born Christian or Muslim (*turco*). Neither showed signs of Christian devotion – no crucifixes, rosaries or devotional images. Marco made fun of miracle stories. Aurora was old, and so it was understandable that she did not leave the house to go to Mass. Other witnesses gave evidence of Marco having a reputation in Venice as a '*turco*', probably circumcised.[46] Hieronyma hinted at disputes between Aurora and relatives, Vincenzo Forno and his sister Franceschina, who herself claimed Aurora and Marco believed in very little. Their mother, Lucietta Forno, a devout Catholic, proved to be the sister of a Venetian physician, Zuan Battista Gemma – Aurora's first husband. He had twice been investigated by the Inquisition, abjuring in 1565 after fostering evangelical beliefs in his pharmacy, the Due Colombini (Two Doves). His activities were investigated again in 1575, a year after he left Venice. By 1599 Gemma was court physician in Cracow, which would explain Aurora's Polish Bible.[47]

Aurora's hostile niece Franceschina revealed that Aurora was the sister of the younger Giovanni Battista Clario (now deceased), member of a notable Friulian family of physicians, and condemned Lutherans. Giovanni Battista Clario senior had abjured in Cividale in 1569. His son became involved with Campanella in the 1590s, suffering investigation and torture with him in Padua before abjuring in Rome in May 1595, vehemently suspected of heresy. On his release he redeemed himself as a good Catholic (with eulogistic epigrams favouring Pope Clement and Cardinal Santoro) and internationally acknowledged physician, court doctor, Count Palatine and Austrian baron.[48]

Despite all the gossip, accusations and information about an extended family of heretics, in 1625 the Venetian court dropped the cases against Aurora and Marco without formal investigation. The inquisitors apparently ignored the implications of Marco being called a *'turco'*, Muslim, and rector Dino's long hostile comment on him. They may have realised that the couple were in part at least victims of neighbourly suspicion of the outside 'other', and family animosities. Aurora's Bible could have been legitimate if it was the version by Jakob Wujk (published in Cracow, 1599), sanctioned by Clement VIII and the Congregation of the Holy Office in their meetings in 1598 to assist a Catholic recovery against Polish Protestants.[49] Furthermore, as noted, Aurora was clearly old. Maybe her late brother had redeemed the family reputation. Her good reputation with local priests outweighed the hostile *fama* among neighbours.

This chapter has illustrated that the inquisitorial process involved complex interrelationships between the inquisitors and their helpers on the one hand, and those under scrutiny on the other, whether the accused or their witnesses. It was not entirely a top-down system. The inquisitors had their wiles and strategies, but some of those facing them could twist and turn, concoct stories, pretend and evade to secure the least bad outcome. They could survive torture, in the interests of 'truth' or to save their skins, even if knowingly guilty. A variety of external social circumstances and presumed *fama* could assist some of the accused, and virtually damn others. *Fama* was particularly important in dealing with a major category of offences, 'superstition and magic' or 'the magical arts', the focus of the next chapter.

CHAPTER 9

✳

THE WORLD OF WITCHCRAFT, SUPERSTITION AND MAGIC

THE SPANISH AND ITALIAN INQUISITIONS ARE OFTEN ASSOCIATED WITH THE early modern 'witch-craze', which in some of today's writing is misleadingly designated as 'women hunting'. Some writers blame 'the Inquisition' for the death of tens of thousands of witches. This is false. Part of the problem arises from a confusion between the 'inquisitorial' method of enquiry and the institutions of the Inquisition, in Iberia and Italy. By the sixteenth century many jurisdictions had adopted variations of the inquisitorial methods of investigation, following medieval ecclesiastical procedures. Undoubtedly, at the hands of untrained or inadequately trained magistrates and investigators, who used uncontrolled methods of torture to extract confessions that almost mandatorily named 'accomplices', many supposed (or real) practitioners of 'magic' were condemned and executed across northern Europe in the later sixteenth and seventeenth centuries. However, in Iberia and Italy during the period of this study, while significant numbers of people were denounced as 'witches', sorcerers and practitioners of (bad) magic, few were condemned to death, and many denunciations were not followed up or were dismissed. In the Italian and Iberian states cases of magic and witchcraft were largely, though not solely, investigated and tried by tribunals of the Inquisition once they were fully established. This last qualification is necessary; as we have seen in Chapter 1, in the later fifteenth and early sixteenth centuries the Dominican inquisitors in northern Italy joined in persecutions of witches that led to significant numbers of burnings.

Although some of the witch-hunting was inaugurated by local secular persons, and some of the worst excesses of torture leading to death sentences were perpetrated by local clergy, learned Dominican inquisitors seemingly supervised, acquiesced, or participated in several investigations. A leading inquisitor like Prierias produced a manual to guide later witch persecution. Once the leadership of the Roman Inquisition was established, and torture was controlled, the persecution of witches diminished. Initially, of course, the dominant inquisitors concentrated on the heresies involving high theology. When these had been largely controlled by the 1570s and the inquisitors turned their attention more to Christian malpractices (such as misusing the sacraments, and sacramentals like holy oil), superstitions and maleficent magical activities, the reading of illicit books and so on, their attitudes to 'witchcraft' were milder, the scepticism greater and the punishments more spiritual than physical.

The comparative mildness of the Inquisition's handling of witchcraft accusations can be explained partly by the inquisitors' good legal training, their guidance by manuals warning that accusations could be triggered by neighbourly animosities, and that some people – particularly women – might be self-deluded and invent experiences. Furthermore, the accusations and claims tended to be about individuals, and not groups. With less pressure than in countries further north and in lay courts to 'confess' under torture, and to name accomplices, the allegations of group activities were minimised. Both the common public and the trained investigators in Italy and Iberia were seemingly less inclined to believe in the sabbat than those from countries further north, whether Catholic or Protestant. This recognition that inquisitors were dubious about the existence of sabbats, group meetings with the Devil and his devilish minions, was stated long ago by one of the pioneering scholars of the Spanish and Italian Inquisitions, Henry C. Lea. In a letter to a friend he wrote: 'It is a very curious fact ... which I have no where seen recognized, that in both Spain and Italy the Holy Office took a decidedly sceptical attitude with regard to the Sabbat and the *Cap. Episcopi*, that preserved those lands from the madness prevailing elsewhere. I have a good many original documents that place this in a clear light and I think will prove a surprise to the demonologists.'[1]

This view has not been absorbed by many commentators on the 'witch-craze' in general, though recent specialists in inquisitional history like Henry Kamen, Gustav Henningsen, John Tedeschi, Brian Levack, Franceso Renda and Maria Sofia Messana have tried to emphasise this scepticism. It does not mean that some of those who appeared before inquisitors did not believe neighbours, or that they themselves might be capable of 'flying off' to sabbats and merely admitted this to please the inquisitor or avoid torture. As Messana argues, Sicily had a proportionately higher number of 'magic' cases because the local population had a more widespread belief in magical powers, for personal benefit or malice. The incoming inquisitors and local bishops feared these beliefs, and cooperated in counteracting them, but were aware that many accusations might be fabricated, especially with extravagant claims about flying and sabbats.[2]

Lea's reference to *Cap. Episcopi* was to a canon *Episcopi*, a church ruling noted from about AD 900 which was absorbed into collections of canon law from the eleventh century onwards, Gratian's collection included. It notably referred to:

> certain wicked women ... who believe that at night, in the company of Diana, goddess of the pagans, and an innumerable multitude of women, they ride on certain beasts, and pass over great distances of the earth in the depth of the night, and obey her commands as their mistress and are summoned to her service on particular nights.

The canon took the view that the night flying was not a physical reality but images of the mind (*phantasmata*), and that it was the Devil who persuaded women they were flying, when they were only moving in spirit. They were 'perverted by Satan', according to the canon. The official scepticism about actual flying could often be discarded by some clergy, as well as tale-tellers. The Devil might displace Diana as the prime mover. The image of witch-flying spread; Robert Bartlett notes a Parisian manuscript of 1451 showing two happy-looking women on broomsticks as possibly the earliest surviving image.[3] Unfortunately the printing of the *Malleus Maleficarum* in 1487 buttressed the idea that women (and men) could fly off to Devil-led sabbats – though its author, Heinrich Kramer, may have written it in a personal battle to overcome doubts that sabbats were merely illusory, and to show that evil spirits really existed.[4] Well-trained inquisitors in Italy (unlike secular magistrates) should have learned to be sceptical of this dream-world, and they reacted accordingly in quizzing those claiming to 'fly off', or being accused of such – though some inquisitors seemed to accept there might be gatherings of night flyers. The aspect of flying was a comparatively rare element in the 'witchcraft' cases they confronted, which were mostly less sinister.

The Roman Congregation and its writers of manuals urged caution about deducing witchcraft or malefice from unfortunate events and deaths. In 1626 Florence seemed to be in a panic about witchcraft – especially harming children in the city and *contado* – and secular officials (especially on the Otto di Balia committee) tried to take the initiative in investigations and prosecutions. The Roman Congregation wrote to the Florentine inquisitor, the nuncio and the archbishop that the issue of witchcraft was leading to miscarriages of justice. Having seen supposed evidence, it concluded: 'these matters are extremely fallacious, and, as daily experience demonstrates, much more real in the imagination of men than in the reality of events; too often every illness whose cause is not immediately discernible, or whose remedy is not readily available is attributed to witchcraft (*maleficia*). . . . the public cry, that in Florence and the *contado* there are many witches (*streghe*) has no real foundation'.[5] A judge on the Otto di Balia, Antonio Maria Cospi, seemed to be fixated on the witch stereotype; Cardinal Millini declared him incompetent. Millini argued that people should not be arrested until there was clear evidence about a crime. Through the seventeenth century the Roman Inquisition showed wariness about Florentine secular pursuers of witches.[6]

Like Millini, Masini's *Sacro Arsenale* ruled that '. . . in prosecuting suspected witches the judge must not reach the point of incarceration, inquisition or torture until the *corpus delicti* is judicially established. Sickness in a person or the presence of a corpse in themselves do not constitute adequate evidence, since infirmity and death do not need to be connected just with malefice (*maleficia*) but can result from a large number of natural causes. The first step, therefore, is to question the physicians who attended the patient.' Guidance from the Roman Inquisition and manuals also now stressed that inquisitors should be suspicious about the claims of accused witches that others were physical participants in a sabbat; they were likely to be hallucinating under the Devil's influence. Also those charged for the first time, if showing a willingness to repent, should be received back into the Church, allocated penances but no harsh penalty, such as the death sentence ordered by secular courts.[7]

Inquisitorial scepticism was shown in the manuals' cautions about 'evidence' in identifying witches, as in the hunting for the Devil's mark which was notoriously used in some Swiss and northern European witch-hunts. In his 1637 handbook *'La prattica di procedere'* dedicated to Cardinal Francesco Barberini, Deodati Scaglia did discuss the shapes that such marks might take on the body (such as astrological symbols), but he was very cautious about using them as evidence, and stated that other proofs were needed. One inquisitorial court in Vicenza in 1616, dealing with a witch from Montagna di Valdagno, did allude to this phenomenon. But secular courts were prone to use the mark as an indicator, as in the Trentino from 1612 to 1615, and the Valtellina had a specialist in hunting Devil's marks, who was called a *ravetta*. The Roman Inquisition regularly warned inquisitors they should rescue those accused by popular or secular magisterial enthusiasm for using such evidence. In a work on the Roman Inquisition published in 1638, Paolo Sarpi stated that 'Concerning malevolent witchcraft (*stregherie malefice*), the most excellent Great Council ordered that they should be punished by the magistrate because the ecclesiastical penalties are not a sufficient castigation for such a great crime (*sclerattezza*)'.[8]

'Superstition' was and is a slippery concept, covering beliefs and practices that bordered on heresy, but it was a less serious sin than heresy. In the fifteenth century canon Martin de Arles (in Pamplona), called it 'superfluous and vain religion pursued in a defective manner in wrong circumstances', but a false religion that could lead the offender into serious heresy. Later Peña in glossing Eymeric declared: 'Superstition is a vice opposed to the correct Christian religion, it is *latria*.' For Peña *latria* meant the honouring and venerating of someone or something other than God, the Virgin Mary, or the saints; if the Devil was involved in any way then the practice became heretical, as also if the offender had acted in clear opposition to Church teaching. Such practices were now better publicised through episcopal legislative warnings, which were supposedly conveyed in parish sermons. As expressed in Venetian inquisitional terminology, superstition covered incantations, charms, or distorted saying of prayers, which might link with healing practices or divination. Much inquisitional time was spent trying to ascertain whether superstitious practices (which would be discouraged and might incur disciplinary penalties) had a devilish element, and so could be punished as magical heresy. For Peña they were heretical if they involved misusing the sacraments, as with 'baptizing of images, or the rebaptizing of a child, or touching (another) with holy oil, or fumigating a skull, or similar such things'.⁹

Stephen Bowd argues that a major change of emphasis occurred in Italy from the end of the fifteenth century in identifying the demonic in superstition, after the earlier emphasis on heresy in the demonic. He points to the interesting example of Maria of Vicenza ('the doctor'), who was living near Brescia and was arraigned by the Brescian inquisitor. No trial records survive, but according to a chronicler she was accused of worshipping the Devil at a sabbat (*ludus*), but further she denied God and Christ and was the recipient of cures from the Devil with whom she celebrated Masses, using the blood of murdered babies. She bewitched thirty boys and girls, leading to the death of half of them. She was executed by mutual agreement of the inquisitor, the bishop and secular authorities. She was the stereotype of the witch (similar to what emerged in the 1495 Rifreddo trials). One might guess that a local superstitious healer ('the doctor'), some of whose child 'patients' had died, who was sceptical about orthodox clergy and sacraments, was induced by questioning and torture to agree that she was such an evil witch.¹⁰

'Witchcraft' was viewed as more extreme than superstition, more specifically involving Devil-inspired evil, intentionally leading to harmful activities, *maleficia*. It could combine folklore, sorcery, demonology, heresy and Christian theology. *Stregoneria* was the normal Italian term for what we call witchcraft, though it could cover non-diabolic superstition as well as diabolic magic. A practitioner, especially female, might be seen to mix beneficial practices (for health, love, finding lost property) with malevolent ones. *Strega* (witch) was (and is) also used more loosely as a term of abuse against an immoral or disliked woman; *strigone* (male witch) was a more focused description of a male practitioner of maleficent magic.¹¹

Chapter 6 and the Tables in the Appendix have indicated the growing concern of inquisitors in cases of superstition and malicious magic. The comparative mildness of inquisitorial punishment has been noted, sometimes in contrast with harsher secular attitudes. Although the Sicilian tribunal is seen as stricter than most mainland Roman tribunals, and it conducted major campaigns against witchcraft – especially alleged '*donne di fora*', those who supposedly flew off at night – it did not hand over any witches to the secular authorities for execution. Inquisitors and bishops very expressly rejected the *Malleus Maleficarum* as a guide, and cast doubts on notions that female or male witches could physically fly off for meetings.¹² Although much of the literature on European witchcraft followed the *Malleus* in stressing that witchcraft was a female occupation, figures for Sicily indicate that many men were involved as well, as *strigoni*; 53 per cent of cases of magic involved women, 47 per cent men. Many men involved were from the clergy or professional orders of society. There is also evidence from Venice and Friuli, though it has been less analysed, of males accused of being witches. While some men were investigated as 'night flyers', whether in Friuli or Sicily, they were more likely to feature in cases of treasure hunting, prognostications through arcane rituals and misuse of the sacraments – as when they were the accomplices of female practitioners of medicinal and love magic. Accusations of magic in society were often levelled among people who were not equals, lay and clerical, and they increased when outside factors such as the plague of 1624 added tensions. Some work on female practitioners in the Veneto and the Kingdom of Naples suggests that women were using magic to demonstrate power and influence in certain localities, as alternatives to priests and doctors. Sometimes acting like female priests, they were vulnerable to accusations both by disappointed customers and by jealous males.[13]

Superstitious or magical practices served many purposes in society, attempting good as well as harm. 'Healing' was a significant factor in the medical sense of having cures for human and animal ills, in helping conception and in the sense of sorting out someone's love-life. Good healing practices were required to counteract the 'bad' witches, whether the latter were hurting people, crops or one's love-life. The healing practices included the use of herbs (which alternative-medicine practitioners today accept as efficacious), potions and unguents – which might incorporate menstrual blood or semen – or the use of talismans and blessed objects. Magic protection could extend as far as protecting people from bullets (nine cases in Friuli, 1611–1785). The magical arts were expected to help forecast the future, find stolen or lost property; here the most cited practices seem to be the casting of a rope, or beans, and looking into a glass carafe, *inghistera* (as already noted in the case of Valeriana Brugnaleschi and her daughter Splandiana Mariano). Clerical help was enlisted and acquired willingly or surreptitiously, for blessing talismans, the umbilical cord (with medicinal value), or pieces of paper on which were written special words or prayers. Lay healers sought holy oil, consecrated wafers, or just blessed water to aid their practices. Clerics assisting the superstitious laity were likely to be more severely punished than the laity themselves. When the 'good' magic seemed to fail, then the denunciations followed.[14]

The rest of this chapter will illustrate what kinds of accusations, confessions and punishments lay behind the various types of cases; and further show how inquisitors differed in approaches to the denunciations. The Appendix of Tables gives an idea of the diversity of magical practices, and the prevalence of accusations in relation to other offences. My choice of detailed examples (mixing the well known and the more obscure) has been influenced by a wish to demonstrate that accusations of superstition and magic (irrespective of the truth of their effectiveness) can reveal a considerable amount about broader social conditions, including the following: animosity or solidarity between neighbours, gender and sexual relations, local healing practices, and rivalries between lay people and clergy.

Playing with the Devil: Group Activities, Imagined or Real?

The Latin word *ludus* was used for supposed group encounters with the Devil and his entourage; it had variously covered organised games such as the Olympics, ordinary playfulness and trickery.[15] It was used to cover what the fifteenth-century investigators above conceived as a witches' sabbat. Johan Huizinga stressed this in his pioneering book *Homo Ludens*, defining play as 'a free activity standing quite consciously outside "ordinary" life as being "not serious", but at the same time absorbing the player intensely and utterly. It is an activity connected with no material interest.... It proceeds within its own proper boundaries of time and space according to fixed rules and in an orderly manner. ... It promotes the formation of social groupings which tend to surround themselves with secrecy and to stress their difference from the common world by disguise or other means.'[16] However, it becomes less orderly than Huizinga saw it, and even deadly serious when in confrontation with the Inquisition. Unlike Huizinga, Ruggiero argues for bringing sex, even with the Devil, into the concept of play. In Venetian court cases secular and ecclesiastical participants used phrases like '*ludendo et trepudiando*' ('playing and sexually enjoying') and '*giocando a letto*' ('playing in bed') for couples disporting, sometimes aided by love potions.[17] In the period of this study we find some elaborate stories woven of ludic encounters with the Devil, while individuals might attempt to trick the Devil for their own ends, or claim they had been tricked by the Devil or his agents. Whatever the impact of suggestive questioning and torture, it seems clear that some men and women genuinely believed in such happenings (in physical encounters or in spirit), or that bargains might be struck with the Devil.

A Brescian correspondent, Giuseppe da Orzinuovo, writing in 1518 to a Venetian friend, as recorded in Sanudo's Diary, summarised what the Brescian inquisitor and bishop had unearthed in the Val Camonica. Witches – *strioni* and *strie* – influenced by arrivals from Albania in particular, had been induced by demonic priests to pursue wealth and pleasure and seek a paradise. 'Rebels against God', promising body and soul to the Devil, assembled in large groups on Monte Tonale to indulge themselves in games (*zuoghi*), and receive powders and unguents, to be used to harm or enchant others and re-shape themselves. They misused and mocked those Christian rituals they attended. Because the Devil had appeared disguised as the Virgin, they believed they could survive the burning when sentenced. But, deceived, they cried out: 'Devil, you have deceived us'. Giuseppe challenged the idea that 'battles' took place. Sanudo reported the castellan of Breno as raising the issue of whether such meetings took place physically (*corporaliter*), or were mere delusions, as canon law texts he consulted suggested was likely from ignorant persons; and so whether they should be burned. The Brescian *podestà*, Piero Tron, managed to interview some of the accused, and concluded that the inquisitorial vicar, Bernardino de Grossis, had used excessive force and deception to induce confessions. Tron reported that some women claimed to have been penetrated front and back by the Devil with a bifurcated penis. Tron told the Council of Ten: 'These all seem rather grave, wondrous, and strange matters to me, which I believe and don't believe.' Elsewhere Sanudo noted the bifurcated penis as an attribute of the Devil.[18] Some forty women and twenty men were burned before the Venetians called a halt. Rather similar 'confessions', and similar doubts as to veracity, were to reappear under the Roman Inquisition, especially in Friuli with *benandanti* battles, and the use of unguents. As we shall see, the investigative procedures were more legalistic, and the punishments milder. The orgiastic fancies largely disappear.

In the mid-sixteenth century conflicting approaches to sabbats become evident, with Inquisition officials closer to Rome more sceptical than those at a distance. In the Kingdom of Naples in 1586–8 Carlo Baldino, a friend of Cardinal Santoro and acting as leading minister for the Holy Office, investigated a number of women claiming to attend sabbats. Much doubt was shown about their veracity, and whether they should be punished, and he abandoned his cases after some lengthy questioning in 1586. But an archiepiscopal vicar, Flaminio Torcella, taking over as chief judge for the Holy Office was more rigorous and tortured some individuals, such as Argenta Amorosa who was accused of diabolic meetings. Torcella imprisoned Baldino's notary in 1588, and only released him on Santoro's orders. When Torcella sought Rome's permission to conclude Amorosa's case, he was promptly told by Cardinal Santa Severina (Santoro) that the witnesses against her and tales of diabolic meetings were unreliable, adding that her withstanding torture for an hour and a half sufficiently purged the allegations. She must be released.[19]

A fertile imagination could produce a fantastic Devil-centred scenario, as with the case of Gostanza da Libbiano, who was living in the village of Bagnio in the Tuscan district of San Miniato (but diocese of Lucca) and was investigated during November and December of 1594.[20] The case well illustrates divergent attitudes and procedures by officials of the Inquisition, and illicit torturing procedures. Gostanza, a sixty-year-old widow and former spinner, had been a well-reputed healer and midwife for over thirty years, and now lived in a community of female relatives. The bishop's *vicario foraneo*, Tommaso Roffia, heard from several witnesses that she had a reputation as 'a witch and sorceress who made medicines and measured cloths'.[21] He then ordered her arrest, questioned her and confronted her with another witness, under threats of torture if she did not tell the truth. The accusations were brought before a Franciscan friar, Mario Porcacchi da Castiglione, a local vicar of the Florentine Inquisition; aged thirty-one, fresh from theological studies, he was in his first responsible post as guardian of the local convent of San Francesco. He was possibly intent on making his reputation. His hearings were attended by Roffia, and various secular officials as witnesses. Gostanza was soon tortured, by the rope (*fune*); she was raised up three *braccia* (arms' length) for the time it took to say a Credo, leading to admissions of various cases of *maleficia* and using incantations in her healing.[22] The inquisitorial vicar was using torture very shortly after starting his questioning, and without permission; since he was handling the case within four days of the bishop's vicar starting proceedings, there was hardly time to secure permission from Florence, let alone Rome. From the beginning the questioning under Porcacchi was in the torture room. Gostanza was driven to say she had done harm to various persons, adults and children.

Then she was asked if she had ever gone at night on a tour with other women who made the same profession as her.[23] She started to talk about going, some twenty-five years before, at the invitation of friends to a feast and dance. Fearing her husband she had gone reluctantly. She was told to invoke a Polletto, not God, who arrived in the form of a goat. Gostanza talked of a beautiful city of the Gran Diavolo, more impressive than Florence, where much feasting and dancing took place. Polletto might appear as a goat, ass or dog, when he took Gostanza to the feasts, moving on the ground but seeming to fly along. She confessed to sucking blood from a child, whose father had seen a large black cat which he had driven off with a stick. She confirmed her confessions when interviewed outside the torture room; secular representatives were again present, and the notary recorded that she was free from any threat of torture, and no guards (*sbirri*) were present. But further sessions were held in the torture chamber where Gostanza had to answer questions about her medical activities, but again about Polletto, whom she then called the Greater Devil ('*il Diavolo Maggiore*'). She answered questions about her celebrations of Mass, about those she harmed, many times drinking the blood of children at Polletto's behest, about those she met at the gatherings. These included a male witch from Siena, a *stregone* or *galatrone*, worse than the others, 'il padrone de' padroni' (given in response to a question whether she knew such a witch). Asked about sex with the Devil she said his semen was cold, not warm like her husband's, and it could not make her pregnant as it emerged watery. However he was a better, more attentive lover than her husband.[24]

The inquisitor of Florence, Dionigi da Costacciaro, when informed of Gostanza's stories or confessions came to investigate. He was at the height of his career, and had earlier been inquisitor in Siena. His interrogations of her took place in the civilian vicar's palace. The tone of his reported questioning suggests scepticism about the validity of her extreme claims, as he urged her not to repeat lies from previous sessions, and not tremble with fear. However, she elaborated on feasting in the Città del Diavolo, and about sexual relations with the Devil, whose caresses made it all more pleasant than sex with her husband; about taking the Sacrament (saved from Easter and Rosary communions) and offering it to the

Devil, who put it in her vagina; about the multitudes who attended the celebrations with the Devil and other demons. After four long interrogation sessions over six days, Gostanza declared that she had been seized aged about eight by shepherds from outside her father's house in Florence and forced into a marriage, and badly treated. A supposedly friendly woman then introduced her to the Devil's gatherings. Two days later during her questioning, having examined her conscience in prison, she suddenly turned round and denied the stories of the House of the Devil, declaring she had made these confessions fearing more torture. The bishop's vicar, Roffia, withdrew from the case and left it to the inquisitors. Porcacchi and inquisitor Dionigi disagreed on their interpretation; the former was convinced Gostanza was guilty of real witch-craft, while the inquisitor judged her 'mad' and a total fabricator. He ordered Gostanza to be released, to pay something towards the cost of keeping her in prison. Property initially confiscated from her was returned. She was to stay away from Bagnio, and not issue medicines to men, women, or animals. She was to tell them where she would reside, which became Rivalto, four miles from Bagnio in the diocese of Volterra. The inquisitor, back in Florence, finally declared to Mario Porcacchi da Castiglione:

> I tell you gossip (*chiacchere*) should not be believed, but the *processo* undertaken, such that in the end it is seen that this poor old woman has said all this under torments, and nothing is true, as she ultimately deposed, and of this we have confirmation by the wife [Lisabetta] of that [late] Menicone, by her named as accomplice, and indeed she has been found a respected woman (*donna da bene*), such that it is not necessary to accept the words of the common public (*parole del vulgo*).[25]

That the bishop's vicar had started the investigation and then brought in the local Inquisition seems to have made it easier for the Florentine Inquisition to curtail the process. Lisabetta, deeply shocked when told she was herself suspect, had been found by the inquisitor to be a convincing witness; he immediately cleared her as innocent at the end of the questioning. Many witnesses testified to Gostanza's contributions as a healer across a large area of Tuscany and the Lucchese Republic, and her willingness to travel to remote areas to help the sick. Her utopian construct was imaginative, and unusual in envisaging a city for the Devil, for most devil-worshipping gatherings were in remote rural areas. Why should she have invented such a scenario to avoid torture? Had this been long part of a fantasy world developed by Gostanza over years as she travelled about, possibly hearing stories based on the *Malleus* or Gianfrancesco Pico's *Strix*, and reacting to sexual frustration? As a child in 1540 had she been influenced by the hanging and burning of four *streghe maliarde*, who were convicted by a San Miniato secular court for killing children?[26] Or was Gostanza's story all constructed in a few days once she had been arrested, hoping that a great fantasy would persuade the tribunal that she was mad, and so release her, as happened? Over long sessions of interrogation she had named a whole range of people, dead and alive, some of whom might be quite readily identifiable. A serious witch-hunt could have ensued had the local inquisitorial vicar acted like his fifteenth-century predecessors. Other inquisitors during this period might have subjected Gostanza to exorcism, as one who was possessed by the Devil. Notably in this case, however, an experienced inquisitor was ready to overrule a younger, but also learned, inquisitorial vicar, and the bishop's vicar.

The worst case of Italian attempts to persecute witches in this period involved individual 'offenders' hounded by secular and episcopal officials. It started in the autumn of 1587 in Triora, a fortified village of about 2,500 inhabitants in the Valle Argentina on the Genoese Riviera. About two hundred people were accused of witchcraft, and of these thirty-two women and one man were tried. But this case was launched by the local lay officials (*anziani*), and was clearly the product of factional infighting, not food shortages as was alleged. The bishop of Albenga's vicar-general took up the case, clearly believing that sabbats and the killing of infants had taken place. Inquisitorial vicars from the Genoese and Albenga tribunals were called to ask questions, and one preached what witches could do; the outcome of their preliminary investigations is unclear. The Genoese Senate intervened and appointed a special commissioner, Giulio Scribani, who transferred the male accused and thirteen of the female accused to Genoese prisons in the summer of 1589. There followed deaths under torture, suicide and death sentences, all condoned by the Genoese Senate. However, the inquisitor called for intervention by the Roman Congregation, so beginning a long legal battle. When Scribani sent more of the women to Genoa for trial, the Inquisition took over and reprimanded the previous judges for too readily believing denunciations of persons for involvement in sabbats, and for cruel treatment of the accused leading to five deaths in prison. Scribani happily stated that one woman had been strangled by the Devil (proved by black spots under her ears). Unfortunately, subsequent inquisitorial evidence is not clear on what happened to the man and thirteen women held in Genoese prisons since 1589. One received a Christian burial in 1595, and was therefore clearly not convicted of heresy. Roman inquisitorial scepticism in this case had prevailed against the credulity and murderous mania of secular and episcopal officials.[27]

The Benandanti, *and* Donne di fora

Those alleged or even claiming to have flown off to sabbats in Friuli were called *benandanti*, while those in Sicily were called *donne di fora*, or *uomini di fora*. Carlo Ginzburg's forays into the records of the Udine Inquisition led to his famous book, highly influential in the anthropology of magic, *I Benandanti* (1966). However, it was not translated (as *The Night Battles*) until 1983, after Ginzburg's *The Cheese and the Worms*, about the miller Menocchio Scandella, had caused a great stir. Ginzburg discovered that from 1574 in Friuli inquisitors investigated a number of cases concerning men and women called *benandanti*. According to their own accounts they were persons marked out and selected because they had been born with the caul (the amniotic membrane). As adults they could leave their bodies at night and fly off in spirit to defend crops against evil witches threatening the harvests. The inquisitors in the early cases were puzzled by such claims, and were fairly open-minded and flexible in their questioning, as demonstrated in the investigations (1575–81) of the first *benandanti*, Paolo Gasparutto and Battista Moducco.[28] However, in Ginzburg's argument, by the mid-seventeenth century the inquisitorial mentality had persuaded the accused and self-denouncing *benandanti* that they were in fact also evil witches, not defenders of the crops. Subsequently Franco Nardon has widened our knowledge of the *benandanti*. Some of them were lay exorcists and healers, who used methods not too dissimilar to the official exorcists, and as such were tolerated by Church authorities in Friuli. These *benandanti* were then exorcised and treated leniently by the inquisitors. Some, especially the females, were claiming to make contact with dead souls.[29] Actual physical gatherings for masquerade rituals, and processions for the dead with humans dressed as animals, may well have occurred. Some who had participated might, possibly under the influence of drug-like herbal concoctions or bad food, have also had ecstatic experiences or dreams, and sensations of flying, while a family member observed their bodies in bed as spirit-less and cold. While men were the first *benandanti* to be investigated, greater attention was soon paid to women – but as healers and competitors with priests, 'night-battling' being an aside for most inquisitors. Nardon has shown that one inquisitor in particular, Giulio Missini from Orvieto (serving Aquileia and Concordia, 1645–53), concentrated on *benandanti*, regarding them as dangerous and among the worst *stregoni*. However, of the 350 accusations of all kinds which he investigated, only twelve involved *benandanti*, while eleven concerned sabbats, pacts or sex with the Devil and sacrilege. Other inquisitors were more intent on controlling local priests involved in magic and necromancy. Missini's case load was dominated by 112 accusations of owning or reading prohibited books, impressive for a region often seen (misleadingly) as remote and backward. A further eighty cases involved divination and the abuse of sacraments.[30]

From 1574 to 1716 eighty-two persons were denounced to the Aquileia and Concordia tribunals for offences that included alleged *benandante* activity; a full trial followed in only thirty-three cases, and only ten males and six females received a formal sentence. Four were imprisoned, including Moducco and Gasparutto. Many were merely admonished, or allocated penances.

Seemingly the harshest treated was Maria Panzona from Latislana, condemned by the Venetian tribunal in 1619 as lightly suspected of heresy, for which she was sentenced to public abjuration, three years in prison and perpetual exile.[31] Originally arrested and imprisoned in 1618 for the theft of handkerchiefs, her behaviour aroused suspicion that she caused illnesses. Initially she was investigated by a Latislana parish priest, who was acting for the Inquisition. She had admitted straightaway to being a '*biandante*', using incantations and strange mixtures to help victims of sorcery by real witches (she named fifteen); Maria ('in the form of a black cat') had personally observed another ('in that of a white cat') sucking blood from humans. Maria, when a 'good night-battler' with like-minded others, had been escorted by cocks and billy-goats, to see 'the woman seated in majesty on the edge of a well, called the abbess', 'in the valley of Josaphat'. Maria's transports to a distant place were, she said explicitly, in spirit; her body remained in bed as if dead. Throughout various interrogations she had been extremely informative and loquacious about her activities. The parish priest contacted the Patriarch of Venice, Francesco Vendramin, with limited details, but enough for him to summon Maria to the tribunal in Venice. There she continued her elaborate accounts. During one session she had an epileptic fit, which she said was common. Having been allocated a lawyer who spent some time trying to make her see her errors, she blamed fits for making her invent these stories; she had never really deserted Christ. She escaped torture because of her physical condition. Having escaped that threat, she reverted to some claims she was a true *benandante*.

As Carlo Ginzburg noted, Maria's confessions in Latislana (being a *benandante* or witch) and Venice (merely a *benandante*) conflicted with each other and were muddled. They were not, however, forced out of her, and one might detect in her a persistent belief over a long period that she was a *benandante*, even if she invented stories about others. The court had little option but to sentence her with some severity, for her obstinacy in holding to strange beliefs: three years in prison followed by banishment from Latislana. But that tribunal paid little credence to claims of sabbats, about which the parish priest had been more credulous. Inquisitor-general Giandomenico Vignuzio, Patriarch Vendramin, nuncio Sigismondo Donati, and *assistenti* Leonardo Mocenigo and Marc'Antonio Loredan agreed on Maria's sentencing. Elsewhere in Europe death would have been the likely punishment.[32]

'Night travellers' were found at the other extreme of Italy. From the Sicilian tribunal records there were seventy-seven investigations involving women and men '*di fora*', known as *brujas* in Spanish. They occurred between 1588 and 1737, mostly in ones or twos. But there were two peak periods, when individual inquisitors took a special interest; thirteen individuals had their trials completed in 1601, under inquisitors Llanes (1594–1618) and Pedro De Hoyo (1598–1602), and twelve in 1640 under Diego Garçia de Trasmiera (inquisitor 1634–55). Pedro De Hoyo, who had been part of the Barcelona tribunal, had come from an extensive visitation in Sardinia between 1596 and 1598, where he had tried to sort out conflicts over the Inquisition in Sassari and the tribunal's parlous state there.[33]

Playing with the Devil: Individuals

From various surviving testimonies of individuals not subject to torture it is clear that some Italians believed it possible to have different kinds of personal relationships with the Devil. In 1590 a young Venetian apprentice perfume maker, Andrea Meri, fell so in love with his master's wife that he decided to write a contract with the Devil:

> ... by means of the present contract ... I obligate myself to the Prince Lucifer and all the princes of Hell. I call him my Lord and am his slave until the final judgement under the agreement and condition that he grant me this grace: that he make Madonna Paolina di Modesta ... be inflamed with love for me. So much so that she will have no content, no repose of her spirit or her body unless she is with me. Morover I pray to those most wise and prudent princes of Hell that they make me this grant. In return I promise my body and my soul at death. I Andrea have written this with my own hand.

We do not know with what confidence Andrea set about writing this. But he seemingly panicked and threw it down the toilet (*necessario*), which took it into a canal, where neighbours found it. The master was informed; after a talk with Andrea he forgave him. But somebody took the contract to the Inquisition. Andrea told the tribunal that he had got the idea from reading Fra Giacomo's *Legendario delle Vite di Santi* (Venice, 1586). He was sentenced to exile from the Republic's territory for three years, and ordered to recite a series of special prayers on Fridays for a year.[34]

Sexual play with the Devil was the key factor in the investigation of the nun Suor Mansueta from the Venetian convent of Santa Croce in 1574.[35] She claimed to have had physical encounters of joy and pain with the Devil. The Inquisition questioned her but never arrived at a formal trial. One of many women in convents unhappy with their position there, she was explicit in describing visits of the Devil in the form of bearded 'Romito' (who sometimes appeared as a porter or chimney-sweep), and the sexual encounters she enjoyed as part of visions. 'I touched him as if he was in fact a man and I felt great pleasure ... and I corrupted myself,' and she enjoyed natural and unnatural sex with him. He tempted her to deny the Trinity, but more especially to leave the convent. A nearly full tribunal (with inquisitor, nuncio and Patriarch all present in person) took a considerable interest in her stories, and were puzzled as to whether she was mad or not. They tried exorcism on her, which she resisted, declaring 'I am not possessed [*inspiritata*]. I have no other spirit than that of the world [*del seculo*].' And almost clowning [*quasi boffonando*], 'If I am mad, bind me!' (The chancellor rather than an ordinary notary took the record, and interestingly interpolated comments into the record.) Mansueta pleaded with the inquisitors to have her released from the convent, 'and have a man for a husband'; for staying there she would lose her soul. Then one of the tribunal said: 'We believe that all you have said is untrue, but you have said it thinking that We because of this must bring you out [of the convent].'[36] The record describes the attempted exorcism in some detail. It took place over several days. Mansueta's body was out of control, and resisting voices came from her as if from the Devil. The exorcist continued to play with the Devil, gradually reducing the amount of her body that the Devil controlled, down to the foot; 'and the body returned to itself'.[37] In February 1575 a note indicates Mansueta was still in the convent, and still 'possessed by demons'. Seemingly she had failed to escape the convent. Was Mansueta a hysterical woman crazed by sexual frustration (as an earlier analyst of her story, Marisa Milani, argued), an 'imprisoned' nun consciously inventing a story to secure release, or one who had had real relations with a porter or chimney-sweep? Venetian nunneries had vulnerable walls, as Mary Laven among others has shown.[38] If Mansueta had been a rational player, she was a very accomplished actress, as demonstrated when the Inquisition handed her over for exorcism.

This example among other things highlights the fact that the Roman Inquisition could adopt a healing role, not just a punitive one. Its record-keeping is valuable here for understanding sexual attitudes and behaviour, exorcisms and also the careful interrogation procedures by a full tribunal.

Healing and Harming

Many persons were denounced to the Inquisition for abuses of healing processes. Clearly, significant numbers of people, especially women, practised the healing arts (what we call 'alternative medicine') and were in demand at all levels of society, as alternatives to expensive university-trained doctors, apothecaries and officially licensed and regulated 'charlatans'. These last – male, usually itinerant, healers – with their medicines or remedies, their contracts with suppliers and patients, were regulated in some areas by *Protomedicato* tribunals (sometimes including notable physicians). These tribunals punished illicit healing, using procedures similar to the Inquisition, and likewise seeking admission of guilt and reconciliation. If, however, superstitious practices were suspected the *Protomedicato* tribunals let the Inquisition's tribunals take responsibility.[39] The unregulated healers might be well-respected married women and widows who became recognised locally as midwives. Others were prostitutes who added healing remedies, love magic and prognostications to their offerings. When some remedy failed, the practitioner might be denounced as a *strega* or *maliarda*. Inquisitors then had to decide whether the perpetrators of healing measures had also used religiously superstitious procedures – by introducing distorted prayers, misusing the sacraments and sacramentals or, worse, invoking the Devil and his agents.

The borderline between acceptable and unacceptable 'popular' healing was fuzzy; much depended on who did the healing, and if appeals for supernatural help were involved, or whether the public reputation of a practitioner suggested she was a witch. As an example where a prior reputation was not an issue, and the accused was cleared of wrongdoing, we have the case of Donato de Quarto from Torre Santa Susanna, who appeared in June 1697 in the bishop of Oria's court held in Francavilla (Puglia), where the bishop was acting as an inquisitor. A farm labourer turned beggar when asthmatic aged sixty-three, Donato was accused of using magic to cure the syphilis of a cooper, Nicola Gargaro, at the latter's request. Donato went to the monastery of S. Francesco di Paolo, had Masses said for his friend, and there had a ribbon blessed in the saint's name. This ribbon he placed on Nicola, also squeezing some sour grapes over his genitals and kidneys, and he may have rubbed him with herbs. Gargaro unfortunately decided this was an attempt at bewitchment, to which Donato responded that he learned this use of grapes as a remedy for a fever patient when he had been in Lecce hospital the year before. The court exonerated him, judging him to know the basics of the faith, and to have used only legitimate prayers.[40] This case illustrates the dubious defining areas between legitimate non-doctoral healing and 'superstition' with evil intent.

Similarly, in the same year in Bologna a prostitute, Virginia de Tomasellis, was investigated for superstitious love practices. It was revealed that she grew plants, notably *erba valeriana*, to which she talked. She made, used and sold an unguent as good for helping pains but also 'good for imprisoning men'. The court was interested because valerian might be used for abortions. Virginia possessed a booklet of secrets, which she could not read. This turned out to be for conjuring tricks, and using invisible ink, *New Rules for Learning Many Beautiful Games*. This last was considered innocent reading matter, so the inquisitor questioned whether Virginia used prayers wrongly, or had an implicit pact with the Devil. She admitted to seeking to know about lovers and future events, declined a defence and put herself at the court's mercy. It decided she was not that bad, and sentenced her to fifteen days of house confinement.[41]

Snippets from the records of the Florentine Inquisition illustrate some attitudes of, and problems posed by, vicarial agents in the province of the inquisitor. In March 1629 Fra Michaele Remededito acting for the Holy Office in Pescia (Tuscany), heard allegations from Costantino de Benedinellis that a certain

Ginevra, wife of Antonio Gaggiollo da Uzzano, knew a medicine to cure eye problems, including those of Costantino's son. It involved using *finochio* (fennel) and *verbenaca* (vervain, *Verbena officianalis*?) in water. Costantino asked whether the medicine was prohibited or licensed. He had given her alms of wine and bread, and he felt no enmity towards her. He declared he confessed at Easter and Christmas. In May 1632 the rector of Fiumalbo, Annibale Bonacchio, acting as vicar for the Florentine inquisitor, received a denunciation against Menga di Nanni of Fiumalbo for theft of wheat, but she also supposedly cured eyes. The notary opaquely annotated that she was '*la maggior strega*', the greater witch. In August the inquisitorial vicar of Pistoia questioned there Alexander Morelli of Fiumalbo, the victim of theft, who declared that he had learned that both Menga and her daughter Maria (servant to his brother) were *streghe*; and they had bewitched him as well as stolen his wheat. Nothing further is recorded. According to another tantalising fragmentary record, in March 1645 the *pievano* of Cammaggiore consulted the Florentine inquisitor: a curate under him had refused absolution to two women who practised *medicina al fuoco salvatico* (for St Anthony's Fire), using salted meat and prayers (Pater Noster and Ave Maria) to make the fire leave the body. They also threw water in the name of God and the Virgin. They often did this, believing they could, and having been taught by persons now dead. *Pievano* Mario Berti wanted to know what he should do about these women, given their poverty. The paucity of surviving inquisitional records for Tuscany means we do not have data to follow up these snippets of information.[42]

In July 1652 Felice de Zabbalis, wife of Portio de Butteris, appeared before Reverend Carlo Cupens (or Crypens), chancellor of the college of the Pieve di San Stefano, and a specially deputed pro-vicar for the Inquisition through the Florentine state. Felice indicated that there was a woman (Margherita) in the public prison of the Vicario di Giustizia who, she learned from a neighbour, had cured a bad hand with a water concoction made from *fusaio* (possibly *fusaggine*, spindle tree, *Euonymus europaeus*), *ditale* (possibly *digitale*, foxglove, *Digitalis purpurea*) and *ago* (pine needle). The application was accompanied by Pater Nosters, Ave Marias and words the patient could not understand. The delator, Felice, and the informant patient visited Margherita in prison to see whether she would repeat the treatment; but Felice decided this was useless. When Felice was questioned by the pro-vicar she clarified the information she had been given, declared she was worried in her conscience, but held no animosity against Margherita. Felice was dismissed after signing the record with a cross, and silence was imposed on her. The pro-vicar wrote to the Holy Office that he had visited Margherita in prison, but resolved to do nothing without the inquisitor's order, though he had banned her from using the medicine again.[43] These examples incidentally exemplify the network of persons assisting the Florentine inquisitor throughout the province.

While most of these healers were women, men could also be practitioners. We have accusations against Giovanni Serrantelli, '*lo stregone di Colle*'. In November 1627 a Florentine citizen, Messer Ottavio Amori, originally from Colle Val d'Elsa and a member of the Florentine Signori Nove council, appeared before the Inquisition 'spontaneously' to say that Serrantelli, having been released from prison (where he had spent some time) in May 1626, had renewed his practice in superstitious medicaments. Ottavio's mother, out in Colle, was very scared of Serrantelli and his father for their *maleficia*, and superstitious, non-canonical healings, where they specialised in treating babies' the more so because her cousin's baby had died as a result. On 15 December a man was questioned about the death of a baby, and Serrantelli himself was quizzed about other deaths, also about calling on the Madonna, and the Madonna di Loreto image, to cure a woman. In May 1626, he had been released from prison on the orders of Cardinal Millini in Rome for the Congregation, provided he desisted from healing superstitiously, and appeared monthly before the Inquisition in Florence. Some documents in the record show Serrantelli did appear there. In March 1628 this order was lifted, as the Inquisition had heard of no more trouble, and Colle was too far away for easy visiting. One has to deduce that Florence was not too worried about Messer Ottavio's complaint![44]

As already noted, Gostanza of San Miniato was seen as an experienced midwife and medical healer; she was respected by many, though some under questioning voiced suspicions. She made various kinds of medicine, especially with betony (*sugo di bettonica, Betonica officinalis*), and used oils, for which she received significant payments. One borderline practice reported was 'measuring the cloths'. A witness, having said that Gostanza had the reputation as *ribalda* and *maliarda*, reported that many came to her house for medical reasons, either the sick or those coming on their behalf, 'and brought there and sent there the cloths so that said *monna* Gostanza would know the illness, who, when they put the cloths in her hands she measures them and handles them and then tells those sent and the sick what to do'. One of the early witnesses reported how Gostanza had forecast the return to health of her boy, after she had inspected his trousers; she had concocted an elaborate medicine (involving cloves, nutmeg and eggs) for him – but he had died.[45] The parish priest who noted Gostanza used oil for healing was unable or unwilling to say whether she used special words; she healed animals as well, but he knew no more. The question of whether she measured the cloths was the one on which she was first questioned by the inquisitorial vicar. Under torture and threat of torture she came to admit this, and that she said words 'in the name of God and the Virgin Mary'.[46]

Measuring of cloths as a diagnostic technique was an accusation made against Angela Reffiletti in Venice in 1638, and one she strongly denied under questioning and in her defence statement. She asserted she was a fully Christian healer who never used superstitious practices. A Cypriot from a noble family, aged thirty-six and married to a Greek apothecary, Zuanne, Angela had clients from various levels of Venetian society. Witnesses attesting to her efficacy declared they came to her when other healers, as well as priests and friars, had not had any success. Her attempts to heal her own husband (after other physicians had proved unhelpful) came under scrutiny. As a healer she used oils to anoint the body, during which she said prayers and made the sign of the Cross. She also used holy water and burned oil (not holy oil) while treating people, as she had learned in the Levant. The inquisitors questioned her on what words she used when healing. She insisted that she only referred to God, the Virgin and the Holy Trinity and reiterated that she lived in a Christian manner, and had priests as her customers, on whom she used holy water. She received payments from some, but treated the poor for free. She was found 'lightly suspect' of heresy, for using holy words in healing, and saying that her special procedures constituted a 'secret'; essentially she was punished for behaving too much like a male priest. Earlier in 1635 Angela had been investigated when Joseph Biondi, whom she had treated for kidney stones by anointing him with oil and signing with the Cross, complained; the inquisitor had then taken no action.[47]

In Venice a number of those sought out, or blamed, as practitioners of magic and healing came from the east, variously designated as Greek, Slav, or Turk. Maria da Ponte (alias Ainis) came from the Greek island of Andros, a Christian who had turned Muslim and married another convert from Coron; neighbours regularly referred to her as *La Turca* (signifying Muslim rather than ethnic origin). Following tribunal investigation in May 1591, the Patriarch absolved her from charges of divination. When in 1591 a Caterina Istriana was under investigation, a witness told the court she had been warned by a friend against Caterina, 'because she told me that this woman was a Slav, I told her that she should watch out because these Slavs and Greeks go by some devilish ways from what I have heard'. The Greek language, spoken and written, clearly had a fascinating, or worrying aspect. Greeks were judged expert in divination, casting the rope (*cordella*), bean-casting and conjuring up images through the *inghistera* (glass flask). They were judged experts in love magic – and in causing or curing impotence.[48]

As Alexandra Bamji's 'Religion and Disease in Venice' makes clear, these female healers in Venice were part of interlocking and cooperative networks of healers, including local parish doctors, apothecaries, regular and secular clergy, who shared supplies and recommended patients to each other when one or another had no success. The Inquisition was ready to accept healers, possibly informally ratify some, but punished those who came too close to behaving as male priest healers, as well as those who used obvious superstitious practices and words.

It was ecclesiastically recognised that diseases could be caused by the Devil as well as nature. According to one noted authority, Francesco Guazzo in his *Compendium maleficarum*, the Devil might especially affect physical and melancholic sickness through producing more black bile. Here the physician would have the greatest difficulty effecting a cure, because as his authority the physician Andrea Cesalpino had argued, the Devil's poison is too subtle and tenacious, too swift and sure in killing, and reaches to the very marrow of the bones.[49] The Devil might be seen as operating directly, or through a human agent, a witch, who might be willingly or inadvertently involved. The Devil might even be behind seemingly beneficial healing, for example by a 'living saint', as was decided by the inquisitor in the case of Suor Giglia di Fino. Patients and even doctors alleged the impact of witchcraft when standard medical treatment failed. Four cases have been found in seventeenth-century Venice where syphilis (the French disease, *morbo gallico, mal francese*) was blamed on witchcraft, as in the case of Angela Castellana.[50]

Love Magic

Inquisitional records show that prostitutes and concubines were widely seen as practitioners of love magic. Love magic and healing also could be combined by them or by women who weren't prostitutes. In the late sixteenth and seventeenth centuries inquisitors and vicars from Modena and Ferrara investigated a number of prostitutes for alleged involvement in love magic. Honest women (*donne oneste*) in these cities would go to prostitutes, sometimes in brothels, for help with their love life. In 1596 Ippolita de Bennis of Ferrara told the court of her visits to the prostitute Moranda Magnanini of Fanano, who performed rituals with incantations for her and other clients. Moranda was described as a *meretrice*, but she had a stable relationship with a Bernardino da Carpi, who had promised to marry her, she claimed.[51] That respectable women were ready to visit the 'dishonest' for such help should be considered when we find the latter lightly punished by the inquisitors for using incantational prayers. Women in desperate need might turn to magical practices as remedies, as we noted with Caterina Erba (see Chapter 8, p.216). Pregnant and seemingly abandoned by her master/lover, she accepted the offer of being taught to throw the rope, stick pins in figures and say spells, to win back his support.

Witness statements in the case of Elisabetta Todesca (Thodesca) in 1652 reveal a *strega* of diverse talents and practices, used primarily for love magic, at the centre of a network of women in Venice. This 'German' woman, who spoke Italian well, came from Trieste according to one witness. She ran a hostelry (*locanda*) where foreigners from locations such as Flanders or Milan stayed, and which attracted residents, largely female, from other parts of Venice. She was denounced by a Flemish sailor's wife living in the parish of San Moise (where many foreigners stayed) for the superstitious practices she engaged in, and for breaking fasting rules for herself and her guests. Using such accoutrements as statues of St Anthony made of blessed wax, blessed candles and fire, Elisabetta conducted experiments and magic to help women over affairs of love. Other witnesses testified that she also threw the *cordella*, said strange words into a mirror and put statues into the fire, or cast beans. One witness said she feared for her life because a certain Prospero (Ciarlatano Todesco, a German charlatan), who often stayed in her house though he was now living in Padua, wanted to punish her for denouncing Elisabetta to the Inquisition. Betta the Greek, who testifyed that Elisabetta ate meat that was prohibited, hinted she was a prostitute as well. Anna Todesca, who had visited the house to compose letters in German for Elisabetta, said the latter cast the *cordella* for her male visitors. A former female servant said Elisabetta blasphemed in German and Italian, but she had not witnessed *stregheria*. Having heard many witnesses, the inquisitor apparently froze the case and did no more.[52]

Some female practitioners of love magic sought help from priests, overtly or by secretly getting a priest to bless some object. Fra Bibone was allegedly brought in to assist Paolina de Rossi. Firstly she had made a concoction of herbs mixed with her menstrual blood and wine, which she had allegedly paid Bibone to 'write' on with the 'secrets' of the consecrational words, '*Hoc est enim corpus meum*' ('This is my Body' from the Mass), before she put it into her would-be lover Battista Giustinian's food. Bibone was also accused of agreeing to bring a consecrated Host to add to the food. He had denied Paolina's story when they were (unusually) put face to face; and torture did not break him.[53] A cleric might himself resort to *sortilegio* and love magic for his own needs. This was the case in 1697 with Ercole Felicin, a friar minor (accused with one Galla, called Madama Marchesa de Scentij), who was interrogated before the inquisitorial vicar in Bologna. Wishing to attract the attention of a certain Giovanna, Felicin had learned (from a male acquaintance) how he should fix his eyes on the loved one's face, say prayers, invoking the Blood of piety, the peace of God, and naming the woman. He learned later, with one Giulia now in his sights, also to try prayers to Saints Peter and Paul, and the Trinity, using lights. Another method was to say '*Hoc est enim corpus meum*' while eating biscuits. Later Felicin used an ampule of reddened oil, and a paper with the psalm *Exaudivi* written on it. The next stage came when he met a French woman from Turin, who taught him how to make a red rose infusion with lemon juice. When questioned whether a good Christian should do such things – implying a pact with the Devil – Felicin replied that he did not believe it right; but he was confused in his passion for the woman. He promised not to repeat such indecency (*porcherie*). He had to abjure vehemently, and do penances (unspecified). The French woman, who had left Bologna, was to be watched.[54]

The use of prayers to Saints Peter and Paul, and the Trinity, was part of the love magic rituals in another Bolognese case in the first semester of 1697, involving Virginia Medelli Cerdoni, and three other females appearing before a court on the orders of their confessor. One of them, Rosa Zanelli, received money for teaching love magic. She denied this was a sin, because it was only a game (*burla*). She wept copiously when seeking forgiveness, as the notary recorded. Another in the group, Benedetta, was helped because her lover was far away in Venice and no longer wrote, and Benedetta's friends were trying to find out whether her lover still wished her well. Under questioning the females showed respect for each other, and said they were basically good. The court decided to warn them severely, allocate penances and dismiss them.[55]

Several historians have drawn on testimonies in inquisitional cases when discussing relations between the sexes, and sexual relations, as practised or desired. Guido Ruggiero has notably revisited the cases before the Venetian tribunal of the abovementioned Suor Mansueta in 1574 who fell in love with the Devil, and in 1573 of Abbot Alessandro Ruiz of Sumaga in Friuli and his former concubine Cecilia Padovano who allegedly practised love magic, by anointing the penis or the vagina with holy oil.[56] As well as illuminating 'love magic', this last case also illustrates the situation of clerical concubinage.[57] Controlling penises was a noted aspect of magical procedures. It was believed that one function of women who practised love magic was to control penises, whether to make them operate beneficially, not operate at all, or even be stolen. Stories of penises being rendered inoperative or being 'stolen' were given prominence by Heinrich Kramer in a comic anecdote in the *Malleus Maleficarum*; a man who claimed he lost his penis was told by a witch he could climb a tree and would find a nest where other witches stored stolen penises, but he was warned against taking a large one that had belonged to a parish priest.[58] (Stories about stolen members still circulate in modern Nigeria, though the 'witch', or *ju-ju* practitioner, might be male.) More realistically it was believed that magical/healing procedures could be used to help men who were unable to consummate a relationship (marital or not). In 1588 the Venetian tribunal investigated Fra Gabriele Garofolo, accused of teaching magic that could 'unbind' penises of newly married men, who claimed that many parishioners suffered from this problem. His remedy: 'Against binding ties it is effective to dissolve some dust from a church bell and drink it with egg or broth while saying a psalm.' He claimed this to be an efficacious procedure, and was approved by the prior of the Augustinian convent, his superior, who assured him it was 'not a superstition'. Magical practices aimed at making couples impotent – by tying knots (*nodi*) – were greatly feared, as documented in the villages around Siena.[59]

Miscellaneous Magic

This section is designed to exemplify further different kinds of magical and superstitious claims or practices hidden behind the statistical categories in the Tables in the Appendix, and to show how the inquisitors reacted – usually mildly.

Clergy, besides helping lay people in their magical practices, might well be involved in magical practices themselves. Their activities might involve more recondite 'secrets' in pursuit of deeper knowledge, as of the future. Capuchin Petro Clodia, on the basis of reports from persons of faith at San Zeno, Verona, denounced various fellow Capuchins in Venice, some of whom he named. He alleged they baptised some 'Virgin papers' and *calamita* (lodestone or magnet), and awaited an angel from Heaven. Lengthy investigations followed, and two friars provided booklets with confessions of what had happened over eight years, to clear their consciences. According to one of them, Fra Silvestro, a Roman Capuchin called Fra Ippolito had arrived claiming he had a secret to secure the spirit of intelligence; the key to this was a white *calamita* which, when blessed, could attract a person for support and benevolence. Many other friars and gentlemen were brought in to learn how to baptise properly. It involved obtaining a black cat's skin, and a black chicken's egg. Some gentlemen became involved, and they had a book for necromancy (*Il centum regum*). Fra Ippolito produced another printed book which he wanted Silvestro to copy, but Silvestro refused; this had certain wheels and characters for telling the future. According to Fra Andrea, Fra Silvestro tried to get an image of the Virgin or an angel to appear, without success. Another witness claimed that several friars and lay people built an altar, offered incense to the Devil, expecting angels, and baptised a *calamita*. On 30 October the tribunal ordered that no Capuchin currently in the Venetian house could leave without its licence. Presumably further enquiries were made, but the outcome remains unknown. The case could have been handed over for discipline by the Order.[60]

Revelations about low-level astrologers emerge in the protracted case of Lucia De Angelis, investigated in Bologna from 1677.[61] Lucia was reappearing before a tribunal, having been exiled by it the previous year in an earlier trial. A widow, aged about forty, she had the reputation of being an astrologer, and *meretrice*. Early on her claim to be pregnant and so deserving release from prison, relayed through a gaoler, was proven false. Many others were brought into the investigation, which persisted for some time. The initial inquisitor Fra Andrea Rovereto was replaced from December 1679 by Fra Tomasso Mazza of Ferrara, who completed the sentencing. Six key figures (four female and two male) also had code names.[62] A number of them claimed/admitted to having met at night, forming a circle to invoke the Devil and practising various *sortilegi* (witchcraft) to determine the future. Lucia Martelli (giving evidence in May 1679) said Marina Terzeta, originally from Venice, taught the *sortilegio* of putting a horseshoe above a house door, in the midst of images of the four Evangelists, then covering all with an image of *Ecce Homo* and periodically saying a psalm for the Office of the Virgin – and so directing this psalm to the great horse that rides through the world. She also taught how to use a black wooden *coronetta* (coronet), saying Pater Nosters and Ave Marias, with hands behind the back, to help damned souls or souls in Purgatory. Marina conversed all night with demons – a practice that went back to 1674. The way Lucia Martelli's evidence is set out in the record as a lengthy deposition suggests she had this well prepared, reacting to numbered points, presumably presented in advance. She had the confidence to declare that what had been deposed to a court official by Lucia De Angelis were lies and 'balls' (*coglionarie*). Lucia, making her defence in April 1679, claimed she was just a poor, ignorant and miserable woman, with none to help her – no family, acquaintances, or money to provide an advocate. Not knowing whether she had committed a defendable crime, she placed herself at the mercy of the inquisitor.

An advocate was provided for her and Martelli, who was given a transcript of the process, and then Lucia de Cavalerijs was added to his case load. The Inquisition in Rome was consulted over verdicts and punishment. Lucia De Angelis was declared guilty of being a notorious astrologer, of breaking an exile order and returning to Bologna without licence. This time she was to be publicly flogged through the usual streets by the ministers of justice, and perpetually exiled. Lucia Martelli was convicted as a long-term diviner; banned from practising this art, she was condemned to exile. She had to provide security (unspecified) that she would not practise again. Marina at some point had left prison (making Martelli fearful), and de Cavalerijs may have escaped punishment pleading illness and stupidity (*donna goffa*), not understanding such matters. Much of this appears as minor superstitious perversion of popular religious practices, with hopes of contacting the deceased, with or without the help of demons or angels. For the Inquisition, dispersing the group was possibly the main concern, not having discovered in them more serious evil intent.

The diversity, and ingenuity, of attempted magical practices, as well as the imagination of those making accusations or claims about meetings with devils, have become evident through the above studies. *Sortilegio* was attempted as much in cities like Bologna and Venice as in rural areas. Those involved were clerical and lay, male and female (even if the latter predominated), and from many levels of society. The inquisitorial punishments were often mild, or non-existent with probationary observation ordered. However, time spent in prison could be lengthy, and torture serious.

CHAPTER 10

CONCLUSION

MANY IMAGES AND IMPRESSIONS HAVE APPEARED IN OUR SURVEY OF THE inquisitions in Italy, of practitioners and victims. We have encountered the horrors of being shamed in an *auto da fé* and the execution of Pietro Carnesecchi; the burning alive of Giordano Bruno; the bonfires of books; the cruel destruction of simple Waldensians under the aptly named 'bad-neighbour' Valerio Malvicino, and inquisitor Michele Ghislieri's encouragement of extermination. We have heard some fantastic story-telling from the accused, of a Great City of the Devil from Gostanza of San Miniato, of good night-battlers flying off to contest evil witches, of sister Mansueta's trysts with the Devil-lover in a nunnery from which she longed to escape. We have learned of strange concoctions and rituals claimed to affect health and love lives, to which claims inquisitors reacted in various ways. Behind all this we have encountered the developed bureaucracy and due legal processes of dedicated inquisitors and their notaries.

The inquisitors ranged from the intransigent hardliners like Gian Pietro Carafa and Michele Ghislieri (who become papal leaders with wider responsibilities), the senior day-to-day operators like cardinals Rebiba, Santoro and Millini who headed the Congregations and whose correspondence has featured in various sections, to the sometimes mild or ambivalent local inquisitors. These included Marino da Venezia in Venice (himself arraigned for undue emollience), Antonio Balducci who dispensed harsh or mild sentences as the occasion warranted in Bologna, Eliseo Masini in Ancona who went on to write an even-handed manual, Dionigi da Castacciaro who was sceptical about Gostanza's stories and Agapito Ugoni who assiduously tested several 'living saints'. Much inquisitorial activity was painstaking, whether trying to elucidate the beliefs and intentions of theological offenders like Giovanni Morone (who survived without being convicted), Pietro Carnesecchi, Mario Galeota, various groups in Bologna in the 1560s, or Miguel de Molinos; the more philosophical/ scientific notions of Antonio Rocco and Galileo Galilei; the misdemeanours of 'a most serious witch', Cristina Collarina; a 'saintly' ascetic and visionary like Maria Janis; a printer like Francesco Valvasense. A careful and prolonged investigation could amount to psychological torture under appalling prison conditions, as with Valvasense.

The Roman Inquisition emerged from a 'medieval' Inquisition that had seen local domination in a few areas, where inquisitors and bishops joined forces and by the fifteenth century were directing their activities more towards witches than Cathars or Waldensians – and in the process giving the Dominicans a bad reputation. The new Inquisition after 1542 developed from that background and the new challenges of reform. Its early evolution was messy and controversial, with power struggles between cardinals in Rome – hardliners against moderates – and between hardliners and some 'softer' Popes (Paul III, Pius IV). Expansion from the centre encountered different attitudes from the other states within Italy, the Republic of Lucca refusing to allow a tribunal under Roman control and the Venetian Republic insisting on a strong power-sharing role. A stand-off with Spain over the Kingdom of Naples left Rome unable to establish an open Inquisition system there, and it had to rely on infiltration into and cooperation with the episcopal establishment, in a way continuing the 'medieval' approach. However, it was not just in this kingdom that the episcopacy continued to play its role in the protection of the faith, and the control of heresy. Given that many bishops from the 1520s to the 1560s had sympathy with some of the ideas of 'reform' – whether from northern Europe or from the hybrid Valdesian and other *spirituali* or evangelist inspirations – they wished to restrain inquisitional severity and undue intrusiveness into personal beliefs. Thereafter inquisitor–bishop relationships varied locally between cooperation and animosity, as has been shown particularly in Ancona and Mantua. Relations between the periphery and the centre have been illustrated by the correspondence of inquisitors in Ancona, Bologna, Mantua and Naples with overseers and cardinals in Rome. Bishops in many areas, and nuncios in northern Italy, shared the responsibility of controlling matters of faith. The inquisitors under the Roman and Spanish Inquisitions did not, therefore, have a monopoly of control.

Research into the operations of tribunals and inquisitors shows that they generally followed fairly clear rules and guidelines, without being dictators. Consultants were brought in locally or in Rome. Guidelines dictated who should be questioned and when, the lines of questioning (which could lead to not following up a question, where a modern prosecutor might), and what kind of heresy accusation could be formulated (or ruled out). From the late sixteenth century, inquisitors led by Cardinal Santoro were self-consciously developing or advocating an 'Inquisition style' for conducting cases that included physical torture. Normally torture was avoided or was introduced late only in cases of real stubbornness, was subject to controls by bishops or the central Holy Office and was time-limited. Where torture was administered early in an investigation, and lengthily, inquisitorial vicars and other deputed officials or episcopal vicars took the lead. Torture under the fifteenth- and early sixteenth-century inquisitors, under Spanish inquisitors in Sicily and secular officials in Lucca, was more prevalent and harsher. However, the added torture for an accused of lengthy delays in dire prison conditions, not knowing how serious the charges might be, should not be underestimated.

Death sentences were not numerous under the Roman Inquisition, and notably rare in cases of witchcraft and magic compared with other courts in Italy and abroad. Of course we find some cruel deaths as in the cases of Pietro Carnesecchi, Giordano Bruno and Francesco Pucci, and a group of *marranos* in Ancona, but some individuals whose heresies seem similar got off more lightly (Mario Galeota and Dionisio Gallo). For others many seemingly heavy sentences – life imprisonment, the galleys, exile, house arrest – were soon modified. The technicalities of 'spontaneous appearances' – whether under pressure or voluntary – generally lessened and shortened the investigative and trial processes, produced plea-bargaining (as with Pietro Gelusio, Francisco Singlitico, or those trying to return to the Catholic faith from their Muslim or Jewish pasts), and lightened the sentences. Parish priests, confessors and nosy neighbours were the prime movers behind particular investigations. Published inquisitorial edicts, and sermons from inquisitors, bishops and other clergy encouraged such denunciations. But inquisitors, their officials and *familiari* were apparently seldom proactive seekers of victims.

Our study of the investigative processes shows that they were not entirely top-down and punitive. Inquisitors could be open-minded on some issues, be puzzled and uncertain how to proceed, and show sympathy for erroneous beliefs deriving from ignorance. Re-education could be as important as punishment, and this was more so once the real scares of 'Lutheranism' (loosely interpreted) and Valdesianism were overcome. Some accused could argue back (and not just because they desired martyrdom). Accused and witnesses clearly could develop strategies to mitigate their position, and avoid serious charges by admitting to minor offences. Public reputation, *fama*, and social standing could affect inquisitors' attitudes and decisions, and the type of punishment. Both accusers and accused could concoct some improbable or impossible stories, whether from conscious strategies or induced by mental disturbances, trances, wishful thinking, maliciousness, sexual frustration, malnutrition, or drugs. We have provided some lengthy summaries of accusations and admissions – shocking or amusing – to indicate what could be believed in the period, what inquisitors had to judge as true or false, devilish, saintly, or misguided.

The targets changed, though there were local variations. By the late 1560s the major theological challenges, which had been upheld by elites in the Church (including some cardinals and bishops) and in aristocratic society, had been essentially overcome. What we have called the 'Carnesecchi Moment' in 1567 allowed for mental and physical shifts of position thereafter, even though significant Lutheran, Calvinist and Valdesian elements could still be uncovered into the 1580s, and the odd adherent emerged throughout the seventeenth century. Inquisitors – and their informants – reverted to concerns about magical and moral issues, though these were treated with less severity than in the pre-1542 world. These worries and considerations persisted through to the eighteenth century, despite the Church's improved education of parishioners, as through Christian doctrine and similar confraternities and sermons. The interactions of Christians with Jews and Muslims (or those converted from non-Christian faiths), and the movements of a few between faiths, have a fascination all of their own both socially and geographically, as well as revealing the inquisitors in cosmopolitan areas to be accommodating and flexible.

The high-profile targets were now the new philosophies, revived and new forms of mysticism (Quietism and Pelaginism), and public expressions of female spirituality. Some of those involved in mysticism and female spirituality were surprisingly harshly treated, whether through the length of their investigation or the final punishment. Behind all these manifestations was the concern among inquisitors and clergy that Rome's authority was being undermined, along with strict clerical, male, leadership. 'Saintly' women, both genuine and fraudulent, were perceived as a threat, unless the Church hierarchy was sure they could be turned into safe role models. The inquisitorial campaigns against mystical religious beliefs and practices, the pursuit of personal 'perfection', were probably effective in limiting their impact.

Much effort went into censorship of ideas promulgated through the printed word, but there were many impediments to effective implementation: lack of manpower to check and survey, and of willing censors; the daring of some publishers and booksellers, especially in Venice, and bookmen trafficking across northern Italy with prohibited books brought in from across the Alps, or by ship into Naples. 'Suspension till amended' often meant a book was no longer available (at least legally). Bishops and other local officials could get in the way of inquisitorial book-hunting, or protect key libraries. The production and reading of vernacular biblical literature were seriously impeded, and some great vernacular literature was bowdlerised (though some scholars involved thought they were improving great masters like Boccaccio or Castiglione). Publication of new philosophical and scientific ideas was also impeded, but not as effectively as used to be alleged. The 'Galileo Affair' has revealed many conflicting attitudes within the Church. His condemnation did not prevent the evolution of new scientific theories in Italy, though other scientists and scholars probably learned from his tactlessness and miscalculations to be more careful about writing for the wider public, and to discuss their ideas with more discretion. The strenuous efforts at censorship in the eighteenth century had a diminishing effect after they were implemented, and ultimately fostered campaigns to close inquisitorial tribunals in different states. Public condemnation by censors or inquisitors could become counter-productive, and induce the pursuit of new books and ideas. Publishers and booksellers in Venice at least proved adept at evading control and censorship in the seventeenth century, just as others in the eighteenth century could readily import books from across the Alps. The great unknown is how much never got written and disseminated for fear of censorship, or was heavily self-censored to make it easier to get a book officially licensed.

The attitude and behaviour of Roman and Spanish Inquisitions toward witchcraft and superstition were milder than those of authorities elsewhere. Witch-hunts did take place in Italy, but essentially when backed by civic authorities, or junior clergy. Where the Inquisition demonstrated harshness and cruelty, it was usually through less-trained assistants. Carlo Borromeo's enthusiasm for burning witches was partly frustrated by both the Roman Congregation and the Milan Senate. Cases of witchcraft and superstition, whatever the reality of specific charges, illuminate the prevalence of folklore beliefs and fears, and non-professional medical remedies.[1] On a wider canvas the inquisitional records provide much intriguing information about social relations, friendly and hostile contacts between neighbours, whether across the canals or around the squares, or *campi*, in Venice, or in Friulian and Tuscan villages; they are also informative about the relationships between those of different religious and ethnic affiliations, especially in port areas or on the northern frontiers.

Was the Roman Inquisition a 'Bloody Tribunal' as outsiders regularly alleged?[2] There were the undoubted horrors of long imprisonment, uncertainty over accusations, accusers and outcomes, the fear of torture and occasionally its actual implementation, and some horrendous burnings. However, these factors should be balanced against the reality that – in comparison with many other courts in Italy and elsewhere – the death sentences were few, the torture rarer, and opportunities for plea-bargaining and accommodations leading to spiritual penances existed. Therefore, we might guardedly answer this question: No. The Inquisitions, when the hardliners won control, contributed to imposing a narrower-minded Catholicism, which lost much of its appeal for Erasmians, Valdesians and those engaged in wider scriptural reading. This form of Catholicism helped discourage some theological and other intellectual debate and writing, but also undesirable superstitious beliefs and practices. Italians remained adept at evasive story-telling and dissimulation. They could deceive tribunals of the Inquisition to ameliorate their vulnerable position, and earn lighter sentences, just as their record can puzzle the historian over what they genuinely believed in matters theological, or attempted to perform in the realms of superstition.

APPENDIX

TABLES OF TYPES OF ACCUSATIONS AND CASES

Table A. Accusations and Denunciations before Inquisition Tribunals in Venice and Friuli, 1547–1720

Venice				Friuli				
Major charge	1547–1585	1586–1630	1631–1720	1557–1595	1596–1636	1637–1676	1677–1716	Major charge
Lutheranism	717	109	77					
Anabaptism	37	0	1					
Heresy in general	68	27	6					
Judaising	34	16	28					
Mohammedanism	10	27	42					
Calvinism	13	18	29					
Greek Orthodoxy	3	8	11					
				3	44	134	56	Apostasy from the faith; includes Lutheran, Anabaptist, Calvinist, Orthodox, Muslim views
Atheism/materialism	1	4	14					
Apostasy	15	17	12					
Heretical propositions	62	26	107	164	102	53	23	Diverse heretical propositions; incl. sexual, moral errors, anticlericalism, lesser blasphemies
Prohibited books	93	48	40	44	48	132	11	Possessing/reading prohibited books
Prohibited meats	23	12	16	120	156	42	7	Prohibited meats
Blasphemy	17	41	61	13	22	20	3	Heretical blasphemy and swearing (*bestemmia*)
Abuse of sacraments	9	12	106	26	17	41	21	Abuse of sacraments
Bigamy	3	7	12	[1]				Bigamy (12 cases, 1611–70)
Concubinage	7	5	4	[2]				Concubinage (1 case, 1596–1611)

Table A. *cont.*

Venice				Friuli				
Major charge	1547–1585	1586–1630	1631–1720	1557–1595	1596–1636	1637–1676	1677–1716	Major charge
Adultery	3	7	0					
Sodomy	5	5	5					
Solicitation	3	22	72	1	4	48	29	Solicitation
Magical arts	59	319	641	62	347	287	77	Magical arts (*magia, stregoneria*)
Offending the Holy Office	10	8	6	14	18	21	4	Offending the Holy Office; incl. prison escape; false witness; ignoring penances; abusing officials
Pretend sanctity	0	1	5					Pretend sanctity (8 cases, 1611–70)
False testimony	14	7	4					False testimony (2 cases, 1611–70)
Illegal Mass	2	4	14					Illegal Mass (1 case, 1611–70)
Miscellaneous; incl. irreverence, sacrilege, irreligiosity	21	66	31	43	43	40	3	Irreverence, sacrilege, irreligiosity
Totals	1,229	816	1,344	490	801	818	234	Totals

Table constructed from Tedeschi and Monter's tables in Tedeschi (ed.), *Prosecution of Heresy*, 'Toward a Statistical Profile', Appendix 1, p. 105, for Venice; and Sarra Di Bert, 'Distribuzione statistica', Table B, for Friuli. The classifications follow different categorisations. For further comparison, figures for some accusations buried in Sarra Di Bert's figures, but identifiable in Tedeschi and Monter's table for Friuli, Appendix 2, p. 106 (but using different period breakdowns), are given in parentheses. Note that the decade 1647–56 saw a major intensification of denunciations, providing 117 of the Prohibited books figure, 30 of the abuse of sacraments, and 287 of that for the Magical arts from the 1637–76 period.

Table B. Break-down of Accusations in the Seventeenth-century before the Venetian Tribunal

Anne Schutte looked at 63 procedural fascicles, some involving more than one person; 23 ended in a sentence, while the others were varyingly fragmentary; some just a denunciation, others with a certain follow-up, questioning witnesses and/or accused, but left pending. She has reclassified some from the way indicated in ASV Index 303.[1]

Main Charge	Number accused	Males	Females
Occult practices	34	10[a]	24[b]
Solicitation	10	10	
Heretical propositions, by Catholics	8	8	
Return to faith of parents	7	6[d]	1[e]
Pretend sanctity	5	2	3
Celebrating Mass when not in Holy Orders	3	3	
Protestants proselytising	2[f]	1	1
Bigamy	2	1	1
Exposition of unconsecrated Host	1	1	
Fleeing Holy Office prison	1	1	
Carrying weapons by Holy Office official	1	1	
Scandalous propositions	1	1[g]	
Printing unlicensed book	1	1[h]	
Not indicated	2	1	1
Total	78	47	31

[a] 1 also with scandalous life
[b] 2 with heretical propositions
[c] 2 with magic, 1 with heretical propositions, 1 with heretical blasphemy and sodomy
[d] 5 to Calvinism, 1 to Judaism
[e] to Calvinism
[f] 1 female French Calvinist, 1 male Swedish Lutheran
[g] Use of improper examples when preaching
[h] Greek Life of saints with a preface

Of the above, 48 were lay persons, 30 ecclesiasts of various kinds, including 12 secular priests, 15 friars and monks, 2 in minor orders and 1 procurator fiscal from the Inquisition.

Table C. Accusations and Denunciations to the Neapolitan Inquisition, 1564–1740

Main charge	1564–1590		1591–1620		1621–1700		1701–1740	
Protestantism	19	(6)	18	(2)	26	(0)	1	(0)
Judaising	41	(0)	8	(1)	20[a]	(0)	0	(0)
Mohammedanism	126	(3)	67	(0)	13	(0)	0	(0)
Heretical propositions	38	(4)	86	(18)	50	(11)	6	(3)
Atheism	4		8		11		1	
Prohibited books	7	(0)	9	(2)	15	(4)	0	(2)
Offences against Sacraments	27	(8)	30	(4)	39	(2)	18	(0)
Offences against vows/precepts	50	(21)	49	(10)	63	(4)	16	(0)
Magical arts	178	(12)	498	(24)	387	(23)	64	(6)
Bigamy	9	(1)	73	(0)	169	(1)	38	(0)
Concubinage	7	(4)	7	(1)	2	(2)	1	(0)
False testimony	39		43		146		13	
Blasphemy	15	(18)	32	(20)	49	(5)	6	(3)
Sacrilege, offence against saints, images, holy places	11	(4)	6	(8)	5	(1)	16	(3)
Offences against Holy Office	16	(2)	39	(8)	4	(0)	2	(0)
Trade in false relics and indulgences	2		12		18[b]		5	
Reconciliation of foreign Protestants	98		3		8		0	
Conversion of Muslims to Christianity	0		9		0		0	
Miscellaneous	48	(1)	24	(13)[d]	61[c]	(0)	9	(0)
Total	735	(84)	1,021	(111)	1,086	(53)	196	(17)

Table taken from Tedeschi and Monter, *Prosecution of Heresy*, Appendix 3, p. 107. The figures in parentheses are secondary charges.

[a] Eight were re-offenders
[b] Some cases did not specify numbers involved
[c] Including repeat offenders, and cases where numbers are not specific
[d] Including cases involving several offenders

Table D. Accusations in Sicily, 1500–1750

Accusations	1501–1550	1551–1600	1601–1650	1651–1700	1701–1750	Males and Females M	F	Total 1500–1750
All Accused								
Judaisers	2,080	25	2	1	2	1,490	620	2,110
Muslims/apostatisers	37	504	478	13	8	921	119	1,040
Protestants	47	353	95	4	0	479	20	499
Alumbrados, Quietists	2	12	25	28	40	79	28	107
Heretical propositions	3	333	240	14	8	545	53	598
Heretical blasphemy	7	237	265	60	11	540	40	580
Magic/witchcraft	6	177	479	157	102	427	494	921
Bigamy	1	158	216	63	47	414	71	485
Sodomy	0	13	0	0	0	13	0	13
Solicitation	0	37	123	12	16	188	0	188
Sacrilegious acts	0	88	90	10	13	182	19	201
Acts against Holy Office	64	144	121	12	15	324	32	356
Crime not given	63	0	0	0	0	42	21	63
Total	2,310	2,081	2,134	374	262	5,644	1,517	7,161
Spontaneous appearances	0	198	396	5	9			599
Death sentences:								
in person	210	42	9	1	3	202	63	265
in effigy	286	33	3	0	1	251	72	323
Torture known to be used						114	29	143

Derived from Del Col, *L'Inquisizione in Italia*, tables on pp. 241 and 243, and Renda, *L'Inquisizione in Sicilia*, 245, 258; commentaries on statistics, sources and complex methods of compiling, Del Col, 241–4, Renda, 240–7.

Of those accused as above, 714 were absolved; 139 had cases suspended and 141 left pending. Those appearing at an *auto* numbered 3,112 (49 per cent of convictions), those condemned in the secret hall, 1,144 (18 per cent), with the method of resolution unclear for others (Renda, 252). The figures for torture will be significantly under-counted, especially as there are virtually no indications for the pre-1550 period (Del Col, 243–4).

Renda indicates that where the social background can be ascertained (for 2,953 cases), there were 905 religious, 474 artisans, 133 shopowners and businessmen, 217 urban workers, 122 rural workers, 71 in public office, 87 nobles, 304 in liberal arts (teachers, physicians, lawyers, etc.), 110 military, 166 sailors, 301 slaves and 51 others (p. 244). Age was indicated for 1,934 (mainly in the sixteenth century), giving 181 under 20, 202 over 50. Nearly half of those under 20 were involved in Christian–Muslim shifts, particularly as male and female slaves. Many of those in their 40s and 50s were accused of sorcery (Renda, 245–6). In terms of origins, known for 6,893 cases, there were 5,545 Sicilians, 538 other Italians (two-thirds from the south, especially Naples and Calabria), 810 foreigners, of whom 333 came from Africa, Asia and Ottoman Europe (including 98 Greeks). Of the 477 Westerners, 188 were Spanish, 103 English, 100 French, 30 German (Renda, 242).

Table E. Malta, 1743–1797. Those Arrested with Case Ended, and Total Number of Allegations*

Completed cases, charges	Male	Female	Total	Total allegations	Allegations
Blasphemy	46	1	47	1,030	Blasphemy
Sorcery	51[a]	1	52		
				883	Witchcraft
Heretical Propositions	6		6	429	Heretical propositions
				116	'heresy'[b]
Solicitation	3		3		
Apostasy	7		7	281	Apostasy
Attempted apostasy	5	1	6		
				3	Greek Orthodoxy
				22	Freemasonry
Bigamy	3	3	6		
Polygamy	2		2	57	Polygamy[c]
Attempted bigamy	1		1		
Prohibited books	2		2	21	Prohibited books
False witness	6		6		
Revealing Holy Office secrets	4		4		
				6	Offences against Holy Office
				56	Offences against sacraments
				102	Not fasting
				43	Illicit life
Other[d]	6		6		
Total	142	6	148	3,059	

[a] Includes a Gaetano Schembri who appeared three times, in 1793, 1795 and 1797; and Pasquale Torregiani, twice, in 1795 and 1796

[b] Catholics joining Protestants

[c] Presumably including bigamy

[d] The other offences were, one each: prohibited meats; tearing holy images (1793); no Easter duty (1793); contempt of church dignitaries (1793); violation of secrecy of the Inquisition (1776, prison keeper); deism (1776, Savoyard)

* Details on 148 completed cases derived from Ciappara, *Society and the Inquisition*, Appendix 3, 518–38; the total allegations or self-denunciations are from his 'Disciplining Diversity', Table 1, using some different classifications.

Abbreviations

AABol	Archivio Arcivescovile, Bologna
AAF	Archivio Arcivescovile, Florence
ACDF	Archivio della Congregazione per la Dottrina della Fede, Rome
APV	Archivio Patriarcale, Venice
ASBol	Archivio di Stato, Bologna
ASV	Archivio di Stato, Venice
b. and B.	*busta*, bundle of archival materials
BAB	Biblioteca Comunale dell'Archiginnasio, Bologna
BCP	Biblioteca Comunale (Augusta), Perugia
DBI	*Dizionario biografico degli Italiani* (Rome, 1960–)
fol(s)	*foglio/fogli*, sheets in manuscripts, with recto (r) and verso (v) to indicate front and reverse side
r	recto (front of manuscript sheet)
St. St.	Stanza Storica, History Room, section of ACDF holdings
SU	Sant'Uffizio (or Sant'Ufficio)
TCD	Trinity College, Dublin
v	verso (reverse of manuscript sheet)

NOTES

Preface

1. The opening to the wider world of scholars of the Archivio della Congregazione per la Dottrina della Fede (ACDF), Rome, was largely thanks to Cardinal Joseph Ratzinger, now Pope Benedict XVI, partly responding to pleas from scholars like Carlo Ginzburg, Andrea Del Col and Peter Godman. Some scholars had been allowed earlier access, usually for very specific purposes and under restricted conditions; see Schutte, 'Recent Studies', 100–5, and citations; Arnold, 'The Archive of the Roman Congregation'; *L'apertura degli archivi del Sant'Uffizio romano*, esp. Cifres, 'L'Archivio storico', on history, contents, prospects for new research, by the current director.
2. Prosperi, *L'Inquisizione romana*, 4 (originally 'L'Inquisizione: verso una nuova immagine?' [1988]).
3. Prosperi, *Tribunali*, 543, and see also xiv–xv. Simon Ditchfield encouraged me to emphasise Prosperi's *positive* views in his paper for the 2007 Renaissance Society of America Conference, 'Adriano Prosperi between *Italia sacra* and *Storia patria*'.
4. Dandelet and Marino (eds), *Spain in Italy*.
5. Benigno, 'Integration and Conflict in Spanish Sicily', 38.
6. Ginzburg, 'Inquisitor as Anthropologist', esp. 158–9, and his 'Microhistory'; Schutte, 'Recent Studies', 98–99, 109 (quoted).
7. Tedeschi, *Prosecution of Heresy*, ix, 8–9; Schutte, 'Recent Studies', 93–5.

Chapter One: The Establishment of the Roman Inquisition in 1542

1. Kadri, *The Trial*, esp. ch. 2, 'The Inquisition'; Dean, *Crime and Justice*, 18–24; Hroch and Skýbová, *Ecclesia Militans*, 16–40; Lambert, *Medieval Heresy*, 176–88 ('Inquisition and Abuse'), and his *The Cathars*, ch. 6, 'The First Inquisitors'; Hamilton, *The Medieval Inquisition*; Roach, *The Devil's World*, ch. 6, esp. 139–44, 'Penance and Procedure'; Brambilla, *Alle origini del Sant'Uffizio*, 89–110 ('Inquisizioni medievali: un solo termine per molti significati'); Stern, *The Criminal Law*, ch. 2 ('Inquisition Procedure').
2. Cowan, *Marriage*; Stern, *The Criminal Law*, esp. 22–6.
3. Bonora, *Giudicare i vescovi*, 50–64.
4. Ginzburg, *Il formaggio e i vermi* (1976), trans. *The Cheese and the Worms* (1980); the full transcripts of the trials and other documents, with commentary published subsequently by Del Col: *Domenico Scandella detto Menocchio* (1990), trans. *Domenico Scandella Known as Menocchio* (1996).
5. Del Col, *Domenico Scandella* (1996), 141–3 and for end results, cx–cxii, 151–65.
6. Tavuzzi, *Renaissance Inquisitors*, 33; Ginzburg, *Night Battles*, 16, 20, 28, 78; Ginzburg, 'Witchcraft and Popular Piety'; Duni, *Tra religione e magia*; Merlo, *Streghe*, on the Rifreddo group.
7. Tavuzzi, *Renaissance Inquisitors*, with Appendix 1 giving the biographical register.
8. Dall'Olio, 'I rapporti tra la Congregazione', 248–9; Tavuzzi, *Renaissance Inquisitors*, ch. 1.
9. Tavuzzi, *Renaissance Inquisitors*, 210.

10. *Ibid.*, 194.
11. *Ibid.*, 29.
12. *Ibid.*, 194–5, Tavuzzi's translation.
13. *Ibid.*, 187–92; Del Col, *L'Inquisizione*, 204–9; Sanudo, *Diarii*, vols 25, 26, 30, 31, regularly copied reports, letters on the events. Tavuzzi's *Prierias* studies Mazzolino da Prierio's whole career and writings.
14. Bowd (ed.), *Vainglorious Death*, quoting 49, 51 (trans. J.D. Cullington), and Bowd's Introduction, esp. xxvii–xl. Bowd's ' "Honeyed flies" and "Sugared Rats" ' elaborates on the Brescian events, and widespread hostility to monks and friars, who were themselves blamed for much of the heresy and superstition in the valleys.
15. Donattini (ed.), *L'Italia dell'inquisitore* (2007), has published thirty papers resulting from the conference and a linked seminar course. Prosperi, 'L'Italia di un inquisitore', Dall'Olio, 'Leandro Alberti, inquisitore e mediatore', Tavuzzi, 'Gli inquisitori di cui fra Leandro Alberti non parla nel *De Viris illustribus ordinis Praedicatorum* (1517)', and Herzig, 'Leandro Alberti and the Savonarolan Movement', are the most relevant for Alberti's inquisitorial context. See also A.L. Redigonda, 'Alberti, Leandro', *DBI* 1 (1960), 699–703; Petrella, 'Nella cella di fra Leandro', on Alberti's reading, from his personal library and San Domenico convent library.
16. Minonzio, ' "Fra Leandro, dolce cosmografo e brusco inquisitore" ', esp. 68–9, 78–9, elucidating the implications of *dolce* in the religious context.
17. Tavuzzi, *Renaissance Inquisitors*, 66–8 (Antonio da Casale), 68–72 (Armellini), 72–7 (Casatossici, and influences on Alberti, 75); Tavuzzi, *Prierias*, 1, 36–7, 88; Dall'Olio, *Eretici*, 59–64 (quoting 63 n33); Del Col, *L'Inquisizione*, 327; Tavuzzi, 'Gli Inquisitori', 49–50 (Antonio da Casale).
18. Henry Kamen's third and latest monograph on the institution and its history, *The Spanish Inquisition* (1997), is the best overall coverage, though paying limited attention to the Sicilian and Sardinian tribunals. What follows is based on this book, ch. 3 'The Coming of the Inquisition'. Monter, *Frontiers of Heresy*, covers Sicily and Sardinia. Messana's excellent *Inquisitori, negromanti e streghe* has a much wider remit about Sicily than the title implies. Alcalá (ed.), *The Spanish Inquisition and the Inquisitorial Mind* has many essays reflecting Spanish views on the Inquisition's attitudes and procedures.
19. Kamen, *Spanish Inquisition*, 49.
20. *Ibid.*, 47.
21. Monter, *Frontiers of Heresy*, 15.
22. For reasons of space only a quick sketch can be given of the reform movements and pro-reform groups in Italy, about which there is considerable valuable literature. Detailed references are limited for this section. My *Church, Religion and Society*, ch. 1 on 'Religious Crises', reflects my starting point, and surveys some literature; Cameron's 'Italy' and Seidel Menchi, 'Italy' are valuable quick guides; Caponetto, *The Protestant Reformation*, is a mine of information and references, but confusing; Hillerbrand (ed.), *The Oxford Encyclopedia of the Reformation* has helpful entries. Studies of key contributors and helpful on wider context as well are the following: Bowd, *Reform before the Reformation*; Fenlon, *Heresy and Obedience in Tridentine Italy*; Gleason, *Gasparo Contarini*; Mayer, *Reginald Pole*, esp. ch. 3, 'The Church of Viterbo?', ch. 5, 'The War of the Saints'; Russell, *Giulia Gonzaga*; Murphy, *Ruling Peacefully: Cardinal Ercole Gonzaga*, esp. ch. 4, 'Gonzaga and the *Spirituali*'; Schutte, *Pier Paolo Vergerio*; Robin, *Publishing Women* on Vittoria Colonna, Giulia Gonzaga and others influenced by Valdés. Benedict et al. (eds), *La Réforme en France et en Italie* has many helpful articles in English, Italian and French. In Italian, Massimo Firpo's *Riforma protestante ed eresie* is the one short, clear book as a guide, and see Del Col, *L'Inquisizione in Italia*, 257–83. Firpo's essays in *Inquisizione romana* are essential for Cardinal Morone and his *spirituali* friends and contacts; and essays in his *Dal sacco di Roma* for Valdés and supporters, and in his '*Disputar di cose pertinente alla fede*' more widely. Dense studies on reform movements or key reform figures and their contacts include: Cantimori, *Eretici italiani*; Firpo, *Vittore Soranzo*; Ginzburg, *Il Nicodemismo*; Peyronel Rambaldi, *Speranze e crisi* (on Modena and Cardinal Morone); Prosperi, *Tra evangelismo e controriforma: G.M. Giberti*, and *L'eresia del Libro Grande* (on Giorgio Siculo); Seidel Menchi, *Erasmo in Italia*.

23. Cameron, 'Italy', 196; Fenlon, *Heresy and Obedience*, 18–21, 29–44.
24. Solfaroli Camillocci, 'Le Confraternite del Divino Amore', and her *I Devoti della Carità*; Black, *Italian Confraternities*, 6, 29, 190–2, 274, and *Church, Religion and Society*, 55–7, 132.
25. Caponetto, *Protestant Reformation*, 19.
26. Peyronel Rambaldi, *Dai Paesi Bassi all'Italia*, for edition and influence, and her *Speranze e crisi*, 256–61; Prosperi, 'L'Italia di un inquisitore', 11.
27. Stefania Pastore, *Un'eresia spagnola*, esp. ch. V, 3, 'Il "Diálogo de doctrina christiana" '; Andrés Martín, 'Alumbrados, Erasmians, "Lutherans", and Mystics'.
28. Massimo Firpo, 'The Italian Reformation and Juan de Valdés', 'Reform of the Church and Heresy', and 'Vittoria Colonna, Giovanni Morone e gli "spirituali" ' (in his *Inquisizione romana* [2005], 131–80); Mayer, *Reginald Pole*, is a key study and entry point into Pole's networks; backed by Mayer, *The Correspondence of Reginald Pole*, esp. vol. 1, *A Calendar, 1518–1546*, and vol. 2, *A Calendar, 1547–1554*; Brundin, *Vittoria Colonna*, esp. ch. 2, 'The Influence of Reform'; Robin, *Publishing Women*; Furey, *Erasmus, Contarini*, 98–117, 122–32, 161–2, 204 n111.
29. Translation with introduction by Ruth Prelowski in Tedeschi (ed.), *Italian Reformation Studies*, 21–102; as guide to spread of influence, see Caponetto, *Protestant Reformation*, 78–88; Del Col, *L'Inquisizione in Italia*, 266–7.
30. Mayer, *Reginald Pole*, 120.
31. On such bishops and inquisitorial controls over them, Bonora, *Giudicare i vescovi*, esp. 150–64, 207–37.
32. Recent indications for the Kingdom of Naples, in Scaramella, 'La Riforma e le *élites*'.
33. Massimo Firpo, *Artisti, gioiellieri, eretici*.
34. Borromeo, 'Il Dissenso religioso', 462; Caponetto, *Protestant Reformation*, 13–15; Del Col, *L'Inquisizione in Italia*, 288–91, and (for Giulio da Milano and early Venetian cases) his 'Organizzazione, composizione e giurisdizione'; John Martin, *Venice's Hidden Enemies*, 9–10, 74, 127.
35. Borromeo, 'Il Dissenso religioso', 481–2; Dall'Olio, *Eretici e inquisitori*, 90–100, esp. 95; Tedeschi, 'Buzio, Giovanni', *DBI* 15 (1972), 632–4. The relevant sitting of the Congregation, 8 August 1553 (ACDF Decreta f.113v), made it clear that all five cardinals present were unanimous in their decision to turn him over to the secular authorities for execution: Carafa, Alvarez de Toledo, Verallo, Puteo and Pighini.
36. Stephen Bowd made this last point in reading my draft chapter; he is considering writing a book on the enigmatic figure of Carafa.
37. Seidel Menchi, 'Italy', 181–2.
38. John Martin, *Venice's Hidden Enemies*, 9, quoting from Giulio's *Esortione al martirio*, and 127 on Nicodemism. On debates about 'nicodemism' and need for reappraisal of its use, Cameron, 'The Reformation in France and Italy', 30–2; Massimo Firpo, '*Disputar di cose pertinente alla fede*', 9 (quoted).

Chapter Two: The Roman Holy Office and Local Tribunals

1. John Martin, 'Introduction: *Renovatio* and Reform', 5, 12.
2. Del Col, *L'Inquisizione in Italia*, 292–4; Prosperi, *Tribunali della coscienza*, 38–9; the Bull is in *Bullarium romanum*... VI (Augustae Taurinorum, 1860), 344–46; Borromeo, 'Il dissenso religioso', esp. 465–6 (quoted); Benzoni, 'Paolo III'.
3. Bellabarba, *La giustizia nell'Italia moderna*, esp. 61–75; Fosi, 'Il governo della giustizia', and her *La giustizia del papa*; Bonora, *Giudicare i vescovi*, esp. 150–64, for assertion of Inquisition powers against episcopal ones in the 1560s; Del Col, 'I rapporti tra i giudici di fede'.
4. Borromeo, 'Il dissenso religioso', 466–8; Dall'Olio, *Eretici e inquisitori*, 160ff.
5. Borromeo, 'Il dissenso religioso', 469–71, for statistics, using ACDF Decreta, 1548–58, ff.1r-22v, 30v-1r; Prosperi, *Tribunali della coscienza*, 125–6; Ambrosini, *Storie di patrizi*, 71–73; Seidel Menchi, *Erasmo in Italia*, 68–72 (Appendix on Nacchianti and Vergerio); Caponetto, *Protestant Reformation*, 145–54, on Vergerio.

6. Borromeo, 'Il dissenso religioso', 471–3, 479; Del Col, *L'Inquisizione in Italia*, 316.
7. Borromeo, 'Il dissenso religioso', 473; Firpo, *Inquisizione romana*, 177–259, esp. p. 195; on Teofilo, see Godman, *The Saint as Censor*, 313 (Docs 1–2); Prosperi, *Tribunali della coscienza*, 142, on Teofilo and Ghislieri.
8. Borromeo, 'Il dissenso religioso', 474; Godman, *The Saint as Censor*, 313; Prosperi, *Tribunali della coscienza*, 133, 223, 239, 272–4; Del Col, *L'Inquisizione in Italia*, 402, 417; Bonora, 'Inquisizione e papato'.
9. Borromeo, 'Il dissenso religioso', 474–5, citing Giuglielmo Dandino, bishop of Imola, Oct. 1550.
10. *Ibid.*, 475; Firpo and Marcatto (eds), *Il processo inquisitoriale*, II/2, 803–12, quoting 804–5.
11. Brunelli, 'Giulio III'; Borromeo, 'Il dissenso religioso', 476.
12. Borromeo, 'Il dissenso religioso', 475–6.
13. Firpo, *Vittore Soranzo*, 466, on these interpretations, 435–68 on the *processo*, diplomatic pressures, sequence of confessions; Del Col, *L'Inquisizione in Italia*, 310–12.
14. Borromeo, 'Il dissenso religioso', 479.
15. Firpo and Marcatto (eds), *Il processo inquisitoriale*, II/2, 805–7 (Muzzarelli, 2 May 1558), 655 (Morone, 3 Nov. 1557); Borromeo, 'Il dissenso religioso', 476–7.
16. Borromeo, 'Il dissenso religioso', 480–2; Dall'Olio, *Eretici e inquisitori*, 90–100, 162–5, 207.
17. Dall'Olio, *Eretici e inquisitori*, 409–10; Del Col, *L'Inquisizione in Italia*, 314.
18. Del Col, *L'Inquisizione in Italia*, 512–14; for the Cardinal's full career, Saverio Ricci, *Il sommo inquisitore*; Borromeo, 'La congregazione cardinalizia'.
19. ACDF Decreta, vols 5–7, covering 1563–7 (vols 6 and 7 being different copies of the minutes for the second half of 1565 to July 1567, with vol. 7 being much harder to decipher!); also St. St., H 6 – f, 'Diversorum ab anno 1602 ad 1631'. This actually copied records for 1602–4, with gaps, then much of 1631; the copyist was clearly unable to read parts of the original, especially names.
20. Fragnito, 'Un archivio conteso', 1,278 n13.
21. ACDF Decreta 6 fols 29v–31r, 14 December 1565.
22. Paolin, 'Gli ordini religiosi e l'Inquisizione', 171–2.
23. ACDF Decreta, vol. 6, fols 130r–131v, Sat. 28 June 1567; A. Pastore, 'Galeota, Mario', *DBI* 51 (1998), 420–3; Scaramella, 'La Riforma e le *élites*', 298, 300.
24. ACDF Decreta, vol. 6, fol. 132r, 3 July 1567.
25. *Ibid.*, fols 63v–64r. To cause confusion some cardinals are indicated by their family name, others by the archbishopric, bishopric, or Roman titular church to which they were attached.
26. Kuntz, *The Anointment of Dionisio*, esp. 48–66 (for the Roman period, with p. 58 on release), 139–76 (trial in Venice, with 175–6 on verdict, and quote), 177–207 (on Venetian prison conditions).
27. 11 July 1566, after reading files of a doctor, Decreta vol. 6, fol. 64v. The cryptic reference to Bishop Alissani may refer to the bishop of Alessano, who was Iacobo Galetto in the period 1560–74.
28. *Ibid.*, fols 65v, 66v–66r, 66v, 67r, 67r–68r and 68rv (in Cardinal Pacheco's palace).
29. Fosi, *La giustizia del papa*, esp. chs III and VI pertaining to the Inquisition's problems in the jurisdictional conflicts; Ditchfield, 'Papal Patchwork Unpicked', is a valuable digest and review of Fosi's book.
30. Del Col, *L'Inquisizione in Italia*, 296, using a list compiled in 1723 by Fra Ermenegildo Todeschini, ACDF St. St., II 2-I; and on Avignon and surrounding French areas, 319–22.
31. Fragnito, 'Central and Peripheral Organization', 22 n23; her ' "In questo vasto mare" ', 5 n9; Del Col (ed.), *L'Inquisizione in Friuli*, 20; Black, *Church, Religion*, 172–3; Biondi, 'Lunga durata e microarticolazione', esp. 78–9; Del Col, *L'Inquisizione in Italia*, 515.
32. Ferri (ed.), *L'Inquisizione romana*, 16–18, 27; on Rodolfo Paleotti (d. 1619), nephew of Archbishop Alfonso Paleotti, also playing a role in Bologna, see Black, *Church, Religion*, 257 n46, 261 n24; Prodi, *Gabriele Paleotti*, I, 40.
33. Dall'Olio, 'I rapporti', 255.
34. Del Col, *L'Inquisizione in Italia*, 322–5; Prosperi, *L'eresia del Libro Grande*, 204–7, 226–33, 437–8 n10.

35. Dall'Olio, 'I rapporti', 249.
36. Tavuzzi, *Renaissance Inquisitors*, 7-8.
37. Prosperi, *Tribunali*, 75-80; Robin, *Publishing Women*, 41, 59-62, 77.
38. Prosperi, *Tribunali*, 103-5, quoting 104.
39. Ibid., 105; Caponetto, *Protestant Reformation*, 132-40; Brambilla, *La giustizia intollerante*, 105-6.
40. Braida, *Il commercio delle idee*, 76-9.
41. Very useful guides exist for the Venetian tribunal in English and Italian; see especially Grendler, *The Roman Inquisition and the Venetian Press*, Section II; Pullan, *The Jews of Europe and the Inquisition of Venice*, Part I; Ruth Martin, *Witchcraft and the Inquisition in Venice*, ch. 1; John Martin, *Venice's Hidden Enemies*, ch. 2; Schutte, *Aspiring Saints*, 26-41; Prosperi, *Tribunali*, 83-103; Del Col, *L'Inquisizione in Italia*, 342-94, and his 'Organizzazione, composizione'. Paolo Sarpi, defender of the Republic during the 1606-7 Interdict Crisis, and major historian of the Council of Trent, provided an early guide to the Venetian Inquisition: 'Sopra l'officio dell'Inquisizione (18 novembre 1613)'.
42. Gaeta, 'Documenti da codici vaticani', esp. 4-13, 30-1 (Doc. VIII), 47-50 (Doc. XXIV); Cardinal Aleandro was sending details to key figures at the Roman Curia, including Pietro Carnesecchi, John Martin, *Venice's Hidden Enemies*, 27, 64-5, 102; Del Col, *L'Inquisizione in Italia*, 290-1; Sarpi, 'Sopra l'officio dell'Inquisizione', 144, 162-3.
43. John Martin, *Venice's Hidden Enemies*, 74; Del Col, *L'Inquisizione in Italia*, 290-1; Massimo Firpo, *Artisti, gioiellieri, eretici*, 130-1.
44. Grendler, *Roman Inquisition*, 40; from 1554 the Doge had been the effective selector, but in 1595 it was decided (by a large majority of the Great Council) that the Collegio should nominate, and the Senate vote on them (removing the leadership of the Doge), 219; Grendler, 'The "tre savii sopra eresia"'; Sarpi, 'Sopra l'officio dell'Inquisizione', 120-3.
45. Seidel Menchi, 'I giudici'.
46. Rowland, *Giordano Bruno*, 94, 229-30, 237.
47. E.g. Ioly Zorattini, *Processi . . . (1561-1570)*, 73-4, a 1568 case introduced a denunciatory letter of 1555 addressed to Giulio Contarini and other *assistenti*.
48. ASV SU 103 nos 2 and 10; Miato, *L'Accademia degli Incogniti*, ch. 3, esp. 135, 155, 157.
49. Ioly Zorattini, *Processi . . . (1548-1560)*, 139 n48, 190, 220, 245, 335; *Processi . . . (1561-1570)*, 64n, 65, 73, 126-7, 131, 142, 147; *Processi . . . 1570-1572*, 42 n9.
50. Ioly Zorattini, *Processi . . . (1570-72)*, 128, trans. Pullan, ' "A Ship with Two Rudders" ', 32.
51. Peruzza, 'L'Inquisizione nello periodo delle riforme settecentesche', 168-71.
52. Grendler, *Roman Inquisition*, 42-8 on lay assistants, quoting 44-5; Del Col, *L'Inquisizione in Italia*, 345, 364.
53. De Vivo, *Information*, 257, 194.
54. Seidel Menchi, 'Inquisitor as Mediator', 184-7; Schutte, 'Un inquisitore al lavoro: Fra Marino da Venezia', esp. 184-6.
55. Schutte, 'Un inquisitore al lavoro: Fra Marino da Venezia', 176-8, 184-6; Francoso's *processo* transcribed in Ioly Zorattini, *Processi . . . (1548-60)*, 67-78; Pullan, *Jews of Europe*, 64, 68, 253, 300.
56. Schutte, 'Un inquisitore al lavoro: Fra Marino da Venezia', 191-3; Seidel Menchi, 'Inquisitor as Mediator', 184-7; Seidel Menchi, *Erasmo in Italia*, 162, 279-80.
57. Del Col, *L'Inquisizione in Italia*, 367-72; Schutte, 'Un inquisitore al lavoro: Fra Marino da Venezia', 189 n84; Grendler, *Roman Inquisition*, 125-6, and 48 n70, on which tribunals generally had Dominican inquisitors and which had Franciscans; Pullan, *Jews of Europe*, 29-30.
58. Davidson, 'Rome and the Venetian Inquisition', and 'Chiesa di Roma'.
59. Del Col, *L'Inquisizione in Italia*, 347, 369-71.
60. Grendler, *Roman Inquisition*, 48 n70.
61. Del Col, *L'Inquisizione in Italia*, 374-91; Del Col, *L'Inquisizione nel patriarcato e diocese di Aquileia*, xv-cclxxii, explains the development of the Inquisition, its procedures and background to the cases transcribed for 1557-9. The head of the archdiocese of Aquileia main-

tained the ancient title of Patriarch instead of being called Archbishop. The head of the Venetian diocese was the only other Patriarch in Italy.
62. Del Col, *L'Inquisizione in Italia*, 381-4, and *L'Inquisizione nel Patriarcato*, xxxix-li, on Cividale problems.
63. Massimo Firpo, *Vittore Soranzo*, 327, 390, 403 (quotes), and see also 316, 388-406, 496-7 on Brugnatelli's work.
64. Del Col, *L'Inquisizione in Italia*, 391-3, summarising his *L'Inquisizione nel Patriarcato*, cxi-cxxxiii on Bergamo problems (using ACDF St. St. sources), my trans., quote from p. cxxxii.
65. Grendler, *Roman Inquisition*, 218. The inquisitor is not named here. See also Sarpi, 'In materia di crear novo inquisitor di Venezia. 29 ottobre 1622', in *Opere*, ed. Cozzi and Cozzi, 1,209.
66. Del Col, *L'Inquisizione in Italia*, 328-31; Romeo, *L'Inquisizione nell'Italia moderna*, 9-10; Prosperi, *Tribunali*, 69-70; Canosa, *Storia dell'Inquisizione in Italia* IV: *Milano e Firenze*, 11-38.
67. Canosa, *Storia dell'Inquisizione in Italia*, IV, 29-38; Maselli, 'Per la storia religiosa dello Stato di Milano', 336; Giannini, 'Fra autonomia politica'.
68. Maselli, 'Per la storia religiosa'; Canosa, *Storia dell'Inquisizione in Italia*, IV, 39-59, 72-3; Del Col, *L'Inquisizione in Italia*, 580-1.
69. Maselli, 'Per la storia religiosa', 339, 344-5, 356-7 (e.g. cases of Bernardo Appiani and Cid); Tedeschi, *Prosecution of Heresy*, 178 n86.
70. For reform movements in Lucca, Del Col, *L'Inquisizione in Italia*, 292, 325-6; Berengo, *Nobili e mercanti*, ch. 7, 'La vita religiosa'; Caponetto, *Protestant Reformation*, esp. 275-82, 287-92.
71. Adorni-Braccesi, *'Una città infetta'*, 319-85, and her 'Il dissenso religioso'. On Vermigli and others, Del Col, *L'Inquisizione in Italia*, 305-6, who cites also M. Firpo, *Riforma protestante*, 123-5; Borromeo, 'Il dissenso religioso', 466-7; Berengo, *Nobili e mercanti*, 408-19.
72. Adorni-Braccesi, *'Una città infetta'*, 340.
73. Del Col, *L'Inquisizione in Italia*, 440.
74. Adorni-Braccesi, 'La magistratura delle *cause delegate*', esp. 280-5.
75. Ibid., 283 n62 (quote), 281-3.
76. Ibid., 285-93. Ginzburg, *I Benandanti* (1974 edn), 30-1. Del Col, *L'Inquisizione in Italia*, 586.
77. Romeo, 'Una città, due inquisizioni'; Scaramella, 'Inquisizione, eresia e poteri feudali'.
78. Scaramella, 'Inquisizione, eresia', 513 n2; ACDF, St. St., LL3a, incartamenta Caserta (unpaginated).
79. Scaramella, 'Inquisizione, eresia', 514 n4, letter of Castelluccio to Cardinal Santa Severina, 26 July 1577, reporting back on his experiences in 1554-5.
80. Ibid., 514. Black, *Church, Religion*, Maps 2-4 and Appendix locate the numerous Italian bishoprics (280-290, with 127 in the Kingdom of Naples).
81. Scaramella, 'Inquisizione, eresia', 514 n5. On Fra Sisto see Del Col, 'Note sull'eterodossia di fra Sisto da Siena'; Scaramella, *Inquisizione, eresie, etnie*, 97-9,114 nn26 and 29, with Bobadilla quoted at p.99.
82. Scaramella, 'Inquisizione, eresia', 514-16. Amabile already recognised this mixed control, *Il Santo Officio* (1891), I, 241; Scaramella, *Inquisizione, eresie, etnie*, 123; Cameron, *Waldenses*, 203, with useful Map VI for location of Waldensian communities. Clear distinctions were not made by many commentators between Waldensians (*Valdesi*), Lutherans and Calvinists.
83. Scaramella, 'Inquisizione, eresia', 517; Scaramella, *Inquisizione, eresie, etnie*, 35, 81 n36; Romeo, *Inquisitori, esorcisti e streghe*, 191-3.
84. Scaramella, *Inquisizione, eresie, etnie*, 128; Del Col, *L'Inquisizione in Italia*, 414-15.
85. Massimo Firpo, *Inquisizione romana* (2005 edn), 174, 223-4. The Neapolitan bishops named included Nicola Maria Carracciolo (bishop of Catania 1537-69, who possessed the *Beneficio di Cristo*), Pietro Antonio di Capua (archbishop of Otranto 1536-79), Nicola Francesco Missanelli (bishop of Policastro 1543-77, author of a tract on justification, and subject to a major investigation in 1563-4, mentioned above [on whom see Del Col,

L'Inquisizione in Italia, 420]); on Alois' widespread influence, Scaramella, 'La Riforma e le élites', 291, 296–300.

86. Massimo Firpo, *Vittore Soranzo*, 69–70; Russell, *Giulia Gonzaga*, 77, 189; Caponetto, *Protestant Reformation*, 330.
87. Scaramella, 'Inquisizione, eresia', 518–19; Black, *Church, Religion*, 9, 179; Massimo Firpo, *Inquisizione romana* (2005 edn), 414.
88. Ricci, *Sommo inquisitore*, 118–19; Scaramella, 'Inquisizione, eresia', 517–18. Borromeo, 'Contributo', 233 and n36 on *processi*; Scaramella (ed.), *Lettere*, XVII, XIX n10, LXXV–LXXVI, LXXXIX, 31 n35, and see 'Baldino' in index for references to him.
89. Discussion relies considerably on Frans Ciappara's books and articles (see Bibliography), some of which he has kindly sent me. Ciappara has effectively mined the Inquisition's records of cases and of correspondence, notably for the eighteenth century; but his referencing sometimes obscures precise dating. Andrew Vella's older (1964), brief and less reliable *The Tribunal of the Inquisition in Malta* has some useful bits. Carmel Cassar, *Society, Culture and Identity in Early Modern Malta* provides the wider context, especially economic, uses some Inquisition material, but says little on the tribunal's roles.
90. Cassar, *Society, Culture*, xl–xliv, 6, 11, with ch. 7 on 'Oral Culture, Literacy, and the Role of Maltese'; a *lingua franca* based on Italian but much else enabled communication in some areas as traders came from Greece, Venice, Genoa, Provence, Catalonia, Sicily, etc. Inquisition cases concerning magic and superstition have proved very illuminating on language issues and Mediterranean folk culture.
91. Ciappara, *Roman Inquisition*, 3–4.
92. Del Col, *L'Inquisizione in Italia*, 621; Bonnici, *Medieval and Roman Inquisition in Malta*, 303–5. Ciappara, *Society and the Inquisition*, 546–8, for a list of Maltese inquisitors.
93. Ciappara, *Roman Inquisition*, 45–52.
94. Ciappara, *Society and the Inquisition*, 326–8.
95. Vella, *Tribunal*, 25–6; Scaramella (ed.), *Lettere*, LXXXIV, 31, on Dusina.
96. Cassar, *Society, Culture*, 18, 27.
97. Vella, *Tribunal*, illustration of Girgenti palace between pp. 16 and 17; Ciappara, *Society and the Inquisition*, 485–95, on prisons.
98. Vella, *Tribunal*, 27–8; he does not give the exact date, but Wignacourt was Grand Master 1601–22 (death): Cassani and Sapia (eds), *Caravaggio: The Final Years*, 66, 71, with pl. 6 (p. 68), Caravaggio's portrait of *Grand Master Wignacourt with a Page* (Louvre).
99. Ciappara, *Roman Inquisition*, 42–8, 85–7, 103–30; his *Society and the Inquisition*, 65–7, 330, 339, 340, 343, 370, 485–95 (on prisons and conditions); his ' "A Spy of Marquis Tanucci" ', 209–10.
100. Vella, *Tribunal*, 31–7; Ciappara, *Society and the Inquisition*, 184–5.
101. Ciappara, *Society and the Inquisition*, esp. 101–14; more widely for eighteenth-century Maltese culture, his *Enlightenment and Reform*.
102. For establishment of the Sicilian tribunal, and for its context in relation to Spain and the Suprema: Monter, *Frontiers of Heresy*, 15–18; Messana, *Inquisitori*, 29–32; Renda, *L'Inquisizione in Sicilia*, 33–51; Leonardi, *Governo, istituzioni, Inquisizione*, ch. II; Canosa, *Storia dell'Inquisizione spagnola in Italia*, 18–50; Zeldes, 'The Former Jews of this Kingdom', esp. 127–71 (1487–1510 period), 171–99 (1511 auto da fé), 199–216 (1516 revolt and recovery).
103. Messana, *Inquisitori*, 33–4; Renda, *L'Inquisizione in Sicilia*, 67–71 (on Albertini); Leonardi, *Governo, istituzioni*, 65, argues for 1547 as a crucial date for hard repression, with royal backing.
104. Messana, *Inquisitori*, esp. 28–9, 593–607 (Appendix tabling the *auto da fé* from 1501 to 1744); Monter, *Frontiers of Heresy*, 59–60; Renda, *L'Inquisizione in Sicilia*, 197–239 (including notes on inquisitors, 233–9); Leonardi, *Governo, istituzioni*, 58–65; Garufi, *Graffiti e disegni dei prigionieri*.
105. Lea, *Inquisition in Spanish Dependencies*, 22–4.
106. Leonardi, *Governo, istituzioni*, 69–70 n30; Borromeo, 'Contributo', 253–4.
107. Renda, *L'Inquisizione in Sicilia*, 23; Messana, 'Inquisitore, Negromanti e Streghe', 54–5.
108. Del Col, *L'Inquisizione in Italia*, 730–1; Renda, *L'Inquisizione in Sicilia*, 170–93, 261–2.

109. For what follows: Del Col, *L'Inquisizione*, 246–52 (including the table, p. 248); Sorgia, 'Sui familiari dell'Inquisizione in Sardegna'; Solinas, *Inquisizione Sarda*, esp. 46–50 ('El real castillo' in Sassari, with illustrations), 55–63, 85–90 (finances); Lea, *Inquisition in the Spanish Dependencies*, 109–19; Sorgia, *Studi sull'Inquisizione in Sardegna*; Canosa, *Storia dell'Inquisizione spagnola in Italia*, Parte Seconda, 'Sardegna'; Borromeo, 'Contributo', 258–74; Rundine, 'Gli inquisitori'.
110. Alberti, *Descrittione*, vol. II, c. 22r; Manconi, 'The Kingdom of Sardinia', esp. 58–60.
111. Monter, *Frontiers of Heresy*, 181.
112. *Ibid.*, 264.
113. Borromeo, 'Contributo', 271: 'aborrescida la inquisición más que el infierno'.
114. A. Stella, 'Arquer, Sigismondo', *DBI* 4 (1962), 302–4; Caponetto, *Protestant Reformation*, 366–8; Del Col, *L'Inquisizione in Italia*, 453; Sorgia, *Studi*, 34–5; Monter, *Frontiers of Heresy*, 130–1 (on Centelles family); Marcocci, 'A proposito dell'immagine dell'Italia nel cinquecento', 288; Massimo Firpo, 'Alcune considerazioni', in his *Dal Sacco di Roma*, 161–220; Amelang, 'Exchanges between Italy and Spain', 440–1.
115. Caponetto, *Protestant Reformation*, 366; Sorgia, *Studi*, 35–7; Spini, 'Di Nicola Gallo'.
116. Canosa, *Storia dell'Inquisizione spagnola in Italia*, 268–80; Sorgia, 'Pietro de Hoyo', in his collected *Studi*, 36–66.
117. Monter, *Frontiers of Heresy*, 286–7.
118. Borromeo, 'Contributo', 267–8.
119. See initially Schutte, 'Recent Studies', 103–5.
120. Black, *Church, Religion*, 43–8; Giordano, 'Sisto V'.
121. Schutte, 'Recent Studies', 105; Gotor, *I beati*, 243–53.
122. Romeo, 'Una città, due inquisizioni', on both the situation in the Kingdom of Naples and within territories of the Roman Inquisition to the north, esp. pp. 65–6, and 55 n30 on developments by the 1620s.
123. ACDF St. St. II 1-I (1 Pezzo), 'Editti generali per tutte le Inquisizioni e per alcune in particolare. 1666–1686'. (In fact, at least one item goes back to 1655.)
124. Fragnito, 'Un archivio conteso', 1276–7.
125. Beretta, 'La Congrégation', 42–7; and see his 'Giordano Bruno e l'Inquisizione'.
126. The following account is based especially on Del Col, *L'Inquisizione in Italia*, 729–40; Romeo, *L'Inquisizione nell'Italia moderna*, 110–17; Peruzza, 'L'Inquisizione', 178; Canosa, *Storia dell'Inquisizione in Italia* V (*Napoli e Bologna*), 133–41 (Naples), IV, 97–108, 192–9 (Lombardy and Tuscany); Dall'Olio, 'I rapporti', 250–1; Renda, *L'Inquisizione in Sicilia*, 175–93.
127. Canosa, *Storia dell'Inquisizione in Italia*, V, (*Napoli e Bologna*), 135.

Chapter Three: How the Tribunals Worked

1. For surveys: Pullan, *Jews of Europe*, esp. chs 7 and 8, with examples from cases of Judaisers; Ruth Martin, *Witchcraft and the Inquisition*, 18–33, on routine procedures, with examples from witchcraft/sorcery cases; Tedeschi, *Prosecution of Heresy*, ch. 5, 'The Organization and Procedures of the Roman Inquisition'; Prosperi, *Tribunali della coscienza*, 194–210, ch. 8, 'Il campo inquisitoriale: le regole'. My general thoughts derive from reading denunciations and *processi* over the years in the Venetian, Bolognese and Florentine archives. Pullan's 'The Trial of Giorgio Moreto' translates the trial transcript of a Christian mariner who frequented the Ghetto, and comments very usefully on the procedures involved in a fairly serious case.
2. Pullan, 'Trial of Giorgio Moreto', 179 n29; cf. Eymeric, *Directorium* (1578 edn), 283–4 and 124–6 for Peña's notes.
3. Lavenia, 'Giurare al Sant'Uffizio'.
4. Pullan, 'Trial of Giorgio Moreto', esp. 175–6; Moreto was banned from visiting the Ghetto; when he was soon found there again he was recalled to the tribunal and made to serve the suspended sentence of three years in the galleys.
5. Rowland, *Giordano Bruno*, 230, 247–8.
6. Tedeschi, *Prosecution of Heresy*, 135–6.

7. BAB B1861 no. 60.
8. Leonardi, *Governo, istituzioni*, 58–65.
9. Finocchiaro, *The Galileo Affair*, 262–76.
10. Beretta, 'La Congrégation', 47–9.
11. Pullan, ' "A Ship with Two Rudders" ', esp. 34, 52–3, and his *Jews of Europe*, 135; Ioly Zorattini, *Processi* ... *(1570–1572)*, 37–209, esp. 151–2, 4 Aug. 1573, petitioning to be moved, if not allowed liberty as an innocent, to relieve financial burden on his friends who were paying especially for doctors and medicine, to have his 1,000-ducat security returned.
12. Kuntz, *Anointment of Dionisio*, 176–207.
13. Ginzburg (ed.), *Pietro Manelfi*, documents Manelfi's evidence to the inquisitors. For ramifications: Caponetto, *Protestant Reformation*, 48, 58, 193, 211, 296–8; John Martin, *Venice's Hidden Enemies*, 99–101, 104–7, 117–21, 145, and his *Myths*, 57–8; Del Col, *L'Inquisizione in Italia*, 282, 327, 338–41; Del Col, *L'Inquisizione nel patriarcato*, 259 n1, 262 n17, on followers who fled after Manelfi's betrayal; Dall'Olio, *Eretici e inquisitori*, 229–30, 355; Scaramella, *Lettere*, LXVII, on Manelfi's notification about heretics in Puglia.
14. Brambilla, 'Il segreto e il sigillo', 123; her *Alle origini del Sant'Uffizio*, 381–402. Her article provides valuable analysis and exemplification from cases across Italy of this complicated situation, and the basis for what follows.
15. Prosperi, *Tribunali*, esp. chs. IX, 'Inquisitori e confessori: prescrizioni', and X, 'Inquisitori e confessori: descrizioni'.
16. Del Col, *L'Inquisizione in Italia*, 765–7; collection in ACDF II 1-l. 'Editti generali ... 1666–1686'.
17. Brambilla, 'Il segreto e il sigillo', 159.
18. *Ibid.*, 142–3, 160–1.
19. ACDF St. St. LL-f, folder (2): 'Differrentiam ...'. Unnumbered, seventeenth century, in haphazard order; includes summaries of issue going back to the sixteenth century.
20. Del Col, *L'Inquisizione in Italia*, 768–9, 454–5 (Sicily).
21. Ciappara, 'Disciplining Diversity', 357–8, 360; Ciappara, *Society and the Inquisition*, 466, Table 9.1.
22. Schutte, 'Un inquisitore al lavoro: Fra Marino da Venezia', 173; Milani, 'L'ossessione secolare di suor Mansueta', esp. 138–9. Limborch's *Historia inquisitionis* (1692) has frontispiece illustrating an inquisitor and notary questioning an accused; reproduced in Martin, *Venice's Hidden Enemies*, 51, and Tedeschi's *Prosecution of Heresy*, opp. p. 136.
23. Guidi, *Ursolina la Rossa e altre storie*, 59–87.
24. Del Col, *L'Inquisizione nel Patriarcato di Aquileia*, CLXXX-CLXXXIII ('Il lavoro dei notai'); Del Col, *Domenico Scandella* (1996 trans.), xlii–xlv, 136 (19 July: 'The last time you were before us, at the end of the session you state you thought you were a philosopher, astrologer and prophet, but that even prophets erred.')
25. Walker, 'Let's Get Lost'; some surviving documents were annotated with instructions on what should be censored in the next version to be passed on (see at notes 45–6).
26. ASV SU b.69, 'Fiorenza Podaccataro', (c. 1592–3?); Plakotos, 'Venetian Inquisition', 201–2. Comments here and elsewhere may be conditioned by my serving on a jury trying a case involving standard English, Polish and a rough Glaswegian, with a voluble proactive Polish interpreter.
27. Davidson, 'Inquisition in Venice and its Documents', and personal discussions.
28. ASV SU b.33, 18 July 1573, 'Paolo Caliari ditto Veronese'.
29. ASV SU b.103; only briefly sampled due to shortage of time, but one version seems to be for the defence; Miato, *L'Accademia degli Incogniti*, 131.
30. Davidson, 'Inquisition in Venice', 124 n28 (on Ghislieri), and 124.
31. Cardini (ed.), *Gostanza*, 204–9.
32. Marc'Antonio Tirabosco, *Ristretto di pratica criminale. Per la formazione di processi ad offesa* (Venice, 1636), 44, as noted by Hacke, *Women, Sex*, 69.
33. BAB B1882, no. 26 (fols 261–267v). Notarial annotation: '*et plangebat fortiter, ostende Mazimam dolorem.*'
34. Ruggiero, *Machiavelli in Love* ('The Abbot's Concubine'), 80.

35. Tedeschi, *Prosecution of Heresy*, 178 n88.
36. Black, *Church, Religion*, 173, using APV 'Criminalia S. Inquisitionis 1586–1599'.
37. ACDF St. St. LL–f, folder (2). See Bibliography for titles, and Chapter 6 for analysis.
38. *Ibid.*, 'Compendio 1598–1635', fol. 6v–7r, 7 May 1626, Jacob Vigevani case, concluding 'ne trovo altro', nothing else found.
39. Ditchfield, 'Tridentine Worship', 211; Borromeo, 'A proposito del *Directorium inquisitorum*', esp. 521–6.
40. Hossain, 'Origins of Inquisitorial Practice', key commentaries on Simancas and Páramo.
41. Hossain, 'Origins of Inquisitorial Practice', 201; Prosperi, *L'Inquisizione romana*, 71–2. For a longer genealogy of 'inquisitors', including Jacob, Elias, King Nebuchadnezzar of Babylon, King Cyrus of Persia, Judas Maccabeus, John the Baptist, Peter Martyr: *Sacro Arsenale* (Genoa and Perugia, 1653), 5–6 (see also under Masini for modern edition).
42. John Martin, *Myths*, 28 (his trans.).
43. Garzoni, *Piazza universale* (1996 edn), 866; Prosperi, *Tribunali*, 156, 163–4; Kamen, *Spanish Inquisition*, 271.
44. Del Col, *L'Inquisizione in Italia*, 770–1; Errera, *Processus in causa fidei*, 264–5 n45, for ten editions; I have used 1653 and 1665 editions in Glasgow University Library, and a modern edition, *Il manuale degli inquisitori* ed. Agnoletto. At end as Decima Parte it provides: 'Avvertimenti utili e necessari ai Giudici della Santa Inquisizione', 249–304, with 330 paragraphs. See Tedeschi, *Prosecution of Heresy*, for references from his index for 'Masini', for uses of this manual on various topics.
45. Carena, *Tractatus de officio* (Cremona, 1642 edn), 338; Tedeschi, *Prosecution of Heresy*, 19 n64, and see his index under Carena for many citations from his manual. Errera, *Processus*, 281. Other editions from Cremona in 1636 and 1668.
46. Del Col, *L'Inquisizione in Italia*, 772; Prosperi, *Tribunali*, 329, 397, 419–20.
47. Tedeschi, *Prosecution of Heresy*, 229–58.
48. Hossain, 'Origins of Inquisitorial Practice', 191.
49. Biondi, 'Lunga durata e microarticolazione', 85.
50. Prosperi, *L'Inquisizione Romana*, 321 (from his 'L'Arsenale degli inquisitori').
51. Del Col, *L'Inquisizione in Italia*, 705–6. Cardinal Francesco Albizzi (1593–1684) was Assessor to the Holy Office from 1635, made Cardinal in 1654; seen by some as an important anti-Jansenist. Tedeschi, *Prosecution of Heresy*, 210, 221 n30; Prosperi, *Tribunali della coscienza*, 83 n57, 84 n59. See *DBI* 2 (1960), 23–6, for Albizzi (by A. Monticone).
52. ASV SU b.80, 'Cristina Collarina', 27 May 1625.
53. Davidson, 'Inquisition in Venice', 126.
54. Pullan, 'Trial of Giorgio Moreto', quoting 168.
55. ASV SU b.33, folder headed '1572–73. Denuncie', sheet dated 6 June 1571, annotated on 9 June. Addressed to 'Al sacro tribunal della inquisisium et alli signori deputati dal nostre principo', it begins: 'E una gran vergogna e sacndolo [sic] inla contra de S. tanrolo che ste feste sia sta la mugier in casa del piova' eche mai Zabia uolesta mandar viia ma col faccor del canselier tegnua parte in casa parte fuora la casa. . . .'
56. Notably Prosperi, *Tribunali*; De Boer, *Conquest of the Soul*; Lavenia, *L'infamia e il perdono*; Black, *Church, Religion*, 103–6.
57. De Boer, *Conquest of the Soul*, 44–5.
58. Del Col, *L'Inquisizione in Italia*, 406–7; quote from Seidel Menchi, 'Origine e origini del Santo Uffizio', 319. See also Prosperi, *Tribunali*, 230–57; Brambilla, *Alle origini del Santo Uffizio*, 403–9.
59. Schutte, 'Recent Studies', 107, endorsing and translating Prosperi, *Tribunali*, 235.
60. Adorni-Braccesi, 'La magistratura', 282 and n58.
61. Prosperi, 'L'Inquisizione', 313; Scaramella (ed.), *Lettere della congregazione*, LXVI, LXVIII; Scaduto, 'Tra inquisitori e riformati'; Prosperi, *Tribunali*, 10–15.
62. Masini, *Sacro Arsenale*, 356 (1705 Rome edn), cited by Prosperi, 'L'Inquisizione', 314–15. For the debates on the subject among moral theologians and others see Lavenia, *L'infamia e il perdono*; Mark Lewis's review of it in *Renaissance Quarterly* 58 (2005), 621–3, and mine in *English Historical Review* 122 (2007), 819–20.

NOTES to pp. 75–83

63. Romeo, *Inquisitori, esorcisti*, 195–6.
64. John Martin, *Myths*, 41–3 (his trans.); Ginzburg, *I costituti di don Pietro Manelfi*, 18, 33, 47, 68–9; Massimo Firpo, 'Reform of the Church', 471. Ginzburg (p. 18) stressed that Tissano should not be confused (as often) with Lorenzo Tiziano, the leading Anabaptist who 'baptised' Manelfi and others. On the exchange of information between inquisitors after Manelfi's revelations, see also Dall'Olio, *Eretici e inquisitori*, 229–30, 312, 355, 412.
65. John Martin, *Myths*, 56 (his trans.); see also Seidel Menchi, *Erasmo in Italia*, 206–8, who identifies the friar as the Benedictine Girolamo Capece, who discussed Erasmus with Tissano in Naples. According to Capece's evidence in Venice in 1553, Tissano had persuaded him that Christ was not God (420–1 nn37–8).
66. John Martin, *Myths*, 55; on Piccolomini, Caponetto, *Protestant Reformation*, 301.
67. Seidel Menchi, 'Inquisitor as Mediator', 178–9.
68. *Ibid.*, 182–3; Seidel Menchi, *Erasmo in Italia*, 279–80; Del Col, *L'Inquisizione in Italia*, 275, 345. John Martin, *Venice's Hidden Enemies*, 166 n39 stresses that successors saw Fra Marino as too lenient.
69. Tedeschi, *Prosecution of Heresy*, 135–41, 172 n75. Peña's updating of Eymeric was adding the right of defence which had been denied by the medieval inquisitors, though in practice sometimes allowed by the fourteenth century; Borromeo, 'A proposito del *Directorium inquisitorum*', 540–1.
70. Tedeschi, *Prosecution*, 175–6 n82.
71. Garzoni, *La piazza universale*, Discorso 63: 'De gli heretici et de gl'inquisitori', 867–8, Discorso 34: 'De' scongiuratori', 493–8 (1996 edn). Tedeschi, *Prosecution*, 176 n83. The Lateran canon Tomaso Garzoni's *Piazza universale* covered all the different kinds of activities, ways of working etc., showing both great learning and hard-hitting comments; first published in 1585. Beatrice Collina, 'Un "cervello universale"', introduction to 1996 edn, LXXXII–LXXXIII as exorcist; Black, *Early Modern Italy*, 79–82, 86.
72. Tedeschi, *Prosecution*, 140, 178 n87, and 179 n89 (his trans.).
73. *Ibid.*, 176–84 (my trans.).
74. *Ibid.*, 175 n81; Ginzburg, *Night Battles*, 110–11.
75. Tedeschi, *Prosecution*, 133, 166 n47, 172 n76, 173 n76, 183 n107.
76. *Ibid.*, 173 n76; Pullan, ' "Ship with Two Rudders" ', esp. 48–51 on Righetto, with now Ioly Zorattini, *Processi . . . (1570–1572)*, esp. for Bariselli's active roles, 20, 131, 136–43, 168, 174–5, 183, 184–5, 268.
77. Ginzburg, *Cheese and Worms*, 7ff, 110; Del Col, *Domenico Scandella*, 139–51; Ginzburg, *Night Battles*, 104, 128; Bonomo, *Caccia alle streghe*, 260.
78. Del Col, *Domenico Scandella*, cx–cxii, 139–51 (transcript), 165; Tedeschi, 'A New Perspective' (1996), 21.
79. McGough, 'Demons, Nature', esp. 220–1 (quote), 237–40. Ruth Martin, *Witchcraft*, discusses Bellina's fuller career as a *strega*, 110–13, 161–2, 182 n58, 221, 252, but ignores this defended charge.
80. Pullan, *Jews of Europe*, 113–14.
81. Dean, *Crime and Justice*, 56–7, 189–91.
82. Tedeschi, *Prosecution*, 141–2, 144, 180–1 nn96–9, 186–7 nn115–20; Masini, *Sacro Arsenale* (Genoa, 1621), 160 (quote), 157; see Roach, *The Devil's World*, 147–9 on medieval inquisitions' qualms about torture and its efficacy.
83. Tedeschi, *Prosecution*, 142 (quoting *Sacro Arsenale*, 154).
84. *Ibid.*, 183 n105 (quoting *Sacro Arsenale*, 155 [my trans.]); BAB 1859 'Consilia et vota in materia S. Officii'.
85. Tedeschi, *Prosecution*, 183–4 n108, with the quotation (my trans.) from a letter of the Roman Congregation to the inquisitor in Saluzzo, March 1626.
86. BAB 1860, fol. 79r; Tedeschi, *Prosecution*, 184 n110 (my trans.).
87. Tedeschi, *Prosecution*, 184 n110 (my trans.).
88. Cardini (ed.), *Gostanza*, 145.
89. Di Simplicio, *Autunno della stregoneria*, 39.
90. Finocchiaro, *Retrying Galileo*, 11.

91. Masini, *Sacro Arsenale* (Genoa, 1625 edn), 162. See Dean, *Crime and Justice*, 57, on the late medieval period.
92. Renda, *L'Inquisizione in Sicilia*, 263–6.
93. Tedeschi, *Prosecution*, 145, 187–9 nn124–8; see John Martin, *Venice's Hidden Enemies*, 180, for a drawing by Domenico Beccafumi (in the Louvre) of hoisting by the *corda*; Ciappara, *Society and the Inquisition*, 441.
94. Tedeschi, *Prosecution*, 188 n124, citing *Sacro Arsenale* (Genoa, 1621), 167, 169; Garrard, *Artemisia Gentileschi*, 20–1, 404, 461–2 ('I am ready to confirm my testimony even under torture and whatever is necessary'); Briggs, *Witches of Lorraine*, 77.
95. See Tedeschi and von Henneberg, 'Contra Petrum Antonium', esp. 266–8; Ciappara, *Society and Inquisition*, 439–40, 527.
96. Firpo and Marcatto (eds), *Il processo*, V, 177–89, esp. 187 (doctor's comment) and for torture session, 188–9, and editorial comment, 41–3.
97. Tedeschi, *Prosecution*, 188 n124, 187 n117 (quoted). Amabile, *Fra Tommaso Campanella*, II, 217–27, III, 498–501 (Doc. 402). Rowland, *Giordano Bruno*, 29, on Campanella's torture.
98. TCD 1226, fols 337v, 343r; Tedeschi, *Prosecution*, 188 n124.
99. Pastore, *Le regole dei corpi*, esp. ch. 5, 'Legittimità e practica della tortura', 101–24, and 70 (Scanaroli), 106 n15 for Palermo notaries, late sixteenth century.
100. Bamji, 'Religion and Disease', 166, cites one case in 1661 involving Lucia Nerivalca, on the island of Arbe, who suffered under feet-burning. For a 1771 Maltese case of a woman tortured over a bigamy charge, Ciappara, *Society and the Inquisition*, 441–2, 533.
101. Ruth Martin, *Witchcraft*, 27 n23, 178; Pullan, *Jews of Europe*, 47, 62, 65, 134 (quote).
102. Ruth Martin, *Witchcraft*, 27.
103. *Ibid.*, 25, 28 (quotes), 130–1, 235.
104. Tedeschi, *Prosecution*, 189 n126; Mercati, *I costituti di Niccolò Franco*, 6.
105. Schutte, 'Un inquisitore al lavoro: fra Marino da Venezia', 182–4.
106. Tedeschi, *Prosecution*, 144, 187 n120, 187 n122 (my trans.).
107. *Ibid.*, 143, 184 n111 (my loose trans.).
108. *Ibid.*, 143, 186 n113 (my trans.).
109. TCD, 1225, fol. 184r; Tedeschi, *Prosecution*, 185 n113 (my trans. from his reading).
110. Tedeschi, *Prosecution*, 143–4 (his trans.); citing Eymeric, *Directorium inquisitorum* (Rome, 1587 edn), 483, with Peña adding it was a 'locus comunis', a commonplace view.
111. Beccaria, *On Crimes and Punishments*, ch. 16 'Of Torture', 39–44, quoting 39. (Original *Dei delitti e delle pene*, 1764.)
112. Tedeschi, *Prosecution*, 189 n129 (my trans.); TCD MS 1226 fol. 184r.
113. Ciappara, *Society and the Inquisition*, 443 and n363 (my trans.). Ciappara does not give a precise date, nor the allegation against Leante. It might be noted that it was the inquisitorial vicar who offended, not a more experienced inquisitor.
114. Tedeschi, *Prosecution*, 152.
115. Finocchiaro, *Retrying Galileo*, 11–12, on levels of condemnation; Favaro, *Le opere*, vol. 19, 404; Finocchiaro (ed.), *Galileo Affair*, 291–2.
116. Black, *Church, Religion*, 178–81, with sources.
117. Messana, *Inquisitori, negromanti*, 593–607; Renda, *L'Inquisizione in Sicilia*, 268–74, listing 114 *autos* between 1501 and 1726.
118. Renda, *L'Inquisizione in Sicilia*, 255–6, 262–3.
119. Gregory, *Salvation at Stake*, quoting 80, 79, 76.
120. Tedeschi, 'A New Perspective' (1996), 17 n4, or (1997) 265 n8.
121. Renda, *L'Inquisizione in Sicilia*, 259–60.
122. Del Col and Milani, ' "Senza effusione di sangue" ', 182; Del Col, *Inquisizione in Italia*, 422.
123. Prosperi, *Tribunali*, 169.
124. Rowland, *Giordano Bruno*, 11–12 (description from a man who also described Bruno's death), 250, 268, 275, 291n.
125. Prosperi, *Tribunali*, 157; Del Col, *L'Inquisizione in Italia*, 435, 439.
126. Dall'Olio, *Eretici e inquisitori*, 275–6, 311–14, 327, 342–4, 355–6, bringing out the extent of Magnavacca's network, and its concern to inquisitors.

127. Prosperi, *Tribunali*, 168; Firpo and Marcatto (eds), *Il processo*, II/2, 619; Del Col, *L'Inquisizione in Italia*, 294–5.
128. Pullan, 'Trial of Giorgio Moreto', 180 n38; Tedeschi, *Prosecution*, 149–51; on Venetian galley sentences, see Viaro, 'La pena della galera'.
129. TCD 1226, fols 10r–21v, esp. 11rv (charges), 14v (sentence), 15r–16r (his confession, ratified 8 Jan. 1581), 19r (copy of the petition for him, 'sette figlioli inutili'), 20r–21v (inquisitor's comments, and 'il remedio compri un schiavo Mahumettano', 21r); see Tedeschi, *Prosecution*, 150–1, 199 n167, to which I have added.
130. Tedeschi, *Prosecution*, 147–9, 194–6 nn153–5.
131. ACDF Decreta vol. 6 (1565–7), vol. 9 (1567–9).
132. *Ibid.*, fols 35r, 130r–131r, vol. 9, fol. 47r.
133. *Ibid.*, vol. 6, fols 29v–31r, 37v–38v.
134. Tedeschi, *Prosecution*, 146, 190 n133, 215, 227 n72 (mixing his and my trans.).
135. *Ibid.*, 146, 190 n134, 176 n82.
136. BAB 1863 no. 65, 17 March 1607, Rome, From Cardinal Arigona; no. 68, 21 April, same; no. 75, 22 June 1607, same, concerning another petition; no. 108, 8 March 1608, from Cardinal (Giovanni Garzia) Mellini, replying to letters of 16 and 20 Feb., now in the house of Lorenzo or Sigismondo, *nipoti* (nephews).
137. Limborch, *Historia inquisitionis* (Amsterdam, 1692), illustrations between pp. 368 and 369; Tedeschi, *Prosecution*, illustrations between pp. 148 and 149; Lea, *Inquisition in Spanish Dependencies*, 22–4. Cover of Rawlings, *The Spanish Inquisition* for Goya example (1818).
138. BAB 1860, no. XXI, 13 June 1571; Dall'Olio, *Eretici*, 330, 376.
139. BAB 1860 no. CXXXVI, 6 June 1573; on Guastavillani, Dall'Olio, *Eretici*, esp. 313, 318–20, 337 n73, 346 n94; TCD 1224, fols 171r–172r (20 Sept. 1567, newer pagination).
140. BAB 1860 no. CLXXXXVIIII, 25 Sept. 1574, Cardinal Pisa; Dall'Olio, *Eretici*, 313, 337n, 346–7, 377; TCD 1224 fols 171rv, 21 Sept. 1567, newer numbering; on Ludovisi earlier, Tedeschi, 'A New Perspective' (1996), 17, trans. from TCD 1224 fol. 201(169v, new numbering, 20 September).
141. Dall'Olio, *Eretici*, esp. 261–70 for the overall career and judgements on Balducci.
142. *Ibid.*, 296, 319–21; Del Col, *L'Inquisizione in Italia*, 434–6, stressing Balducci's 'discreet work of persuasion'.
143. Dall'Olio, *Eretici*, 321–6.
144. *Ibid.*, 322–3; ACDF St. St. EE 1-b, Balducci letters to Cardinal Rebiba.
145. BAB 1860, Littere Sacrae Congregationis, 1571–6, no. LXIX, 12 March 1572, Cardinal of Pisa to Inquisitor [Balducci]. Dall'Olio, *Eretici*, 375 n169.
146. Battistella, *Santo Officio . . . Bologna*, 66, 70, Appendix no. 9; Dall'Olio, *Eretici*, 154–5 with n119, 286–7, 323 n41, 374–5. On Aldrovandi, also Prodi, *Il cardinale Gabriele Paleotti*, II, 231, 539–43.
147. Del Col (ed.), *L'Inquisizione in Friuli*, 33; Del Col, *L'Inquisizione in Italia*, 347, Venier appealed to be moved to Venice, 444 on Iechil.
148. Prosperi, 'L'Inquisizione in Italia' (1997), 297–8, and *Tribunali*, 146, 157, 162, 165–8; Caponetto, *Protestant Reformation*, 237–8, 244–6 (for Fanino), 210–11 (Benedetto del Borgo), 271–4, 312 (Lando); Del Col, *L'Inquisizione in Italia*, 323 (Fanino and Crespin).
149. Prosperi, *Tribunali*, 180–93.
150. Ciappara, *Society and the Inquisition*, 548; his *Roman Inquisition*, 103–30.
151. Ciappara, *Roman Inquisition*, 107, 112; Borromeo, 'Contributo', 255–8; Bennassar, 'Un tribunal inquisitorial mal connu', 122; Garufi, *Fatti e personaggi*, 214, and Canosa, *Storia dell'Inquisizione spagnola in Italia*, 177.
152. Biondi, 'Lunga durata', 85–9; Prosperi, *Tribunali*, 184–8, listing the different offices under inquisitors in Modena and Ferrara. For staffing throughout the Venetian Republic in the mid-eighteenth century: Del Col, *L'Inquisizione in Italia*, 704–5; Peruzza, 'L'Inquisizione nel periodo delle riforme', esp. Appendix, 180–6.
153. Peruzza, 'L'Inquisizione nel periodo delle riforme', 172–5.
154. Maselli, 'Per la storia religiosa dello stato di Milano', 351–2.
155. ACDF St. St. EE 3-a, *passim*.

156. *Ibid.*, 13 Aug. 1698, Congregation's copy of the complaint; 26 Aug. 1698, inquisitor Fra Gio. Francesco Orselli, Fermo, to cardinals.

Chapter Four: How the Inquisitors Worked

1. Prosperi, 'Il "budget" di un inquisitore'; Del Col, *L'Inquisizione in Italia*, 755–6.
2. For Campeggi, Niccolò del Finale and Costabili, their activities in Ferrara and Modena pursuing followers of Siculo, Prosperi, *L'eresia del Libro Grande*, esp. 260–3, 282–4, 444 nn21–3; Del Col, *L'Inquisizione in Italia*, 428–30 (with Campeggi's continuing work in Mantua against Endimio Calandra).
3. ASBol Corporazioni Soppresse (Demaniale), vol. 1/7589, folder, 'Copia delli Conti Mandati a Rome il 26 Gen. 1695, per tutto l'anno 1694'. Dall'Olio, *Eretici*, 296, on the episcopal pension for inquisition. Bologna became a metropolitan archbishopric from 1582. Lavenia, 'I beni dell'eretico. I conti dell'inquisitore', and his 'Gli ebrei e il fisco dell'Inquisizione'.
4. ASBol Corp. Sopp., 5/7593, 6/7594, 7/1595 (bound as one). Eighteenth-century records of various financial aspects, fols 1r, 2r, 14r. See Dall'Olio, *Eretici*, 322–3 on Righetti.
5. ASBol Corp. Sopp. Buste 5-7/7593–5, fols 84v–85v.
6. ACDF St. St. DD 2–b, fols 592–594v, 684r–686v.
7. *Ibid.*, fols 133r–227rv, *passim*. Letters are not bound in strict chronological order. The way letters were folded and tightly bound in clumps within a very fat volume means that sides 3–4 (which may just contain the details of the addressee, but may be the continuation of a longer letter and/or some summary or gloss made once the letter reached Rome) may be some distance away. See Fosi, *La Giustizia*, 90–1, who mistakenly says Masini stayed in Ancona until June 1611. The pagination is modern.
8. ACDF St. St. DD 2–b, fols 142rv, 143rv (Osimo, 30 April 1608), fols 150rv, 151r, 5 and 15 Sept. (Rocca Contrada).
9. *Ibid.*, fols 133r + 240v, Ancona, 11 Feb., Cardinal Conti to Cardinal Arrigoni, forwarded to Benevento where Arrigoni was visiting; fol. 14r, 22 May, Masini to Arrigoni.
10. *Ibid.*, fols 159rv, 23 Nov., fols 166r–167v + 206rv, 9 Oct. See below, Chapter 6, note 16.
11. *Ibid.*, fols 142r, 30 April, 160r, 23 Nov., 161rv + 213rv, 20 Nov.
12. *Ibid.*, 30 April from Osimo, 142r and 143rv; 9 Oct. from Ancona, 166rv and 167rv + 206v; 27 Nov. from Ancona, 159rv and 160r.
13. *Ibid.*, fol. 159rv, 23 Nov.
14. *Ibid.*, fols 134rv + 239rv, 14 Feb. 1608, Ancona, to Cardinal Millini, Rome.
15. *Ibid.*, fols 134rv. On the back page (fol. 239v) is a summary of the two issues; with the comment annotated, dated 21 Feb.
16. *Ibid.*, fol. 139r, 20 April, Ancona; Beretta, 'La Congrégation', 44–5, using Carena, *Tractatus de officio* (Cremona, 1655 edn), 105–22, on bigamy as heresy.
17. ACDF St. St. DD 2–b, fols 161rv, 19 Nov.
18. *Ibid.*, fols 143rv, 30 April.
19. *Ibid.*, fols 150rv, 5 Sept., 151r, 15 Sept.
20. *Ibid.*, fol. 156r, 3 April, Ancona, with attached print, 157r. On Fra Fulgentio Manfredi see: Bouwsma, *Venice and the Defense of Republican Liberty*, 401, 488–9, 500–1; Cozzi, *Venezia barocca*, 99–100, 108. On Crosta, ACDF St. St. DD 2–b, fol. 159r, 23 Nov.
21. ACDF St. St. DD 2–b, fols 147rv and continued 227rv, Ancona, 17 April. See below on Archangelo Calbetti. Loreto and Recanati were in this period united under one bishop (but had been separate 1586–91). Macerata had been united with Recanati in 1571, but put under Fermo from 1589; Black, *Church, Religion*, 238, 244, 274.
22. ACDF St. St. DD 2–b, fols 161rv + 213r, 20 Nov.; Livia's bail money was higher presumably because she was the leading practitioner of superstitious medical remedies! On 23 Nov. the inquisitor asked the cardinal to arrange for the civil prosecution over the security given for Francesco of Montemarciano and his wife, same fol. 160r.
23. *Ibid.*, fols 165r, 9 Oct., 172r, 27 Nov., and 173rv, 7 Dec. 1608.

24. *Ibid.*, fols 286rv + 294rv, 31 Dec. 1608, Ancona.
25. *Ibid.*, fols 439rv, 30 May 1611, Sassoferrato, on learning he has been made prior; 450r, 16 June; 452r, 3 July, Fra Giovanni Maria announces his arrival two days after Calbetti left for Bologna.
26. Del Col, *L'Inquisizione in Italia*, 429; Prosperi, *Tribunali*, 150; Pagano, *Il processo*, 54–6: 'si fa per la via de martirii'.
27. Prosperi, 'L'Inquisizione', 301, and *Tribunali*, 128, 138.
28. Chabod, *Lo stato e la vita religiosa*, 356–7, Doc. 82, pp. 459–60 (Chiarini's frightening experience, and called *'fra poltrone, fra beccho'* – 'cowardly, goat-like'); Doc. 80, pp. 455–8 (Senate conditions for cooperation).
29. Romeo, 'Una città, due inquisizioni', 60–3, quoting 61: the words of the inquisitor's notary, a priest.
30. Prosperi, 'L'Inquisizione', 316 (with quote), and *Tribunali*, 400, 415–16, 518–19 (same quote).
31. Burkardt, 'L'Inquisition et les autorités locales'.
32. *Ibid.*, 110; Paolin, 'Gli ordini religiosi', esp. 174–81.
33. ACDF St. St. DD 2–b, fol. 14r; Fosi, *La giustizia del papa*, 90
34. ACDF St. St. DD 2–b, fols 343r + 430r, 9 April 1610, Macerata.
35. *Ibid.*, fols 243r + 337v, 13 Dec.1613, Fra Archangelo to Cardinal Millini.
36. *Ibid.*, fols 342rv + 429rv, 16 April 1610, Macerata; fols 434rv + 513v, 16 December 1611, Macerata, bishop to Roman Congregation ('Per il S.to Uff.o'), an unusual addressee, since normally the leading cardinal is named, but the bishop may have been less aware of who was in charge than an inquisitor).
37. *Ibid.*, fols 703rv + 772v, 9 Jan. 1614. Iesi. Fra Vincenzo Maria da Bologna *lettore Dominicano*, and Vicario del S. Ufficio di Iesi, to Cardinal Millini.
38. *Ibid.*, fols 708r + 767v. Iesi, 9 Jan. 1614. Bishop of Iesi, to Sig.e Pro'n., Rome.
39. *Ibid.*, fols 731rv + 744rv. Last Jan. 1614. Iesi. Bishop of Iesi to Sig.e Pro'n., Rome; ibid., fol. 633r, 20 Dec. 1613, bishop of Iesi to Cardinal Millini; fols 703rv + 772v; 9 Jan. 1614, Fra Vincenzo Maria da Bologna, *lettor Dominicano* and Vicario del S. Ufficio di Iesi, to Millini; fols 700r + 775v, 28 Dec. 1613, Bologna, Fra Archangelo Calbetti, Provinciale, to Inquisitor General, Ancona.
40. Fontaine, 'Making Heresy Marginal'; Murphy, 'Rumors of Heresy'.
41. Deutscher, 'Role of the Episcopal Tribunal of Novara'.
42. Tedeschi, *Prosecution* ('The Question of Magic'), 229–58 in general, and 185 n112 for specific points.
43. Messana, *Inquisitori, negromanti*, 20–1.
44. Dall'Olio, *Eretici*, 266–7, 288–91.
45. AABol Ricuperi Attuariali, Foro Archivescovili vol. 249 (AB86) contains several complex cases involving Pensabene.
46. Dall'Olio, *Eretici*, 371 (Pensabene), 275, 314, 344 n87 (Magnavacca), 326–9 (Panzacchi); Del Col, *L'Inquisizione in Italia*, 435–6.
47. AAB vol. 249, 95v–105r.
48. Reported ACDF St. St. EE 1–b, c, 97r, Balducci to Rebiba, 13 Sept.; Dall'Olio, *Eretici*, 329 n60.
49. Dall'Olio, *Eretici*, 329 n60, 375 n171.
50. Dall'Olio, 'I rapporti', 250.
51. Based on my own sampling of Bolognese correspondence in BAB Lettere Sacrae Congregationis B1860 (1571–6), B1863 (1601–10), B1871 (1661–7), as well as Dall'Olio, 'I rapporti', who covered B1860–1.
52. BAB, B1860, no. CCI, 10 Feb. 1575, trans. from Dall'Olio's transcription, 'I rapporti', 255.
53. Dall'Olio, 'I rapporti', 256; BAB, B1861, no. 141, 18 Sept. 1591; B1860 nos CCXV and CCXVI, 22 Sept. and 8 Oct. 1575. On Oddoni (or Odoni): Seidel Menchi, *Erasmo in Italia*, 83–4, 356 (seen as 'one of the generation of 1510'); Dall'Olio, *Eretici*, 74–8, 412–13.
54. BAB 1860, nos. CLXXVI, 15 Feb., CLXXVII, 17 Feb., CLXXVIII, 20 Feb. 1574; partly discussed in Battistella, *Santo Officio Bologna*, 67, but muddling quotations from nos CLXXVII–CLXXVIII.
55. Tedeschi, *Prosecution*, 58–9 and 64n, translating from BAB 1860, fol. 156, 3 Oct. 1573.

56. BAB 1861 no. 60, 24 Feb. 1607: '. . . si procede avanti alla sped. ne co' debiti termini di guistitia [sic]'; no. 61, 3 March. On Vicari, Battistella, *Santo Officio Bologna*, 30 n2, 48 n3.
57. BAB 1861, no. 66, 31 March, and no. 87, 15 Sept. 1607; no. 56, 20 Jan. 1607.
58. De Vito, *Information*, 246.
59. Scaramella (ed.), *Le lettere* transcribes 1,029 letters from Rome; pp. 130–1 Doc. 263 (26 Feb. 1593), for the Ferrante bigamy case. On the concern with bigamy in Naples, see Scaramella, *Inquisizioni, eresie*, ch. 7, 'Controllo e repressione ecclesiastica della poligamia a Napoli'.
60. Scaramella (ed.), *Le lettere*, 184–5 Doc. 361 (2 Nov. 1595) for Rosso; p. 49 Doc. 115 (18 Sept.1579) for Leona; 187 Doc. 366 (5 Jan. 1596, '*alligando di esser carico di figlie femine et familia inutilia*'), 98 Doc. 219 (9 Aug. 1591), 102 Doc. 227 (22 Nov. 1591), 131 Doc. 264 (12 March 1593), the first mention that Musella had sent a petition to Rome concerning his family burdens, whose veracity the archbishop should test, 189 Doc. 372 (16 March 1596) for Musella; Canosa, *Storia . . . V: Napoli e Bologna*, 43–4 for Leona.
61. Scaramella (ed.), *Le lettere*, 46, 51, 54–5, doc. nos 109 ('*principale instruttrice in constringere il diavolo nella glassa*'), 120, 129 (for Portella), 151 Doc. 298. (for Gran Turco, '*sospetto di apostasia della santa fede . . . al demonio*').
62. Scaramella (ed.), *Le lettere*, 166–70, 171, 180–1 (7 July 1595 to 30 Dec. 1595). Camillo Borghese was still dealing with di Silva in Aug. 1603, and there had been problems in April 1599 over him paying his penalty of 500 *scudi* to the hospital for incurables in Naples; the bishop of Caserta, acting as an inquisition official, was ordered to seize Giovanni di Silva's property if he didn't pay up, pp. 374, 272.
63. Prosperi, *Tribunali*, 181–2; see my forthcoming article 'Confraternite e l'Inquisizione' for Prosperi (ed.), *Dizionario dell'inquisizionie*, vol. 1 (forthcoming).
64. Black, *Italian Confraternities*, 76–7.
65. *Ordini, privilegi et indulgenze* (Mantua, 1595). See below, note 68.
66. ACDF St. St. DD 2-b, fol. 440r, 18 Aug. 1611. Ancona, Fra Gio. Maria da Bologna.
67. *Ibid.*, fols 546r + 549v. 2 June 1612, il rettore et banca della Croce segnata. Ancona, to Cardinal Arrigone.
68. ACDF St. St. LL 4-f, large folder (2). 'Differentiam vertentem inter RRV Episcoporum Mantua, et Crocesignatos', 1637–1659. (These dates in the index are misleading, at both ends.) This is a somewhat disorganised collection of sub-folders, some numbered, with copies of letters and documents from earlier, and other, places, including the *ordini* cited above, note 65. The disagreements rumbled on until 1678.
69. Renda, *L'Inquisizione in Sicilia*, 217: 'En este isla mas facilmente se hallarán cien testigas para provar una mentira, que dos para provar una verdad', and p. 379.
70. Messana, *Inquisitori, negromanti*, 40–3; Renda, *L'Inquisizione in Sicilia*, 105–16.
71. Renda, *L'Inquisizione in Sicilia*, 129–30, 216–25.
72. *Ibid.*, 130–2; Messana, *Inquisitori, negromanti*, 43–7.

Chapter Five: The Carnesecchi Moment

1. Massimo Firpo, 'Teologia, storia', in his '*Disputar*', 227–46, esp. 228, 232 (quoted).
2. This account is based on: Russell, *Giulia Gonzaga*, utilising the Carnesecchi–Gonzaga correspondence, now accessible in ACDF, supplementing Firpo and Marcatto, *I processi inquisitoriali di Pietro Carnesecchi (1557–1567)* (4 vols), which transcribed and annotated surviving *processi* records, and other documents, while the editors provided an extensive 'Nota Critica' to vol. I and vol. II/1; Rotondò, 'Carnesecchi, Pietro'; Caponetto, *Protestant Reformation*, esp. 56–7, 263–9, 311–12.
3. While the *processo* was annulled 'perpetual silence' was imposed; but Carnesecchi sent Giulia Gonzaga a copy of the *sentenza* on 8 June 1561. Firpo and Marcatto, 'Nota Critica', in *I processi inquisitoriali di Pietro Carnesecchi*, I, XCIII–IV, and LXXXIII–XVII on conflicting views on how Carnesecchi should be treated.
4. Russell, *Giulia Gonzaga*, esp. 56–60 (on Carnesecchi's background), 157 n96 (on Venice's non-involvement); Del Col, *L'Inquisizione in Italia*, 402–3, 425–31.

5. Russell, *Giulia Gonzaga*, 127–8, 138; letters of 4 June 1558, 29 April and 7 Jan. 1559 (her trans. from originals in ACDF Storia Storica files). These all became part of the *processo* against Carnesecchi: Firpo and Marcatto, *I processi*, II/3 1151, II/2 573, 433 ('bruciato' was coded as 81 96 99 82 88 98 93, and Donna Giulia this time as 69). The June letter ended by noting that he had been told 'they wanted to give the *corda* to Morone [coded as H] ... which Donna Giulia [oo] cannot believe. And enough of this' (II/3, 1152, my trans.). Carnesecchi ratified the deciphering in his subsequent testimony.
6. Russell, *Giulia Gonzaga*, 151–4; Schutte, 'The *lettere volgari*', 659–60.
7. Firpo and Marcatto, *I processi*, II/2, 433–4, referring to a letter received 'that spoke of [oo = Giulia] dying willingly, accompanied by such a friend as he . . .'.
8. Russell, *Giulia Gonzaga*, 155, translates part of Carnesecchi's 12 June 1557 letter to her giving news of these persons; it was incorporated in the October 1566 trial record, from which I have expanded and altered Russell's quotes (Firpo and Marcatto, *I processi*, II/1, 268–9).
9. Russell, *Giulia Gonzaga*, 156, 158, Firpo and Marcatto, *I processi*, I, 44–5, as explained in May 1560 at the start of his next trial.
10. Russell, *Giulia Gonzaga*, 157–62.
11. *Ibid.*, 171, with my addition of the last sentence, from Firpo and Marcatto, *I processi*, II/2, 455. Confronted on 13 November 1566 with this letter of 21 January 1559, Carnesecchi ratified the court's deciphering, declared that his advice had been not to keep prohibited books, except those of Valdés, but 'intended she should be cautious not to allow those books to be found in her possession'. Robin, *Publishing Women*, 18–26, on co-authorship.
12. Firpo and Marcatto, *I processi*, II/1, 49; partly used Russell, *Giulia Gonzaga*, 203.
13. Russell, *Giulia Gonzaga*, 202, to which I have added from *I processi*, II/1, pp. 47–8.
14. Firpo, 'Teologia, storia', 240; Firpo and Marcatto's 'Nota Critica' to *I processi*, II/1, XXXIV–V; see also Russell, *Giulia Gonzaga*, 59–60; Firpo and Simoncelli, 'I processi inquisitoriali', 59.
15. Russell, *Giulia Gonzaga*, 60, trans. from Firpo and Marcatto, *I processi*, II/3, 1,346, to which I have added the last sentence of the main quotation; the full letter is given on pp. 1,256–60, with the comments on Pacheco, and the postscript on pp. 1,259–60. Pacheco seems not to have been part of this lesser investigation, presided over by Cardinal Santa Severina [Santoro], see p. 1,263; on the latter's role in the final Carnesecchi case, Ricci, *Il sommo inquisitore*, esp. 222–32.
16. Russell, *Giulia Gonzaga*, esp. 76–90.
17. Firpo and Marcatto, *I processi*, II/3, 1,192–3 (21 April), 1,195–1,200 (23 April). The editors note that Carnesecchi's signature of ratification is not appended to either of these records, as would be expected. See Russell, *Giulia Gonzaga*, 204, who only says he was tortured on the 23 April, but quotes from the record for 21 April.
18. Firpo and Marcatto, *I processi*, II/3, 1,237–62, eleven letters, some just expressing a wish for clothing and such things.
19. Russell, *Giulia Gonzaga*, 204–5; Firpo and Marcatto, *I processi*, esp. II/3, 1,359–60 (24 April), with pp. 1,336 ff. on the letter smuggling.
20. Del Col, *L'Inquisizione in Italia*, 425–8; Black, *Church, Religion*, 178–81 (Carnesecchi and *autos*); Russell, *Giulia Gonzaga*, 207; Robin, *Publishing Women*, 160–1, quoting a diarist's description.
21. Firpo and Marcatto, 'Nota Critica', *I processi*, I, III, citing the Florentine ambassador in Rome, Francesco Babbi, to his duke, 6 Feb. 1546; the advice was for him not to appear in Rome, even if innocent, because the Pope 'in these times with him and any other suspect of these heresies would use rigour'.
22. Firpo and Marcatto, *I processi*, II/3, 1,374, clause 34; Caponetto, *Protestant Reformation*, 311.
23. Rotondò, 'Carnesecchi, Pietro'; Del Col, *L'Inquisizione in Italia*, 425–8, for Carnesecchi, and see the name index for some others; Caponetto, *Protestant Reformation*, esp. 56–7, 311–12; Ambrosini, *Storie di patrizi*, esp. 51–2, 180, 225–6, 230–5, 263–4.
24. Ditchfield, 'Innovation and its Limits'.
25. Black, *Religion, Society*, 179–80; Russell, *Giulia Gonzaga*, 79–80, 167, 181–2, 190–6; Firpo and Marcatto, *I processi*, II/3, 1,159 (Gonzaga to Carnesecchi, 26 Aug. 1564, Russell's trans.), and II/2, 930–1 (8 June 1561, shown at trial session of 24 Jan. 1567, my trans.). The Israelite allusion was to '*Ecce vere Israelita, in quo dolus est*', John 1:47 ('Behold an Israelite, in whom is no guile'),

on which Carnesecchi was asked to comment: 'I wished to allude to that difference there used to be between Jews and Gentiles, understanding the Jews as the absolved and the Gentiles those contumacious before the holy Inquisition'; Prosperi, 'Galeota, Mario', *DBI* 51 (1998) 420–3.
26. Black, *Religion, Society*, 179–81; Caponetto, *Protestant Reformation*, 263–9; Del Col, *L'Inquisizione in Italia*, 428–31.

Chapter Six: Diverse and Changing Targets

1. See in general Kamen, *The Spanish Inquisition* (1965); his 'Marxist' version, modified in his *Inquisition and Society* (revised edn, 1986), and his *The Spanish Inquisition* (1997); Lea, *The History of the Inquisition of Spain*; Rawlings, *The Spanish Inquisition*, but not mentioning the islands.
2. Seidel Menchi, *Erasmo in Italia*.
3. Messana, *Inquisitori, negromanti*, 35–6.
4. Dean, *Crime and Justice*, 137; on flexible definitions of sodomy, and divergent views on which courts should investigate it and other sex crimes, Black, *Early Modern Italy*, 198–9, 201, and *Church, Religion*, 51, 195–6; Davidson, 'Theology, Nature and the Law'; Scaramella, 'Controllo e repressione'; Siebenhüner, ' "M'ha mosso l'amore": bigami e inquisitori'.
5. Schutte, 'I processi dell'Inquisizione', esp. 159–62.
6. ASV SU b.103, 'Rocco, Antonio'; Black, *Early Modern Italy*, 199; Muir, *Cultural Wars*, 80–3.
7. Del Col, *L'Inquisizione in Italia*, 772–84.
8. Ciappara, *Society and the Inquisition*, Table 9.1, p. 466. The four inquisitors sampled covered the years 1754–9, 1760–6, 1785–93, 1793–8.
9. Stow, 'Church, Conversion and Tradition', 27–8.
10. Del Col, *L'Inquisizione in Italia*, 772–3, 789–90; Luigi Firpo, 'Esecuzioni' for these old figures.
11. Del Col, *L'Inquisizione in Italia*, 781–2.
12. Rawlings, *Spanish Inquisition*, 115.
13. Levack, *The Witch-Hunt*, 21–6; cf. Briggs, *Witches of Lorraine*, 52 (trying to relate deaths to the size of population, putting Italy at the low end), and Barstow, *Witchcraze*, Appendix B (focusing on gender balances).
14. Fosi, *La giustizia*, 117–23; Ditchfield, 'Papal Patchwork Unpicked', 523–4.
15. Cozzi, 'Religione, moralità'; Derosas, 'Moralità e giustizia'; Horodowich, *Language and Statecraft*, esp. ch. 2, 'Regulating Blasphemy'; her 'Civic Identity'.
16. ACDF St. St. DD 2-b, fols 166rv, 9 Oct. 1608, Ancona. It is not clear whether the blasphemer confused the words for orifices, or whether he is suggesting St. Paul had a whore.
17. ASV SU b.103 'Contra Iov. Paulum Sorratinum', 10 April 1646, and b.106 'Contra Francisum Matthei', 2 Dec. 1653.
18. De Vivo, *Information*, 150.
19. BAB B1882, 'Processi del S. Ufficio di Bologna, Tomo 1 del 1697', no. 35 (fols 333–334v).
20. *Ibid.*, no. 24 (fols 229–252r, with blank pages).
21. ACDF St. St. DD 2–b, fols 2rv, 23 April 1607. Cagli, Fra Cherubino Arcangelo to Cardinal Pinelli. The annotation in Rome said the accusation should be read to the Congregation. See Fosi, *La giustizia*, 120, with a shorter quotation.
22. ASV Busta 80, 'Gervasio'; Black, *Church, Religion*, 110, also citing a case in 1594 in the Patriarch's court, where a jealous husband seems to have persuaded his wife to denounce her confessor, the *piovano* of San Simone, but where the charges were withdrawn and the priest exonerated: APV, 'Criminalia S. Inquisitionis 1586–99', fols 85–102, 'S. Simone'.
23. ASV SU b.69, 'Contra fratrem Augustinum Altomonte . . ., 8 Feb. 1592'.
24. Romeo, *Amori proibiti*; Black, *Church, Religion*, 108–9; Peruzza, 'L'Inquisizione nel periodo delle riforme settecentesche', 152–3.
25. ASV SU b.33 'Dominicus Longinus portator Farina', 14 and 29 Nov. 1573. 'Volta carta, e varda su'l messal,/ che torvare il Papa, che buzera/ Il Gardenal da ca colonna/ Chi cazza in culo il Papa ghe perdona'. A separate sheet has it with variant spellings.

26. John Martin, *Myths*, 62–82, esp. 62–7, 72, 76.
27. ASV SU b.103 'Joannis Jons. Q. Jois. De Saxonia', 24 March 1639, and 'Fugarola Lodovico', 10 July 1646; AAF S. Uffizio Filze 2–3, fols 55–7. Plakotos, 'The Venetian Inquisition', 174 n5, noted several other cases involving Protestant converts, in ASV SU bb.86, 88, 97, 98.
28. Black, *Early Modern Italy*, 154–5, and sources; Siegmund, *The Medici State and the Ghetto of Florence*; Ioly Zorattini, 'Jews, Crypto-Jews and the Inquisition', and 'Ebrei e S. Uffizio a Venezia'; Davis and Ravid (eds), *The Jews of Early Modern Venice*; Stow, 'Church, Conversion and Tradition'.
29. Rothman, 'Becoming Venetian'; Caffiero, ' "Caccia agli Ebrei" ', and her *Battesimi forzati*, esp. 21–34 on the Roman *Casa*, and interactions with the Holy Office.
30. ASV SU b.94, Iseppo Bon; see Pullan, *Jews of Europe*, 54, 64–5, 98, 121–2, 289, 301–2, also using b.91 for Andrea Nunciata, now transcribed in Ioly Zorattini, *Processi . . . (1636–1637)*, 31–93.
31. ASV SU b.59; Black, *Early Modern Italy*, 156–7; Pullan, *Jews of Europe*, 1612; Ruggiero, *Binding Passions*, 118–19, 249; on the *inghistera* technique of divination, and other Venetian cases, Ruth Martin, *Witchcraft*, 113–19.
32. TCD Ms 1225 fols 1r–6r (with 3rv for sentence); Tedeschi, 'Jews and Judaizers', 180. His transcription, my translation.
33. Pullan, *Jews of Europe*, 47, 61 (quote), 62, 65–6, 77, 96, 113–14, 134 (torture quote), 137–8.
34. Pullan, ' "A Ship with Two Rudders" ', 37–8; now transcribed Ioly Zorattini, *Processi . . . (1579–1586)*, who transcribes his name as Cyhan Saruc. 'Io ho havuto ditto Gaspare per marano per publica voce et fama e ho inteso dire che deto Gaspare è marano. Et marano come ho ditto è quello che navega con doi timoni, idest perché non sono né Hbrei né christiani' (p. 204).
35. Ioly Zorattini, *Processi . . . (1579–1586)*; Pullan, *Jews of Europe*, 230–40; Black, *Italian Confraternities*, 268–9, and 'Early Modern Italian Confraternities', 73; Boccato, 'Risvolti familiari'.
36. The following is based on Plakotos, 'The Venetian Inquisition', 103–18, analysing transcripts in Ioly Zorattini *Processi . . . (1585–1589)*; see also Pullan, *Jews of Europe*, esp. 47, 49–50, 64–5, 78, 129, 136–8, 140, 215–17.
37. Ioly Zorattini, *Processi . . . 1585–1589*, 100–1, 119–20 (circumcision), 109–12 (torture).
38. Plakotos, 'The Venetian Inquisition', 117–18; Ioly Zorattini, *Processi . . . 1585–1589*, 136–44, 157–64.
39. Pullan, *Jews of Europe*, 69, 78, 129, 172, 216–17, 221.
40. Natalie Davis, *Trickster Travels*, 19, 38, 63, 78, 224.
41. Plakotos, 'The Venetian Inquisition', esp. ch. 1, 'Witnesses before the Inquisition and Perceptions of Crypto-Judaism', which closely analyses witness statements in cases recorded by Ioly Zorattini, *Processi*.
42. Ioly Zorattini, *Processi . . . (1578–1596)*, esp. 96, 212 (Margharita), 296, 298 (Matteo); Plakotos, 'The Venetian Inquisition', 38–40 – our combined translations.
43. Ioly Zorattini, *Processi . . . (1548–1560)*, 152; Plakotos, 'The Venetian Inquisition', 22.
44. Plakotos, 'The Venetian Inquisition', 24–5; Ioly Zorattini, *Processi . . . (1642–1681)*, 182.
45. ACDF St. St. DD 2-b, fols 588r + 690v. 27 Dec. 1612. Fra Gio. Maria da Bologna, Ancona, to Card. Millini (the back sheet summarises the letter; there is no indication of the action taken).
46. Wheatcroft, *Infidels*, esp. 65–76, 101, 146–7.
47. Pullan, ' "A Ship with Two Rudders" ', 45–6; Ioly Zorattini, *Processi . . . (1570–1572)*, 43 (Diego Ortis de Vega, witness, 7 Oct. 1570), 107–8 (Alvaro de Caçeres): ' "Valgate el diablo, este parece deschapelhado" . . .'.
48. ACDF St. St. LL–f, folder (2): 'Differrentiam . . .'. A lot of pages are unnumbered; early on a four-page background paper is provided by the inquisitor, leading him to compile summaries of how in the past his predecessors had treated the issue.
49. ACDF St. St. LL–f, folder (2): besides the unpaginated sheets there are two numbered folders: 'Compendio, e nota delle Cause . . . 1598 sino all'Anni 1635 inclusive.' 'Sommario e Nota . . . dall'Anno 1636, sino all'Anno 1684'.
50. *Ibid.*, 'Compendio 1636–1685', fols 4rv, 14 March 1640, Vidal Meli, other Jews and Diamante. *Ibid.*, 'Compendio 1598–1635', fols 9v–10r, 13 Aug. 1635, case of Moise Special and the *puttana* Chara, who changed her admissions at various stages while she remained in prison.

51. *Ibid.*, cases mentioned 4 Feb. 1620, 29 March 1627, 16 June 1638.
52. *Ibid.*, 'Compendio 1598–1635', fols 4r, 28 Sept. 1623, 4rv, 7 Oct. 1623, 'Compendio 1636–1685', fols 8v–9r.
53. *Ibid.*, 'Compendio 1636–1685', 9v, 29 Oct. 1666; 12v, 26 April 1677. The inquisitor speculated on the causal relationship at the end of his first 'Compendio', fol. 11r.
54. ACDF St. St. LL 4 – f, among unnumbered pages there is a two-page Note or Letter, dated on the third page, 19 April 1685, after the bishop's death; part of copied documents. Many individuals named Norsa appeared over the decades.
55. Ricci, *I Turchi alle porte*, esp. 54, 86–7.
56. My knowledge of this topic owes much to supervising Georgios Plakotos' Ph.D. thesis, 'The Venetian Inquisition and Aspects of "Otherness" ', a fascinating pioneering work on Muslim/Christian relations and the Ottoman world.
57. Tedeschi, *Prosecution*, 41 n41.
58. Ciappara, 'Disciplining Diversity', 356.
59. Plakotos, 'Venetian Inquisition', 181–2 (on instructions to inquisitors in Adria and Venice), 182–3, 189 (his trans. from the 'Prattica'); Tedeschi, *Prosecution*, 212, 230–1.
60. Plakotos, 'Christian and Muslim Converts', 127; his 'The Venetian Inquisition', ch. 4.
61. Miculian, 'Storia della riforma in Istria', esp. 207–11.
62. Minchella, 'I processi' for what follows.
63. Plakotos, 'Christian and Muslim Converts', 130.
64. Minchella, 'I processi', 11, 17 n29.
65. *Ibid.*, 26–7.
66. *Ibid.*, 27–31.
67. Schutte, *Aspiring Saints*, for excellent coverage.
68. Malena, *L'eresia dei perfetti*, 6–7.
69. Schutte, 'Pretense of Holiness', 301.
70. Tellechia Idígoras, *El proceso*, esp. XVI–XXVI, XLVII–L on mystical ideas, the *Guía*, Albizzi's investigation, 3–45, summary of witness statements and evidence, 48–52, sentencing.
71. Signorotto, *Inquisitori e mistici* for the whole Pelagini movement, with 253–8 on Borri; Del Col, *L'Inquisizione in Italia*, 666–9; Petrocchi, *Il Quietismo*, 32–5, 113 n34; Malena, *L'eresia dei perfetti*, 242–5, 250–2, on Pelagini-Quietist connections. For the overlap between cases of Quietism and sexual misconduct, Barbierato, *Politici e ateisti*, esp. 208–11.
72. Tomizza, *Heavenly Supper*, and Signorotto, *Inquisitori e mistici*, 242–4, on Janis; Ciammitti, 'One Saint Less', on Mellini.
73. Gentilcore, *Healers and Healing*, 168–74. Not listed by Schutte, 'Pretense'.
74. Schutte, 'Pretense'.
75. See also Petrocchi, *Il Quietismo italiano*, 86–9; Renda, *L'Inquisizione in Sicilia*, 165–70.
76. Del Col, *L'Inquisizione in Italia*, 661.
77. Schutte, ' "Piccole donne" ', 288; *DBI* 40 (1991), 'Di Marco, Giulia', 78–81.
78. Tomizza, *Heavenly Supper*, for the full story by a novelist using trial records; Schutte, *Aspiring Saints*, 15–16, 116–20, 168–71, 206; her ' "Piccole donne" ', 292–3; Black, *Church, Religion*, 170.
79. Schutte, *Aspiring Saints*, esp. 13–15, 87–8, 125–31, 137, 164–7, 190–2, 207–11, 216, 225–6; Schutte, *Cecilia Ferrazzi*, and her 'Inquisition and Female Autobiography'.
80. Schutte, ' "Questo non è il ritratto" '.
81. Black, *Church, Religion*, 82–8, 127, 169; Schutte, *Aspiring Saints*, 12–13, 162–4, 192–3; her ' "Piccole donne" ', 297–9.

Chapter Seven: Censorship

1. Godman, *Saint as Censor*, 232, 233.
2. Hellyer, *Catholic Physics*, esp. 45–6 (on hypothesising, and probabilities), 90–113 ('The Physics of the Eucharist'); Neil Safier, review in *Pacific Historical Review* 77 (2008), 489–90, of Antonio Barrera-Osorio, *Experiencing Nature: The Spanish American Empire and the Early Scientific Revolution* (Austin, TX, 2006).

3. Fragnito, 'Central and Peripheral Organization of Censorship', is a valuable introduction to this topic; pp.14–16 on this background.
4. Tavuzzi, *Prierias*, 75–8 (on the Master's roles, and Mazzolini's appointment), 104–15 (Mazzolini versus Luther).
5. Godman, *Saint as Censor*, 8–9.
6. *Ibid.*, 34–6.
7. Borromeo, 'Il dissenso religioso', 482–5; Godman, *Saint as Censor*, 314.
8. Prosperi, *L'Inquisizione romana*, 365 (from his 'Censurare le favole).
9. Godman, *I Segreti dell'Inquisizione*, 74; Del Col, *L'Inquisizione in Italia*, 405; Bujanda (ed.), *Index des Livres Interdits*, VIII, *Index de Rome, 1557, 1559, 1564*, 27–39.
10. Fragnito, 'Central and Peripheral', 17–18; Bujanda (ed.), *Index*, VIII, 51–4, on *Moderatio*, 59–99 on 1564 Index.
11. Canosa, *Storia dell'Inquisizione*, IV: *Milano e Firenze*, 129–33.
12. Infelise, *Libri proibiti*, 76.
13. Schutte, 'Recent Studies', 103–5; Fragnito, 'La censura libraria', 167; Frajese, *Nascita dell'Indice*, 102; Fragnito, 'Un archivio conteso', esp. 1,282–6, 1,296–1304 on Brisighella and Pico struggles, 1,292–5 on expurgatory index; Godman, *Saint as Censor*, 173–4, 208 (calling him Brisinghella).
14. Fragnito, 'Central and Peripheral', esp. 18–20, her *La Bibbia al rogo*, 121–42, on the 1560–1590s period; Black, *Church, Religion*, 43–4 (congregations), 181–6 (censorship).
15. Godman, *Saint as Censor*, 20–1; his *I segreti dell'Inquisizione*, 84–5.
16. ACDF Indice 1, I Diarii, II (1607–20), fols 3v–5r, 8r–9r.
17. Van Boxel, 'Cardinal Santoro', 30–3.
18. Baldini, 'Il pubblico della scienza', esp. 184–94.
19. ACDF Decreta vol. 6 fols 29v–31r.
20. Del Col, *L'Inquisizione in Italia*, 405, 532–3; Infelise, *Libri proibiti*, 33–4.
21. Rozzo, 'Italian Literature on the Index', 201; Bujanda (ed.), *Index*, IX, 914–31, photo of Preface, Rules and Observations of 1596 edition, and vol. VIII 802–22, for the same from the 1564 Index.
22. *Index Librorum Prohibitorum* ... (Rome, Camera Apostolica 1596 ... 1632), copy in Biblioteca Comunale, Perugia; I also consulted the 1596 Rome Paolo Manutius, and 1570 Venice, Regazolam, editions in the same library; Black, *Church, Religion*, 182–3; G. Lavina, 'Capiferro Maddaleni, Francesco', *DBI* 10 (1968), 525–7. For a translation of Capiferro's 15 May 1620 corrections of Copernicus' *De Revolutionibus*: *The Galileo Affair*, ed. Finocchiaro, 200–2.
23. Fragnito, 'Central and Peripheral'; her *La Bibbia al rogo*, 143–71; Del Col, *L'Inquisizione in Italia*, 531–3.
24. Fragnito, 'Central and Peripheral', 19–20; her *Proibito capire*, 48–72, modifying Godman, *Saint as Censor*, 171–2, with 451–5 (documents).
25. Lopez, *Inquisizione, Stampa*, 161–6, 199–205.
26. See excellent chapters in Fragnito (ed.), *Church, Censorship and Culture*, which I reviewed in *Renaissance Studies* 17 (2003), 122–5.
27. Rozzo, 'Italian Literature on the Index', for an assault on vernacular literature; Fragnito, 'Central and Peripheral', 27–33, lists numerous authors and works subject to attack; Prosperi, *L'Inquisizione romana*, 345–84.
28. Rozzo, 'Italian Literature', 201, 205.
29. Donati, 'A Project of "Expurgation" '.
30. Del Col, *L'Inquisizione in Italia*, 537–9.
31. Savelli, 'The Censoring of Law Books'.
32. Fragnito (ed.), *Church, Censorship and Culture*, her 'Introduction', 10, and Savelli, 'The Censoring of Law Books', 232.
33. Baldini, 'Condemnation of Astrology'.
34. Infelise, *Libri proibiti*, 72–3.
35. Lopez, *Inquisizione, stampa*, 215–18.
36. Fragnito, 'Central and Peripheral', 20–7 (quoting 27).

37. Ibid., 35–6; Black, 'Perugia and Post-Tridentine Church Reform', 443; Cecchini, *La Biblioteca Augusta*, 1–38, 147 (Capuchins as borrowers and slow returners of books, including works of philosophy, a Hebrew grammar, and 'Il Jansensio sopra i salmi'), 212, 228–9, 397 (inquisitors), 361–2 (Melanchthon), 371–2 (Erasmus); BCP Ms 195 (D13), 'Indice di libri prestati', esp. fols 20–2, 49, 53, 91 (borrowings in 1590s); Ms 186 (D4), 'Ricordi domestici e note di libri prestati', Podiani's autograph for c. 1579–1614 (muddled), fols 34–5, 44 for religious borrowers; Ms 3081, 'Index librorum Bibliotheche Augustae a Prospero Podiani donata', including prices for some volumes; he donated about 7,000 printed texts, and many Mss. Godman, *Saint as Censor*, 30, 40, 327–8; McCuaig, *Carlo Sigonio*, 73, 75, 93–4, 266–8.
38. Fragnito, 'Central and Peripheral', 26.
39. ACDF Indice, Epistolae III, fols 287rv + 300v, 24 May 1596; Fra Domencio Istriani da Pesaro to Agostino Valier, Cardinal of Verona; fols 289r + 298r, 6 June, same to same. Fragnito, *Proibito capire*, 196 n9, 254 n193.
40. Fragnito, 'Central and Peripheral', 35 and note (quote), 26–7 (quotes).
41. Ibid., 35; her *Proibito capire*, 225; Assereto, 'Inquisitori e libri'.
42. Rozzo, 'Il rogo dei libri', with some illustrations.
43. Grendler, *Roman Inquisition*, 120–1; Robin, *Publishing Women*, 58.
44. Rozzo, 'Il rogo dei libri', 24, 31n99.
45. Ibid., illustrations on p. 27. King James version: 'Many of them also which used curious arts brought their books together, and burned them before all men.'
46. Barbierato, '*La rovina di Venetia*', 22–41.
47. Savelli, 'The Censoring of Law Books', 252–3.
48. Prosperi, 'La Chiesa e la circolazione della cultura', 156–7; also on expurgation problems, Frajese, *Nascita dell'Indice*, 102–7, 115–20; Fragnito, 'Aspetti e problemi'.
49. Fragnito, 'Central and Peripheral', 40.
50. Balsamo, 'How to Doctor a Bibliography', 66; Burke, *The Fortunes of* The Courtier, 102.
51. Fragnito, 'Central and Peripheral', 32, 40–1, 44; Balsamo, 'How to Doctor a Bibliography', 70; Donati, 'A Project of "Expurgation" ', 146, 149–50.
52. Rozzo, 'Italian Literature', 210–14; Burke, *Fortunes of* The Courtier, 102–6, and Appendix 1 for 153 editions of *The Courtier*, including translations, 1528–62.
53. Rozzo, 'Italian Literature', 194, 200, 203, 215–16; Fragnito, *Proibito capire*, 160–3, and 87–9 on Costabili more widely.
54. Tedeschi, 'A Sixteenth-Century Italian Erasmian'; Seidel Menchi, 'Whether to Remove Erasmus'; Fragnito, 'Central and Peripheral', 30–1; Godman, *From Poliziano to Machiavelli*, Appendix, 'Machiavelli, the Inquisition and the Index', esp. 325–8; Ricci, *Il sommo Inquisitore*, 350, 355, 386; Bujanda (ed.), *Index*, vol. 9, 350; Black, *Church, Religion*, 184–5.
55. Rozzo, 'Italian Literature', 204; Fragnito, 'Central and Peripheral', 25.
56. Barbieri, 'Tradition and Change in the Spiritual Literature', 115.
57. Ibid., 117; Black, *Church, Religion*, 58, 162, 184, 254 n46; Fragnito (ed.), *Church, Censorship*, her 'Introduction', 6–7; Balsamo, 'How to Doctor a Bibliography', detailed on the *Biblioteca selecta*, quoting 67, 68; Prosperi, 'La Chiesa e la circolazione', 152–5, on Possevino and *coltura*.
58. Fragnito, 'Central and Peripheral', 38–9, 48.
59. Fragnito, *Proibito capire*, 248–9; on Forty-Hour devotions, Black, *Church, Religion*, 216–17 and refs.
60. Finocchiaro (ed.), *The Galileo Affair*, 35–6, 206–18, 227–8, 304; Shea and Artigas, *Galileo in Rome*, 132–65; Shank, 'Setting the Stage', 75–81; Drake, *Galileo at Work*, 319–20, 335–40.
61. Barbieri, 'Tradition and Change', 125–8; Fragnito, *La Bibbia al rogo*, and *Proibito capire*; Infelise, *Libri proibiti*, 36; Del Col, 'Il controllo della stampa'; Massimo Firpo, *Artisti, gioiellieri, eretici*, esp. 100–16 (Brucioli), and his 'Lorenzo Lotto and the Reformation'.
62. Fragnito, *La Bibbia al rogo*, 108.
63. Barbieri, 'Tradition and Change', 127–31; Fragnito, *La Bibbia al rogo*, 108–9, 125–7, 291–2; her *Proibito capire*, 90–2, 100, 103, 110–12, 128, 207, 266; Del Col (ed.), *Domenico Scandella*, 52.
64. Fragnito, *Proibito capire*, 214–15, 225.

65. *Ibid.*, 216–22, 226; her *Bibbia al rogo*, 200–2, 294–6.
66. Godman, *Saint as Censor*, 70–2, 230.
67. Bowd (ed.), *Vainglorious Death*, lxiii.
68. Grendler, 'The Destruction of Hebrew books', quoting 130; Godman, *I segreti*, 127–8; Stow, 'The Burning of the Talmud'.
69. Ioly Zorattini, *Processi . . . (1561–1570)*, 139–72; Grendler, *Roman Inquisition*, 143–4.
70. Parente, 'The Condemnation of the Talmud', esp. 191–3; Frajese, *Nascita dell'Indice*, 127–31.
71. Raz-Krakotzkin, 'The Censor as a Mediator'.
72. *Ibid.*, 53–7; van Boxel, 'Cardinal Santoro and the Expurgation'.
73. Barbierato, 'La rovina di Venetia'.
74. Lopez, *Inquisizione, stampa*, 350–5 (inventories of Neapolitan bookshops, and banning order); Grendler, *Roman Inquisition*, 280–4, 289 (Meietti's international publishing and trading).
75. Scaramella (ed.), *Lettere*, CX–CXI and 25 (doc. 58) (Rebiba's order); Lopez, *Inquisizione, stampa*, 275–300 (*processo* and book inventories); Seidel Menchi, *Erasmo in Italia*, 346, 463 n23.
76. Grendler, *Roman Inquisition*, esp. 57n, 108–10, 188, 192–3 (for Donzellino), 186–95 (for Longo), 164–7, 185, 319 (for Ziletti), and 99–100, 185–6, 190–3, 311–14 (for Valgrisi family); Seidel Menchi, *Erasmo in Italia*, 344; De Frede, 'Tipografi, editori'.
77. Infelise, *Prima dei giornali*, 24.
78. Del Col, *L'Inquisizione in Italia*, 543; Campbell (ed.), *Oxford Dictionary of the Renaissance*, 590, 746.
79. Del Col, *L'Inquisizione in Italia*, 543–4; Baldini, 'Condemnation of Astrology', 91; his 'Il pubblico della scienza', 187 n43; Campbell (ed.), *Oxford Dictionary of the Renaissance*, 215; Scaramella (ed.), *Lettere* 25 (no. 58, 21 June 1574), 112 (no. 237, 20 April 1592); Ricci, *Sommo inquisitore*, 400–1.
80. Saverio Ricci, *Giordano Bruno*, for an extensive, well-rounded, modern study (2000), with Foa, *Giordano Bruno* (1998), as a valuable short guide; both helpful on the *processi*. In English, Yates highlighted the abstruse philosophical aspects of Bruno as magus and memory-man (*Giordano Bruno and the Hermetic Tradition; The Art of Memory*). Rowland's stimulating and well-rounded *Giordano Bruno* appeared when completing this text, with valuable comments on his writings as well as his inquisitorial experiences. On the partially surviving records of investigations and trials: Luigi Firpo, 'Il processo di Giordano Bruno' articles (1948 and 1949); Del Col, *L'Inquisizione in Italia*, 545–8; Mercati, *Il sommario del processo di Giordano Bruno*, which summary was produced at the end of the Roman process to facilitate final decision making, indicating which delators and witnesses supported which of the final thirty-one accusations against Bruno, and see Beretta, 'Giordano Bruno e l'Inquisizione romana' on this document.
81. Foa, *Giordano Bruno*, 7–20, on this nineteenth-century context and the statue.
82. This was an obscure accusation by Giovanni Mocenigo, whose testimony has to be treated with caution, Foa, *Bruno*, 37; Rowland, *Giordano Bruno*, 71–86.
83. Luigi Firpo, 'Il processo' (1948), 553–4; Ricci, *Giordano Bruno*, esp. 486–91; Foa, *Giordano Bruno*, 41, 47, 54; Rowland, *Giordano Bruno*, 226 on Mocenigo's wife, 227–9 quoting from the first letter of denunciation.
84. Luigi Firpo, 'Il processo' (1948), 558 n2, and see Mercati, *Il sommario*, 102, delator Muzengus (= Mocenigo), on Solomon's mistresses, and that the Church was wrong to make a sin of this, which served nature well.
85. Luigi Firpo, 'Il processo' (1948), 558–69.
86. Yates, *Giordano Bruno*, 350–3; see also Beretta, 'Giordano Bruno', 35–7, on Bruno's philosophical style opposing 'the inquisitorial style'.
87. Luigi Firpo, 'Il processo' (1949), 16; Rowland, *Giordano Bruno*, 246–8, on Fra Celestino's allegations.
88. '*forma corporis per se et essentialiter*', Luigi Firpo, 'Il processo' (1949), 37, 38 (quote), 39; Foa, *Giordano Bruno*, 60–3; Godman, *Saint as Censor*, 176–8, on the heresy, and he adds on the relationship, 'The cardinal-inquisitor and the heretic spoke the same language – a religious language, whose truth-claims were absolute and whose conclusions were uncompromising.' This may explain Bruno's final decision to overcome fear, and not compromise truth by

abjuring. Rowland, *Giordano Bruno*, 256–60, on Bellarmino, and summaries of the accusations.
89. Luigi Firpo, 'Il processo' (1949), 45–50; Foa, *Giordano Bruno*, 59–65; Beretta, 'Giordano Bruno', 45–9; Yates, *Renaissance and Reform*, 147, reviewing a translation of *La Cena de le Ceneri*; Rowland, *Giordano Bruno*, 271–6, sentence and death.
90. Ricci, *Sommo inquisitore*, 414–15.
91. Ricci, *Giordano Bruno*, 417, 458, 520–1, 528; Foa, *Giordano Bruno*, 95–6, Ricci, *Sommo inquisitore*, 401–6.
92. Foa, *Giordano Bruno*, 96–101; Ricci, *Sommo inquisitore*, 415–20, judges Campanella feigned madness. Amabile, *Fra Tommaso Campanella*, passim, but esp. vol. II, 119–327 on 1600-2 trial, vol. III, doc. 395 (pp. 457–61), summary of indictment; doc. 402 (pp. 498–501) on *veglia* torture session, 4 June 1501; doc. 403 (pp. 502–3) concerning his *pazzia* (madness). For intellectual and pro-Henri IV political strategy links between Bruno and Campanella see Yates, *Giordano Bruno*, ch. xx, 360–97, and her *Renaissance and Reform*, 130–8.
93. Finocchiaro, *The Galileo Affair*, translates the central documents from and surrounding the inquisitorial investigations, with a useful, crisp introduction, chronology and biographical glossary. Drake's *Galileo at Work* is a useful biographical study. Blackwell's *Behind the Scenes at Galileo's Trial* has a pithy outline analysis of the 1633 trial, 1–27 ('The Legal Case at Galileo's Trial: Impasse and Perfidy'). Speller's inelegant *Galileo's Inquisition Trial Revisited* analyses many controversies; Finocchiaro's *Retrying Galileo, 1633–1992* impressively digests the subsequent changing attitudes to the investigations of Galileo. McMullin (ed.), *The Church and Galileo*, has several valuable essays based on recent research and debate, some used below.
94. Poppi, *Cremonini, Galilei*, 55–61 (doc. V), P[i]agnoni's denunciation, 21 April 1604, in front of the inquisitorial vicar Cesare Lippi de Mordáno, the inquisitorial fiscal, the episcopal vicar-general and a judge as secular *assistente*. The *'puttana'*, Marina Gambi, was the mother of his three children.
95. Muir, *Cultural Wars*, 35–8, 40–4; Poppi, *Cremonini, Galilei*, 42–4 (Doctor Camillo Bellono, 12 April 1604, main denunciation of Cremonini's teaching about mortality), 55–61, 81–2 (Signoria, 16 June, asserting his being a good Catholic, and obeying the rules on teaching, and asking the inquisitor to impose silence on the *processo*, and not proceed further), 86 (Paduan Rettori to Doge on fear of student tumult if Cremonini was arraigned), 88–93 (undated Cremonini self-defence to Signoria); Davidson, 'Unbelief and Atheism in Italy', 75–7. See also Shank, 'Setting the Stage', with 66 and notes on Cremonini and Galileo.
96. Muir, *Cultural Wars*, 39–40.
97. Finocchiaro, *Galileo Affair*, 299; Pagano (ed.), *I documenti*, 219, 17 May 1611.
98. Finocchiaro, *Galileo Affair*, 134–5; Caccini's deposition was put before the Inquisition's Congregation, 2 April, when the Pope ordered that the Florentine inquisitor be sent a copy and told to question named witnesses, Pagano (ed.), *I documenti*, 221.
99. Finocchiaro, *Galileo Affair*, 146–7.
100. Favaro (ed.), *Opere*, 12 (1902), 175–6, Piero Pini (Rome) to Galileo (Florence), 2 May 1615; McMullin, 'The Church's Ban on Copernicanism, 1616', esp. 150–4 (on Index decree), 174–82 (Bellarmino's attitudes and roles); Blackwell, *Behind the Scenes*, 4, 55–6.
101. Finocchiaro, *Galileo Affair*, 147–53, 259; Fantoli, 'The Disputed Injunction'.
102. Finocchiaro, *Galileo Affair*, 67–9; Favaro (ed.), *Opere*, 12 (1902), 171–2: 'contentarsi di parlare *ex suppositione* e non assolutamente, come io ho sempre creduto che habbia parlato il Copernico'. Shea and Artigas, *Galileo in Rome*, 35–6, 69–74, 83–4; Drake, *Galileo at Work*, 245–56.
103. Blackwell, *Galileo, Bellarmine and the Bible*, 45–8.
104. On Barberini and Galileo in this period, Shea and Artigas, *Galileo in Rome*, 32, 46–7, 64–5, 72–3; Drake, *Galileo at Work*, 287–92. Maffeo and Galileo exchanged letters about a comet and a new *Discorso* about it in 1619, Favaro (ed.), *Opere*, 12 (1902), 461–3.
105. Finocchiaro, *Galileo Affair*, 204–6, 303; Westfall, *Essays on the Trial*, 59–60; Beretta, 'The Documents of Galileo's Trial', 217–18.
106. Both documents are in the ACDF Index, Protocolli, EE. Redondi (with limited access to the volume before the 1998 opening) spotted the possible importance of the document he called

G3, generating heated debate with his *Galileo eretico* (1983) and *Galileo Heretic* (1987), giving the text (427–9 and 333–5 respectively). Mariano Artigas, looking more freely at the volume containing G3, spotted another analysis of *The Assayer*, naming it EE 291 after its volume and folio numbers (possibly written by the Jesuit Melchior Inchofer). Accessible and short discussions of both documents, possible authorship and dates, and implications: Artigas, Rafael Martínez and William R. Shea, 'New Light on the Galileo Affair?', with Latin text of EE 291, and translation; see also now Speller, *Galileo's Inquisition Trial Revisited*, 117–23; Finocchiaro, *Retrying Galileo*, 362–3, on Redondi; Blackwell, *Behind the Scenes*.

107. Shank, 'Setting the Stage', 79; Finocchiaro, *Galileo Affair*, 218–221, for full Report.
108. Drake, *Galileo at Work*, 342–3.
109. Finocchiaro, *Galileo Affair*, 256–62, 277–81, 286–93, transcribes his four interrogations (12, 30 April, 10 May, 21 June), his defence (10 May), sentence and abjuration (22 June).
110. *Ibid.*, 147–8 (called 'Special Injunction'); Fantoli, 'The Disputed Injunction', 119–20 (Segizzi Injunction); Blackwell, *Behind the Scenes*, 4–6; Speller, *Galileo's Inquisition Trial Revisited*, 94–110.
111. Finocchiaro, *Galileo Affair*, 218–22 (reports), 355 n64 (comment), 319–21 (biographical profiles); Redondi, *Galileo Heretic*, 78, 249–55; Speller, *Galileo's Inquisition Trial*, 229–54 ('The Biased Answers of the Consultants'). Blackwell, *Behind the Scenes*, Appendix One, translates Inchofer's fully published (1633) Treatise, *Concerning the Motion or Rest of the Earth and the Sun*, sparked by having analysed Galileo's *Dialogue*.
112. Westfall, *Essays on the Trial*, 74, 82 n71; Drake, *Galileo at Work*, 350–1; Speller, *Galileo's Inquisition Trial*, emphasises Francesco Barberini's support for Galileo, from early in Urban VIII's pontificate to the 1632–3 crisis, with Ambassador Niccolini dealing with him, e.g. pp.115–23, 167–71, 219–26, 266–8, 304–5.
113. Blackwell, *Behind the Scenes*, 13–16 ('The Plea Bargain'); Finocchiaro, *Galileo Affair*, 276–7.
114. Finocchiaro, *Galileo Affair*, 287, referring back to his comment 'that therefore to proceed with certainty one had to resort to the determination of more subtle doctrines, as one can see in many places in the *Dialogue*'; Drake, *Galileo at Work*, 351.
115. Blackwell, *Behind the Scenes*, 18–21 ('The False Summary Report').
116. Finocchiaro, *Galileo Affair*, 287–91, 363 n87; his *Retrying Galileo*, 43–6, quoting Descartes' letters to Mersenne, November 1633, February and April 1634; Redondi, *Galileo Heretic*, 260–1; Heilbron, 'Censorship of Astronomy', 284–5; Beretta, 'Galileo, Urban VIII'.
117. Sobel, *Galileo's Daughter*, 300, 366n, 368–9; Drake, *Galileo at Work*, 353–6; Cioni, *Documenti Galileiani*, 41–7; Cochrane, *Florence in the Forgotten Centuries*, 215; Garrard, *Artemisia Gentileschi*, 37–8, 383–4 (Letter 9, from Naples, 9 Oct. 1635); Speller, *Galileo's Inquisition Trial*, 349–64, on the aftermath.
118. Redondi, *Galileo Heretic*, 266–71; Finocchiaro, *Retrying Galileo*, 26–42 ('Promulgation and Diffusion of the News'), with 372 n15 on uncooperative inquisitors.
119. Cochrane, *Florence*, 181–2, 226–8.
120. Redondi, *Galileo Heretic*, 261; Heilbron, 'Censorship of Astronomy'.
121. Grendler, *Roman Inquisition*, passim.
122. Del Col, *L'Inquisizione in Italia*, 540.
123. Bouwsma, *Venice and the Defense*, 358–64, on Sarpi's background, and chs. VII–IX on the Interdict, and the men and ideas involved; Black, *Church, Religion*, 48–54, with sources.
124. Bouwsma, *Venice and the Defense*, 497.
125. ACDF Indice Diarii II (1607–20), ff. 1rv (6 July), 1v–2r (20 July), 2v–3v (10 Aug., when it delayed sending a positive decree on the booksellers).
126. De Vito, *Information*, esp. 207, 214, 216 (Table 6.1 on Interdict-related pamphlets), 235–6.
127. *Ibid.*, 239–40.
128. BAB B1863, nos 30 (10 June 1606), 32 (27 June), 43 (16 Sept.), 44 (23 Sept.), 49 (28 Oct.), 56 (20 Jan. 1607, on nunneries), 63 (10 March, from the Master of the Palace). On Fra Paolo as the longest-serving Bolognese inquisitor (1606–43d), dying in odour of sanctity, Battistella, *Il Santo Officio . . . Bologna*, 30, 48.
129. BAB B1863, no. 49, 28 Oct.1606.

130. ASV SU b.103, nos 2 and 10 respectively. The author sampled the latter (bulky) bundle, discovered on the last day of a visit to the ASV; both have since been discussed in Miato, *L'Accademia degli Incogniti*, esp. ch. 3, and briefly but usefully by Infelise, 'Books and Politics in Arcangela Tarabotti's Venice', on both of which much of what follows is based.
131. Del Col, *L'Inquisizione in Italia*, 555–6, 640.
132. Dialeti, 'The Debate about Women' (Glasgow Ph.D., 2004, supervised by the author).
133. Infelise, 'Books and Politics', 67. This was a version of an older Latin work, *Disputio nova contra mulieres*, 1595: Dialeti, 'The Debate about Women', 163–5.
134. Tarabotti, *Che le donne siano della spezie degli uomini*, ed. Panizza. Tarabotti's *La tirannia paterna* was to be put on the Index in 1651: *Paternal Tyranny*, ed. Panizza, 'Introduction', 27.
135. ASV SU b.103, 2 and 21 April 1648; Infelise, 'Books and Politics', 68.
136. Miato, *L'Accademia degli Incogniti*, 142, 146.
137. See esp. ASV SU b.103, 'Valvasense', 9 June 1648, witness Marcus Ginamuthus.
138. Infelise, 'Books and Politics', 60–1; also on Vitelli and Pallavicino, Perocco, 'Prose Production in Venice', 82–5; Infelise, *Libri proibiti*, 83.
139. Infelise, 'Books and Politics', 68 (Thomas Simpson's translation of the article); see also Miato, *L'Accademia degli Incogniti*, 128–30, 124–5 (applying to the guild of booksellers, printers and binders, *Arte dei libreri, stampatori e ligatori*).
140. Miato, *L'Accademia degli Incogniti*, 158–9.
141. Ibid., 162–6; Infelise, 'Books and Politics', esp. 69–72.
142. ASV SU b.103, 27 Feb. 1635; 3 Nov. 1648; 20 July 1552, with attachments; Muir, *Culture Wars*, 80–3, translating part of the 1648 denunciation. Miato, *L'Accademia degli Incogniti*, 88–9, 181, 267, quotes some of the 1648 record (p. 89). Barbierato, *Politici e ateisti*, 174–6, 272, 283–7.
143. Perocco, 'Prose Production', 85–6.
144. Delpiano, *Il governo della lettura*, building on her 'Per una storia della censura ecclesiastica', (see my forthcoming review for the *Journal of Modern History*); Costa, *Thomas Burnet e la censura pontificia* (my review in *Renaissance Quarterly* 59 [2006], 1,295–7). Chadwick's *The Popes and European Revolution*, 323–32, remains useful and readable.
145. Delpiano, *Il governo*, 12–13, 25–6, 45; Prosperi, *Tribunali*, 543–5, 465 (quote).
146. Extensively covered by Franco Venturi, notably in *Settecento riformatore*, vol. I, *Da Muratori a Beccaria*; II, *La Chiesa e la Repubblica dentro loro i limiti*; V, 1 and 2, *L'Italia dei lumi*. In English his essays in *Italy and the Enlightenment*, as ch. 4, 'Enlightenment versus the Powers of Darkness', and ch. 10, 'The Enlightenment in the Papal States'.
147. Di Rienzo and Formica, 'Tra Napoli e Roma', esp. 205–6, 210–11, 226–30.
148. Delpiano, *Il governo*, 80–92; Godman, *I segreti*, 203–27.
149. Delpiano, *Il governo*, 90–1, also on Lazzeri, 99, 103–4 (against Voltaire), 113–14 (against Gorani), 139–40 (librarian, and helping with reorganisation of the Index), 246 (against Beccaria); see Godman, *I segreti*, 231–6, on reforming the Index, though it spells his name Lazzari. On Gorani: Infelise, *I libri proibiti*, 116–17, and Venturi, *Settecento riformatore*, V/1, 500–1 (Verri's view), 501–11 (the book).
150. Delpiano, *Il governo*, 131.
151. Costa, 'La Congregazione dell'Indice e Jonathan Swift'; Delpiano, *Il governo*, 78–9, 138; Mazzotti, 'Newton for Ladies', 143–5, on Crudeli and Freemasons.
152. Delpiano, 'Per una storia', 507; her *Il governo*, 88 n39, 149, 125 and n135, 135, 266 (quoting the Spanish ex-Jesuit Juan Andrés on *Clarissa* in 1785), 60–5.
153. Delpiano, *Il governo* 72, 141–7, 154, and see her fig. 2 for the decree about burning Voltaire's *La Pucelle d'Orleans*, Jan. 1757.
154. Delpiano, 'Per una storia', 505–6; her *Il governo*, 61, 148–9, 102–3 (with quote on Beccaria).
155. Ibid., 103, 113.
156. Ibid., 92–8, quoting 96–7.
157. Braida, *Il commercio delle idee*, esp. 85–6, 112, 124, 150–2, 254–64; Delpiano, *Il governo*, 155–67.
158. Delpiano, *Il governo*, 168–9, 174–7.
159. Del Col, *L'Inquisizione in Italia*, 694–8; Chadwick, *The Popes and European Revolution*, 404–6; Delpiano, *Il governo*, 78 n7, 91, 147, 249–50; Venturi, *Settecento riformatore*, I, 24–5, 308, II, 8n, 118; Infelise, *L'editoria veneziana*, 150–1, 110 n135.

160. Del Col, *L'Inquisizione in Italia*, 689–93; Casini, 'Crudeli Affair'; Pasta, 'Fermenti culturali e circoli massonici', 459–66; Venturi, *Settecento riformatore*, I, 55–8, 308–9.
161. Morelli Timpanaro, *Tomasso Crudeli*, I, 73–5, docs 59 and 6, doc. 274, p. 396, I, 285–7, II, 713–14, 716, for terminology used about Freemasons, regarded sometimes as atheists.
162. Casini, 'Crudeli Affair', 138.
163. Morelli Timpanaro, *Tomasso Crudeli*, II, 705–6 (some key accusations). For his denials, and some admissions, vol. II, 715–31.
164. *Ibid.*, II, 740–9, I, 396–7, doc. 274, 25 July 1740, the congregation ratifying the sentence, and confinement to Poppi; see II, 670–1 (imprisonment, health).
165. Casini, 'Crudeli Affair', 151–2; Di Rienzo and Formica, 'Tra Napoli e Roma', 218.

Chapter Eight: Inquisitors, Accused and Witnesses

1. For the problems of interpreting court records, whether inquisitorial or other, but relevant to our discussions here: Cohen and Cohen, *Words and Deeds*, on the Roman governor's court records; Davis, *Fiction in the Archives*, especially about framing petitions, in a French context; Kuehn, 'Reading Microhistory'; Laven, 'Testifying to the Self', on nuns' evidence to a Venetian court; Pullan, 'The Trial of Giorgio Moreto'; Sbriccoli, 'Fonti giudiziarie e fonti giuridiche', with Grendi, 'Sulla "storia criminale" '.
2. Prosperi, *Tribunali*, 203–4.
3. Cardini (ed.), *Gostanza*.
4. Ruggiero, *Binding Passions*, 111–12, 122–4; Ruth Martin, who only mentions the wall-measuring aspect and treats her as a teacher of the trick, in *Witchcraft*, 103, 218 n15, 220 n18.
5. ASV SU b.80, 'Cristina Collarina', 1625.
6. *Ibid*: 'ma spero che Di breve a Dio piagendo saro costi tra tanto a V.S. caro mio, coze bassio la Dolce bocha con li cadDdDi mani, et altra cosa tanta Dolce ame.' (5r, first letter); 'mi nostricho a guisa D salamanDra con il vivo focho Del canDiDo suo peto biastimanDo che mi causa . . .' (8r, fourth letter).
7. Prosperi, *Tribunali*, 194–5, 357, and 'L'Inquisizione in Italia' (1997), 308.
8. John Martin, *Myths*, 33, his trans. from Vergerio's *La historia di M. Francesco Spiera*, followed by mine from Prosperi, *L'eresia del Libro Grande*, 122.
9. Del Col, *L'Inquisizione in Italia*, 350–3; Prosperi, *L'eresia del Libro Grande*, 102–22, and his *Tribunali*, 164–5; Caponetto, *Protestant Reformation*, 48–9.
10. Prosperi, *Tribunali*, 168–9.
11. Russell, *Giulia Gonzaga*, 118–19 (her trans.); Dall'Olio, 'Gonzaga, Giulia', 785. While Archbishop Gian Pietro Carafa of Naples was deeply suspicious of her, he may have drawn back in pursuing her on Reginald Pole's advice to 'win her with courtesy, since there was no better way', and her cousins Ercole and Ferrante Gonzaga were powerful in Church and State; Russell, *Giulia Gonzaga*, 120–1.
12. Russell, *Giulia Gonzaga*, 131; Schutte, 'The *lettere volgari*', 659–60.
13. Seidel Menchi, 'Inquisitor as Mediator', 182–3.
14. BAB B1882, 'Processi del S. Ufficio di Bologna, Tomo 1 del 1697', e.g. nos 26 (Virginia Medelli Cerdoni and others), 31 (Virginia de Tomasellis and Magdalena Passavini).
15. Davidson, 'Inquisition in Venice', 128, 'Felino Giuseppe' case, witness on 29 Oct. 1580 (my translation).
16. Schutte, ' "Saints" and "Witches" ', 161–3.
17. BAB B1882, Case 12, ff. 134r–8, 24 Feb. 1697. Supposedly she had said 'sia maledetto quella Razzasfondradona che pose la Quaresima, et il digiunare'. Boerio, *Dizionario*, 652, under 'Sfondradon'. See Pomata, *Promessa di guarigione*, 272–3, or *Contracting a Cure*, 136–7; she avoided translating *Razzasfondraddone*, though she uses '*razza*' in inverted commas, which she translated as 'breed'.
18. Davis, *Fiction in the Archives*.
19. Plakotos, 'Christian and Muslim Converts', 131, 139 (quote), 141 (quote), his translations from ASV SU b.72, 'Giorgio Iuririch'; his 'The Venetian Inquisition', 195, 200, 215 (last quote).

20. Plakotos, 'Christian and Muslim Converts', 133, using ASV SU b.98, 'Martino Velincovich'. (Plakotos does not give the dates, but in 'The Venetian Inquisition', 195, discusses several cases from b.98 which are in the 1640s.)
21. Plakotos, 'Venetian Inquisition', 200–1, 'Fiorenza Podaccataro' (his trans.); his 'Christian and Muslim Converts', 139, on Balkan interpreters.
22. Masini, *Sacro Arsenale*, 147 (Rome, 1705 edn, 952), cited by Prosperi, *Tribunali*, 357, my trans.
23. John Martin, *Venice's Hidden Enemies*, 213–14.
24. Prosperi, *Tribunali*, 356–8, and (virtually same text) 'L'Inquisizione', 310–12.
25. AABol Ric. Att., vol. 249, fols 98r–v, 104r (Isabella), 100r–103r (Giulio). For a fuller picture, Dall'Olio, *Eretici*, 316, 326–30, 343 n83, 366 n146.
26. Dall'Olio, *Eretici*, 342–3; Diana was giving evidence in May 1567, as a widow. Pelegrino and Urselina's testimony in 1563–4 in Modena, and Pietro Antonio da Cervia's interrogations in Feb. and June 1567 in Bologna, are translated in Tedeschi and von Hennenberg, 'Contra Petrum Antonium a Cervia', 245–68, see esp. 246–9 (Varanini), 260–2 (soldiers' discussions), 264 (Panzacchi house and women).
27. Wickersham, ' "He was obnoxious': Lay Denunciations and the Roman Inquisition" ' (pre-publication paper), at notes 29–31.
28. Tedeschi and von Hennenberg, 'Contra Petrum Antonium a Cervia', 266–8; Dall'Olio, *Eretici*, 322–3.
29. Kuntz, *Anointment of Dionisio*, ch. 5.
30. Bonora, 'Heresy of a Venetian Prelate'; John Martin, '*Renovatio* and Reform', 14.
31. Ambrosini, *Storie di patrizi*, 114 n49; Alvise di Tommaso Mocenigo earlier had often served as one of the *Savii sopra l'eresia*, assistants to the Inquisition; confusingly a relative Alvise di Marin Mocenigo had appeared voluntarily before the Venetian tribunal in 1565, and abjured various Lutheran ideas he had once accepted, deceived by the Devil, *ibid.*, 110–12.
32. Bonora, 'Heresy of a Venetian Prelate', 220.
33. *Ibid.*, 221 n47.
34. Schutte, 'Fra Marino da Venezia', 178–81, quoting, p. 179, evidence of *pre* Giacomo Parmesanus (from Parma, so an outsider), 31 July 1548.
35. Schutte, 'Fra Marino da Venezia', 179 n50.
36. ACDF St. St. DD 2-b, fols 716r + 759v, 9 June 1614, Rocca Contrada, canon Fornito to inquisitor-general of Ancona.
37. *Ibid.*, fols 715r + 760v.19 June 1614, Ancona. Fra Gio. Maria. Summarised in Rome, but without comment; fols 714r + 761v. 3 July 1614, Fra Giov. Maria da Bologna. Ancona; fol. 729r, 17 July 1614, Ancona. Fra Gio Maria.
38. *Ibid.*, fol. 151r, 15 Sept. 1608.
39. John Martin, *Myths*, 23–4, 32–3, 70, and his *Venice's Hidden Enemies*, 85, 90, 131–2, 137–9, 164–5, 170 for his wider career and beliefs.
40. De Vivo, *Information*, 112.
41. Briggs, *Witches of Lorraine*, 59–60, and ch. 6, 'Reputations and Communal Reactions', for an exemplary study of the damaging effects on a range of cases.
42. Merlo, *Streghe*, 12, 15–16; John Martin, *Myths*, 90.
43. ACDF St. St. LL 4-f, 'Compendio 1598–1635', fols 5r, 6v–7r; Horodowich, 'The Gossiping Tongue' valuably considers good and bad *fama* in Venice.
44. ASV SU b.80 'De Domo Marco, Gemma Aurora', April 1625; on 29 April the main session was before the nuncio, Patriarch and Inquisitor-General, and two *assistenti*. Some evidence was taken in Treviso and incorporated into the Venetian hearing. Giorgios Plakotos first alerted me to this file and the discussion below derives from our joint efforts, transcriptions and translations. See his 'The Venetian Inquisition', 29; Ambrosini, 'Between Heresy and Free Thought', 86–9, has covered some aspects also. On 'turco' meaning Muslim see Chapter 6.
45. ASV SU b.80, 29 April 1625, Sebastiano Dino, canon regular of S. Salvator, rector of Sovernigo.
46. *Ibid.*, 17 April testimony of Hieronyma de Scuti, aged fifty-eight; Antonio and Franceschina Valvasor, 15 April.

NOTES to pp. 229–38 295

47. Ambrosini, 'Between Heresy and Free Thought', 87–8, 235 nn10–11; John Martin, *Venice's Hidden Enemies*, 140.
48. *DBI*, vol. 26, 138–41, 'Clario, Giovanni Battista' (L. Firpo), on both, but mainly Clario junior, and vol. 17, 371–401, esp. 376, 'Campanella, Tommaso' (L. Firpo); Ambrosini, 'Between Heresy and Free Thought', 87–8, 237 n12; Caponetto, *Protestant Reformation*, 160 (on Clario senior); Del Col, *L'Inquisizione . . . Aquileia*, 163 n14 (Clario senior).
49. Fragnito, *La Bibbia*, 218–19 and n47; Ambrosini, 'Between Heresy and Free Thought', 236 n8.

Chapter Nine: The World of Witchcraft, Superstition and Magic

1. *Minor Historical Writings and Other Essays by Henry Charles Lea*, ed. A.C. Howland (Philadelphia, PA, 1942), 3; as cited by Tedeschi, 'Toward a Statistical Profile', 124 n62.
2. Messana, *Inquisitori, negromanti*, 83, 87.
3. Bartlett, *The Natural and the Supernatural*, 79–85 (quote 79–80, illustration 82).
4. Briggs, *Witches of Lorraine*, 33–5. This recent book, as well as being a thorough study of one of the areas of intense witch-persecution, summarises much work on European witch-hunting, and has many insights into how to study trial records. Levack, *The Witch Hunt*, for a good European-wide survey; Barstow, *Witchcraze*, on the 'violence against women' debates.
5. Tedeschi, 'A New Perspective' (1996), 22–3, and (1997), 258, my addition of the last sentence to his translated quotation. See also his 'Inquisitorial Law and the Witch', for the inquisitions' use of inquisitorial processes, and unprofessional usage by other courts, with uncontrolled torture.
6. Prosperi, 'Inquisitori e streghe nel seicento fiorentino', Postfazione to Cardini (ed.), *Gostanza*, 217–50, esp. 220–2.
7. Tedeschi, 'A New Perspective' (1996), 22–3, or (1997), 258, trans. (marginally modified by me) from *Sacro Arsenale* (Bologna 1665 edn), 206.
8. Tedeschi, *Prosecution* ('The Question of Magic and Witchcraft in two Inquisitorial Manuals'), 238–9, 254 nn60–2; his 'A New Perspective' (1996), 24, and (1997), 259, 268 n34, adding the quotation from Sarpi (my trans.).
9. Ruth Martin, *Witchcraft and the Inquisition*, 124, 69, 60, quoting from Eymeric, *Directorium* (1973 edn), 367, 358–9.
10. Bowd, ' "Honeyed flies" and "sugared rats" '; Merlo, *Streghe*.
11. Ruth Martin, *Witchcraft and the Inquisition*, 3; Italian was rich in terminology for those practising magic; some other names apparently used instead of *streghe* and *donne di fora* for female witches include: *lamie, malefiche, strie, masche, basche, talamasche, fattucchiere, arpie, megere, maliarde, diavolesse, invocatrici di demoni* and *cultrici di Satana*, see Benazzi and D'Amico, *Il libro nero*, 277.
12. Renda, *L'Inquisizione in Sicilia*, ch. XII.
13. Messana, *Inquisitori, negromanti*, 85–8, 95–6; cf. Ruggiero, *Binding Passions*; Gentilcore, *From Bishop to Witch*; Romeo, *Inquisitori, esorcisti e streghe*; Di Simplicio, *Inquisizione, stregoneria, medicina*, and his *Autumno della stregoneria*; O'Neil, 'Magical Healing, Love Magic'.
14. Ruth Martin, *Witchcraft and the Inquisition*, is valuable on various kinds of superstitions and techniques of divination, exemplified by rich Venetian records; for *inghistera*, 113–19, the sieve (*cribo*), 119–21, bean-casting, interpreting the rope (*cordella*), 121–4, charms and incantations, 124–39, healing methods, 139–47; Di Simplicio, *Inquisizione, stregoneria, medicina*, for the healing aspects, especially from Siena.
15. For interesting contextualisation, linking literary ideas and an inquisitorial interest: Ruggiero, *Machiavelli in Love*, esp. ch. 2, 'Playing with the Devil: The Pleasures and Dangers of Sex and Play'.
16. Huizinga, *Homo Ludens* (1955 edn), 13; Ruggiero, *Machiavelli in Love*, 42, 230 n3.
17. Ruggiero, *Machiavelli in Love*, 48–50.
18. Sanudo, *Diarii*, XXV, cols 602–8, 548, 588, 639–40, discussed by Bowd, ' "Honeyed Flies" and "sugared rats"'.

19. Romeo, *Inquisitori, esorcisti,* 3–24, with Santa Severina's letter (18–19); Del Col, *L'Inquisizione in Italia,* 579–80.
20. Cardini (ed.), *Gostanza la strega di San Miniato;* a full transcript is provided (130–213), while Franco Cardini, Silvia Mantini, Silvia Nannipieri, Arianna Orlandi and Marilena Lombardi contribute to the introduction of the background and analysis; and Adriano Prosperi provides an afterword on 'Inquisitori e streghe nel seicento fiorentino'. The diocese of Lucca was larger than the Republic of Lucca (having no Roman Inquisition tribunal); San Miniato was part of the Lucca diocese (until it headed a new diocese 1622–4), but was covered for inquisitional purposes by the Florentine inquisitor. See Black, *Church, Religion,* 65, 192; Del Col, *L'Inquisizione in Italia,* 584–6; Mantini, 'Gostanza da Libbiano'.
21. Cardini (ed.), *Gostanza la strega di San Miniato,* 133: 'alcuni dicano che detta monna Gostanza è strega et maliarda con fare medicine et misurare li panni'. *Maliarda,* sorceress, does not seem a common term; *misurare li panni* was a method of diagnosis, see later.
22. *Ibid.,* 145.
23. *Ibid.,* 148.
24. *Ibid.,* esp. 159, 162, 166.
25. *Ibid.,* esp. 168, 172–3 (the Devil and husband compared as lovers), 182–3, 204, 207–9, 210.
26. *Ibid.,* 112–28; Mantini, 'Gostanza', 159.
27. Del Col, *L'Inquisizione in Italia,* 582–3; Romeo, *Inquisitori, esorcisti,* 30–1; Ferrario, *Triora* (a bilingual study of wider contexts, but appendix documents are only in Italian), esp. 243–50.
28. Transcripts in Appendix to Ginzburg, *Night Battles.*
29. Nardon, *Benandanti e inquisitori,* esp. 179–88; his 'Benandanti "funebri": le processioni'; John Martin, *Myths,* 96. Cf. Margheria Ciucchi in the Mugello, *meretrice,* learning from another prostitute how to say prayers, so that souls of the executed might appear; a self-confession to the Tuscan Inquisitor-General, AAF SU Filza 2–3, no. 73, 3 Dec. 1639. She was dismissed with a promise to do salutary penances.
30. Nardon, *Benandanti e inquisitori,* 136–8, tables.
31. *Ibid.,* 138.
32. Ginzburg, *Night Battles,* esp. 99–106, 180 n44 (for a case in Lucca where epilepsy did not save a witch from burning); Nardon, *Benandanti,* esp. 112–16, 190 (for a spirit/body statement).
33. Messana, *Inquisitori, negromanti,* 75, 550–69; Renda, *L'Inquisizione in Sicilia,* 432–3, suggests a hundred were investigated, but he is more interesting when detailing a few intriguing cases, and their possible influences on beliefs, 418–49; Sorgia, 'Pietro de Hoyo', 31–66, in his *Studi sull'Inquisizione in Sardegna.* For survival of the *benandante* idea into the twentieth century, Ferrario, *Triora,* 93–8 (Italian), 196–201 (English).
34. Ruggiero, *Binding Passions,* 88–90.
35. Ruggiero, *Machiavelli in Love,* 54–9, 234–5 nn35–9, and Milani, 'L'ossessione secolare'. While the transcript sets this out as a continuous narrative, there is a note on the record by the chancellor Fra Vittore that she was prompted by some questions.
36. Milani, 'L'ossessione secolare', 142–7.
37. Ruggiero, *Machiavelli in Love,* 65–70.
38. Laven, *Virgins of Venice,* esp. ch. 10, 'Between Celibates', and ch. 11, 'Chastity and Desire'; Sperling, *Convents and the Body Politic,* esp. 148–63; Black, *Church, Religion,* 150–61.
39. Gentilcore, 'A Tale of Two Tribunals', on the comparisons; more broadly on medical controls and practices, his *Healers and Healing* and *Medical Charlatanism.*
40. Gentilcore, *From Bishop to Witch,* 134–5, 139–40, 157 n27.
41. BAB 1882, no. 31 (fols 306–329v), with *Regola nuova d'imparare molti e beliss. giuochi . . .,* bound, in eight printed pages.
42. AAF SU Filza 2–3, fol. 38, 26 March 1629, fols 46–47r, 8 May 1632. The further action is not known.
43. *Ibid.,* fol. 137, 1 July 1652.
44. *Ibid.,* fols 5–34 (but with blank pages, and muddled microfilming of the record).
45. Cardini (ed.), *Gostanza la strega di San Miniato,* 132–3 (child's trousers, and medicine), 136–8; Mantini, 'Gostanza', 144–6.

46. Cardini (ed.), *Gostanza la strega di San Miniato*, 144–5, and 79–80 (Marilena Lombardi on betony, nutmeg, etc., used in popular remedies).
47. Bamji, 'Religion and Disease', 7–16, 157, 225. For another case of 'measuring', along with healing, see that of Marietta Colonna in 1638, who claimed to have inquisitional approval for her healing practices; she might be the same as Marietta *greca* arraigned in 1622: Ruth Martin, *Witchcraft*, 143, 187–8; see Bamji, 'Religion and Disease', 16, 45, 50, 173–4.
48. Plakotos, 'Christian and Muslim Converts', 137, and 'The Venetian Inquisition', 180, 184; Ruth Martin, *Witchcraft*, 231–3; see above, note 14 on techniques.
49. Gentilcore, *Healers and Healing*, 161, quoting Andrea Cesalpino, *De Daemonum investigatione* (Florence, 1580), ch. 16.
50. McGough, 'Demons, Nature', 237–40.
51. Ghirardo, 'Marginal Spaces of Prostitution', 96, 101–2.
52. ASV SU b.106, 'Elisabetta Thodesca', 16 July 1652.
53. ASV SU b.63; Ruth Martin, *Witchcraft*, 25, 28, 130–1, 235.
54. BAB B1882, 'Processi del S. Ufficio di Bologna, Tomo 1 del 1697', no. 23 (fols 221–225v).
55. *Ibid.*, no. 26 (fols 261–267v). Notarial annotation: '*et plangebat fortiter, ostende. maximam dolorem.*'
56. Ruggiero, *Machiavelli in Love*, chs 2 and 3.
57. Di Simplicio, *Peccato, penitenza, perdono*, ch. 6, on clerical concubinage, based on Sienese cases; Black, *Church, Religion*, 108–9.
58. Stephens, 'Witches Who Steal Penises'.
59. Ruggiero, *Machiavelli in Love*, 24, 226 n14; Gentilcore, *From Bishop to Witch*, 217; Di Simplicio, *Autunno della stregoneria*, 69–71.
60. ASV SU b.80, 'Contra fris. Capucinos', 17 September 1592; Ruth Martin, *Witchcraft*, 96, also citing another Capuchin case from 1647.
61. BAB B1886 'Processi sortilegi e imposture, 1676–1679': 'Lucia De Angelis', starting 14 May 1677. Limited archival time prevented my full study of the very lengthy record, so comments are the product of sampling.
62. The codes were given on a loose, inserted sheet: Lucia De Angelis = Berta; Lucia Martelli = Sibilla; Lucia de Cavalerijs = Ottavia; Marina Terzeta = Media; Michele Taguarino = Sinfonia; Gerolomao Trebigla = Bruto.

Chapter Ten: Conclusion

1. Gri, *Altri Modi* and 'L'uso delle fonti inquisitoriali'; Ioly Zorattini, 'Gli archivi del Sant'Ufficio'.
2. Valente, '*Bloody Tribunal.* L'immagine dell'Inquisizione'.

Appendix: Tables of Types of Accusations and Cases

1. Schutte, 'I processi dell'Inquisizione', 163–4.

BIBLIOGRAPHY

A Brief Reading Guide

The Bibliography that now exists for covering the inquisitions in early modern Italy is daunting. The lengthy one given here only represents what I have been able to cover in a few years and to incorporate in the references. With rare exceptions I have included only what has been cited; more has been sampled than appears here. For those who want to follow up the topics in minor ways, I am here highlighting some books that I consider particularly useful, and readable; firstly in English, bearing students and general readers in mind, and then in Italian for those able to utilise that language, but who are not specialists in the Inquisition or Italian religious-social history. I have been mindful of both the utility and readability of the Italian recommendations for non-Italians.

For those reading in English and needing a wide introduction to early modern Italy and the Catholic Church, I would suggest Gregory Hanlon's *Early Modern Italy 1550–1800* (2000) along with my *Early Modern Italy: A Social History* (2000), then my *Church, Religion and Society in Early Modern Italy* (2004), with Michael Mullett's *The Catholic Reformation* (1999) providing a wider European context. Antony D. Wright's *The Early Modern Papacy* (2000) is the crucial modern work on the popes. For the Roman Inquisition the essays by John Tedeschi in his *The Prosecution of Heresy* (1991) were fundamental to my early work on the Inquisition, and they remain extremely valuable. The surviving Venetian archival material generated a collection of informed and readable monographs that provide introductions to inquisitorial operations, and to specialist targets: John Martin's *Venice's Hidden Enemies* (1993), on largely artisan challengers to Catholic orthodoxy; Ruth Martin's *Witchcraft and the Inquisition in Venice* (1989), on the whole range of 'superstitions'; Brian Pullan's *The Jews of Europe and the Inquisition of Venice* (1983); Guido Ruggiero's essays in *Binding Passions: Tales of Magic, Marriage and Power* (1993), for love magic, neighbourly relations and suspicions; and Paul Grendler's *The Roman Inquisition and the Venetian Press* (1977).

The key volume on censorship, taking advantage of accessibility to the Roman archive (ACDF), is the collection of essays edited by Gigliola Fragnito, *Church, Censorship and Culture in Early Modern Italy* (2001). The translations of Carlo Ginzburg's major works, *The Cheese and the Worms*, about an idiosyncratic Friulian miller, and *The Night Battles*, about men and women initially claiming to battle at night with evil forces, are highly readable insights into inquisitorial cases and targets. The problems of deciding between saintly women and frauds receive excellent illustration and analysis by Anne Jacobson Schutte in her *Aspiring Saints* (2001), while extracts from a very lengthy case have been edited by her in *Cecilia Ferrazzi: Autobiography of An Aspiring Saint* (1996), which has proved a good seminar text. Despite harsh criticisms from Massimo Firpo, Camilla Russell's *Giulia Gonzaga and the Religious Controversies of Sixteenth-Century Italy* (2006), can be recommended to those not totally immersed in the scene and problems of defining Italian reform, for insights into some interlocking groups of reformers, and the background to the final trial and execution of a leading 'heretic', Pietro Carnesecchi. Henry Kamen's *The Spanish Inquisition: An Historical Revision* (1997) provides the most accessible study of the Spanish system and attitudes, though largely ignoring Sicily and Sardinia. William Monter's *The Frontiers of Heresy: The Spanish Inquisition from the Basque Lands to Sicily* (1990) helps with comparative analysis, and Sicily.

In Italian the indispensable guide, informative, analytical, well balanced and clear for a general reader as well as specialist, is Andrea Del Col's *L'Inquisizione in Italia* (1999). Giovanni Romeo's pocket-sized *L'Inquisizione nell'Italia moderna* (2002) is an effective and enticing introductory overview; as in the same Laterza series is Mario Infelise's *I libri proibiti* (2006 edn), for censorship issues. Elena Brambilla' clear and average length *La giustizia intollerante: inquisizioni e tribunali confessionali in Europa (secoli IV–XVIII)* (2006) is valuable for a broad context. Selecting initiatory, less daunting, examples from the heavyweight modern contributors, I suggest Gigliola Fragnito's pioneering use of ACDF records in *La Bibbia al rogo* (1997), for the fraught debates over allowing the Bible in translation, and its implications; and her *Proibito capire. La Chiesa e il volgare nella prima età moderna* (2005), for further exemplary use of ACDF material on censorship. Saverio Ricci's *Il sommo inquisitore. Giulio Antonio Santori tra autobiografia e storia* (2002) readily illustrates many issues from one of the dominant inquisitors. Patrizia Delpiano's *Il governo della lettura* (2007) valiantly uses

ACDF's Index and Holy Office sources (and much more) to exemplify eighteenth-century attempts to combat threats from enlightenment writers, but also subversive fiction, and reading for pleasure.

From the two heavyweight scholars who have massively contributed to modern knowledge and interpretation of the Roman Inquisition, the easiest examples are: Massimo Firpo's *Riforma protestante ed eresie nell'Italia del cinquecento* (1993), and *Vittore Soranzo vescovo e eretico. Riforma della Chiesa e Inquisizione nell'Italia del cinquecento* (2006); Adriano Prosperi's collected essays, *L'Inquisizione romana. Letture e ricerche* (2003), and *L'eresia del Libro Grande. Storia di Giorgio Siculo e della sua setta* (2000). Modern approaches to cases of superstition are well exemplified by Oscar Di Simplicio, as in his *Inquisizione, stregoneria, medicina. Siena e il suo stato (1580–1721)* (2000), and Giovanni Romeo, *Inquisitori, esorcisti e streghe nell'Italia della Controriforma* (1990). Franco Cardini's *Gostanza, la strega di San Miniato* (1989/2001) is a fascinating case study, for the mentalities of accusers, inquisitors and story-telling accused. Franco Nardon's *Benandanti e inquisitori nel Friuli del seicento* (1999) provides a wider context for Carlo Ginzburg's *I Benandanti* (translated as *The Night Battles*). Maria Sofia Messana's *Inquisitori, negromanti e streghe nella Sicilia moderna (1500–1782)* (2007), though long and dense, is valuable for cases of superstition, and wider Sicilian context. Irene Fosi's informative and readable *La giustizia del papa. Sudditi e tribunali nello Stato Pontificio in età moderna* (2007) puts the inquisitorial activity in the legal and governmental contexts of the Papal State, and links with episcopal activity. Guido Dall'Olio's *Eretici e inquisitori nella Bologna del cinquecento* (1999) is a profound study of the second city of the Papacy, the great university city, during the mid-century crises, making some use of the ACDF archive as it opened, as well as rich Bolognese sources.

Full Bibliography
Archival Sources

Bologna

Archivio Arcivescovile [AABol]

Ricuperi Attuariali, Foro Archivescovili vol. 249 [AB86], '1567. Criminalis 1457 BS Ant.s Balzan.s Not.s'.

Archivio di Stato [ASBol]

ASBol Corporazioni Soppresse (Demaniale), vols 1/7589 [Ex San Domenico], 16th–18th cent. Documents; 5/7593, 6/7594, 7/1595 [bound as one]. 18th-century records of various financial aspects.

Biblioteca dell'Archiginnasio [BAB]

B1546, Malta; B1859 'Consilia et Vota in Materia S. Officii', 15th–16th cent.; B1860 Lettere Sacrae Congregationis 1571–1576; 1861 Lettere ... 1577–1594; B1863 Lettere ... 1601–1610; B1866 Processi Sortilegi e imposture, 1676–1679; B1871 Lettere ... 1661–1667; B1882 Processi del S. Ufficio di Bologna, Tomo 1 del 1697; B1883 Processi del S. Ufficio di Bologna. Tomo II del 1699; B1888 Processi contro Eretici per Affettata Santità [17th cent.]; B1897 Lettere varie del S. Officio, 1652–1705; B1898 Carte diverse de S. Ufficio di Bologna la più parte comprendenti corrispondenza d'ufficio 1626–1760; B1909 Lettere di diversi al padre Inquisitore del S. Ufficio di Bologna, 1653–1679.

Dublin

Trinity College Library [TCD]

Ms 1224–1277. *Sentenze* from Rome and peripheral tribunals, 1564–1659; *Atti* concerning suits in local tribunals, 1625–1789. Some available on old microfilms in Glasgow Univeristy Library. I have used Mss. 1224, 1225, 1226, 1227 (Reels 8 and 9); (see Abbott, *Catalogue of the Manuscripts*, esp. 243–51).

Florence

Archivio Arcivescovile [AAF]

Sant'Uffizio, SU Filza 2–3 (together on microfilm).

Perugia

Biblioteca Comunale Augusta [BCP]

Ms 3081, 'Index librorum Biblioteche Augustae a Prospero Podiani donata'; Ms 195 (D13), 'Indice di libri prestati'; Ms 186 (D4), 'Ricordi domestici e note di libri prestati', c. 1579–1614 (muddled).

Rome

Archivio della Congregazione per la Dottrina della Fede [ACDF]

St. St. DD 2-b, Inquisizione dello Stato Pontificio (Ancona e altre città delle Marche); St. St. EE 1-b; St. St. EE 3-a, Patentati dell'Inquisizione di Gubbio, Ancona, Fabriano, Faenza, Perugia etc., 1693–1701; St. St. GG-a, b, Inquisizione di Bergamo, 1557–1679; St. St. H 6-f 'Diversorum ab anno 1602 ad 1631'. Raccolta di Verbali delle Congregazioni 'Coram Ill. Mis. D.nis' e 'Coram Sanctissimo'; St. St. II 1-l. 'Editti generali per tutte le Inquisizioni e per alcune in particolare. 1666–1686'. St. St. LL 2-g, h, Raccolta di lettere patenti concedenti facoltà di leggere, ecc. Libri proibiti, e di assolvere dall'eresia. 1684–1768; St. St. LL 4-f, folder (2): 'Differrentiam vertem inter Episcopum, et Inquisitorem Mantue. In cognoscendis causis commmercij carnalis inter Judeos, et Mulieres Christianorum, et e contra.' 'Compendio, e nota delle Cause, e spontanee Comparitioni d'Hebrei di Commercio carnale con donne Christiane fatte nell'Inquisitione di Mantua, dall'anno 1598, sino all'Anni 1635 inclusive.' Sommario e Nota delle Spontanee Comparitione, e Cause fatte nel S. Off.o di Mantua, di commercio Carnale di Hebrei con Christiani, dall'Anno 1636, sino all'Anno 1684.'; St. St. O 3-e, Atti contro il P. Giacinto da Casale Monferrato per la stampa di un libro (1618–1619) e contro delle nuove confraternite (1668–1672).

Decreta vols 5 (July 1563–May 1564), 6 (July 1565–Aug. 1567), 7 (Jan. 1565–July 1567), 9 (1567–1571).

Indice 1, I Diarii II (1607–20).

Indice III, Epistolae III.

Venice

Archivio di Stato, Venice [ASV]

Savii all'Eresia (S. Uffizio). [SU] See Indice 303, compiled 1870 by Luigi Passini and Giuseppe Giomo. Buste (b.) 13, 33, 59, 63, 67, 72, 80, 94, 103.

Archivio Patriarcale [APV]

Criminalia Sanctae Inquisitionis buste 1–2, for 1589–99.

Printed Sources and Secondary Literature

Abbott, T.K., *Catalogue of the Manuscripts in the Library of Trinity College, Dublin* (Dublin and London, 1900; reprint 1980).

Accati, L., 'Lo spirito della fornicazione: virtù dell'anima e virtù del corpo in Friuli fra '600 e '700', *Quaderni storici* 41 (1979).

Adorni-Braccesi, Simonetta, 'Il dissenso religioso nel contesto urbano lucchese della Controriforma', *Città Italiane del '500* (1988), 225–39.

— 'Una Città infetta'. *La Repubblica di Lucca nella crisi religiosa del cinquecento* (Florence, 1994).

— 'La magistratura delle *cause delegate* nella Repubblica di Lucca: eresia e stregoneria (secoli XVI–XVIII), in Del Col and Paolin (eds), *L'Inquisizione romana; metologia* (2000), 273–94.

Alberti, Leandro, *Descrittione di tutta d'Italia, et isole pertinenti ad essa. . . . Nuovamente ristampata, et con somma diligenza reuista et correcta. Con le sue tavole copiosissime* (Venice, 1596).

Alcalá, Angel (ed.), *The Spanish Inquisition and the Inquisitorial Mind* (New York, 1987).

Alfonso de Castro, *see* Castro

Amabile, Luigi, *Fra Tommaso Campanella. La sua congiura, i suoi processi e la sua pazzia*, 3 vols (Naples, 1882).

— *Il Santo Officio dell'Inquisizione a Napoli* (Città di Castello, 1892). Two vols in one, but separate pagination. Vol. 1, ch. III, 84–347 on 'L'Inquisizione a tempo de' Vicerè Spagnuoli'; vol. II, ch. IV, 3–112 on 'Seguito dell'Inquisizione de' Vicerè Spagnuoli, poi a tempo degli Austriaci, e della Monarchia', followed by 'Documenti', 1–98, in separate pagination.

Ambrosini, Federica, *Storie di patrizi e di eresia nella Venezia del '500* (Milan, 1999).

— 'Between Heresy and Free Thought, between the Mediterranean and the North: Heterodox Women in Seventeenth-Century Venice', in A. Cowan (ed.), *Mediterranean Urban Culture 1400–1700* (Exeter, 2000), 83–94.

Amelang, James S., 'Exchanges between Italy and Spain: Culture and Religion', in Dandelet and Marino (eds), *Spain in Italy*, 434–55.

Andrés Martín, Melquiades, 'Alumbrados, Erasmians, "Lutherans" and Mystics: The Risk of More "Intimate" Spirituality', in Alcalá (ed.), *The Spanish Inquisition*, 457–94.

L'Apertura degli archivi del Sant'Uffizio romano (Roma, 22 gennaio 1998) (Rome, 2000).

Arnold, Claus, 'The Archive of the Roman Congregation for the Doctrine of the Faith (ACDF): An Initial Overview of its Holdings and Scholarship to Date', in Wendehorst, *The Roman Inquisition, the Index and the Jews* (2004), 155–68.

Artigas, Mariano, Martínez, Rafael and Shea, William R., 'New Light on the Galileo Affair?', in McMullin (ed.), *The Church and Galileo*, 213-33.
Assereto, Giovanni, 'Inquisitori e libri nella Genova del seicento', in Livio Antonielli et al. (eds), *Per Marino Berengo. Studi degli allievi* (Milan, 2000), 322-48.
Audisio, Gabriel (ed.), *Inquisition et Pouvoir* (Aix-en-Provence, 2004).
Baldini, Ugo, 'Il pubblico della scienza nei permessi di lettura di libri proibiti delle Congregazioni del Sant'Ufficio e dell'Indice (secolo XVI); verso una tipologia professionale e disciplinare', in Stango (ed.), *Censura ecclesiastica* (2001), 171-201.
— 'The Roman Inquisition's Condemnation of Astrology', in Fragnito (ed.), *Church, Censorship* (2001), 79-110.
Balsamo, Luigi, 'How to Doctor a Bibliography: Antonio Possevino's Practice', in Fragnito (ed.), *Church, Censorship* (2001), 50-78.
Bamji, Alexandra, 'Religion and Disease in Venice, c. 1620-1700' (Cambridge Ph.D, 2007).
— 'The Control of Space: Dealing with Diversity in Early Modern Venice', *Italian Studies* 62/2 (2007), 175-88.
Barbierato, Federico, *Politici e ateisti. Percorsi della miscredenza a Venezia fra sei e settecento* (Milan, 2006).
— *'La rovina di Venetia in materia de' libri prohibiti'. Il libraio Salvatore de' Negri e l'Inquisizione veneziana (1628-1661)* (Venice, 2007).
Barbieri, Edoardo, 'Tradition and Change in the Spiritual Literature of the Cinquecento', in Fragnito (ed.), *Church, Censorship* (2001), 111-33.
Barbieri, Edoardo and Zardin, Danilo (eds), *Libri, biblioteche e cultura nell'Italia del cinque e seicento* (Milan, 2002).
Barstow, Anne Llewellyn, *Witchcraze: A New History of the European Witch Hunts* (San Francisco, CA, and London, 1994).
Bartlett, Robert, *The Natural and the Supernatural in the Middle Ages* (Cambridge, 2008).
Battistella, Antonio., *Il S. Officio e la riforma religiosa in Friuli* (Udine, 1895).
— *Il Santo Officio e la riforma religiosa in Bologna* (Bologna, 1905).
Beccaria, Cesare, *On Crimes and Punishments and Other Writings*, ed. Richard Bellamy (Cambridge, 1995).
Bellabarba, Marco, *La giustizia nell'Italia moderna* (Rome and Bari, 2008).
Benazzi, Natale and D'Amico, Matteo, *Il libro nero dell'Inquisizione. La riconstruzione dei grandi processi* (Casale Monferrato, 2006, pb).
Benedict, Philip, Seidel Menchi, Silvana, and Tallon, Alain (eds), *La Réforme en France et en Italie. Contacts, comparaisons et contrastes* (Rome, 2007).
Benigno, Francesco, 'Integration and Conflict in Spanish Sicily', in Dandelet and Marino (eds), *Spain in Italy*, 23-44.
Bennassar, Bartolomé, 'Un Tribunal inquistorial mal connu: le tribunal de Sardaigne', in *Foi, Fidélité, Amitié en Europe à la periode moderne (Mélanges offerts à Robert Sauzet)* (Tours, 1995).
Benzoni, Gino, 'Paolo III', in *Enciclopedia dei Papi*, III (2000), 91-101.
Berengo, Marino, *Nobili e mercanti nella Lucca del cinquecento* (Turin, 1965).
Beretta, Francesco, 'L'archivio della Congregazione del'Sant'Ufficio: bilancio provvisiorio della storia e natura dei fondi d'antico regime', in Del Col and Paolin, *L'Inquisizione romana: metologia* (2000), 119-44.
— 'Giordano Bruno e l'Inquisizione romana: considerazioni sul processo', *Bruniana e Campanelliana* 7 (2001), 20-3.
— 'La Congrégation de l'Inquisition et la censure doctrinale au XVIIe siècle', in Audisio (ed.), *Inquisition et Pouvoir* (2004), 41-54.
— 'The Documents of Galileo's Trial: Recent Hypotheses and Historical Criticism', in McMullin (ed.), *The Church and Galileo* (2005), 191-212.
— 'Galileo, Urban VIII, and the Prosecution of Natural Philosophers', in McMullin (ed.), *The Church and Galileo* (2005), 234-61.
Biondi, Albano, 'Lunga durata e microarticolazione nel territorio di un ufficio dell'Inquisizione: il "Sacro Tribunale" a Modena (1292-1785)', *Annali dell'istituto storico italo-germanico in Trento*, 8 (1982), 73-90.
Biondi, Albano and Prosperi, Adriano (eds), *Libri, idee e sentimenti religiosi nel cinquecento italiano* (Ferrara and Modena, 1987).
Black, Christopher F., 'Perugia and Post-Tridentine Church Reform', *Journal of Ecclesiastical History* 35 (1984), 429-51.
— *Italian Confraternities in the Sixteenth Century* (Cambridge and New York, 1989, and 2003 reprint).
— 'Early Modern Italian Confraternities: Inclusion and Exclusion', *Historein* 2 (Athens, 2000), 65-86.
— *Early Modern Italy: A Social History* (London and New York, 2001).
— *Church, Religion and Society in Early Modern Italy* (Basingstoke, 2004).
— 'Confraternite e l'Inquisizione. Italia', in Prosperi and Tedeschi (eds), *Dizionario dell'Inquisizione*, vol. 1 (forthcoming).
Blackwell, Richard J., *Galileo, Bellarmine and the Bible* (Notre Dame, IN, and London, 1991).

— *Behind the Scenes at Galileo's Trial: Including the First English Translation of Melchior Inchofer's* 'Tractatus syllepticus' (Notre Dame, IN, 2006).
Boccato, Carla, 'Risvolti familiari e attività di impresa intorno al "marrano" Gaspar Ribiera', in Ioly Zorattini (ed.), *L'Identità dissimulata* (2000), 311–20.
Boerio, Giuseppe, *Dizionario del dialetto veneziano* (2nd edn, Venice, 1856, anastatic reprint Florence, 1993).
Bonnici, Alexander, *Medieval and Roman Inquisition in Malta* (Malta, 1998).
Bonomo, Giuseppe, *Caccia alle streghe: la credenza nelle streghe dal sec. XIII al XIX con particolare riferimento all'Italia* (Palermo, 1971).
Bonora, Elena, 'Inquisizione e papato tra Pio IV e Pio V,' in Guasco and Torre (eds), *Pio V* (2005), 49–83.
— 'The Heresy of a Venetian Prelate: Archbishop Filippo Mocenigo', in Delph et al. (eds), *Heresy, Culture* (2006), 211–29.
— *Giudicare i vescovi: La definizione dei poteri nella Chiesa postridentina* (Rome and Bari, 2007).
Borromeo, Agostino, 'Contributo allo studio dell'Inquisizione e dei suoi rapporti con il potere episcopale nell'Italia spagnola del cinquecento', *Annuario dell'istituto storico italiano per l'età moderna e contemporanea*, XXIX–XXX (1977–8), 219–76.
— 'A proposito del *Directorium inquisitorum* di Nicolas Eymerich e delle sue edizioni cinquecentesche', *Critica Storica* 20 (1983), 499–547.
— 'Il dissenso religioso tra il clero italiano e la prima attività del Sant'Ufficio romano', in Sangalli (ed.), *Per il cinquecento religioso italiano* (2003), II, 455–85.
— 'La Congregazione Cardinalizia dell'Inquisizione (XVI–XVIII secolo), in Borromeo (ed.), *L'Inquisizione* (2003), 323–44.
Borromeo, Agostino (ed.), *L'Inquisizione. Atti del simposio internazionale. Città del Vaticano, 29–31 ottobre 1998* (Vatican City, 2003).
Bouwsma, William J., *Venice and the Defense of Republican Liberty* (Berkeley and Los Angeles, CA, 1968).
Bowd, Stephen, *Reform before the Reformation: Vincenzo Querini and the Religious Renaissance in Italy* (Leiden, Boston, MA, and Cologne, 2002).
— ' "Honeyed flies" and "sugared rats": Witchcraft, Heresy and Superstition in the Bresciano, 1454–1535', in S[teve].A. Smith and Alan Knight (eds), *The Religion of Fools? Superstition Past and Present* (Oxford, 2008), 134–56.
Bowd, Stephen (ed.), and Cullington, J. Donald (trans. and annotator), *Vainglorious Death: A Funerary Fracas in Renaissance Brescia* (Tempe, AZ, 2006).
Braida, Lodovica, *Il commercio dell idee. Editoria e circolazione del libro nella Torino del settecento* (Florence, 1995).
Brambilla, Elena, *Alle origini del Sant'Uffizio: Penitenza, confessione e giustizia spirituale dal medioevo al XVI secolo* (Bologna, 2000).
— *La giustizia intollerante: inquisizioni e tribunali confessionali in Europa (secoli IV–XVIII)* (Rome, 2006).
— 'Il segreto e il sigillo: denunce e comparizione spontanee nei processi inquisitoriali', in Peyronel Rambaldi (ed.), *I Tribunali* (2007), 111–61.
Briggs, Robin, *The Witches of Lorraine* (Oxford, 2008).
Brundin, Abigail, *Vittoria Colonna and the Spiritual Poetics of the Italian Reformation* (Aldershot and Burlington, VT, 2008).
Brunelli, Giampiero, 'Giulio III', in *Enciclopedia dei papi*, vol. III (2000), 111–21.
Bujanda, J.M. de, *Index des Livres interdits* (Geneva), vol. VIII (1990): *Index de Rome 1557, 1559, 1564. Les primeurs index romains et index du Concile de Trente*; vol. IX (1994): *Index de Rome 1590, 1593, 1596, Avec étude des index de Parme 1580 et Munich 1582*, by J.M. de Bujanda, Ugo Rozzo, Peter G. Pietenholz, Paul F. Grendler; vol. X (1996): *Thesaurus de la Littérature interdite au XVIe siècle: Auteurs, ouvrages, editions*.
Burkardt, Albrecht, 'L'Inquisition et les autorités locales: Casale Monferrat en 1628', in Audisio (ed.), *Inquisition et Pouvoir* (2004), 89–117.
Burke, Peter, *The Fortunes of* The Courtier (Cambridge, 1995).
Caffiero, Marina, ' "La caccia agli Ebrei". Inquisizione, Casa dei Catecumeni e battesimi forzati nella Roma moderna', in *Le Inquisizioni cristiane e gli Ebrei* (2003), 503–37.
— 'Un rapport à trois. L'Inquisition romaine, les papes et les juifs aux XVIIe et XVIIIe siècles', in Audisio (ed.), *Inquisition et Pouvoir* (2004), 219–32.
— *Battesimi forzati. Storie di Ebrei, Cristiani e converti nella Roma dei papi* (Rome, 2004).
— 'Gli ebrei sono eretici? L'Inquisizione romana e gli ebrei tra cinque e ottocento', in Peyronel Rambaldi (ed.), *I Tribunali* (2007), 245–64.
Cameron, Euan, 'Italy', in Andrew Pettegree (ed.), *The Early Reformation in Europe* (Cambridge, 1992), 188–214.
— *Waldenses: Rejections of Holy Church in Medieval Europe* (Oxford, 2000).
— 'The Reformation in France and Italy to c. 1560: A Review of Recent Contributions and Debates', in Benedict et al., *La Réforme* (2007), 17–33.

Campbell, Gordon (ed.), *The Oxford Dictionary of the Renaissance* (Oxford, 2003).
Canosa, Romano, *Storia dell'Inquisizione in Italia dalla metà del cinquecento alla fine del settecento* (Roma: vol. I: *Modena* [1986]; II: *Venezia* [1987]; III: *Torino e Genova* [1988]; IV: *Milano e Firenze* [1988]; V: *Napoli e Bologna. La procura inquisizioriale* [1990]).
— *Storia dell'Inquisizione spagnola in Italia* (Rome, 1992, reprint 2002).
Cantimori, Delio, *Eretici italiani del cinquecento. Ricerche storiche* (Florence, 1939; reprinted 1967).
Caponetto, Salvatore, *The Protestant Reformation in Sixteenth-Century Italy*, trans. Anne C. Tedeschi and John Tedeschi (Kirksville, MO, 1999).
Cardini, Franco, *Gostanza, la strega di San Miniato* (Bari, 1989; 2001 pb edn).
Carena, Cesare, *Tractatus de Officio Sanctissimae inquisitionis* (1631; Cremona 1668).
Casini, Federico, 'The Crudeli Affair: The Inquisition and Reason of State', in Peter Gay (ed.), *Eighteenth-Century Studies in Honour of A.M. Wilson* (Hanover, NH, 1972), 133-52.
Cassani, Silvia, and Sapio, Maria (eds), *Caravaggio: The Final Years* (National Gallery, London, exhibition catalogue, 2005).
Cassar, Carmel, *Society, Culture and Identity in Early Modern Malta* (Msida [Malta] 2000).
Castro, Alfonso de, *De iusta haereticorum punitione* (1549).
Cecchini, Giovanni, *La Biblioteca Augusta del Comune di Perugia* (Rome, 1978).
Chabod, Federico, *Lo stato e la vita religiosa a Milano nell'epoca di Carlo V* (Turin, 1971; originally 1936-7). Includes, 231-502, *Per la storia religiosa dello Stato di Milan durante il dominio di Carlo V. Note e documenti* (from 2nd edn, Rome 1962).
Chadwick, Owen, *The Popes and European Revolution* (Oxford, 1981).
Ciammitti, Luisa, 'One Saint Less: The Story of Angela Mellini, a Bolognese Seamstress (1667-17?)', in Edward Muir and Guido Ruggiero (eds), *Sex and Gender in Historical Perspective* (Baltimore, MD, and London, 1994), 141-76.
Ciappara, Frans, *The Roman Inquisition in Enlightened Malta* (Malta, 2000).
— *Society and the Inquisition in Early Modern Malta* (Malta, 2001).
— ' "A Spy of Marquis Tanucci": Inquisitor Antonio Maria Lante', *Melita Historica* 13/2 (2001), 209-20 (Malta Historical Society Offprint, 2003).
— *Enlightenment and Reform in Malta 1740-1798* (Sta Venera, Malta, 2006).
— 'Disciplining Diversity: The Roman Inquisition and Social Control in Malta, 1743-98', in Kate Cooper and Jeremy Gregory (eds), *Discipline and Diversity: Papers Read at the 2005 Summer Meeting and the 2006 Winter Meeting of the Ecclesiastical History Society* (Woodbridge, 2007), 354-65.
Cifres, Alejandro, 'L'Archivio storico della Congregazione per la Dottrina della Fede', in *L'Apertura* (1998), 73-84.
— 'Lo stato attuale dell'archivio romano del Sant'Uffizio', in *L'Inquisizione e gli storici* (2000), 27-34.
Cioni, Michele, *I documenti Galileiani del S. Uffizio di Firenze* (Florence, 1996).
Città italiane del cinquecento tra Riforma e Controriforma (Lucca, 1988).
Cochrane, Eric, *Florence in the Forgotten Centuries, 1527-1800* (Chicago, IL, and London, 1973).
Cohen, Thomas and Cohen, Elizabeth, *Words and Deeds in Renaissance Rome: Trials before the Papal Magistrates* (Toronto, 1993).
Concilium Tridentinum. Diariorum Actorum Episularum Tractatum. Nova Collectio edidit Societas Georresiana, vol. 12 (Freiburg, 1930).
Costa, Gustavo, 'La Congregazione dell'Indice e Jonathan Swift (documenti sulla ricezione italiana di *A Tale of a Tub*)', *Paratesto* 1 (2004), 145-65.
— *Thomas Burnet e la censura pontificia (con documenti inediti)* (Florence, 2006).
Costa-Zalessow, Natalia, 'Tarabotti's *La semplicità ingannata* and its Twentieth-Century Interpreters: With Unpublished Documents Regarding its Condemnation to the Index', *Italica* 78 (2001), 314-24.
Cowan, Alexander, *Marriage, Manners and Mobility in Early Modern Venice* (Aldershot and Burlington, VT, 2007).
Cozzi, Gaetano, 'Religione, moralità e giustizia a Venezia: vicende della magistratura degli Esecutori contra la Bestemmia (secoli XVI-XVII)', *Ateneo Veneto* 29 (1991), 7-95.
— *Venezia barocca. Conflitti di uomini e idee nella crisi del seicento veneziano* (Venice, 1995).
Cozzi, Gaetano (ed.), *Stato, società e giustizia nella Repubblica veneta (sec.xv-xviii)* (Rome, 1980).
— *Gli Ebrei e Venezia, secoli XIV-XVIII. Atti del Convegno . . . 1983* (Milan, 1987).
Dall'Olio, Guido, 'I rapporti tra la Congregazione del Sant'Uffizio e gli inquisitori locali nei carteggi bolognesi (1573-1594)', *Rivista Storica Italiana* 105 (1993), 246-86.
— *Eretici e inquisitori nella Bologna del cinquecento* (Bologna, 1999).
— 'Gonzaga, Giulia', *DBI* 57 (2001), 783-7.
— 'Leandro Alberti, inquisitore e mediatore', in Donattini (ed.), *L'Italia dell'inquisitore* (2007), 27-39.
Dandelet, Thomas J. and Marino, John A. (eds), *Spain in Italy: Politics, Society and Religion 1500-1700* (Leiden and Boston, MA, 2007).

Davidson, Nicholas S., 'Chiesa di Roma ed Inquisizione veneziana', in *Città italiane* (1988), 283-92.
— 'Rome and the Venetian Inquisition in the Sixteenth Century', *Journal of Ecclesiastical History* 39 (1988), 16-36.
— 'Unbelief and Atheism in Italy, 1500-1700', in Michael Hunter and David Wootton (eds), *Atheism from the Reformation to the Enlightenment* (Oxford and New York, 1992), 55-85.
— 'Theology, Nature and the Law: Sexual Sin and Sexual Crime in Italy from the Fourteenth to the Seventeenth Century', in Trevor Dean and Kate J.P. Lowe (eds), *Crime, Society and the Law in Renaissance Italy* (Cambridge, 1994), 74-98.
— 'The Inquisition in Venice and its Documents: Some Problems of Method and Analysis', in Del Col and Paolin (eds), *L'Inquisizione romana* (2000), 117-31.
Davis, Natalie Zemon, *Fiction in the Archives: Pardon Tales and their Tellers in Sixteenth-Century France* (Cambridge, 1988).
— *Trickster Travels: A Sixteenth-Century Muslim between Worlds* (New York, 2006).
Davis, Robert C., and Ravid, Benjamin (eds), *The Jews of Early Modern Venice* (Baltimore, MD, and London, 2001).
Dean, Trevor, *Crime and Justice in Late Medieval Italy* (Cambridge, 2007).
De Boer, Wietse, *The Conquest of the Soul: Confession, Discipline and Public Order in Counter-Reformation Milan* (Leiden, Boston, MA, and Cologne, 2001).
De Frede, Carlo, 'Tipografi, editori, librai italiani del cinquecento coinvolti in processi di eresia', *Rivista di Storia della Chiesa in Italia* 23 (1969), 21-53.
Del Col, Andrea, 'Note sull'eterodossia di fra Sisto da Siena: I suoi rapporti con Orazio Brunetto e un gruppo Veneziano di "Spirituali" ', *Collectanea Francescana*, 47 (1977), 27-64.
— 'Il controllo della stampa a Venezia e i processi di Antonio Brucioli (1548-1559)', *Critica Storica* 17 (1980), 457-510.
— 'Organizzazione, composizione e giurisdizione del tribunali dell'Inquisizione romana nella repubblica di Venezia (1500-1550)', *Critica Storica* 25 (1988), 244-94.
— *Domenico Scandella Known as Menocchio: His Trials before the Inquisition (1583-1599)*, trans. John and Anne C. Tedeschi (Binghampton, NY, 1996).
— 'Strumenti di ricerca per le fonti inquisitoriali in Italia nell'età moderna', *Società e Storia* 75 (1997), 143-67, 417-24.
— *L'Inquisizione nel Patriarcato e Diocesi di Aquileia, 1557-1559* (Montereale Valcellina, 1998).
— 'Osservazioni preliminari sulla storiografia dell'Inquisizione romana', in Cesare Mozzarelli (ed.), *Identità italiana e cattolicesimo. Una prospettiva storica* (Rome, 2003), 75-137.
— *L'Inquisizione in Italia. Dal XII al XXI secolo* (Milan, 2006).
— 'I rapporti tra i giudici di fede in Italia dal medioevo all'età contemporanea', in Peyronel Rambaldi (ed.), *I Tribunali* (2007), 83-110.
Del Col, Andrea (ed.), in collaboration with Aldo Colonello and Giovanna Paolin, *L'Inquisizione in Friuli. Mostra storica* (Trieste and Montereale Valcellina, 2000).
Del Col, Andrea and Milani, Marisa, ' "Senza effusione di sangue e senza pericolo di morte". Intorno alcune condanne capitali delle inquisizioni di Venezia e di Verona nel settecento e a quelle veneziane del cinquecento', in Mario Rosa (ed.), *Eretici, esuli e indemoniati nell'età moderna* (Florence, 1998), 141-96.
Del Col, Andrea and Paolin, Giovanna (eds), *L'Inquisizione romana in Italia nell'età moderna. Archivi, problemi di metodo e nuove ricerche* (Rome, 1991).
Del Col, Andrea and Paolin, Giovanna (eds), *L'Inquisizione romana: metologia delle fonti e storia istituzionale. Atti del seminario internazionale. Montereale Valcellina ... 1999* (Trieste and Montereale Valcellina, 2000).
Delph, Ronald K., Fontaine, Michelle M., and Martin, John Jeffries (eds), *Heresy, Culture, and Religion in Early Modern Italy: Contexts and Contestations* (Kirksville, MO, 2006).
Delpiano, Patrizia, 'Per una storia della censura ecclesiastica nel settecento. Aspetti e problemi', *Società e Storia* 27 (2004), 487-530.
— *Il governo della lettura. Chiesa e libri della lettura* (Bologna, 2007).
Derosas, R., 'Moralità e giustizia a Venezia nel '500-'600: gli esecutori contra la Bestemmia', in Cozzi (ed.), *Stato, società*, 431-528.
Deutscher, Thomas, 'The Role of the Episcopal Tribunal of Novara in the Suppression of Heresy and Witchcraft', *Catholic Historical Review* 77 (1991), 403-21.
De Vivo, Filippo, *Information and Communication in Venice: Rethinking Early Modern Politics* (Oxford, 2007).
Dialeti, Androniki, 'The Debate about Women and its Socio-Cultural Background in Early Modern Venice' (Ph.D. Thesis, University of Glasgow, 2004).
Di Rienzo, Eugenio and Formica, Marina, 'Tra Napoli e Roma: censura e commercio librario', in Anna Maria Rao (ed.), *Editoria e cultura a Napoli nel XVIII secolo* (Naples, 1998).
Di Simplicio, Oscar, *Peccato, penitenza, perdono, Siena 1575-1800* (Milan, 1994).

— *Inquisizione, stregoneria, medicina. Siena e il suo stato (1580–1721)* (Monteriggioni [Siena], 2000).
— *Autunno della stregoneria. Maleficio e magia nell'Italia moderna* (Bologna, 2005).
Ditchfield, Simon, 'Adriano Prosperi between *Italia Sacra* and *Storia patria*' (paper for the 2007 Renaissance Society of America Conference).
— 'Innovation and its Limits: The Case of Italy (ca. 1512–ca. 1572), in Benedict *et al.* (eds), *La Réforme* (2007), 145–60.
— 'Papal Patchwork Unpicked' [review article], *Journal of Early Modern History* 11 (2007), 519–25.
— 'Tridentine Worship and the Cult of Saints', in R. Po-Chia Hsia (ed.), *The Cambridge History of Christianity*, vol. 6: *Reform and Expansion 1500–1600* (Cambridge, 2007), 201–23, 640–3 (bibliography).
Dizionario biografico degli Italiani (Rome, 1960–). [*DBI*]
Donati, Claudio, 'A Project of "Expurgation" by the Congregation of the Index: Treatises on Duelling', in Fragnito (ed.), *Church, Censorship* (2001), 134–62.
Donattini, Massimo (ed.), *L'Italia dell'Inquisitore. Storia e Geografia dell'Italia del Cinquecento nella Descrittione di Leandro Alberti* (Bologna, 2007).
Drake, Stillman, *Galileo at Work: His Scientific Biography* (Chicago, IL, and London, 1981 edn).
Duni, Matteo, *Tra religione e magia. Storia del prete modenese Guglielmo Campana (1460?–1541)* (Florence, 1999).
Enciclopedia dei Papi (Rome), vol. III (2000).
Errera, Andrea, *Processus in causa fidei. L'evoluzione dei manuali inquisitoriali nei secoli XVI–XVIII e il manuale inedito di un inquisitore perugino* (Bologna, 2000).
Eymeric, Nicolau and Peña, Francisco, *Directorium inquisitorum* (Rome, 1585 edn used).
Fantoli, Annibale, 'The Disputed Injunction and its Role in Galileo's Trial', in McMullin (ed.), *The Church and Galileo* (2005), 117–49.
Favaro, Antonio (ed.), *Le opere di Galileo Galilei*, 20 vols (Florence, Barbèra, 1890–1909; reprints 1929–39, 1968).
Fenlon, Dermot, *Heresy and Obedience in Tridentine Italy: Cardinal Pole and the Counter-Reformation* (Cambridge, 1972).
Ferrario, Ippolito Edmondo, *Triora. Anno Domini 1587. Storia della stregoneria nel Ponente Ligure: A History of Witchcraft in Western Liguria* (Genoa, 2005).
Ferri, Andrea (ed.), *L'Inquisizione romana in diocesi di Imola. Inventario del fondo inquisitoriale presso l'archivio diocesano di Imola* (Imola, 2001).
Finocchiaro, Maurice A., *Retrying Galileo, 1633–1992* (Berkeley, CA, and London, 2005).
Finocchiaro, Maurice A. (ed.), *The Galileo Affair: A Documentary Collection* (Berkeley, CA, 1989).
Firpo, Luigi, 'Il processo di Giordano Bruno', *Rivista storica italiana* 60 (1948), 542–97, 61 (1949), 5–59.
— 'Esecuzioni capitali in Roma (1567–1671)', in *Eresia e Riforma nell'Italia del cinquecento. Miscellanea I* (Florence and Chicago, IL, 1974), 307–42.
Firpo, Massimo, *Riforma protestante ed eresie nell'Italia del cinquecento* (Rome and Bari, 1993).
— 'The Italian Reformation and Juan de Valdés', *Sixteenth Century Journal* 27 (1996), 353–64.
— *Dal Sacco di Roma all'Inquisizione. Studi su Juan de Valdés e la Riforma italiana* (Alessandria, 1998). Especially: 'Il problema storico della Riforma italiana e Juan de Valdés', 61–88; 'Juan de Valdés tra *Alumbrados* e "Spirituali", note sul Valdesianismo in Italia', 89–117; 'Il *Beneficio di Christo* e il Concilio di Trento (1542–1546)', 119–45; 'Alcune considerazioni sull'esperienza religiosa di Sigismondo Arquer', 161–220.
— *Artisti, gioiellieri, eretici. Il mondo di Lorenzo Lotto tra Riforma e Controriforma* (Rome and Bari, 2001).
— *'Disputar di cose pertinente alla fede' Studi sulla vita religiosa del cinquecento italiano* (Milan, 2003). Especially: 'La Riforma italiana del cinquecento. Le premesse storiografiche', 11–66; 'Eresia e l'inquisizione in Italia (1542–72)', 197–208; 'Teologia, storia e politica nell'ultimo processo inquisitoriale di Pietro Carnesecchi (1566–67)', 227–46.
— *Inquisizione romana e Controriforma. Studi sul Cardinale Giovanni Morone (1509–1580) e il suo processo d'eresia* (Bologna, 1992; expanded edn, Brescia, 2005). Especially: 'Gli "spirituali", l'Accademia di Modena e il formulario di fede di 1542: Controllo del dissenso religioso e Nicodemismo', 55–129; 'Vittoria Colonna, Giovanni Morone e gli "spirituali" ', 131–80; 'Il primo processo inquisitoriale contro il cardinale Morone (1552–53)', 243–314.
— *Vittore Soranzo vescovo e eretico. Riforma della Chiesa e Inquisizione nell'Italia del cinquecento* (Rome and Bari, 2006).
— 'Lorenzo Lotto and the Reformation in Venice', in Delph *et al.* (eds), *Heresy, Culture* (2007), 21–36.
— 'Reform of the Church and Heresy in the Age of Charles V: Reflections of Spain in Italy', in Dandelet and Marino (eds), *Spain in Italy* (2007), 457–87.
Firpo, Massimo and Marcatto, Dario (eds), *Il processo inquisitoriale del cardinale Giovanni Morone*, 6 vols (Rome, 1981–95).
— *I processi inquisitoriali di Pietro Carnesecchi (1557–1567)*, 2 vols in 5 parts (Vatican City, 1998–2000).
Firpo, Massimo and Pagano, Sergio (eds), *I processi inquisitoriali di Vittore Soranzo (1550–1558)* 2 vols (Vatican City, 2004).

Firpo, Massimo and Simoncelli, Paolo, 'I processi inquisitoriali contro Savonarola (1558) e Carnesecchi (1566-1567): un proposto di interpretazione', *Rivista di storia e letteratura religiosa* 18 (1982), 200-52.
Flori, Maria Chiara, 'Eresia e scandolo nel '600: la biblioteca di Pandolfo Ricasoli', *Rinascimento* 44 (2004), 379-408.
Foa, Anna, *Giordano Bruno* (Bologna, 1998).
Fontaine, Michelle M., 'Making Heresy Marginal in Modena', in Delph et al. (eds), *Heresy, Culture* (2006), 37-51.
Fosi, Irene, 'Il governo della giustizia nello Stato Ecclesiastico fra centro e periferia (secoli XVI-XVII)', in A. Jamme, O. Poncet, (eds), *Offices et Papauté (XIVe-XVIIe). Charges, hommes, destins* (Rome, 2005), 216-22.
— *La giustizia del papa. Sudditi e tribunali nello Stato Pontificio in età moderna* (Rome and Bari, 2007).
Fragnito, Gigliola, *La Bibbia al rogo. La censura ecclesiastica e i volgarizzamenti della Scrittura (1471-1605)* (Bologna, 1997).
— 'La censura libraria tra Congregazione dell'Indice, Congregazione dell'Inquisizione e Maestro del Sacro Palazzo (1571-1506)', in Rozzo (ed.), *La censura libraria* (1997), 163-75.
— 'Aspetti e problemi della censura espurgatoria', in *L'Inquisizione e gli storici* (2000), 161-78.
— ' "In questo vasto mare . . .": La censura ecclesiastica tra la fine del cinquecento e i primi del seicento,' in Stango (ed.), *Censura ecclesiastica* (2001), 1-35.
— 'Central and Peripheral Organization of Censorship', in Fragnito (ed.), *Church, Censorship* (2001), 13-49.
— *Proibito capire. La Chiesa e il volgare nella prima età moderna* (Bologna, 2005).
— 'Un archivio conteso: le "carte" dell'Indice tra Congregazione e Maestro del Sacro Palazzo', *Rivista Storica Italiana* 119 (2007), 1,276-1,318.
Fragnito, Gigliola (ed.), *Church, Censorship and Culture in Early Modern Italy* (Cambridge and New York, 2001).
Frajese, Vittorio, *Nascita dell'Indice. La censura ecclesiastica dal Rinascimento alla Controriforma* (Brescia, 2006).
Furey, Constance, *Erasmus, Contarini and the Religious Republic of Letters* (Cambridge and New York, 2005).
Gaeta, Franco, 'Documenti da codici vaticani per la storia della Riforma in Venezia. Appunti e documenti', *Annuario dell'istituto storico italiano per l'età moderna e contemporanea* 7 (1955), 5-53.
Garrard, Mary D., *Artemisia Gentileschi* (Princeton, NJ, 1989).
Garufi, Carlo Alberto, *Fatti e personaggi del'Inquisizione in Sicilia* (Palermo, 1978).
— *Graffiti e disegni dei prigionieri dell'Inquisizione* (Palermo, 1978).
Garzoni, Tomaso, *La piazza universale di tutte le professioni del mondo* (1585), ed. Paolo Cherchi and Beatrice Collina, 2 vols (Turin, 1996).
Gentilcore, David, *From Bishop to Witch: The System of the Sacred in Early Modern Terra d'Otranto* (Manchester and New York, 1992).
— *Healers and Healing in Early Modern Italy* (Manchester and New York, 1998).
— *Medical Charlatanism in Early Modern Italy* (Oxford, 2006).
— 'A Tale of Two Tribunals', in John Jeffries Martin (ed.), *The Renaissance World* (New York and London, 2007), 605-20.
Ghirardo, Diane Yvonne, 'Marginal Spaces of Prostitution in Renaissance Ferrara', in Dennis Looney and Deanna Shemek (eds), *Phaeton's Children: The Este Court and its Culture in Early Modern Ferrara* (Tempe, AZ, 2005), 87-127.
Giannini, Massimo Carlo, 'Fra autonomia politica e ortodossia religiosa: il tentativo d'introdurre l'Inquisizione "al modo di Spagna" nello stato di Milano (1558-1566)', *Società e Storia* 91 (2001), 79-134.
Ginzburg, Carlo, *I Benandanti: stregoneria e culti agrari tra cinquecento e seicento* (Turin, 1966); trans. *The Night Battles: Witchcraft and Agrarian Cults in the Sixteenth and Seventeenth Centuries*, trans. John and Anne Tedeschi (Baltimore, MD, 1983).
— *I costituti di don Pietro Manelfi* (Florence and Chicago, IL, 1970).
— *Il Nicodemismo: simulazione e dissimulazione religiosa nell'Europa del '500* (Turin, 1970).
— *Il formaggio e i vermi, Il cosmo di un mugnaio del '500* (Turin, 1976); trans. *The Cheese and the Worms: The Cosmos of a Sixteenth-Century Miller*, trans. John and Anne Tedeschi (Baltimore, MD, and London, 1980).
— *Myths, Emblems, Clues*, trans. John and Anne C. Tedeschi (London and Sydney, 1990). Especially: 'The Inquisitor as Anthropologist', 156-64, 220-1; 'Witchcraft and Popular Piety: Notes on a Modenese Trial of 1519', 1-16, 165-70.
— 'Microhistory: Two or Three Things that I Know about It', *Critical Inquiry* 20 (1993), 10-35.
Giordano, Silvano, 'Sisto V', in *Enciclopedia dei papi*, III, 210-22.
Gleason, Elisabeth G., *Gasparo Contarini: Venice, Rome and Reform* (Berkeley, CA, 1993).
Godman, Peter, *From Poliziano to Machiavelli: Florentine Humanism in the High Renaissance* (Princeton, NJ, 1998).
— *The Saint as Censor: Robert Bellarmine between Inquisition and Index* (Leiden, Boston, MA, and Cologne, 2000).
— *I segreti dell'Inquisizione*, trans. Marco Papi and Clara Ghibellini (Milan, 2004).
Gotor, Miguel, *I beati del Papa. Santità, Inquisizione e obbedienza in età moderna* (Florence, 2002).

Gregory, Brad S., *Salvation at Stake: Christian Martyrdom in Early Modern Europe* (Cambridge, MA, and London, 1999).
Grendi, E., 'Sulla "storia criminale": risposta a Mario Sbriccoli', *Quaderni Storici* 73 (1990), 267-75.
Grendler, Paul F., *The Roman Inquisition and the Venetian Press (1510-1605)* (Princeton, NJ, 1977).
— 'The Destruction of Hebrew Books in Venice', *Proceedings of the American Academy for Jewish Research* 15 (1978), 103-30.
— 'The "tre savii sopra eresia" 1547-1605: A Prosopographical Study', *Studi Veneziani* 3 (1979), 283-303.
Gri, Gian Paolo, 'L'uso delle fonti inquisitoriali in ambito demo-antropologico', in Del Col and Paolin (eds), *L'Inquisizione romana: metologia* (2000), 73-89.
— *Altri modi. Etnografia dell'agire simbolico nei processi friulani dell'Inquisizione* (Montereale Valcellina, 2001).
Guasco, Maurilio and Torre, Angelo (eds), *Pio V nella società politica del suo tempo* (Bologna, 2005).
Guidi, Oscar, *Ursolina la Rossa e altre storie. Inquisitori e streghe tra Lucca e Modena nel XVI secolo*. Introduction by Franco Cardini (Lucca, 2007).
Hacke, Daniela, *Women, Sex and Marriage in Early Modern Venice* (Aldershot, 2004).
Hamilton, Bernard, *The Medieval Inquisition* (London, 1981).
Heilbron, John L., 'Censorship of Astronomy in Italy after Galileo', in McMullin (ed.), *The Church and Galileo*, 279-322.
Hellyer, Marcus, *Catholic Physics: Jesuit Natural Philosophy in Early Modern Germany* (Notre Dame, IN, 2005).
Henningsen, Gustav, Tedeschi, John, and Amiel, C. (eds), *The Inquisition in Early Modern Europe: Studies on Sources and Methods* (Dekalb, IL, 1986).
Herzig, Tamar, 'Leandro Alberti and the Savonarolan Movement in Northern Italy', in Donattini (ed.), *L'Italia dell'Inquisitore* (2007), 81-95.
Hillerbrand, Hans (ed.), *The Oxford Encyclopedia of the Reformation*, 4 vols (Oxford and New York, 1996).
Horodowich, Elizabeth, 'Civic Identity and the Control of Blasphemy in Sixteenth-Century Venice', *Past and Present* 181 (2003), 5-33.
— 'The Gossiping Tongue: Oral Networks, Public Life and Political Culture in Early Modern Venice', *Renaissance Studies* 19 (2005), 22-45.
— *Language and Statecraft in Early Modern Venice* (New York and Cambridge, 2008).
Hossain, Kimberley Lynn, 'Was Adam the First Heretic? Diego de Simancas, Luis de Páramo and the Origins of Inquisitorial Practice', *Archive for Reformation History/Archiv für Reformationsgeschichte* 97 (2006), 184-210.
Hroch, Miroslav and Skýbová, Anna, *Ecclesia Militans: The Inquisition*, trans. Janet Fraser (Dorset Press, np, 1990).
Huizinga, Johan, *Homo Ludens: A Study of the Play Element in Culture* (Boston, MA, 1955).
Index Librorum Prohibitorum ... (Rome, Camera Apostolica, 1596 ... 1632).
Index librorum prohibitorum ... *Benedicti XIV* (Rome, 1758).
Infelise, Mario, *L'editoria veneziana nel '700* (Milan, 1989; upated edn, 1999).
— *I libri proibiti. Da Gutenberg all'Encyclopédie* (Rome and Bari, 1999; 8th edn, 2008).
— *Prima dei giornali. Alle origini della pubblica informazione* (Rome and Bari, 2002; 2nd edn, 2005).
— 'Books and Politics in Arcangela Tarabotti's Venice', in Weaver (ed.), *Arcangela Tarabotti* (2006), 57-72.
Le inquisizioni cristiane e gli Ebrei. Tavola Rotonda nell'ambito della conferenza annuale della ricerca (Roma, 20-21 dicembre 2001) (Atti dei Convegni Lincei 191, Rome, 2003).
L'Inquisizione e gli storici: Un cantiere aperto. (Tavola Rotonda ... giugno 1999), (Rome, 2000).
L'Inquisizione romana in Italia nell'età moderna. Archivi, problemi di metodo e nuove ricerche (Rome, 1991).
Ioly Zorattini, Pier Cesare, *Processi del S. Uffizio di Venezia contro Ebrei e Giudaizzanti*, 9 vols (Florence, 1980-99).
— 'Gli archivi del Sant'Ufficio come fonti per la storia della mentalità e della cultura delle minoranze etnico-religiose', in Del Col and Paolin (eds), *L'Inquisizione romana* (2000), 189-201.
— 'Jews, Crypto-Jews and the Inquisition', in Davis and Ravid (eds), *The Jews of Early Modern Venice* (2001), 97-116.
— 'Ebrei e S. Uffizio a Venezia: tre secoli di storia', in *Le Inquisizioni cristiane e gli Ebrei* (2003), 219-33.
Ioly Zorattini, Pier Cesare (ed.), *L'identità dissimulata. Giudaizzanti Iberici nell'Europa Cristiana dell'età moderna* (Florence, 2000).
Kadri, Sadakat, *The Trial: A History from Socrates to O.J. Simpson* (London, 2006).
Kamen, Henry, *The Spanish Inquisition* (London, 1965).
— *Inquisition and Society in Spain in the Sixteenth and Seventeenth Centuries* (revised edn, London, 1985).
— *The Spanish Inquisition: An Historical Revision* (London, 1997).
Kuehn, Thomas, 'Rereading Microhistory: The Example of Giovanni and Susanna,' *Journal of Modern History* 61 (1989), 512-34.
Kuntz, Marion Leathers, *The Anointment of Dionisio: Prophecy and Politics in Renaissance Italy* (University Park, PA, 2001).

— 'Venice and Justice: Saint Mark and Moses', in Delph et al. (eds), *Heresy, Culture* (2006), 151–68.
Lambert, Malcolm D., *Medieval Heresy: Popular Movements from the Gregorian Reform to the Reformation* (2nd edn, Oxford, 1992).
— *The Cathars* (Oxford, 1998).
Laven, Mary, *Virgins of Venice: Enclosed Lives and Broken Vows in the Renaissance Convent* (London, 2002).
— 'Testifying to the Self: Nuns' Narratives in Early Modern Venice', in Mulholland and Pullan (eds), *Judicial Tribunals* (2003), 147–58.
Lavenia, Vincenzo, 'I beni dell'eretico. I conti dell'inquisitore. Confische, stati italiani, economici del Sacro Tribunale', in *L'Inquisizione e gli storici: Un cantiere aperto* (2000), 47–94.
— 'Gli ebrei e il fisco dell'Inquisizione. Tributi, esproprie e multe tra cinque e seicento', in *Le inquisizioni cristiane e gli Ebrei* (2003), 325–56.
— *L'infamia e il perdono. Tributi, pene e confessione nella teologia morale della prima età moderna* (Bologna, 2004).
— 'Giurare al Sant'Uffizio. Sarpi, l'Inquisizione e un conflitto nella Repubblica di Venezia', *Rivista Storica Italiana* 118 (2006), 7–50.
Lea, Henry C., *The History of the Inquisition of Spain*, 4 vols (New York, 1906–7).
— *The Inquisition in the Spanish Dependencies* (New York, 1908).
Leonardi, Melita, *Governo, istituzioni, Inquisizione nella Sicilia spagnola. I processi per magia e superstizione* (Acireale-Roma, 2005).
Levack, Brian, *The Witch-Hunt in Early Modern Europe* (2nd edn, London and New York, 1995).
Limborch, Phillipp van, *Historia inquisitionis* . . . (Amsterdam, 1692).
Lopez, Pasquale, *Inquisizione, stampa, censura nel Regno di Napoli tra '500 e'600* (Naples, 1974).
McCuaig, William, *Carlo Sigonio: The Changing World of the Late Renaissance* (Princeton, NJ, 1989).
McGough, Laura J., 'Demons, Nature or God? Witchcraft Accusations and the French Disease in Early Modern Venice', *Bulletin of the History of Medicine* 80/2 (2006), 219–46.
McMullin, Ernan, 'The Church's Ban on Copernicanism, 1616', in his (ed.) *The Church and Galileo* (2005), 150–90.
McMullin, Ernan, (ed.), *The Church and Galileo* (Notre Dame, IL, 2005).
Malena, Adelisa, *L'eresia dei perfetti: Inquisizione romana ed esperienze mistiche nel seicento italiano* (Rome, 2003).
Manconi, Francesco, 'The Kingdom of Sardinia: A Province in Balance between Catalonia, Castile and Italy', in Dandelet and Marino (eds), *Spain in Italy* (2007), 45–72.
Mantini, Silvia, 'Gostanza da Libbiano, guaritrice e strega (1534–?)', in Ottavia Niccoli (ed.), *Rinascimento al femminile* (Rome and Bari, 1998 edn), 143–62.
Marcocci, Giuseppe, 'A proposito dell'immagine dell'Italia nel cinquecento. La *Descrittione di Tutta Italia* di Leandro Alberti e la cartografia rinascimentale', in Massimo Donattini (ed.), *L'Italia dell'inquisitore* (2007), 273–98.
Martin, John, *Venice's Hidden Enemies: Italian Heretics in a Renaissance City* (London and Berkeley, CA, 1993).
— *Myths of Renaissance Individualism* (Basingstoke, 2004).
— 'Introduction: Renovatio and Reform in Early Modern Italy', in Delph et al., *Heresy, Culture* (2006), 1–17.
Martin, Ruth, *Witchcraft and the Inquisition in Venice 1550–1650* (Oxford, 1989).
Maselli, Domenico, 'Per la storia religiosa dello Stato di Milano durante il dominio di Filippo II: l'eresia e la sua repressione dal 1555 al 1584', *Nuova Rivista Storica* 54 (1970), 317–73 [same as, item I in his *Saggi di storia ereticale lombarda al tempo di S. Carlo* (Naples, 1979), 11–88].
Masini, Eliseo, *Sacro Arsenale, overo prattica dell'officio della Santa Inquisizione, ampliata* (Genova, 1625) [See also under *Sacro Arsenale* . . .]. Modern edition: *Il manuale degli inquisitori ovvero pratica dell'officio della Santa Inquisizione*, preface by Attilio Agnoletto (Milan, 1990).
Mayer, Thomas F., *Reginald Pole: Prince & Prophet* (Cambridge, 2000).
— *The Correspondence of Reginald Pole. Vol 1. A Calendar, 1518–1546: Beginnings to Legate of Viterbo; Vol. 2, A Calendar, 1547–1554: A Power in Rome* (Aldershot, 2002 and 2003).
Mazzotti, Massimo, 'Newton for Ladies: Gentility, Gender and Radical Culture', *British Journal for the History of Science*, 37(2) (2004), 119–46.
Medici, G.C., 'Cesare Carena, giurista cremonese del secolo XVII', *Archivio storico lombardo* 57 (1930), 297–330.
Mercati, Angelo, *Il sommario del processo di Giordano Bruno, con appendice di documenti sull'eresia e l'Inquisizione a Modena nel secolo XVI* (Vatican City, 1942).
— *Il costituti di Niccolò Franco* (Vatican City, 1955).
Merlo, Grado Giovanni, *Streghe* (Bologna, 2006).
Messana, Maria Sofia, *Inquisitori, negromanti e streghe nella Sicilia moderna (1500–1782)* (Palermo, 2007).
Miato, Monica, *L'Accademia degli Incogniti di Giovan Francesco Loredano. Venezia (1630–1661)* (Florence, 1998).

Miculian, Antonio, 'Storia della Riforma in Istria', in Branca, Vittore, and Graciotti, Sante (eds), *L'Umanesimo in Istria* (Florence, 1983) 203–14.
Milani, Marisa, 'L'ossessione secolare di suor Mansueta. Un esorcismo a Venezia nel 1574', *Quaderni Veneti*, fasc. 7 (1988), 129–53.
Minchella, Giuseppina, 'I processi del Sant'Ufficio di Aquileia e Concordia per apostasia all'Islam contro i soldati della fortezza di Palma (1605–1652)', *Metodi e ricerche* 24/1 (2005), 7–31.
Minonzio, Franco, ' "Fra Leandro, dolce cosmografo e brusco inquisitore, leccardo del arrosto di carne umana". I rapporti tra Leandro Alberti e Paolo Giovio e l'ombra inquieta della memoria tra Giovanfrancesco Pico e Giovanni Mainardi', in Donattini (ed.), *L'Italia dell'inquisitore* (2007), 51–79.
Miranda, Salvador, 'The Cardinals of the Holy Roman Church', www.fiu.edu/~miranda/cardinals.htm
Monter, William, *The Frontiers of Heresy: The Spanish Inquisition from the Basque Lands to Sicily* (Cambridge and New York, 1990).
Monter, E. William and Tedeschi, John, 'Towards a Statistical Profile of the Italian Inquisitions: Sixteenth to Eighteenth Centuries', in Henningsen *et al.* (eds), *The Inquisition in Early Modern Europe* (1986), 13–32, 130–57.
Morelli Timpanaro, Maria Augusta, *Tomasso Crudeli. Poppi 1702–1745. Contributo per uno studio sulla Inquisizione a Firenze nella prima metà del XVIII secolo*, 2 vols (Florence, 2003).
Muir, Edward, *The Cultural Wars of the Late Renaissance: Skeptics, Libertines and Opera* (Cambridge, MA, and London, 2007).
Mulholland, Maureen and Pullan, Brian (eds), with Anne Pullan, *Judicial Tribunals in England and Europe, 1200–1700: The Trial in History*, vol. 1 (Manchester, 2003).
Murphy, Paul, 'Rumors of Heresy in Mantua', in Delph *et al.* (eds), *Heresy, Culture*, (2006) 53–67.
— *Ruling Peacefully: Cardinal Ercole Gonzaga and Patrician Reform in Sixteenth-Century Italy* (Washington D.C., 2007).
Murray, Alexander, 'Counselling in Medieval Confession', in *Handling Sin: Confession in the Middle Ages*, ed. Peter A. Biller and Alastair J. Minnis (York, 1998), 63–77.
Nardon, Franco, *Benandanti e inquisitori nel Friuli del seicento. Prefazione di Andrea Del Col* (Trieste, 1999).
— 'Benandanti "funebri": le processioni dei morti nei documenti inquisitoriali', in *L'incerto confine. Vivi e morti, incontri, luoghi e percorsi di religiosità nella montagna friuliana* (Udine, 2001), 173–80.
O'Neil, Mary, 'Magical Healing, Love Magic and the Inquisition in Late Sixteenth-Century Modena', in Stephen Haliczer (ed.), *Inquisition and Society in Early Modern Europe* (London and Sydney, 1987), 88–114.
Ordini, privilegi et indulgenze della venerabile compagnia della Santissima Croce di Mantova (Mantua, per Tomaso Ruffinello, l'anno 1595. Con licentia de' Superiori), 42 pp. (Copy bound in with Mss docs: ACDF St. St. LL 4–f, folder (2).
Pagano, Sergio M. (ed.), *I documenti del processo di Galileo Galilei* (Vatican City, 1984).
— *Il processo di Endimio Calandra e l'Inquisizione a Mantova nel 1567–68* (Rome, 1991).
Pagano, Sergio M. and Ranieri, Concetta, *Nuovi documenti su Vittoria Colonna e Reginald Pole* (Vatican City, 1989).
Paolin, Giovanna, 'Gli ordini religiosi e l'Inquisizione: analisi di un rapporto', in Del Col and Paolin (eds), *L'Inquisizione romana: metologia* (2000), 169–86.
Parente, Fausto, 'The Condemnation of the Talmud', in Fragnito (ed.), *Church, Censorship* (2001), 163–93.
Pasta, Renato, 'Fermenti culturali e circoli massonici nella Toscana del settecento', in Gian Mario Cazzaniga (ed.), *Storia d'Italia. Annali 21. La Massoneria* (Turin, 2006), 447–83.
Pastore, Alessandro, 'Galeota, Mario', *DBI* 51 (1998), 420–3.
— *Le regole dei corpi. Medicina e disciplina nell'Italia moderna* (Bologna, 2006).
Pastore, Stefania, *Un'eresia spagnola. Spiritualità conversa, alumbradismo e Inquisizione (1449–1559)* (Florence, 2004).
Perocco, Daria, 'Prose Production in Venice in the Early Seicento', in Weaver (ed.), *Arcangela Tarabotti* (2006), 73–87.
Peruzza, Morena, 'L'Inquisizione nel periodo delle riforme settecentesche: il caso veneziano', *Ricerche di storia sociale e religiosa* 46 (1994), 139–86.
Petrella, Giancarlo, 'Nella cella di fra Leandro: prime ricerche sui libri di Leandro Alberti umanista e inquisitore', in Barbieri and Zardin (eds), *Libri, biblioteche* (2002), 85–135.
Petrocchi, Massimo, *Il Quietismo italiano nel seicento* (Rome, 1948).
Peyronel Rambaldi, Susanna, *Speranze e crisi nel cinquecento modenese: Tensioni religiose e vita cittadina ai tempi di Giovanni Morone* (Milan, 1979).
— *Dai Paesi Bassi all'Italia. 'Il sommario della Sacra Scrittura'. Un libro proibito nella società italiana del cinquecento* (Florence, 1997).
Peyronel Rambaldi, Susanna (ed.), *I Tribunali della Fede: continuità e discontinuità dal medioevo all'età moderna* (Turin, 2007).

Plakotos, Georgios, 'The Venetian Inquisition and Aspects of "Otherness": Judaizers, Muslim and Christian Converts (16th–17th Century)' (Ph.D., Glasgow, 2004–5).
— 'Christian and Muslim Converts from the Balkans in Early Modern Venice: Patterns of Social and Cultural Mobility and Identities', in Raymond Detrez and Pieter Plas (eds), *Developing Cultural Identity in the Balkans: Convergence vs. Divergence* (Brussels and Berne, 2005), 125–45.
Pomata, Gianna, *Contracting a Cure: Patients, Healers and the Law in Early Modern Bologna* (Baltimore, MD, and London, 1998); trans. of her *La promessa di guarigione: Malatti e curatori in antico regime* (Rome and Bari, 1994).
Poppi, Antonino, *Cremonini, Galilei e gli inquisitori del Santo a Padova. Nuovi documenti d'Archivio* (Padua, 1993).
Prodi, Paolo, *Il cardinale Gabriele Paleotti (1522–1597)*, 2 vols (Rome, 1959–1967).
Prosperi, Adriano, *Tra evangelismo e controriforma: G.M. Giberti (1495–1543)* (Rome, 1969).
— *Tribunali della coscienza. Inquisitori, confessori, missionari* (Turin, 1996).
— 'L'Inquisizione in Italia', in Mario Rosa (ed.), *Clero e società nell'Italia moderna* (Rome and Bari, 1997), 275–320.
— 'La Chiesa e la circolazione della cultura nell'Italia della Controriforma. Effetti imprevisti della censura', in Rozzo (ed.) *La censura libraria* (1997), 147–61.
— *L'eresia del Libro Grande. Storia di Giorgio Siculo e della sua setta* (Milan, 2000).
— *L'Inquisizione romana. Letture e ricerche* (Rome, 2003). Especially: 'L'Inquisizione: verso una nuova immagine?', 3–27; 'Per la storia dell'Inquisizione romana', 29–68; 'Il "budget" di un inquisitore. Ferrara 1567–1672', 125–40.
— 'L'Italia di un inquisitore', in Donattini (ed.), *L'Italia dell'Inquisitore* (2007), 3–25.
Prosperi, Adriano, and Tedeschi, John (eds), *Dizionario dell'Inquisizione*, 4 vols (Pisa, forthcoming c. 2009).
Pullan, Brian S., ' "A Ship with Two Rudders": Righetto Marrano and the Inquisition in Venice', *Historical Journal* 20 (1977), 25–58.
— *The Jews of Europe and the Inquisition of Venice 1550–1670* (Oxford and Totowa, NJ, 1983).
— 'The Trial of Giorgio Moreto before the Inquisition in Venice, 1589', in Mulholland and Pullan (eds), *Judicial Tribunals* (2003), 159–81.
Rawlings, Helen, *The Spanish Inquisition* (Oxford, 2006).
Raz-Krakotzkin, Amnon, 'The Censor as a Mediator: Printing Censorship and the Shaping of Hebrew Literature', in Wendehorst (ed.), *The Roman Inquisition* (2004), 35–57.
Redingonda, Abele L., 'Alberti, Leandro', *DBI* 1 (1960), 699–703.
Redondi, Pietro, *Galileo eretico* (Turin, 1983), trans. as *Galileo Heretic*, by Raymond Rosenthal (Princeton, NJ, 1987).
Renda, Francesco, *L'Inquisizione in Sicilia. I fatti. Le persone* (Palermo, 1997).
Ricci, Giovanni, *I Turchi alle porte* (Bologna, 2008).
Ricci, Saverio, *Giordano Bruno nell'Europa del cinquecento* (Rome, 2000).
— *Il sommo inquisitore. Giulio Antonio Santori tra autobiografia e storia (1532–1602)* (Rome, 2002).
Roach, Andrew P., *The Devil's World: Heresy and Society 1100–1300* (Harlow, 2005).
Robin, Diana, *Publishing Women: Salons, the Presses and the Counter-Reformation in Sixteenth-century Italy* (Chicago, IL, 2007).
Romeo, Giovanni, 'Una "simulatrice di santità" a Napoli nel '500: Alfonsina Rispola', *Campania sacra* 8–9 (1977–8), 159–218.
— 'Una città, due inquisizioni: l'anomalia del Sant'Ufficio a Napoli nel tardo '500', *Rivista di storia della letteratura religiosa* 24 (1988), 42–67.
— *Inquisitori, esorcisti e streghe nell'Italia della Controriforma* (Florence, 1990).
— *L'Inquisizione nell'Italia moderna* (Bari and Rome, 2002; 3rd edn, 2006).
— *Amori proibiti. I concubini tra Chiesa e Inquisizione* (Rome and Bari, 2008).
Rothman, E. Natalie, 'Becoming Venetian: Conversion and Transformation in the Seventeenth-Century Mediterranean', *Mediterranean Historical Review* 21 (2006), 39–75.
Rotondò, Antonio, 'Carnesecchi, Pietro', *DBI* 20 (1977), 466–76.
Rowland, Ingrid D., *Giordano Bruno: Philosopher/Heretic* (New York, 2008).
Rozzo, Ugo, 'Il rogo dei libri: Appunti per una iconologia', *Libri e documenti* 12 (1986), 7–32.
— 'Italian Literature on the Index', in Fragnito (ed.), *Church, Censorship* (2001), 194–222.
Rozzo, Ugo (ed.), *La censura libraria nell'Europa del seccolo XVI* (Udine, 1997).
Ruggiero, Guido, *Binding Passions: Tales of Magic, Marriage and Power at the End of the Renaissance* (New York and Oxford, 1993).
— *Machiavelli in Love: Sex, Self and Society in the Italian Renaissance* (Baltimore, MD, 2007).
Rundine, Angelo, 'Gli inquisitori del tribunale del Santo Ufficio di Sardegna (1493–1718)', *Archivio Storico Sardo* 39 (1998), 227–63.
Russell, Camilla, *Giulia Gonzaga and the Religious Controversies of Sixteenth-Century Italy* (Turnhout, 2006).

Sacro Arsenale ouero prattica dell'officio della Santa Inqvisitione. Di nuouo corretto, et ampliato (Genoa and Perugia, 1653). [*See also* under Masini]
Sacro Arsenale ouero prattica dell'officio della Santa Inqvisitione. Nuouamente corretto, ed ampliato (Bologna, 1665).
Sangalli, Maurizio (ed.), *Per il cinquecento religioso italiano. Clero cultura società. Att. del Convegno internazionali di studi, Siena, 27–30 giugno 2001, Introduzione di Adriano Prosperi*, 2 vols (Rome, 2003).
Sanudo, Marin, *I Diarii*, 58 vols (Venice, 1879–1903).
Sarpi, Paolo, 'Sopra l'Officio dell'Inquisizione', in *Scritti giurisdizionalistici*, ed. G. Gambarin (Bari, 1958), 119–212.
— *Opere*, ed. Gaetano and Luisa Cozzi (Milan and Naples, 1969), esp. for 'In materia di crear novo inquisitor di Venezia. 29 ottobre 1622', 1,198–1,211.
Sarra Di Bert, Mariangela. 'Distribuzione statistica dei dati processuali dell'Inquisizione in Friuli dal 1557 al 1786. Tecniche di ricerca e risultati', *Metodi e ricerche* 7/1 (1988), 5–31.
Savelli, Rodolfo, 'The Censoring of Law Books', in Fragnito (ed.), *Church, Censorship* (2001), 223–53.
Sbriccoli, Mario, 'Fonti giudiziarie e fonti giuridiche. Riflessioni sulla fase attuale degli studi di storia del crimine e della giustizia criminale', *Studi Storici* 29 (1988), 491–501.
Scaduto, Mario, 'Tra inquisitori e riformati: le missioni dei Gesuiti tra i Valdesi della Calabria e delle Puglie. Con un carteggio inedito del Card. Alessandrino (S. Pio V) 1561-1566,' *Archivum Historicum Societatis Iesu* 15 (1946), 1–76.
Scaramella, Pierroberto, 'Inquisizione, eresia e poteri feudali nel Viceregno napoletana alla metà del cinquecento', in Sangalli (ed.), *Per il cinquecento religioso italiano* (2003), II, 513–21.
— 'Controllo e repressione ecclesiastica della poligamia a Napoli in età moderna: dalle cause matrimoniali al crimine della fede (1514–1799)', in Seidel Menchi and Quaglione (eds), *Transgressioni* (2004), 443–501.
— *Inquisizioni, eresie, etnie, dissenso religioso e giustizia ecclesiastica in Italia (secc. XVI–XVIII)* (Bari, 2005).
— 'La Riforma et le *élites* nell'Italia Centromeridionale (Napoli e Roma)', in Benedict *et al.*, *La Réforme* (2007), 283–308.
Scaramella, Pierroberto (ed.), *Le lettere della Congregazione del Sant'Ufficio ai tribunali di fede di Napoli 1563–1625* (Trieste and Naples, 2002). *Prefazione* by John Tedeschi, V–XI.
Schutte, Anne Jacobson, 'The *lettere volgari* and the Crisis of Evangelism in Italy', *Renaissance Quarterly* 28 (1975), 639–88.
— *Pier Paolo Vergerio: The Making of an Italian Reformer* (Geneva, 1977).
— 'Un inquisitore al lavoro: fra Marino da Venezia e l'Inquisizione veneziana', in *I Francescani in Europa tra riforma e controriforma* (Naples, 1987), 165–96.
— ' "Questo non è il ritratto che ho fatto io": Painters, the Inquisition, and the Shape of Sanctity in Seventeenth-Century Venice', in Peter Denley and Caroline Elam (eds), *Florence and Italy: Studies in Honour of Nicolai Rubinstein* (London, 1988), 419–31.
— 'Inquisition and Female Autobiography: The Case of Cecilia Ferrazzi', in Craig A. Monson (ed.), *The Crannied Wall: Women, Religion and the Arts in Early Modern Europe* (Ann Arbor, MI, 1992), 105–18.
— ' "Piccole donne", "grandi eroine": Santità femminile, "simulate" e "vera", nella Italia della prima età moderna', in Lucetta Scaraffia and Gabriella Zarri (eds), *Donna e fede: Santità e vita religiosa* (Rome, 1994), 277–301.
— 'I processi dell'Inquisizione veneziana nel seicento: la femminilizzazione dell'eresia', in Del Col and Paolin (eds), *L'Inquisizione romana* (2000), 159–73.
— *Aspiring Saints: Pretense of Sanctity, Inquisition and Gender in the Republic of Venice, 1618–1750* (Baltimore, MD, and London, 2001).
— 'Pretense of Holiness in Italy: Investigations and Prosecutions (1581–1876)', *Rivista di Storia e Letteratura Religiosa* 37 (2001), 299–321.
— ' "Saints" and "Witches" in Early Modern Italy', in Schutte, Thomas Kuen, Silvana Seidel Menchi (eds), *Time, Space and Women's Lives in Early Modern Europe* (Kirksville, MO, 2001), 153–64.
— 'Recent Studies of the Roman Inquisition', in Christopher Ocker *et al.* (eds), *Politics and Reformations: Histories and Reformations. Essays in Honor of Thomas A. Brady Jr.* (Leiden and Boston, MA, 2007), 91–111.
Schutte, Anne Jacobson, (ed.), *Cecilia Ferrazzi: Autobiography of an Aspiring Saint* (Chicago, IL, 1996).
Seidel Menchi, Silvana, *Erasmo in Italia 1520–1580* (Turin, 1987; reprint 2001, with 'Postilla' of 1990).
— 'Characteristics of Italian anti-clericalism', in Peter S. Dykema and Heiko A. Oberman (eds), *Anticlericalism in Late Medieval and Early Modern Europe* (Leiden, 1993), 271–81.
— 'Italy', in Bob Scribner, Roy Porter and Mikuláš Teich (eds), *The Reformation in National Context* (Cambridge, 1994), 181–201.
— 'I tribunali dell'Inquisizione in Italia: le tappe dell'esplorazione documentaria,' in Del Col and Paolin (eds), *L'Inquisizione romana* (2000), 75–85.

— 'Whether to Remove Erasmus from the Index of Forbidden Books: Debates in the Roman Curia, 1570-1610', *Erasmus of Rotterdam Society Yearbook* 20 (2000), 19-33.
— 'Origine e origini del Santo Uffizio dell'Inquisizione romana (1542-1559)', in Borromeo (ed.), *L'Inquisizione* (2003), 291-321.
— 'I giudici dell'Inquisizione romana: inquisitori e vescovi, commissari, nunzi, cardinali, papi', *Cromohs* 10 (2005), 1-7. (www.cromohs.unifi.it/11).
— 'The Inquisitor as Mediator', trans. John Jeffries Martin of her 'Inquisizione come repressione', in Delph et al. (eds), *Heresy, Culture* (2006), 173-92.
Seidel Menchi, Silvana, and Quaglione, Diego (eds), *Transgressioni. Seduzione, concubinato, adulterio, bigamia (XIV-XVIII secolo)* (Bologna, 2004).
Shank, Michael H., 'Setting the Stage: Galileo in Tuscany, the Veneto and Rome', in McMullin (ed.), *The Church and Galileo* (2005), 57-87.
Shea, William R. and Artigas, Mariano, *Galileo in Rome: The Rise and Fall of a Troublesome Genius* (Oxford and New York, 2003).
Siebenhüner, Kim, ' "M'ha mosso l'amore": bigami e inquisitori nella documentazione del Sant'Uffizio romano (secolo XVII)', in Seidel Menchi and Quaglione (eds), *Transgressioni* (2004), 503-33.
Siegmund, Stefanie B., *The Medici State and the Ghetto of Florence: The Construction of an Early Modern Jewish Community* (Stanford, CA, 2006).
Signorotto, Gianvittorio, *Inquisitori e mistici nel seicento italiano. L'eresia di Santa Pelagia* (Bologna, 1989).
Sobel, Dava, *Galileo's Daughter* (London, 1999).
Solfaroli Camillocci, Daniela, 'Le confraternite del Divino Amore. Interpretazioni storiografiche e proposte attuali di ricerca', *Rivista di storia e letteratura religiosa* 27 (1991), 315-32.
— *I Devoti della Carità. Le confraternite del Divino Amore nell'Italia del primo cinquecento* (Naples, 2002).
Solinas, Luigi, *Inquisizione Sarda nel'600 e'700. Denunce al Santo Officio* (Dolianova, 2005).
Sorgia, Giancarlo, *Studi sull'Inquisizione in Sardegna* (Sassari, 1961).
— 'Sui familiari dell'Inquisizione in Sardegna', *Studi storici e giuridici in onore di Antonio Era* (Padua, 1963), 397-406.
Speller, Jules, *Galileo's Inquisition Trial Revisited* (Frankfurt am Main and Oxford, 2008).
Sperling, Jutta Gisela, *Convents and the Body Politic in Late Renaissance Venice* (Chicago, IL, and London, 1999).
Spini, Giorgio, 'Di Nicola Gallo e di alcune infiltrazioni in Sardegna della riforma protestante', *Rinascimento* 2 (1951), 145-78.
Stango, Cristina (ed.), *Censura ecclesiastica e cultura politica in Italia tra cinquecento e seicento* (Florence, 2001).
Stephens, Walter, 'Witches Who Steal Penises: Impotence and Illusion in *Malleus Maleficarum*', *Journal of Medieval and Modern Studies* 28/3 (1998), 495-529.
Stern, Laura Ikins, *The Criminal Law System of Medieval and Renaissance Florence* (Baltimore, MD, and London, 1994).
Stow, Kenneth, *Jewish Life in Early Modern Rome* (Aldershot and Burlington, VT, 2007), esp. no. I, 'The Burning of the Talmud in 1553' (reset and updated), and no. V, 'Church, Conversion and Tradition: The Problem of Jewish Conversion in Sixteenth-Century Italy'.
Tarabotti, Arcangela, *Che le donne siano della spezie degli uomini*, ed. and introduced by Letizia Panizza (London, 1994).
— *Paternal Tyranny*, ed. Letizia Panizza (Chicago, IL, and London, 2004).
Tavuzzi, Michael, *Prierias: The Life and Works of Silvestro Mazzolini da Prierio (1456-1527)* (Durham, NC, and London, 1997).
— 'Gli inquisitori di cui fra Leandro Alberti non parla nel *De viris illustribus ordinis Praedicatorum* (1517)', in Donattini (ed.), *L'Italia dell'inquisitore* (2007), 41-50.
— *Renaissance Inquisitors: Dominican Inquisitors and Inquisitorial Districts in Northern Italy, 1474-1527* (Leiden and Boston, MA, 2007).
Tedeschi, John, 'Buzio, Giovanni', *DBI* 15(1972), 632-4.
— *The Prosecution of Heresy: Collected Studies on the Inquisition in Early Modern Italy* (Binghamton, NY, 1991). The most important essays are as follows: 1. 'Preliminary Observations of Writing a History of the Roman Inquisition'; 3. 'Inquisitorial Sources and their Uses'; 4. 'Towards a Statistical Profile of the Italian Inquisitions', with E. Monter; 5. 'The Organization and Procedures of the Roman Inquisition'; 6. 'The Roman Inquisition and Witchcraft: An Early Seventeenth-Century "Instruction" on Correct Trial Procedure'; 7. 'The Question of Magic and Witchcraft in Two Inquisitorial Manuals of the Seventeenth century'; 9. 'Florentine Documents for a History of the *Index of Prohibited Books*'; 10. 'A Sixteenth-Century Italian Erasmian and the Index'.
— 'A New Perspective on the Roman Inquisition' (1996), in Jesús Martínez de Bujanda (ed.), *Le Contrôle des Idées à la Renaissance. Actes du colloque de la FISIER tenu à Montréal en septembre 1995* (Geneva, 1996), 15-30.

— 'A New Perspective on the Roman Inquisition' (1997), in Cesare Mozzarelli and Danilo Zardin (eds), *I tempi del Concilio. Religione, cultura e società nell'Europa tridentina* (Rome, 1997), 253–69.
— 'I documenti inquisitoriali del Trinity College di Dublino provenienti dall'archivio romana del Sant'Ufficio', in Del Col and Paolin (eds), *L'Inquisizione romana* (2000), 145–68.
— 'Jews and Judaizers in the Dispersed Archives of the Roman Inquisition', in Wendehorst (ed.), *The Roman Inquisition* (2004), 177–97.
Tedeschi, John (ed.), *Italian Reformation Studies in Honor of Laelius Socinus* (Florence, 1965).
Tedeschi, John (with William Monter), 'Toward a Statistical Profile of the Italian Inquisitions, Sixteenth to Eighteenth Centuries', in Tedeschi, *Prosecution*, 89–126.
Tedeschi, John, and von Henneberg, J., 'Contra Petrum Antonium a Cervia relapsum et Bononiae concrematum', in Tedeschi (ed.) *Italian Reformation Studies in Honor of Laelius Socinus* (Florence, 1965), 243–68.
Tellechia Idígoras, Ignacio, J., *El proceso del Doctor Miguel Molinos* (Rome, 2005).
Tomizza, Fulvio, *Heavenly Supper: The Story of Maria Janis*, trans. A.J. Schutte (Chicago, IL, and London, 1991).
Valente, Michaela, '*Bloody Tribunal.* L'immagine dell'Inquisizione romana nella controversistica europea tra sei e settecento', in Peyronel Rambaldi (ed.), *I tribunali della fede* (2007), 231–43.
Van Boxel, Piet W., 'Cardinal Santoro and the Expurgation of Hebrew Literature', in Wendehorst (ed.), *Roman Inquisition* (2004), 19–34.
Vella, Andrew P., *The Tribunal of the Inquisition in Malta* (Malta, 1964).
Venturi, Franco, *Settecento riformatore* (Turin, 1969–90), esp. vol. I, *Da Muratori a Beccaria (1730–1764)* (1969); vol. II, *La Chiesa e la Repubblica dentro i loro limiti (1758–1771)* (1976); vol. V, 1 and 2, *L'Italia dei lumi, 1764–1790* (1987, 1990).
Viaro, A., 'La pena della galera: la condizione dei condannati a bordo delle galere veneziane', in Cozzi (ed.), *Stato, società* (1980), vol. 1, 379–430.
Walker, Jonathan, 'Let's Get Lost; on the Importance of Itineraries, Detours and Dead-ends', *Rethinking History* 10 (2006), 573–97.
Weaver, Elissa B. (ed.), *Arcangela Tarabotti: A Literary Nun in Baroque Venice* (Ravenna, 2006).
Wendehorst, Stephan (ed.), *The Roman Inquisition, the Index and the Jews: Contexts, Sources and the Jews* (Leiden and Boston, MA, 2004), including his 'The Roman Inquisition, the Index and the Jews: New Perpsectives for Research', 201–14.
Westfall, Richard S., *Essays on the Trial of Galileo* (Vatican City, 1989).
Wheatcroft, Andrew, *Infidels: A History of the Conflict between Christendom and Islam* (London, 2003, and 2004 rev. edn).
Wickersham, Jane, ' "He was obnoxious": Lay Denunciations and the Roman Inquisition', forthcoming article, advance reading of April 2006 version. Based on paper to the Sixteenth-Century Studies Conference, Pittsburg, PA, October 2003.
Yates, Frances A., *Giordano Bruno and the Hermetic Tradition* (London and Chicago, IL, 1964).
— *The Art of Memory* (London and Chicago, IL, 1966).
— *Renaissance and Reform: The Italian Contribution. Collected Essays* II (London and Boston, MA, 1983), ch. 10 on Giordano Bruno.
Zarri, Gabriella, *Le sante vive* (Turin, 1990).
Zarri, Gabriella (ed.), *Finzione e santità tra medioevo et età moderna* (Turin, 1991), including her ' "Vera" santità, "simulata" santità. I potesi e riscontri', 9–36.
Zeldes, Nadia, *'The Former Jews of this Kingdom': Sicilian Converts after the Expulsion, 1492–1516* (Leiden and Boston, MA, 2003).

INDEX

The Index does not list all named individuals among the accused, witnesses or minor local officials, only the most significant ones and those named more than once; some minor passing references to localities are also omitted. All named inquisitors are included. Cardinals are listed under family name, and with cross-references where they are also named from episcopal diocese (e.g., Cardinal of Pisa = Rebiba). Inquisitors were often designated by Christian name and place or origin (*da*, from, Bologna, Siena etc.), as named in their Order, even if they had a family name, but I have tried to give both family name and original city where ascertainable. Many outside the elites had no family name in this period, though they likewise might be distinguished by birth place, a characteristic, or father's first name, using '*di*' (son of). Names might be spelled differently within the same document, and I have sometimes included a variant to assist identification. Modern historians are listed if named with emphasis in the text. Capitalised 'Reformer/Reform' indicates those under strong suspicion, or convicted; lower case 'reformer' for those advocating organisational, moral and other reforms, and/or theological ideas short of condemnation. Notes like 'blasphemer', 'witch', indicate accusation, not necessarily conviction, or my acceptance of guilt!

Aaron di Rafael Francoso, Judaiser, 34
abitello, and *sanbenito*, tunics 42, 49–50, 90, 94–5, 143; *and see* Glossary
Accademia degli Segreti, Naples, 182
Adria, inquisition tribunal, 27, 36, 286 n59
Agostino Altomonte da Brissignano, friar, solicitation charges, 139
Agrippa, Cornelius, sceptic, writer on high magic, censored, 167, 168, 169
Albani, Alessandro, Cardinal, and Giannone's mis-treatment, 206
Alberti, Leandro, inquisitor (Bologna) and writer, 8–9, 13, 35, 50–1, 61
Albertini, Arnaldo, inquisitor (Sicily), 49
Albizzi, Francesco, Cardinal inquisitor, 71, 154 (on Molinos), 276 n51
Alciati, Andrea, jurist, and censorship, 165, 171
Aldrovandi, Canon Teseo, and Ulisse (botanist), and censorship, 97
Aleandro, Girolamo, Cardinal, nuncio, and inquisition, 16, 31
Alessandria, inquisition, 27, 30
Alessandrino, Cardinal, *see* Ghislieri
Alexander VII (Fabio Chigi), inquisitor, Pope 1655–67, 46

Alfabeto cristiano, by Valdés and Giulia Gonzaga, 13–14, 125
Algarotti, Francesco, Freemason, censored, 203
Alissani, bishop (probably = bishop Iacobo Galetto of Alessano), 26, 270 n27
Allen, Walter, Cardinal, amending the Talmud, 178
Ambrogi, (Paolo) Antonio, inquisitor (Florence), and Freemasons, 206
Alois, Giovanni Francesco, Valdesian, 44–5
Alonso, de Hojeda, and Spanish Inquisition, 10
Alumbrados, Spanish mystics, 13, 131–2, 136, 154; *see* Glossary
Alvarez, Juan de Toledo, Cardinal and inquisition, 17, 20, 22, 23
Anabaptism and Anabaptists, 9, 35, 44, 61, 75–7, 98–9, 132, 134, 277 n64
Ancona, 142, 176, 226; inquisition, 26, 27, 29, 104–9, 111–13, 115, 120, 135–6 (executions), 137, 146–7, 150, 226–7, 255, 256
Andrea Nunciata (alias Abram Teseo), convert, 143, 146

Andreassi, Giorgio, nuncio (Venice), 16, 31
Angelo da Faenza, inquisitor (Bologna), 116
Angelo da Venezia, Franciscan, witness, inquisitor, 31, 34
Annibale di Capua, archbishop of Naples, 118–19, 143, 182
Antoniano, Silvio, Cardinal, prefect of Index, 173
Antonio da Casale, inquisitor, 8
Antonio *marangone* (carpenter), boastful Lutheran, 31
Aquileia, Patriarchate of, 223, 271 n61; and inquisition tribunals, 36–7, 134–5, 176, 201, 242, Table A, 260–1; *see also* Concordia, Portogruaro, Udine
Archivio della Congregazione per la Dottrina della Fede [ACDF], vii, ix, xii, 101, 115, 200, 267 n1 (for Preface)
Aretino, Pietro, satirist; obscenity and censorship, 85, 165, 168, 169, 180–1, 187
Armellini, Girolamo da Faenza, inquisitor, 8
Arquer, Giovanni Antonio, necromancy, 51; Sigismondo, son, Sardinian Reformer, 51
Arrigoni, Celestino, da Verona, Capuchin, witness against Bruno, 184
Arrigoni (or Arigoni), Pompeo, Cardinal inquisitor, 79, 94, 104–6, 111, 116–17, 196
Asteo, Girolamo, inquisitor (Pordenone), 3–4
Asti, inquisition, 27
atheism and alleged atheists, 4, 134, 181, 200, 201–2, 205
auto da fé, autos, 10, 40, 48–9, 52, 89, 98, 122, 123, 128 and 130 (Carnesecchi), 132, 255, 264; *see* Glossary
Avignon, and inquisition, 27, 55, 135 (death sentences), 197

Bachaud, Francesco, nuncio in Turin, 30
Badia, Tommaso, Dominican reformer, Cardinal, 15, 16
Badoer, Giovanni, *podestà* of Brescia, 6–7
Badoer, Girolamo, denouncer, 71–2
Baldini, Gianfrancesco, Somaschian, eighteenth-century censor, 202–3
Baldino, Carlo, inquisitor, archbishop of Sorrento, 43–5, 238 (sceptical about sabbats)
Balducci (or Balduzzi), Antonio, da Forlì, inquisitor (Bologna) and *Commissario*, 91, 95, 96–7, 114–15, 116, 220, 221–2, 255
Bamji, Alexandra, historian, 249
Barbarigo, Gregorio (St) Cardinal, and 'pretend saints', 93, 157
Barberini, Antonio, Cardinal, Urban VIII's brother, 193

Barberini, Francesco, Cardinal, Urban VIII's nephew, 70, 88, 148, 234; and Galileo, 191–2, 291 n112
Barberini, Maffeo, Cardinal *see under* Urban VIII
Bariselli, Benedetto, defence lawyer, 79
Baronio, Cesare, Cardinal, historian, 162, 172
Baruch, Chaim (or Chayn Saruc), Jewish consul, on converts, 144, 228
Basenghi, Marcantonio, Bologna Reformer, and *abitello* problem, 95
Basilio da Castelluccio, priest persecuting *Valdesi*, 42
Batti, Giacomo, Venetian bookseller's trials, 196–9
beata/beato, and beatification, 53, 132; Congregation of Beati, 69; *see* Glossary;
Beccadelli, Ludovico, archbishop, nuncio (Venice), 32, 175
Beccaria, Cesare, against torture and capital punishment, 88, 202, 204
Bellarmino, Roberto, Cardinal inquisitor, 158, 162, 177, 178, 181, 185; and Giordano Bruno, 184–5; and Galileo, 187–9, 195
Belluno, inquisition, 36, 71, 169, 194
Bembo, Pietro, Cardinal and writer, 15
benandanti ('Night Battlers'), 79, 238, 241–4, 296 n33; *and see* sabbats
Benedetto del Borgo (or d'Asolo), executed Anabaptist, 61, 98–9
Benedict XIV (Prospero Lambertini), Pope 1740–58, 201–2
Beneficio di Cristo, condemned best-seller, 9, 14, 44, 89, 124, 129, 130, 159, 227–8, 272 n85
Beretta, Francesco, historian, 53–4
Bergamo, 13, 15, 22–3, 28, 66–7, 125, 155, 160; inquisition, 8, 27, 36, 37, 100, 109, 137, 156
Bernardino da Feltre, Franciscan, burns the Talmud, 177
Bernardino de Grossis, inquisitor (Brescia), harshness against witches, 238
Bernardo da Como, on torture, 83
Bertano, Pietro, Cardinal, 124
Bertinoro, bishopric and inquisition, 28
Besançon, 27; bookmen from, in Italy, evading censorship, 205
Betti, Bartolomeo, trial mishandled, 93–4
Bible in vernacular, and suppression, 3, 12, 31, 133, 158, 162–3, 164–9, 175–7, 178, 193, 202 (rules relaxed 1758), 229–30 (Polish version)
Bibone, Fra Felice, and love magic, tortured, 84, 251 (and Paolina de Rossi)

bigamy, 49, 105, 106, 118, 130
bishops' and their vicars' relations with
  inquisitors, 3, 7, 8, 11, 13–15, 16, 18, 19, 20,
  20–1 (arrest of bishops), 22, 24, 27, 42–5
  (in Kingdom of Naples), 46 (Malta), 48–52
  (Sicily and Sardinia), 53, 54, 56, 62–3, 73
  (Carlo Borromeo), 74–5 (confession
  issues), 82, 96 (Balducci and Paleotti), 102,
  104, 107–8 (Masini), 110 (violent conflict),
  111–13 (Ancona inquisitors' problems),
  113–15 (cooperation), 120–1 (over
  confraternities), 148–9 (Mantua example),
  232, 235, 238 (Gostanza case), 246, 256,
  258; handling Index and censorship,
  159–64, 166–7, 173, 194
blasphemy, 49, 70, 105, 107, 110, 131, 132–3,
  136–8, 177, 213, 220 (family
  denunciation), 251, 284 n16 (on sexual
  terminology)
Bobadilla, Nicolàs, Jesuit, and *Valdesi*, 42, 74
Boccaccio's works censored, 162, 165, 168,
  171–2, 258
Bodin, Jean, political theorist, censorship,
  164, 168
Bologna, 5, 9, 15, 16, 23, 109, 115, 142, 169;
  inquisitors, investigations and trials, 8–9,
  13, 20, 25, 27–8, 55, 59, 76, 79, 82, 84, 91,
  93–4, 94–5 (*abitello*), 104, 117, 119, 135
  (death sentences), 137, 155, 165, 167, 170,
  196, 205, 215, 220–1 (Panzacchi case),
  246, 251–2 (love magic), 253–4 (sorcery),
  255; *and see* Balducci
Bonforno, Erffrim (or Ephraim), Jew involved
  in Collarina case, 210
Bonomo, Pietro, episcopal reformer, 17
book-burning, 13, 103, 158, 160–1, 166–7
  (Naples display), 168–9, 176, 177–8
  (Jewish books), 179, 196, 201, 202, 203;
  illustrations of, 169
Borelli, Giovanni Alfonso, 'Galileian', evades
  censorship, 194
Borghese, Camillo, Cardinal inquisitor, 118;
  and see Paul V
Borghese, Scipione, Cardinal, 117
Borgia, Gasparo, Cardinal inquisitor, 192
Borri, Francesco Giuseppe, physician,
  Pelaginian, 155
Borromeo, Agostino, historian, 20
Borromeo, Carlo (St), Cardinal archbishop of
  Milan, 30, 38–9, 73, 101, 179, 259; and
  witchcraft, 39, 259
Bowd, Stephen, historian, xii, 235, 269 n36
Boxel, Piet van, historian, 178
Bracciolini, Poggio, his *Facezie* censored, 165
Brasi, Augusto, Master of Sacred Palace, 162

Brembati, Achille, ambassador, 37
Brescia, 6–8, 15, 154, 156, 177; inquisition,
  6–8, 27, 36, 235, 237–8 (Val Camonica
  witches' games)
Brucioli, Antonio, Bible translator, 12, 163,
  175, 180
Brucioli, Francesco, publisher, 163
Brugnaleschi, Valeria, sorcery, pro-Jews,
  143, 236
Brugnatelli, Giovanni Battista, apostolic vicar-
  general, 37
Bruno, Giordano, burned heretic, 91, 181,
  182–6, 189, 191–2, 207, 223, 255, 257,
  289 n80
Bucer, Martin, and influence, 15, 128
Buoncompagni, Giacomo, Duke of Sora,
  mediating censorship, 167
Burkardt, Albrecht, historian, 111
Burnet, Thomas, works censored, 202–3
Busi, Nicolo, blasphemer, 137
Buzio, Giovanni da Montalcino, trials and
  execution, 16, 23, 88

Cacatossici, Giorgio da Casale, inquisitor and
  writer, 8
Cacciarda, Lucia, burned witch, 8
Caccini, Tommaso, Dominican against
  Galileo, 187–8, 193
Cagliari, archbishop of, on Sicilians, 121
Cagliari, Sardinian inquisition centre, 50–1;
  and reform groups, 51–2
Calabria, and Campanella, 186; Valdesians,
  45; Waldensians, 15, 43, 74–5
Calandra, Endimio, follower of Siculo,
  109, 130
Calbetti, Arcangelo, inquisitor, 108–9,
  111–13
Calepin, Girolamo, Venetian printer, 172
Calvin and Calvinists, 9, 13–15, 18, 28, 29, 31,
  38, 41, 44, 49, 51–2, 57, 98–9, 128–9, 132,
  134, 137 (prayer to), 141, 152, 153
Calvo, Diego, inquisitor (Sardinia), 51
Cameron, Euan, historian, 43
Campanella, Tomasso, philosopher, trials, and
  torture, 79, 84, 186, 191, 207, 230
Campeggi, Camillo, inquisitor (Ferrara),
  102–3, 280 n2
Canal, Cristoforo, blasphemer, 33
Canale, Antonio da, Venetian *assistente*, 32,
  198–9
Canons Regular of San Salvatore, Bologna,
  and heterodox groups, 97
Canopolo, Antonio, archbishop of Oristano
  (Sardinia), challenges inquisition powers,
  50, 52

Canossa, Gasparre, escaping Reformer, 91
Cantimori, Delio, historian, vii
Capece, Girolamo, Benedictine, Erasmian, 76–7, 277 n65
Capiferro, Francisco, secretary to Index Congregation, and his *Elenchus*, 163
Capodistria (or Capo d'Istria), 20, 27, 36
Caponetto, Salvatore, historian, 99
Capponi, Giovanni Battista, and prohibited books, tortured, 80–1, 85, 143–4 (pro-Jews)
Capua and heresy problems, 15, 43
Capuano, Alvise, on dissimulation, 215
Caracciolo, Domenico, marchese of Villamarino, Viceroy of Sicily, 50, 54
Caracciolo, Galeazzo, marchese di Vico, reformer, 15, 93, 129
Carafa, Beatrice, defender of *Valdesi*, 45
Carafa, Francesco, nuncio (Venice), 33
Carafa, Gian Pietro, Cardinal and Pope Paul IV (1555–9), viii, 11, 12, 14, 16, 18, 19, 39, 224, 255, 293 n11; *see* Paul IV
Carafa, Mario, archbishop of Naples, 182
Caravia, Alessandro, goldsmith, poet and reformer, 15
Carena, Cesare, manual writer, 70–1, 78, 82, 86, 204
Carlo Emanuele III of Savoy, anti-Papacy, and Giannone, 205–6
Carnesecchi, Pietro, burned heretic, 22, 44, 68, 87, 89, 122, 123–30, 214, 223, 224, 255, 257
Carpegna, Giulio, inquisitor (Malta), 55
Casale Monferrato, 207; inquisition tribunal, 27, 89, 110–11
Casani, Alessio da Fivizzano, Augustinian, Lutheran suspect, 16
Caserta, and Valdesian group, 14, 44–5, 282 n62 (bishop)
Casolo, Giacomo Filippo, and Pelagianism, 154–5
Castenario, Ambrogio, smith, against death sentences for faith, 91
Castiglione, Baldesar, his *The Courtier* and censorship, 77, 165–6, 171, 258
Castro, Alfonso de, writer on heresy, 69–70
Cataneo, Rocco, nuncio's auditor (Venice), 33, 214–15
Cateau Cambrésis, Treaty of (1559), 11, 12, 30, 38, Map 1
Cathars, 2, 4, 30, 256
Cavra, Bartolomeo, painter, images of condemned, 103
Ceneda, inquisition, 27, 36

censorship, 30, 34, 35, 48, 52, 54–5, 65, 100, 107, 115, 158–207, 258–9; *see also* Index; Master of the Sacred Palace
Centelles, Gaspar, executed 'Lutheran', 51–2
Cento, 114–15, 137–8, 220–1; and Santa Croce confraternity, 119–20
Cervera, Mateo, inquisitor, 48–9
Cervini, Marcello, Cardinal inquisitor, and Pope 1555, 20
Cesena, bishopric and inquisition, 28, 115
Chanforan, and Waldensians, 15
Charles Bourbon, King of Naples, 50
Charles V, Holy Roman Emperor, and earlier King Charles I in Spain, 32, 38, 45, 48–9, 132
Charles VI (Habsburg Emperor), 52
Cheevers, Sara, prisoner of Maltese inquisition, 48
Cherubino Arcangelo d'Urbino, Dominican, on prevalence of blasphemy, 138
Chiari, Isidoro, Benedictine reformer, 12
Chiarini, Giovanni Battista, inquisitor (Cremona), 109–10, 281 n28
Chiavello, Carlo, multiple heresy, galley sentence, 92
Ciampoli, Giovanni, papal secretary, pro-Galileo, 174, 190
Ciappara, Frans, historian, xii, 46, 47, 151, 273 n89
Ciccarelli, Antonio, theologian, and literary censorship, 171
Cid, Nicola, bribing gaolers, 39–40
Ciocchi del Monte, Cardinal, *see* Julius III
circumcision, problems over, 141, 145–8, 150, 152–3
Cisneros, Francisco Jiménez de, Cardinal Inquisitor General, 48–9
Cividale, inquisition, 27, 36–7, 230
Clario, Giovanni Battista, and son, Friulian physicians, condemned Lutherans, 229–30
Clement VII (Giulio de'Medici), Pope 1523–34, 16, 123
Clement VIII (Ippolito Aldobrandini), Pope 1592–1605, 24, 52, 158, 230; and 1596 Index, 160–1, 163, 165, 175; and Bruno's sentence, 185
Clement XI (Francesco Albani), Pope 1700–21, 166
Clement XII (Lorenzo Corsini), Pope 1730–40, 50, 206 (attacks Freemasonry)
Clement XIII (Carlo Rezzonico), Pope 1758–69, 204
Clozio, Bonaventura, da Casalmaggiore, Franciscan, acquitted, 34

Coen, Giacob, Jewish convert to Christianity via inquisition, 147
Collarina, Cristina, witchcraft case, 71–2, 148, 210–12, 255
Colonna, Ascanio, noble reformer, 15
Colonna, Marcantonio, Cardinal, and Index, 176–7, 178
Colonna, Marco Antonio, prince of Tagliacozzo, Viceroy of Sicily, 121
Colonna, Marietta, healer, 297 n47
Colonna, Vittoria, poet and reformer, 14, 15
Como, and inquisitors, 6, 23, 27, 38, 55, 109, 111, 119, 193
Concini, Bartolomeo, Medicean agent in Rome, 127
Concordia, inquisition, 27, 36, 63, 98, 134, 135, 241; *and see* Aquileia
confessions and confessors, 72–8
confraternities, 144, 147, 175; and Inquisition, 103, 114, 119–22, 147; and catechumens, 142, 147, 152; and Janis, 156
Congregations, at centre of papal government, 20, 24, 161; *see under* Index, Inquisition
Consorti, Massimo de', boastful Lutheran, 225–6
Constantini, Niccolò, inquisitor, 6
consultants, and inquisition reports, 26, 45, 57–8, 59, 69, 76, 79–80, 82, 83, 93, 100, 117, 140, 173, 174, 184, 224; on Galileo's writings, 188–9, 190–1; on eighteenth-century books, 202–4
Contarini, Gasparo, Cardinal, reformer, xv, 1, 12
Contarini, Giulio di Zorzi, Venetian *assistente*, 33, 271 n47
Conti, Carlo, Cardinal bishop of Ancona, 104–6, 112
conversos, 10, 13, 48–9, 50, 132, 136, 142, 154; *and see* Judaisers
Copernicus and Copernican theory, 163, 174, 181, 184–5, 188–94 (and Galileo)
Corner, Carlo, Venetian reformer, 129
Cortese, Gregorio, Benedictine reformer, 12, 15
Cosenza, 181; and Waldensians, 42, 43
Cosimo I de'Medici, Duke, then Grand Duke of Tuscany, 29, 128–9, 169
Cospi, Antonio Maria, Florentine judge, and witch stereotype, 233
Costabili, Paolo, inquisitor (Ferrara), Master of the Sacred Palace, and Boccaccio, 171–2, 176
Costacciaro, *see* Dionigi da
Crema, 8, 142, 170; and inquisitors, 8, 27, 36, 55, 111

Cremona, 178, 205; inquisition, 8, 40, 70, 109, 119, 121, 152
Cremona, Gian Franco, inquisitor (Milan), 55
Cremonini, Cesare, philosopher, 134, 187, 200, 290 n95
Crocesignati, confraternities supporting inquisition, 100, 119–21
Crosta, Girolamo, da Osimo, pursued anti-papalist, 107, 108
Crudeli, Tommaso, Freemason, 203, 206–7
Cubelles, Domenico, bishop and inquisitor, 46–7
Curione, Celio Secondo, Calvinist, 21, 40, 213–14

Da Canal, Marcantonio, Venetian reformer, 129
Dall'Occhio, Antonio, inquisitor (Aquileia), 201
Da Ponte, Andrea, Venetian reformer, 129
D'Ávalos, Alfonso, Governor of Milan, 38
Davidson, Nicholas, historian, xii, 66
death sentences, figures, 48, 89, 135–6; Table D, 264
De Boer, Wietse, historian, 73
defence and defence lawyers, 26, 33, 58–9, 66, 78–81, 82–3, 117, 123–4, 139, 145, 243, 254
Defoe, Daniel, books censored and burned, 201
De La Cruz, Isabel, *beata*, 132
Del Col, Adriano, historian, xii, 37, 63, 65, 134, 135, 155, 162–3
Della Casa, Giovanni, nuncio (Venice) and writer, 32, 35, 77, 213
Della Porta, Giambattista, polymath, varied treatment by censors, 182
Delpiano, Patrizia, historian, 200–1
Descartes, Renée, philosopher, on Galileo condemnation, 192, 193
De Vos, Maerten, painter, illustrates book-burning, 163
di Capua, *see* Annibale di Capua, Pietro Antonio di Capua
Diego Garcia de Trasmiera, inquisitor (Sicily), and night-flyers, 244
Diodati, Giovanni, and Calvinist Bible, 176
Dionigi, Bartolomeo, da Fano, biblical *Compendio* banned, 175
Dionigi da Costacciaro, inquisitor (Florence), and Gostanza case, 209, 239–40, 255
Dionisio Gallo, heretical prophetic preacher, 26, 60, 223, 257
dissimulation, 76–7, 212–17, 219, 227, 259; *see* Nicodemism
Ditchfield, Simon, historian, viii, xii, 129

Domenichi, Lodovico, poet, investigated, 29
Domenico Gerosolominato (formerly Shmuel Vivas), expurgating Jewish texts, 178
Dominicans (Order of Preachers), roles as inquisitors and censors, 3, 4, 5–9, 10–11, 12, 21–2, 25, 28, 29, 35, 42, 59, 74, 102–4, 110, 119, 159, 172, 231, 256; and Galileo, 181, 187–8
Dominico Longino, and anti-papal song, 140
Donà, Francesco, Doge of Venice, 31–2
Donati, Sigismundo, nuncio (Venice), 243
Donato de Quarto, magic for syphilitic cure, 246
Donzellini, Girolamo, physician and book trader, executed, 180
Dotti, Gaspare, inquisitor, 22
Druda, Andrea, blaspheming canon, 138
Dumoulin (or Du Moulin), Charles, anti-papal work and censorship, 166
Duzina (or Dusina), Pietro, inquisitor, 47

Egidi, Clemente, inquisitor (Florence), and Galileo's *Dialogue*, 175, 193
Elisabetta Todesca, multi-talented witch (*strega*), 250–1
Emanuele Filiberto, Prince of Savoy, 30
Encyclopédie, censored, 204
English Protestants in Italy, 48, 106, 132, 207; Table D, 264
Episcopi canon, and night-flying, 232–3
Erasmus's works and Erasmians, viii, 12–13, 15, 17, 34, 51–2, 98, 116, 131–2, 259; censorship and evasion, 160–1, 163, 167, 172, 180, 183
Erba, Caterina, magical practices, and her court ploy, 216, 250
Ercolani, Astorre and Nicolò, Bolognese Valdesians, 96
Errera, Andrea, historian, 70
Este, Ercole d', Duke of Ferrara, 102
Evans, Katherine, prisoner of Maltese inquisition, 48
executions, 28, 44, 49, 51–2, 86, 88–90, 98–9, 103, 104, 114–15, 128 (Carnesecchi), 132, 135–6 (statistics), 136 (non-Italian comparisons), 180 (bookmen), 184–5 (Bruno), 185–6 (Pucci), 187, 222; *and see* death sentences
exorcism, 156, 157, 241–3, 245
Eymeric, Nicholas, medieval manual writer, 68–9, 71, 87, 234, 245, 277 n69; *see also* Peña

Facchinetti, Giovanni Antonio, nuncio (Venice), 33, 91–2

Faenza, 99; inquisition, 27–8, 99, 119, 121, 130, 193
fama (reputation) and gossip, 2, 224–30, 240
familiari (familiars), 47, 49–50, 52, 57, 99–100, 102, 121–2, 258
Fanini, Fanino da Faenza, Calvinist, executed, 28, 98–9
Farinacci, Prospero, writer on heresy, 71
Felicin, Ercole, Bologna priest, love magic, 251
Felipe de Nis, *see* Nis
Feltre, inquisition office, 36
Ferdinand II, as King of Aragon, Sicily and Sardinia, but V of Castile, viii–ix, 9–10, 48
Ferdinand III, King of Sicily, abolishes Inquisition, 50
Fermo, inquisition, 27, 101
Ferrara, 142, 145, 148, 182; inquisition, 27, 102–3, 115, 117, 135, 193, 214, 221, 250
Ferrari, Giulio da Cremona, inquisitor, 39
Ferrazzi, Cecilia, condemned *affettata santa*, 93, 156–7
Figino, Giacomo, inquisitor (Casale), 110–11
Filomella, Paolo da Venezia, inquisitor (Venice), 16, 31
Filonardi, Marcello, and opposition to vernacular Bibles, 164
Finocchiaro, Maurice, historian, 82–3
Fioretti della Bibbia, censorship problems, 175–7
Firpo, Massimo, historian, viii, 126
Flaminio, Marcantonio, Reform writer, 9, 12, 14, 44, 124, 129
Florence, i, ii, 12, 32 (nuncio), 123, 129, 165; Ghetto and Jews, 142–3, 148; inquisitors, 16, 27, 29, 78, 86–7, 110, 119, 141, 233; and censorship, 169, 170–2, 175; and Crudeli, Freemasons, 203, 206–7; and Galileo, 174–5, 187–93; and Gostanza case, 209–10, 238–41; and healing magic, 246–8
Florio, *see* Tissano
Folengo, Teofilo, Benedictine reformer, 12
Fondi, centre for Valdesians, 45
Fontantini, Benedetto da Mantova, and *Beneficio di Cristo*, 14
Fonzio, Bartolomeo, Reformer, strangled, 90–1
Forlí, bishopric and inquisition, 28
Forniti, canon in Rocca Contrada, problem of young female penitent, 226–7
foro esterno and *foro interno* (*see* Glossary), 20, 62, 73–4, 75–6, 176
Forteguerri, Niccolò, Cardinal, his poem *Ricciardelli* best-seller after Indexed, 204
Foscarari, Egidio, bishop (Modena), inquisitor and book censor, 22, 113, 125, 159–60, 227–8

Foscarini, Paolo Antonio, Carmelite, defender of Copernicanism, 188–9
Fragnito, Gigliola, historian, 162
Franciscans, as inquisitors and helpers, 3, 5, 29, 35, 206
Franco, Niccolò, libellous writer, tortured, 85–6; censored, 165, 180
Franco, Veronica, poet, 165
Freemasons, attacked, 203, 206–7, 293 n161
Frezza, Antonio, bigamist, tortured, 82
Frigimelica, Francesco Antonio, da Padova, inquisitor (Belluno), 71
Friuli, tribunals and case characteristics, 36–7, 134, 139, 147, 150–1, 176, 180, 184, 235–6, *and see* Table A, 260–1; and *benandanti*, 238, 241–3; magic and bullets, 236; *see also* Aquileia, Concordia, Portogruaro, Spilimbergo, Udine

Gaiano, Paolo, evangelical, Nicodemist, 227–8
Galeota (or Galeotta), Mario, Valdesian, 23, 25, 26, 130, 255, 257
Galilei, Galileo, 59, 82–3, 88, 92, 134, 158–9, 170, 174–5 (licensing the *Dialogue*), 181, 183, 185, 186–94 (main investigations and trial), 201–3, 207, 255, 258
Gallicciolo, Bassano, inquisitor (Mantua), 68, 148–9, 228
Gallo, *see* Dionisio Gallo
Gallo, Antonio Maria, bishop of Osimo, 111
Gallo de Iglesias, Giovanni and Nicolo, Sardinian Calvinists, 51–2
Gambara, Gian Francesco, Cardinal inquisitor, 25–6, 126
Garofolo, Gabriele, Bologna priest, magic to unbind penises, 252
Garzoni, Tomaso, writer, inquisition helper?, 70, 78, 277 n71
Gasparutto, Paolo, *benandante*, 242
Gazzani, Marcantonio, Bologna painter, anti-Trinitarian, 91
Gei, Bartolomeo from Cadoro, Venetian bookman, 181
Gelusio, Pietro, Dominican, Zwingli influenced, 77, 257
Gemma, Aurora, accused of Lutheranism (with husband Marco da Domo), Polish connections, 229–30; Zuan Battista Gemma, first husband, physician, evangelical, 229–30
Geneva, influences, exile refuge, 14, 15, 30, 31, 38, 39, 41, 44, 52, 98–9, 129, 133, 136,180, 183, 205–6

Genoa, Divine Love Oratory, 1, 12; inquisition, 6, 27, 55, 70, 104, 168–9, 207; Triora trial, 241
Genovesi, Antonio, political economist, co-operates with censor, 202
Gentileschi, Artemisia, painter, 84 (tortured), 193 (and Galileo)
Geremia da Trepide, Augustinian Reformer, 16
Geremia da Udine, inquisitor (Siena), 160
Gesualdo, Alfonso, archbishop of Naples, and censorship, 165
Ghislieri, Michele, inquisitor, Cardinal ('Alessandrino'), and Pope Pius V (1565–72), viii, 17, 22–3, 28, 30, 43–4, 67, 74–5 (against Waldensians), 54, 115, 118, 125, 130, 169, 256; *see also* Pius V
Giannone, Pietro, excommunicated for anti-clerical writings, 205–6
Giantis, Elisabetta, love magic, 209–10
Giglia di Fino, tertiary nun, 'living saint'?, 155, 250
Ginzburg, Carlo, historian, x, 3, 241–3
Giorgio da Tira [Tyre], bigamist, 105–6
Giovan Domenico di Giovanni (alias Gran Turco), 119
Giovanni, a Croat, as a 'Turk', reconverts, 152–3
Giovanni Antonio da Foiano, inquisitor (Bologna), 116
Giovanni Maria da Bologna, inquisitor (Ancona), 109, 114, 226–7
Giovanni Paolo da Cremona, inquisitor (Ancona), 111
Giovio, Paolo, writer, 9
Girello, Geronimo, inquisitor (Padua), 76
Girolamo da Lodi, inquisitor (Brescia) and apostolic *commissario*, 6–7, 28
Giulia di Marco, Neapolitan, spirituality and sexuality, 156
Giulio della Rovere (or Giulio da Milano), Augustinian, and Lutheranism, 16, 18, 31
Giuseppe da Orzinuovo, Brescian, on Val Camonica witches, 237
Giustiniani, Marc'Antonio, and son Antonio, publish Hebrew books, 177
Giustiniani, Paolo and Tommaso, calling for reforms, 1, 12–13
Godman, Peter, historian, 158, 289 n88
Goito (Mantua), Crocesignati confraternity, 121
Gonzaga, Eleonora, reform supporter, 15
Gonzaga, Ercole, reforming bishop and cardinal, 14, 17, 109, 113
Gonzaga, Ferrante, Governor of Milan, mixed attitudes to inquisitors, 109, 214

Gonzaga, Giulia, and promotion of Valdés, 13, 15, 44–5, 76, 89, 124, 125, 139, 293n11; and Carnesecchi, 124–30, 214–15
Gorani, Giuseppe, his *Il Vero dispotismo* condemned, 202
gossip, *see fama*
Gostanza (Libbiano) da San Miniato, accused witch, 58, 67, 80, 82, 209–10, 238–41 (the Great Devil story), 248 (healer), 255
Goya, painter of inquisition scenes, vii, 94, 279 n136
Grassi, Orazio, Jesuit mathematician, and Galileo's *Assayer*, 189
Greco, Orazio, bishop of Lesina, against Valdesi, 42
Greeks, and Greek, 66, 67, 214–15; value of language and associated skills, and magic, 249, 251, 297 n47; Greek Orthodoxy, 31, 77, 141, 150, 152–3, 215, 217
Gregory XIII (Ugo Buoncompagni), Pope 1572–85, 45, 151, 167, 223
Gregory, Brad, historian, 89–90
Griani d'Urcisioni, Aurelio, rescues Ghislieri from attack, 109
Grimani, Giovanni, Cardinal, 14, 17, 23, 37
Grimani, Girolamo di Marin, Venetian *assistente*, 33
Grisons, and heretics, 16, 38–9, 51, 76
Guanzelli, Giovanni Maria, 'bungler' as censor, 161
Guardia, Waldensian centre, and massacre, 43
Guastavillani, Girolamo, Bolognese Valdesian, 85
Guazzo, Francesco, *Compendium maleficarum*, devil and illness, 250
Guazzo, Stefano, his *Civil Conversation*, 77
Gubbio, inquisition, 27
Guidiccioni, Bartolomeo, Cardinal and inquisition, 16
Guiscardi (or Viscardi), Traiano, grand chancellor of Casale, suspect heretic, 110–11

Henri of Navarre, Henri IV of France, Italian admirers of, 182–3 (Bruno), 186 (Pucci)
Heremio de Tripedibus, Sicilian Lutheran, executed, 132
heresy, types and degrees of, 2–3, 54, 88, 134, 140, 161–2
Holy Office, *see* Inquisition Congregation
Huizinga, Johan, *Homo Ludens*, 237

Imola, inquisition tribunal and bishop, 27, 28, 61, 119

Imperiolo (Pyrrho), bishop of Iesi, opposes Ancona inquisitor, 112–13
Impoccio, Angelo, Capuchin, pro-Infidels, 166–7
Inchofer, Melchior, Jesuit mathematician, on Galileo's *Dialogue*, 191
Incogniti, Academy of, Venice, 196–7; *see* Loredan
Index, Congregation of, 20, 25, 43, 53, 59, 115, 158–64, 169–72, 181–2, 189, 191, 195, 202, 204
Indexes of Prohibited Books, 71, 158–78; correction and expurgation problems, 169–78, 177–8 (Jewish texts); confronting the Enlightenment, 200–5; 1559 Index ('Pauline'), 125, 162–3, 165, 169, 172, 175; 1564 Index ('Tridentine'), 160–3, 172, 178; 1596 Index ('Clementine'), 158, 163, 165–6, 168–70, 175, 178; 1758 Index, 202; 1786 Index, 169
Infelise, Mario, historian, 162
Innocent VIII (Giovanni Battista Cybò), Pope 1484–92, 1487 Bull and censorship, 159
Innocent XII (Antonio Pignatelli), inquisitor, Pope 1691–1700, 46
inquisitio, defined, 1–4
inquisition archives and records, vii, ix, xii, 36, 46, 53, 55, 56, 65–8, 97, 107, 116, 120
Inquisition, Congregation of (or Holy Office), development of, 5, 19–26 (main structures), 45, 115, 150–1 (policy on Islamic apostasies), 160–2 (censorship), 202 (on book-burning in eighteenth century), 233–4 (attitudes to witchcraft); *and see key cases* Bruno, Campanella, Carnesecchi, Galeota, Galileo, Mocenigo, Pucci; general instructions, and links with tribunals, 5, 29, 35, 37, 45, 53, 59, 68, 73–4, 78–9, 81, 87, 83–4, 94–5, 98–9 (death sentences), 104–13 (dealing with Ancona), 114, 115–19 (especially dealing with Bologna and Naples), 149–51, 156, 157, 184, 187, 206, 233 (Florence's panic over witchcraft), 241 (curbing Genoese witch-hunt); *and see leading corresponding cardinals* Arrigoni, Millini, Rebiba, Santoro; some specific meetings of Congregation, 22–6, 80, 162–3, 190, 192
inquisition, conversions via, 26, 141, 143, 149–50 (general); 57, 141 (from Calvinism); 57, 66, 149–53 (from Islam); 141–2, 147 (from Judaism); 141 (from Lutheranism); 77, 152 (from Greek Orthodoxy)

inquisition, finances, 52, 95–6, 101, 102–4
inquisition, local tribunals, list of, 27 (from which see indexed places); and closures, 47–8, 50, 52, 54–5
inquisition, manuals, 56, 64, 67, 68–71, 78, 81–2, 83, 87, 113–14, 149, 151, 204, 208–9, 233–5
Inquisition, Spanish, vii–ix, 9–11, 52–3, 75, 114, 131–2, 136 (statistics); and censorship, 159, 160; *and see* Sardinia, Sicily
inquisition style (*stilo*), 53–4, 75, 79, 82, 186, 256, 289 n86
inquisitors assaulted, threatened, 28, 38, 109–11, 121–2
interpreters and court translators, 48, 65–6, 218–19
Iolanda, Duchess of Savoy, 6
Iseppo Bon, Giacomo Fransoso (alias Moses Israel and Francesco Maria Leoncini), multiple conversions, 142–3
Istriani, Domenico, da Pesaro, inquisitor (Bologna), on censorship problems, 168
Iuiririch, Giorgio, from Bosnia, negotiated conversion story, 217–18

Janis, Maria, 'living saint'?, 155–7, 255
Jews, 7, 10–11, 26, 29, 31, 33, 46, 48, 50, 63, 103, 106, 131–2, 142–3 (Ghettos), 177–8 (Jewish books destroyed or censored); close relationships with Christians, 63, 68, 71, 72, 85, 141–9, 210–12; admiration for, 89, 143–4; *and see* Judaisers
Judaisers, and *conversos*, 6, 10, 13, 33, 34, 42–3, 47, 48–9, 50, 89, 118, 131–2, 135–6, 141–7, 186
Julius III (Ciocchi del Monte), cardinal, Pope 1550–55, 21, 22–3 (hostility to Carafa), 61

Kramer, Heinrich (alias Institoris), 6, 233, 252; *see Malleus Maleficarum*

Lando, Ortensio, Erasmian, utopian, executed, 98–9
Lauerio, Dionisio, Cardinal and inquisition, 16
Laven, Mary, historian, 245
Lazzeri, Pietro, Jesuit, librarian, consultant to Index, 202
Lea, Henry, historian, 49, 232
Lecco (Lombardy), heretics, 100–1; witchcraft, 39
Leni, Matteo, printer in Venice, denounces Valvasense, 197, 199
Leo X (Giovanni de' Medici), Pope 1513–21, and censorship, 159

Leona, Angela, Judaiser, 118
Licet ab initio, foundation Bull for Inquisition, 16–17, 19–20
Limborch, Phillipp van, *Historia Inquisitionis* (1692) and illustrations, 94, 275 n22, 279 n137
Lippi, Cesare, professor, inquisitorial vicar (Florence), pro-Galileo, 187
Lippomano, Alvise, bishop (Bergamo), 37
'Living saints', 'pretend saints' and *Perfetti*, x, 93, 153–7, 224, 250
Livorno, 143, 150, 207
Llanes, inquisitor (Sicily), and night-flyers, 243–4
Locati, Umberto, inquisitor (Pavia and Piacenza), manual writer, 69, 71, 208–9
Lombardy, Duchy of (or Duchy of Milan), and inquisition, ix, 8, 10–11, 38–40, 73, 100–1, 201; see Map 3; *see also* Como, Crema, Cremona, Milan, Novara, Pavia, Tortona
Longo, Pietro, bookman, drowned, 180
Lorca, Alfonso, inquisitor (Sardinia), 51
Loredan, Bernardino, Venetian reformer, 129
Loredan, Giovanni Francesco, his Academy of Incogniti, and illegal publications, 197–200
Loredana, Bellina, prostitute, witchcraft charges, 80
Lorenzo da Bergamo, inquisitor (Cyprus), 77, 214–15
Lorini, Niccolo, Dominican against Galileo, 188
Lorraine, Duchy of, and witch-hunts, 84, 228
Lotto, Lorenzo, painter and reformer, 15, 175
love magic, 57, 67, 85, 142–3, 209–10 (Giantis case), 211, 216 (Erba case), 236, 246, 249, 250–2
Luca dell'Iadra, Dominican persecutor of *Valdesi*, 42
Lucatelli, Eustacchio, bishop, papal confessor, favours Machiavelli, 172
Lucca, Republic of, ix, 15, 17, 40–1, 61, 176, 204, 238, 240, 296 n20; independent inquisition tribunal, 19, 27, 40–1, 47, 74, 256–7
Ludovisi, Antonio, Bolognese Valdesian, and *abitello*, 95
Luis de Páramo, inquisitor (Palermo), manual writer, 69
Luther's works and 'Lutheranism', 1, 9, 11, 12–18, 21–2, 31–2, 34, 42–3, 44, 49, 51–2, 61, 68, 75–6, 76–7, 88–9, 109–10, 123, 128–9, 131–2, 140–1, 152, 153, 159, 160, 176, 183–4, 185, 214–15, 225–6, 229–30, 257–8; 134 (loose use of *luterano*), 146 (*luterano* and *marrano* confused)

Macerata, bishop of (Galeazzo Moroni), and inquisitors, 108, 111–12, 280 n21
Machiavelli's works, censored, 160, 162, 165, 168–9, 171–2, 180, 195–6
Maculano, Vincenzo, da Firenzuola, Commissary General, and Galileo compromise, 192
Madruzzo, Cristoforo, Cardinal inquisitor, 14–15, 224
magic and superstition, see Chapter 9; categories and terminology, 134, 234–5, 295 nn11 and 14; accusations, attitudes and cases, 41 (Lucca), 50–1 (Sardinia), 62, 70–1 (manuals), 80–1 (Loredana case), 85 and 233–4 (use of torture for), 132, 143, 185 (Bruno), 209–10 (Elisabetta Giantis' varied techniques), 249–50 (Elisabetta Todesca), 258; 'baptising' and signing objects, 83, 251, 253; 'binding' penises, 252; healing and harming magic, 245–9; *inghistera*, carafe, technique, 143, 236; 'measuring' cloths and clothes, 238, 248–9; rope trick (*cordella*), 211, 216, 249–51; *see also* love magic, witchcraft, and witch-hunts
Magnavacca, Marco, anti-Trinitarian, strangled, 91
Malerbi, Nicolò, Bible translator, 175
Malleus Maleficarum (Heinrich Kramer), 6, 71, 233, 236, 240, 252
Malta, ix, 27, 45–8; Inquisition in, ix, 54, 55, 69, 84, 88, 99–100 (staffing), 147, 150–1 (inter-faith problems), *and see* Table E, 265; Knights of St John, 27, 45–7
Malvicino, Valerio, Dominican pursuer of Waldensians, 43–4, 255
Manelfi, Pietro, Anabaptist, 9, 35, 61, 76, 277 n64
Manfredi, Fulgentio, anti-papal propagandist, portrait, 107
Mantua, 15, 27, 108, 113, 256; Crocesignati confraternity, 118–21; inquisition, 63, 89 (*autos*), 94–5, 104; Jewish–Christian relations, 63, 68, 147–9, 157, 228
Maracco, Giacomo, chasing heretics in Friuli, 36
Marco da Domo, accused of Lutheranism (with wife Aurora Gemma), 229
Margarita, called La Mora da Casale, alleged sorceress, resisting torture, 88
Maria Geltruda, Quietist, burned (Palermo), 155
Mariano, Splandiana, sorceress, 143, 236
Marini (or Marino), Giambattista, poet, censored, 162 (*Opera Poetica*), 197–8

Marino (Venier) da Venezia, inquisitor (Venice), 33–5, 77, 86, 215, 225–6, 255
marranos, 135–6, 142, 144, 228; *and see* Baruch, *conversos*, Judaisers
Martin, John, historian, 19
Martire, Pietro, *see* Vermigli
Masini, Eliseo, as inquisitor: in Ancona, 104–9, 137, 227, 256, 280 n7; in Genoa, book-burning, 168–9, 176; in Mantua, 149; his *Sacro Arsenale* manual, 70–1, 78, 81–4, 86, 149, 219, 228, 233–4, 256
Massarelli, Angelo, secretary to Council, 21
Master of the Sacred Palace, Rome (*Maestro del Sacro Palazzo*), and censorship, 5, 17, 20, 22, 24, 26, 53, 62, 159–60, 161–2, 164, 171–2, 174, 176, 178, 188, 196, 202, 204–5
Mattei, Francesco, blasphemer, 137
Mazza, Tomasso, inquisitor (Bologna), astrology case, 253–4
Mazzolini, Silvestro da Prierio (Prieras), manual writer, 6, 7, 9, 159
Medici, Domenico, inquisition consultant, 79
Melanchthon's influence, and censored, 12, 18, 77, 132, 134, 167, 180, 183, 215
Mellini, Angela, 'living saint'?, 155
Menghini, Tommaso, inquisitor (Ferrara), manual writer, 70
Menocchio, *see* Scandella
Merenda, Apollonio, Valdesian, 23, 129
Meri, Andrea, contract with the Devil, 244
Merse, Walter, Scot, burned alive, 91
Messana, Maria Sofia, historian, 89, 232
Messina, inquisition trials and sentencing, 89
Michelangelo Buonarroti, and reform, 14
Milan, 38–40, 73, 109–10, 119, 154–5 (church of Santa Pelagia, and Pelaginism), 160 (1538 Index), 170, 178, 179 (Borromeo chasing banned books), 203, 205; inquisition, 27, 29, 38–40, 54–5, 70, 112, 151, 154–5 (Borri trial); *and see* Borromeo, Lombardy
Milani, Marisa, historian, 245
Millini (or Millino, or Mellini), Gian Garzia, Cardinal inquisitor, 53–4, 105–6, 111–12, 120–1, 147, 188, 233, 255
Milton, John, poet, visits Galileo, 193
Minchella, Giuseppina, historian, 151
Mingozzi, Antonia, coached evidence, 217
Mirabino, Angelo, inquisitor (Venice), 141
Mirandola, and 1522–3 witch-hunt, 8–9
Missanelli, Nicola Francesco, bishop of Policastro, reformer, 26, 272 n85
Missini, Giulio, da Orvieto, inquisitor (Friuli), 200, 242

Mocenigo, Alvise di Marin, abjured Lutheranism, 294 n31
Mocenigo, Alvise di Tommaso, Doge and former *assistente*, 223, 294 n31
Mocenigo, Filippo, archbishop of Nicosia, diplomat, philosopher, debates with inquisitors, 223–4
Mocenigo, Giovanni, denounces Bruno, 183–4
Modena, 4–5 (records), 6, 15, 16, 22, 27, 61, 113, 119, 142, 207 (Freemasons); inquisitors and trials, 4–5, 28, 54, 55, 63, 65, 87, 98 (Anti-Trinitarians), 100 (staff and familiars), 103, 112, 114–15, 135 (figures), 221, 228
Modena, Giacomo, denounces Batti, 197–8
Moducco, Battista, *benandante*, 242
Molinos, Miguel de, and Quietism, 50, 154–5, 255
Moncada, Juan de, Sicilian Viceroy, 48
Montesquieu, and censors, 202, 205
Montichiari, Francesco, inquisitorial and episcopal vicar, 110
Morandi, Innocenzo, inquisitor (Bologna), lazy?, 116
Morando, Domenico, tortured, 84
Moreto, Giorgio, mariner, Christian in Ghetto, 58, 60, 72, 274 nn1, 4
moriscos, Muslim converts, 46, 50, 63, 66, 136, 149–53
Morone, Giovanni, Cardinal, as heresy suspect, 14, 16, 17, 20, 22–6, 29, 68, 79, 84, 91, 97, 113, 124–6, 128–9, 255
Musella, Giuliano, da Casamassima, necromancer, and galley sentence, 118
Muslim faith, admiration for, 143, 150; willing or forced conversions to, 150–3, 217–19; *and see moriscos*
Muzzarelli, Girolamo, inquisition and papal consultant, 22–3, 61

Nacchianti, Giacomo, suspected bishop, 15, 20
Nani, Agostino, Venetian *assistente*, 33
Naples, Kingdom of, ix, 1, 11, 12, 13, 23, 26, 32, 33, 41–5, 46, 50, 54, 130, 164; inquisition system, and cases, ix, 19, 27, 41–5, 47, 61, 63 (spontaneous appearances), 70, 88–9, 116, 118–19, 134–5, 143 (Raguante), 150, 156 ('living saints'), 182 (Della Porta), 186 (Bruno), 238 (sabbats feared), 256; *autos*, 89, 130; Campanella, 79, 84, 186; censorship via bishops, 166–7, 179, 182, 183; Valdesian worries, 13–14, 61, 133, *and see* Galeota,

Gonzaga, Valdés and Valdesianism; Enlightenment issues, 201–5, 207, and Giannone, 205–6. Statistics, 134–5, 150, and Table C, 263. *See also* Annibale di Capua, *Valdesi* (Waldensians)
Nardon, Franco, historian, 242
Negri, Francesco, and *Tragedia del libero arbitrio*, influential on evangelicals, 98
Negri, Salvatore de', Venetian seller of prohibited books, 169, 179
Niccolini, Francesco, Tuscan ambassador, and Galileo, 190–1, 292 n112
Nicodemism, 18, 22, 226, 227
Nicolo de Elmis, advocate, 72
Nicolo di Elmi, witness in Collarina case, 210–11
Nicosia, 36, 219, 223
night-flying, 41, 232–3, 235–6, 239, 241–4 (*benandanti*, *donne di fora*, and *brujas*); *and see* sabbats
Nis, Felipe de (or Filipe, alias Solomon Marcos), crypto-Jew, and family, 144
Norlengo, David, Jew, self-confesses sexual misconduct, 148
notaries, and inquisition services, 26, 27, 32, 37, 43, 44, 47 (a murder), 49, 52, 56–7, 64, 65–8 (and their records), 79, 83–5 (recording torture), 85, 100, 112, 114, 143, 148, 209, 213, 215, 217–18 (helping accused and witnesses?), 222, 239, 245, 247, 252, 275 n22, 281 n29
Novara, and witchcraft, 6, 27, 88, 113
nuncios, inquisitorial roles, 7, 16, 20, 29, 30, 31–4 (Venice roles), 47, 64, 100 (Venice), 144, 160, 185, 188, 200, 211, 213, 233, 243, 244–5, 256, 294 n44
Nuzzi, Cesare, archiepiscopal vicar against inquisitor, 110

Ochino, Bernardino, Capuchin, Reform preacher, 13, 15, 20, 21, 38, 40, 77, 126, 129
Oddoni, Giovanni Angelo, Erasmian, 116
Oradino, Costanzo, Bolognese canon, and imprisonment, 94
Oratory of Divine Love, xv, 1, 13
Oreggi, Agostino, Jesuit, report on Galileo's *Dialogue*, 191
Oria, bishop of (Tommaso Maria Franza), his court in Francavilla (Puglia), 246
Orselli, Giovanni Francesco, inquisitor (Fermo), 280 n156
Orsi, Giuseppe Agostino, Master of the Sacred Palace, on *Encyclopèdie*, 204
Orsini, Camillo, noble reformer, 15

Ottoman Empire, and Turks, 46, 66, 121, 141–2, 144, 146, 149–53 (converts), 173, 217–19 (soldiers, converts), 223, 264 (see note in Table D, 264); *see also moriscos*; 'Turk'
Ovid, works censored, 175–6, 180

Pacheco, Francisco, Cardinal inquisitor, 24, 126, 270 n32
Padua, and university, 61, 104, 134, 142, 181–2, 186 (Campanella), 195 (Sarpi), 205–6; inquisition tribunal, 27, 34, 36, 76 (Tissano), 80–1 (Capponi), 168 (book burning), 169–70 (censorship), 180, 187 (Cremonini and Galileo), 194, 196, 199, 230
Paduano Grasso, censored, 21
Paleotti, Gabriele, bishop/archbishop of Bologna, Cardinal, 96–7, 114, 161
Paleotti, Rodolfo, bishop of Imola, on inquisition power, 28, 270 n32
Palermo, 60; inquisition 16, 48, 49 (prisons), 54, 60, 69, 85, 89 (*autos*), 121, 155 ('pretence of sanctity')
Pallavicino, Ferrante, Venetian academician, executed in Avignon, 197–9, 200
Palma (or Palmanova), Venetian fortress, inter-faith conversions, 152–3
Panigarola, Francesco, preacher, 176
Panzacchi, troublesome Bologna family, 114–15, 220–1
Panzona, Maria, from Latislana, *benandante*, 243
Paolina de Rossi, love magic, tortured, 251
Paolo Veronese, painter and inquisition record, 66
Papini, Girolamo, inquisitor, 28
Paris, Matthew, as heretic, 162
Parisio, Pier Paolo, Cardinal and inquisition, 16
Parma, inquisition, 27, 29, 55, 170, 203
Paruta, Paolo, Venetian ambassador, writer, 37
Pasqualigo, Angela Maria, 'living saint', 157
Pasqualigo, Zaccaria, Theatine, on Galileo's *Dialogue*, 191
Passaro, Naples bookseller, 179–80
Patrizi, Francesco da Cherso (born Franjo Petrić), philosopher, and Index, 181–2, 223
Paul III (Alessandro Farnese), Pope 1534–49, 1, 11, 17, 19–21 (1542 Bull and Inquisition), 82, 124, 256
Paul IV, (Gian Pietro Carafa), Pope 1555–9, *see also under* Carafa, viii, 22, 35, 40, 73, 85–6, 124–5, 125 (Index), 128, 136, 160 (censorship); *see* Indexes (1559)

Paul V (Camillo Borghese), Pope 1605–21, 53, 70, 82, 188, 194–6 (Venice Interdict)
Pavesi, Giulio, Dominican, attacking Waldensians, 43–4
Pavia, 5, 38; inquisitors, 27, 70, 119, 151, 196, 205, 209
Pedro de Hoyo, inquisitor (Sardinia and Sicily), 52, 243–4
Pelagini, and *pelaginismo*, 133, 154–5, 156, 258
Peña, Francisco, manual writer, 68–9, 71, 78, 81, 83, 234–5, 277 nn69 and 110; *see* Eymeric
penises, controlling and 'unbinding', 252; Devil's, 238
Penitentiary court, 20
Pensabene, Cristoforo, canon, assists Bologna inquisition and bishop, 114–15, 220
Peretti, Felice, da Montalto, Franciscan, inquisitor (Venice), 35; *see* Sixtus V
perfetti, select group of medieval Cathars, 2; *see* 'Living saints'
Perinetti, Bonventura, da Piacenza, inquisitor, 169
Pero, Giovanni Antonio, da Chiavenna, burned in effigy, 116
Perugia, inquisition, 27, 108, 168, 170 (censors); Podiani's library, 167
Pesenti, Antonia, 'living saint'?, 155–6
Peter Leopold, Grand Duke of Tuscany, 55
Petrarca, Francesco (Petrarch), works censored, 165, 171
Philip II of Spain, 11, 38, 41–2, 51
Piacenza, inquisitors, 8, 25, 69, 84, 109, 112, 170
Piagnoni (or Pagnoni), Silvestro, denounces Galileo, 188
Piccolomini, Ascanio, Cardinal archbishop of Siena, hosts Galileo, 192–3
Piccolomini, Bartolomeo Carli, on dissimulation, 77
Pico, Giovanni Francesco, lord of Mirandola and writer, 8, 240 (*Strix*, on witchcraft)
Pico, Paolo, secretary to Index Congregation, 161, 164
Piedmont, under House of Savoy, and inquisition, 30, 201, 205, Map 3; *see also* Mondoví; Saluzzo; Turin, Vercelli
Pietro Antonio da Cervia, Reformer, tortured, 84, 221–2, 294 n26; *and see* Panzacchi
Pietro Antonio di Capua, bishop of Otranto, and reform, 13, 15, 20, 22, 23, 272 n85
Pietro Aretino, *see* Aretino
Pietro da Saronno, inquisitor (Siena), 160–1

Pietro Martire, *see* Vermigli
Pighini, Sebastiano, Cardinal inquisitor, 23, 269 n35
Pignatelli, Giulio, Marchese of Cerchiaro, impedes inquisition, 45
Pinelli, Domenico, Cardinal inquisitor, 138
Pinzi, Giovanni Battista, abbot, and prohibited books, 205
Pisa, 1, 51, 61, 111, 175, 193 (Galileo supporters); inquisition tribunal, 27, 41, 71, 110, 187 (Galileo), 205, 213; Archbishop of Pisa, in 1619, Francesco Bonciani, 111, in 1649, Scipio Panneschieshi d'Elci, 199
Pisa, Cardinal of, *see* Rebiba
Pisenti, Agostino, defence lawyer, 3, 79–80
Pistoia, inquisition activity under Florence, 86–7, 247
Pius IV (Giovanni Angelo de' Medici), Pope 1559–65, 22, 29, 35, 38, 124, 126, 160
Pius V (St), (Michele Ghislieri), Pope 1565–72, *see also under* Ghislieri; viii, 22, 47, 68, 88, 91, 109, 110, 124, 129, 130 (Carnesecchi), 161, 169, 209, 256
Plakotos, Giorgios, historian, 151, 217, 286 n56
plea-bargaining, 22–3, 64, 77–8 (Galileo), 217–19
Podacataro, Fiorenza (alias Titiia), needed interpreter, 66, 218–19
Podiani, Prospero, library in Perugia, 167, 288 n37
Poetin, Francesco, da Vicenza, accused tailor, 33–4
Polacco, Giorgio, confessor, exorcist, 156–7
Pole, Reginald, Cardinal, xv, 13–14, 17–18, 20, 22–3, 68, 123–4, 126, 129, 293 n11
Policastro, bishop of, *see* Missanelli
Poma, Gaspar, Sardinian Reformer, pretend Jew, 50
Pompeo da Loiano, leader of Reform group in Bologna, 95
Pompeo, Lucchese perjuror, 41
Pomponazzi, Pietro, philosopher, 187
Porcacchi, Mario, da Castiglione, inquisitorial vicar, Gostanza case, 209, 238–40
Portella, Beatrice, and confining the Devil, 118–19
Portogruaro, inquisition tribunal, 27, 98; *and see* Aquileia
Possevino, Antonio, Jesuit, 30; his *Biblioteca Selecta*, 173
Pozzuolo, bishop of (Giovanni Matteo Casaldo), 76–7
Pratello, Francesco, Franciscan inquisitor (Pisa), assaulted, 110

'pretend saints', *see* 'living saints'
Prieras, *see* Mazzolini
prisons and prison sentences, 22–4, 47, 51, 59–60, 75, 92–3, 94, 95–6, 108 (and bail problem), 114, 148–9, 182–6 (Bruno and fellow prisoners), 186 (Campanella), 199, 205–6 (Giannone), 206–7 (Crudeli), 225, 247, 254
Priuli, Alvise, reformer, 129
Priuli, Girolamo, Doge of Venice, 24–5
Priuli, Lorenzo, Patriarch of Venice, 172
Prohibited Books, *see* Index
Prosperi, Adriano, historian, vii–viii, 19, 98, 201, 208–9, 213
Protestants, *see under* Anabaptism; Bucer; Calvinism; Lutheranism; Melanchthon
protomedicato tribunals, and healers, 245–6
Pucci, Francesco, philosopher, Reformer, decapitated, 185–6, 257
Puglia, 42, 74–5, 93 (*Valdesiani*), 155 (Suor Giglia), 246; and *Valdesi*/Waldensians, xv, 15, 25
Pulci, Luigi, his *Morgante maggiore* censored, 172
Puteo, Giacomo, Cardinal inquisitor, 23, 269 n35

Quaderti, Andrea, blaspheming dice-player, 137–8
Querini (or Quirini), Vincenzo, calling for reforms, 1, 12, 15
Quietists, *see* Molinos

Raguante (or Raguantes), Laura, convert to Judaism, 143
Raimondi, Giovanni Battista, inquisitor (Venice), 198, 200
Rangone, Giovanni, and Mantua reformers, 15
Ravenna, bishopric and inquisition, 28, 61, 120–1, 205
Raz-Krakotzkin, Amnon, historian, 178
Rebiba, Scipione, called Cardinal of Pisa, Cardinal inquisitor, 24, 25, 30, 39, 42, 82, 95–8 (and inquisitor Balducci), 101, 116, 118, 127, 180, 182, 223 (criticised by Filippo Mocenigo), 255
Reffiletti, Angela, Cypriot, Venetian healer, and 'measurer' of cloths, 248–9
Reggio Emilia, inquisition, 198, 200
Renato, Camillo, Reformer, 79
Renda, Francesco, historian, 50, 88–9, 122, 232
Renée (Renata) d'Este, Duchess of Ferrara, Calvinist, 28, 99
Renier, Andrea, Venetian noble, denounces lover (Erba), 216

Reumano, Giovanni, Cardinal inquisitor, 125
Ribeiro, Gaspare (or Gasparo Ribiera), and family, Christian or Jew?, 144, 146, 285 n34
Riccardi, Niccolò, Master of the Sacred Palace, and Galileo, 174–5
Ricchini, Tomasso, Master of the Sacred Palace, censorship, 205
Richardson, Samuel, his *Pamela* and *Clarissa* banned, 203
Rifreddo, witch trials, 5, 228, 235
Righetti, Peregrino (or Pellegrino), painter, executed, 103–4
Righetto, Adam (alias Enriques Nuñes), Judaiser, 33, 60, 79, 275 n11
Rimini, inquisition, 27, 119, 120–1
Rinaldo (or Rinaldini), Flaminio, over-lengthy case, 59, 79, 117
Rioli, *see* Siculo
Risposa, Alfonsina, visionary, long imprisonment, 155–6
Rocca Contrada (under Ancona), investigated by Masini, 204, 207, 226
Rocco, Antonio, and mortality of the soul, obscene writings, 134, 200, 255
Rodriguez, Cristoforo, Jesuit and inquisitorial role, 74
Roffia, Tommaso, episcopal vicar, Gostanza case, 209, 238–40
Roman Inquisition, *see* Inquisition
Romano, Marco, Naples bookseller, 179–80
Rome, 5, 11 (Sack of 1527), 42 (bishops resident in), 88–9 (*autos*), 124 (crowd destroys records, 1559), 130 (Galeota at *auto*), 142 (Ghetto); Academy of Gli Arcadi, and censors, 202; Academy of Lynxes (*Lincei*), and Galileo, 174, 182, 187; book-burning, 169, 177; booksellers, 21–2, 205; Campo dei Fiori, 16, 91, 128 155, 177, 183 (Bruno statue), 185 (Bruno's burning); Governor's court and prisons, 20, 24, 184, 185; executions, 23, 88–9, 98, 135–6 (numbers of); S. Maria sopra Minerva (Dominican and inquisition centre), 21, 24, 128, 186; *see also* Index, Inquisition entries
Romualdo, Fra, Quiestist, burned (Palermo), 155
Rosario, Virgilio, Cardinal inquisitor, 125
Rota (or Ruota), Benedetto, troublesome ex-inquisitor (Casale), 110–11
Rovereto, Andrea, inquisitor (Bologna), astrology case, 253
Rovigo, heretics, 15, 61; inquisition office, 36, 61, 86
Ruggiero, Guido, historian, 67, 237, 252

Ruis (or Ruiz), Alessandro, abbot, and concubine, 67–8, 252
Ruzzante's play *La Moscheta*, 12

sabbat (*ludus*), 7, 39, 41, 52, 79, 232–5 (and inquisitorial scepticism); playing with the Devil, 235, 237, 238–44
Sacro Arsenale, *see* Masini
Sagredo, Piero, Venetian *assistente*, 32, 198
saints, 'living', 'pretend', x, 93, 131, 153–7, 224
Saliceti, Giacomo, Bolognese weaver, executed, 23
Salmerón, Alfonso, Jesuit and Waldensians, 43
Salonica, 144
Saluzzo, 5, 6; inquisitorial tribunal, 27, 30, 277 n85
salvation by faith alone (*sola fide*), Italian support for doctrine, xv, 1, 12–14, 16, 17, 31, 98, 130
sanbenito, *see* abitello
Sanfelice, Giovanni Tommaso, reform bishop, 15, 125
San Miniato, trial of Gostanza in, 209–10, 238–41, 296 n20
San Sisto, Waldensian centre, massacre, 43
Santa Severina, Cardinal, *see* Santoro
Santoro (or Santori), Giulio, archbishop of Santa Severina (sometimes called Cardinal Santa Severina), Cardinal inquisitor, 24, 25, 43, 44–5, 82 (on inquisition 'style'), 109, 116, 118–19, 130, 223, 224, 230, 238 (scepticism about sabbats), 255, 256; Congregation of the Index and censorship, 43, 162, 164, 172, 178, 182, 184–6 (Bruno)
Sanudo (or Sanuto), Marino, Venetian diarist, 7, 237–8
Sardinia, and inquisition, ix, 9–12, 48–53, 54, 59, 73, 114, 131–2, 150, 244
Sarpi, Paolo, Servite, writings on the inquisition, and Interdict, 31, 57, 71, 107, 163, 169–70, 195–6, 206, 234 (on witchcraft)
Sarsina, bishopric and inquisition, 28
Sassari, Sardinian inquisition centre, 51, 52 (*autos*), 244
Savelli, Giacomo, Cardinal inquisitor, 79, 92, 118–19, 224
Savonarola, Girolamo, burned as heretic, 1, 11; his book-burning, 165, 172; his later supporters, 9, 172, 180; works censored, 163, 172
Savoy, House of, *see* Piedmont, Turin
Scaglia, Deodato, bishop, manual writer, 70, 324

Scaglia, Desiderio, bishop, inquisitor, manual writer, 70, 114, 151–2
Scanaroli, Giovanni Battista, his treatise on prisons, 85
Scandella, Domenico (Menocchio), miller, heretic, 3–4, 65, 79–80, 98, 242
Scaramella, Pierroberto, historian, 42, 43–4
Schellino, Aurelio, da Brescia, inquisitor (Venice), 227–8 (Gaiano case)
Schoppe, Kaspar, witness for Bruno's execution, 185
Schutte, Anne Jacobson, historian, 34, 64, 133, 155, 262
Sclender, Alessandro, samples three religions, 153
Scotti, Bernardino (or, Bernardo, Cardinal Trani), Cardinal inquisitor, 25, 26, 126
Scribani, Giulio, Genoese civilian witch-hunter, 241
Scrofa, Modesto, inquisitor (Como), 6
Scullica, Teofilo da Troppea, censor, 21–2
Sebastian, Bartolomé, inquisitor (Sicily), 132
Segizzi (or Seghizzi), Michelangelo, and injunction against Galileo, 190–1
Seidel Menchi, Silvana, historian, 17
self-denunciation, *see* spontaneous appearances,
sentencing, range of, and conditions affecting, 90–9; *see also abitelli*; *autos*; death sentences; executions
Seripando, Girolamo, Augustinian reformer and Cardinal, 15, 20, 43–4, 91
Severi, Francesco, da Argenta, physician follower of Siculo, beheaded, 103
Sfondrati, Francesco, Cardinal inquisitor, 20–1
Sfondrati, Paolo Emilio, Cardinal inquisitor, 188
Sicily, viii–ix, 9–11, 15, 131–2, 142, 150, 151, 161; Spanish inquisition in, 11, 19, 48–50, 52–3, 54, 59, 73, 83, 89 (sentencing and *autos*), 114, 121–2 (confraternities for familiars), 132, 138, 161 (uses Roman Indexes), 256–7; its attitudes to witchcraft, 232, 235–6, and night-flyers, *donne di fora* or *brujas*, 241, 243–4, 264, Table D
Siculo, Giorgio (or, Rioli), executed Reformer, 28, 103, 214
Siena, 15, 51, 77, 142, 175, 192; inquisition activity, 27, 34, 135 (statistics), 155 ('living saints'), 239, 252
Sigonio, Carlo, historian's compromise with censors, 167
silent prayer, as problem, 133, 154–5, 165–6
Simancas, Diego (or Iacobo), manual writer, 69, 71, 81, 90

Singlitico, Franzino, bargain with inquisitor, 77–8, 214–15 (questioned), 257
Sion, Giovanni, *benandante*, 79
Sirleto, Guglielmo, Cardinal, prefect of Index, 161, 178
Sixtus IV (Francesco della Rovere), Pope 1471–84, 10
Sixtus V (Felice Peretti), Pope 1585–90, 53, 161, 164; *see under* Peretti
sodomy, 35, 52, 133, 134–5, 147, 176 (by Cain and son), 198 (Pallavicino praises), 200 (Rocco discusses)
Soleri, Lorenzo, inquisitor, influences the *Malleus Maleficarum*, 6
solicitation, priestly, 52, 110, 131, 133, 138–9
Sommario della Sacra Scrittura, 12–13
Sondrio (Valtellina), and witch trials, 6
Soraggio, witch-hunt, 65, 88, 228
Soranzo, Vittore, condemned bishop (Bergamo), 13, 15, 17, 22–3, 28, 37 (death), 44, 67, 68, 109, 125, 129
Sorratini, Giovanni Paolo, blasphemer, 137
Spadini, Giovanni Antonio, inquisitor (Bologna), on censorship problems, 167–8
Spalato (Split), 36
Spannocchi, Diofebo, militant Bologna Protestant, 96–7
Spiera, Francesco, notary, reformer, and dissimulation, 213
Spilimbergo (Friuli), Lutherans in, and Consorti case, 225–6
Spina, Barolomeo, inquisitor and writer, 6
spirituali, *see* Glossary; 18, 44, 124–5, 130, 214, 256 *and see* Valdesians
Spoleto, 77; inquisition tribunal, 27
spontaneous appearances, 44, 60–3 (with statistics), 75, 91, 126–7 (Carnesecchi and his interpretation), 135, 141, 148–9 (by Jews), 151–3, 197, 205, 206, 217, 242, 248, 267
stregoneria, streghe, see witchcraft and witches
Suor (Sister) Mansueta, troubled nun, 64, 244–5, 252, 255
superstitions, Chapter 9; concepts, 234–6; *see* magic, witchcraft
Swift, Jonathan, his *The Tale of a Tub* censored, 203
syphilis, and witchcraft, 11, 246, 250

Tagliavia d'Aragona, Simone (or Cardinal Terranova), and Index, 170–1
Talmud, attacks on, 164, 177
Tarabotti, Arcangela (alias Galerana Barcitotti), Venetian nun, writer, 197
Tavuzzi, Michael, historian, 5–6

Tedeschi, John, historian, xi, 70, 135, 232
Telesio, Bernardino, philosopher, and Index, 181–2
Tiepolo, Agostino, Venetian reformer, 129
Tiepolo, Giovanni, Venetian Patriarch, 211
Tiepolo, Paolo, Venetian ambassador, 223
Tirabosco, Marc'Antonio, manual writer, 67
Tissano (or Tizzano), Lorenzo (alias Benedetto Florio), and his diverse heresies, 75–6, 277 nn64 and 65
Tiziano, Lorenzo, Anabaptist, 277 n64
Toledo, Francisco, Jesuit, quoted on Inquisition's excessive rigour, 223
Tolossenti, Antonio, Maltese vicar, reprimanded, 88
Torcella, Flaminio, inquisition judge for Naples, harsh on witches, 238
Torquemada, Tomá de, Spanish inquisitor-general, 10–11, 48
Tortona, inquisition, 27
torture, vii, 1, 2–4, 6, 8–10, 26–7, 32–3, 38, 41, 43–4, 48–9, 52, 58, 62, 81–8 (methods and conditions), 82, 96–7, 103, 111, 113–14, 118, 127–8 (Carnesecchi), 140, 144, 145, 183 (Della Porta), 186 (Campanella), 209, 221–2 (Pietro Angelo da Cervia), 228, 230, 233, 235, 238–41 and 248 (Gostanza), 243, 251 (Bibone), 256–7; types of torture, 41, 83–6, 97, 222, 278 nn91, 94 and 100
Traballesi, Giuliano, painter, illustrates book-burning, 169
Tragagliolo, Albert, inquisitor, and Bruno's Roman trial, 184
Tramezzino, Francesco, Roman bookseller, 19–20
Trani, Cardinal, *see* Scotti
Trent, Council of [meeting 1545–7, 1550–1, 1562–3], 17, 21, 38, 62, 113, 120, 126, 129, 160, 161, 163, 194; *see* Indexes, 1564 Index (Tridentine)
Trevisan, Giovanni, Venetian Patriarch, 141
Treviso, inquisition, 27, 29, 36, 98–9 (executions), 229, 294 n44
Triora (Genoa), witch trials, 79, 241
Turin, 30, 32 (nuncios), 119, 120, 205 (book trade); inquisition, 27, 30, 205–6 (Giannone)
'Turk' (*'turco'*) meaning Muslim, 151–3, 229–30, 249
Tuscany, Medici state, 2, 29, 193; inquisition in, 29, 55, 201, 296 n29; *see also* Florence, Galileo, Pisa, San Miniato, Siena

Udine, 15; heretics, inquisition, 27, 36–7, 55, 91, 98, 134–5 (statistics), 152, 155, 200, 207 (Freemasonry and magic linked), 241–2, 244
Ugoni, Agapito, inquisitor (Venice), and 'living saint' trials, 155, 255
Ugoni, Giovan Andrea, and Brescia reform, 15
Urban VIII (Maffeo Barberini), Pope 1623–44, 198; and Campanella, 186; and Galileo, 174–5, 187, 189
Usimbardi, Usimbardo, bishop (Colle Val d'Elsa), and nuns' reading, 176–7

Vagnola, Pietro, varied Protestant beliefs, 86
Val Camonica, heretics and witches, 6–8, 154 (Pelagini), 237
Val Chiavenna, heretics, 39
Valdés, Juan de, Spanish Reformer, viii, 1, 11, 13–14, 38, 124–6, 214 *and see Valdesiani*
Valdesi (Waldensians, followers of Waldo), *see* Glossary; 4, 6, 15, 30, 42–5, 132, 255–6, 272 n82
Valdesiani (Valdesians, followers of Juan de Valdés), Glossary, ix, 1, 9, 14–15, 16, 18, 23, 25, 44–5, 51–2, 61, 75–6, 77, 95, 103, 123–30, 132, 134, 214, 256, 257–8, 259; *see* Carnesecchi, Galeotta, Gonzaga (Giulia), Pole
Valgrisi family, Venetian bookmen, fined, 181
Valier, Agostino, Cardinal, and Index, 158, 168, 173–4, 175, 176–7
Val Mescolina, and witchcraft, 39
Valtellina, and heretics, 6, 16, 39, 101
Valvasense, Francesco, Venetian bookman, and censorship, 32, 66, 179, 196–200, 255
Velincovich, Martino (alias Ossiman), from Croatia, negotiated conversion, 218
Vendramin, Francesco, Patriarch of Venice, 194–5, 243
Vendramin, Pietro, consultant and manual editor, 140
Venetian Republic and Venice, general: 1, 6–8, 12, 22–3, 90–2, 100, 123–5 (Carnesecchi), 160 (early Index), 194–200, 207–8; Ottoman contacts, 152–3, 217–19; *see also benandanti*, Bergamo, Brescia, Ceneda, Cividale, Concordia, Padua, Portogruaro, Treviso, Udine, Verona, Vicenza
Venice, general: Avogaria di Comune tribunal, 2; Bestemmia tribunal, 133, 136–7, 177; Casa dei Catecumeni, 142, 152; Council of Ten, 7, 33, 35, 65–7, 90–2, 134, 238; Ghetto, 72, 141–4; Inquisitori dello Stato (state inquisitors), 65–6; Interdict Crisis 1606–7, 33, 107, 117, 163, 194–5; nuncios (papal legates), 31–3, 35–6, 91–2, 100, 140–1, 160,

211–12, 213–14; Patriarchs in, 32, 35–6, 140, 156, 172, 211–12, 213–14; as Reform centre, 15–16, 17, 21, 31–2, 35 and 61 (Anabaptists), 129 (Carnesecchi's contacts)
Venice, inquisition tribunal in, general: 27, 29, 31–7, 55, 57, 60–1 (prisons), 66–7, 72–3, 79–80 (legal defences), 85 (torture), 90, 117–18, 133–8 and Table A, 260–1) (statistics), 227–8 (gossip), 234–8 (superstition and witchcraft), 256; inquisitorial *assistenti* (*Tre Savii sopra eresia*), 32–3, 66, 85, 100, 139, 140–1, 195, 198, 211, 243, 290 n94, 294 n44; investigations and trials, 5, 21, 23, 26 (Gallo), 31, 33–5, 60–1 (Righetto), 64, 66–7, 68, 71–2, 75–6, 77–8, 79–80, 90–1, 98, 117–18, 137 (blasphemers), 138–9, 140–1 (solicitation accusations), 141–7 (Judaisers and Jewish–Christian relationships), 152–3 (reconciling Muslim converts), 155–7 ('living saints'), 173–4, 179–81 (bookmen), 182, 183–4 (Bruno), 196–200 (bookmen, Valvasense and Batti), 200 (Rocco), 209–10 (Giantis), 210–12 (Collarina), 213–14 (Spiera), 214–15 (Singlitico), 215–16 (Erba), 217–19 (negotiated conversion cases), 223, 225–6, 227–8 (Gaiano), 229–30 (Aurora Gemma and Marco da Domo), 243 (Panzona, *benandante*), 244 (Meri), 244–5 (Suor Mansueta), 249 (non-Italians and healing magic), 250–1 (Elisabetta Todesca), 251 (Fra Bibone), 252, 253
Venier, *see* Marino da Venezia
Veraldo, Ambrogio, convicted Sardinian Calvinist, 52
Verallo, Girolamo, Cardinal inquisitor, 22, 23, 269 n35
Vercelli, 6, 27
Vergerio, Pier Paolo, bishop (Capodistria), Reformer, 15, 17, 20–1, 31, 34, 36–7, 79, 176, 213–14
Vermigli, Pietro Martire (Peter Martyr), Reformer, 13, 20, 40, 44, 126, 129
Verona, 142 (Ghetto), 253; inquisition, 27, 29, 36, 55, 78–9, 87

Verri, Pietro, Enlightenment writer, 202
Vicari, Paolo, da Garessio, inquisitor (Bologna), 94, 117, 196
Vicenza, 15, 61, 143, 180; inquisition, 27, 29, 33, 36, 84, 189, 234
Vidua, Francesco, Reformer, 87
Vignuzzi (or Vignuzio), Giovanni Domenico, inquisitor (Venice), 173–4, 243
Vincenzi, Francesco, priest, 155, 156
Vincenzo Maria da Bologna, inquisition vicar (Iesi), 112
Virginia de Tomasellis, Bologna prostitute and herbal magic, 246
Visconti, Raffaello, Dominican, favours Galileo, 174
Vitelli, Francesco, nuncio in Venice, on Pallavicino book, 198
Vitello, Pellegrina, tortured, 83
Viterbo, as reform centre, 14–15, 123
Vittori, Girolamo, Bolognese Valdesian leader, 95, 96, 103
Vittorio Amedeo II, of Savoy, 30
Vittoriosa (formerly Birgu), Malta's inquisition centre, 47
Voglia, Alessandro, necromancer, 105

Waldensians, *see Valdesi* and Glossary
Wignacourt, Alof de, Grand Master of Knights of St John, 47, 273 n98
witchcraft and witches, and witch-crazes, *see* Chapter 9, *and* magic and superstition; and sabbats. Accusations and episodes: pre-1542 witch-hunts, 4–5, 6–9, 50–1, 237–8 (Val Camonica, 'games', 1518); Borromeo and witchcraft, 39, 259; Collarina, 210–12; gender divisions, 136, 235–6, 251; Giantis case, 209–10; hunt for Devil's mark, 234; Lucca cases, 41; Soraggio trials, 88

Zacchia, Laudivio, Cardinal inquisitor, 192
Zane, Paolo, bishop of Brescia, and witches, 7
Zara (Dalmatia), inquisition, 27, 36
Zarlati, Francesco, accused notary, 213
Ziletti, Francesco, Venetian bookman, 180
Zwingli's influence, 31, 77

www.ingramcontent.com/pod-product-compliance
Lightning Source LLC
Chambersburg PA
CBHW021932290426
44108CB00012B/817